Ancient Literacies

Ancient Literacies

The Culture of Reading in Greece and Rome

EDITED BY

William A. Johnson and Holt N. Parker

OXFORD
UNIVERSITY PRESS

OXFORD
UNIVERSITY PRESS

Oxford University Press, Inc., publishes works that further
Oxford University's objective of excellence
in research, scholarship, and education.

Oxford   New York
Auckland   Cape Town   Dar es Salaam   Hong Kong   Karachi
Kuala Lumpur   Madrid   Melbourne   Mexico City   Nairobi
New Delhi   Shanghai   Taipei   Toronto

With offices in
Argentina   Austria   Brazil   Chile   Czech Republic   France   Greece
Guatemala   Hungary   Italy   Japan   Poland   Portugal   Singapore
South Korea   Switzerland   Thailand   Turkey   Ukraine   Vietnam

Copyright © 2009 by Oxford University Press, Inc.

First published by Oxford University Press, Inc. 2009
198 Madison Avenue, New York, New York 10016
www.oup.com

First issued as an Oxford University Press paperback, 2011

Oxford is a registered trademark of Oxford University Press.

Library of Congress Cataloging-in-Publication Data
Ancient literacies : the culture of reading in Greece and Rome / edited by William A. Johnson and
Holt N. Parker.
    p. cm.
Includes bibliographical references and indexes.
ISBN 978-0-19-979398-3 (pbk)
1. Transmission of texts—Greece. 2. Transmission of texts—Rome.
3. Books and reading—Greece. 4. Books and reading—Rome. 5. Literacy—Greece.
6. Literacy—Rome. I. Johnson, William A. (William Allen), 1956– II. Parker, Holt N.
Z1003.5.G8A53 2009
302.2′24409495—dc22   2008020329

Figures 2.1–2.6, 2.8b, and 2.9 are printed courtesy of the Trustees of the American School of Classical
Studies at Athens. Permission to reproduce Figure 2.7 granted by the German Archaeological
Institute; photograph by Eva-Maria Czakò, negative no. D-DAI-ATH-Kerameikos 6147, all rights
reserved. Permission to reproduce the squeeze in Figure 2.8a was kindly granted by the Centre for
Ancient Documents, Oxford University. Figures 4.1–4.5 were drawn by Nate Bullock. Figures 10.1
and 11.2 are printed courtesy of the Egypt Exploration Society. Figure 11.1 was drawn by John Wallrodt.
Figure 12.1 is printed courtesy of the Getty Museum: Gift of Mr. and Mrs. Halsted B. Vander Poel.
Research Library, The Getty Research Institute, Los Angeles, California (2002.M16). Figure 12.3
is printed by permission Luciano Pedicini, fotografo.

Printed in the United States of America

Acknowledgments

On April 28–29, 2006, the University of Cincinnati convened a Semple Symposium under the rubric "Constructing 'Literacy' among the Greeks and Romans." That conference was the origin of the volume in your hands, and first thanks must therefore go to the Louise Taft Semple Fund, whose financial generosity made the conference possible, and to Louise Taft Semple herself, to whose memory we dedicate this book. We hope to have succeeded in forwarding her wish "to make vital and constructive in the civilization of our country the spiritual, intellectual, and aesthetic inheritance we have received from Greece and Rome" (establishment document, Louise Taft Semple Fund). We also thank the many colleagues and students and friends who formed such a lively and invested audience during the two days of the conference. But this is no simple volume of proceedings, and we must also express our gratitude to the contributors, who not only gave splendid lecture presentations, but took seriously the charge to refashion their talks into chapters for this book and also graciously received and responded to editorial demands for further revision. Finally, it is a pleasure to record the contributions of our graduate assistants: Jamie Reuben, who adroitly managed the myriad details of organizing the Semple Symposium, Austin Chapman, who has done a masterly job in proofreading and other aspects of the production of the book, and Dana Clark, our helpmeet in the final stages of production.

William A. Johnson
Holt N. Parker

Contents

PART III: INSTITUTIONS AND COMMUNITIES

PART IV: BIBLIOGRAPHICAL ESSAY

PART V: EPILOGUE

Illustrations

Abbreviations

ATL:	Meritt, B.D., H. D. Wade-Gery, and M. L. McGregor. 1939–1953. *The Athenian Tribute Lists.* Princeton.
CIL:	*Corpus Inscriptionum Latinarum.* 1863–. Berlin.
FPL-Blänsdorf:	Blänsdorf, Jürgen. 1995. *Fragmenta poetarum Latinorum epicorum et lyricorum praeter Ennium et Lucilium.* 3rd ed. Leipzig.
IG:	*Inscriptiones Graecae.* 1873–. Berlin.
ILLRP:	Degrassi, A. 1957–1963. *Inscriptiones Latinae Liberae Rei Publicae.* Florence.
IvE:	*Inschriften von Ephesos.* 1979–1981. *Inschriften griechischer Städte aus Kleinasien* 11–17. Bonn.
LIMC:	*Lexicon Iconographum Mythologiae Classicae.* 1981. Zurich.
LTUR:	Steinby, Eva Margarita. 1993–2000. *Lexicon topographicum urbis Romae.* Rome.
MP3:	*The Mertens-Pack³ Database Project,* URL=http://promethee.philo.ulg.ac.be/cedopal/index.htm.
OCD:	Hornblower, Simon, and Antony Spawforth, eds. 2003. *Oxford Classical Dictionary.* 3rd ed. Oxford.
ORF:	Malcovati, E. 1955. *Oratorum Romanorum Fragmenta.* 2nd ed. Turin.
PIR²:	*Prosopographia Imperii Romani.* 1933. 2nd ed. Berlin and Leipzig.
PSI:	Papiri greci e latini. (Pubblicazioni della Società Italiana per la ricerca dei papiri greci e latini in Egitto). Florence.
RIB:	Collingwood, R. G., and R. P. Wright. 1995. *The Roman Inscriptions of Britain.* 2nd ed. Gloucestershire.
SEG:	*Supplementum Epigraphicum Graecum.* 1923. Leiden.
TLL:	*Thesaurus Linguae Latinae.* 1900–1990. Leipzig.

Contributors

Trained at New York University and at Harvard, BARBARA BURRELL has dug at sites across the Mediterranean, including Spain, Italy, Greece, Turkey, and currently in Israel, where she is Field Director for the Promontory Palace Excavations at Caesarea Maritima. Her specialties include Roman provincial coins, Greek epigraphy of Asia Minor, and Hellenistic and Roman imperial architecture, art, and history. Her major work on cities that built temples to the imperial cult, *Neokoroi: Greek Cities and Roman Emperors*, appeared in 2004. She is currently Associate Professor of Roman Archaeology at Brock University, as well as Associate Research Professor of Classics at the University of Cincinnati.

FLORENCE DUPONT is Professor of Classics at the University Paris Denis-Diderot. With interests in Roman theater (tragedy and comedy) and the anthropology of Roman culture, her research now focuses on ethnopoetics. In 2007 she founded the *Groupe de recherches en ethnopoétique* (GREP). She is the author of many books and articles. Her most recent books include *L'orateur sans visage, essai sur l'acteur romain et son masque* (2000), *Façons de parler grec à Rome* (2003), coauthored with Emmanuelle Valette-Cagnac, and *Aristote ou le vampire du théâtre occidental* (2007).

JOSEPH FARRELL is Professor of Classical Studies at the University of Pennsylvania, where he teaches courses on Latin literature and Roman culture. He is the author of *Vergil's* Georgics *and the Traditions of Ancient Epic* (1991), of *Latin Language and Latin Culture from Ancient to Modern Times* (2001), and of papers on various aspects of Latin literature.

SIMON GOLDHILL is Professor of Greek at Cambridge University. He has published extensively on Greek literature from Homer to the late antique, but specializes on Greek tragedy. His current research projects include a five-year program, *Abandoning the Past in Victorian Britain*, and a three-year project, *Art and Law in Modern Society*. His most recent books are *How to Stage Greek Tragedy Today* (2007) and *Jerusalem, City of Longing* (2008).

THOMAS HABINEK, Professor of Classics at the University of Southern California, is a specialist in Latin literature and Roman cultural history. His many publications include *The Colometry of Latin Prose* (1985), *The Politics of Latin Literature* (1998), and *The World of Roman Song* (2005), winner of the Classics and Ancient History Award presented by the Association of American Publishers. He is currently investigating the potential impact of new developments in neuroscience, cognition, and evolution on issues and problems in the humanities.

GEORGE W. HOUSTON is Professor of Classics Emeritus at the University of North Carolina at Chapel Hill. His research interests include Latin literature, Latin epigraphy, Roman technology, and libraries and book collections in the Roman world. He has published extensively on ancient libraries, including papers on the personnel of public libraries (*TAPA* 2002), public libraries in the city of Rome (*MEFRA* 2006; with T. Keith Dix), and book collections in Egypt (*GRBS* 2007). He is currently at work, with T. Keith Dix, on a book-length study of the contents and management of book collections in the Roman world.

WILLIAM A. JOHNSON is Associate Professor of Classics and Head of Department at the University of Cincinnati. He works broadly in the cultural history of Greece and Rome, with particular interest in ancient books, readers, and reading. Among his many articles is the winner of the 2000 Gildersleeve Prize, "Towards a Sociology of Reading in Classical Antiquity." *Bookrolls and Scribes in Oxyrhynchus*, a close study of ancient papyrus bookrolls, was published in 2004, and he is presently completing a volume, *Readers and Reading Culture in the High Empire*, for Oxford University Press.

KRISTINA MILNOR is Associate Professor of Classics at Barnard College in New York City. She is the author of *Gender, Domesticity, and the Age of Augustus: Inventing Private Life* (2005), which won the 2006 Goodwin Award of Merit from the American Philological Association. Her research interests include early imperial prose and poetry, feminist theory and gender studies, and the intersection of material and literary cultures. She has published articles on Plautus, Sulpicia, Livy, the graffiti art movement in the 1970s, and Barbie®. She is currently working on her second book, on literary graffiti from Roman Pompeii.

DAVID R. OLSON is University Professor Emeritus of the Ontario Institute for Studies in Education at the University of Toronto. He is author of *The World on Paper: The Conceptual and Cognitive Implications of Writing and Reading* (Cambridge University Press 1994), *Psychological Theory and Educational Reform* (2003), and *Jerome Bruner* (2007). He is editor with Nancy Torrance of the forthcoming *Cambridge Handbook of Literacy*.

HOLT N. PARKER is Professor of Classics at the University of Cincinnati and Fellow of the American Academy in Rome. He has published on Sappho, Sulpicia, sexuality, slavery, sadism, and spectacle.

ROSALIND THOMAS works on literacy and orality in ancient Greece. She has written *Oral Tradition and Written Record in Classical Athens* (1989), and *Literacy and Orality in Ancient Greece* (1992). Her research interests also include Greek law and the polis, Greek medicine, and historiography. Her most recent book is *Herodotus in Context. Ethnography, Science and the Art of Persuasion* (2000). She is Tutorial Fellow and University Lecturer in Ancient History at Balliol College, Oxford.

SHIRLEY WERNER taught at Rutgers University and the University of California, Irvine, and served as the American Fellow to the Thesaurus linguae Latinae in Munich. She has published on Latin poetry and manuscripts. She works as the Associate Director of the American Office of *L'Année philologique* and has recently joined the editorial board of the journal *Vergilius* as Bibliographical Editor.

PETER WHITE is Professor of Classics at the University of Chicago. He has written extensively on the relationship between Latin literature and the structure of Roman society during the Late Republic and Early Empire. His books include *Promised Verse: Poets in the Society of Augustan Rome* (1993), for which he received the American Philological Association's Goodwin Award for Merit in 1995. He is currently completing a book about Cicero's letters.

GREG WOOLF is Professor of Ancient History at the University of St Andrews. He has written on European prehistory, the cultural history of the Roman provinces, the Roman economy, and Roman religion. Along with Alan Bowman he edited *Literacy and Power in the Ancient World* (1994) and contributed a chapter on the subject to the *Cambridge Ancient History*. He is currently working on patterns of cultural change in Roman antiquity, and on science in the Roman world.

Ancient Literacies

1

Introduction

William A. Johnson

A previous generation of scholars made ancient Greece a point of central focus in arguments concerning literacy. In these earlier accounts (one thinks in particular of Jack Goody, Eric Havelock, and Walter Ong), literacy was isolated as a primary agent of change in the "Greek revolution"—what Brian Street has dubbed the "autonomous model"—in which the introduction of an alphabetic writing system, in and of itself, is said to bring about various consequences for society and culture.[1] Such determinist accounts are now generally discredited, both at large and among most classicists.[2] Yet little has arisen to take its place. Classicists have only slowly begun to take advantage of the important advances in the way that literacy is viewed in other disciplines (including in particular cognitive psychology, sociolinguistics, and socio-anthropology).[3] The most widely referenced general book remains William Harris' *Ancient Literacy* (1989), a thoughtful, immensely learned, and important book, which, however, focuses narrowly on the question of what percentage of people in antiquity might have been able to read and write.[4]

The moment seems right, therefore, to try to formulate more interesting, productive ways of talking about the conception and construction of "literacies" in the ancient world—literacy not in the sense of whether 10 percent or 30 percent of people in the ancient world could read or write, but in the sense of text-oriented events embedded in particular sociocultural contexts.[5] The volume in your hands was constructed as a

1. Goody 1963, 1977; Havelock 1963, 1986; Ong 1982; Street 1984.
2. See summary and critique in Street 1984, 44–65; Thomas 1992, 15–28; Olson 1994, 1–20, 36–44; Johnson 2003, 10–13.
3. For overviews of the tendencies, see in this volume Thomas (chapter 2: for Classics) and Olson (chapter 15: for a broader view), and the bibliographical essay by Werner (chapter 14).
4. Harris 1989; reactions collected in Humphrey 1991.
5. UNESCO has defined *literacy* in terms of the illiterate: someone "who cannot with understanding both read and write a short simple statement on his everyday life" (quoted in Harris 1989, 3). But sociological researchers have proposed definitions with a much broader cast to the net: for example, Shirley Heath (1982, 50) speaks of "literacy events" as "occasions

forum in which selected leading scholars were challenged to rethink from the ground up how students of classical antiquity might best approach the question of literacy, and how that investigation might materially intersect with changes in the way that literacy is now viewed in other disciplines. The result is intentionally pluralistic: theoretical reflections, practical demonstrations, and combinations of the two share equal space in the effort to chart a new course. Readers will come away, therefore, with food for thought of many types: new ways of thinking about specific elements of literacy in antiquity, such as the nature of personal libraries, or the place and function of bookshops in antiquity; new constructivist questions, such as what constitutes reading communities and how they fashion themselves; new takes on the public sphere, such as how literacy intersects with commercialism, or with the use of public spaces, or with the construction of civic identity; new essentialist questions, such as what "book" and "reading" signify in antiquity, why literate cultures develop, or why literate cultures matter.

SITUATING LITERACIES

Rosalind Thomas's opening essay ("Writing, Reading, Public and Private 'Literacies': Functional Literacy and Democratic Literacy in Greece") serves as an introduction and overview of the inquiry. Her essay takes as its starting point the observation that we need to speak of a multitude of "literacies" that play out in different ways in different contexts. She focuses on the ways that different uses of reading and writing are embedded in specific institutions in classical Athens, such as the distinct uses of literacy in banking and other commercial activities, the use of names and lists in citizenship activities, and the particular needs and uses of reading and writing among Athenian officials. Her aim is to tease out specific literacy practices that can be associated with separate social, economic, and political groups.

Along somewhat similar lines, Greg Woolf in his essay ("Literacy or Literacies in Rome?") focuses on inscribed objects under the Roman empire, and what they tell us about the uses of literacy in specific social and commercial contexts; but also what such uses say more generally

---

in which written language is integral to the nature of participants' interactions and their interpretive processes and strategies"; Brian Street (1988, 61) of "literacy practices," referring thereby to "both behaviour and conceptualisations related to the use of reading and/or writing"; and R. D. Grillo (1989, 15) of "communicative practices," in which he includes "the social activities through which language or communication is produced," "the way in which these activities are embedded in institutions, settings or domains which in turn are implicated in other, wider, social, economic, political and cultural processes," and "the ideologies, which may be linguistic or other, which guide processes of communicative production." These are summarized and discussed further in Street 1993, 12–13; Johnson 2000.

about the "joined-up" relationship between private uses of writing and literacy practices as they are developed by the state.

Barbara Burrell ("Reading, Hearing, and Looking at Ephesos") examines more literally the situating of inscribed writing in its context, as she explores the complex relationship between inscriptions and public space in the great plaza in Ephesus known, in particular, for the Library of Celsus. Texts, architecture, and décor of public buildings are considered in tight, reflective relationship to one another; and she charts as well an evolving readers' response over time as new dedications and new structures are added to the plaza such that it ultimately becomes a hallmark of the intersection of Hellenic and Roman culture.

Simon Goldhill's essay ("The Anecdote: Exploring the Boundaries between Oral and Literate Performance in the Second Sophistic"), by contrast, focuses on literary culture. He explores the sudden popularity of "anecdote" in the Second Sophistic and how that speaks to the ways that literate practices can be situated in oral performance in distinct social settings. The anecdote as a written form is seen as emblematic of the literary culture of the time, a characteristic packaging of material that is best understood in relation to actual oral practices among the literary elite. As an originally oral form that can be written down, and once written down memorized and recirculated orally, the anecdote becomes a normative means whereby a bookish, highly educated elite compete in the symposium and other contexts.

Thomas Habinek ("Situating Literacy at Rome"), looking at the Roman evidence, also emphasizes the interdependence of oral and literate as he tries to situate writing in what he sees as the predominate oral culture at Rome. In a broad-ranging essay, he looks at writing (1) diachronically, sketching an account of the early use of writing for assertion of status and Roman identity; (2) synchronically, describing what is at stake socially in the mastery of literate practices; and (3) ontologically, examining the "embodied" character of writing, whereby writing is seen not as a representation of speech but as something material, and thus with its own opportunities but also its own strictures and constraints.

BOOKS AND TEXTS

The three essays that follow focus on working out the relation between book and text, a longstanding and productive area of inquiry in Classics. Florence Dupont ("The Corrupted Boy and the Crowned Poet or The Material Reality and the Symbolic Status of the Literary Book at Rome") explores in nuanced fashion the nature of the symbolic status and function of the bookroll. Her interest lies in the tension between the fragile physical book and the ways in which the text—the "fictive utterance" for which the book acts as vehicle—can escape that fragility. For Dupont, the literary book by Alexandrian times is in concept no more than a container, a copy of something composed in the past; and this conceit is one that Catullus and the Augustan poets use to advantage, as they strive to establish themselves among the ones who are *qui primus*, the "first" to create the foundational, "consecrated" text that is preserved so as to be imitated and commented on, thus sealing their status as canonical authors, worthy of the Greeks.

Joe Farrell ("The Impermanent Text in Catullus and Other Roman Poets") is likewise interested in the emphasis in the Roman poets on the fragility of the physical bookroll. For Farrell, too, this emphasis entails a paradox, but of a different sort. He wishes, rather, to focus on the curious way in which the poets, even while recognizing material texts as the vehicle for gaining a wide and lasting audience, repeatedly express anxieties over the corruptibility and "impermanence" of the physical text. The image of the bookroll is linked, in Catullus and others, with the ceremonial presentation copy, and thereby, he argues, attracts association with anxieties over public reception of the work and the alienation of the work from the poet's control; for these reasons, the image of the bookroll is inherently ambivalent, and the increasing emphasis on "song" and "singer" in the Augustan poets a fitting, if also strictly anachronistic, turn.

Holt N. Parker's essay ("Books and Reading Latin Poetry") also focuses on the image of the book and its reception, but from a different strategic angle. This essay is written as a challenge to the sometimes careless comfort with which Romanists speak of "orality" and "performance" when speaking of classical Latin poetry. Although acknowledging the importance of recitations, entertainments at dinner parties, and use of professional lectors, Parker advocates a return to the *communis opinio* of an earlier era, namely, that such communal activities were preparatory or complementary to "the unmarked case of private reading." In a wide-ranging analysis, he questions the notion that Augustan Rome was an "oral society" in any meaningful sense, and underscores the poets' own statements about their expectations for a readership divorced from performance, and extending in time and space.

INSTITUTIONS AND COMMUNITIES

Several essays examine the social institutions or communities in which literate practices may be said to be "embedded." George Houston ("Papyrological Evidence for Book Collections and Libraries in the Roman Empire") surveys the papyrological evidence for personal libraries and book collections under the empire. Along the way he has much of interest to say about the activity of book collecting and the people who did this collecting. General conclusions emerge, however tentatively, about the nature of book collecting and use over time: there seems a distinct tendency toward collections garnered together mostly in a limited time period, with specific goals (such as accumulation of philosophical texts), followed then by use, with only occasional augmentation or maintenance, over a succession of generations.

In similar fashion, Peter White ("Bookshops in the Literary Culture of Rome") surveys what we know of ancient bookshops and booksellers in Rome. Again, investigation of details leads to discovery. As an institution, bookshops had a commercial identity that differentiated them from other small shops, because they were concentrated in a small sector of the city, had distinctive conventions of sale, and fostered special types of literate sociability. The modes of engagement with texts are themselves of interest, because they privilege the use of a book as a commodity—there is value, for example, in being able to size up a book for its antiquity or authorship, without attention to substantive content. But the central role of niche players, such as *grammatici*, in bookshop society is yet more striking, a demonstration of how "hyper-literacy converted into social performance" facilitated social movement and allowed non-elite to gain entry to the highest literary circles in Rome, moving thereby into positions of considerable social authority.

Kristina Milnor ("Literary Literacy in Roman Pompeii: The Case of Vergil's *Aeneid*") looks at the placement and function of literary texts written as graffiti on the walls of Pompeii. Taking Vergil as a sample set, she explores "literary literacy" for the variety of ways it speaks to the interests and attitudes of the ancient writers and readers. Her theoretical stance is explicitly localizing, avoiding universal explanations in favor of a focus on the unique character of each text in its context, as she tries to tease out, in particular, the writers' view of the relationship between Vergil's text and their own act of inscribing. The specific interpretations lend themselves nonetheless to a general conclusion: the use of canonical literary texts seems to open the door to a special kind of discourse, by which the Vergilian tags function less as a cultural product and more as a means of cultural production ("less facts than acts and... aware of themselves as such").

William Johnson ("Constructing Elite Reading Communities in the High Empire") similarly insists on a focus on particulars and specific contexts as a means to work towards more general conclusions. Taking Gellius's *Attic Nights* as an illustrative example, he presents a methodology for exposing the sociology of certain types of reading events in the *Nights*, including both reading in groups and reading alone, as he explores the "nuts and bolts" of how a specific reading community makes use of texts. This then leads to conclusions about the ideological components of reading events. At basis, his theoretical angle is constructivist, that is, he sees the ancient literary text as a vehicle by which the ancient writer (in this case Gellius) and the ancient community ("Gellius's world," in his terms) not only construct "best practice" ways for using texts but also construct defined significances for different types of reading events.

BIBLIOGRAPHICAL ESSAY AND EPILOGUE

Shirley Werner's bibliographical essay and index ("Literacy Studies in Classics: The Last Twenty Years") give a convenient, quick overview of the last generation of literacy studies in Classics, followed by a topical index and the bibliography itself. Defining the boundaries of "literacy studies" can be at times a task more pragmatic than theoretical; the omission of books and articles on orality in the Homeric epics, for example, will surprise no one who pauses to think through the consequences. Chronological limits are arbitrary, but rooted in the conviction that William Harris's work (1989) marked a turning point in literacy studies in Classics. Harris's bibliography is extensive, even though it does not claim to be comprehensive, and we thus agreed to take the last year of Harris's active collecting, 1987, as an approximate boundary in Werner's bibliographical assemblage.

By way of coda to the collection, David Olson offers an essay ("Why Literacy Matters, Then and Now") with both a review of the last couple of generations of work in literacy as it impinges on Classics, and his own take on the relationship between the objectification of written text and linguistic features of quotation. Building on ideas developed in his earlier work, Olson sees writing as neither equivalent to speaking nor utterly divorced from speaking. Specifically, he sees written text to share with quoted expressions (whether written or spoken) the characteristic that the understanding of illocutionary force—how the utterance is intended to be taken—is something that needs to be added in order for the expression to be understood. The distance between expression and understanding leads, in the case of written texts, to a range of reading competencies, and Olson isolates the fully competent reader as one who is not only "critical" (grasping the author's attitude) but "reflective" (understanding both the author's attitude and the reader's own perception of that attitude). This trained ability to separate the attitude of an utterance from the propositional content has important cognitive consequences, since one can then use language to reflect on language in "pure thought" fashion; and this then helps account for why writing is so important in the development of modern thought and the growth of literate traditions.

As we try to step back from this sampling for the larger view, the first thing to notice is what is not there. No one in this group is speaking of, or in terms of, gross estimations of the literate population. Harris (1989) seems to have marked a turning point in that, however one evaluates his conclusions, he seems to have put paid to that line of inquiry. Similarly, there is an interesting, perhaps surprising, lack of emphasis on the long-central set of scholarly debates on the importance of "orality" and "performance" for ancient literacy;[6] and in any case the

---

6. Perhaps because study of orality and performance has become a subdiscipline itself, rather than a point of distinction in literacy studies.

nature of the questions raised along these lines (see Goldhill, Habinek, Parker) are a far remove from the likes of Eric Havelock and Walter Ong.

What we find instead is an intense interest in particulars. In what may be taken as a *leitmotiv* of our current generation of scholarship, local variation is found to trump generalizing tendencies. Where generalities are put forward, these tend to be tentative, with deep alertness to the probability of real, essential exceptions among individual examples. Even an overarching cognitive theory (Olson) is grounded in recognition of different types of readers, of real exceptions, that is, to the working theoretical principle. It is this urgent attention to local variation that led us to take over the plural of Thomas's essay, *Ancient Literacies*, for the title of this book.

There are other striking tendencies, again consistent with some dominant themes of our scholarly era. Texts, reading, and writing are seldom considered in and of themselves. Books are taken as symbolic materialities, having strong social valuation. Reading and writing are events, to be analyzed in broad and deep context, carrying social and cultural valuation, embedded in particular institutions or communities. Several themes repeat themselves, with variation, time and again: the sociology of literacy; the importance of deep contextualization; the necessity to see literacy as an integrative aspect within a larger sociocultural whole. It is this strong set of themes that conditioned our subtitle to this volume, *The Culture of Reading in Greece and Rome*.

As said at the outset, this volume speaks, intentionally, with disparate voices. And yet within the whole one can, I think, sense a strong movement away from earlier work in ancient literacy, work in our view gone stagnant, toward a rich field of new inquiries that frame books, readers, and reading more clearly and interestingly within study of the culture that produced them.

BIBLIOGRAPHY

Goody, J. 1977. *The Domestication of the Savage Mind*. Cambridge.
——— and I. Watt. 1963. "The Consequences of Literacy." *Comparative Studies in Society and History* 5: 304–45. Republished in *Literacy in Traditional Societies*, ed. J. Goody (Cambridge, 1968), 27–68.
Grillo, R. D. 1989. *Dominant Languages: Language and Hierarchy in Britain and France*. Cambridge.
Harris, William V. 1989. *Ancient Literacy*. Cambridge, Mass.
Havelock, Eric A. 1963. *Preface to Plato*. Cambridge.
———. 1986. *The Muse Learns to Write: Reflections on Orality and Literacy from Antiquity to the Present*. New Haven.
Heath, Shirley Brice. 1982. "What No Bedtime Story Means: Narrative Skills at Home and School." *Language in Society* 11: 49–76.
Humphrey, J. H., ed. 1991. *Literacy in the Roman World*. Journal of Roman Archaeology, Supplementary Series 3. Journal of Roman Archaeology 19. Ann Arbor.

Johnson, William A. 2000. "Towards a Sociology of Reading in Classical Antiquity." *AJPh* 121: 593–627.
——— . 2003. "Reading Cultures and Education." In Peter C. Patrikis, ed., *Reading
between the Lines: Perspectives on Foreign Language Literacy*. New Haven.
Olson, D. R. 1994. *The World on Paper: The Conceptual and Cognitive Implications
of Writing and Reading*. Cambridge.
Ong, Walter J. 1982. *Orality and Literacy: The Technologizing of the Word*. London
and New York.
Street, Brian V. 1984. *Literacy in Theory and Practice*. Cambridge.
——— . 1988. "Literacy Practices and Literacy Myths." In Roger Saljo, ed., *The
Written World: Studies in Literate Thought and Action*. Berlin.
——— , ed. 1993. *Cross-Cultural Approaches to Literacy*. Cambridge.
Thomas, Rosalind. 1992. *Literacy and Orality in Ancient Greece*. Cambridge.

Part I

SITUATING LITERACIES

2

Writing, Reading, Public and Private "Literacies"

Functional Literacy and Democratic Literacy in Greece

Rosalind Thomas

In 1997 a UNESCO conference was convened to help reformulate policy on illiteracy in the modern world. The final statement on the "Making of a Literate Society" stressed that "current research and practice has shown that in order to bring about cultural and social transformation, literacy must be seen as an activity embedded in social and cultural practice";[1] that literacy is not something that is simply "delivered" but something to be employed, and employed in diverse ways for activities which are meaningful in some way for individuals and communities; some campaigns failed because they were "carried out without proper regard to the language, knowledge and learning needs of the individuals and communities involved."[2]

For literacy to take root in a society, it has to have meaning, it needs to have obvious and valuable uses, to be "relevant" or empowering in some way; and it needs to be in a language that is actually used by the people learning to read. Both conference and volume embraced the idea of "multi-literacies," an awkward neologism but one that attempts to underline the fact that reading and writing tend to be learned and given meaning in a particular social, political, and cultural context. They tend to be learned and used in quite specific tasks, not necessarily transferred by their users across these boundaries. Some modern literacy campaigns had tended to assume that "literacy" meant Western literacy and literate habits in a Western language, though literacy in other languages for often quite different contexts and functions might exist (half-hidden to outside observers) along-side Western literacy. A multitude of literacies needs to be recognized alongside the ideals and habits of standard Western literacy and the potential

---

1. Olson and Torrance 2001, xii, taken from the draft policy statement.
2. Olson and Torrance 2001, xiii, also from the policy statement. Note esp. ch. 9 in that volume on Pulaar literacy in a Senegalese community.

advantages that that can bring. There is thus a fascinating tension between the obvious fact that writing makes certain activities possible or easier, and that different potentials are seized upon by different communities. In some, writing means bureaucracy, control, and oppression by the state, in others an enabling skill that frees an individual's creative potential.

This is the direction of research at the moment. Rather than see "literacy" as an independent, separable skill, researchers as well as teachers in the field tend to wish to see it more as an embedded activity—or to see a tension between the social context and the potentialities of writing. All this makes it both more interesting and more difficult to discern the social positioning of different kinds of literacies and their relation to individual empowerment or to power of any kind, such as community or bureaucratic empowerment.

The situation in the Greek world contributes to and enhances this more complex picture of "literacies" rather than literacy. Moreover, the insights of researchers able to study living societies can suggest further questions and potential interpretations, and therefore enrich the way we approach the Greek written evidence: this Greek evidence is often fragmentary and by definition it obscures the unwritten side of life, privileging the written. It might be tempting to look for a general, overall picture of Greek literacy and literate habits. Yet it is misleading to talk simply in these terms, or to talk of percentages of "literates," for that presupposes a certain definition of literacy, one that irons out variety and complexity. The percentages of "literates" in modern Britain changes depending on whether you define literacy as being able to read three words on a page, an Inland Revenue form, or a work of literature (we see ancient equivalents of these below). It thus seems more useful to talk of the uses writing is put to, and of different types of literacy. Pressing the insights of modern research into twentieth-century literate practices, some of it in turn influenced by research into the ancient world, I therefore wish to try further to isolate and define some specific literacies or subgenres of literacies from the Greek evidence. In particular, can we isolate for the Greek world at least some separate social, economic, or political groups with different practices, habits, and assumptions about writing? As part of this aim, this paper will discuss (a) various types of written text and the form of literacy they presuppose; (b) closely related, different levels of literacy and uses of literacy, and in the process, (c) consider the relation between social advancement and type of literacy. It will seek constantly to bear in mind the possibility of change in both— too much is said, still, about literacy in the ancient world as if evidence for one period tells us about the situation a hundred years later or earlier.[3]

---

3. Sickinger 1999, for instance, is puzzlingly unwilling to acknowledge the possibility and extent of change over the period of Athenian democratic politics. Pébarthe 2006 is important, appearing too late for full discussion here, but he also occasionally underplays large gaps of time and the likelihood of development over time.

I hope that this will circumvent the all-or-nothing approach to ancient literacy that sometimes occurs, and suggest a profitable way of thinking about the different forms of literacies around in a society where—as almost all would agree—various social, cultural, or political groups approached writing with differing purposes and attitudes. This is a rather different approach from William Harris's use of the term "craftsman's literacy" to denote the literacy of a skilled craftsman in early modern Europe.[4] It also attempts to be more specific than the vague all-embracing term functional literacy (see below) often used to denote literacy of a mundane kind.

First, two preliminary points: further discoveries both of informal and formal epigraphic writing mean that new and often surprising texts are bound to appear, and our discussion must be provisional. We may think, for instance, of the recent discovery of an extraordinary "archive" at Argos: in a small sanctuary annex a series of stone "chests" were found, of which four still contained "an estimated 120 to 150 inscribed bronze plaques," dating to second half of the fifth or early fourth century B.C. They seem to record sums of money either borrowed from, or deposited with, the goddess Athena by institutions or groups in the polis—the temple effectively performing the role of central bank.[5] Or the new laws and lead curse tablets appearing in Greek-speaking Sicily, the small but steady appearance of lead letters.[6] Second, it is an obvious point but one that needs constantly to be borne in mind, that our evidence for writing inevitably privileges the literate: written texts have some chance of preservation, and activities, hopes, prayers, rituals, that were not committed to writing disappear from sight. It is the combination both of written and of nonwritten activity that tells us about the place of writing in the totality of ancient experience.

As with most other practices in the Greek world, city-states had local specialisms in their use of writing. Even with the selective preservation of evidence, we can discern, for instance, that Camarina's inhabitants went in for extensive use of lead tablets for curses, as did those of Selinous.[7] Lead survives, it is true, yet even so, a local augmentation of this use of lead is

---

4. See W. Harris 1989, 8: "By craftsman's literacy, I mean not the literacy of an individual craftsman but the condition in which the majority, or a near-majority, of skilled craftsmen are literate, while women and unskilled laborers and peasants are mainly not, this being the situation which prevailed in most of the educationally more advanced regions of Europe and north America from the sixteenth to the eighteenth century"; cf. also p. 61.

5. See *JHS Archaeological Reports* 2003–4, pp. 19–20: texts being published by Prof. Kritsas.

6. Curses from Camarina and Selinous: Dubois 1989 *IGDS*, nos. 29–40 and pp. 124ff. Laws from Himera: Brugnone 1997; and from Selinous: Jameson, Jordan, Kotansky 1993. Note also the Mappa di Soleto: *Daily Telegraph* Nov. 18, 2005.

7. Selinous curses: mid-sixth century to end of fifth century, Dubois 1989 *IGDS* nos. 29–40; Camarina curses: c. 450 or later 5th century—and Dubois 1989 *IGDS* pp. 124ff. Contracts in lead seem to appear later.

visible in Athens, where curse tablets were adapted for the peculiar local need against opponents in the democracy's law courts. Athens produced inscriptions in stone on a grand scale, dwarfing other classical cities: to a large extent this must be linked to her democratic constitution, yet even so other democracies were not so extravagant in stone—Syracuse (were their decrees on bronze?), or Argos, which had a form of democracy in the fifth century, or Taras, which has left no public inscriptions at all.

We will look more closely at Athens, whose rich evidence allows us to discern a range of literate habits. What types of literacies, what different social contexts or political habits of literacy can we discern? Cribiore, for instance, has recently emphasized the importance of "signature literacy" in Greco-Roman Egypt.[8] What about Athens? And how are different literacies linked to the various social or political aspirations of her citizens?

Here "functional literacy" rears its head, and it will be a recurrent element in this paper. Yet the very term *functional literacy* seems increasingly inadequate. Though it is a term that we all (myself included) take refuge in to mean in a vague way "enough literacy to get by," that evades the question what exactly *is* enough literacy to get by, in what circumstances and for whom? Whether someone's literacy is adequate (functional) depends on the surrounding needs and uses of writing. In a modern Western society functional literacy—enough literacy to function adequately—requires a large range of skills and increasingly a basic computer literacy of the kind necessary (for instance) to access information, or to initiate applications. What is the line between just being able to manage, and being able to manipulate writing and written skills so well that someone can prosper? In ancient Athens, the line at which someone is seriously disadvantaged by poor writing skills can be drawn very low, but that does not mean that he was on an educational and political level with the elite. The educated elite, who overlapped considerably with the political leaders, had advanced literacy and cultural attainments that included *mousike*, music, literary knowledge, and literary composition. We therefore need to examine evidence for differing literacy skills alongside the surrounding social or political demands for writing.

We will concentrate on aspects of financially related literacy and democratic literacy, omitting more literary kinds of literacy, not least the increasing use of writing for composing speeches in the late fifth and fourth centuries. Starting with banking literacy, we will look at minimal citizen literacy ("name literacy") in Athens' early democracy; then the case of the merchant and the possibility of commercial literacy or list literacy; and finally return to the question of types of citizen literacies in Athens, considering both list literacy, this time in public inscriptions, and the literacy of the official. Some of these overlap, but I hope that this

---

8. Cribiore 2001. Pébarthe 2006 prefers to stress the extensive *use* of writing (in Athens), esp. ch. 2, minimizing social and professional distinctions.

makes possible a nuanced and flexible picture of several overlapping literacies, and illustrates the point that to examine "functional literacy" we need an ever-shifting, sliding scale of literate attainments.

BANKING

I start with banking because interesting evidence implies that banks in Athens of the fourth century (at least) had peculiar habits in their exploitation of the written word. At least this type of writing use needed explaining to the big democratic audience listening to [Demosthenes] 49, *Against Timotheus*, in such a way as to imply that it was quite unfamiliar to most Athenians. Probably dating to 362 B.C., the action was undertaken in order to recover money lent to the prominent politician Timotheus by Pasion, the famous slave-turned-banker and father of Apollodorus, the writer of the speech. Initially we are told that when Timotheus was in danger of a death sentence, Pasion lent him a large sum without security (οὔτε . . . ἐπ᾽ ἐνεχύρῳ) and without witnesses—for him to repay when he wished (49.2). Other large payments followed. But when Timotheus was back and in the political limelight again, he refused to pay unless forced by law, and Apollodorus needs in the speech to go through the list of moneys lent and the dates: "Let no one wonder that I know accurately," he continues. "For bankers are accustomed to write out memoranda (ὑπομνήματα γράφεσθαι) of the money they lend, and for what, and the payments a borrower makes (καὶ ὧν ἄν τις τιθῆται), in order that his receipts and his payments should be known for the accounts (*logismos*)" (49.5).

Apollodorus continues with a blow-by-blow account of dates of payment, names of the men who receive the money, the very precise sums passed over, and the reasons for the loan. Much revolves around these details. At chapter 43, Timotheus challenged him before the arbitrator to bring *ta grammata* from the bank, and demanded copies, sending someone to the bank to examine the records and make copies. At chapter 59f. we return again to the peculiar methods of the banks, carefully explained to the audience—which turn out to be simply that the debt is noted at the precise time money is paid out.

There are remarks elsewhere about banking practice—special pleading perhaps—such as the accusation made in Isocrates that Pasion reneged on the agreement with his Black Sea client to keep his money in Athens secret (Isocrates XVII, esp. 7–10, 19–20).[9] Alongside these fascinating

---

9. There is less here on the workings of the bank: Isoc. XVII 7 for agreement; 7–10 speaker in cahoots with banker to pretend he has no money in the bank; 19–20, further (written) agreement to keep things under wraps. Cf. also [Dem] LII, for example, 4, 6, 24, 27. Pébarthe 2006, 103–9 approaches this from a rather different angle.

hints that banks might be enjoined to keep matters hidden as well as keeping records, we are dealing with a species of literate practices, a kind of literate environment, which is special to the bank and this realm of professional activity. It is not unique, for in other areas people made lists, probably agreements. But the whole amounts to a genre of literacy, and it needs explaining to the audience. The jury is subject to a barrage of other rhetorical arguments about court practice and life in general that are not presented in the speeches as unfamiliar. But banking literacy is presented as operating under special conventions, a subgenre of literacy, a fact we may obscure by talking simply of "functional literacy" or "literacy" in general.

THE CITIZEN: NAME LITERACY

Let us take a step back to a precise category of citizen: what kind of writing needs did a citizen have who was not politically prominent but went to the Assembly, even the jury-courts? Was there a democratic minimum in the mid-fifth century (ostracism?) and perhaps a different minimum in the restored democracy of the fourth century?

Ostracism was the only time a citizen had to write to perform his basic democratic functions in the fifth century: a name on a sherd to vote someone into exile. Much discussed of course, it seems to assume every citizen could write a name (as Vanderpool [1973] believed). The mass of ostraka found in the Agora, and then the further 8,500 found in the Kerameikos, dating to the 470s, offer unusually rich direct evidence for such writing citizens. Attention focuses on the mass of 190 ostraka conveniently found together naming Themistokles and written out neatly in fourteen identifiable hands.[10] Were they prepared for convenience or vote-rigging, for wavering voters who might be swayed by having a prepared vote thrust into their hands, or simply for illiterates? We do not really know, but the anecdote about Aristeides and the illiterate voter (Plut. *Aristeides* 7.7–8) shows that the Greeks were well aware of the possibility— and the irony—of an illiterate having to get someone, even the man he hated, to help write the name. Further careful research on joining ostraka shows several ostraka from the same pot written out in the same hand both against the same politician, and against different politicians: as Brenne points out from the Kerameikos ostraka, the implication is that they were prepared in advance, probably by a "scribe," but not necessarily as part of a concerted effort against the one candidate.[11] Other ostraka with the name painted before firing imply preprepared names. Phillips has also recently canvassed the idea, building on a suggestion of Vanderpool's, that more scribal hands are visible in the ostraka, especially when the pottery is of a

---

10. Broneer 1938.
11. See Brenne 1994, esp. 16–20 on the Kerameikos ostraka.

high grade.[12] But again, are these simply helpful scribes? There is still considerable ambiguity, but the evidence seems to be growing that many more sherds were preprepared, for whatever reason, to be given ready-made to the voters. (These ambiguities are perhaps reminiscent of the recent phenomenon of the mass e-mail protest.)

The varying quality and especially poor quality of many sherds is in itself revealing, a point Phillips has emphasized. Though scratching on pottery is not that easy, it is clear that some writers found the process far harder than others, though the material was the same for all. The published ostraka do show dramatic variation in the quality and confidence of handwriting, spelling, omitted letters, badly formed or back-to-front letters. Of the examples in Phillips' article, figures 11 and 12, which read *ΚΛΕΟΦΝ* (with omega omitted) are such examples, and figure 1 (*Τεισανδρος Ισαγορο*) has writing that is wavering boustrophedon but with the sigmas the wrong way round. Mabel Lang's edition of the Agora ostraka (1990) gives many more examples in which essential vowels or consonants are missing.[13] The following are some examples, all from *Ostraka*, written with lowercase letters in the modern convention, without the missing letters added in:

> *Ostraka* no. 89 (Lang 1990, fig. 4): *Βουταλιανα ho μαρθονιος Βυταλιονα*—with *Βυταλιονα* crossed out and alpha missing in "marathonios." (See figure 2.1.)

Figure 2.1 Athenian Agora XXV, *Ostraka*, no. 89.

no.1061 (Lang 1990, fig. 27): *Χονθιπος Αριφρονος* (for *Χσ{α}νθιπος Αριφρονος*). Note omitted alpha; also single pi and rho.

no.1097 (Lang 1990, fig. 29): *Ματισηνς hιφοχρατος*—with four-bar sigma the wrong way round.[14] (See figure 2.2.)

---

12. Phillips 1990.

13. Lang 1990: omitted letters listed pp. 16–17. Note also Lang 1982 on writing and spelling.

14. For an alternative reading of the first word, see Lang's edition, ad loc.

Figure 2.2 Athenian Agora XXV, *Ostraka*, no.1097.

no.768 (Lang 1990, fig. 23): Θμισθοε Φρεαριος—an attempt at
Θεμισθοκλες Φρεαριος. Spindly, uncertain writing. (See figure 2.3.)

Figure 2.3 Athenian Agora XXV, *Ostraka*, no.768.

no.762 (Lang 1990, fig. 23): Θεμσθοκλες Φρεαριος—written retrograde,
but the sigmas still face forward; iota missing in Themistokles' name.
Far less impressive on the sherd than the modern text implies. (See
figure 2.4.)

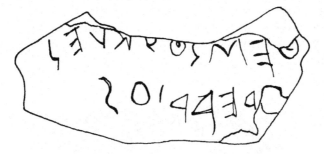

Figure 2.4 Athenian Agora XXV, *Ostraka*, no.762.

no.198 (Lang 1990, fig. 9): *hιπποκρατ*[ ] *Αλμεονιδος*. K omitted in Alkmeonidos. The sherd reads from left to right, then upside down as the sherd is
turned around. The sigma at the end of the patronymic and the form
(*alkmeonidos*) is wrong (writer thinking of Alkmeonos?).[15] (See figure 2.5.)

Figure 2.5 Athenian Agora XXV, *Ostraka*, no.198.

By contrast, no. 1065 (Lang 1990, fig. 27), the much quoted couplet
against Xanthippos ("This ostrakon says Xanthippos son of Ariphron
does most wrong of the accursed leaders") is an elegiac couplet, and the
small, neat handwriting is that of a confident writer well used to forming
letters and constructing written texts. (See figure 2.6.)

These extreme examples seem to be attempts by men quite unaccustomed to writing the simplest message, and the fact that the grammar is
occasionally awry—some give the patronymic in the nominative, not the

15. See Lang 1990, no. 198 for discussion.

correct genitive[16]—suggests the same. In a period such as this in which a standard orthography is not developed, let alone taught comprehensively, we might partly be seeing individuals' representations of what they

Figure 2.6 Athenian Agora XXV, *Ostraka*, no.1065.

thought they heard. As Lang and Threatte have investigated, quite a few of the "misspellings" or deviations may be indications of actual pronunciation.[17] But many must simply be labeled "graphic error," to use the polite term of Threatte, and he points out that it is in general in the private texts, as opposed to the big public inscriptions, that one finds the greatest variety of spelling. A further fascinating suggestion about missing letters has been made by Wachter, who examined more fully the possible patterns in missing letters as a way of analyzing when a lapse is a mistake or reflects pronunciation.[18] He finds that the omitted vowel after a particular consonant is very often the vowel occurring after that consonant in the Greek name for the consonant (e.g., ε is often omitted after *theta*), thus a form of "abbreviated writing" and a common "semi-mistake" generated by the fact of learning the alphabet from the letter names (thus *theta* is thought to equal the sound *th* + *e*). This helps explain the omission of ε in Themistokles' name, yet the other examples cited above do not fit this pattern—numbers 89, 1061, 1097, 768, and 762 are

16. Lang 1990, 17 has found 15 cases of this. See further Lang 1990 for lists of omitted syllables, extra letters and so forth, and below for Wachter 1991.
17. Threatte 1980, 395–407—"graphic error" at p. 398; Lang 1982, 1990.
18. Wachter 1991 (who was unable to use the Agora publication).

still simply wrong. In other words, we find carelessness and semi-literacy, revealing, one may imagine, real unfamiliarity with letters.

The political implications are interesting: quite a few of those exercising their democratic rights found writing hard and unfamiliar in the early fifth century, when most of these ostraka originate (480s and 470s). They can barely write. Unlike the modern damaged ballot papers, this does not seem to matter. We are dealing with the early days of democracy, it is true, so perhaps this is not surprising, but we may remember that those who cast their sherd in an ostracism were, by definition, the active citizens. This probably changed as the democracy gathered steam and more and more documents were produced. But at the basic level of participation by listening to Assembly debates, even listening in the jury-courts, this very poor, basic acquaintance with writing was adequate. The juror needed to recognize his name on his *pinakion*, when these are introduced in the fourth century (perhaps the first and most basic type of reading, joyfully practiced, to judge from children today!). "Functional literacy," then, in the sense of enough literacy to function in the democratic process, could have been extremely basic in the 480s, even 460s.

But in a way, that is not the point, or only half the point. The Sausage-seller in the *Knights* is jokingly declared appropriate as *prostates tou demou* because he has no education (*mousike*) except his letters and those barely at all; it would be still better if he had none (*Knights* 188–93). Ostracism only indicates a bare minimum, and that not fully attained. Someone who could barely read or write would have to listen to others reading out proposed laws—not debarred completely, that is absolutely true, but less able to use his initiative in certain areas as the democracy developed in the late fifth and fourth centuries: less able, for instance, to check lists of suspect Athenians as more lists were put up on the Acropolis (we return to lists below), unable to read details on mortgage stones without taking someone along, unable to draft a proposal without help. Gossip, oral communication, heralds, and announcements were all essential; much could and was conveyed by these methods, but the "slow writer," to use the term of Roman Egypt, could hardly be equal to a member of the educated elite in their ability to master every aspect of the political system, especially as the elite could probably manipulate written texts with relative ease as well as compose eloquent speeches. The poor writers of the 480s and 470s ostraka will have become increasingly left behind as the democracy developed its more complex use of decrees and written record (and indeed the elite will have had to differentiate itself as this low-level literacy became more common). By the 380s, say, one hundred years later, there were simply more written records around, and the illiterate therefore probably excluded from more.

As for the juror in the fourth century, a member of a central element of the democracy, his identity as juror was now established in writing with the *pinakia*, small plaques of bronze with the juror's name and a letter or symbol, many of which have been found in the Agora. There were also coin-shaped bronze tokens.[19] The fourth-century juror thus had his written badge, as it were. The courts were an environment in which written texts were used—written testimonies, laws, and decrees were read out—but it seems unlikely that jurors were required to read anything themselves as part of their duties. Two amusing remarks occur in fourth-century speeches. In Apollodorus' *Against Makartetos*, [Dem] 43.18, the speaker goes into the family relationships of Hagnias' family necessary for this complex inheritance case of the mid-fourth century. He says he was intending to write the genealogy out on a board, but those farther away would be at a disadvantage, therefore word of mouth would be fairer, and he proceeds with the spoken word. This is both tantalizing and suspicious, the only hint, so far as I know, that a written text might be set up in the courts to be read: Apollodorus leaves out some significant items of genealogy, and given the complexity of this case, he may have benefited from a certain lack of clarity! The balance between rhetoric and fact here is unclear. He can flatter the jurors while advancing his own case.

In the second, dating to 330, Aeschines reminisces with nostalgia about jurors of the old days of the restored democracy (III, *Against Ctesiphon* 192): they often told the clerk, he claims, to read the laws and the motion again (as appropriate for cases of illegal proposals). Nowadays, though, he continues, jurors treat the clerk reading τὸ παράνομον (statement of illegality) as if they were hearing an incantation of something of no concern to them (ὥσπερ ἐπῳδὴν ἢ ἀλλότριόν τι πρᾶγμα) and thinking of something quite different. Even here jurors in the present and idealized past are envisaged as listening carefully or listening carelessly (cf. Cleon, in Thuc. III 38), and careful attention to a written text is manifested by asking the clerk—in this idealizing picture—to read out the text again.

Athenian jurors, then, could function as jurors with only the most basic literacy skills, for example, recognition of names. Some would have a more complex level of literacy, some less. By the late fifth and early fourth centuries, they were partaking of a democratic system with valued written law, produced numerous inscriptions for public display, and they heard the written texts read aloud:[20] one would expect from this that some of these other written practices would become more embedded for more of the active citizen body than they had been in the 480s. At the very least they were partaking, if aurally, in the manifestations of a political system that included these written texts. As the Agora graffiti seem to confirm (*Athenian Agora* vol. XXI), this would mean that more citizens were reading and writing in relatively simple ways. The "democratic minimum" for an Athenian citizen in courts or assembly, however, could have remained the ability to read or write little more than names.

19. See Boegehold 1995; also Boegehold 1960.
20. This seems to become more common as the fourth century progresses: see Thomas 1989, ch. 1, esp. 60ff., 83ff.

COMMERCIAL LITERACY? THE CASE OF THE MERCHANT

"Commercial literacy" is another case in point. It is increasingly tempting to suspect a subgenre of writing use and written techniques that can best be called commercial literacy. Because the Greeks had adapted the alphabet from the Phoenicians who were traversing, settling, and trading across the Mediterranean, we would expect the current uses of writing—which included some form of commercial use—to be adopted along with the alphabet itself. Even more telling are the lead letters increasingly coming to light from the Black Sea settlements and Southern France, and dating considerably later to c. 500 and after. They indicate a sphere of commercial activity and writing that hitherto had to be deduced from the archaeological and literary evidence, for traders did not seem to leave direct written evidence themselves. Wilson has examined this growing body of evidence to argue that some traders at least were literate enough to write letters, and perhaps even write contracts, in the late archaic period.[21] Van Berchem has used fascinating Near Eastern evidence to supplement the Greek and press the possibility that written contracts were adopted by Greeks from the Phoenicians, and by implication even earlier than our explicit evidence.[22]

Lead letters are rather hard to date, and much still remains obscure. The Berezan lead letter is dated to c. 500 B.C., as is the Emporion letter.[23] Moreover, it is clear that the letters belong to a world of traders, buyers, and sellers, on the edge of the Greek world, but unclear that this is a specifically commercial literacy. Most of these letters seem to be crisis letters, letters about circumstances and problems arising within a group engaged in various commercial activities, and there is much about seizure of goods or people. The Berezan letter was sent by Achillodorus to his son to say that he has been seized and so have the goods he was carrying; the Olbia letter is about seizure of goods.[24] But we may compare the fourth-century Attic letter from a slave in dire circumstances in a foundry—the letter recently published by Jordan, with the convincing argument that it is from a slave (but written *by* a slave too?) by Edward Harris.[25] A crisis letter is not uniquely commercial, clearly, and we should also note that the creation of a continuous prose letter with a degree of narration is more complicated than the banker's list. Yet the surroundings and circumstances of their activities may have made written messages between traders rather necessary—the long distances and times to cross them, suspicion of intermediaries, perhaps even language barriers that might distort messages. Antiphon in *Herodes*, V 53, gives a "persuasive definition" of the written message as opposed to

21. Wilson 1997–8.
22. Van Berchem 1991.
23. Bravo 1974 for the publication of the Berezan letter; for the Emporion letter, Sanmartí and Santiago 1987 and 1988.
24. See Wilson 1997–8, 38.
25. E. Harris 2004.

the messenger: written messages, he says, are used only when it is necessary to conceal the message from the bearer, or else for a very long message. This is an attempt at special pleading, but it must have sounded plausible. In crisis and suspicious circumstances, the letter's ability to cross distances and time, and transcend messengers, would be very handy.

One letter contains peremptory instructions from a business man or maritime trader: the Emporion letter, found in Northeast Spain (see note 23 above), has an impatient tone of command surrounding the transactions and its contents. It is tempting to see this as a particular subgenre of writing for commercial activity—the written instructions from one person to another.

We may also wonder about the use of writing for receipts, loans, or contracts, all of which need to be carefully distinguished from a letter that is simply from a trader. The seven Corcyrean lead tablets of the early fifth century possibly record maritime loans.[26] A puzzling lead tablet mentioning guarantors, conflict, and the attempted sale of an ox was found in Sicilian Gela (c. 480–450 B.C.).[27] And as van Berchem and Wilson argue, we have evidence of a surprisingly sophisticated use of writing, the written contract, in one of these lead documents, the Pech-Maho tablet (so far this is the only lead document that can probably count as a contract, though see below). The Pech-Maho tablet is particularly revealing, because it involves an agreement between people of different origins, as is clear from the names.[28] Witnesses are invoked, a guarantee (ἐγγυητήριον) and an *arrabon*, a form of pledge that is handed over at a named location.

> "So-and-so (*perhaps* Kyprios) bought a boat [from the] Emporitans. He also bought [three (?) more] (*i.e., from elsewhere*). He passed over to me a half share at the price of 2 1/2 *hektai* (each). I paid 2 1/2 *hektai* in cash and two days later personally gave a guarantee (ἐγγυητήριον). The former (*i.e., the money*) he received on the river. The pledge (*arrabon*) I handed over where the boats are moored. Witness(es): Basigerros and Bleruas and Golo.biur and Sedegon; these (were) witnesses when I handed over the pledge. But when I paid the money, the 2 1/2 *hektai*, .auaras, Nalb. .n." (Chadwick's 1990 translation of revised text)

It is very tempting to wonder if the written contract developed early among traders on the edges (both geographical and ideological) of the Greek world precisely because of the mobility of the trader, the fluidity of business, the absence of a secure and permanent base, and of security in land; and above all, the need to make agreements with strangers Greek and

26. See Calligas 1971, Wilson 1997–8.

27. Dubois, *IGDS* no.134, for text and commentary; *LSAG*, 2nd ed., Gela, Q (p. 461): note the past tenses.

28. For the Pech-Maho tablet: Lejeune and Pouilloux 1988; Lejeune, Pouilloux and Solier 1988; revised text and interpretation, Chadwick 1990. Cf. also Rodríguez Somolinos 1996. Faria 2007, 170 reads Eleruas, an Iberian name, for Bleruas.

non-Greek. Writing might seem to offer an extra, unchangeable proof of agreement in which witnesses might be thought not totally trustworthy.[29]

But even in the Pech-Maho document it is not writing alone that gives the contract its security. There are three forms of guarantee mentioned, including witnesses: apparently every attempt is made to buttress and secure the transaction. It is also interesting that the "contract," if that is what it really is, is couched in the form of a narrative of past actions, unlike later Greek contracts. This is fascinating because it implies that the conventions and technicalities of what a transaction entailed might have developed slowly and in quite different form in different places.[30] The important aim was for trust and security to be established: the written word was molded to that aim in whatever form seemed appropriate.

If we compare the Athenian situation, the written contract between individuals appears relatively late in our evidence, first in a speech delivered in 390 B.C. No one would imagine that this was therefore the first example for the Athenians, and Millett has pointed out that because oratory provides us with our main evidence for contracts in Athens, we are therefore confined to speeches of the late fifth and fourth centuries.[31] It may be that the written contract for private individuals was at least known in the fifth century, as Millett and Stroud suggest, but it seems too easy to assume that fully formed written contracts were ubiquitous throughout the fifth century and everywhere in an "all-or-nothing" model. These practices will develop: the Pech-Maho tablet is couched in narrative form; Athens itself continued to use the very primitive *horoi* as mortgage stones. Besides, trust in writing cannot be simply assumed to override trust in witnesses. As Antiphon puts it in his first speech, a dying man anxious to name his murderer will call witnesses from his friends and relatives and tell them who the murderer was; failing that he will write and use slaves as witnesses (I 28–30). Writing might be called upon when personal trust was lacking.

We may also need to consider more emphatically a distinction between contracts made between private individuals acting independently in far corners of the Mediterranean, and contracts made between an Athenian citizen and the polis in which legal safeguards and procedures were available.[32] A contract's usefulness depends on the degree of trust and the nature of the guarantees or penalties. It is possible that in Athens the state led the way in the use of written agreements—for instance, in tax leases—and Athenian officials were sufficiently confident of the machinery of the polis and had faith in its power of redress. It is difficult at the moment to reach further certainty: it would be unwise to posit a universal system.

29. Wilson 1997–8 esp. good on this, esp. pp. 48ff.: following Millett 1991, written contract developed first in Athens in banking.

30. We may tentatively wonder if it is even a contract in the usual later sense or some hybrid.

31. Millett 1991, 259–60 n. 27; Stroud 1998, 46–7. See now Pébarthe 2006, 94–103.

32. *Pace* Stroud 1998 and van Berchem 1991.

A further element in the Pech-Maho tablet suggests an even greater distance between its world and that of Athens. The *arrabon* in the document, the object of pledge, is a Semitic loanword, and we may naturally guess that this form of pledge was learned from the Phoenicians along with the word. This suggests that areas with extensive Greek-Phoenician interaction might well have developed the business contract in a form quite different from that visible in later Athenian evidence (Greeks in certain places may have been more open than others to the Near Eastern form of contract).[33] It may be unwise to class the Pech-Maho document simply and straightforwardly with the Athenian documents as "written contracts," ignoring the differing compulsions and habits of thought. As Stroud emphasized in discussing the Athenian Grain-Tax law, Athenian contracts used the future indicative (and imperative);[34] the Pech-Maho document gives an account of a series of guarantees in the past tense. It may well be, with more evidence, that the earliest "written contracts" turn out to be more like written accounts of pledges and witnessing already made.

Be that as it may, we can see then that from the point of view of functionality, the trader had more use of literacy as written contracts became more normal, more acceptable; and these letters indicate more command of continuous writing than do simple lists. As in late Ptolemaic Egypt, even a "slow writer" might be at an advantage compared to the illiterate, but *only if* his habits and business could be progressed by making written records or contracts. Signatures, after all, were not yet required in classical Greece.

LIST LITERACY: "FUNCTIONAL LITERACY" AND THE COMMERCIAL LIST

Similarly with the list. Who used lists of sums of money, lists of articles, goods, lists of people? We should surely expect that by the late fifth century commercial habits of literacy—buying, selling, counting receipts—may have begun to make use of the list, and more so in the next century.[35] It is extremely difficult at present to suggest periods or stages of development, but the ostrakon list from Athens of the mid fourth century, found in the Kerameikos, may be used as a possible example of what I mean (see figure 2.7).[36]

33. Van Berchem is rather vague on this (his main thesis is that the Greeks learned to use written contracts from the Phoenicians).

34. Stroud 1998, 45–6.

35. Goody 1977 argued that the list was a quintessentially literate creation; this seems exaggerated because the earliest Greek poetry has great liking for lists, albeit in continuous verse.

36. Johnston 1985 for *ed. pr.*

Figure 2.7 Kerameikos ostrakon inv. 2242, DAI.

Here we see a double list with names and numerals in the Attic form, and some extra entries squashed in, on the inner side of a base of a wide plate. It dates to around the mid-fourth century. The text is unique: "there is no close or even vague parallel in any medium" as the editor Alan Johnston says (1985, 296), though individual elements occur elsewhere. Each column consists of lists of names, mostly abbreviated, then a neat colon [:], then a number, another colon, then another number, usually half of the first (for example, 28:14). The names mostly look like slaves' names and the likely scenario suggested by Johnston is that this is a list of slaves, days worked, and the payment for the use of these slaves; or alternatively, the payment made by the slaves to their master from their income, which seems (on this interpretation) to be half an obol per day.[37] A month is given, and archon, which suggests that the list refers to activities in this month.

37. Johnston 1985, 305–6.

Though it is unique, and extremely puzzling to us, it is not actually a complicated text. Although we need careful decipherment, it must have been obvious for the writer. The writing is confident and neat, the layout pretty clear. There is a system here, even a system of punctuation, and the added notation of "E" (the editor suggests this signaled a completed transaction). It is well organized and looks like a text written by someone who knows what he is doing (is it, for instance, his own system of punctuation?). As for its date, c. 350 B.C., it is much later than the ostraka we looked at earlier, and we cannot read this system back 100 years earlier or even more. But this may be a glimpse into the mundane "functional" literacy of a commercial kind in Athens of the high classical period; this may be a rare example of a type of list literacy that was used and usable in a commercial establishment of slaves, or leasing of slaves. It is exceptionally functional and easily legible: no continuous prose, no words running on without word division, no problem working out names and numbers.[38] One can perhaps wonder if much of the day-to-day literacy—if it existed— of traders, bankers, potters, small-manufacturing establishments, looked somewhat like this by the mid-fourth century.

LISTS AND LEGIBILITY IN THE PUBLIC SPHERE: THE CITIZEN

This brings us to the list in the public sphere and back to Athens. I would like to emphasize the list as a separate type of writing and writing use that is relevant to public documents as well as private, and "list literacy" as an interesting subcategory of literacy use. Lists are interesting for our purposes for several reasons. They have been said to be a quite separate entity from oral communication (Goody [1977] argued that the list was a quintessentially literate artifact, not a naturally occurring phenomenon in an entirely oral society, though early Greek poetry is not entirely unable to give lists of names). Lists on stone are very common indeed in classical Athens. They are usually—but not always—set out in list form, names one below another rather than continuously along the same line, and therefore they are exceptionally clear and easy to read (see, for instance, the First Stele from the Athenian Tribute Lists, figure 2.8b, and the fragment from the list of 440/439, figure 2.8a). In the Greek writing system the list is unusual in not having words running on continuously: there would be no difficulty separating words. If Saenger is right about the connection of silent reading with separated words,[39] lists

---

38. It is interesting, as Threatte points out (1980, 74ff., esp. 82) that punctuation and interpuncts were apparently seen as especially useful for setting off numerals even in public texts, which usually avoided them.

39. Saenger 1997.

Figure 2.8a Fragment of IG i³ 272.

lie in an interesting category, for lists *do* separate the words. Lists on stone and whitened boards form an intriguing subgroup of inscriptions that are important for any discussion of the extent to which the big public inscriptions were widely read.

Some publicly displayed lists were certainly widely consulted by Athenians because they are referred to, some repeatedly, in Athenian lawsuits. These include the list of public benefactors who murdered Phrynichus and helped overturn the oligarchy mentioned in Lysias 13, *Against Agoratus*,

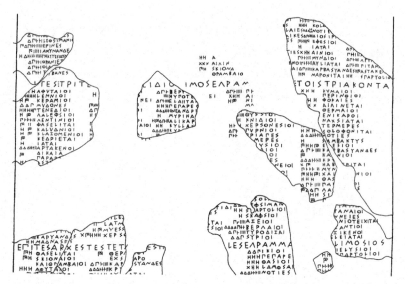

Figure 2.8b ATL vol. I, plate IV, First Stele (obverse), List 3.

70–72, the list of public debtors, much checked,[40] the list of men owing equipment to the city,[41] the list of traitors read out by Lycurgus,[42] the list of Plataians granted citizenship set up on stone on the Acropolis near the "Temple of the Goddess" ([Dem] 59.105). Isocrates mentions other lists put up on *sanides* by 353 (*Antid.* 237), and there was a much disputed wooden list of the cavalry under the Thirty (Lys. XVI 5–7).

Andocides' *On the Mysteries* quoted the decree of Patrocleides of 405 B.C., which arranged for an erasure of names from incriminating documents in the panic of 405 (Andoc. I 77–79). It is not clear how many of these were on publicly displayed lists on stone or wood, but even so, the number of lists available seems impressive—some perhaps mainly for officials, others for public consumption. The decree mentions the list of deserters, those tried for homicide or guilty of massacre or attempted tyranny, or those listed as one of the Four Hundred. Chapter 77 also mentions those "listed" or "registered" (περὶ τῶν ἐγγεγραμμένων) with the Praktores or with the Treasurers of Athena and other Deities or with the Basileus, those *atimoi* for debt or guilty of administration. All these people listed are to have an amnesty, and their names erased, except those categories described (I 78) as "all those listed on *stelai*" (πλὴν ὁπόσα ἐν στήλαις γέγραπται) as deserters,

40. [Dem.] 58.14–16, 48, 51; [Dem.] 25 (*Ag. Aristogeiton*) 69–70, referring to it as "the *sanis* with the goddess."

41. Dem. 47 (*Ag. Evergos*) 22, a stele.

42. Lycurgus, *Leocr.* I, 117–119.

those tried for homicide by the various homicide courts and convicted, those guilty of massacre or attempted tyranny. It is those guilty of particularly heinous crimes who are, not surprisingly, the ones exempt from the generous and forgiving impetus of the decree. These documents are various in form, but several do seem to be lists, some public, exemplary memorials, some held by officials.

Many other lists were made, including lists of people, lists of property, lists of tribute contributions: some seem very deliberately designed to be easily legible. The remarkable list of those rewarded for supporting democracy at the time of the Thirty gives a broadly spaced list of names and occupations, superbly legible and clearly laid out (IG ii^2 10, now Rhodes-Osborne no. 4). There were the lists of the war dead, the lists of the sixtieth of the tribute paid to Athena, the list of allies and newly calculated payments made in 425, the lists of the confiscated property of the Hermokopidai inventoried elegantly and at length under the name of each malefactor.[43] The First Fruits decree of 434 B.C. orders that a wooden tablet (*pinakion*) should be made listing the weights of grain dedicated as First Fruits of the Greek states and arranges for copies to be set up in the Eleusinion and Bouleuterion, and a list of dedicators is to be inscribed onto the votive offerings made out of the financial proceeds (IG i^3 78, ML 73, lines 26ff., 43–4; by contrast, the fourth-century law about First Fruits, IG ii^2 140, is much less preoccupied with making lists). The Callias decree(s) (IG i^3 52, ML 58) arranged for lists to be put on *stelai* of the treasures being handed over, and future practice (lines 21ff.; though these would probably not be laid out in list form). Payers and defaulters of tribute were to be listed according to the Cleinias decree of 448/7 (IG i^3 34, ML 46), and so on. Many, though not all of these, were to be displayed in public.

Were there, then, different levels of "democratic literacy" and different types of "democratic document"? We may wonder whether these carefully arranged lists on stone and wood were deliberately intended to be especially legible, more easily deciphered than most other documents and inscriptions.[44] We may also suspect that they were indeed more readily read than most other inscriptions. This impinges on the wider question of the role of public inscriptions, which we cannot pursue here, the main questions concerning (a) whether pre-Hellenistic inscriptions constitute the "authoritative" text, either theoretically or *de facto*; (b) their relation to archive texts; (c) the combination of symbolic value and value as a living item of reference; and (d) whether they were widely read (and by whom)?[45] People do go up and search for a name on one of the

43. See Pritchett 1953–6 for detailed treatment.
44. This develops a suggestion made in Thomas 1989, 66; lists also discussed in Thomas 1994, 41–2, à propos the power of the state.
45. See esp. Rhodes 2001; Sickinger 1999; Boffo 1995; Thomas 1989 ch. 1 and 1992 ch. 7; Stroud 1998, 46ff.—all intertwined with the question of how the archives were used.

exemplary lists on the Acropolis like the wooden tablet of state debtors (see examples above, pp. 31–2). Searching a single name on a simple list in list form would be far easier than reading a continuous text. Can we also imagine people seeking the name of a relative on the lists of war dead (as with the Vietnam War Memorial in Washington)? Descendants of the Plataians granted citizenship may have showed the ancestor's name on the Acropolis stele, perhaps what is envisaged in [Dem.] 59.105. Leodamas denied that he was ever on the stele of traitors (ὅτι ἦν στηλίτης), and that the name had been erased by the Thirty (Arist. *Rhet.* II 1400a 32–6). People looked at these lists.

The layout of some of these stone lists implies a deliberate decision to produce them in list form, one item below another (see fragment from the Attic stelai, IG i³ 422, figure 2.9). The alternative, which one also sees, is to run together the list of items (e.g., in an inventory) as a continuous text in dense, continuous lines. It is tempting to think that those in proper list form—more expensive in stone, one assumes—were designed to be more easily read by those who were less educated, not skilled readers. The "Athenian Tribute Lists" listing the sixtieth of the tribute paid on to Athena as a tithe ally by ally are superbly set out so that every name is clear: was it hoped that the tribute-payers (or their envoys) would like to be able to check their communal entry easily on the list for Athena?—at least if it was not on the top of the two-meter-high inscription (see figures 2.8a, 2.8b). Such lists throw into relief the many other inscriptions that are devoted to lists or accounts that are not written in list form at all: inventories of temple treasures tend to be written out continuously in full lines.[46] The first of the *poletai* ("sellers") inscriptions listing the confiscated property of those convicted of sacrilege in 415 was laid out in list form, very clear to the eye (figure 2.9), yet the long, impressive *poletai* inscriptions of the fourth century are dense, continuous prose.[47] Perhaps we see here the difference between a big, exemplary public text inviting people to read it and check the malefactors, and documents that were more the technical documents of a board of officials, which they need to publish on stone to show that they had done their job. Why was the list form abandoned in these *poletai* inscriptions? Or were the "Attic Stelai" the expensive exception, meant as the widely visible memorial of crime and punishment? There at least seem to be different levels of legibility for public "democratic documents." The punitive power of the list probably plays a large part here.

46. Cf. (e.g.) IG ii² 120, of 362/1, a list in continuous prose form of objects in the Chalkotheke (or IG i³ 123). Cf. D. Harris's interesting discussion (1994) of the inventory lists of the Parthenon and public accountability; and D. Harris 1995.

47. Helpfully collected in Langdon 1991; Pritchett 1953–6 for the "Attic stelai."

Figure 2.9 Fragment of IG i³ 422, col. III.

Dedications and dedicatory inscriptions are also interesting in this connection, that of public accessibility. As Keesling has recently pointed out, the inscriptions on the Athenian Acropolis dedications are very well spaced, very clear, and are unjustly ignored in discussion about literacy and access to inscriptions.[48] In particular, she notes the prominence of the name of the dedicator in such inscriptions, usually first in the line, the name of the sculptor in a separate line, and the continuing presence of punctuation even as it drops out of fifth-century Athenian decrees. The clarity and simplicity of these dedications is certainly very striking—as are many victory dedications elsewhere, one might add—and we can imagine

48. Keesling 2003.

that someone with the mere rudiments of letters might be able to figure out the name. We may be back again to "name literacy," the recognition of names—your own name if not someone else's—in inscriptions, an easy kind of literacy that was more widespread, and known to be more wide-spread, than the ability to read a long continuous text.

Perhaps, then, we can isolate name literacy and list literacy as impor-tant types of literacy to which some inscriptions deliberately catered: we can perhaps see in Athens an attempt to make certain inscriptions more accessible than others, easier to read, with more space and separ-ation of words—particularly dedications and the big public exemplary lists. After all, there seems no trace of the ideal of universal education in the modern sense at Athens, despite the democracy (law-court speeches talk of the institutions of democracy as educational).[49] This still leaves the enigma of the great stoichedon inscriptions of Classical Athens: very clear, very beautiful, very expensive, and laid out in a grid plan that gives little visual help with divisions of words, phrases, clauses, or sentence structure, though the clarity of the letters is superb.[50] What we can at least see in the list inscriptions, as well as the dedications, is that there *could* be an attention to layout of the words on the stone that made it very much easier for citizens or noncitizens to figure out the words. It is not hard to see why dedicators should wish to publicize the name of the dedicator, and we can speculate about why certain lists get the clarity of layout they do.

The increase in inscriptions recording Athenian decrees of the people will have at least provided a powerful image of Athenian democracy on stone for the illiterate or barely literate, and anyone attending the Assem-bly could hear them read out. Athenian public inscriptions do seem to follow a democratic ideal of publicity,[51] though as with even modern laws on freedom of information, theory and practice could diverge spectacu-larly. Athenians at the low end of the educational scale may have been encouraged to read by the increasing number and presence of such exem-plary lists in the midst of their city. "Name literacy" and "list literacy" would probably be the simplest forms of literacy. The "functionality" of someone's literacy is related to the society in which it operates, thus in Ptolemaic Egypt many could sign their name but little more, because signatures were often necessary in everyday life. As the democracy be-came more dependent on written records, name literacy and list literacy would be ever less impressive or useful by themselves.

49. Plato's view that schooling was necessary for boys and girls in *Laws* III was radical; equally radical, Phaleas of Chalcedon favored equal education, Arist. *Pol.* II, 1266b31–35.

50. See, for instance, the Methone decrees, photographed clearly in *ATL*, vol. II, plate 1.

51. See Hedrick's very useful survey of epigraphic evidence, 1999 (and note Teisamenos' decree, And. I 83–4); Hedrick 2000.

ATHENIAN OFFICIALS AND THE CHANGING DEMOCRACY: THE LITERACY OF THE OFFICIAL

Many other spheres in the Athenian democracy involved writing, of course, written records and a degree of literacy, and the degree to which this was so changed in the course of its long history. The literacy of officials is another type of literacy we need to examine: by this I mean the type of literacy needed by Athenians active enough to hold some form of office, whether chosen by lot from the top three property classes like members of the *boule* (council), the archons, the various officials in the Athenian empire and elsewhere, or those chosen by election like the generals. As before, we have two related questions, the nature of the written texts made and the types of literate habits that are assumed and then encouraged by the very existence of these records. We need constantly to bear in mind that the Athenians must have developed and altered their use of writing over this period. The radical democracy established from the 460s continued to evolve with further changes on its restoration in 403. Its hallmarks included the wide distribution of power and responsibility, relying on the use of the lot, and the one-year-long tenure of office, which means a relatively large number of Athenians must have participated actively. Because the system in 350 B.C. had evolved considerably since c. 450 B.C., the needs of functional literacy will also have changed.

It is essential to differentiate groups of Athenians and types of literacy partly because some discussions of the Athenian use of written documents tend implicitly to merge all Athenians together as well as different periods.[52] It may also be a way toward resolving the dilemma hinted at above that many inscriptions in the late fifth and fourth century imply that written records were increasingly being made, while at the same time the speeches actually delivered in the democratic organs of government give the impression that the Athenian *demos* mostly got its information orally,[53] and many inscriptions were disregarded or not referred to far less than scholars might expect. Inscriptions were carefully and expensively made but they are often referred to as having exemplary and symbolic value—not a negligible value—as well as for their factual or executive content.[54] One interesting possibility is that new circumstances may have generated the need for new uses of writing or more records, and these new uses may then have generated expectations for more, or embedded new ideas about writing.

52. Sickinger 1999 does not entirely do this, but seems at times to be moving in this direction: see note 54 below, and Thomas 2003; and remarks in Thomas 1992, 133–4.
53. For example, Dem. 47.44 refers for proof of an earlier *boule*'s decision to those who were in the *boule* that year, and anyone sitting beside them, not to written records.
54. See Thomas 1989, 49ff.; also Rhodes 2001, with provisos; and the Introduction to Rhodes and Osborne 2003, p. xiii.

For instance, the developing Athenian empire seems to have generated administration and some documents, possibly rather simple, to achieve better tribute collection. When a decree mentions the special making of records, this may either be because these special records are a new type of record now being introduced for this purpose, or because the decree simply mentions every stage of a normal and everyday procedure. The former seems more plausible. An interesting case study, the Cleinias decree (IG i^3 34) of 448/7 B.C. tried to reduce corruption in the tribute collection:[55] as the decree describes, *symbola* or identification seals are agreed with each city to prevent fraud; the amount each ally pays is written down on a tablet (*grammateion*) in the city itself and sealed with the *symbolon*. The document is read out in the Athenian Boule when the money is actually delivered—the pile of money supposedly tallying with the *grammateion*. Then the Hellenotamiai (officials responsible for the Athenian tribute) are to read out to the Assembly those cities that paid the full tribute (lines 18–22). Receipts for tribute go to the cities (ἀντιγραφσομένος), and the same officials try to obtain the missing payments. Certain officials, probably the Hellenotamiai, record the tribute on a whitened *pinakion*, listing city by city (lines 43–45). There are also lists of tribute defaulters on the *pinakion* in the *boule*, and in the last fragmentary section the *boule* may be to "publish" these (ἐπιδεῖχσαι) to the people (lines 58–60).

What, then, does this mean in practice for the literate habits of the *boule*? A lot of people are making lists. The 500 *bouleutai* as a body are responsible for receiving and keeping various lists of tribute payers and defaulters, and along with Hellenotamiai they supervise the new system of *symbola*. Can we deduce more? The decree devotes much detail to spelling out the system of *symbola*, and how the *grammateion* containing the full sum owed is brought into the *boule* and read out with the money: it sounds as if this is new and relatively unfamiliar. Members of the *boule* are essential in this attempt to tighten up by creating more documentation. Much could be read out by clerks and slaves,[56] but *bouleutai* may have needed enough working "list literacy" to deal with these documents, which sound as if they consisted mainly of lists of names with numbers alongside. Some officials (clerks) have to make and write out the lists. This sounds primarily like list literacy for both clerks and *bouleutai*.

It is instructive to try to imagine what other literate practices are involved in other similar decrees. We hear elsewhere of records being made of debts of tribute, and we can get a snapshot of energetic list making in connection with the tribute.[57] The Kleonymos decree of 426/5 (IG i^3 68)

---

55. Cf. also important article by Pébarthe 1999 (which seems, however, to underplay the possible novelty here); developed in Pébarthe 2006.

56. Rhodes 1972, 136–42 discusses secretaries, clerks, and public slaves connected with the *boule*.

57. See Thomas 1994, 47: including Methone's owed tribute, IG i^3 61, lines 9, 14–15; Neapolis is to give the generals the money owed and the generals are to record

arranges for Hellenotamiai to make lists on a *sanis* of tribute defaulters and to put the list up in front of some public building (18ff.). The Coinage Decree toward the end of the current text says that the *epistatai* in the mint are to erect a public notice (on a stele) listing what seems to be the amount of money of foreign origin received.[58] The Kallias decrees of 434/3 B.C. (IG i[3] 52) involve the sums owed by the state to the gods: more lists are to go up. The *logistai* are to calculate "what is owing to the gods precisely." The Prytaneis with the *boule* are to repay the money, and they are to cancel records of debts as they are repaid, "after seeking both the *pinakia* and *grammateia* and wherever other claims are written down." Priests, who would tend to come from the elite, and other officials are to produce the written records. The money returning to the gods is counted out on the Acropolis before the (500) *bouleutai*—quite a sight, one imagines. Treasurers of the Other Gods (selected by lot from the top two classes) take the money and make records on a stele: money coming in, and money still owed to the gods, by individual deity.

It is obvious here that a *degree* of literacy is involved for all concerned: Prytaneis of the *boule*, the *boule* generally, Treasurers, and priests. Records of debts have to be sought, deciphered, added together and computed, and with repayment, more lists and records made, both of payments and of remaining debts. There is a lot of listing. Anyone completely unable to read or write would be out of place, one supposes, though one could imagine an illiterate *boule* member sitting quietly at the back and listening carefully; the ambitious and active would have to have a basic ability, for documents are being sought, new documents made, all to ensure financial probity. The Secretary of the Boule had an enormous role, as did the public slaves in the archives. What does this kind of literacy look like? It seems again to be very list-oriented: preambles must be understood, then the list of debts incurred or payments, with numerals. A degree of numeracy is important, and that with the awkward Attic numeral system which used the alphabet both visually and aurally (*thus* $\Delta = \delta\acute{\epsilon}\kappa\alpha = 10$; *but* $\Delta\Delta = \epsilon\check{\iota}\kappa o\sigma\iota = 20$). An Athenian incapable of even this kind of literate activity could presumably only remain the most mundane observer. To be able to risk being chosen by lot as envoy to the allies or treasurer by the late fifth century, an Athenian citizen must have had some facility with this type of literacy and numeracy—even if there were clerks and slaves to help.

It is this, perhaps, that we are looking for as functional democratic literacy in the mid-to-late fifth century—and part of the point stressed here is that there is a sliding functionality as the polis extended its use of written texts. A facility with making lists of tribute defaulters has little to do with the ability to compose elegant sentences and write them down,

the sums, IG i[3] 101, lines 25–30, with other records of moneys paid to be made and handed to the boule, lines 39–40.

58. The new fragment from Aphytis does not alter this: SEG LI (2001), 55.

still less in composing and recording verse (i.e., *mousike*). But it was the type of literacy needed by an Athenian active enough in the democratic machinery to enter the *boule* or take up a position of responsibility as an official, a magistrate (for which *thetes* were excluded). I would tentatively call it "officials' literacy," a literacy rather different from the ability to write a name for an ostracism.

As the democracy developed, so did its processes and the Boule itself took on more duties. The democracy in the fourth century is quite distinct from that of the fifth, as is well known.[59] It is therefore inconceivable that one should consider literacy practices implied in the fourth-century democracy as automatically similar or parallel to those of the fifth.[60] Even within the fourth-century democracy, a period, after all, of several decades, one would expect a certain degree of change, as I think we can see. The Boule alone acquired more responsibility and the democracy in general moved more power to committees and subgroups from the Assembly, whereas the Assembly had commonly voted over even tiny details in the first flush of radical democracy in the fifth century. Various groups of officials like the *poletai* ("sellers") leave extensive stone records of their activities. One assumes that these were helped by secretaries, but it is hard to avoid the impression that a fully active member of any of these groups must have been literate enough to deal with accounts, instructions, and decrees where necessary (drafting, checking, etc.), though always with the proviso that secretaries were there to read things out as one of their main tasks. In a way, these activities may be more of the same in literacy terms, but one would guess that as such documents became more extensive, the *boule* members themselves would gradually become more familiar and experienced, if they were not already (we may perhaps compare Brian Stock's concept of "textual community" [1983] but for a context of democratic Athenian officialdom). The degree of "functional" familiarity with written texts will now necessary have changed.

The remarkable Grain Tax Law of 374/3 should be mentioned here. Stroud's publication of this newly discovered inscription points out the relatively complicated set of activities the Ten men are expected to complete to sell the grain coming in from the Grain Tax (which is a tax in kind), and to ensure that the Athenians have grain.[61] These men are chosen by election from the Assembly which underlines the democratic importance of the law and its provisions. Stroud suggests that the law was

59. For example, Hansen 1991, Rhodes 1972; note also Eder 1995.
60. A problem with Sickinger's book (1999) is that although he patiently shows many cases in which the orator will have had to delve into the archives to find a decree, or get someone to do so, he reads back on a priori grounds a mass of document-making and keeping from the fourth to the fifth century, and from the fifth to the sixth in a way which seems to sidestep the great political, cultural, and social changes occurring over the periods in question. See Thomas 2003.
61. Stroud 1998.

meant to be discussed and consulted extensively on the stone, though this might be necessary only for a relatively elite group of grain dealers rather than the mass of the Athenian citizenry.[62] It is also interesting that the Ten men are to be elected rather than chosen by lot, a sign of their importance,[63] and one supects that was also meant instinctively as a check against getting by lot someone incompetent and incapable of carrying out these important functions for the city. These functions would indeed involve a degree of what we called above commercial literacy, not to mention considerable know-how about the workings of the grain market. We seem to return here to the commercial literacy and list literacy that we have been finding relatively important.

There is more research to be done on the relative appearance and accessibility of the big public inscriptions, particularly in the fourth century.[64] There are cases in which relevant inscriptions are clearly not read by all who would benefit, as well as the opposite; and cases in which inscriptions are clearly meant to have powerful paradigmatic and symbolic force, whether they are carefully read in detail or not (see note 54 above, p. 37). What we may be seeing in these developments of the democracy's administration is a growing reliance on written documents,[65] which meant that even semi-literates or illiterates would be surrounded by lists and accounts if they were active enough to be on the *boule*, or its sub-committees. I have called this tentatively "officials' literacy." There would have been a sliding scale of growing competence in this as the democracy developed in which merely adequate ability in the 470s was outclassed in the next fifty years, and so on.

This is quite different from the skills needed to compose and write out a speech in good Attic. It is also at a distance from the level of education of the elite envisaged by Plato when he assumed that the "*achoreutos*," the man unskilled in singing in a chorus, was uneducated. In some ways these men with "officials' literacy" would have had a certain power through their supervision even of tribute lists, perhaps all the more annoying if it were perceived as a new (and inferior) kind of literacy by the traditionally educated elite. These were different types of literate practices, and there was a gulf between them. Each was linked to a series of attitudes to writing and its uses. The demagogues parodied in the *Knights* tended to possess one kind of literacy, whereas the ideal of the civilized gentleman who traditionally provided the leaders embraced another.

---

62. Stroud 1998, 47; cf. Thomas 1992, 138–9 on central importance of the publicly displayed laws and decrees.

63. Stroud 1998 passim, esp. 70–1.

64. See (for example) Liddel 2003, and judicious remarks in Rhodes 2001.

65. As argued in Thomas 1989, ch. 1, seeing a significant sea change by the mid-fourth century; Pébarthe 2006 would put this earlier but accepts some escalation in the latter half of the fourth century.

CONCLUSION: LITERACY AND LITERACIES IN ATHENS

To return to the problem of functional literacy, what it means at any point, and how it might relate to individual aspirations and ambitions: the really ambitious in fifth- or indeed fourth-century Athens needed far more than list literacy or any level of education that left him without the ability to compose speeches and speak eloquently off the cuff. But we can see at a less elevated level a range of different literacy practices, of which we have isolated banking literacy, list literacy, name literacy, and officials' literacy. A similar range of literacies can be recognized nowadays from text messaging, for example, to the literacy of Parliamentary clerks, or legal secretaries. As the democracy developed in Athens, there was increasingly a need for anyone active as an official, magistrate, or *boule* member to be familiar, or at least not uncomfortable, with writing down the basic decisions and accounts of the democracy, with keeping or reading accounts. The relation to the spoken word changed. By their very layout, the written records we have discussed show degrees of accessibility and legibility, some exceptionally well presented in list form, others not. This perhaps reflects a recognition that some Athenians were more likely to read certain inscriptions than others.

Between the faltering or illiterate ostraka of the 480s and 470s and the more sophisticated record keeping of the mid-to-late fourth-century democracy, the very active democratic citizen (and I stress "active") will have had to change. What worked as "functional literacy" in the democracy of the 470s was not so functional two generations later, let alone three or four. It is interesting how much Athenian document keeping boils down to lists and I have suggested list literacy as a genre of literacy very relevant to ancient Greece. But the elite stayed well ahead: literary education developed in turn; the truly ambitious needed to learn the skills of oratory. The juror whose literacy extended only to recognizing his *pinakion* will have become outclassed. The upwardly mobile needed to learn still more in a kind of cultural (and political?) inflation. In the fourth century, ever more elaborated forms of verbal skill, written or not, were the supreme educational goal.

BIBLIOGRAPHY

Boegehold, A. 1960. "Aristotle's *Athenaion Politeia* 65, 2: The 'Official Token.'" *Hesperia* 29: 393–401.

———. et al. 1995. *The Athenian Agora: Results of Excavations Conducted by the American School of Classical Studies.* Vol. 28: *The Lawcourts at Athens: Sites, Buildings, Equipment, Procedure, and Testimonia.* Princeton.

Boffo, Laura. 1995. "Ancora una volta sugli 'archivi' nel mondo greco: conservazione e 'pubblicazione' epigraphica." *Athenaeum* 83: 91–130.

Bravo, B. 1974. "Une lettre sur plomb de Berezan: colonisation et modes de contact dans le Pont." *DHA* 1: 110–87.

Brenne, Stefan. 1994. "Ostraka and the Process of Ostrakophoria." In W. D. E. Coulson et al., eds., *The Archaeology of Athens and Attica under the Democracy:*

Proceedings of an International Conference Celebrating 2500 Years since the Birth of Democracy in Greece, Held at the American School of Classical Studies at Athens, December 4–6, 1992, 13–24. Oxbow Monographs 37. Oxford.

Broneer, O. 1938. "Excavations on the North Slope of the Acropolis, 1937." *Hesperia* 7: 161–263.

Brugnone, A. 1997. "Legge di Himera sulla ridistribuzione della terra." In *Società e cultura nella Sicilia antica*, 262–305. Special number of *La Parola del Passato* 52. Naples.

Calligas, P. 1971. "An Inscribed Lead Plaque from Korkyra." *ABSA* 66: 79–94.

Chadwick, J. 1990. "The Pech-Maho Lead." *ZPE* 82: 161–6.

Cribiore, R. 2001. *Gymnastics of the Mind: Greek Education in Hellenistic and Roman Egypt*. Princeton.

Davies, J. K. 2003. "Greek Archives: From Record to Monument." In M. Brosius, ed., *Ancient Archives and Archival Traditions: Concepts of Record-Keeping in the Ancient World*, 323–43. Oxford Studies in Ancient Documents. Oxford.

——. 2005. "The Origins of the Inscribed Greek Stela." In P. Bienkowski, C. Mee, and E. Slater, eds., *Writing and Ancient Near Eastern Society: Papers in Honour of Alan R. Millard*, 283–300. Journal for the Study of the Old Testament, Library of Hebrew Bible/Old Testament Studies 426. New York.

Dubois, Laurent. 1989. *Inscriptions grecques dialectales de Sicile: contribution à l'étude du vocabulaire grec colonial*. [*IDGS*] Collection de l'École française de Rome 119. Rome.

Eder, Walter, ed. 1995. *Die athenische Demokratie im 4. Jahrhundert v. Chr.* Stuttgart.

Faria, A. Marques de. 2007, "Crónica de onomástica paleo-hispânica (13)," *Rivista Portuguesa de arqueologia* 10: 161–187.

Goody, Jack. 1977. *The Domestication of the Savage Mind*. Cambridge.

Hansen, Mogens H. 1991. *The Athenian Democracy in the Age of Demosthenes: Structures, Principles and Ideology*. Trans. by J. A. Crook. The Ancient World. Oxford.

Harris, Diane. 1994. "Freedom of Information and Accountability: The Inventory Lists of the Parthenon." In R. Osborne and S. Hornblower, eds., *Ritual, Finance, Politics. Athenian Democratic Accounts Presented to David Lewis*, 213–25. Oxford.

——. 1995. *The Treasures of the Parthenon and Erechtheion*. Oxford Monographs on Classical Archaeology. Oxford.

Harris, Edward M. 2004. "Notes on a Lead Letter from the Athenian Agora." *HSPh* 102: 157–70.

Harris, William V. 1989. *Ancient Literacy*. Cambridge, MA.

Hedrick, Charles W. 1999. "Democracy and the Athenian Epigraphical Habit." *Hesperia* 68: 387–439.

——. 2000. "Epigraphic Writing and the Democratic Restoration of 307." In P. Flensted-Jensen, T. H. Nielsen, and L. Rubinstein, eds., *Polis and Politics: Studies in Ancient Greek History Presented to Mogens Herman Hansen on his Sixtieth Birthday, August 20, 2000*, 327–35. Copenhagen.

Jameson, Michael H., David R. Jordan, and Roy D. Kotansky. 1993. *A 'Lex Sacra' from Selinous*. Greek, Roman, and Byzantine Monographs 11. Durham, N.C.

Johnston, A. 1985. "A Fourth Century Graffito from the Kerameikos." *MDAI(A)* 100: 293–307.

Jordan, David R. 2000. "A Personal Letter Found in the Athenian Agora."
    Hesperia 69: 91–103.
Jordan, David R. 2003. "A Letter from the Banker Pasion." In Jordan and Traill
    2003: 23–39 (Appendix A: Corpus of Personal Letters on Lead).
—— and John Traill, eds. 2003. *Lettered Attica: A Day of Attic Epigraphy:
    Proceedings of the Athens Symposium, 8 March 2000.* Publications of the
    Canadian Archaeological Institute of Athens 3. Athens.
Keesling, C. 2003. "Rereading the Acropolis Dedications." In Jordan and Traill
    2003: 41–54.
Lang, Mabel. 1976. *The Athenian Agora: Results of the Excavations Conducted by
    the American School of Classical Studies at Athens.* Vol. 21: *Graffiti and Dipinti.*
    Princeton.
——. 1982. "Writing and Spelling on Ostraka." In *Studies in Attic Epigraphy,
    History and Topography Presented to Eugene Vanderpool by Members of the
    American School of Classical Studies,* 75–87. Hesperia Supplement 19. Prince-
    ton.
——. 1990. *The Athenian Agora: Results of the Excavations Conducted by the
    American School of Classical Studies at Athens.* Vol. 25: *Ostraka.* Princeton.
Langdon, Merle. 1991. "Poletai Records." In G. V. Lalonde, M. K. Langdon, and
    M. B. Walbank, eds., *The Athenian Agora: Results of the Excavations Conducted
    by the American School of Classical Studies at Athens.* Vol. 19: *Inscriptions:
    Horoi, Poletai Records, Leases of Public Lands.* Princeton.
Lawall, Mark Lewis. 2000. "Graffiti, Wine Selling, and the Reuse of Amphoras in
    the Athenian Agora, ca. 430 to 400 B.C." *Hesperia* 69: 3–90.
Lawton, Carol L. 1995. *Attic Document Reliefs: Art and Politics in Ancient Athens.*
    Oxford Monographs on Classical Archaeology. Oxford.
Lejeune, Michel and Jean Pouilloux. 1988. "Une transaction commerciale ioni-
    enne au Ve s. av. J.-C. à Pech-Maho." *CRAI* 1988: 526–36.
M. Lejeune, J. Pouilloux, and Y. Solier. 1988. "Étrusque et ionien archaïques sur un
    plomb de Pech Maho (Aude)," *Revue archéologique de Narbonnaise* 21: 19–59.
Liddel, Peter. 2003. "The Places of Publication of Athenian State Decrees from
    the 5th Century BC to the 3rd Century AD." *ZPE* 143: 79–93.
Millett, Paul. 1991. *Lending and Borrowing in Ancient Athens.* Cambridge.
Morgan, Teresa J. 1999. "Literate Education in Classical Athens." *CQ* 49: 46–61.
Olson, David R. and Nancy Torrance, eds. 2001. *The Making of Literate Societies.*
    Malden, Mass.
Pébarthe, Christophe. 1999. "Fiscalité, empire athénien et écriture: retour sur les
    causes de la guerre du Péloponnèse." *ZPE* 129: 47–76.
——. 2006. *Cité, démocratie et écriture: histoire de l'alphabétisation d'Athènes à
    l'époque classique.* Culture et cité 3. Paris.
Phillips, David J. 1990. "Observations on Some Ostraka from the Athenian
    Agora." *ZPE* 83: 123–48.
de Polignac, François. 2005. "Usages de l'écriture dans les sanctuaires du
    haut archaïsme." In V. Dasen and M. Piérart, eds., Ἰδίᾳ καὶ δημοσίᾳ. *Les cadres
    « privés » et « publics » de la religion grecque antique: actes du IXe colloque du
    Centre International d'Étude de la Religion Grecque Antique (CIERGA), tenu à
    Fribourg du 8 au 10 septembre 2003,* 13–25. Kernos, Supplément 15. Liège.
Pritchett, W. K. 1953–6. "The Attic Stelai." Pts. 1 and 2. *Hesperia* 22 (1953):
    225–99; 25 (1956): 178–317.
Rhodes, P. J. 1972. *The Athenian Boule.* Oxford.

——. 2001. "Public Documents in the Greek States: Archives and Inscriptions." Pts. 1 and 2. *G&R* 48: 33–44; 136–53.

—— and Robin Osborne, eds. 2003. *Greek Historical Inscriptions: 404–323 BC.* Oxford.

Rodríguez Somolinos, Helena. 1996. "The Commercial Transaction of the Pech-Maho Lead: A New Interpretation." *ZPE* 111: 74–8.

Saenger, Paul. 1997. *Space between Words: The Origins of Silent Reading.* Figurae: Reading Medieval Culture. Stanford.

Sanmartí, E., and Rosa A. Santiago. 1987. "Une lettre grecque sur plomb trouvée à Emporion (Fouilles 1985)." *ZPE* 68: 119–27.

——. 1988. "Notes additionnelles sur la lettre sur plomb d'Emporion." *ZPE* 72: 100–2.

Sickinger, James P. 1999. *Public Records and Archives in Classical Athens.* Studies in the History of Greece and Rome. Chapel Hill.

Stock, Brian. 1983. *The Implications of Literacy: Written Language and Models of Interpretation in the Eleventh and Twelfth Centuries.* Princeton.

Stroud, R. S. 1998. *The Athenian Grain-Tax Law of 374/3 B.C.* Hesperia Supplement 29. Princeton.

Thomas, Rosalind. 1989. *Oral Tradition and Written Record in Classical Athens.* Cambridge Studies in Oral and Literate Culture 18. Cambridge.

——. 1992. *Literacy and Orality in Ancient Greece.* Key Themes in Ancient History. Cambridge.

——. 1994. "Literacy and the City-State in Archaic and Classical Greece." In A. Bowman and G. Woolf, eds., *Literacy and Power in the Ancient World*, 33–50. Cambridge.

——. 2003. *JHS* 123: 230–1. Review of Sickinger 1999.

Threatte, L. 1980–96. *The Grammar of Attic Inscriptions.* 2 vols. Berlin.

van Berchem, D. 1991. "Commerce et écriture: l'exemple de Délos à l'époque hellénistique." *MH* 48: 129–45.

Vanderpool, E. 1973. "Ostracism at Athens." *Lectures in Memory of Louise Taft Semple: Second Series, 1966–1970*, 215–70. Cincinnati.

Wachter, Rudolf. 1991. "Abbreviated Writing." *Kadmos* 30: 49–80.

Wilson, Jean-Paul. 1997–8. "The 'Illiterate Trader'?" *BICS* 42: 29–56.

3

Literacy or Literacies in Rome?

Greg Woolf

A great deal is now agreed about Roman uses of writing. It is certain that relatively few individuals possessed that broad set of skills in creating and using texts that today we term full literacy. It is also clear that a far greater proportion of the population of the Roman empire could make use of texts than was the case in most ancient societies.[1] That the Roman world was once awash with documents is also clear, even if hardly any have survived. Papyri from interior Egypt and other arid areas of the Roman Near East; waterlogged writing tablets from Vindolanda and other military sites; ritual inscriptions on stone and on lead from all over the empire; the vast number of brick stamps, potters' marks, and other epigraphy on *instrumentum domesticum*; graffiti on *ostraka* and standing structures: all substantiate the impression given by a mass of literary and legal sources, and by the abundant textual relics of the Vesuvian cities. Writing was in widespread use throughout the empire. Texts were produced, stored, and referred to in vast numbers. The precious remains of genuine documents—contracts, wills, *vadimonia*, and the like—together with monumental epigraphy, show that writing was also accorded a certain authority per se, not unlike the authority that written documents possess in our own societies.[2] We can go further. Writing articulated the complex economic and administrative systems on which the empire, its cities, and their inhabitants depended. The Roman empire, and its societies, could not have functioned without it.

My aim in this chapter is to ask some questions about how this situation came about. I want in particular to raise questions about how different uses of writing were related to each other in the Roman world. Should we envisage a range of literacies—literary, commercial, religious, military, and so on—differentiated by the social location of those who

---

1. Harris 1989 firmly established the limitations of literacy. The studies gathered in Humphrey 1991 and Bowman and Woolf 1994 (largely in response to Harris) did not challenge this central contention. For other ancient literacies see the studies gathered in Schousboe and Larsen 1989 and Gledhill, Bender, and Larsen 1988.
2. Meyer 2004 for a recent exploration of this.

possessed them, by the methods and institutions through which they were imparted and acquired, by the languages and kinds of text they dealt in, and the uses to which they were put? This idea has been a powerful way of making sense of the diversity of the uses of writing in some societies,[3] but I shall argue that it has relatively limited applicability to the case of Rome. In attempting to understand how the Roman empire came to be such a literate society I shall focus in particular on how writing practices associated with the state were related to private uses of texts. I shall argue that Roman literacies were much more closely connected— much more joined up—than in many other premodern societies.

1. EMPIRE AND THE EXPANSION OF ROMAN LITERACY

How precisely was Roman imperialism related to the growth and elaboration of literacy?

Comparison is less helpful than it might be. It is generally true to say that the use of writing systems of some sort or another seems always to have been an essential component of state formation.[4] No early states seem to have managed without writing technology of some kind or other, and writing is rare in societies without the state. Administrative uses are in some cases the first uses of writing attested. Writing has been seen by some as a way of coordinating increasingly complex societies, and by others as a common tool of domination. When early states became empires, we might expect that their writing systems, too, might become more elaborate.

But when individual cases are considered, what is really striking is the variety of ways in which writing was employed by ancient regimes. Take scribal literacy, for example. It seems that in many societies those who were richest, most powerful, and most respected were not in fact those with the greatest command of texts. This was probably the norm in the Bronze Age states of the Old World from western Asia to China, and it has recurred on several occasions since. The European Middle Ages are often cited in this context, and a good case may now be made for the dependence of modern elites on e-clerisies expert in handling the now essential communicative media and the arcane languages in which modern software is written. Most often in antiquity a range of uses of writing were combined. The emperors of Achaemenid Persia made use of a (low status) scribal class who composed tablets and letters in Elamite and

3. Street 1984 is a classic demonstration of this technique, as are many of the papers he gathered in Street 1993.
4. For establishing all this, the works of Goody (especially 1968 and 1986) and of Ong (e.g., 1982), together with the observations of Lévi-Strauss 1955, 260–70, remain fundamental.

Aramaic on clay tablets and papyrus. The Iranian elite themselves were not particularly defined by their facility with letters.[5] The Persians also made other uses of writing. The Old Persian script was actually created during the construction of the monumental inscriptions at Behistun that proclaim a religious, ethnic, and imperial ideology in the language spoken by the new rulers of the Near East (alongside versions in Babylonian and Elamite). The combination of large-scale palace literacy with royal edicts on papyrus and a monumental epigraphy strongly suggests that writing was already accorded an innate authority per se. The Persians ruled too over many peoples who placed slightly different authority in texts: the priestly families of Egypt continued to monopolize knowledge of hiero-glyphic writing; the Greek cities of Persian Asia Minor played a key role in the creation of prose literatures on medicine, history, and philosophy; and the Jews of Babylonia and the rebuilt city of Jerusalem alike were placing increased emphasis on the scriptures written in exile. No simple model of the relationship between empire and writing can adequately capture this complexity.

At Rome too, imperial expansion coincides—to put it in neutral terms—with an enormous increase in the complexity of writing practices. However measured, they reached a high watermark during a long second century C.E. This is true of monumental epigraphy and mundane texts.[6] (The generation of literary works is less easy to quantify, but a good case may be made, too, for an expansion of this kind of writing in the same period on the basis of surviving Greek literature at least, especially if medical texts are included.) Because few of these uses can be traced back to the origins of Roman literacy in the seventh century B.C.E.,[7] we may deduce that the growth of the Roman state was accompanied—another neutral expression—by an *elaboration* as well as an expansion of writing and reading practices.

None of this proves, however, that Roman political expansion was associated with changes in writing practices in a straightforward way. From the Republic, there was a tradition that some forms of knowledge were originally restricted to aristocratic priests and that the publication of the public calendar in writing was a populist blow against their authority. It has been suggested that the prestige sometimes attached to the order of *scribae* reflects this situation.[8] Yet Rome never had anything approximat-ing to scribal literacy on the Near Eastern model, and the story can equally

5. D. M. Lewis 1994 explores this.
6. On epigraphy see MacMullen 1982, discussed by Meyer 1990 and Woolf 1996 (neither account winning widespread support). For the correlation with *instrumentum domesticum* and graffiti, see Fulford 1994. Harris 1993, 9 characterizes the period in which *instrumentum domesticum* was being produced in its greatest quantities as "between the very late Republic and the mid-3rd century AD."
7. Cornell 1991 is right to note how little we know about these earliest phases.
8. Purcell 2001 for both points. For the status of scribes in Etruria cf. Colonna 1976.

be told to show the democratizing potential of writing. The inclusion in much *popularis* legislation of clauses requiring its prominent publication in places "from which it may be clearly read," even if borrowed from the epigraphic mannerisms of democratic Athens, strongly suggests some Romans at least regarded writing as something that might empower the masses and hold their rulers to account.

A stronger case for connections between imperialism and the expanded use of writing can be made for the early empire.[9] The *a priori* argument seems a powerful one. As states grow, their demands on their subjects expand. State bureaucratization often stimulates greater document use among its subjects. The more the state puts its faith in written documentation, the more its citizens and subjects have to do the same.[10] Did this not happen in the Roman provinces? In one formulation

> one reason for the growth of literacy was the confrontation of Roman subjects with Roman power. Subjects wrote petitions and did so in amazing numbers. They learned the language of the conquerors in order to borrow the conqueror's power, and to help protect themselves from exploitation.[11]

This is wonderfully illustrated for the Roman empire by the personal archive of the Jewish woman named Babatha, found in the Cave of Letters on the shore of the Dead Sea and dating to the early second century C.E.[12] Babatha's papers comprised thirty-five documents written in Greek, Nabatean, and Aramaic or a mixture of these languages, with occasional transliterated Latin terms for Roman institutions. The archive included documents relating to the sale of land, dates and probably also wine, various marriage contracts and probably details of a dowry, a bequest, a court summons, various notices of deposits and loans, a court summons and a deposition, petitions, and an extract from the minutes of the council of Petra relating to the guardianship of her son. Much of this was generated by private transactions—both commercial and disputes arising from her complicated family life. But it was the recourse to law, and to civic and provincial administration, that generated this mass of material, which she kept with her until her death in the disturbances arising from the Bar Kokhba war.

Yet again we may choose to emphasize either the power of the state to entrap its subjects in webs of documentation or the potential opened up

---

9. For a recent exploration of this theme see Draper 2004.

10. Clanchy 1993, for example, argues that the Norman conquest led to a fundamental shift in attitudes toward and uses of writing in England, but also shows that this was simply an accentuated form of a phenomenon that can be traced all over Europe as centralizing states encroached on local societies.

11. Hopkins 1991, 137. Hopkins went on to show from Egyptian examples how the use of tax receipts, the recruitment of locals as part-time tax collectors, and the development of official archives combined to empower those with the skills to use written texts of this kind and disadvantage those who did not acquire those skills.

12. N. Lewis 1989.

by these strategies of control to those subjects who were able to master writing or gain access to those who had. This is a very different situation to that in, say, the Achaemenid empire. If we turn for a moment to literary production, here, too, recent scholarship has made less of the exclusive social circles from which almost all ancient authors emerge and more of the observation that it is hard to find a text written in the imperial period that does not "write back" to empire.[13] Literary texts claim authority independent of the state from a variety of sources: from divine inspiration, on the basis of philosophical argument, or simply by inserting themselves in a canon that predates the emperors. Writing was at best a technology that might be employed by subject as well as ruler. Perhaps it was even more important to subjects than it was to rulers, given the emperors' greater capacity to claim a monopoly of violence and ceremony.

More indirect links are more plausible. For instance, the appropriation of elite writing practices by a wider social circle has sometimes been explained as being part of the process through which a new urban culture emerged during the middle Republic. Take, for example, this interpretation of the complex lore and practices that surrounded the popular Roman game of dicing (*alea*).

> The *ars aleatoria* is essentially a cultural skill. The surrounding of quite simple games with complex intellectual paraphernalia is a familiar phenomenon. The passionate and exclusive detail with which the culture of the racegoer or football supporter is maintained, forming a kind of parody academic system, is an obvious case; it might be seen as a calque on a fact-based education curriculum as the perverted numeracy of the train-spotter is on the elementary mathematics and science of the same educational philosophy. The cultural panoply of the game of *alea* is likewise an offshoot of the world of élite literary culture, or *literae*.[14]

The idea of a calque or parody implies that popular knowledge is in some respects secondary to that mastered by the social elite.[15] This may well have been the case in ancient Rome. The Roman élite played *alea*, but not all *alea* players had access to the educational curriculum described by Quintilian or documented in the schoolbooks.[16] The kind of cognitive skills required for the game were developed in one context—élite education—and then entered wider circulation through other less socially circumscribed activities. But it was the fact that the adopters were already familiar with these skills that made the transfer possible. An indirect

13. A theme of Goldhill 2001.
14. Purcell 1995, 31.
15. Secondary in sequence clearly, but there is often an implication, too, of inappropriate appropriation, or a debasement consequent on vulgarization. As Purcell makes clear, *aleatores* ranged in status from emperors to the soldiers at the foot of the cross.
16. For comparison of which, see Morgan 1998, Cribiore 1996.

consequence of empire had been the creation of a complex urban world, one where even the essentials of life had to be obtained through the retail market, where many sold their labor, rented accommodation, and were as a consequence functionally numerate. Public notions of time, weights, measures, and the calendar ordered daily life, as law and custom ordered the city. Navigating the rules of these games was, for those acclimatized to this urban world, literally child's play. An advantage of the terms *calque* and *parody* is that they emphasize the agency of the adopters, whether they were slaves imitating their masters, the free poor their rich neighbors, or provincials those Romans they encountered in the provinces.[17] Once again, it is the ease with which the relatively powerless could obtain and use these skills that is striking.

2. FROM ARISTOCRATIC HOUSEHOLD TO IMPERIAL BUREAUCRACY

Too little is known of the earliest stages of gaming or education in Rome to be certain of the exact sequence of imitation and appropriation. But when we turn to Rome's development of an administrative literacy, it is much clearer that no component of what evolved into the complex governmental system of Babatha's day can be shown to predate analogous uses of writing in the private sphere. Put otherwise, it seems very likely that in ancient Rome, empire learned how to use writing from private individuals, rather than the other way around.

The many roles played by literacy in Cato's *On Agriculture* illustrates this perfectly. His preface already plays imaginative games with the supposedly mundane subject matter of farming.[18] Cato also repeatedly recommends the use of writing to manage the farm. These uses form a link between his self-idealizing moralizing account and the records kept for his eyes by his educated *vilicus*. Cato—orator, historian, landowner—offers a type, and his treatise with its detailed lists, its didactic prose, and its precise formulae to be uttered in various farming rituals, displays him as the master of all those literacies he needs to exercise mastery at home as in the state. From about the same period are the first traces of a law of agency that explicitly envisages the use of a *lex praeposita* that all parties could inspect, a document that established the extent to which a bailiff or any other individual nominated as an *institor* could act on behalf of their principals (often in effect their masters or former masters).[19] Writing of

17. But see Horsfall 2003, 64–74 for criticism of views that translate social hierarchies into hierarchies of culture.

18. Gratwick 2002; cf. Reay 2005 for the self-consciously literary self-production of Cato in the *de Agricultura*.

19. Aubert 1994.

institores the Roman jurists conceived of a mass of written communications linking them and their principals: these included reports, queries, written instructions, and even a form of written dismissal. We should probably also envisage the Republican *vilici* of urban *insulae*, pottery workshops, and farms using writing as a means of storing information for actual or potential auditing. This was certainly the case in the Appianus estate of third century C.E. Egypt, the accounts of which were so detailed they included the cost of the papyrus on which they were written.[20] Because financial records, even if often compiled by slaves, ex-slaves, and free *institores*, have to be potentially auditable and comprehensible to landowners, this is not really scribal literacy. Likewise, because these documents linked the richest men in the community with their slaves and agents, this is not an example of commercial literacy or craftsman's literacy.[21] Roman landowners had good reason not to permit the development of segregated literacies. The joined-up nature of Roman writing practices—so different from those of Achaemenid Persia or Anglo-Norman England—owed a good deal to the fact that the landowning classes of Rome also formed the political and military elite.

Perhaps the aristocratic household was the key node, the place where most forms of writing came together. If so, then slavery was the key institutional and cultural context. Slaves educated their masters' children and kept records of their property; they transcribed literary compositions and compiled business letters alike. They kept complex accounts (*rationes*) and must have managed some information systems if only in connection with enterprises like leasing property or ensuring that individual businesses were adequately supplied and made a reasonable return. As managers of remote farms and productive enterprises, some slaves and ex-slaves received their instructions and returned accounts in written form.[22] As domestic slavery, supported by ever more complex legal instruments, emerged as the key managerial mechanism for private and public business alike, so writing provided its essential operating system.

Magistrates, and especially those serving away from Rome, relied on their trusted slaves to assist them in their official functions. The "short account of the entire empire," passed on to the senate with Augustus's will, famously itemized not only the empire's financial and military resources but also those members of his *familia* from whom more detailed *rationes* might be sought.[23] The imperial household is just the best attested example of the use of domestics to conduct public business.

The long-term consequences can only be sketched here. Societies in which multiple literacies coexist, distinguishable by language, function,

20. On which Rathbone 1991.
21. Harris 1989 for explanation of these terms.
22. Aubert 1994 for all this.
23. Suetonius, *Divus Augustus* 101.

and social milieu, have often been attested.[24] Rome was not one of them. As a result, transactions were easier between loosely embedded writing practices.[25] New usages were easily developed. The marshaling of writing to serve innovations in law and cult are cases in point. Different kinds of text often used the same writing materials. Papyrus was used and reused for administrative and literary purposes, for accounts and schoolbooks, for sacred and profane writing, and it was written on in a number of languages. Literacy approached the status of generalized skill that it has in our societies. As a result, those who learned to read in the army might make use of the skill in commerce and the *literati* could read—and be astonished by—religious tracts emerging from unfamiliar sources. The state innovated, too—for example, in creating "sacrifice certificates" in the third century C.E. But in general, the power of this generalized literacy was most widely felt beyond the narrow realm of administration.

3. WHAT ROMANS WROTE

It is important to appreciate the textual background noise out of which some of our longest and most complex texts emerge. Most ancient texts were short. Less often noticed, their very shortness meant that many required very particular reading skills. Like the highly abbreviated labels on food packaging today, many ancient texts were formulaic and required the reader to supply a good deal of knowledge. Most of the difficulties involved today in the study of what epigraphists term *instrumentum domesticum* derive from our lack of that knowledge.[26]

It is difficult to compile an exhaustive account of all the kinds of writing produced in the Roman empire, but there is a pretty complete inventory for one province, and that is Roman Britain. The province was hardly typical; indeed, it was probably poorer than most in terms of writing. The military zone accounts for most of the stone epigraphy, in which funerary slabs and votive altars predominate.[27] Very low levels of urbanism, the poverty of monumental epigraphy, and the very limited evidence that euergetistic monumentality ever took root, together with the near complete absence of Britons from the ranks of attested imperial elite, make it likely literacy levels were always relatively low, however we

---

24. Street 1984 for the classic statement of this.

25. Bowman 1991, 123–7.

26. *Instrumentum domesticum* is conveniently characterized by Harris 1993, 7, as "most kinds of inscribed portable objects from Roman antiquity, and its major categories are held to be amphora inscriptions, brick- and tile-stamps, makers' names on terracotta lamps, and stamps and graffiti on *terra sigillata*."

27. Biró 1975 for discussion and maps. Harris 1989, 268 shows Britain has the third lowest density of inscriptions per 1,000 km^2 in the western provinces. For discussion of the reasons see Mann 1985.

measure them.[28] There have been some indicative studies of the graffiti from the province, which demonstrate that graffiti were more common on military than civil, on larger than on smaller sites, and on urban than on rural sites, and are more often to be found on high status ceramics such as *terra sigillata* than on coarseware.[29] A thin spread of writers and readers, then, concentrated very much where we would guess. Yet the great advantage of beginning from Romano-British material is that whatever can be shown about the use of writing in this poorest of prospects provides a minimum standard of what we can expect in other provinces.

The other advantage, naturally, is that the combination of intense scholarly activity and the manageable quantities of data involved have allowed a more complete inventory than for any other part of the empire. The two volumes of *Roman Inscriptions of Britain* (*RIB*) total respectively the entirety of the monumental epigraphy and almost all the remaining writing from the province.[30] Curse tablets from Bath and Uley need to be added, along with the stylus and ink tablets from Hadrian's Wall and a handful of other finds mostly from London. When coin legends are added we have a pretty good idea of the total extant remains from Roman Britain.

How representative are these remains of what once existed? This is a difficult question to answer, especially in brief. But we can be reasonably certain that if most writing vanished long ago, there is no particular reason to imagine any complete categories are missing except for those on the most perishable materials, chiefly, that is, papyrus. Presumably there were once school copies of major Latin and perhaps Greek classics, and perhaps major private collections of books. By late antiquity, when there is ample evidence of Christianity in Britain, copies of scripture at least must have circulated. Equally there must also have been a vanished mass of documentation for private commercial contracts—traders and business deals are well attested for the province—but only rare examples survive, like the recently discovered bill of sale that once accompanied a slave woman sold into Britain from Gaul.[31]

The second volume of *RIB* has been published in eight fascicules over the course of the last decade, and it deals with all inscribed objects except for monumental lapidary epigraphy. An abbreviated table of contents would read as follows, fascicule by fascicule:

1. The Military Diplomata; Metal Ingots; Tesserae, Dies; Labels; and Lead Sealings

---

28. On the low penetration of euergetism see Blagg 1990.
29. Evans 1987 with 2001, 33–4 and see *RIB* II fascicules 7 and 8. Raybould 1999 collects a mass of relevant material. See also Hanson and Conolly 2002, Pearce 2004.
30. Fulford 1994 for an important review of both, pointing out the broad similarities of the chronology of monumental and mundane writing.
31. Tomlin 2003.

2. Weights, Gold Vessels, Silver Vessels, Bronze Vessels, Lead Vessels, Pewter Vessels, Shale Vessels, Glass Vessels, Spoons
3. Brooches, Rings, Gems, Bracelets, Helmets, Shields, Weapons, Iron Tools, Baldric Fittings, Votives in Gold, Silver and Bronze, Lead Pipes, Roundels, Sheets and Other Lead Objects, Stone Roundels, Pottery and Bone Roundels, Other Objects of Bone
4. Wooden Barrels, Stilus-Tablets, Objects of Wood, Leather, Oculists' Stamps, Wallplaster, Mosaics, Handmills, Stone Tablets, Stone Balls, Stone Pebbles, Small Stone Votives, Miscellaneous Objects of Stone, Jet, Clay Figurines, Clay Objects, Antefixes, Tile-Stamps of Legion II Augusta, of Legion VI Victrix, of Legion IX Hispana, of Legion XX Valeria Victrix, Tile-Stamps of the Auxiliaries
5. Tile Stamps of the Classis Britannica; Imperial, Procuratorial and Civic Tile Stamps; Stamps of Private Tilers, Inscriptions on Relief-Patterned Tiles and Graffiti on Tiles
6. Dipinti and Graffiti on Amphorae, Dipinti and Graffiti on Mortaria, Inscriptions in White Barbotine, Dipinti on Coarse Pottery, Samian Barbotine or Moulded
7. Graffiti on Samian Ware/Terra Sigillata
8. Graffiti on Coarse Pottery Cut before and after Firing, Stamps on Coarse Pottery

The gaps are obvious, but what we do have is rather interesting. These texts can be broadly classified as follows. The smallest group are those that emanate from the actions of the state. The military *diplomata* are the main examples here, along with some of the lapidary epigraphy from the two walls, on milestones and the like. These are highly formulaic, made use of standard abbreviations, and include most of our longest documents. The *diplomata* are a rare trace from this end of the empire of those personal archives of official documents, which are more fully represented from Egypt and other arid environments where papyri and parchment have survived.

A second group, also quite small in number, are texts or numbers integral to the manufactured objects. The numbers and signs on gaming tokens are a case in point, and some (although not all) of the writing on coins could be included. These objects provide evidence for habits of thought and practice we mostly associate with the complex world of urban communities, but one that was equally present in the quasi-urban environments of the camps.[32] They were the tools and toys of people quite used to using numbers and letters, weights and measures in their everyday life, people who picked up a new format of text as easily as the computer literate today pick up a new application.

A third group, much more numerous, are those marks generated in the making, transportation, and perhaps retailing of objects. Stamps on tiles

---

32. Purcell 1995 on the cognitive and cultural implications of Roman gambling.

and amphorae come into this category, along with the painted labels on amphorae. I will return to these below, but for the moment I want to note simply that they are typically highly abbreviated and often make considerable use of symbols, especially numerals.

A fourth and final group, very numerous indeed, are short texts on portable objects that are not integral to their use. Most of these are objects of some value, so metal vessels are more likely to have writing on them than ceramic, and terra sigillata than other local wares. These are all very short and do not generally use abbreviations. They vary enormously in nature from elegant labels engraved on silver spoons at the time of their manufacture to scratched graffiti added long after, some of which are pretty clearly not real words. But almost all of these seem to link an object with a person, usually human but occasionally a god. The same could, of course, be said for almost all religious uses of writing.[33] But whereas curse tablets, votive inscriptions, and altars—most of them also votives—tend to be highly formulaic, the majority of texts on portable objects are *not*.

4. INSTRUMENTUM DOMESTICUM

Instrumentum domesticum and the names added to personal objects together make up the bulk of surviving writing from the Roman world.

Instrumentum domesticum—my third category, the kind of texts we find on objects of mass production like bricks, tiles, and amphorae—is characterized by very short, highly abbreviated texts that often make use of symbols (including numerals). If there is a case to be made for a specialized literacy in antiquity it is in the understanding of these symbols, their codes, and the protocols according to which they were ordered.

Something similar could be said of monumental inscriptions, although they were not mass produced in any meaningful sense. The family resemblance between monumental epigraphy and the labels and stamps used by manufacturers and traders is perhaps another sign of how connected up different Roman literacies were. Inscriptions, too, made frequent use of numbers, often to indicate dates and ages but also to identify military units or sums of money; often these are accompanied by standard symbols denoting particular units of quantity, currency, or time. Inscriptions and stamps alike also often make careful use of standardized layouts. Actual quotes or shared signs—apart from numbers—are rare of course: what we are observing is rather a shared set of cultural conventions about how to produce short, precise, and meaningful texts, legible to strangers. Those conventions, too, form part of the logic evoked by gaming boards, legal documents, and ephemeral military records. Appropriate formatting

---

33. Beard 1991, 44–8 for the prominence of names in religious inscriptions and some suggestions about its significance.

makes documents easier to read or scan quickly. Standardized formats
reduce the number of words needed, and present the viewer with something like an ideogram of reference. Many tombstones, for example,
proclaim their subject before one word is read. So, too, do votive altars.
So does the standard form of a Roman letter. All this was perhaps
particularly useful in a world where many had relatively limited reading
skills, and also where some readers had to handle large numbers of
documents.

Like monumental inscriptions, the labels on *instrumentum domesticum*
did not make many demands on a reader. A small recognition vocabulary
probably sufficed, and the general content must have been pretty predict-
able. They did, however, demand a knowledge of the particular format
and of the abbreviations used. Take the well-known Dressel 20 globular
amphorae from Baetica.[34] These were used for the most part for trans-
porting olive oil to distant locations, among them Rome—where their
fragments make up most of Monte Testaccio—the Rhineland camps, and
Roman Britain, where they are the most frequent type of transporter
amphorae. These amphorae have been much studied by epigraphists
because of the highly formulaic nature of the texts on them. There are
variations, but the standard set of texts includes a graffito on the base and
a stamp on the shoulder, both made before the amphora was fired, and
then up to four painted labels listing the weight of the amphora empty, its
weight full, the estate of origin, the names of those involved in checking it
and perhaps the names of the merchants taking it on. Each kind of label
appears in exactly the same position on the amphora. The precise interpretation of these stamps and labels is debated mostly because they are
so abbreviated. What is not debated is that they show considerable
effort being made to monitor quantities and origins of each vessel,
or rather of its contents. Some see in this a highly evolved fiscal or
regulatory scheme organized by the state. But it seems more likely that
we are seeing attempts by a chain of individual and largely independent
economic agents to avoid fraud and guarantee the identity, provenance,
and quality of the contents. It is impossible to open a vessel once
sealed and pretty difficult to tell how much of the weight you buy
is ceramic and how much is contents. Between the olive orchards of
Andalusia and consumers on Hadrian's Wall or on the Rhine there were
many stages of shipment, transhipment, and perhaps of purchase and
resale. The painted labels in the end offered the final purchasers some
sort of guarantee.

The Baetican amphorae are unusual in some respects, but versions of
this technology of labeling recur in other contexts. Olive oil does not last

---

34. Peacock and Williams 1986, 136–40 for a short introduction; Blázquez and
Remesal 1980 and 1983 for the production in general; Rodriguez-Almeida 1993 for a
recent account of the epigraphy.

long, even sealed, and consumers want it fresh, so there are no dates on
Dressel 20 amphorae. Wine is different. Consular years were occasionally
painted on containers used for fine wine that might be laid down. The
prefiring stamps and graffiti on amphorae offered different kinds of guarantee. Many related to the management of the production processes by
which these vessels were made. The study of ceramic production is
making clearer and clearer how often potters working individually came
together to share facilities like kilns.[35] Control marks on brick, tiles, and
amphorae were often designed to enable different producers to keep
separate products that were visually hard to distinguish. This reflects an
increasing tendency to standardize size and appearance of products—to
the extent that when petrographic analysis was first employed on wine
amphorae it revealed completely unsuspected diversities of provenance
among vessels classified typologically as identical. None of this uniformity
was the product of mechanized or automated processes, and there can
have been few practical advantages, the main exception being in helping
stack and store large consignments. The development of Italian wine
amphora types in the Western empire shows a concern by Italian producers to duplicate the physical appearance of the vessels in which more
prestigious Greek wines—like those of Cos—were imported, followed by
a concern by provincial producers to replicate styles that had become
associated with central Italian production. I emphasize two points. First,
amphora makers tried increasingly hard to conform on canonical types.
Second, writing was a vital means of allowing distinction among these
products, and a guarantee of the quantities and qualities that this uniformity claimed.

All this is so natural to us—living in a world of standardized sizes and
obsessive commodity labeling—that it takes an effort to step back and see
how remarkable and unusual it was in antiquity. Much exchange took
place directly between maker and consumer, or through a single inter-
mediary, even in classical times. The history of labels on container amphorae can easily be traced back to the Bronze Age. But before the
Hellenistic period they rarely did more than specify contents or ownership. The more complex systems seem to have originated chronologically
in the late third or early second century B.C.E.

It is tempting to connect this with some contemporaneous developments
in the Mediterranean economy. These might include the appearance of
the *villa*; the creation of *macella*—retail food markets in Rome and its
colonies; the development of the Roman law of agency that made it possible
to regulate *institores*; the boom of public contracts noted by Polybius,
exemplified in censorial building projects and by the provisioning of
Roman armies overseas; and by the apparent mushrooming in the trade of

35. Pucci 1981, Fülle 1997 on Arretine, Peacock 1982, 114–28 in general.

that most characteristic commodity, the slave. The notion of a slave mode of production is not widely subscribed to in the form originally proposed, but it is very clear that slaves and ex-slaves played key roles in the organization of new and more complex forms of production and exchange.[36] What we are observing is the emergence of new social forms that were not only more complex than before, but which extended further in space and time than their predecessors. Writing was an essential tool for moving goods, information, and people within this system.

New conditions of this kind required the production of new kinds of people, too, even among the free. Texts of the kind under discussion are designed for strangers to read. It is a truism of epistolography that letters inscribe within themselves the identity of the author (as she or he wishes to present it) and that of the recipient (again as the author chooses to shape it). *Tituli picti* and amphora stamps are the opposite. Their communicative effect, like that of labels on commodities today, is anonymizing. Although they claim a certain authority, through their conformity to formatting rules, through the precision of their detail, perhaps through their orthography, they are generally depersonalized. They do, however, presume a particular quality of literate competence on the part of readers, who must not only be able to read but also must understand the complex conventions of labeling. A skilled amphora reader must have known just where to look for a key bit of data, could "skim-read" hundreds of amphorae on the dockside knowing that an anomalous one would stand out, must be able to follow the clues in detail once suspicion is aroused. For Baetican amphorae, this competence must be shared from Rome's northern frontier to the Tiber emporion, and from London to Seville. The almost complete absence of whole words other than proper names, or of grammar, caters perfectly to readers who do not share a spoken language. Standard European food labeling is almost equally legible to French, Irish, Italian, Polish, and Greek consumers. So, too, was amphora-ese.

During the second century B.C.E., if not before, the Roman empire had become a world of fixed quantities. One monetary system dominated most of it, a single legal system had increasing range, and a set of common basic weights and measures was becoming widespread. Even in those parts of the empire where educated elite members studied Greek in school and used it in public life, there was a wide understanding of Latin. Interactions with strangers were easier and more important than ever before. The writing practices encoded in this most common form of texts expressed and responded to this feature of imperial culture, and of course promoted it further.

---

36. Rathbone 1983 suggested that this might profitably be seen as the extension of the use of highly specialized and educated domestic slaves into new spheres of the economy.

5. NAMES AND THINGS

Alongside this proliferation of texts written for strangers with limited
but precise reading skills, there was a parallel expansion in the marking
of objects with the names of individual persons. These two tendencies
might seem contradictory at first, the one anonymizing objects of
exchange, the other personalizing possessions. It is possible to see
several ways in which the two practices might have fitted together.
First, the same general period of economic growth that was manifested
in increased production and exchange brought modest prosperity to
many sectors of society. Second, the need for readers evoked by the
increased use of writing increased the numbers of those who were familiar
with writing and so able to use it. Third, the very ubiquity of writing as
a source of authority of various kinds must have increased the sense
in which it was believed to be powerful and effective. Again there are
plentiful modern parallels in the proliferation of signage in public and
institutional space. Less easy to test is the possibility that the increasing
complexity of the Hellenistic Mediterranean, the higher levels of mobility, and the growing size of urban populations may have provided an
incentive to inscribe one's identity on treasured possessions as an antidote
for *anomie*.

The practice of labeling one's possessions is very ancient, of course,
and is still with us. Children today find that the capacity to personalize
objects is one of the most attractive features of writing when that
skill is first acquired. We still label more possessions than we expect
to lose. Presents are inscribed, books of condolence signed, and the
mystique of the autograph signature as a final validation is only just
beginning to be eroded by electronic media. Personal names are among
the oldest and commonest types of graffiti from the archaic Mediterranean.[37] Writing is a powerful means of extending one's self, of investing
it in objects and (through their use) of expanding one's participation in
the world.

Writing is not the only means of doing this. A mass of recent Melanesian
anthropology has been concerned with the way the production of some art
objects serves as a means of dispersing personhood among those who use,
give, and receive them.[38] Dispersed personhood is one of the means by
which relationships are asserted and acknowledged, relationships that link
distant communities but also create authoritative accounts of past relations, in a word, of society. The materiality of the inscribed objects I have
been discussing means they, too, may be considered in this way, as objects
in which personhood is inscribed, stored, communicated and shared.
Objects of this kind are possessed by their owners in more than one sense.

37. R. Thomas 1992, 56–61.
38. Gell 1998 is most often cited; see also N. Thomas 1991.

Was there anything especially Roman about the fixing of personal names through writing? That personal names are particularly common in monumental epigraphy is well known. Roman epitaphs are more likely than most Greek ones to map out a whole complex of relationships between the deceased and her or his survivors.[39] It has been suggested that leaving one's name inscribed in a sanctuary was one way of asserting membership of a particular religious community.[40] The joined-up nature of Roman literacies perhaps makes it all the more likely that some at least felt that inscribing their possessions with their name might fix their place in a world that was ever expanding and less and less personalized.

6. WRITING, SOCIETY, AND THE STATE

It is time to return to writing and the state and the question with which this chapter began, whether or not the undoubted growth in the use of writing in the Roman and Hellenistic Mediterranean was a by-product of the state's increased dependency on the written word. The broad lines of an answer are clear. The growing complexity of social and economic relations and the increased reach of the institutions developed to facilitate them provided many opportunities for literates. New forms of document emerged, along with new kinds of readers well equipped to use them. A few—such as legal formulae or the labels on Dressel 20 amphorae—were highly specialized. But the peculiar conditions of Roman alphabetic literacy, and in particular the centrality of the aristocratic slave household in most of these webs of exchange, held Roman literacies together. There was no real fragmentation of writing practices, no specialized literacies, and the practices of writing—in particular the use of complex formats, of a set of graphic symbols, and of particular resonances associated with personal names—moved easily between different genres of text. Roman writing practices, in brief, were joined up.

How did the writing practices of the state fit into this? Here it is possible to draw on a recent and very thorough body of research on precisely this subject, generated by the research project *La mémoire perdue* centered on the École française à Rome.[41] In the course of a collaborative project investigating the use of documentation for public and private purposes by Romans, extensive investigations were carried out of the use of texts in a range of spheres including banking, census,

---

39. Woolf 1996.

40. Beard 1991.

41. This project, under the direction of Claude Nicolet, set out to investigate a range of vanished public and private Roman archives. The principal publications are Demougin 1994, Moatti 1998, 2000, and 2001. The project developed ideas adumbrated in Nicolet 1988. Moatti 2004 is in some respects a successor project.

colonization and land distribution, taxation, senatorial and magisterial business, the archiving of laws, the management of grain distributions, the movement of goods, religious archives, personal documentation, and the regulation of individual mobility. The majority of contributions concerned either the activities of the state or private activities in which the state had a special interest.

One thing that emerged clearly was a more vivid than ever picture of Rome's dependence on writing to articulate the enormously complex operations on which its government and economy relied. Moving grain from Egypt to Rome, for example, involved paperwork transactions at the Egyptian granaries where the *sitologoi* issued receipts to suppliers, then a new set of receipts issued by captains of the transport vessels, lists of grain dispersed, inscribed seals on shipments, written contracts between shippers and the state, some form of harbor control in Portus, documents to manage the Roman warehouses.[42] None of this includes the complex private paperwork used by great Egyptian estates to keep track of local spending on casual labor, materials and transport, and revenue from rental and sale, nor the equally complex paperwork of the *frumentationes* at Rome through which a good deal of state grain found its way to the consumer.[43] Equally the process of colonization involved not just the original law but also the compilation of lists of volunteers, lists of properties assigned, cadastral documents providing an official map of the territory in question, additional books, notes and *commentarii*—apparently formal annotations explaining the assignment. Many of these would potentially be of use in any subsequent legal dispute, and some would be important for the census.[44] Examples of this kind could be multiplied.

It is clear not only that great quantities of texts were produced by almost every major project in which the state was involved, but also that creating documentation was commonly seen as an essential part of any such operation. A "documentary mentality" pervaded Roman action of this kind, so that when some new scheme was developed—the Gracchan grain distributions, for example—it was assumed by all that this would generate records. Again, this sort of procedure is so familiar to us that we forget that it is alien to many societies. It is all the more surprising, then, that another of the clear conclusions of the project was that although record making was ubiquitous, hardly any efforts were made to store information in forms in which it could be conveniently recovered.[45] Roman archives were haphazard. Anecdotes from the age of Cicero

42. Rickman 1998.

43. On the use of writing on the Egyptian estates see Rathbone 1991, 331–87. On the paperwork associated with grain distributions see Virlouvet 1995.

44. Moatti 1993.

45. Moatti 1993, 99; cf. Culham 1989.

make clear that the only place that records of ancient decisions or actions could be found were in the private archives of those families with consular and censorial ancestors, that the documentation created by colonial enterprises did not find its way back to Rome, that there were few copies even of laws and senatorial edicts.[46] There are several instances from the imperial period of central government finding it hard to track down records of its own actions, from the efforts needed to replace the 3,000 inscriptions allegedly lost when the Capitol was burned in 68–69 to the difficulties facing compilers of the Theodosian Code. It is less clear how much this was due to a lack of desire to store and retrieve information and how much it was simply the incompetence of those responsible for doing so. Either way, if Rome was indeed bureaucratic in the sense of creating paperwork, there is little sign that government made much use of its records for long after they had been generated.[47]

This documentary mentality was clearly in place by the late Republic. The growth of the state promoted first by the *populares* and then by their opponents generated a mass of new texts and new categories of texts. The emperors would add more. Colonization and the census were much older, but it is unclear how far back these operations involved intensive documentation. *La mémoire perdue* found plenty of evidence from the early second century B.C.E., together with some indications that the amount of documentation generated by the state increased dramatically in the last century B.C.E.[48] Military uses of texts were not covered directly by this project, but Polybius's account of the Roman army shows the regular use of texts in routine operations such as the watch.[49] Although our detailed knowledge of military documents does not predate the Augustan reforms, it is clear that Caesar made extensive use of writing to coordinate his operations in Gaul. It is difficult to imagine Pompey's campaigns against the pirates not requiring something similar. Roman coins, also not surveyed by the project, bore short legends from the early third century B.C.E.

46. Culham 1989, Nicolet 1994, Moatti 1993.

47. The term bureaucracy has been revived by Nicolet 1994 to refer to Rome, and one achievement of the project is certainly to show Roman government was not amateurish or primitive. It does not follow that Roman government was bureaucratic in the Weberian sense in which the term is often used, and Saller's arguments (1982) for a strong patrimonial element remain strong. Many of the documents to which Suetonius had access as *ab epistulis* in Hadrian's court seem precisely the kind of personal and private documents that many great senatorial families held.

48. Nicolet 1994 writes of first century B.C.E. Rome as "fortement 'paperassière'" and supposes fiscality after 167 B.C.E. must have required significant documentation. Moatti 1993 traces the documentation of colonization back to the early second century B.C.E. but thinks it increased over the last century B.C.E. Lo Cascio 2001 suggests the census began to collect more information after 179 B.C.E. Purcell 2001 sees key changes in the order of scribes in the early second century B.C.E.

49. Best 1966–7, Harris 1989, 166–7.

All this may be compared to the evidence for private uses of writing. The period in which *instrumentum domesticum* was produced in the greatest quantities ran from the late Republic to the middle of the third century C.E. But stamps already appeared on Greco-Italic amphorae produced in the early second century B.C.E. Cato's *On Agriculture* (composed around 160 B.C.E.) takes for granted extensive use of writing for running a farm and for commercial contracts. It may be inferred that the property classes were already keeping private archives of written tablets in case of legal challenge from this point.[50] As some became involved in taking state contracts, for which Polybius also attests the importance, these private uses of writing will have intersected with the needs of the state. But it is difficult to say that most of these uses were responses to a bureaucratization of Roman government. The Roman *ius civile* was growing in complexity and volume over this period, too, to cope with the new demands made on it by the same processes of growth. By the end of the last century B.C.E. it had developed a body of what was, in effect, commercial law, a set of instruments that enabled agency, partnership, and contracts of various kinds to be formed. Most or all of these involved extensive use of writing. But these innovations, mostly introduced by the praetor's edict, were essentially responsive. It was the transformation of the Roman economy that provided the stimulus.[51] More generally, it seems the private uses of writing develop rather gradually from the needs of landowners whose activities and interests were increasingly complex. As more owned multiple properties, produced goods for sale, made increasing use of slave and ex-slave managers, and relied more and more on formal legal arrangements, so the need to develop new uses of writing grew. For those who were mostly concerned with commercial lending or trade, for example in the growing international trades in slaves and food, these needs were more acute.

If we ask what role the state played in all this, there seem broadly two acceptable answers. One is that the Roman state's needs evolved alongside those of its most powerful citizens. The other is that when those powerful citizens took time away from managing their farms and urban properties, and from engaging in contracts to supply the growing metropolis and its growing armies, they adapted existing private solutions to the more complex tasks they faced as leaders of colonies, legislators, and generals. That Roman literacies were joined up will have helped enormously. Perhaps choosing between these two answers is only a matter of emphasis. But a strong case can be made that the documentary explosion of official texts in Rome during the last two centuries B.C.E. represents an appropriation, for the needs of the state, of writing practices developed first of all to suit the private needs of its citizens.

---

50. Meyer 2004, 36–43 on this.
51. Morel 1989 offers the best account of this.

ACKNOWLEDGMENTS

This chapter is much improved by the comments of other participants at the Semple symposium. My thanks to them and to the editors, whom I must also thank for their extreme patience and careful critique of an earlier version. Mike Fulford's (1994) review article of *RIB* II suddenly made clear a correlation of which I had been only dimly aware. I am also grateful to the editors of the *Cambridge Ancient History* who commissioned me to contribute a chapter on literacy to volume XI and to Alison Cooley for inviting me to comment on the Roman Archaeology Conference panel that became Cooley 2002. This chapter develops some ideas that first appeared in both places.

BIBLIOGRAPHY

Adams, J. N. 1994. "Latin and Punic in Contact? The Case of the Bu Njem Ostraka." *JRS* 84: 87–112.

Aubert, J.-J. 1993. "Workshop Managers." In Harris 1993: 171–81.

——. 1994. *Business Managers in Ancient Rome: A Social and Economic Study of Institores, 200 BC–AD 250.* Leiden.

Beard, M. 1991. "Writing and Religion: Ancient Literacy and the Function of the Written Word in Roman Religion. Question: What Was the Role of Writing in Graeco-Roman Paganism?" In Humphrey 1991: 35–58.

Best, E. E. 1966–7. "The Literate Roman Soldier." *CJ* 62: 122–7.

Biró, M. 1975. "The Inscriptions of Roman Britain." *AArchHung* 27: 13–58.

Blagg, T. F. C. 1990. "Architectural Munificence in Britain: The Evidence of Inscriptions." *Britannia* 21: 13–31.

Blázquez, J. M., and J. Remesal, eds. 1980. *Producción y comercio del aceite en la antigüedad Congresso I.* Madrid.

——, eds. 1983. *Producción y comercio del aceite en la antigüedad Congresso II.* Madrid.

Bowman, A. K. 1991. "Literacy in the Roman Empire: Mass and Mode." In Humphrey 1991: 119–31.

——. 1994. "The Roman Imperial Army: Letters and Literacy on the Northern Frontier." In Bowman and Woolf 1994: 109–25.

—— and G. Woolf, eds. 1994. *Literacy and Power in the Ancient World.* Cambridge.

Clanchy, M. T. 1993. *From Memory to Written Record: England 1066–1307.* 2nd ed. Oxford.

Colonna, G. 1976. "Scriba cum rege sedens." In *L'Italie pré-romaine et la Rome républicaine: Mélanges Jacques Heurgon,* 187–96. Rome.

Cooley, A., ed. 2002. *Becoming Roman, Writing Latin? Literacy and Epigraphy in the Roman West.* Journal of Roman Archaeology, Supplementary Series 48. Portsmouth, RI.

Corbier, M. 2006. *Donner à voir, donner à lire: mémoire et communication dans la Rome ancienne.* Paris.

Cornell, T. 1991. "The Tyranny of the Evidence: A Discussion of the Possible Uses of Literacy in Etruria and Latium in the Archaic Age." In Humphrey 1991: 7–34.

Cribiore, R. 1996. *Writing, Teachers, and Students in Graeco-Roman Egypt*. American Studies in Papyrology 36. Atlanta.

Culham, P. 1989. "Archives and Alternatives in Republican Rome." *CPh* 84: 100–15.

Demougin, S., ed. 1994. *La mémoire perdue: à la recherche des archives oubliées, publiques et privées, de la Rome antique*. Publications de la Sorbonne. Série Histoire Ancienne et Médiévale 30. Paris.

Draper, J. A., ed. 2004. *Orality, Literacy, and Colonialism in Antiquity*. Semeia Studies 47. Leiden.

Evans, J. 1987. "Graffiti and the Evidence of Literacy and Pottery Use in Roman Britain." *AJ* 144: 191–204.

——. 2001. "Material Approaches to the Identification of Different Romano-British Site-Types." In S. James and M. Millett, eds., *Britons and Romans: Advancing an Archaeological Agenda*, 26–35. Council for British Archaeology Research Report 125.

Fink, R. O. 1971. *Roman Military Records on Papyrus*. Philological Monographs of the American Philological Association 26. Cleveland.

Fulford, M. G. 1994. "The Monumental and the Mundane: A Common Epigraphic Tradition." *Britannia* 25: 315–18.

Fülle, G. 1997. "The Internal Organization of the Arretine Terra Sigillata Industry: Problems of Evidence and Interpretation." *JRS* 87: 111–55.

Gell, A. 1998. *Art and Agency: An Anthropological Theory*. Oxford.

Gledhill, J., B. Bender, and M. T. Larsen, eds. 1988. *State and Society: The Emergence and Development of Social Hierarchy and Political Centralisation*. One World Archaeology 4. London.

Goldhill, S., ed. 2001. *Being Greek under Rome: Cultural Identity, the Second Sophistic and the Development of Empire*. Cambridge.

Goody, J. R., ed. 1968. *Literacy in Traditional Societies*. Cambridge.

——. 1986. *The Logic of Writing and the Organization of Society*. Cambridge.

Gratwick, A. 2002. "A Matter of Substance: Cato's Preface to the *De agri cultura*." *Mnemosyne* 55: 41–72.

Hanson, W. S., and R. Conolly. 2002. "Language and Literacy in Roman Britain: Some Archaeological Considerations." In Cooley 2002: 151–64.

Harris, W. V. 1989. *Ancient Literacy*. Cambridge, MA.

——, ed. 1993. *The Inscribed Economy: Production and Distribution in the Roman Empire in the Light of* Instrumentum Domesticum. *The Proceedings of a Conference Held at the American Academy in Rome on 10–11 January, 1992*. Journal of Roman Archaeology, Supplementary Series 6. Ann Arbor.

Hopkins, K. 1991. "Conquest by Book." In Humphrey 1991: 133–58.

Horsfall, N. 2003. *The Culture of the Roman Plebs*. London.

Humphrey, J. H., ed. 1991. *Literacy in the Roman World*. Journal of Roman Archaeology, Supplementary Series 3. Ann Arbor.

Levi-Strauss, C. 1955. *Tristes Tropiques*. Paris.

Lewis, D. M. 1994. "The Persepolis Tablets: Speech, Seal and Script." In Bowman and Woolf 1994: 17–32.

Lewis, N. 1989. *The Documents from the Bar Kokhba Period in the Cave of Letters: Greek Papyri*. Jerusalem.

Lo Cascio, E. 2001. "Il *census* a Roma e la sua evoluzione dall'età 'Serviana' alla prima età imperiale." *MEFRA* 113: 565–603.

MacMullen, R. 1982. "The Epigraphic Habit in the Roman Empire." *AJPh* 103: 233–46.

Mann, J. C. 1985. "Epigraphic Consciousness." *JRS* 75: 204–6.

Meyer, E. A. 1990. "Explaining the Epigraphic Habit in the Roman Empire: The Evidence of Epitaphs." *JRS* 80: 74–96.

———. 2004. *Legitimacy and Law in the Roman World*: Tabulae *in Roman Belief and Practice*. Cambridge.

Moatti, Claude. 1993. *Archives et partage de la terre dans le monde romain (II s. avant—1 après J.-C.)*. Collection de l'École française de Rome 173. Rome.

———, ed. 1998. *La mémoire perdue: recherches sur l'administration romaine*. Collection de l'École française de Rome 243. Rome.

Moatti, Claudia, ed. 2000. "La mémoire perdue III: recherches sur l'administration romaine: le cas des archives judiciaires pénales." *MEFRA* 112: 647–779.

———, ed. 2001. *Les archives du census: le contrôle des homes. Actes de la table ronde, Rome, 1er décembre 1997.* 2001. *MEFRA* 113.2: 559–764.

———, ed. 2004. *La mobilité des personnes en Méditerranée de l'antiquité à l'époque moderne: procédures de contrôle et documents d'identification*. Collection de l'École française de Rome 341. Rome.

Morel, J.-P. 1989. "The Transformation of Italy, 300–133 BC: The Evidence of Archaeology." *Cambridge Ancient History* VIII. 2nd ed. Cambridge.

Morgan, T. 1998. *Literate Education in the Hellenistic and Roman Worlds*. Cambridge.

Nicolet, C. 1988. *L'inventaire du monde: géographie et politique aux origines de l'Empire romain*. Paris.

———. 1994. "À la recherche des archives oubliées: une contribution à l'histoire de la bureaucratie romaine." In *La mémoire perdue* (1994): v–xviii.

Ong, W. J. 1982. *Orality and Literacy: The Technologizing of the Word*. London.

Peacock, D. P. S. 1982. *Pottery in the Roman World: An Ethnoarchaeological Approach*. London.

——— and D. F. Williams. 1986. *Amphorae and the Roman Economy: An Introductory Guide*. London.

Pearce, J. 2004. "Archaeology, Writing Tablets and Literacy in Roman Britain." *Gallia* 61: 43–51.

Pucci, G. 1981. "La ceramica italica (terra sigillata)." In A. Giardina and A. Schiavone, eds., *Società romana e produzione schiavistica II*, 99–121. Rome.

Purcell, N. 1995. "Literate Games: Roman Urban Society and the Game of *Alea*." *P&P* 147: 3–37.

———. 2001. "The *Ordo scribarum*: A Study in the Loss of Memory." *MEFRA* 113: 633–74.

Rathbone, D. W. 1983. "The Slave Mode of Production in Italy." *JRS* 73: 160–8.

———. 1991. *Economic Rationalism and Rural Society in Third-Century AD Egypt*. Cambridge.

Raybould, M. E. 1999. *A Study of Inscribed Material from Roman Britain: An Inquiry into Some Aspects of Literacy in Romano-British Society*. British Archaeological Reports BS 281. Oxford.

Reay, B. 2005. "Agriculture, Writing, and Cato's Aristocratic Self-Fashioning." *ClAnt* 24: 331–61.

Rickman, G. E. 1998. "Problems of Transport and Storage of Goods: 'Les traces oubliées'." In *La mémoire perdue* (1998): 317–24.

Rodriguez-Almeida, E. 1993. "Graffiti e produzione anforaria della Betica." In Harris 1993: 95–106.

Saller, R. P. 1982. *Personal Patronage under the Early Empire*. Cambridge.

Schousboe, K., and M. T. Larsen, eds. 1989. *Literacy and Society*. Copenhagen.

Stock, B. 1983. *The Implications of Literacy: Written Language and Models of Interpretation in the Eleventh and Twelfth Centuries*. Princeton.

Street, B. V. 1984. *Literacy in Theory and Practice*. Cambridge.

——, ed. 1993. *Cross-Cultural Approaches to Literacy*. Cambridge.

Thomas, N. 1991. *Entangled Objects: Exchange, Material Culture, and Colonialism in the Pacific*. Cambridge, MA.

Thomas, R. 1992. *Literacy and Orality in Ancient Greece*. Cambridge.

Tomlin, R. S. O. 2003. " 'The Girl in Question': A New Text from Roman London." *Britannia* 34: 41–51.

Virlouvet, C. 1995. *Tessera frumentaria: Les procédures de la distribution du blé public à Rome*. Bibliothèque des Écoles françaises d'Athènes et de Rome 286. Rome.

Woolf, G. D. 1996. "Monumental Writing and the Expansion of Roman Society." *JRS* 86: 22–39.

4

Reading, Hearing, and Looking at Ephesos

Barbara Burrell

This chapter takes the title of the conference at which it was presented[1] literally, by trying to "construct literacy." It examines a series of buildings in a particular locale, each with its own inscriptions, structure, and decor. This gives an advantage rare in reconstructing ancient "reading experiences": whereas most Greek and Latin texts, literary and even epigraphic, are not in their original condition or context, many monumental inscriptions and the buildings they stood on can be reconstructed in something close to their original form, as they can in this case, at Ephesos.

Further, I want to apply reception theory to the buildings as well as to their texts.[2] I hope to show how each structure's combination of architecture, sculpture, and inscriptions had particular purposes, and how the reading of each by a series of elite viewers led to new dedications, again with new perceptions and receptions, and thus new concepts of the space they stood in, over a period of centuries. Following this process will show how a combination of text, architecture, and decor made one particular spot a focus and intersection of Hellenic and Roman culture.

The scene is the city of Ephesos during the Roman empire. This is not just because Ephesos has been well-excavated and published for the past hundred years, though that is reason enough. It is also a particularly good place to study bilingualism in Greek and Latin. To the Greeks, the city had an impeccable Hellenic background as one of the first settlements of the Ionian migration, founded by Androklos, son of Kodros the king of Athens. It was the home of Herakleitos, Hipponax, and of Zenodotos, the first head of the Library at Alexandria.[3] In the Roman period, it was an important

1. *Constructing Ancient "Literacy" among the Greeks and Romans*, a Semple Symposium held at the University of Cincinnati on April 28–9, 2006.

2. Elsner 1996 and Corbier 2006 for relationships between written text and monuments in Roman culture; thanks to Fergus Millar for pointing me toward the latter. For the power of inscriptions, Woolf 1996 and Alföldy 2003, and for the power of decor, von Hesberg 2003, all mainly on Italy and the West. A useful collection on the aesthetics of reception is Jauss 1982. Holtorf 2007 applies reception theory to monuments and archaeology.

3. For a general introduction, Knibbe 1998.

harbor and crossroads for trade; there was an organization of resident
Romans at Ephesos by the first century B.C.E.[4] Augustus himself designated
it as the Asian center where Romans were to worship the deified Caesar
and Roma.[5] It was the chief headquarters of the proconsul of Asia; by
the third century, governors were required to make their first landfall at
Ephesos.[6]

A recent study of bilingual Greek and Latin inscriptions from all over
the province shows that Ephesos has revealed far more such inscriptions
than any other city.[7] In fact, when one looks at public civic inscriptions,
Ephesos has more bilinguals than all the other cities of Asia (which
ancient tradition numbered at 500, perhaps actually over 300) combined:
nineteen honorific bases, whereas the rest of the province has a total of
six; fifteen public dedications, whereas the rest of the province has ten.[8]
And among building inscriptions, the greatest concentration of bilinguals
in the city of Ephesos was at one particular locus, the plaza just south of
the great Hellenistic Agora (figure 4.1).

Plainly this was an important crossroads. Three roads met here: one
from the harbor and the central city, at the north; one from the Magnesian
gate to the east; and one from the west, perhaps leading from Ortygia,
birthplace and festival site of Ephesos's patron god Artemis. It is natural
that important people wished to place their buildings and monuments
where they would be seen, and Ephesos was a place whose builders
and benefactors were not just locals, but the elite citizens of other
cities, Roman officials, and even emperors.[9] Of course, one cannot say
who or how many actually stood before these dedications to read their
inscriptions, or gaze at the statues.[10] Most no doubt gave them a hurried
glance, with the literate subconsciously reading a word or two, and getting
a vague impression of the rest. What is important is that the dedicators
built as if their gifts would be seen, and their messages received as
intended. Also, it is likely that those who commissioned further buildings
to stand in this space paid close attention to what was already there, and
what it said. In the metropolis of Ephesos, the desires and decisions of

4. *IvE* 658, supplemented by Knibbe, Engelmann, and İplikçioğlu 1989, 235–6.

5. Burrell 2004, 59.

6. Ulpian, *Digest* 1.16.4.5, by ruling of Caracalla.

7. Figures taken from Kearsley 2001, though I consider the Library of Celsus a public
dedication more than a sepulchral inscription. Note that Ephesos provides almost a third
(34) of the 109 listed bilingual epitaphs.

8. Reynolds 1995; Sartre 1995, 212.

9. Winter 1996, 233–4.

10. On varied receptions of statuary, Edwards 2003; on reading inscriptions, Corbier
2006, 47, 87. Thanks to Peter Bing (2002) for his thoughts on epigram reading, though
I believe that epigram inscriptions were occasionally read despite the dearth of descriptions
of this process in classical literature. Ancient inscriptions' effects may have been largely
subliminal, like modern billboards; this does not stop advertisers from putting up billboards.

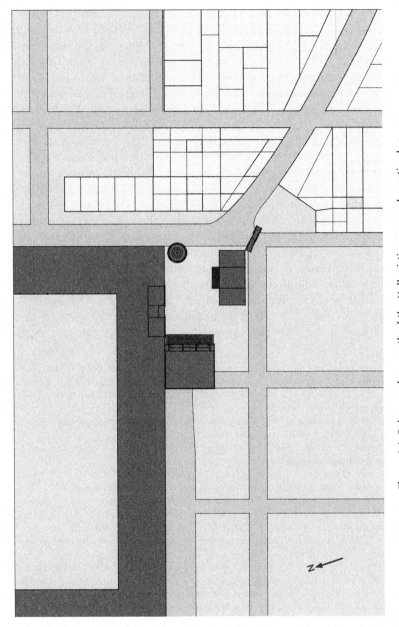

Figure 4.1 Ephesos, plaza south of the Hellenistic agora: schematic plan.

initial builders would be received by a wide audience of varied elites, who furthered and modified that reception with their own dedications.[11]

The building that seems to have determined the area's bilingual future was the South Gate of the Agora, often called the "Gate of Mazaeus and Mithridates." Figure 4.2 shows what the area might have looked like after this gate was added, at the start of the first century C.E., though this and the following reconstructions are necessarily speculative, meant to give an impression of the topography as a whole rather than be archaeologically precise for each structure. The Gate's inscription was originally set with large bronze letters, making it quite legible even from a distance.[12] In Latin, the two exotically named freedmen honor their patrons, Augustus and Agrippa, each with his wife. One reads the three-line Latin inscription on the attic of the left arch (Augustus's) first, then its counterpart on the right arch (Agrippa's), then, below them, the single Latin line of the two dedicators across both the protruding arches. The two-line Greek dedication, on the attic of the recessed arch in the center, was probably meant to be read last. It was written in the characteristic Greek style of evenly spaced letters, whereas the Latin inscription lengthened its "I"s and separated words with points, and sometimes with wider spaces.[13]

As a gravestone found elsewhere specifies that Mithradates [sic] was the freedman of Agrippa, Mazaeus must have been the freedman of Augustus.[14] Indeed, each freedman's name stands on the part of the gate dedicated to his own patron, and the two parts of the gate were

11. For the variety of elites in Asia, Campanile 2004b; for the semiotics of bilingualism on public monuments, for example, Adams 2002; for the siting of inscriptions and gradual specialization of certain sites, Corbier 2006, esp. 35–9. Halfmann 2001, 93–106, is provocative but has some crucial errors.

12. *IvE* 3006: Imp. Caesari Divi f. Augusto pontifici / maximo, cos. XII, tribunic. potest. XX et / Liviae Caesaris Augusti

M. Agrippae L. f. cos. tert. imb. [sic] tribunic. / potest. VI et / Iuliae Caesaris Augusti fil. Mazaeus et Mithridates patronis.

Μαζ[αῖο]ς καὶ Μιθριδάτης / [τοῖς] πά[τ]ρωσι καὶ τῶι δή[μωι].

On bronze letters as an Augustan innovation, Rose 2005, 29, 55. Kearsley (2001, 124–5 no. 121, 154) assumes that Mithridates passed into the *familia* of Augustus, but see infra n. 14. On the use of *cognomina* only, Chantraine 1967, 53–4, 103 n. 14; Weaver 1972, 37–8. The Persianized names lead Halfmann (2001, 29–31) to see the men's origins in eastern Anatolia or Syria, though slaves' names were given by the master and did not necessarily reflect reality; cf. Dench 2005, 73, 296.

13. Few publications of bilingual building inscriptions consider whether the Latin and Greek portions were cut by the same person or workshop, or what artistic effect the contrast (or any induced similarity) in writing styles between the two languages might have had. One certain example of a single artist, or at least workshop, cutting both Greek and Latin is an advertisement for monumental inscriptions in both languages from Sicily, *IG* 14.297/*CIL* 10.7296; Ireland 1983, 221–2.

14. *IvE* 851; Kearsley 2001, 15–16 no. 19. The difference in spelling makes P. Scherrer's theory that the gate enclosed gravesites for Mazaeus and Mithridates in its wings (cited in Thür 1997, 73–5; Scherrer 2000, 138; Cormack 2004, 225) less likely. On the other hand, the Latin inscription gives Agrippa the misspelled title Imb(erator), though Augustus's title is correctly abbreviated on his half of the gate.

Figure 4.2 Reconstruction of plaza at start of first century C.E., showing Gate of Mazaeus and Mithridates and Round Monument; view from east.

even produced by different teams of sculptors.[15] Augustus's titulature dates the monument precisely to 4/3 B.C.E., though at that time Agrippa had been dead for nine years. As Julia, his widow, was currently married to Tiberius, the inscription delicately calls her "daughter of Augustus." Statues of the imperial personages, and later of their descendants Lucius and likely Gaius Caesar, stood above.[16] In the central part, the briefer Greek inscription states that Mazaeus and Mithridates dedicate the building to the *Demos* of Ephesos as well as to their patrons.

There are further bicultural aspects to this monument. For one thing, it is a Roman triumphal arch, or rather, a pair of arches, a design completely new to this city, resembling the arch of Susa in Italy, built only a short time before.[17] When removed from Roman traditions of commemoration, such arches have little function except to support and glorify statues of imperial personages, as these in fact do. In plan, however, the Ephesos Gate is a typical Greek propylon, its U-shape and triple passageway tracing its ancestry back to Mnesikles' Propylaia on the Athenian akropolis.[18] It is architecturally as well as textually bilingual. The meld of the two is very smoothly done for being so novel, but we should remember that Rome derived its basic architectural forms from Greece in any case.[19]

How did Mazaeus and Mithridates want viewers to read this monument? They put their Very Important Patrons to the fore, in a monumental format proper to them as Roman rulers, whereas the freedmen dedicators' names are without qualification or titulature, and their Greek inscription is central, but recessed.[20] Glorifying their patrons gives the freedmen a place where ordinarily they would have had none. Mazaeus and Mithridates are not known to have held any imperial, provincial, or civic office, and freedmen, even wealthy ones, would have had a hard time among the freeborn elites of Ephesos were it not for their imperial connections.[21]

15. Rose 1997, 172–4 no. 112.

16. *IvE* 3007, Latin inscription for base of statue of Lucius Caesar.

17. Kader 1996, 259–60; the arch at Susa is dated 9/8 B.C.E. For Roman traditions of arch building, Beard 2007, 45–6, 101.

18. Alzinger 1974, 9–16; Ortaç 2002, 175–7, 179–81.

19. Colledge (1987) discusses the gradual progress by which truly foreign architectural styles may be absorbed and domesticated. Note that the architectural influences are not limited to Roman or Greek, as the decor of the side niches of the gate may derive from the "Syrian pediment" (Hornbostel-Hüttner 1979, 200; infra, n. 45).

20. The dedication to the imperial personages is a Hellenic formula, rather than being in the Roman tradition, in which triumphant generals erected their own arches. At Rome, arch dedications were changing from Roman to Hellenic style at just this time: Wallace-Hadrill 1990.

21. On imperial freedmen in Asia Minor, and their rise specifically in early Augustan times, Smith 1993, 8–10; Reynolds 1995, 398–9. Kearsley (2001, 154, 156) may paint too rosy a picture.

What messages would have been received from this gate? Its "reading communities" would have been varied. For those from Italy whose first language was Latin, the stocky arches, their inscriptions, and the powerful figures (now missing) atop them would have been a powerful proof that they were now on top, that their culture and traditions were taking hold all over the world. Nonetheless, any Romans who stood here were traveling, living in, or governing the East, and it is likely that they would have comprehended the Greek inscription as well.[22] Asians literate in Latin were no doubt fewer, especially this early, though there would be some, especially if they aimed to climb the ladder in Rome.[23] Even those who only spoke and read Greek would certainly recognize the features and costumes of Augustus and his family from many other statues and monuments.[24] The receding but central Greek inscription would have filled in some of the gaps in a reassuring fashion, and it adds the People of Ephesos to the dedicatees, so the great tradition of the polis is adhered to.

About sixty years after this gate was made, a two-aisled stoa about 150 meters long was added to the east side of the Agora (figure 4.3). It is interesting that the benefactors who supplied the funds for this enormous project saw fit to put their names, not on the long face of the building, on the main street from the theater, but on its end, near the Gate of Mazaeus and Mithridates. Once again, the dedicators make their inscription bilingual, with the Latin likely coming first, below the stoa's triglyph frieze, the Greek below that. Though both are incomplete, they said pretty much the same thing: that the building was dedicated to Artemis Ephesia, the deified Claudius, Nero (with his name Germanicus later scratched out), Agrippina Augusta, and the city of the Ephesians. Neither preserves the name of the male dedicator, though the Greek version gives the name of his wife, Claudia Metrodora, and the fact that he built it from his own funds.[25] Metrodora became not just a benefactor but the eponymous magistrate of Chios, so perhaps lived there after her husband's death.

22. Swain 1996, 389 n. 48; Wallace-Hadrill 1998; though note Reynolds (1995, 396) on non-Greek-speaking governors; Eck (2004) on Latin as a language of power, but also on government communications in Greek and possibly other native languages.

23. Majbom Madsen 2002, 99, 103–105; Jones 2005, 265, 268–69. According to Cassius Dio (60.17.4), the emperor Claudius stripped a Lycian of Roman citizenship because he couldn't understand Latin. For Eastern experts in Roman law using Latin, Swain 1996, 392 n. 17, Millar 1999.

24. On portrait statue dedications and receptions by provincial clients, see Tanner 2000, 46–50; Stewart 2003, 84–5, 90–1, 157–69.

25. *IvE* 3003: Dianae Ephesiae, Divo Clau[dio, Neroni Claudio Caesari Augusto [[Germa]nico]], Agrippinae Aug[ustae], civita[ti Ephesiorum] / [----- cum Claudia Metro]dora uxor[e].

['Ἀρτέμιδι 'Εφεσίᾳ, θεῷ Κλαυδίῳ, Νέρωνι Κλαυδίῳ Καίσαρι Σεβαστῷ [[Γερμανικῷ]], 'Αγριππείῃ Σ[ε]βασ[τῇ, τῷ 'Εφεσίων δήμῳ] / [----- ἐκ τ]ῶν ἰδίων κατασκευάσας ἀνέθηκεν σὺν Κλαυδίᾳ Μητροδώρᾳ τῇ γυναικί.

Halfmann 2001, 37; Kearsley 2001, 129 no. 155. Dated 54–59 C.E.

Figure 4.3 Reconstruction of plaza late in first century C.E., with addition of Neronian Hall; view from east.

Her brother Tiberius Claudius Phesinus from Teos, likely her original home as well, became chief priest of the provincial temple of the Augusti at Ephesos in 90 C.E.[26] Usually when both dedicators are Easterners, even if Roman citizens, the dedications are just in Greek. Was Metrodora's husband a Latin speaker from the West? Or was the dedication so strongly attracted by the nearby gate of Mazaeus and Mithridates that it ended up bilingual? We can only hope for additional data that will tell us.

The Neronian Hall's effect on its readers must have been quite different from that of the Gate of Mazaeus and Mithridates. First, the architectural parallelism made it evident that the two inscriptions on the stoa were equivalents, rather than statements of different things. That the Latin inscription came first, was higher on the building, and was in larger letters (with interpuncts), was usual, and just showed the pecking order. This time the building's architecture has no tinge of the Roman, but that is to be expected, as the design of the end of the stoa had to reflect that of the whole, which was plain Doric. Though a new construction, it is unmistakably an extension of the Greek Agora.

Before the Neronian Hall stood an older, round monument on a tall base. Stairs had to be added to make a passable transition between it, the new Neronian Hall, and the Gate of Mazaeus and Mithridates. There are several guesses about what this monument was. From the parts that have been found, dated by ornament style to the second half of the first century B.C.E., it was a small tholos with a conical roof. It has been restored by Friedmund Hueber, chief engineer and architect of Ephesos, as a combination water clock, tower of the winds, and water organ, with a nest of trumpets coming out of the roof; he did not indicate exactly how this would have worked.[27] Jobst saw the monument as a heroon, one of several such along the "Embolos" street leading off to the east; there is a similar circular podium for an intramural tomb at Aphrodisias.[28] It is also possible that it was a fountain, as there were holes and grooves for piping in roof and column fragments that may have belonged to it. Unfortunately, no inscription for it has yet been found.

Originally this area was a major east-west street flanking the Agora, and on its other side was a late Hellenistic peristyle house. But the new

26. Campanile 1994, 42–3; van Bremen 1996, 71–5, 84, 154, 195, 291–2, 309; Kearsley 1999.

27. Hueber (1997a, 70–3, 1997b, 267) based his theory on a mid-first-century B.C.E. inscription (*IvE* 3004) which states that a *horologeion* was at "the middle of the Agora." But at the time of that inscription, the area in which the round monument stood was not yet a plaza, but a street; it may have become part of the Agora later, by the time of the burial of Dionysios of Miletos there (see below). The remains of what may be a contemporary water-clock in Pergamon look very different from the building at Ephesos: Radt 2005. On Hellenistic and later water clocks, Wikander 2000, 363–9.

28. Jobst 1983, 184–98; on the "Embolos" heroa, infra n. 61. Cormack 2004, 173, on the Aphrodisias tomb.

additions of the Gate of Mazaeus and Mithridates and then the Neronian
Hall led to a complete change in the area's function. For one thing, soon
after the Gate's construction its floor level had to be raised and culverts
installed under it, as rain erosion was washing down the hillside to the
south and east and getting into the Agora.[29] Raising the floor level of
the Gate meant that wheeled traffic could no longer pass through it into
the Agora, but had to veer off and take the northbound street instead. This
isolated the space in front of the Gate, making it more of a pedestrian
thoroughfare than a through street. Perhaps now people began to gather
here for meetings, speeches, or legal proceedings which did not require the
large spaces offered by the great square Agora. By the early second century,
new benefactors recognized and furthered the change in the area by
eliminating the peristyle house, blocking the westward street, and building
a third bilingual monument here, the Library of Celsus (figure 4.4).

This is one of the best preserved and best known libraries of the ancient
world, as well as the most photographed spot in all Ephesos.[30] But
familiarity may mask what a very unusual building it is. It was built in
honor of Tiberius Julius Celsus Polemeanus, one of the first easterners to
become consul at Rome, in 92 C.E. When he died, his son, Tiberius Julius
Aquila, himself consul in 110, began the project, and when the son died
soon after, it was finished by his heirs. The family of Celsus likely came
from Sardis, not Ephesos, so Aquila had chosen to put his father's monument and burial place at Ephesos, a rival city, rather than their ancestral
home. He placed it where his father had enacted one of the greatest
offices of his life: after his suffect consulship, Polemeanus had returned
to his province as its highest Roman official, as Proconsul of Asia in 106/7.
Was this spot chosen, at sacrifice of a rather large house and at considerable expense, because this was close to where Celsus had enacted some of
his responsibilities as proconsul?

The front of the library bears a Greek dedication written only on the
lower story and on the largest of the three fasciae of the front-facing
architrave, making it legible and comprehensible to a viewer standing
before the building, with no need to follow along the sides of the facade's
aediculae.[31] This inscription is unusual in naming Celsus in the accusative, as if the building were a statue base; it then states that Aquila built

---

29. Inscription of [Herakleides] Passalas, who altered the Gate of Mazaeus and
Mithridates to keep floods out of the Agora and keep the "Triodos" passable: Knibbe,
Engelmann, and İplikçioğlu 1993, 123–4 no. 13. See Knibbe and Langmann 1993, 55;
Engelmann 1995, 87 n. 33; Halfmann 2001, 31–2.

30. Wilberg et al. 1953; Strocka 1981, esp. 322–9; 2003; Hoepfner 2002. Thanks to
George Houston for information and advice on libraries during and after the conference.

31. IvE 5101: Τι. Ἰούλ[ιον Κέλσον Πολεμαιανὸν] ὕπατον ἀνθύπατον Ἀσίας· Τι. Ἰούλιος
Ἀκύλας ὕπατος ὁ υἱὸς κατεσκεύασεν τὴν βιβλιοθήκην, [τὸ ἔργον ἀπα]ρτ[ι]σάν[τ]ων τῶν Ἀκύλα
κληρ[ονόμων, ἐπιμε]ληθέντος Τι. Κλ. Ἀριστίωνος, γʹ ἀσιάρχου.
For all inscriptions of the Library of Celsus, Keil in Wilberg et al. 1953, 61–80.

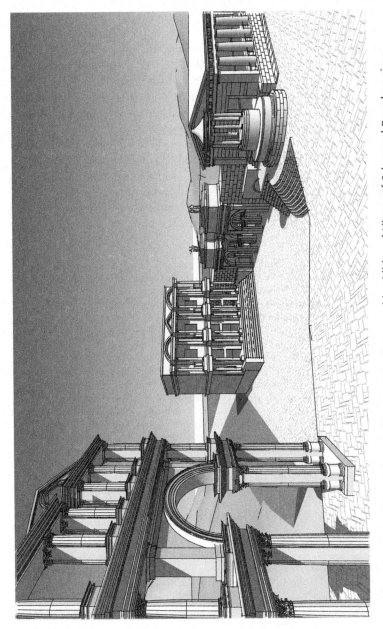

Figure 4.4 Reconstruction of plaza at mid-second century C.E., with addition of Library of Celsus and Propylon; view from southeast.

the library and his heirs finished it.[32] The building was in fact a heroon, enclosing Celsus's sarcophagus in a crypt directly below the library's vaulted central apse, which likely held his statue.[33] A long foundation document, again in Greek but this time dedicated more normally to Celsus in the dative, stood to the right of the center door, and stated the conditions of the bequest, as well as amounts given for construction and purchase of books, specifying that Celsus's statues were to be crowned three times a year.[34] This inscription would have taken more effort to read, as it was over a statue niche and stood 4.80–6.30 meters from floor level; though its 24 closely written lines began with letters 4.5 cm tall, they dwindle to 2 cm at the bottom.

The bilingual aspect comes to the fore—literally—on the bases of two equestrian statues of Celsus that flanked the library staircase. Their inscriptions, in Latin on the right, Greek on the left, both show Celsus's name and his most important titles (consul and proconsul of Asia) on the front, whereas those entering the library would see the long sides listing Celsus's official career to either side as they climbed the stairs.[35] The

32. Ma (2007, esp. 220) discusses the meaning behind the use of the accusative for statues, which may be extended to this building: "The honorific formula and decree, in their determination to speak of civic culture, say 'Look around you.'"

33. Neudecker (2004, 303–4) on library as heroon, though he misattributes the sarcophagus to Aquila. For intramural burial, infra n. 61.

34. *IvE* 5113: [Τιβ. Ἰουλίῳ Κέλσῳ] Πολεμαιανῷ ὑπάτῳ / [ἀνθυπάτῳ τῆς Ἀσί]ας Τιβ. Ἰούλιος Ἀκύλας / [Πολεμ]αιανός, ὕπατος, ὁ υἱὸς τὴν Κελσι/[αν]ὴν βιβλιοθήκην κατ[ε]σκεύασεν ἐκ τῶν / [ἰδίων] σὺν παντὶ τῷ κόσ[μ]ῳ καὶ ἀναθήμασι / [καὶ βυβ]λίοις· κατέλιπε δὲ κ[αὶ] εἰς ἐπισκευὴν αὐτῆς / [καὶ ὠνὴ]ν βυβλίων ✕ μ[υρι]άδας δύο ἥμισυ· ἐξ ὧν ὑφῇ/[ρέθη᾿β ἐπιε]τῇ, ὥστ[ε μενόντων τῶν] ἀρχαίων ✕ δισμυρίων ᾿γ / [ἀπὸ τῶν κατ᾿ ἔτος γιγνομέν]ων τόκων ἐπισκευ/[άζεσθαι τὴν βιβλιοθήκην κ]αὶ τοὺς προσμένον/[τας αὐτῇ λανβάνειν ✕ - ἃ αὐτοῖ]ς χορηγη[θ]ήσεται ἐπὶ / [τῇ γενεθλίῳ τοῦ Κέλσου ἡμέρα εἰ]ς ἀεί· κ[αὶ ὁμοίως] / κατὰ δια[θήκην τοῦ Ἀκύλα κατ᾿ ἔτος ἀγορ]άζ[εσθαι νέα] / βιβλία· ὁμοίως καὶ στεφανοῦσθ[αι τοὺς ἀνδριάντας] / [αὐ]τοῦ τρὶς [τ]οῦ ἐνιαυτοῦ· ὁμοίω[ς κοσμεῖσθαι τὰς] / [ἄλ]λας ε[ἰκόνα]ς κατ᾿ ἔ[τος] ἐν τῇ ἑο[ρτῇ τοῦ Κέλσου?] / [ἐπιτελεσθείσης ἀπὸ τῶν ✕᾿β, ἃ] ὑφηρέθη, ὑπ᾿ α]ὐτῶν τῶν / [κληρονόμων τῆς λοιπῆς ἐπισκευῆς καθιερώθη] ἡ βιβλιο/θήκη τῇ τοῦ Κέλσο[υ ἑορτῇ ?, ὥστε μηνὸς -------ὠνο]ς ἑπτα/καιδεκάτῃ τῶν χρη[μάτων ..] .σ[..........τῶ]ν ἐνγεγρ[αμμέν]ων / κατὰ τὸ ῥητὸν τῆς διαθήκης μή[τε γραφὰς ? μήτε] κατ[α]ρήσ[εις ? μήτε] / ἀναλώματα ἐπιγενήσεσθαι αὐ[τοῖς, ἐντελὲς] ἀπαρτισάντων τῶν / τοῦ Ἀκύλα κληρονόμων τὸ ἔργο[ν, ἐπιμεληθέ]ντος κατὰ διαθήκην / Τιβ. Κλαυδίου Ἀριστίωνος, τρὶς [ἀσιάρ]χου.

35. *IvE* 5102, front: Τι. Ἰούλιον Τι. υἱὸν Κορνηλία / Κέλσον Πολεμαιανόν / ὕπατον ἀνθύπατον Ἀσίας / χειλίαρχον λεγιῶνος γ᾿ /

Right side: Κυρηναϊκῆς, καὶ ἀγορανόμον καταλεγέντα ὑπὸ θεοῦ Οὐεσπασιανοῦ, / στρατηγὸν δήμου Ῥωμαίων, πρεσβευτὴν θεοῦ Οὐεσπασιανοῦ καὶ θεοῦ / Τίτου ἐπαρχειῶν Καππαδοκίας Γαλατίας Πόντου Πισιδίας Παφλαγονίας / Ἀρμενίας, πρεσβευτὴν θεοῦ Τίτου καὶ Αὐτοκράτορος Σεβαστοῦ λεγιῶνος δ᾿ / Σκυθικῆς, ἀνθύπατον Πόντου καὶ Βειθυνίας, ἔπαρχον αἱραρίου στρατιωτικοῦ, / πρεσβευτὴν Αὐτοκράτορος Καίσαρος Σεβαστοῦ ἐπαρχείας Κιλικίας, γενόμενον δὲ καὶ / ἐπὶ ἔργων δημοσίων τῶν ἐν Ῥώμῃ, Τι. Ἰούλιος Ἀκύλας Πολεμαιανὸς ὕπατος τὸν ἑαυτοῦ πατέρα, ἀπαρτισάντων / τῶν κληρονόμων Ἀκύλα.

IvE 5103, front: Ti. Iulio Ti. f. Celso / Polemaeano cos. / procos. Asiae Ti. Iulius / Aquila cos. f./

Left side: Ti. Iulio Ti. f. Cor. Celso Polemaeano, cos., procos. Asiae, trib. legionis III / Cyrenaicae, adlecto inter aedilicios ab divo Vespasiano, pr(aetori) p(opuli) R(omani), leg

format traditional to each language is used correctly and with some ease; for example, Celsus's name is in the dative in the Latin, accusative in the Greek. Interestingly, despite some small differences, the two bases' close spacing, circular rounded letters, and tendency to end lines at word endings make them look remarkably similar; the Latin retains its long "I"s and interpuncts, but even the Greek gets interpuncts in its attention-getting front first line, for Celsus's name. Save for the right hand statue base, all the other inscriptions on the building were in Greek.

The Library carried explicit messages about Celsus, not just in text, but in statues and decor. In addition to the one in the inner apse and the equestrian pair on the outside, at least three other statues of Celsus and one of Aquila stood on Greek-inscribed bases in the upper story of the monument, likely wearing the various costumes of their offices. An over-life-sized statue of a laurel-crowned man in full general's outfit with senator's shoes is likely one of those (Celsus commanded the fourth legion Scythica under Titus and Domitian).[36] The twelve fasces of Celsus's proconsular office, with hooded axes, are carved among the decorative scrollwork on six of the pilasters flanking the doors into the building, and in the labeled niches between stood figures of his personified Wisdom (*Sophia*), Excellence (*Arete*), Knowledge (*Episteme*), and another quality (replaced by a late antique inscription of the Forethought, *Ennoia*, of one Philippos). These are not the virtues usually trumpeted for emperors or portrayed on coins and honorific shields, but the literary ones that hailed the crowning of Homer on the Relief of Archelaos.[37] They heroize a man for his high Hellenic culture. The statues now set up in the reconstructed niches are copies, but not of the originals, which were likely destroyed in a third-century earthquake. They were replaced with miscellaneous females, including a reused Hygieia, and can't tell us what attributes identified *Sophia* or *Arete*.[38]

(ato) Aug(ustorum) / divorum Vespasiani et Titi provinciae Cappadociae et Galatiae Ponti / Pisidiae Paphlagoniae Armeniae Minoris, leg(ato) divi Titi leg(ionis) IIII Scythicae, procos. / Ponti et Bithyniae, praef(ecto) aerari militaris, leg(ato) Aug(usti) pro pr(aetore) provinciae Ciliciae, XVviro s(acris) f(aciundis), cur(atori) / aedium sacrarum et operum locorumque publicorum populi Romani, Ti. Iulius Aquila Polemaeanus cos. / patrem suum, consummaverunt heredes Aquilae.

Kearsley 2001, 51–3 no. 73 gives texts and English translations of the two statue bases, though she calls them the "epitaph" of Tiberius Julius Celsus Polemaeanus.

36. Eichler in Wilberg et al. 1953, 57–9 Abb. 101; Smith 1998, 73–5. For portrait statues' dedication and reception, supra n. 24.

37. Both *Sophia* and *Arete* appear in the relief of Archelaos of Priene, ca. 130 B.C.E., for which see Pinkwart 1965, 72–5, and Newby 2007, 158, 175. A statue of *Arete* stood next to Ptolemy in the procession of Ptolemy II as described by Kallixeinos of Rhodes in Athenaeus, *Deipnosophistae* 5.201d. For the iconography of Celsus's virtues, infra n. 38.

38. This is not accounted for by J. C. Balty in his articles in *LIMC*, s.v. "Arete," "Ennoia," and "Episteme"; but noted by M. Xagorari s.v. "Sophia."

The front of the Library is built in a style that might be called "New Asian Roman." It features tall Composite columns, an order that may have been seen as particularly Italian, at the lower story, where they would be noticed more than the smaller and more standard Corinthian columns that stood above.[39] Monolithic column shafts, of purple-veined marble from central Phrygia, give the Library a striking resemblance to a Roman-style theater stage, like the one Ephesos had recently installed in its own theater.[40] The columns were not just rare, but cut to specially ordered heights; one wonders whether Celsus, who served as *curator operum locorumque publicorum populi Romani* under Domitian, had made some contacts at the imperial quarries and passed them on to his son.[41] The sheer expense was obvious, as the facade has no practical function whatever; the three-story interior as restored, with its niches for bookcases, does not even correspond to the two-story exterior. Certainly all this was meant to draw the attention, to make a new civic space; it is so theatrical that it may have envisioned an audience before it. Its architecture, texts, and sculpture glorify Celsus as a figure worthy of emulation by all who stood here; but by the preponderance of the messages, his Roman offices seem the result of his Greek virtues.[42] It was aimed at a Hellenized and cultivated audience, and it proved to be a magnet for it.

That the plaza was now designated a separate space is shown by the fact that it soon received another gate, marking off its southeastern corner as the Gate of Mazaeus and Mithridates marked off its northwestern one (figure 4.4). This is often called "Hadrian's Gate," but there is little basis to the name. Only fragments of the Greek dedication inscription on the two lower of its three architraves have been found, and they could refer to either Trajan or Hadrian.[43] The Composite capitals are much like those of the Library of Celsus, and they must come close to it in time. Another Greek inscription on it dedicates the paving of a street that led from it, and calls it "Propylon."[44] But the most elaborate side, with brecciated

39. Onians 1988, 42–8, 53–6.
40. *IvE* 2034, dedication of the skene under Nero or Domitian (Burrell 2004, 62).
41. Both Hueber (1997a, 77–81) and Barresi (2003, 377–80) posit the influence of Trajan's Forum and the Bibliotheca Ulpia on the Ephesian building, but the architectural resemblance is not strong, and whether Trajan's Column was planned as his gravesite during his lifetime is itself problematic: Davies 2000, 30–4. For new views on the Bibliotheca Ulpia and its placement, Meneghini 2002a, b.
42. On cultured senators, Jones 2005. The Library of Celsus could also have been the meeting place for a deliberative body, as when the Roman Senate met in the Latin library in the sanctuary of Apollo on the Palatine (Corbier 2006, 163–79). This would have augmented its role in the development of the plaza as a center for speech, leading up to the Auditorion, below; but unfortunately no traces of such a use were found in the Library, whose original interior fittings had been stripped out in late antiquity.
43. *IvE* 329 (3): ---]νῶι Καίσ[αρι---
The Propylon is published by Thür (1989, inscriptions discussed pp. 69–75).
44. *IvE* 422A: . . .]ς πλατείας τῆς ἀπὸ τοῦ προπύλο[υ / γρ]α[μ]ματεύοντος τοῦ [δήμου . . .

columns that again echo the Library of Celsus, was that seen from the plaza. Though named a propylon, it is not "before" anything but a road, aiming more south than west toward the sacred site of Ortygia. The Propylon is structurally a Roman triumphal arch, but instead of copying an Italian model, it is so tall and thin as to be two-dimensional, with a Syrian-style pediment at the top, unusual on arches, but known on other Hadrianic buildings at Ephesos. Its closest match is the Arch of Hadrian in Athens, which is similar in design, though the Ephesos Propylon may well be the earlier of the two.[45] There is just enough room for statues to stand on the lower level: on a late inscribed base propped against the Propylon, one Demeas boasts of having taken down the image of the *daimon* Artemis and put up a Christian cross instead.[46] We know nothing else of the decor, or whether it had any Latin inscriptions. If there was a statue of the city goddess Artemis on the Propylon, she might have been accompanied by a statue of the emperor, as on the Gate of Mazaeus and Mithridates; the goddess and the emperors cohabit on almost every building dedication in Roman Ephesos, and their silver and gold images were set up together in the theater and carried in processions all around the city.[47]

After the Propylon was built, a new building was added to the plaza (figure 4.5). Its foundation, which is all we have, takes the shape of a shallow U, with a broad staircase on the front. This used to be called the "Altar Building," not just from a slight resemblance to altar-courts like that of Zeus at Pergamon, but because sculptural blocks of the so-called Parthian monument were found nearby and attributed to it. Now other pieces of that monument have been found elsewhere; also, the 70-meter length of its frieze would barely fit on this shallow foundation, whose walls offer just under 75 meters of display space.[48] In default of this, fragments found near the theater, possibly from another displaced altar depicting amazon(s), have also been associated with the foundation, though the argument is not compelling.[49]

45. The term "Syrian" for a pediment with arched entablature does not necessarily indicate ethnicity or origin, as Butcher (2003, 290) pithily observes. For the Arch of Hadrian in Athens, Willers 1990, 68–92. Note that, like the Ephesos Propylon, the two sides of the Arch of Hadrian also mark outer limits, not entry: when one reads the inscription for the "city of Hadrian" on the east side, that region is behind, not before, the viewer. This directionality is not noted by the otherwise theoretically loaded Gheorghiu, 2003.

46. *IvE* 1351; Thür 1989, 129–31.

47. G. Rogers 1991.

48. Oberleitner 1999. Though Thür (1989, 26) previously accepted the Parthian Monument's 170 C.E. date for the U-shaped building, only noting that its socle that butts against (and thus postdates) the Propylon may not have been from its first phase, she now (with Pyszkowski-Wyzykowski 2006, 155) says that the U-shaped building is earlier than the Propylon. This contradicts excavation evidence (Jobst 1983, 215–29).

49. Thür 2005. *IvE* 3059, a statue base of a priestess of Artemis found during excavations in the Agora, should not be taken to identify a "sacred place of Artemis on the Embolos," and

Figure 4.5 Reconstruction of plaza in late second century C.E., with addition of building that may be the Auditorion; view from northeast.

A hint at this building's function is offered by an inscription carved on the left center pillar of the Gate of Mazaeus and Mithridates in the early third century C.E.[50] It records that the city, using the bequest of one Julia Potentilla, constructed a paving in front of the "Auditorion" and the Library of Celsus. A new paving was indeed installed in the plaza around 200 C.E., and one could stand beside the Auditorion inscription and look out onto it. This inscription is the sole case yet known where the Latin word "auditorium" has been transliterated into Greek, bypassing such cognates as "akroaterion" for a lecture or meeting hall, or "dikasterion" for a hall of justice.[51] In spoken language, this would be called "code-switching," the sudden use of a foreign phrase in speech of another language, though in this case it is transliterated, the letter forms remaining Greek. So the Auditorion inscription differs from the independent or closely translated bilinguals that we have seen so far, though a transliteration of an official Roman term also occurs on the Greek version of Celsus's equestrian statue base, in which the Latin version's "aerarium" becomes Greek "airarion."[52]

From this choice of the Latinate "auditorion" rather than a Greek term, it has been postulated that the building in question was named from its particular Roman use, in other words, that it was the courtroom for the proconsul of Asia and his consilium.[53] The inscription on the gate faces onto the plaza, and if the Auditorion had a front pavement shared with the Library of Celsus, it must have faced onto the plaza, too. But it cannot be the Neronian Hall, on the right: its two doors leading into two long separate passages would have ill accommodated a tribunal or a courtroom full of standing people, much less the seating that most of our texts place in Roman auditoria.[54]

thus to justify restoring an altar of Artemis here (Thür 2005, 359, citing Knibbe 1991); the relevant (end) part of the base's inscription, lines 11–13 after a vacant line, reads: ὁ ἱερὸς τόπος Ἐμβολει/τῶν τῶν παρὰ τῇ κυρίᾳ ἡμῶν θεᾷ Ἀρτέμιδι, that is, "the sacred place of the Emboleitans who are at the side of our mistress the goddess Artemis." The "sacred place" is the base itself, as shown by the nominative typical of *topos* inscriptions, whereas the rest refers to the dedicators who live on that street and their allegiance to the goddess.

50. *IvE* 3009: ἀγαθῇ τύχ[ῃ] / ἡ πόλις τὸ σύστρω[μα] / τὸ πρὸ τοῦ αὐδειτωρίου / καὶ τῆς Κέλσου βιβλιοθή/κης κατεσκεύασεν ἐκ προ/σόδων κληρονομίας / Ἰου[λία]ς Ποτεντίλλης.
Potentilla's bequest extended to other projects as well: see *IvE* 2041, 2042; van Bremen 1996, 195, 320.

51. Tamm 1963, 8–23. Infra n. 52. Note *SEG* 17 (1960) 759, a bilingual inscription that records a hearing held by the emperor Caracalla in Antioch: the Latin portion sets the scene in the aud(itorium), whereas the Greek refers to it as a *dikasterion*.

52. Mason 1974, 5, 7–8, 20; Leiwo 1995, 300–1; Adams and Swain 2002, 3–7.

53. Engelmann 1993.

54. *Pace* Kearsley 2001, 129. The excavators at first thought that the Auditorion consisted of the steps at the east of the plaza, and the space enclosed by them: Alzinger 1970, 1633, where he posits that Dionysios of Miletos founded the Auditorion. This notion changed due to further excavation in the 1980s: Jobst 1983, 154–64.

Hueber has suggested that the U-shaped building is the Auditorion.[55] His restoration is not impossible, but the side aisles are too narrow to be used, the vaulted central space is so imaginary that no roof has been drawn in on its reconstruction, and the result resembles a Renaissance pavilion like the Loggia dei Lanzi in Florence. One wonders how legal cases could have been heard there; certainly the postulated statue of an emperor at the back would have had to be replaced by the proconsul's tribunal. Hueber also downplays the fact that the building's interior is only about 19 feet deep. In Rome, basilicas used as courtrooms were both enclosed and far larger, as they needed to accommodate the magistrate, his consilium, and all the jurors; in Asia as in Rome, juries of a hundred are known.[56]

The U-shaped building's ground plan resembles the type of exedra decorated with columns that is found on gymnasium palaestrae in Asia Minor, and has been incorrectly termed "Kaisersaal." I have argued elsewhere against the supposed association between these rooms and imperial cult, and have been looking for the real function(s) for such exedrae.[57] It is likely that at least some of them were lecture rooms for the men of learning whose natural haunts were gymnasia. Though we know of no other use of the word "auditorion" than the Ephesos inscription, we know of a few akroateria in Asia Minor, and two are specifically in gymnasia.[58] Like the building in the plaza, gymnasium exedrae had support for an aediculated column display—like that on the front of the Library of Celsus—on three walls, and were unwalled but columned on the broad fourth side. This would have provided seating for honored guests—or jurors—in the interior, but also allowed standees to listen to the declamation from the pavement beyond.

As no other building that shared a pavement with the Library of Celsus seems as appropriate—indeed, as no other building other than the ones mentioned has yet been found, though surprises are always possible with further excavation—the U-shaped building is likely to have been the Auditorion mentioned in the inscription. But even if its function and official status was Roman, its design probably met specifically Asian desires. We know that those who brought cases before the governor of Asia's tribunal took care to employ professional orators to argue for them, and that fans of these sophists would travel far and wide to hear them.[59]

55. Hueber 1997a, 83–5. Thanks to Elizabeth Riorden for her thoughts on the architecture.

56. Philostratus, *Lives of the Sophists* 1.22, section 524. On the provincial justice system of Asia, see Burton 1975.

57. Burrell 2006.

58. At Chios (*IGRR* 4.1703) and at Aigai in Aeolis (Ameling et al. 1995, 427–8 nos. 357, 357 [A]). See also Robert 1937, 79–80; Delorme 1960, 324–5; Hellmann 1988, 243; Korenjak 2000, 31.

59. Philostratus, *Lives of the Sophists* 1.22, section 525: as an old man, Dionysios of Miletos traveled from his home in Ephesos to the assize court held in Sardis to hear Polemon

Perhaps, then, this open-fronted Auditorion was designed so that the stars of the Second Sophistic could display their talents to crowds beyond the lawcourt.[60]

In fact, an earlier sophist had found his final resting place in this very plaza. In 1967, excavators cleared a late antique ramp that led up from the Gate of Mazaeus and Mithridates over what had previously been the steps of the Neronian Hall. Tucked under the ramp, they found a sarcophagus, still with its original lead lining and the bones within. If it had been moved to build the ramp, it hadn't gone far. The name of the honored dead was inscribed on the front: Titus Claudius Flavianus Dionysios, and under the central rosette, his profession: *Rhetor*.[61] A base for a bronze statue of this man was found close by: he was the famous sophist Dionysios of Miletos, who spent the last part of his life speaking and teaching in Ephesos.[62] Philostratos confirms that the Ephesians buried Dionysios with the greatest of honors, for his grave was in the most important part of the Agora.[63] Philostratos would have known; he came to Ephesos several times, to visit a later but equally famous sophist, Damianos. So in the second century this plaza may have been considered not just part of the Agora, but its most important part. Perhaps this particular spot was chosen because it was where Dionysios and his fellow orators practiced and displayed their art, close by the new, theatrical Library of Celsus, and once it was built, in the Auditorion. The plaza certainly contained other monuments to both

of Smyrna defend a wealthy Lydian in danger of losing his property. Philostratos calls the courtroom "dikasterion." On languages and ethnicities of sophists and orators, Puech 2002, 32; on the languages of the courtroom, Eck 2004, 14–16. Note the debate between the orators C. Sallius Aristainetos and L. Egnatius Victor Lollianus in a trial before Caracalla at Antioch (Puech 2002, 132–134, 332, and supra n. 51): their words are quoted in Greek within the body of the Latin inscription.

60. A provocative summary of the worlds of the Second Sophistic is Whitmarsh (2005). See Korenjak 2000, 27–33, 44–6, 96–100, for the varied scenes of sophistic display, including auditoria and akroateria, the crowds they might have held, and those crowds' adulation. Lucian's *On the Hall* describes the *oikos* used for (this) oration as large and high, with east-facing doors, windows, a marble statue of Athena in a shrine (as in some libraries), mythological paintings, and a magnificent gilt ceiling.

61. *IvE* 426: *T. Κλαύδιος / Φλαουιανὸς / Διονύσιος / ῥήτωρ*. See Jobst 1983, 163–4, 211–12; Jones 2005, 263. Burial within the city was an honor rather frequently granted at Ephesos, especially along the "Embolos" that connects this plaza to the city's eastern Agora: Knibbe and Langmann 1993, 54; Thür 1995 and 1997, 69–75. For intramural burial in this and other cities of Asia, see Cormack 2004, 44–9, 222–3, though on 48 she states that Celsus, rather than his son, donated the funds for the library. It is interesting that both Hadrian (*Digest* 47.12.3.5) and Antoninus Pius (*HA Antoninus Pius* 12.3) forbade burials within cities; I thank Mark Atwood for this observation.

62. Puech 2002, 229–32, no. 98, which emends lines 2 and 4 of *IvE* 3047:
[ἡ βουλὴ καὶ] ὁ δῆμος / [T. Κλ.] Φ[λαουιαν]ὸν Διονύσιον / [τὸν] ῥήτορα καὶ σοφιστὴν καὶ / [δ?ὶ]ς ἐπίτροπον τοῦ Σεβαστοῦ / Κλ. Εὔτυχος τὸν ἑαυτοῦ πάτρωνα.
Supra n. 54 for Dionysios as possible founder of the Auditorion.

63. *Lives of the Sophists* 1.22; Engelmann 1995 and 1996.

sophists and governors: here Damianos himself put up a statue of the Proconsul Marcus Nonius Macrinus in 170/71, calling him "savior of the province" (though the largest lettering was used for Damianos's own name).[64] In the Auditorion of Ephesos, Roman government and Asian oratory were intermingled, inseparable.

What do we have, then, when the whole plaza is assembled, just before the earthquake in 262 that may have sent all the delicate architecture and statues tumbling? A developing story of the intersection between Greek and Roman culture. It begins with a startling novelty, introduced by a new element in provincial society; this it absorbs, translates into its own traditions, and domesticates. Buildings attract further building, texts attract texts, whether on those buildings or standing around them, clustered in a new civic nexus which in the process became a focus for speech as well.[65] This cluster at Ephesos emphasizes and aggrandizes a burgeoning Helleno-Roman cultural ideal.

These buildings, sculptures, and texts are not simple products of "Romanization," a concept that has lately been examined, dissected, and widely rejected.[66] If Greek and Roman were polar opposites (and I do not think they were), these monuments at Ephesos would all fall somewhere between the two.[67] The earlier ones, like the Gate of Mazaeus and Mithridates, are hybrids from which disparate elements can be isolated, but the Library of Celsus is a blended architecture that its viewers probably read, not as "Greek" or "Roman," but as "modern" and "expensive" and "theatrical," its hero as "cultured" and "official" and "important."

Those who were inspired by these buildings toward further building came from various elites. There was certainly the directing class of the city: magistrates, priests, liturgists, and other benefactors, from the first century C.E. increasingly acquiring Roman citizenship.[68] Imperial freedmen got a look in too, especially in the times of Caesar and Augustus. From the last third of the first century onward, once Ephesos got its first

64. *IvE* 3029. For Damianos and his inscriptions, Puech 2002, 190–200. She observes of this one (199, no. 84) that it painstakingly translates the Latin formulae ("avec leurs gérondifs déconcertants") of Macrinus's offices and priesthoods into Greek, but is not so careful at numbering Roman legions: it makes Macrinus *tribunus laticlavius* of XVII, one of Varus's legions, wiped out in 9 C.E. and never reconstituted.

65. Van Nijf 2000 on clustered benefactors' inscriptions and the prominence they give to dedicators as well as dedicatees; cf. the dedication by Damianos, supra n. 64.

66. For example, Woolf 1992 and 1994; Freeman 1993 and 1997; Mattingly 1997; Majbom Madsen 2002. Dench (2005, esp. 30–5, 61–92, 166–221) shows the difficulty of even defining what it is to be "Roman."

67. For example, Whitmarsh (2001) studies the complexities of Roman Greek "cultural identity" through literature. I do not advocate the theory of "harmonious cultural equilibrium" that Woolf (1994, 117) warned against, but emphasize that architecture was less ideologically "loaded" than, for example, language, law, and literary culture (ibid. 127–8).

68. Campanile 2004a.

provincial imperial temple, there were the chief priests, priestesses, and functionaries who served it, many of them from other cities of Asia.[69] Then there were the orators, sophists, philosophers, and grammarians, not just from Hellenic lands but from the exotic West: Favorinus, the famous Gallic orator, made his headquarters at Ephesos, like Dionysios, Damianos, and other world-class teachers. Of course there were incoming Roman citizens: merchants, the governors, their families, staff, and soldiers; as time went on, these were as likely to be from Asia or further east as from Italy, Gaul, or Spain. And all of these could intersect with one another: a Roman governor (or emperor) more comfortable speaking Greek, an Ephesian who was a senator in Rome, or a sophist who came from Gaul to teach Greek oratory and became citizen-benefactor of Ephesos. And this is not to ignore the people coming in from the countryside, some of whom may have still spoken Carian or Phrygian;[70] or travelers from outside the Empire, to whom the writing on the monuments may have been a blur next to the commanding statues and dazzling marbles.

If this chapter shows anything, it is the benefit of reconstructing reading experiences in the fullest contexts possible. Ephesos offers a "vertical stratigraphy" of buildings, sculptures, and texts, and to read its development from (transcribed) inscriptions alone would have been as limiting as restoring the architecture and sculpture without the inscriptions. Because in the city of Ephesos, though there was no monument without its text, there was also no text without its monument.

ACKNOWLEDGMENTS

Illustrations by Nate Bullock with assistance from Tim Callan, with thanks to Elizabeth Riorden for her advice.

BIBLIOGRAPHY

Adams, J. N. 2002. "Bilingualism at Delos." In J. N. Adams, M. Janse, and S. Swain, eds., *Bilingualism in Ancient Society: Language Contact and the Written Text*, 103–27. Oxford.

—— and S. Swain. 2002. "Introduction." In J. N. Adams, M. Janse, and S. Swain, eds., *Bilingualism in Ancient Society: Language Contact and the Written Text*, 1–20. Oxford.

---

69. Burrell 2004, 60–6.

70. Rural residence did not necessarily mean being illiterate in Greek, however: see de Hoz 2006. *Pace* Mitchell 2000, 120–1, Strabo's mention (12.4.6) of the disappearance of most local languages and ethnic identities in Roman times should not be uncritically applied beyond the areas of Bithynia about which he was writing.

Alföldy, G. 2003. "Die Repräsentation der kaiserlichen Macht in den Inschriften Roms und des Imperium Romanum." In L. de Blois, P. Erdkamp, O. Hekster, G. de Kleijn, and S. Mols, eds., *The Representation and Perception of Roman Imperial Power: Proceedings of the Third Workshop of the International Network Impact of Empire (Roman Empire, c. 200 B.C.–A.D. 476), Netherlands Institute in Rome, March 20–23, 2002*, 3–19. Amsterdam.

Alzinger, W. 1970. "Ephesos B." In *RE* Supplement 12: 1588–1704.

——. 1974. *Augusteische Architektur in Ephesos*. Österreichisches Archäologisches Institut, Sonderschriften 16. Vienna.

Ameling, W., K. Bringmann, and B. Schmidt-Dounas. 1995. *Schenkungen hellenistischer Herrscher an griechische Städte und Heiligtümer, 1: Zeugnisse und Kommentare*. Berlin.

Barresi, P. 2003. *Province dell'Asia minore: Costo dei marmi, architettura pubblica e committenza*. Rome.

Beard, M. 2007. *The Roman Triumph*. Cambridge, Mass.

Bing, P. 2002. "The Un-Read Muse? Inscribed Epigram and its Readers in Antiquity." In M. A. Harder, R. F. Regtuit, and G. K. Wakker, eds., *Hellenistic Epigrams*, 39–66. Hellenistica Groningana 6. Leuven.

Burrell, B. 2004. *Neokoroi: Greek Cities and Roman Emperors*. Cincinnati Classical Studies N. S. 9. Leiden.

——. 2006. "False Fronts: Separating the Aedicular Facade from the Imperial Cult in Roman Asia Minor." *AJA* 110: 437–69.

Burton, G. 1975. "Proconsuls, Assizes and the Administration of Justice under the Empire." *JRS* 65: 92–106.

Butcher, K. 2003. *Roman Syria and the Near East*. Los Angeles.

Campanile, M. 1994. *I sacerdoti del koinon d'Asia (I sec. a.C.-III sec. d.C.): Contributo allo studio della romanizzazione delle élites provinciali nell'Oriente greco*. Biblioteca di studi antichi 74, Studi ellenistici 7. Pisa.

——. 2004a. "Appunti sulla cittadinanza romana nella provincia d'Asia: i casi di Efeso e Smirne." In G. Salmeri, A. Raggi, and A. Baroni, eds., *Colonie romane nel mondo greco*, 165–85. Minima Epigraphica et Papyrologica. Supplementa 3. Rome.

——. 2004b. "Il fine ultimo della creazione: élità nel mondo ellenistico e romano." In *Mediterraneo Antico: Economie, Società, Culture* 7(1): 1–12.

Chantraine, H. 1967. *Freigelassene und Sklaven im Dienst der römischen Kaiser: Studien zu ihrer Nomenklatur*. Forschungen zur antiken Sklaverei 1. Wiesbaden.

Colledge, M. 1987. "Greek and Non-Greek Interaction in the Art and Architecture of the Hellenistic East." In A. Kuhrt and S. Sherwin-White, eds., *Hellenism in the East*, 134–62. London.

Corbier, M. 2006. *Donner à voir, donner à lire: Mémoire et communication dans la Rome ancienne*. Paris.

Cormack, S. 2004. *The Space of Death in Roman Asia Minor*. Wiener Forschungen zur Archäologie 6. Vienna.

Davies, P. 2000. *Death and the Emperor: Roman Imperial Funerary Monuments, from Augustus to Marcus Aurelius*. Cambridge.

de Hoz, M. 2006. "Literacy in Rural Anatolia: The Testimony of the Confession Inscriptions." *ZPE* 155: 139–44.

Delorme, J. 1960. *Gymnasion: Étude sur les monuments consacrés a l'éducation en Grèce (des origines à l'Empire romain)*. Bibliothèque des écoles françaises d'Athènes et de Rome ser. 1, fasc. 196. Paris.

Dench, E. 2005. *Romulus' Asylum: Roman Identities from the Age of Alexander to the Age of Hadrian.* Oxford.

Eck, W. 2004. "Lateinisch, Griechisch, Germanisch...? Wie sprach Rom mit seinen Untertanen?" In L. de Ligt, E. Hemelrijk, and H. Singor, eds., *Roman Rule and Civic Life: Local and Regional Perspectives. Proceedings of the Fourth Workshop of the International Network Impact of Empire (Roman Empire, c. 200 B.C.– A.D. 476), Leiden, June 25–28, 2003,* 3–19. Amsterdam.

Edwards, C. 2003. "Incorporating the Alien: The Art of Conquest." In C. Edwards and G. Woolf, eds., *Rome the Cosmopolis,* 44–70. Cambridge.

Elsner, J. 1996. "Inventing Imperium: Texts and the Propaganda of Monuments in Augustan Rome." In J. Elsner, ed., *Art and Text in Roman Culture,* 32–53. Cambridge.

Engelmann, H. 1993. "Celsusbibliothek und Auditorium in Ephesos (IK 17, 3009)." *ÖJh* 62: 105–11.

———. 1995. "Philostrat und Ephesos." *ZPE* 108: 77–87.

———. 1996. "Philostrat und die Agora von Ephesos." *Arkeoloji Dergisi* 4: 33–6.

Freeman, P. 1993. "'Romanisation' and Roman Material Culture." *JRA* 6: 438–45.

———. 1997. "Mommsen to Haverfield: The Origins of Studies of Romanization in Late 19th-c. Britain." In D. Mattingly, ed., *Dialogues in Roman Imperialism: Power, Discourse, and Discrepant Experience in the Roman Empire,* 27–50. Journal of Roman Archaeology, Supplementary Series 23. Portsmouth, R.I.

Gheorghiu, D. 2003. "Massive Walls and Decorated Entrances: An Archaeological Approach to Pre-Modern Architecture." In G. Malm, ed., *Toward an Archaeology of Buildings: Contexts and Concepts,* 119–24. BAR International Series 1186. Oxford.

Halfmann, H. 2001. *Städtebau und Bauherren im römischen Kleinasien: Ein Vergleich zwischen Pergamon und Ephesos.* Tübingen.

Hellmann, M.-C. 1988. "À propos d'un lexique des termes d'architecture grecque." In D. Knoepfler, ed., *Comptes et inventaires dans la cité grecque. Actes du Colloque international d'épigraphie tenu a Neuchâtel du 23 au 26 septembre 1986 en l'honneur de Jacques Tréheux,* 239–61. Geneva.

Hoepfner, W. 2002. "Die Celsus-Bibliothek in Ephesos." In W. Hoepfner, ed., *Antike Bibliotheken,* 123–6. Mainz.

Holtorf, C. 2007. "The Reception History of Monuments." https://tspace.library.utoronto.ca/citd/holtorf/2.4.html (as of October 15, 2007).

Hornbostel-Hüttner, G. 1979. *Studien zur römischen Nischenarchitektur.* Studies of the Dutch Archaeological and Historical Society 9. Leiden.

Hueber, F. 1997a. *Ephesos: Gebaute Geschichte.* Mainz am Rhein.

———. 1997b. "Zur städtebaulichen Entwicklung des hellenistisch-römischen Ephesos: Phylen, Embolos, Olympieion, Horologeion, Statthalterpalast, Auditorium, Parthermonument, Marienkirche." *IstMitt* 47: 251–69.

Ireland, R. 1983. "Epigraphy." In M. Henig, ed., *A Handbook of Roman Art: A Comprehensive Survey of All the Arts of the Roman World,* 220–33. Ithaca, N.Y.

Jauss, H. 1982. *Toward an Aesthetic of Reception.* Trans. T. Bahti. Minneapolis.

Jobst, W. 1983. "Embolosforschungen I." *ÖJh* 54: Beibl. 149–242.

Jones, C. 2005. "Culture in the Careers of Eastern Senators." In W. Eck and M. Heil, eds., *Senatores Populi Romani: Realität und mediale Präsentation einer Führungsschicht. Kolloquium der Prosopographia Imperii Romani vom 11.–13.*

Juni 2004, 263–70. Heidelberger althistorische Beiträge und epigraphische Studien 40. Stuttgart.

Kader, I. 1996. "'Romanisierende' Tendenzen in der frühkaiserzeitlichen Architektur des syrischen Raums im Spiegel der Bogenmonumente: Dargestellt am Tetrapylon von Latakia." In B. Funck, ed., *Hellenismus: Beiträge zur Erforschung von Akkulturation und politischer Ordnung in den Staaten des hellenistischen Zeitalters. Akten des Internationalen Hellenismus-Kolloquiums, 9.–14. März 1994 in Berlin*, 255–68. Tübingen.

Kearsley, R. A. 1999. "Women in Public Life in the Roman East: Iunia Theodora, Claudia Metrodora and Phoebe, Benefactress of Paul." *Tyndale Bulletin* 50: 189–211.

——, ed.; with the collaboration of T. Evans. 2001. *Greeks and Romans in Imperial Asia: Mixed Language Inscriptions and Linguistic Evidence for Cultural Interaction until the End of* A.D. *III*. Inschriften griechischer Städte aus Kleinasien 59. Bonn.

Knibbe, D. 1991. "Das 'Parthermonument' von Ephesos: (Parthersieg)altar der Artemis (und Kenotaph des L. Verus) an der 'Triodos.'" In *Berichte und Materialien, Österreichisches Archäologisches Institut*, 1: 5–18.

——. 1998. *Ephesus: Geschichte einer bedeutenden antiken Stadt und Portrait einer modernen Grossgrabung im 102. Jahr der Wiederkehr des Beginnes österreichischer Forschungen (1895–1997)*. Frankfurt.

——, H. Engelmann, and B. İplikçioğlu. 1989. "Neue Inschriften aus Ephesos XI." *ÖJh* 59: Beibl. 162–238.

——, H. Engelmann, and B. İplikçioğlu. 1993. "Neue Inschriften aus Ephesos XII." *ÖJh* 62: 113–50.

—— and G. Langmann. 1993. *Via Sacra Ephesiaca I. Berichte und Materialien, Österreichisches Archaologisches Institut*, 3. Vienna.

Korenjak, M. 2000. *Publikum und Redner: Ihre Interaktion in der sophistischen Rhetorik der Kaiserzeit*. Munich.

Leiwo, M. 1995. "The Mixed Languages in Roman Inscriptions." In H. Solin, O. Salomies, and U.-M. Liertz, eds., *Acta colloquii epigraphici Latini, Helsingiae 3.–6. sept. 1991 habiti*, 293–301. Helsinki.

Ma, J. 2007. "Hellenistic Honorific Statues and Their Inscriptions." In Z. Newby and R. Leader-Newby, eds., *Art and Inscriptions in the Ancient World*, 203–20. Cambridge.

Majbom Madsen, J. 2002. "The Romanization of the Greek Elite in Achaia, Asia and Bithynia: Greek Resistance or Regional Discrepancies?" *Orbis Terrarum* 8: 87–113.

Mason, H. 1974. *Greek Terms for Roman Institutions: A Lexicon and Analysis*. American Studies in Papyrology 13. Toronto.

Mattingly, D. 1997. "Dialogues of Power and Experience in the Roman Empire." In D. Mattingly, ed., *Dialogues in Roman Imperialism: Power, Discourse, and Discrepant Experience in the Roman Empire*, 7–24. Journal of Roman Archaeology, Supplementary Series 23. Portsmouth, RI.

Meneghini, R. 2002a. "Die 'Bibliotheca Ulpia.'" In W. Hoepfner, ed., *Antike Bibliotheken*, 117–22. Mainz.

——. 2002b. "Nuovi dati sulla funzione e le fasi costruttive delle biblioteche del Foro di Traiano." *MEFRA* 114: 655–92.

Millar, F. 1999. "The Greek East and Roman Law: The Dossier of M. Cn. Licinius Rufinus." *JRS* 89: 90–108.

Mitchell, S. 2000. "Ethnicity, Acculturation and Empire in Roman and Late Roman Asia Minor." In S. Mitchell and G. Greatrex, eds., *Ethnicity and Culture in Late Antiquity*, 117–50. London.

Neudecker, R. 2004. "Aspekte öffentlicher Bibliotheken in der Kaiserzeit." In B. Borg, ed., *Paideia: The World of the Second Sophistic*, 293–313. Berlin.

Newby, Z. 2007. "Reading the Allegory of the Archelaos Relief." In Z. Newby and R. Leader-Newby, eds., *Art and Inscriptions in the Ancient World*, 156–78. Cambridge.

Oberleitner, W. 1999. "Das Partherdenkmal von Ephesos." In H. Friesinger and F. Krinzinger, eds., *100 Jahre österreichische Forschungen in Ephesos*, 619–31. Vienna.

Onians, J. 1988. *Bearers of Meaning: The Classical Orders in Antiquity, the Middle Ages, and the Renaissance*. Princeton.

Ortaç, M. 2002. "Zur Veränderung der kleinasiatischen Propyla in der frühen Kaiserzeit in Bauform und Bedeutung." In C. Berns, H. von Hesberg, L. Vandeput and M. Waelkens, eds., *Patris und Imperium: Kulturelle und politische Identität in den Städten der römischen Provinzen Kleinasiens in der frühen Kaiserzeit. Kolloquium Köln, November 1998*, 175–85. Babesch Supplement 8. Leuven.

Pinkwart, D. 1965. *Das Relief des Archelaos von Priene und die "Musen des Philiskos."* Kallmünz.

Puech, B. 2002. *Orateurs et sophistes grecs dans les inscriptions d'époque impériale*. Paris.

Radt, W. 2005. "Eine antike Wasseruhr im Gymnasion von Pergamon." *IstMitt* 55: 179–90.

Reynolds, J. 1982. *Aphrodisias and Rome: Documents from the Excavation of the Theatre at Aphrodisias Conducted by Professor Kenan T. Erim, Together with Some Related Texts*. London.

——. 1995. "The Latin Inscriptions of Asia Minor." In H. Solin, O. Salomies, and U.-M. Liertz, eds., *Acta colloquii epigraphici Latini, Helsingiae 3.–6. sept. 1991 habiti*, 393–402. Helsinki.

Robert, L. 1937. *Études anatoliennes: Recherches sur les inscriptions grecques de l'Asie Mineure*. Paris.

Rogers, G. 1991. *The Sacred Identity of Ephesos. Foundation Myths of a Roman City*. London.

Rose, C. B. 1997. *Dynastic Commemoration and Imperial Portraiture in the Julio-Claudian Period*. Cambridge.

——. 2005. "The Parthians in Augustan Rome." *AJA* 109: 21–75.

Sartre, M. 1995. *L'Asie Mineure et l'Anatolie: d'Alexandre à Dioclétien (IVe siècle av. J.-C./IIIe siècle ap. J.-C.)*. Paris.

Scherrer, P., ed. 2000. *Ephesus: The New Guide*. Rev. ed. Turkey.

Smith, R. R. R. 1993. *The Monument of C. Julius Zoilos*. Mainz am Rhein.

——. 1998. "Cultural Choice and Political Identity in Honorific Portrait Statues in the Greek East in the Second Century A.D." *JRS* 88: 56–93.

Stewart, P. 2003. *Statues in Roman Society: Representation and Response*. Oxford.

Strocka, V. 1981. "Römische Bibliotheken." *Gymnasium* 88: 298–329.

——. 2003. "The Celsus Library in Ephesus." In *Ancient Libraries in Anatolia: Libraries of Hattusha, Pergamon, Ephesus, Nysa. The 24th Annual Conference, Libraries and Education in the Networked Information Environment, June 2–5, 2003, Ankara, Turkey*, 33–43. Ankara.

Swain, S. 1996. *Hellenism and Empire: Language, Classicism, and Power in the Greek World, AD 50–250*. Oxford.

Tamm, B. 1963. *Auditorium and Palatium: A Study on Assembly-rooms in Roman Palaces during the 1st Century* B.C. *and the 1st Century* A.D. Stockholm Studies in Classical Archaeology 2. Stockholm.

Tanner, J. 2000. "Portraits, Power, and Patronage in the Late Roman Republic." *JRS* 90: 18–50.

Thür, H. 1989. *Das Hadrianstor in Ephesos*. Forschungen in Ephesos 11/1. Vienna.

——. 1995. "The Processional Way in Ephesos as a Place of Cult and Burial." In H. Koester, ed., *Ephesos Metropolis of Asia: An Interdisciplinary Approach to its Archaeology, Religion, and Culture*, 157–99. Valley Forge.

——. 1997. "Girlandensarkophag und Porträt eines Kaiserpriesters im Fund- und Primärkontext—Bestandteile eines Ehrengrabes am Embolos?" In H. Thür, ed., *" . . . und verschönerte die Stadt . . . ": Ein Ephesischer Priester des Kaiserkultes in seinem Umfeld*, 65–75. Vienna.

——. 2005. "Altarstudien aus Ephesos." In B. Brandt, V. Gassner, and S. Ladstatter, eds., *Synergia: Festschrift für Friedrich Krinzinger*, 1: 355–62. Vienna.

——, with A. Pyszkowski-Wyzykowski. 2006. "Das Partherdenkmal in Ephesos: Aspekte der Bauforschung." In W. Seipel, ed., *Das Partherdenkmal von Ephesos: Akten des Kolloquiums, Wien, 27.–28. April 2003, veranstaltet vom Institut für Kulturgeschichte der Antike der Österreichischen Akademie der Wissenschaften und der Antikensammlung des Kunsthistorischen Museums Wien*, 142–57. Milan.

van Bremen, R. 1996. *The Limits of Participation: Women and Civic Life in the Greek East in the Hellenistic and Roman periods*. Amsterdam.

Van Nijf, O. 2000. "Inscriptions and Civic Memory in the Roman East." In A. Cooley, ed., *The Afterlife of Inscriptions: Reusing, Rediscovering, Reinventing and Revitalizing Ancient Inscriptions*, 21–36. Bulletin of the Institute of Classical Studies Supplement 75. London.

von Hesberg, H. 2003. "Römisches Ornament als Sprache. Die sanfte Gegenwart der Macht." In L. de Blois, P. Erdkamp, O. Hekster, G. de Kleijn, and S. Mols, eds., *The Representation and Perception of Roman Imperial Power: Proceedings of the Third Workshop of the International Network Impact of Empire (Roman Empire, c. 200* B.C.—A.D. *476), Netherlands Institute in Rome, March 20–23, 2002*, 48–68. Amsterdam.

Wallace-Hadrill, A. 1990. "Roman Arches and Greek Honours: The Language of Power at Rome." *PCPS* 216: 143–81.

——. 1998. "To Be Roman, Go Greek: Thoughts on Hellenization at Rome." In M. Austin, J. Harries, and C. Smith, eds., *Modus Operandi: Essays in Honour of Geoffrey Rickman*, 79–91. Bulletin of the Institute of Classical Studies Supplement 71. London.

Weaver, P. 1972. *Familia Caesaris: A Social Study of the Emperor's Freedmen and Slaves*. Cambridge.

Whitmarsh, T. 2001. *Greek Literature and the Roman Empire: The Politics of Imitation*. Oxford.

——. 2005. *The Second Sophistic*. Greece & Rome: New Surveys in the Classics 35. Oxford.

Wikander, O., ed. 2000. *Handbook of Ancient Water Technology*. Leiden.

Wilberg, W., M. Theuer, F. Eichler, and J. Keil. 1953. *Forschungen in Ephesos 5/1: Die Bibliothek*. Vienna.

Willers, D. 1990. *Hadrians panhellenisches Programm: Archäologische Beiträge zur Neugestaltung Athens durch Hadrian.* Basel.

Winter, E. 1996. *Staatliche Baupolitik und Baufürsorge in den römischen Provinzen des kaiserzeitlichen Kleinasien.* Asia Minor Studien 20. Bonn.

Woolf, G. 1992. "The Unity and Diversity of Romanization." *JRA* 5: 349–52.

——. 1994. "Becoming Roman, Staying Greek: Culture, Identity and the Civilizing Process in the Roman East." *PCPS* 40: 116–43.

——. 1996. "Monumental Writing and the Expansion of Roman Society in the Early Empire." *JRS* 86: 22–39.

5

The Anecdote

Exploring the Boundaries between Oral and Literate
Performance in the Second Sophistic

Simon Goldhill

It may seem paradoxical to focus on the period of the Second Sophistic to try to understand the boundary between the oral and the literate. If any era of Greek culture seems far removed from the world of Homeric bards and the ideological investment classicists have made in orality as an explanatory category, it must be the Greek literature of the Roman empire. This is a world not just of the book, but of the very big book.

Athenaeus—to start with a paradigmatic *mega biblion* of this period[1]—praises Larensis, the host of the *Deipnosophistae*, because he has amassed in his private library more books than anyone else in history (I.3a): "he surpassed all those who prompt wonder for their collecting." It is piquant and telling that *thauma*, the driving force of Herodotean history and its heirs, should here be lavished on the book collectors of yore (named as Polycrates, Peisistratus, Eucleides, Euripides, Aristotle—all figures who had other, rather more pressing claims to fame, it might be thought). In a similar vein, he praises Galen because he published more books on philosophy and medicine than any of his predecessors (1.1e–f), and describes the assembled company coming in to dinner dragging bundles of scrolls, as if going to a picnic with piles of bedding (1.4b). Whereas Socrates stood barefoot in the street before Agathon's party, and Alcibiades crashes in with a flute-girl on each arm, these diners, like parodic Classics professors, struggle to carry their reference works in with them. And, despite its Platonic framing device ("Were you present, Athenaeus, at the noble party of those known as the Deipnosophistae?" [1.1f-2a]), the dialogue opens in the style of *Habilitationsschrift* with a summary of previous books about dining and symposia—a gesture more reminiscent of the academic polemic of a Strabo than the party fun epitomized in the dirty dancing of Xenophon's *Symposium*. This is a very bookish culture indeed.

---

1. For an introduction to Athenaeus, see Braund and Wilkins 2000.

A single and simple pair of contrasting images will make the point most vividly. When the embassy comes upon Achilles before his tent in Book IX of the *Iliad*, he is famously celebrating the famous deeds of men, singing the *klea andron*. For oral theorists this is an archetypal moment of representation, or even of bardic self-representation.[2] The hero in pursuit of his own glory sings of the glory of past heroes. Poetry preserves the past only in and through oral performance (as oral scholars would say), and the poet lets us see Achilles as the subject and object of song at once. As the bard sings of Achilles singing of the famous deeds of men, the bard's performance takes its place in the chain of performances constructing *kleos* across the generations.

This can be put in contrast with a delightful moment from Libanius's autobiography, a work that combines the whingeing of Aelius Aristides with the self-obsession of Cicero and occasionally the narrative flair of Achilles Tatius.[3] Libanius is being harassed by a drunken oaf from town, who throws stones at him while he marches to give his lectures and threatens him with more severe aggression. The oaf, with violence on his mind, comes looking for Libanius in the very temple where he is sitting by a pillar and reading to himself the speeches of Demosthenes. Libanius sits absolutely still, and the oaf fails to spot him. "I owe my life," writes Libanius, "to the Gods of Literature (*theoi logioi*), who saved me." For Libanius, reading Demosthenes can save your life.

This heroic tale of a life threatened and saved by divine force self-consciously plays off its Homeric antecedents. The image of the fourth-century orator sitting quietly not in a military camp but in a temple (a place of study, performance, and meeting), reading the great orator of the other fourth century, is as carefully constructed an image as the Homeric picture of Achilles by the tent. His lightly ironic reference to the "gods of literature" seals the image of Libanius as the Muses' favored son and heir of the great tradition of Greek culture, Greek literary culture. As we read Libanius, we are also being asked to see ourselves as participating in a chain of performance—the cultural inheritance of books and reading—and to see Libanius as a hero of this tradition.

The contrast between Achilles and Libanius at all levels is telling, but it certainly epitomizes how far from any simple ideal of orality we have progressed. Whereas Achilles strums the lyre and sings, Libanius carries his well-worn copy of Demosthenes. Whereas Achilles as hero performs a song that embodies the logic of the fame he himself seeks through heroic

---

2. See Nagy 1974, 244–55; Nagy 1979, 94–117; Segal 1994, 85–109, 113–41; Lynn-George 1988; Redfield 1975, 1–41; Goldhill 1991, 72–93—all with further bibliographies.

3. Libanius, writing in the second half of the fourth century, is obviously later in date than most temporal definitions of the Second Sophistic era, even when taking into account the well-known difficulties of defining the Second Sophistic as a period or even as a coherent movement. But with his highly self-aware look backward to Greek tradition, he captures in elegant form the tradition he wishes to see himself as embodying.

action, Libanius writes himself as a hero in his own story of the intellectual tradition of Greek rhetoric.

Now, as my mention of the famous orator and teacher Libanius should
make absolutely plain, the performance of rhetoric is integral to our
understanding of the Second Sophistic—and to the self-representation
of the authors of the period.[4] Standing up and speaking is a route to
power and influence in this era as much as it is in the classical city—for
all that the frames of such influence have changed radically. As ambas-
sadors, sophists, or teachers, oral performance is a sine qua non of self-
representation in this period, and an education in oratory is integral to
paideia, the formation of cultural norms through institutional training.
Maud Gleason's work *Making Men* has been justly influential on this topic,
and her analysis of the self-fashioning of the orator has shown the important interaction of training, performance, and public status through oratory
in Empire culture.[5] From a different angle, the satirist Lucian revels in
displaying and poking fun at the orator's walk, talk, and self-importance,
for all that he is a self-professed success story, a success story that precisely
demonstrates the transformative powers of a *paideia* through Greek rhetoric.[6] There can be no doubt that rhetorical performance is a fundamental
aspect of the social and intellectual life of this period.

But it would be hard to call such performances a sign of orality, if by
orality we mean a category opposed to literacy. It would make as much
sense to categorize political speeches of George W. Bush, the current
president, as oral. His speeches may be delivered orally, but they are
some of the most written and rewritten performances imaginable—
which makes them all the more frightening. And I expect that the speeches
of the great rhetoricians of the Empire were also written and rewritten,
certainly in the form that they have come down to us. Literacy does not in
any way preclude oral performance, but *grounds* it: an orator's speech is
grounded in rhetorical theory (including the recognition that an audience,
too, knows the tropes of presentation); it is grounded in a utilization of
past models—the great speeches of the past, the exempla read in history
books, the figures of tragedy or epic; and a speech also may manipulate a
set of quotations of laws or other literature, all written material absorbed through reading. Hence the ideological power of Libanius's self-
representation as a reader of Demosthenes. Oratory's oral performance is
fully informed by reading and writing. It is only in the grimly and falsely
named "chat rooms" of modern cyber hell that literacy has actually totally
silenced the oral. But when I say that the interest of this chapter is in
exploring the boundaries between the literate and the oral, I am not

4. Gleason 1995; Bowersock 1969; Anderson 1989; Anderson 1993; Goldhill 2001;
Whitmarsh 2001.
    5. Gleason 1995.
    6. Goldhill 2002, 60–107.

referring to the evident necessity for orators and sophists to write the spoken and to speak the written.

Nor am I going to focus on the oppressive nature of Atticism. In modern literacy studies, particularly in the last fifteen years or so, there has been a great deal of work on the potentially oppressive nature of literacy training in Western schools.[7] This research is aimed at explaining why certain groups, ethnic minorities in the main, in so-called advanced and wealthy urban environments appear to be repeatedly disadvantaged in schools. It has explored how verbal patterns in, say, black or Hispanic use of English are not recognized in the classroom, and how certain patterns of social behavior in black culture—not asking children questions, for example, or, more importantly, not expecting answers to be given by children to non-family members—disadvantages them when they enter an environment where answering questions promptly is at a premium.[8]

Although some of this research seems to me to have some awkward political manipulation in it, it is useful for reminding us how we could look at the strange and forced world of Second Sophistic linguistic performance. Although scholars continue to argue with great ferocity about levels of Atticism in this or that piece of late prose,[9] we should not allow such discussion to obscure the sociopolitical impact of what appears to have become a linguistic environment imbued with an aggressive and self-aware scrutiny. Plutarch tells us firmly that we should accustom ourselves to shout out "No! Error!" if we hear a mistake of pronunciation or grammar in conversation.[10] Lucian records with a more self-deprecating irony how he had used the wrong word one morning when greeting his patron at the *salutatio*. "I began to sweat and went pink with embarrassment, and was all over the shop in my confusion. Some of those present thought I had made an error, naturally enough; others that I was babbling from age; others thought it was a hangover from yesterday's wine-drinking."[11] Lucian captures with amusing poignancy the shame of a public verbal slip in the presence of his patron, without even a Plutarch to correct him loudly.

Literacy, in the form of the carefully trained and practiced world of Attic speech, constantly polices the boundary of verbal performance. The performance of oral speech is regulated and ordered by the institutions of literacy in the Second Sophistic as much as in the secondary schools of America. There is a continuity between Plutarch's essays on "How to listen to lectures," "On garrulousness," "How a young man should listen to poetry," "How to tell a flatterer from a friend," and Philostratus's

---

7. Good summary of this in Collins and Blot 2003—with extensive bibliography.
8. See Heath 1983.
9. See the useful work of Swain 1996.
10. *How to Study Poetry* 26b.
11. Lucian *pro lapsu* (64).1.

interests in "pure Attic," or Galen's comments on good Greek, or
Lucian's angst- and humor-filled satires on obsessive interest in Atticism
(along with his own brilliant forays into Herodotean Ionic Greek), or the
critical essays on the prose style of orators by Dionysius of Halicarnas-
sus.[12] The profusion of normative texts on how to write and speak Greek
reveals the anxieties and hesitations of social intercourse as well as the
ideals and nostalgia of the Second Sophistic.

It seems to me that this fascinating interplay between literate training
and verbal performance has not been fully explored for the Second
Sophistic. But in this chapter, I am interested rather in pursuing what
seems to me to be a phenomenon that has not been much discussed in
classical studies or elsewhere, which I will call for the moment "the
anecdote." By "the anecdote" I mean a short and pointed narrative,
often of a biographical nature and rarely attributed to an author. Before
I move on to look at what is at stake in such a term, and why I think it is
helpful for us in understanding both the circulation of knowledge in
Empire culture and the boundaries between literacy and orality, let me
clarify some of the formal constraints on what is meant by the term
"anecdote."

The fact that it is a narrative and usually has no author distinguishes the
anecdote from the quotation. Athenaeus collects quotations: they are
metrical when in verse, attributed to an author, and any discussion or
use of them shows considerable attention to precise verbal usage. From
the fifth century B.C.E. onward the circulation of quotations is a sign of
cultured and cultivated performance, whether it is Demosthenes quoting
Sophocles in court or Plato's Socrates quoting Simonides.[13] Athenaeus is
the limit case of the logic of the prestige of the quotation. Not only is his
book comprised largely of quotations, but he also quotes Clearchus, who
tells the story of Charmus the Syracusan, who would quote a verse or
proverb for any course of any dinner ("Thus for fish he'd say, 'From the
salt depths of the Aegean I come' "—Euripides *Trojan Women* 1 [I. 4a]).
Ulpian would never taste any item without asking if a word was found in
literature or not. (He would ask *keitai ê ou keitai*: "Source or no source?"
and hence was known as *Keitoukeitos* [I. 1e].) The practice of citation is
discussed in this text, just as citations contribute so much to its form. For
centuries of Greek culture, being *mousikos* or *paideutos* means having
poetry at your beck and call: and as the prisoners in Syracuse found,
it, too, can save your life.[14]

The *chreia* is closer to the anecdote, and this tradition has received
some attention, not least from the scholars exploring the relationship

---

12. See Goldhill 1999, 69–76; Goldhill 2002, 60–107; Whitmarsh 2001.
13. Fine discussion in Ford 1999.
14. Plutarch *Nikias* 29. It should be no surprise that this story is a Second Sophistic
attestation not found in Thucydides.

between Christianity and ancient philosophy.[15] The *chreia* is usually a single sentence or brief exchange culminating in a witty or profound put-down. It is associated with Cynic philosophy in particular, the biting, dog-like retort: "Diogenes is to be praised for rubbing away on his genital organ in public and saying to the bystanders, 'If only it were as easy to rub away hunger.'"[16] This is not philosophy as Plato would understand it: there is no question of giving a *logos* and constructing an extended dialectical argument toward truth. Nor is it perhaps quite as David Sedley describes it, "a practical approach to life";[17] at least this example of Diogenes is unlikely to prove practical in any normal city, ancient or modern. It is closer perhaps to what Foucault would probably call a stylistics of living: an attitude. It captures a view of the world not through rules or argument but through exemplary expression. Most historians believe that the sayings of Jesus circulated separately from the narrative biographies of the Gospels precisely in this form of the *chreia*: hence one motivation for the considerable interest in them.

For the purposes of my argument today, perhaps the most relevant Second Sophistic example of the *chreia* tradition is Lucian's *Demonax*, which, although it has the form of a biography, contains at its core fifty examples of Demonax's put-downs (Lucian 9.12–62).[18] Each is a brief paragraph or sentence. There is no structure to the list, no chronology or narrative. Most importantly, each is offered as an example of his "pithy and witty expressions" (9.12) and is available for recirculation as a discrete *exemplum* of how the Cynic philosopher faced (down) the world. This probably looks back to the tradition of collected material, oral and then written, on Pythagoras—the exemplary sage. His sayings, as the master of the sect, were collected and circulated, and used as part of the group formation of the sect. Demonax may not have a sect, but in Lucian's biography of him, he has a gospel for any future disciples.

The *chreia* can prove in this way a serious and effective form of circulating a way of doing things. It is not by chance that so many hagiographic saints' lives, at the point of martyrdom, turn to the witty put-down as a form of assertion of authoritative control. The *chreia* has the advantage of being memorable, short, and, above all, powerful—a sign of power, and repeated as a demonstration of power. Hence its effectiveness in circulation. The *chreia* will turn out to be an important model for my argument because it shows how powerful an ideological tool—an educative or persuasive form—the brief and pointed remark can be in practice. It circulates a view of the world with striking efficiency.

15. See Hock and O'Neil 1986; 2002 (and Kennedy 2003, for translations of the *progumnasmata*). Also Mack and Robbins 1989; Mack 1987; Robbins 1988. Good background in Morgan 1998; Cribiore 2001.

16. Plutarch *de Stoic. repugn.* 21, 1044b.

17. Sedley 1980, 5.

18. On *Demonax*, see Branham 1989, 57–63.

The anecdote differs from the *chreia*, however, in that it is not committed in the same way to the single witticism, nor is it quite so precisely linked to the construction of the subject who knows, at least in the sense that the anecdote, unlike the *chreia*, need not be not such a vivid demonstration of the power or persona of the speaker. That the anecdote as a form is part of a construction of a view of the world, however, will be a central claim of my argument shortly.

The third collection of material that seems an interesting frame for understanding the anecdote is paradoxography.[19] This is a genre particularly associated with Empire literature—the collection of surprising facts about nature. So Aelian's book *On the Nature of Animals* begins, "That a human being is wise and just and takes particular care of his children and shows fitting consideration for his parents, seeks sustenance for himself, protects himself against plots, and has all the other gifts nature has endowed him with, is perhaps no paradox—*ouden paradoxon*." This of course is a priamel to the "remarkable fact" that animals, the *alogoi*, do have similar qualities. And the book is structured as a series of usually short paragraphs capturing in each case a remarkable fact about the animal world, such as the remarkable information that if a horse steps on the footprint of a wolf it will go numb, and if you were to throw the vertebra of a wolf under a four-horse chariot team in full flight, it will come to a complete standstill as if frozen, because the horses have stepped on the vertebra (1.36).

We see how this sort of material might become part of the discourse of the *pepaideumenoi* of Empire in Achilles Tatius's novel *Leucippe and Cleitophon*. The lovers are traveling together in Egypt and observing the hippopotamus (4.4). A general, one Charmides, has fallen in love with Leucippe, and as they watch the hippopotamus, he tells them of the Indian Elephant, which he says has a manner of birth which is really a *paradoxos*, a remarkable and strange thing. This leads to the story that an elephant's breath is a cure for a headache. "Now the elephant knows of its restorative powers and does not open its mouth without a fee: like a quack doctor, it demands its payment first. If you pay up, it agrees and fulfils its side of the bargain, unfurling its jaws, opening wide, and admitting the human as far as is desired. It knows it has sold its odour." Platonic scholars will not be surprised that a figure called Charmides should come up with a headache story, because Plato's pretty-boy Charmides has a headache in the beginning of the dialogue of the same name, which leads to Socrates' erotic encounter with him. Here another hopeful but destined-to-fail erotic encounter with a Charmides turns to headache cures. But the use of the *paradoxos* is paradigmatic. Wise guys, involved in chatting up a girl, and in competition with each other, roll out a well-turned image of a paradox of nature to enthrall and seduce the mind of

19. Rommel 1923 is a starting point.

the listener. Having a few good paradoxes up your sleeve can save your love life.

Indeed, when the hero of the novel is trying first to seduce the heroine, he wanders with his confidant, Satyrus, in a garden where he can have a conversation about the erotics of nature and be overheard by Leucippe and her slave. He has been told that he must approach her indirectly (as young girls do not like direct dirty talk). So he speaks loudly about how nature is full of examples of bizarre but touching erotic desires. His list of surprising facts culminates with the story of the viper, a land snake, and the moray eel, a sea snake. The viper, he says, goes down to the shore and hisses a signal, and the moray climbs out of the water but waits until the land snake has disgorged his poison before she comes to him for a kiss (Ach. Tat. 1.18). The same fact of nature is told in Aelian (*de nat. anim.* 1. 50): "the male viper, in his frenzy for copulation, goes to the sea, and like a party-goer plays a pipe outside his lover's door to get entrance, the snake hisses a summons to his lover." Although Aelian was writing after Achilles Tatius, this gives us a good indication of how Aelian might have been used: read, filleted for good examples, and reused to cut a figure about town by the *pepaideumenos* in conversation. So, Achilles Tatius's slightly different version of the paradox, which highlights his character-istic focus on kissing, shows also how such paradoxical paragraphs can be reworked to fit a more precise set of circumstances.

The anecdote is not necessarily paradoxical, even in the weak sense of the paradox seen in Aelian, and it usually involves humans rather than animals or the natural world; but the use of the paradox in the novel and collections of *paradoxa* like Aelian's *On the Nature of Animals* do give us an important insight into how the short paragraph can function as an object of exchange in the conversation of the *pepaideumenoi* and as an object of collection by authors—for reuse by the *pepaideumenoi*. The characters in the so-called sophistic novels often seem to converse by swapping neatly reworked extracts from such written collections. When a character in Heliodorus delivers a brief paragraph on the evil eye, which echoes extremely closely a paragraph in Plutarch, classical scholars have traditionally argued whether Heliodorus is echoing Plutarch specifically, or whether both had a source in common.[20] What is obscured by such an argument is the fact that Heliodorus shows us a sophisticated character quoting from earlier written texts in conversation.

Now I have suggested that the quotation, the *chreia*, and the paradox are particularly useful frames for understanding the anecdote within Greek literary tradition, but we should not think of these forms as being absolutely discrete genres, although they are often discussed as such. One

---

20. See *Aeth.* 3.7.4–5; Plutarch *Sympotic Questions* 680cff, with Dickie 1991. Plutarch's work is, as discussed below, both a collection of *logoi* and designed for reuse, so we should not be surprised to see similar material in a later author.

simple case will show how they can overlap. The sophist Favorinus, since Maud Gleason's *Making Men*, has become a familiar figure on the Second Sophistic circuit. The most celebrated story of Favorinus comes from Philostratus's *Lives of the Sophists* (1.8). "He used to say in the ambiguous style of an oracle, that there were in his life story three paradoxes: A Gaul, he had become Greek; a eunuch, he had been tried for adultery; he had argued with the emperor and lived." This is a quotation, attributed to Favorinus himself. It is noted for its style as well as its content. It consists of three paradoxes, and the word Philostratus uses here is precisely *paradoxa*. And the remark is a *chreia*, a witticism, a one-liner, that captures in exemplary form an attitude to the world: a worldview that loves paradox, as befits the sophist, revels in rhetorical flair, self-presentation with panache, and a self-consciously oblique stance to the norms of society.

We should not, then, imagine that the quotation, the *chreia*, and the paradox are easily separable genres. I have separated them for heuristic purposes (as well as taking account of the fact that this follows current scholarship and some ancient organizations of knowledge). Each will prove helpful in understanding the anecdote as a form and the way that the anecdote performs as a circulation of knowledge.

The boundaries between Greek and Roman forms of discourse in this period are now a topic of considerable and sophisticated discussion in the contemporary academy, and need particular care here. Greek writers often fail to indicate any knowledge of Latin or Latin literature. When they do so, it is often with a disclaimer, itself often disingenuous.[21] Roman writers use knowledge of Greek as a sign of sophistication—and also use knowledge of Greek as a sign of lack of good Roman values. It is interesting to note, therefore, how hard it is to render *chreia* or *paradoxa* into Latin. Both words are usually transliterated or left in Greek, and often glossed, especially in Stoic texts, to indicate their Greek origin. Cicero, when he uses the term *paradoxon*, does so only to explain how he has translated this Greek term, in its technical Stoic usage, into Latin as "mirabilia" or "admirabilia." The Latin word "(ad)mirabilia," with its sense of wonder or amazement, adds a quite different note to the Greek term and shows a discomfort with the Greek notion, even or especially as Greek philosophy becomes Latin thinking.[22] Quintilian points out (*de inst. orat.*1.9.3) that a *chria* (transliterated) is basic to rhetorical training: a *chria*, a brief moralistic sentence, acts as a "theme" for the budding orator. Hence, some call such "themes" *chreiodes* (in Greek letters), "useful" (a pun designed to show the normative thrust of the

---

21. *Locus classicus* is Plutarch on his own poor Latinity, which is often rather naively read by critics: *Life of Demosthenes* 1–2, with Jones 1971, 80–7. General background in Swain 1996 and Goldhill 2001.

22. See Cicero *Fin.* 4.27.74, *Acad.* 2.44.136, *Paradoxa Stoicorum, proem* 4.

chria).[23] Interestingly, he concludes by pointing out that Latin rhetoricians do not match up to their Greek counterparts: "Cetera maioris operis et spiritus Latini rhetores reliquendo necessaria grammaticis fecerunt: Graeci magis operum suorum et onera et modum norunt," "Roman rhetoricians by leaving out the remaining work of greater weight and seriousness have made a compulsory burden for the teachers: the Greek rhetoricians better understand the weight and manner of their own works" (1.9.6). I am not sure I understand the full thrust of Quintilian's complaint here, but when Roman writers note their debt to Greek, or, as here, their insufficiency in comparison with the Greeks, such explication is often a sign of unease. The *synkrisis* of Greek and Latin rhetoric/oratory, at a theoretical and practical level, articulates a self-aware cultural difference as well as patterns of inheritance, imitation, and similarity.

The word in Latin rhetorical writing that goes to the heart of the nexus of ideas mapped by the Greek words *chreia*, *paradoxa*, and quotation, is *exemplum*. Rebecca Langlands has recently expressed with great clarity and insight the role of the *exemplum* in Latin thinking about *pudicitia* and, in particular, the continuing role of the *exemplum* from rhetorical theory through to the historians and the poets of the Augustan and post-Augustan periods.[24] Valerius Maximus provides a thematically organized collection of *exempla*, each of which is available either as a theme for *declamatio* (like a *chria*) or for use as a proof or example in a *declamatio*. The *exemplum* is an institutionalized, packaged narrative form, which is used and reused as an element of Roman discourse. It is close to what I will be calling an anecdote in the Greek tradition, though the anecdote is less formally recognized and therefore circulates knowledge in a different manner. The difference between Greek and Roman forms of organizing and circulating knowledge is another area where further research is needed—but cannot here be pursued.

With that much framing we are ready to turn to look at what I am calling the anecdote in Second Sophistic culture. I will begin once again with Philostratus's *Lives of the Sophists*. The *Lives of the Sophists* is two moderately short books, which collect together in a similar manner to a modern biographical dictionary the figures Philostratus thinks worthy of

---

23. See Seneca *Ep.* 33.7: Ideo pueris et sententias ediscendas damus et has quas Graeci chrias vocant, quia complecti illas puerilis animus potest, qui plus adhuc non capit.

A schoolboy catechism from Oxyrhynchus reads as follows:

What is the chreia?
A concise reminiscence associated with some character.
Why is the chreia a reminiscence?
Because it is remembered so that it may be recited...
Why is it called "chreia"?
Because of its being useful....

24. Langlands 2006.

the title of sophist, and one or two he doesn't. Many of these entries are very brief and are little more than markers of identification. Take Carneades (1.4): "Carneades of Athens was also enrolled among the sophists, for though his mind had been equipped for the pursuit of philosophy, yet in virtue of the force and vigour of his orations he attained an extraordinarily high level of eloquence." A single sentence allows the reader to give Carneades a place on his or her mental map of the classical city's intellectual world, and to find a way of relating him to the book's introduction, which has outlined the difference between philosophy, rhetoric, and sophistry. It gives Carneades a characterization, to be recognized and used in conversation by the readers of Philostratus. If you hear or use the name Carneades, you know at least what sort of a figure he was and what you might say about him: "I find the force and vigor of his orations brought his rhetoric to such a degree of excellence that he belies his training as a philosopher." That could save your social life at a dinner party. That is, I am suggesting that such short written, anecdotal paragraphs are not just a history of sophists, but also constitute a handbook for the discursive performance of the *pepaideumenoi* in Empire culture.

There are also longer lives, and the longest of all is that of Herodes Atticus. This is not organized like a traditional biography, however, but epitomizes how continuous narrative is sucked into the orbit of the anecdote. The life is organized as a set of discrete paragraphs, each of which is easily excerptable for retelling. So immediately after a paragraph on his beneficence and some praise for the canal cut through the isthmus of Corinth (552), we move straight into a paragraph on the man called "Heracles of Herodes." There is no connection beyond a *de*. "As for the man they call Heracles of Herodes..." (552), and the text shifts into another story. There is no evident thematic link between the two paragraphs, except that both are about Herodes Atticus. It is just another story. We are given a physical description of Heracles, and details of his diet. As you might expect from his name, he is a marvelous physical specimen who wrestles wild boars and wolves and mad bulls, but, unlike the real Heracles, this modern macho man lives mainly on milk, though occasionally he eats enough barley for ten men (553). This is a sort of rustic hero, who suitably enough claims Marathon, the *genius loci*, as his father (553).

It is Heracles' speech that especially amazes Herodes (554):

"τὴν δὲ δὴ γλῶτταν," ἔφη ὁ Ἡρώδης, "πῶς ἐπαιδεύθης καὶ ὑπὸ τίνων; οὐ γάρ μοι τῶν ἀπαιδεύτων φαίη." καὶ ὁ Ἀγαθίων "ἡ μεσογεία," ἔφη, "τῆς Ἀττικῆς ἀγαθὸν διδασκαλεῖον ἀνδρὶ βουλομένῳ διαλέγεσθαι, οἱ μὲν γὰρ ἐν τῷ ἄστει Ἀθηναῖοι μισθοῦ δεχόμενοι Θρᾴκια καὶ Ποντικὰ μειράκια καὶ ἐξ ἄλλων ἐθνῶν βαρβάρων ξυνερρυηκότα παραφθείρονται παρ' αὐτῶν τὴν φωνὴν μᾶλλον ἢ ξυμβάλλονταί τι αὐτοῖς ἐς εὐγλωττίαν, ἡ μεσογεία δὲ ἄμικτος βαρβάροις οὖσα ὑγιαίνει αὐτοῖς ἡ φωνὴ καὶ ἡ γλῶττα τὴν ἄκραν Ἀτθίδα ἀποψάλλει."

"What about your speech?" asked Herodes. "How were you educated, and by whom? For you do not seem to me to be one of the uneducated." "The interior of Attica," Agathion replied, "a good schooling for a man who wants to converse. For the Athenians in the town take in youths, flooding in to work from Thrace and Pontus and other barbarian races, and their own speech is corrupted by them, more than they can encourage them towards proper speech. The interior is pure—no barbarians; their speech is healthy and their language has the twang of perfect Attic."

Although Heracles/Agathion is a rustic fellow, he speaks well: he has clearly been educated, become cultured, *epaideuthês*, and is indeed not uneducated/uncultured, *apaideutos*. The answer is that he speaks the very best Attic Greek because he comes from the very interior of Attica, the best teacher there is. The Athenians have allowed all sorts of other Greeks and barbarians to come into the city to work for money, with the result that their own speech has been corrupted (*paraphtheirontai*), when you might have expected the barbarians to move toward proper speech (*euglôttian*) by contact with Athenian language. The interior, however, is *amiktos*, "pure," "untouched by barbarians"; it is healthy, *hugiainei*, and consequently the voice and tongue "twang the best of Attic" (*apopsallei*— a difficult word here to translate).[25] Hercules combines Second Sophistic obsessions: he is a living paradox about the purity of Attic Greek, with a *chreia* on his lips.

There are several things to say about this charming passage. First of all, notice that Herodes Atticus, the *pepaideumenos* of *pepaideumenoi*, the man to know, is given a lesson on how to speak Greek. Knowing as we do the privileged status of good Attic speech and the scrutiny and care with which language use was policed, it is a neat irony that the most sophisticated member of the elite is impressed by the Greek of a rustic man of the country: Dio of Prusa's *Euboicus* plays plenty of games with the delights of rural innocence in contrast with urban dissatisfactions, but even in that speech "pure Attic" is not one of the blessings of the bucolic haven. If you want to be able to converse, *dialegesthai*, this story suggests that it is not the elegant symposium or gymnasium or festival, those traditional sites for dialogue, that will prepare you, but a life untouched by the city—something none of Philostratus's readers can have. The game with the values of being *asteios* versus *agroikos* is neatly turned. Heracles goes on to laugh at drama festivals and at athletics in a way that Herodes recognizes as "philosophical" (553–4), thus further separating himself from the world of the leisured classes. He inhabits a world that the readers of Philostratus cannot share. "Best Attic," "pure Attic," with all the moral valuing of health and purity, is set beyond the purchase of the

---

25. It is used at Lycophron 407 apparently to refer to the springing of a trap, hence my translation "twang" to get the sense both of the mousetrap springing and the lyre sounding out.

sophisticated: even a Plutarch, it is suggested, accustomed to shout "No! Error!,", is like a rube before this paragon of uneducated learning.

So the biographical narrative here slips easily into neat packages of anecdote, a story for repetition (as I have just done, of course); we have a collection of discrete stories rather than a continuous tale of growth or development of character. But the anecdote also works because it is a tale that talks, like a *chreia*, to the educated: it uses and plays with their fantasies of escaping the taints of the modern city, and reaching back to a lost past of purity, when men were men and Greek was Greek.

There are in the Second Sophistic amid the very big books a considerable number of volumes in what one might call anecdotal form—like Aelian's *On the Nature of Animals* or Philostratus's *Lives of the Sophists*. Particularly interesting, I think, is the trend toward collecting mythological stories into consolidated volumes. It is always dangerous to generalize about "Greek myth," especially over a long time span. But one could say that the literature of the classical city—drama and history and philosophy—loved to explore the normative power of the inherited and circulating stories of the past, whereas the Hellenistic poets in turn were fascinated by the increasingly obscure and baroque details of the tradition, and by the work of myth in the new Hellenic world of the Hellenistic kingdoms. In the same spirit, it is striking that in the prose of the Second Sophistic, mythic examples are generally taken from a far more restricted range of stories, and told in a far more conventional manner. (The danger of such claims would be instantly evident if one turned to poetry and included Nonnus, say, in the literature of Empire.) In this period, Apollodorus collects and attempts to systematize the vast profusion of Greek myths within a coherent genealogy and narrative—reducing each story to a bare and schematized form. Earlier, Parthenius had packaged myths in neat parcels for a Roman audience. Ptolemaius Chennus seems to have put together a collection of mythic fantastical trivia to titillate his audiences.[26] I would like to suggest that there is a significant synergy between these collections of mythic "anecdotes," the restriction of scope and range of mythic examples in use, and an attitude to the past and the rhetoric of the past in Empire Greek culture. Forming a collective mythic culture is important not just for the curriculum of the *enkuklios paideia*, but for creating an empire-wide Hellenic identity. The value of the local inevitably changes in Empire, and with it the value of local myth, especially the more bizarre and disturbing stories. With the increasing globalization of Greek culture—Hellenization—comes a broadening and flattening of what is recognized as the shared knowledge that will signal

---

26. The *New* or *Strange History* (*Kaine Historia*) also known as the *Paradoxos Historia*, "Paradoxical History," epitomized in Photius *Bibliotheca* 146a–153b [190] and put into context by Bowersock 1994, 24–7, who reminds us that Philo of Byblos also wrote a *Paradoxical History* (*FGH* III, C, 790, F 12–13).

Greekness. The uncertain degree to which such an observation depends
on contemporary cultural understandings or illuminates modern culture
is one of the many issues that makes generalizations about Greek myth
so dangerous.

There is also a back history to this trend toward the anecdotal. As with
so much in the Second Sophistic, it starts with one of their great heroes of
the classical city, Xenophon. Xenophon is the first word not just of Arrian
on hunting, but also of Eunapius's *Lives of the Philosophers*. Xenophon
is cited again and again in the Second Sophistic. He is a richly varied figure
in the imagination of Empire culture and admired for that very richness
of influence as much as for his specific qualities as a philosopher or a
historian. The big book on Xenophon's influence remains to be written—
though Tim Rood has managed to write a very fine exposition of the fate
of two words of Xenophon over the ages.[27]

The work of Xenophon that is particularly important for the history of
the anecdote is the *Memorabilia*. This is four books of stories about
Socrates, very loosely linked around the general claims that "Socrates
was good," "Socrates was useful," and with an explicit apologetic agenda.
Each story is short, rarely more than a long paragraph, and can be told in
any order. This unparalleled literary form is in striking contrast to Plato,
whose accounts of his master's thought seem to have become longer and
longer and more and more complexly integrated. I would like to suggest
that the *Memorabilia* might well have been designed for fragmented
sympotic use rather than just for reading. That is, any paragraph could
have been chosen and recited at a symposium, putting into circulation a
set of brief stories, any one of which could be told elsewhere. This is in
part how the image of Socrates built up in public discourse. The simple
language, often with a *chreia*-like conclusion, is designed for retelling.
(The symposium is only one forum for such recirculation, of course.)
Plato gives one version of how dialogues start from oral performance in
his *Symposium*, with its nesting of narrators: were you there, who did you
hear it from and so forth, which became a *topos* of dialogue writing;
but Xenophon offers another model of how a written text could enter
discourse: as fragmented anecdotes.

Plutarch's *Sympotic Questions* reveals a different strand of what I am
calling the anecdotal. *Sympotic Questions* is a very big book, Plutarch's
longest, but, unlike Plato's *Symposium*, it is completely morselized into
discrete elements that could be read in any order and that seem designed
for reuse in a symposium of one's own. Like Athenaeus, Plutarch, too,
notes how there is a long list of predecessors, philosophers mainly, who
have thought fit to record what was said at a famous symposium (I proem
[612d]). But his is specifically a collection of "what's needed" (τὰ
ἐπιτήδεια) (I proem [612e]), and offered so that sympotic *logos* can

27. Rood 2004.

prevent the dissolution of the drinkers through drink and bring the right social qualities of relaxed friendship—"if people engage in it properly," ἄν τις ἐμμελῶς ἅπτηται (IV proem [660c]). You must get your sympotic conversation right. So Plato's combination of seriousness and play is explicitly a *paradeigma* bequeathed by tradition to be followed still (VI proem [686d])—Book VIII is, suitably enough, conversations from a celebration of Plato's birthday—and conversations no less than friends need to be of proven quality and worth (δεδοκιμασμένους) before they can be admitted to a symposium (VII proem [697d]). The proems (except the last) each talk about the suitability of particular topics for the symposium, just as the dialogues demonstrate how to go about engaging in such topics. Plutarch's *Sympotic Questions* offers a normative version of sympotic behavior for the *pepaideumenoi*: it is a guide and handbook to social discourse, which can be used and reused by selective performance.

We may read Philostratus's *Erotic Letters* or even the letters of Aelian and Alciphron in the same light. Each of these collections produces discrete moments of narrative—an anecdote captured through the lens of a letter—and no more. Even when more than one letter seems to be connected in theme, as with the first five of Alciphron's *Erotic Letters*, each letter takes a well-known anecdote from the fourth-century city and turns it into a letter from one of the participants in the story. As I have discussed elsewhere, Philostratus's *Erotic Letters* are best seen as "a manual for self-expression as a Greek lover within the tropology of classical eros"—a handbook in how to present oneself as a lover.[29] Handbooks are the archetypal way of packaging a culture under threat, circulating knowledge in restricted units as a gesture toward tradition, as that tradition feels

Plutarch's famous comment in the *Lives* that you can see the character of a great man by his casual remarks or in a small action as much as by his world-changing deeds offers something of a theoretical underpinning for the turn toward anecdotal biographical narrative in the *Sympotic Questions*. (This, too, is something he learned from Xenophon.) His symposium brings together Greeks and Romans at the same table, just as his *Lives* specifically juxtapose and compare Greek and Roman heroes (and are the source of so many anecdotes). Whereas Athenaeus's dinner party of sophists creates one idealized image of Greek culture at work, a world where everyone fully embodies literate Greek culture, Plutarch's didacticism sits on the boundary of Greek and Roman culture. He addresses Sossius Senecio in each book; they are entertained at Mestrius Florus's house; Romans take part in the conversation. The text represents the sort of elite occasion in Empire society for which reading Plutarch's *Sympotic Questions* is a suitable preparation.[28]

---

28. I wish to record how much I have learnt on this from conversations with Jason Konig, whose forthcoming book on late sympotic literature is eagerly awaited.

29. Goldhill (forthcoming).

increasing need to use such fragments to bolster against ruin. A dictionary of cultural literacy. It is a pattern that Classics as a discipline is all too familiar with.

I am suggesting that in Empire culture, parallel to the high level of literacy with its concomitant focus on the book, there is another current whereby information becomes increasingly divided into anecdotal form for oral circulation. What the *pepaideumenoi* swap in dialogic exchange—with all the competitiveness that such exchanges can have in this male agonistic environment—is the brief paragraph of paradox, strange tale, telling a story. Whereas the heroes of oral poetry tell myths, the elite of the Empire tell a neat story about the peacock or what Diogenes said to Alexander. The anecdote is the *muthos* of literate culture.[30] The glue and ideological underpinning of literate exchange. It is where the literate and the oral meet.

At one level, this sort of oral performance could certainly tend firmly toward the literate. We are told in Athenaeus (1.4c) of one Calliphanes, called son of Parabrukon, Mr. Voracious, who wrote down and learnt the first three lines of a host of poems and speeches, so that he could get a reputation for *polumatheia* by reciting a suitable quotation at any moment in a symposium. This shows us how reading and learning underpinned performance in the oral environments of the symposium or of less formal exchanges. At another, more general level, the circulation or dissemination of such packaged information is key to the construction of *paideia*, the culture and education that binds the elite into a social group. We are accustomed to thinking of the *enkuklios paideia* as the training that ties together the upper echelons of society. But it also involves a discursive frame, which is made up in part of the anecdotes which define and delimit the normal, *to eikos*, by their careful exposition of the strange or unexpected. Because anecdotes depend on an agreed recognition and acceptance of the ordinary in order to have their *frisson* of the surprise, anecdotes perform the ideological function of linking a speaker and an audience in a shared normative frame. Even as they allow competition by the exchange of wittier, more bizarre, more striking anecdotes. Anecdotes thus enable the elite to perform *paideia* at an everyday and oral level—to place themselves socially. A life becomes a set of brief tales, to be retold. As Horace put it, *heu fabula quanta fiebam*.

The anecdote is an oral form that can be written down, or it can be written down and then recirculated orally. It crosses the boundaries between oral and literate in a way that shows the interdependence of both spheres. It plays an integral role in the construction of the ordinary and the creation of a normative perspective on the world. It organizes knowledge in a very particular, packaged way. The Second Sophistic is the period of

---

30. See Beard 1993 on how *declamationes* may play such a role in Roman discourse (with Kaster 2001).

Greek culture in which the anecdote seems to come into its own as a form, at least to judge from the literary evidence, our only evidence, in which the collection of discrete short tales or examples becomes a prevalent style of writing. This happens at the same time that the range of traditional mythic narratives is drastically restricted in subject matter, exposition, and detail. No one could sensibly deny that the Second Sophistic is a culture that privileges literacy in its dedication to *paideia*, but that makes the role of the anecdote and its link into oral performance all the more interesting.

BIBLIOGRAPHY

Anderson, G. 1989. "The Pepaideumenos in Action: Sophists and Their Outlook in the Early Empire." *ANRW* II.33.1: 79–208.

——— . 1993. *The Second Sophistic: A Cultural Phenomenon in the Roman Empire.* London.

Aune, D., ed. 1988. *Greco-Roman Literature and the New Testament.* Atlanta.

Beard, M. 1993. "Looking (Harder) for Roman Myth: Dumézil, Declamation and the Problems of Definition." In F. Graf, ed., *Mythos in mythenloser Gesellschaft: Das Paradigma Roms*, 44–64. Stuttgart.

Bowersock, G. 1994. *Fiction as History: Nero to Julian.* Berkeley.

Branham, B. 1989. *Unruly Eloquence: Lucian and the Comedy of Traditions.* Cambridge, Mass.

Braund, D., and J. Wilkins, eds. 2000. *Athenaeus and His World: Reading Greek Culture in the Roman Empire.* Exeter.

Collins, J., and R. K. Blot. 2003. *Literacy and Literacies: Texts, Power, and Identity.* Cambridge.

Cribiore, R. 2001. *Gymnastics of the Mind: Greek Education in Hellenistic and Roman Egypt.* Princeton.

Dickie, M. 1991. "Heliodorus and Plutarch on the Evil Eye." *CP* 86: 17–29.

Ford, A. 1999. "Reading Homer from the Rostrum: Poems and Laws in Aeschines' *Against Timarchus*." In S. Goldhill and R. Osborne, eds., *Performance Culture and Athenian Democracy*, 231–56. Cambridge.

Gleason, M. 1995. *Making Men: Sophists and Self-Presentation in Ancient Rome.* Princeton.

Goldhill, S. 1991. *The Poet's Voice: Essays on Poetics and Greek Literature.* Cambridge.

——— . 1999. "Literary History without Literature: Reading Practices in the Ancient World." *SubStance* 28: 57–89.

——— , ed. 2001. *Being Greek under Rome: Cultural Identity, the Second Sophistic and the Development of Empire.* Cambridge.

——— . 2002. *Who Needs Greek? Contests in the Cultural History of Hellenism.* Cambridge.

——— . Forthcoming. "'Drink to Me Only with Thine Eyes': Philostratus' *Erotic Letters*." In E. Bowie and J. Elsner, eds., *Philostratus.* Cambridge.

Heath, S. 1983. *Ways with Words: Language, Life, and Work in Communities and Classrooms.* New York.

Hock, R., and E. O'Neil, eds. 1986. *The Chreia in Ancient Rhetoric.* Vol. 1: *The Progymnasmata.* Atlanta.

——— , eds. 2002. *The Chreia and Ancient Rhetoric*. Vol. 2: *Classroom Exercises*. Atlanta.

Jones, C. 1971. *Plutarch and Rome*. Oxford.

Kaster, R. 2001. "Controlling Reason: Declamation in Rhetorical Education in Rome." In Yun-Lee Too, ed., *Education in Greek and Roman Antiquity*, 317–337. Leiden.

Kennedy, G. 2003. *Progymnasmata: Greek Textbooks of Prose Composition and Rhetoric*. Leiden.

Langlands, R. 2006. *Sexual Morality in Ancient Rome*. Cambridge.

Lynn-George, M. 1988. *Epos: Word, Narrative and the* Iliad. Atlantic Heights.

Mack, B. 1987. "Anecdotes and Arguments: The Chreia in Antiquity and Early Christianity." *Occasional Papers, Institute for Antiquity and Christianity* 10. Claremont, CA.

——— and V. Robbins. 1989. *Patterns of Persuasion in the Gospels*. Sonoma, Calif.

Morgan, T. J. 1998. *Literate Education in the Hellenistic and Roman Worlds*. Cambridge Classical Studies. Cambridge.

Nagy, G. 1974. *Comparative Studies in Greek and Indic Meter*. Cambridge, Mass.

——— . 1979. *The Best of the Achaeans: Concepts of the Hero in Archaic Greek Poetry*. Baltimore.

Redfield, J. 1975. *Nature and Culture in the Iliad: The Tragedy of Hector*. Chicago.

Robbins, V. 1988. "The Chreia." In D. Aune, ed., *Greco-Roman Literature and the New Testament*, 1–23. Atlanta.

——— . 1989. "Pronouncement Stories and Jesus' Blessing of the Children." *Semeia* 29: 42–74.

Rommel, H. 1923. *Die naturwissenschaftlich-paradoxographischen Exkurse bei Philostratos, Heliodoros und Achilleus Tatios*. Stuttgart.

Rood, T. 2004. *The Sea! The Sea! The Shout of the Ten Thousand in the Modern Imagination*. London.

Sedley, D. 1980. "The Protagonists." In M. Schofield, M. Burnyeat, and J. Barnes, eds., *Doubt and Dogmatism*, 1–19. Oxford.

Segal, C. 1994. *Singers, Heroes, and Gods in the Odyssey*. Ithaca.

Swain, S. 1996. *Hellenism and Empire: Language, Classicism, and Power in the Greek World*, AD 50–250. Oxford.

Whitmarsh, T. 2001. *Greek Literature and the Roman Empire: The Politics of Imitation*. Oxford.

6

Situating Literacy at Rome

Thomas Habinek

In 1997 Emmanuelle Valette-Cagnac published her Paris dissertation on the anthropology of reading in the Roman world.[1] This important study opened the way to a new understanding of what its author calls "the practices and rituals" of reading in relationship to those of speaking and writing. Valette-Cagnac reminds us of the privileging of the oral over the written in Roman law, of the range of ways in which a text can be enunciated, as characterized by such Latin verbs as *recito, pronuntio,* and *canto,* and of the interdependence of speaking, writing, reading, and performing in the production of verbal utterances in the Roman world.[2] Like William Johnson, in his article "Towards a Sociology of Reading in Classical Antiquity," published in 2000, Valette-Cagnac shifts attention from text to practice, from writing to reading, and from a schematic distinction between orality and literacy to a more nuanced account of the varieties of both.[3]

A year after Valette-Cagnac's work appeared, Rudolf Wachter published an equally important study of the relationship between Pompeiian epigraphical verses and the surviving elegiac poetry of Propertius, Tibullus, and Ovid, making the surprising but compelling argument that both sets of texts could be understood as building on a tradition of orally transmitted verse in elegiac couplet.[4] Wachter's paper, the title of which can be translated as "Oral Poetry in an Unexpected Context," does not argue for or against the importance of writing in the production of so-called literary elegiac, but it does remind us of the role of hearing and

---

1. Valette-Cagnac 1997.
2. On the last-mentioned point, see also Habinek 2005a.
3. W. A. Johnson 2000. On reading, rather than writing, as the skill effecting the cognitive and social changes that accompany the spread of literacy, see Olson 1994. Morrison 1987 makes the important distinction between alphabetic literacy, which he associates with classical Greece, and textual literacy, which he regards as the contribution of late antiquity and the early Middle Ages. He makes no mention, however, of the conflicted efforts of the Romans in the direction of textual literacy.
4. Wachter 1998.

vocalizing in the transmittal of turns of phrase, metrical patterns, sound effects, and the like. More generally, Wachter's paper speaks to the way in which elite artistic forms, then as now, routinely derive their energy from popular traditions of singing, speaking, dancing, and depicting—a point that will become relevant later in this chapter. Working outside the mainstream of classical studies, linguist B. G. Campbell in 2001 further complicated our understanding of the relationship between reading, writing, and listening in a monograph entitled *Performing and Processing the* Aeneid. There Campbell demonstrates that various stylistic features of Vergilian epic can best be understood if we recognize that the poem is to be processed orally. The suppression of anaphoric in favor of deictic pronouns, the use of conjunctions for structural as opposed to strictly syntactic purposes, the foregrounding of key ideas: these and other features make for a text that is easy for a listener to process the first time through. Of course skeptics may still claim that all this shows is that Vergil wrote his poem to make it seem like something that could be read aloud, a "fiction of orality," as it were; but thanks to Campbell, Johnson, and others, the burden of proof would seem once and for all to be on those who want to turn classical Roman audiences into medieval monks or modern scholars. In Campbell's case, we seem to have confirmation of the argument Eduard Fraenkel made long ago that Vergil could not have written the *Aeneid* without first listening to Roman oratory.[5]

All of the works just cited—and the list could go on—demonstrate the untenability of traditional accounts of Roman literacy. Literacy and orality are not mutually exclusive in Rome or in any other culture; nor can Rome's adoption of writing and reading be positioned on some imaginary continuum between archaic Greek song culture and medieval scholasticism or early modern print culture. Rome interacted with its Greek, Etruscan, and Oscan neighbors, and we surely must consider the possibility that its literacy practices were affected by theirs. But this is far from saying that Rome partakes in a teleological movement culminating in us— where reading and writing are concerned, or anything else for that matter. Literacy must be situated at Rome, or better, in various specific contexts at Rome.[6] The present paper aims to begin the project of situating Roman literacy by viewing it from three perspectives—diachronic, synchronic, and, for lack of a better term, ontological. How does the social impact and significance of literacy at Rome change over time? How do the uses of literacy at Rome differ from those found in other ancient societies? What do Roman practices of reading and writing tell us about the Roman understanding of what writing is and is not?

5. Fraenkel 1926/7.
6. For the concept of literacy as a "situated practice," see Barton et al. 2000.

1. WRITING, PROPERTY, AND THE MATERIALIZATION OF SOCIAL RELATIONS

If we consider the spread of writing and reading practices at Rome, perhaps the first question to come to mind is, why did it take so long? Rome did not develop a literary culture in the sense of professional authors, a preserved and transmitted canon, and intertextual reference and critique until the late third century B.C.[7] Yet the Romans—or at least some Romans—would have had access to writing probably as early as the first part of the eighth century.[8] It is worth recalling that among the earliest examples of Greek writing are the EUOIN or (less likely) EULIN inscription on a pot unearthed in the cemetery at Osteria dell'Osa near Gabii, in Latium, now generally dated to the first quarter of the eighth century B.C.,[9] and the slightly later Nestor's cup inscription from Pithekoussai—an island whose location in the Bay of Naples made it a jumping-off point for Greek contacts up and down the Italian seacoast.[10] Written Latin makes its appearance, depending on whom you believe and how you interpret certain texts, as early as the seventh century, with the Duenos inscription, which was found at Rome in the late nineteenth century.[11] The early Latin alphabet resembles, and was perhaps shaped by, that of the Etruscans, who of course had their own literacy practices before, during, and after the emergence of Rome as a major power in central Italy. It is worth noting that preserved Etruscan writing is largely formulaic in nature, a feature suggesting that the significance of Etruscan texts could have been apparent even to those not familiar with their exact meaning, somewhat the way trademarks today can be meaningful across linguistic boundaries. The issue of writing in the earliest period of Roman history, its prevalence, use, and significance, usually gets wrapped up in scholarly debates over the credibility of the later Roman historiographic tradition—an odd development, because there is no particular reason to believe that a society's memory can only be preserved in documentary

---

7. See Habinek 1998, 34–68; Rüpke 2000; Sciarrino 2004.

8. For a compendium of the earliest instances of writing in Latium see Smith 1996, 233–6; also important are Colonna 1980 and Cornell 1991. Note also the joint research project on pre-Roman literacy, based at University College London and described online at http://www.ucl.ac.uk/ancient-literacy/.

9. Ridgway 1996; Peruzzi 1998.

10. On the cultural significance of Pithekoussai (Ischia) see Camporeale 2000, passim; Whitley 2001, 126–33; for discussion of the Nestor's cup inscription, see Watkins 1976, Faraone 1996.

11. CIL 1.2.4 = *ILLRP* 1.2; discussed Ernout 1973, 7–9. Other candidates for earliest Latin inscription include the Vetusia inscription on a silver bowl from the Bernardini tomb, now housed at the Villa Giulia in Rome; and the Praenestine fibula (*ILLRP* 1.1; Ernout 1973, 1–2), displayed at the Museo Etnografico L. Pigorini, also in Rome. Controversy over the authenticity of the latter continues apace, with recent opinion appearing to incline toward authenticity: see, for example, Hartmann 2005, 67–106.

form and, equally, no particular reason to think that preserving a record of a society's past is the only function to which writing can be put.

Following the lead of Simon Stoddart and James Whitley's excellent article on "The Social Context of Literacy in Archaic Greece and Etruria," we may consider a different, more socially grounded approach to early Roman literacy, both in relation to literacy in other Mediterranean cultures and in relation to later developments at Rome.[12] Stoddart and Whitley's analysis of the relative frequency of different uses of writing in different cultural/geographical contexts (Athens, Crete, Etruria) and at different periods of time (half centuries from 700 to 450 B.C.) allows them to draw reasonable inferences about the variable social and ideological significance of writing in different times and places. Although critics are right to note that such interpretations are subject to the "tyranny of the evidence" (especially the disappearance of instances of writing on perishable material), the fact that such tyranny operates with the same force in different archaic contexts and time periods suggests that *relative* conclusions about uses of literacy—such as those drawn by Stoddart and Whitley—are valid, even if no absolute account of prevalence or full enumeration of uses of writing can be provided.[13]

Table 6.1, then, reproduces the data as organized by Stoddart and Whitley, showing the sources of surviving Greek writing from Crete and Attica and of surviving Etruscan writing from northern (less urbanized) and southern (more urbanized) Etruria. Noting the high proportion of dipinti and graffiti at Athens, Stoddart and Whitley argue that "Writing [there] was very much connected to the needs of individuals to record their names publicly, and thereby to display their virtue and skills. For such inscriptions to be effective, a fairly wide literary audience is pre-supposed. This contrasts sharply with the role that writing played in Crete." There, they suggest, the disproportionate emphasis on promulgation of law codes is meant "to mystify them," to make them seem "immutable and unchanging."[14] In the case of the Etruscan material, they link differential patterns of use to different degrees of urbanization in northern and southern Etruria.

Table 6.2 summarizes results of my own preliminary and admittedly incomplete survey of uses of writing in early Rome and surrounding areas. The database consists of all the inscriptions for which dates are provided by Degrassi in his compendium of Inscriptions of the Free Roman Republic (*Inscriptiones latinae liberae rei publicae*), as well as more recent discoveries compiled in the Dutch school's edition of the Lapis Satricanus.[15] Only inscriptions found in central Italy are included, and only those

12. Stoddart and Whitley 1988.
13. Cornell states his objections at Cornell 1991, 7–10.
14. Stoddart and Whitley 1988, 766.
15. Stibbe et al. 1980, especially the compilation by Colonna at pp. 53–70.

Table 6.1. Sources for Greek and Etruscan Writing

	700–650	650–600	600–550	550–500	500–450
Crete					
Dedications	0	16	0	0	5
Gravestones	0	1	0	1	3
Legal	0	2	4	12	5
Graffiti	1	1	0	3	0
Dipinti	0	0	0	0	0
Athens and Attica					
Dedications	4	5	14	115	211
Gravestones	0	2	7	46	?
Legal	0	0	0	2	4
Graffiti	73	81	200+	200+	200+
Dipinti	4	4	200+	200+	200+
South Etruria					
Dedications	0	0	0	4	
Gravestones	0	3	5	113	
Legal	0	0	0	0	
Graffiti					
Dedicatory	3	5	59	63	
Possessive	25	52	45	45	
Dipinti	0	0	0	1	
Single letters	10	13	47	52	
North Etruria					
Dedications	0	0	0	0	
Gravestones	0	2	3	5	
Legal	0	0	0	0	
Graffiti					
Dedicatory	0	0	0	0	
Possessive	1	10	6	5	
Dipinti	0	0	0	0	
Single letters	1	3	61	10	

Source: Following Stoddart and Whitley 1988.

that record at least some use of the Latin language or a close dialectal variant. The table shows uses of inscriptions roughly comparable to those found in Greece and Etruria, listed by percentage for the given historical period. There are two versions of the last column (for the first century B.C.), one excluding *tesserae* (inscribed bits of bone and ivory) and *glandes* (sling bullets), the other including them.[16]

16. The *tesserae nummulariae* (*ILLRP* 2.987–1063) are bits of bone or ivory that verify the contents of the container to which they are affixed: see Andreau 1999, 80–9. *Glandes* (*ILLRP* 2.1088–1120) are sling bullets inscribed with curses or threats against the enemy. Many surviving examples are from the siege of Perugia in 43–42 B.C. The numbers of both, which are cheap and easy to produce, distort the ratios of different uses of writing, especially those involving display of status. For this reason, I have tabulated uses both with and without the tesserae and glandes.

Table 6.2. Sources for Roman Writing

	Before Third Cent. B.C.	Third/Second Cent. B.C.	First Cent. B.C.	First Cent. B.C. Incl. Tesserae and Glandes
Precious objects				
Incised	28%	1%	1%	1%
Dipinti	0	1%	0	0
Gravestones				
Non-elite	0	2%	9%	6%
Elite	0	16%	3%	2%
Dedications	38%	21%	30%	18%
Boundaries	22%	10%	5%	3%
Other legal	0	3%	2%	1.5%
Commemorative	11%	13%	34%	20%
Fasti	0	1%	1%	>1%
Milestones	0	14%	1%	1%
Acta of collegia	1%	17%	12%	7%
Sortes	0	0	3%	2%
Tesserae	0	0	26 items	22%
Glandes	0	0	11 items	6%

Despite the superficiality of the survey, certain trends may be observed. In terms of movement over time, we note the drop in frequency of inscription on precious objects—a practice that seems to have characterized aristocratic gift exchange in archaic Latium and Etruria.[17] We may note as well the steady upturn in funerary and commemorative uses, the latter instances for the most part recording the contributions of individuals or corporations to the public good (repair of aqueducts, construction of temples, etc.). Such changes, together with the use of writing by soldiers (in the case of the *glandes*) and on lots may well testify to an expansion of literacy.

More striking is the contrast between this chart and those provided for Attica and Etruria. What seems to emerge is a distinctly Roman use of writing for two purposes, one of which we might call proprietarial, as in the marking of territory or indications of ownership and financial responsibility (this is what most of the *tesserae* seem to be about);[18] the other of which speaks to a particular form of sociability—dedications overwhelmingly to other people, not to the gods, commemorative inscriptions that are, despite their boastfulness, concrete manifestations of social obligations and aspirations.

17. See Cristofani 1984.
18. See the discussion by Andreau 1999, 80–9, following the earlier interpretation of R. Herzog.

With respect to the latter phenomenon, we may recall Lotte Hedeager's argument, advanced in her discussion of status markers in north European iron-age societies, that the prevalence of status assertion corresponds to periods of insecurity and social change: in other words, there is less need to display your wealth or status if no one is challenging it.[19] Following that logic, we might read from the Roman results relative security about status in the early period, coupled with insecurity about property lines, and the reverse—insecurity about status, security about property—in the later centuries. It is worth noting that of the dedications in the earliest period, six are by anonymous donors to deities; the only one that names people as both donor and recipient (namely, the Lapis Satricanus) is the exception that proves Hedeager's rule, for within a few years of its placement in the temple of Mater Matuta, the structure was burned by a rebel army, the dedication overthrown, and the inscription buried in the foundation of a new building.[20] Competitive display by newly emergent elites (e.g., the family inscriptions of the Scipiones, *CIL* I, pp. 11–15) can be understood as further illustration of the connection between status assertion and status insecurity, although in this case the status that is insecure is one that is still sought after: will past achievements entitle the clan and its descendants to extend their authority forward in time?

More generally, the tentative results offered here for epigraphic writing in the Roman republic provide an interesting prequel to Elizabeth Meyer's and Greg Woolf's discussions of the relationship between epigraphic writing and social status under the early empire in their articles of 1990 and 1996 respectively. The concern to "fix an individual's place within history, society and the cosmos," as Woolf puts it,[21] although it certainly intensified during the Augustan era and subsequent periods of social and cultural change, has its roots in the competitive, inclusive, and contested nature of Roman identity evidenced from earlier periods of history, perhaps especially the end of the third and beginning of the second centuries B.C., precisely the era in which Roman literary culture took form. Epigraphic display both advances one's position in intra-Roman struggles for status and secures one's position in the ever-strengthening Roman community. In answer to the question, why did an expanded literate culture take so long to develop at Rome, one answer might be, because that's how long it took for the Romans to require clarification of their status and identity as Romans.[22]

19. Hedeager 1992.
20. For the history and interpretation of the inscription see, among others, Versnel 1980, Coarelli 1995, Habinek 2005a, 37–40.
21. Woolf 1996, 29.
22. It might also be argued that the Roman inscriptional habit of the late Republic derives in part from the influence of Hellenistic Greek inscriptions. In general I find such arguments unpersuasive on their own, because they deny the recipient culture's agency in choosing which practices to be influenced by and under what circumstances. Even if Greek

2. WRITING, RITUALIZATION, AND MASTERY

The use of writing to assert status leads to a second line of inquiry, which considers writing as a more generalized practice, encompassing epigraphic as well as literary and economic uses. What is it about writing that allows it to operate as an effective assertion of status? We can see the link in the case of monumental writing, in which the size, expense, and permanence of the monument itself speak to the status of its agents: the inscription on the monument, as Woolf notes, specifies or disambiguates the monument's symbolic significance.[23] But writing, as writing, does more than just disambiguate. In monuments of varying sizes as well as in literary texts, writing amplifies the persona of the writer, extending his reach as it were; and it constitutes a mode of ritualization that generates new agencies and new opportunities for mastery.

The first function, that of amplification and extension of persona, I have already discussed in an earlier study, in which I argue that the inscription and circulation of a text extends the efficacy of the authorizing performance, thereby anchoring literary production even more securely in the elite cultural contexts from which it emerges.[24] Republican-era inscriptions corroborate this association of writing with extensibility, albeit in a context quite different from that of literary production. For example, in the case of the *tesserae nummulariae* (*ILLRP* 2.987–1063), bits of bone or ivory verifying that so-and-so the slave or freedman of so-and-so inspected the contents of the container, there is a double extensibility: from the authorizing practice, presumably the verification of the metallic content of the coins, to the written certification, but also from the master to the slave or freedman. Recent scholarship has shown how Latin authors, not to mention Roman law, take for granted what might be called the prosthetic nature of the slave, his or her function as an extension of masterly agency.[25] To strike a slave is to strike his master; to tell a free man to dig a ditch is in fact to tell him to have his slaves dig a ditch, as the very language of Vergil's *Georgics* and of Roman agricultural treatises makes clear.[26] The *tesserae* exactly capture this sense of the slave

inscriptions (like Greek literature) provide an object for Roman emulation, we must still account for the choice to emulate within the framework of Roman cultural needs and objectives.

23. Woolf 1996.
24. Habinek 1998, 103–21, discusses the parallel between literary and epigraphic practices.
25. Reay 2003, 2005.
26. For example, at Vergil *Georgics* 2.230–2, the second person singular of the verb in the expressions "you will identify" (*capies*), "you will replace" (*repones*), and "you will flatten" (*aequabis*) clearly encompasses both master (the immediate addressee of the poet) and his slaves. Cf. *Georgics* 2.259–60; 2.274–5, Varro *De Re Rustica* 1.23: all examples from Reay 2005.

as an extension of the master's power or in this case credit, but they do so through the medium of writing.

As it turns out, writing is also routinely associated with slaves in other contexts in the Roman world, sometimes in the practical sense that a slave will function as copyist or amanuensis; but also ideologically in that writing is associated with the body, with submission to an externally imposed system of constraints, and thus treated as socially inferior to the free exercise of the voice. Horace's association of his book of poems with a cultivated slave (*Epl.* 1.20.1–2 etc.) is just one manifestation of this widespread phenomenon.[27] But there's a certain paradox in the association of writing with slavery, because writing, at least in the sense of composing, can also serve to authorize the agency of the writer.

To explain this latter process we can draw upon a large body of theoretical work on the practices of ritualization. The term *ritualization* is borrowed from scholars of religion, such as Catherine Bell, who in turn have borrowed it from ethologists, or students of animal behavior.[28] In the case of animal behavior, ritualization refers to the process whereby part of a natural sequence of actions comes to stand for the whole of the sequence and, eventually, for something else entirely.[29] Thus the ruffling of feathers that naturally precedes a bird's flight comes to signify a need to fly, as in a warning sign, but also to signify ability to fly as in a mating dance. Perceptual iconicity, as it is sometimes called, is thus the foundation of semiotics.[30] When applied to human behavior, ritualization refers to the making special of otherwise everyday activities through the stylization, intensification, or repetition of some natural aspect of the activity. Thus bodily movement can be ritualized into dance (*ludus*), a meal ritualized into a sacred banquet (*epula*) or a dinner party (*convivium*), everyday speech (*locutio*) ritualized into prayer, poetry, or song (*carmen*). As with animal ritualization, so with human, the signifying power of the ritualized act can be dislodged and carry over into other spheres of activity besides that in which it originated. For Bell, this tendency for the power of ritualization to "spill over" into other contexts explains how it is that ritualization generates agency—a mastery of certain patterns of action or speech that obtains beyond the immediate ritual sphere, as, for example, when a priest's authority extends beyond the confines of a liturgy or a skilled speaker's charisma and influence have an impact beyond the immediate occasion of speech making.

---

27. For further discussion and examples see Habinek 2005a, 146–9; Habinek 2005b. More generally on slavery in the Roman literary imagination, see Fitzgerald 2000.

28. See Bell 1992, 88–9 on the history of the term. The transfer from ethology to religious studies is marked by the essays gathered in *Philosophical Transactions of the Royal Society*, series B, 251 (1966). Ritualization is also a key concept in discussions of the origin of language: see Wilcox 1999.

29. For example, Wilson 1975, 594.

30. Brandon 1996, 85–105.

In *The World of Roman Song*, I argue that mastery of the ritualization of speech into song is an important means through which the agency of the free elite male is established and reestablished within the Roman world.[31] The master of special speech—whether an orator, a *vates*, or a poet—has a power that extends beyond the power to speak or sing well, an authority that obtains even outside the immediate context of public verbal production. We might now consider the possibility that writing extends the process of ritualization and thus opens new avenues for mastery. Once writing is available, it is potentially part of the process of production of special speech or song. And indeed we know from rhetorical handbooks, poetic self-reference, and so on that writing was used in the preparation of speech— as indeed was the process of reading the writings of others.[32] Like the bird ruffling its feathers, reading and writing are each aspects of speech production that can come to signify the process as a whole. Mastery of literacy practices thus creates new agencies within the realm of special speech or song whose authority spills over into other areas of social interaction. To inscribe a version of a eulogy, as in the third and second century Scipionic epitaphs, or to textualize a speech—a practice that began at least as early as Cato the Elder (see *ORF* 8.173–5)—is not just to preserve a version for possible future reperformance. It is also to demonstrate mastery of a ritualized practice and thereby constitute an agency that extends beyond the immediate context of reading, speaking, and writing.

The practice of writing other kinds of literary texts has similar effect. The written version is not strictly speaking the telos of the process of composition. Rather, reading and writing make more special the already special practices of composing and reciting; they create—or attempt to create—a further level of mastery beyond the mastery implicit in the production of special speech. The problem, as already indicated, is that reading and writing can never quite break free of their association with embodiment, their slavishness, as it were, and thus do not destroy the centrality of the voice and orality. Nonetheless, mastery of reading and especially writing as ritualized practices constitutes an agency that has validity in situations where the voice cannot be heard—namely across time or space—and thus makes such practices available for the effective assertion of status. Oddly enough, then, it is because of writing's role in the reproduction of oral culture at Rome that it becomes a means for "fix[ing] an individual's place within history, society and the cosmos."[33] It is both writing's capacity to disambiguate the symbolism of art and

---

31. Habinek 2005a, esp. 34–57.

32. On the use of writing in the production of speech, see Cic. *De Or.* 1.150 (*stilus optimus et praestantissimus dicendi effector ac magister.* "the pen is the best and most distinguished improver and teacher of public speaking"); Quintilian *Inst. Or.* 10.3; Catull. 50; Hor. *Serm.* 1.4.129–39, 1.10.72–4. Small 1997, 177–80 collects examples of the use of written excerpts of prior works in the production of new ones.

33. Woolf 1996, 29.

monument (a capacity shared with spoken language, too, we should recall) and its own status as ritualized practice that account for its persistent use in monuments of dedication and commemoration as well as its privileged position within the predominantly oral culture of the Roman elite.

3. WRITING OF LANGUAGE, WRITING AS LANGUAGE

Having asked why it takes literacy so long to spread at Rome, and what is at stake socially in the mastery of practices of literacy, we can complicate matters still further by asking yet another large and not strictly answerable question: what is at stake in our own privileging of literacy as a means of access to ancient cultures more generally and to Rome specifically? My participation in a volume on literacy has an ironic aspect to it, in that my own recent work has emphasized the limitations imposed by a scholarly focus on practices of symbolization, of which spoken and written language are important examples.[34] I accept the conclusion of much recent research in evolutionary biology and neuroscience, namely, that the capacity for bodily imitation precedes and sustains the capacity for symbolization, especially the production of language.[35] Both mimesis and symbolization make it possible for human beings to gain access to information accumulated by other members of the species, to trade representations, to imagine and to deceive—activities that as a group differentiate humans from other species.[36] Yet, as Paul Connerton has written, at least since the Enlightenment (if not before), inscribing practices (i.e., writing or other practices that lend themselves to interpretation as writing) have constituted the privileged, incorporating practices the neglected, dimension of hermeneutics.[37] To give a full account of the transmittal of knowledge across time historians must develop ways to recover the history carried by bodies as well as that carried by texts and to identify the mimetic regimes that shape and structure action with or without the assistance of ideologies carried by language and other symbolic means. In this context, both orality and literacy are privileged cultural practices that need to be decentered, or at least supplemented, if we are to understand ancient and other cultures as fully as possible.

34. Habinek 2005a, 2005c. On language as an embodied process see more generally M. Johnson 1990, Johnson and Lakoff 1999.

35. See, for example, Donald 1999, Wilcox 1999, Donald 2001, Arbib 2002, Iacoboni 2005.

36. I leave aside the complex and ongoing debates over the representational capacities of other species. All that is necessary for my argument is acceptance of the view that the activities listed in the text in their clustering and their frequency differentiate human beings from all or virtually all other species.

37. Connerton 1989.

Yet if embodied mimetic practices merit consideration on their own terms, nonetheless attention to them can broaden and enrich our understanding of modes of symbolization, including writing. Let us consider, for example, Nicholas Purcell's suggestive article "Literate Games," which examines inscribed game boards (the so-called *lusoriae tabulae*) and the culture of gaming surrounding them—a set of objects, scripts, and practices that mark the intersection of the embodied and the symbolic.[38] In his analysis of the culture of gaming, Purcell draws many plausible inferences concerning the role of competition, windfalls, economic and social aspirations, and so forth; but when it comes to writing, he sees the game boards as evidence of a quasi-literary culture surrounding and parasitical upon the practices of the truly literate and literary elites. It seems possible to argue, however, that the influence runs in the opposite direction; or perhaps better that the playfulness of the script on the game boards and certain kinds of play in literary texts are manifestations of the same underlying attitude to writing, which treats it not just as an expression of speech but also as a distinctive means of graphic communication that entails strictures and constraints not characteristic of spoken language. As Ken Morrison puts it in his discussion of the emergence of modern forms of textuality, "meaning inheres as much in our patterns of textual organization as it does in the structures of linguistic usage."[39] Text and language constitute "separate but co-operative loci of meaning."[40]

Of the many pieces of surviving material evidence pertaining to gaming in the Roman world, a group of *lusoriae tabulae* constructed around a pattern of six words of six letters each invites particular attention.[41] In addition to their stereotyped arrangement (two words per line, often with an intervening rosette or other mark), the *tabulae* contain similar messages inviting the reader/user to relax, play, and so on. For example, the pavement of the Forum at Timgad contains the inscription

VENARI	LAVARI
LVDERE	RIDERE
OCCEST	VIVERE
(To hunt	to bathe
To play	to laugh
This is	to live)[42]

Another inscription, from Trier, reads

38. Purcell 1995.
39. Morrison 1987, 243.
40. Morrison 1987, 268.
41. Twenty-one such tablets are recorded in the slightly differing collections of Lamer 1927, Austin 1934 and 1935, Ferrua 1946, and Purcell 1995. For full bibliography see Purcell 1995, 18. Ferrua includes several inscriptions too fragmentary to determine for certain if they follow the three-by-twelve pattern.
42. Purcell 1995, 24.

PARTHI   OCCISI
BRITTO   VICTVS
LVDITE   ROMANI
(Parthians slain
Briton   conquered
Play   Romans!)[43]

Certain phrases occur on the *tabulae* with sufficient frequency to appear formulaic: for example, *circus plenus* ("the circus is full") and *ludere nescis* ("you don't know how to play"). The arrangement of the letters on the surviving tablets suggests that they may mark positions for movement of game pieces across the playing space.[44] As a player moves his game piece from position to position he also moves from letter to letter of a message exhorting him and the other participants to relax, play, enjoy the defeat of the Picts, and so on. It seems worth noting in this context that one of the popular board games from antiquity—perhaps the one called *latrunculi*, or "little bandits"—is known to have thirty-six pieces (the same as the number of places on the *tabulae*) while another was called *duodecim scripta*, or "twelve written things"[45] (twelve, like thirty-six, being a multiple of six). A certain self-consciousness with respect to the interrelated processes of reading, writing, and playing can thus be seen to have characterized at least one familiar type of Roman board game.

Word games comparable to those on the *lusoriae tabulae* can also be found among the poems of the *Anthologia Latina*, which expressly attribute them to "twelve sages" or *sapientes* (Riese 1894, c. 495–506). In the poetic context, the challenge of producing sayings consisting of six words of six letters (familiar from the *lusoriae tabulae*) is intensified, in that the sayings must also comprise dactylic hexameters. Examples include a saying attributed to Pompilianus:

Irasci victos minime placet, optime frater
(it ill behooves losers to grow angry, dearest brother)

—*Anth. Lat.* 498

and this one assigned to Basilius

Lusori cupido semper gravis exitus instat
(a player's greed always brings a bad outcome)

—*Anth. Lat.* 501

43. Lamer 1927, 2010; Purcell 1995, 25.
44. Ferrua 1946, 54 followed by Purcell 1995, 19. It is also possible that each letter marks a different spot for the landing of dice.
45. The term *duodecim scripta* is attested Cic. *De Or.* 1.217. Mart. 14.17 and Ov. *Tr.* 2.477 may refer to the same game. Ov. *Ars* 3.357–66 alludes to the title "duodecim scripta" while also referring to playing pieces called *latrunculi*. His remarks, as well as the possibility of organizing thirty-six places into three lines, has led some to see *latrunculi* and *duodecim scripta* as referring to the same game, a possibility denied by Austin 1934 and 1935.

Self-referentiality about the playfulness of writing provides an additional
link between the board games and the manuscripts' word games: forms of
lud- or *lus-* occur on eleven of twenty-one *tabulae* and in five of the twelve
monostichs. Such insistence on play is unlikely to be accidental. In the
Latin language, the term *ludus*, or "play," refers to the ordering of the
body according to externally imposed schemes and patterns (as in ritual
performance, gladiatorial training, school exercises, and even sex) and, in
many cases, to the ordering of writing according to arbitrary rules and
conventions.[46] For example, the *ludus poeticus* of Catullus and Calvus in
Catullus 50 takes place through writing (*scribens*, 50.4) on tablets (*in meis
tabellis*, 50.2) and consists of submission to metrical and perhaps sexual
rhythms (*ludebat numero modo hoc modo illoc*, 50.5). In the works of
Vergil, Horace, and other poets as well, the terms *ludus* and *ludere* refer
to responsive singing, as in a challenge match, or more generally to the
poet or other performer's submission to externally imposed standards and
patterns of genre, meter, and style.[47]

These writing games, which cross boundaries between the literary and
the nonliterary, the textual and the inscriptional, and the symbolic and
the embodied, can be compared to yet another set of interrelated graphic
practices, ones that construct and transmit meaning through the arrangement of letters at cross-purposes to the usual pattern of reading left to
right. Figure writings, acrostics, and palindromes share with board games,
metrical play, and the like an insistence on the users' recognition of the
arbitrariness of writing practices and of the materiality of their own
perceptual processes. Although they communicate symbolically (i.e.,
transmit meaning), they do so only by calling attention to the nonsym-
bolic, embodied aspects of writing, reading, and playing.

Figure 6.1 presents one of the *tabulae iliacae* found near Bovillae in
Latium and dated to the reign of Augustus. (The *tabulae iliacae* are a
group of low reliefs dating to the early principate, many but not all of
which, illustrate scenes from the *Iliad*.)[48] This one, known as the Tabula
Iliaca Capitolina, provides a particularly striking example of the visual
playfulness that characterizes much ancient writing—epigraphic and
otherwise. Here the letters of the text have been organized into the
form of an altar. If the reader starts at the center and follows the line
of letters horizontally or vertically in any direction, she or he receives
the same message: *aspis akhilleos theodoreos kat' homeron* ("the shield
of Achilles by Theodorus following Homer"). Note, as well, that the

46. Habinek 2005a, 116–22, 132–50; cf. Piccaluga 1965.

47. For responsive song and dance, see Pl. *Curc.* 295–6, Hor. C. 2.12.17–9, Verg. *Ecl.*
7.5–17. For adherence to metrical or other formal constraints, see Hor. C. 1.32.1–5, *Ep.*
2.2.141–4, Ov. *Am.* 3.1.27–8, *Tr.* 2.59, *Ciris* 19–20.

48. On the *tabulae iliacae* in general and the *Tabula Iliaca Capitolina* in particular see
Horsfall 1979, who recommends Sadurska 1964, which I have not yet seen.

Figure 6.1 Tabula Iliaca Capitolina (MDAI(R) vi (1891) pl. v).

words at the bottom of the depicted "altar" constitute a palindrome: *iereiaierei*. Either way they read "the priestess to the priest."

We can understand the *tabulae iliacae* as part of a more widespread interest in acrostics, word-squares, and palindromes that characterizes—again—both literary and nonliterary writing.[49] As is well known, acrostic plot summaries survive from antiquity for most of the plays of Plautus, such as the following that precedes the text of the *Pseudolus*:

> Praesentis numerat quindecim miles minas
> Simul consignat symbolum, ut Phoenicium
> Ei det leno qui eum cum relicuo adferat.
> Venientem caculam intervortit symbolo
> Dicens Syrum se Ballionis Pseudolus
> Opemque erili ita tulit; nam Simmiae
> Leno mulierem, quem is supposuit, tradidit.
> Venit harpax verus: res palam cognoscitur
> Senexque argentum quod erat pactus reddidit.

> (A soldier counts out fifteen minae in ready money
> At the same time he seals a token, so that the pimp
> Will hand over Phoenicium to the person who approaches with the
>   remainder [i.e., of the token].
> Pseudolus intercepts the soldier's servant coming with the token
> Claiming that he is Syrus, slave of Ballio.
> Thus he aided his master's [son]. For the pimp
> Handed over to Simmia the woman whom he [Pseudolus] supplied instead
> The true plunderer arrives: the affair becomes public knowledge
> And the old man made good on the money that was pledged.)

The content of the plot summary, here as elsewhere, sacrifices a strict logic of explanation (e.g., the identity of Ballio with the *leno*, the importance of the master's son within the action) to the generation of a visual pattern that expresses the title of the play. As one scholar puts it, the acrostic summary is "really only intelligible if one already knows the play."[50]

The presence of acrostics in the didactic poetry of Aratus and Vergil has also received widespread acknowledgement by scholars. In these instances, the acrostics seem to reinforce, rather than obscure the linguistic meaning of the text. One Aratean acrostic emphasizes a characteristic, fineness or *leptotes*, that unites subject matter (the crescent moon) and poetic style (note λεπτή across and down):

---

49. For a survey of Greek and Latin acrostics, including a number of epigraphic examples, see Courtney 1990.
50. Willcock 1987, 95.

λεπτὴ μὲν καθαρὴ τε περὶ τρίτον ἦμαρ ἐοῦσα
εὔδιός κ' εἴη, λεπτὴ δὲ καὶ εὖ μάλ' ἐρευθὴς
πνευματίη· παχίων δὲ καὶ ἀμβλείῃσι κεραίαις
τέτρατον ἐκ τριτάτοιο φόως ἀμενηνὸν ἔχουσα
ἠὲ νότου ἀμβλύνετ' ἢ ὕδατος ἐγγὺς ἐόντος.

(If slender and clear around the third day, the moon signals
Fair weather. If slender and quite red
There will be wind. If thick and with blunted horns
Having weak light the fourth night following the third,
Then she is made blurry either by the south wind or by a coming storm.)[51]
                                                                    —Aratus, *Phaen.* 783–7

Another, playing on forms of the Greek words for "all" (*panta, pasa*:
πάντα, πᾶσα), is found in the section of the *Phainomena*, that deals with
the full moon:

πάντῃ γὰρ καθαρῇ κε μάλ' εὔδια τεκμήραιο·.
πάντα δ' ἐρευθομένη δοκέειν ἀνέμοιο κελεύθους·
ἄλλοθι δ' ἄλλο μελαινομένη δοκέειν ὑετοῖο.
Σήματα δ' οὐτὰρ πᾶσιν ἐπ' ἤμασι πάντα τέτυκται·
ἀλλ' ὅσα μὲν τριτάτῃ τε τεταρταῇ τε πέλονται

(When the full moon is clear, forecast fair weather;
If red, expect an onslaught of wind.
When darkened with spots here and there, expect rain.
But not all signs fit all days:
The signs for the third and fourth day foretell ...)
                                                                    —Aratus, *Phaen.* 802–6

Still others, found in the immediately succeeding lines, note the role of
half-phases of the moon by highlighting the term *mese* (μέση), which asks
to be read in two manners (down and up), and in two halves in each of
two appearances.[52] As the text explains, the first half points to the full
moon, and the full to the second half:

μέσφα διχαιομένης, διχάδος γε μὲν ἄχρις ἐπ' αὐτὴν
σημαίνει διχόμηνον, ἀτὰρ πάλιν ἐκ διχομήνου
ἐς διχάδα φθιμένην· ἔχεται δέ οἱ αὐτίκα τετρὰς
μηνὸς ἀποιχομένου ...

---

51. This and subsequent translations are heavily adapted from Mair and Mair 1955 and
Kidd 1997. See Lombardo 1983 for a translation built around an acrostic containing the
English word "slight."

52. The *lepte* acrostic was first spotted by J. M. Jacques (see Jacques 1960); on *pasa* see
Levitan 1979; on *mese* Haslam 1992.

(Up to the half moon, signs of the half tell up to mid-month,
and in turn from mid-month
To the waning half. Next comes the fourth day from the end of the month
Followed by the third of the succeeding month.)

                                                        —Aratus, *Phaen.* 807–10

A Vergilian acrostic, which follows a pattern identifiable elsewhere in
Latin poetry of employing the first two letters of verses some distance
apart, seems to be a signature of sorts: PUblius VErgilius MAro.[53]

luna revertentis cum primum colligit ignis,
si nigrum obscuro comprenderit aera cornu,
MAximus agricolis pelagoque parabitur imber;
at si virgineum suffuderit ore ruborem,
VEntus erit: vento semper rubet aurea Phoebe.
sin ortu quarto (namque is certissimus auctor)
PUra neque obtunsis per caelum cornibus ibit,
totus et ille dies et qui nascentur ab illo
exactum ad mensem pluvia ventisque carebunt.

(The moon, when first she gathers her recovering lights,
If she embraces the dark sky obscurely with her crescent,
An enormous rainstorm will come to pass for farmers and those at sea.
But if a maiden blush suffuses her face,
Wind will there be: golden Phoebe always reddens in face of the wind.
And if in the fourth quarter (for this is a most reliable indicator)
Unblemished she passes through the heavens,
That day and all that follow until the end of the month,
Will not be troubled by rain or wind.)

                                                        —Verg. G. 1.427–35

It seems unlikely that the Latin quasi-acrostic is accidental,
because it appears in a passage of the *Georgics* that deals with comparable
subject matter as the locus of the Aratean acrostics (i.e., the phases
of the moon). The phrase *certissimus auctor* (either "most reliable
indicator" or "most assured author") points the reader to the authorial
self-reference, and language describing the reddening of the moon (*ruborem*,
G. 1.430; *rubet*, G. 1.431) could reinforce the rubrication of key letters.[54]
Vergil would have had precedent for some sort of authorial acrostic within
the Latin tradition, if we trust Cicero's indication that the early Latin poet

53. Brown 1963, Haslam 1992.
54. The acrostic, mesostich, and telestich found at *Anthologia Latina* 214 Riese (205
Shackleton Bailey) are rubricated or reddened in a late seventh or early eighth century
manuscript. On rubrication see also Courtney 1990.

Ennius himself composed an acrostic on his name: QVINTVS ENNIVS
FECIT ("Quintus Ennius wrote this," Cic. *Div.* 2.111–2).

Also relevant is the signature acrostic by the otherwise unknown
author of a Neronian-era mini-epic, the *Ilias Latina*:

> Iram pande mihi Pelidae, Diua, superbi
> Tristia quae miseris iniecit funera Grais
> Atque animas fortes heroum tradidit Orco
> Latrantumque dedit rostris uolucrumque trahendos
> Illorum exsangues, inhumatis ossibus, artus.
> Confiebat enim summi sententia Regis,
> †Protulerant† ex quo discordia pectora pugnas,
> Sceptriger Atrides et bello clarus Achilles.

> (The wrath of proud Achilles, reveal, O Goddess, to me,
> How it heaped fierce pyres for the miserable Greeks
> And sent strong souls of heroes down to Orcus
> Giving their limbs over to dogs and birds of prey,
> Bloodless, with bones uninterred.
> Thus decreed the judgment of the supreme king
> From when discordant hearts . . . . . battles,
> The scepter-bearing son of Atreus against Achilles renowned in war.)
> —*Ilias Latina*, 1–8[55]

> Sed iam siste gradum finemque impone labori
> Calliope, uatisque tui moderare carinam,
> Remis quem cernis stringentem litora paucis,
> Iamque tenet portum metamque potentis Homeri.
> Pieridum comitata cohors, summitte rudentes
> Sanctaque uirgineos lauro redimita capillos
> Ipsa tuas depone lyras. Ades, inclita Pallas,
> Tuque faue cursu uatis iam, Phoebe, peracto.

> (But now halt your progress and put an end to labor,
> Calliope, and steer the ship of your poet
> Whom you see skirting the shore with his paltry oars,
> Until—just now!—he reaches the harbor and finish-line of great Homer.
> You, Pieridan cohort, loosen the mast-line,
> And wreathing your youthful hair with sacred laurel,
> Lay down your lyres. Be at hand, noble Pallas,
> And you, dear Phoebus, show favor to your poet
> Who has completed his prescribed course.)
> —*Ilias Latina*, 1063–70

---

55. For text and interpretation of this and the subsequent passage see Scaffai 1982.
Scholars have proposed various substitutes for *protulerant* (line 7) that complete the acrostic
and match the sense of the passage.

Although the acrostic requires slight emendations in both parts (substitution of a verb beginning with the letter *v* in verse 7, transposition of the word *remis* from the end to the beginning of verse 1065), it is generally accepted as complete and intentional: ITALICVS SCRIPSIT.[56]

Like figure writing and acrostics, palindromes, too, invite a use of writing contrary to the normal practices of left-to-right reading. ROMA OLIM MILO AMOR (*CIL* iv. Suppl. 8297), reads one such palindrome ("Rome once Milo love"). Another, playing as often on the relationship between *Roma* (Rome) and *Amor* (Love), reads *Roma tibi subito motibus ibit amor* ("Rome, to you love will come with sudden passion"; Sid. Ap. *Ep.* 9.14). Such palindromes share with acrostics and figure writing an insistence that the reader/viewer defamiliarize his own processes of visual perception and interpretation: indeed, unlike the acrostics, which can at times layer one form of meaning production on another, it is hard to see what function the palindromes have other than that of calling attention to writing's insistence on arbitrary patterns of visual perception.[57]

Reading and writing's role in the process of defamiliarizing one's own language is at the heart of recent cognitive approaches to literacy and its effects on the literate subject. As David Olson notes, learning to read requires the adoption of an objective or analytical stance towards language.[58] What I am arguing here is that certain instances of writing—and the reading processes they invite—require the adoption of a self-aware stance toward one's own processes of perception. Literacy defamiliarizes the word. These processes potentially defamiliarize our perceptual relationship to the world.

A little-noticed passage of the Roman scholar Varro's treatise on the Latin language suggests an awareness of both versions of defamiliarization—of the word and of the world. Varro's text gives instructions for drawing up a chart that maps the declension of the Latin adjective *albus, -a, -um* in its thirty-six forms (the term for the color "white," as adapted to nouns of masculine, feminine, and neuter gender respectively, in both singular and plural: *De Lingua Latina* 10.22, 10.44).[59] The resulting matrix would have the following appearance:[60]

---

56. Scaffai 1982, Courtney 1990.

57. In their reliance on and confutation of normal means of visual processing, acrostics and palindromes are to be differentiated from the widespread use of anagrams, or "words under words" in Latin literature. These latter are oral/auditory in their processing and thus accessible even to illiterate audiences of literature. For discussion of Latin anagrams, see Starobinski 1979, Ahl 1985.

58. Olson 1994. On the cognitive aspects of ancient literacy, especially in relationship to memory, see Small 1997.

59. I follow the text of Taylor 1996. On the use of the term *ordo* to describe Varro's chart or matrix, see Taylor 1978.

60. Cf. Lamer 1927, 1977.

albus	albi	albo	album	albe	albo
alba	albae	albae	albam	alba	alba
album	albi	albo	album	album	albo
albi	alborum	albis	albos	albi	albis
albae	albarum	albis	albas	albae	albis
alba	alborum	albis	alba	alba	albis

Read across, the chart gives the forms of *albus* in the six cases of the Latin language (nominative, genitive, dative, accusative, vocative, and ablative). The first row gives the masculine singular forms, the second row the feminine singular forms, and so on. Read down, the chart provides a summary of adjectival forms to be drawn on in the syntactic contexts communicated by Latin case: thus all of the nominative forms are together, all of the genitive, and so on. The chart gives order to the naturally occurring forms of language, as one would expect in a text strongly influenced by Stoic theories of language.[61] One can also imagine that such a chart was useful in pedagogical contexts, regularizing the forms of the language for the native speaker, introducing and summarizing them for the new learner. Learning the declension of a single form of the adjective (e.g., the masculine plural) across its various cases invites an analytical approach to the language, one that focuses on the possible transformations of a given word. It's a useful method for learning to read or otherwise decode: figuring out where a form "fits" on the chart will tell the reader its case and number, information he needs if he is to parse its function in the sentence. In contrast, learning the declension of the adjective in clusters of cases would seem to be more useful for the speaker or writer (i.e., the producer of language): he or she already knows the use or syntax he has in mind and instead must apply the correct gender and number to match the gender and number of the governing substantive. In a sense, the duality of the chart captures the duality of the user as both subject and object of language.

But there is more, for Varro expressly tells us that the chart is arranged according to the format of a *tabula lusoria*: "as is customary on a tablet, on which they play 'little bandits'" (*ut in tabula solet, in qua latrunculis ludunt, Ling. Lat.* 10.22). Varro thus links the graphic chart of adjectives to other instances of the defamiliarization of perception via writing. Reading, writing, and even speaking become a kind of self-aware game requiring submission to rules and constraints that vary in large part according to one's position on the board. Although such self-awareness applies to speaking, it comes into being through the encounter with writing and through the interplay of different processes of visual perception (left to right versus top to bottom).

---

61. For the Stoic background to Varro's work (and his occasional misuse of it), see Blank 1994.

One last instance of visual/verbal interplay invites yet another set of reflections on the materiality of writing and the impact of its form on the awareness of the reader. An Eudoxan (or pseudo-Eudoxan) verse acrostic, *Eudoxou tekhne* ($EY\Delta O\Xi OYTEXNH$), from the back of Pap. Louvre 1, dated to the early second century B.C., is of special interest because it illustrates both alphabetic and numerological virtuosity. As Nicholas Horsfall has noted, the iambic preface contains "twelve lines (one per month, as line 6 observes) and 11×30 days in the month $+ 35 = 365$ letters (that is, the days in a Great Year, as line 8 observes)."[62] The pattern is not unique to Eudoxus: a similar numerology marks the Propertian *Monobiblos*, which describes an entire year (*totus annus*) of a waxing and waning love affair with a woman named for the goddess of the moon (Cynthia) in the same number of couplets as there are days in a lunar year.[63] In each instance, the graphic transmission of language calls attention to one aspect of its own materiality: the enumerability of letters in the one case, of verses in the other. Moreover, the significance of the respective numbers 365 and 354 would obtain regardless of the content of the texts transmitted by the letters and verses. Here language in effect disambiguates writing: it makes us aware that the significance of the production of specifically 365 verses is to be found in the equivalence to the number of days in a solar year.

The use of modes of symbolization disconnected from speech seems particularly appropriate for works by Aratus, Vergil, Eudoxus, and Propertius that make reference to the movement of heavenly bodies and their relationship to terrestrial experience. Speech, writing, and the movement of the stars are related to one another as systems of communication, but each follows its own internal logic. Indeed, some ancient schools of thought, especially Stoicism, provided explicit theorization of the "sympathy" between cosmic and microcosmic systems of signs and therefore of the possibility of divining meaning from both.[64] In the Stoic view at least, the connection is not one of metaphor or symbolization, but of embodiment—the subtle and dynamic movement of the *pneuma* throughout the cosmos and the impact of all bodies on all other bodies.[65] In this, as in other contexts, we might regard Stoicism as the rationalization and intensification of more widespread, "folk" understandings of the world, such as those made manifest in the games and other practices outlined here.

The traditional way of viewing graphic word games is to see them as "trivial" and "bizarre"; as learning gone haywire; in particular, as deformations of the natural function of writing.[66] Clearly they can be understood

62. Horsfall 1979, 31; for the text of Ps.-Eudoxus, see also Blass 1997.

63. Habinek 1982.

64. This view was especially popular among Roman Stoics, as evidenced by Cicero, Vergil, and Seneca. See, for example, Schiesaro 1997, Rosenmeyer 1989.

65. Sambursky 1959.

66. For the expressions "trivial" and "bizarre" see Horsfall 1979, 29 and again 1979, 32.

differently. These tours de force are further instances of the propensity among the Romans to intensify the constraints upon writing beyond what is needed for the communication of speech. As Julia Kristeva reminds us in her study *Language: The Unknown*, writing can be understood as a distinct language, in the sense that it, too, generates meaning through differentiation.[67] Its material is graphic, whereas the material of speech is phonetic. Her observation is easy to accept in dealing with, for example, Peruvian knot writing, or Egyptian hieroglyphics. But it is relevant to understanding writing in the Roman world as well. Without a doubt, writing can have a second order function as transcription of speech, but the prevalence of that function today should not blind us to the ways in which writing exists and operates independent of speech. Paradoxically, it was by cultivating and intensifying this independence, through the sorts of phenomena presented here, that the Romans—and some Greek counterparts—sought to constrain writing's potential as a liberatory technology. We are accustomed to think of writing as offering the advantage of communication unbound to context. By turning writing into a visual game, the Romans restrain this liberatory potential and re-embed writing in the specific and the concrete. Whether we regard such word games as residue of a more primitive or magical approach to script[68] or as virtuoso performance by a hyperliterate elite, the result is the same. They constitute a vivid reminder of the incommensurability of ancient approaches to writing with those characteristic of other times and places. By paying attention to the embodied, self-referential, and freely constrained aspects of writing in the Roman world we gain access to features of ancient culture not carried by language alone and we refine our understanding of the difference between writing at Rome and writing in other contexts past and present.

Viewed historically, the spread of writing in the Roman world correlates with and sustains changing configurations of property, status, and identity. Viewed synchronically, especially in its relationship to speaking, Roman writing helps to confer agency upon the writer, to differentiate him or her from others, as master from slave, and to expand the literate ego beyond the confines of the here and now of speech production. At the same time, in separating writing from its connection with speech, using it to defamiliarize processes of visual and auditory perception, at least some Romans expose the materiality of the word, its groundedness in the realm of the phenomenal. Roman writing, to be sure, is an aid to signification. But more often than we are accustomed to acknowledge, it denies the freedom of the signifier and limits production of meaning to direct encounters with the very system of inscription recognized as such.

---

67. Kristeva 1989, esp. 23–30. Her observations on writing systems can be supplemented by Morrison's discussion of textual organization: Morrison 1987.
68. As intimated by Benjamin 1999 and Courtney 1990.

BIBLIOGRAPHY

Ahl, F. 1985. *Metaformations: Soundplay and Wordplay in Ovid and Other Classical Poets*. Ithaca, N.Y.

Andreau, J. 1999. *Banking and Business in the Roman World*. Trans. J. Lloyd. Cambridge.

Arbib, M. 2002. "The Mirror System, Imitation, and the Evolution of Language." In C. Nehaniv and K. Dautenhahn, eds., *Imitation in Animals and Artifacts*, 229–280. Cambridge, Mass.

Austin, R. G. 1934. "Roman Board Games, I." *G&R* 4: 24–34.

———. 1935. "Roman Board Games, II." *G&R* 4: 76–82.

Barton, D., M. Hamilton, and R. Ivanič, eds. 2000. *Situated Literacies: Reading and Writing in Context*. Literacies. London.

Bell, C. 1992. *Ritual Theory, Ritual Practice*. Oxford.

Benjamin, W. 1999 (written in 1933). "On the Mimetic Faculty." In *Selected Writings*, vol. 2, 720–2. Cambridge, Mass.

Blank, D. 1994. "Analogy, Anomaly and Apollonius Dyscolus." In S. Everson, ed., *Language*, 149–165. Companions to Ancient Thought 3. Cambridge.

Blass, F. 1997 (1887). "Eudoxi ars astronomica qualis in charta aegyptiaca superest." Keil Universitätsprogramm für das Sommersemester, 1887. Reprinted *ZPE* 115: 79–101.

Brandon, R. 1996. *Concepts and Methods in Evolutionary Biology*. Cambridge.

Brown, E. L. 1963. *Numeri Vergiliani: Studies in* Eclogues *and* Georgics. Collection Latomus 63. Brussels.

Campbell, B. G. 2001. *Performing and Processing the* Aeneid. Berkeley Insights in Linguistics and Semiotics 48. New York.

Camporeale, G. 2000. *Gli Etruschi: Storia e civiltà*. Turin.

Coarelli, F. 1995. "Vino e ideologia nella Roma arcaica." In O. Murray and M. Tecusan, eds., *In Vino Veritas*, 196–213. London.

Colonna, G. 1980. "Appendice: le iscrizioni strumentali latine del VI e V secolo a. C." In Stibbe et al. 1980: 53–70.

Connerton, P. 1989. *How Societies Remember*. Themes in the Social Sciences. Cambridge.

Cornell, T. 1991. "The Tyranny of the Evidence: A Discussion of the Possible Uses of Literacy in Etruria and Latium in the Archaic Age." In J. Humphrey, ed., *Literacy in the Roman World*, 7–34. Journal of Roman Archaeology, Supplementary Series 3. Ann Arbor.

Courtney, E. 1990. "Greek and Latin Acrostichs." *Philologus* 134: 3–13.

Cristofani, M. 1984. "Iscrizioni e bene suntuari." *Opus* 3: 319–24.

Degrassi, A. 1972. *Inscriptiones latinae liberae rei publicae*. 2 vols. Florence.

Donald, M. 1999. "Preconditions for the Evolution of Protolanguages." In M. Corballis and I. Lea, eds., *The Descent of Mind: Psychological Perspectives on Hominid Evolution*, 138–154. Oxford.

———. 2001. *Mind So Rare: The Evolution of Human Consciousness*. New York.

Ernout, A. 1973. *Recueil de textes latins archaïques*. Paris.

Faraone, C. 1996. "Taking the 'Nestor's Cup Inscription' Seriously: Erotic Magic and Conditional Curses in the Earliest Inscribed Hexameters." *ClAnt* 15: 77–112.

Ferrua, A. 1946. "Tavole lusorie scritte." *Epigraphica* 8: 53–73.

Fitzgerald, W. 2000. *Slavery and the Roman Literary Imagination*. Cambridge.

Fraenkel, E. 1926–7. "Vergil und Cicero." *Atti e Memorie di R. Accademia Virgiliana di Mantova* n. s. 19–20: 217–227.

Habinek, T. 1982. "Propertius, Cynthia, and the Lunar Year." *Latomus* 41: 589–96.

———. 1998. *The Politics of Latin Literature: Writing, Identity, and Empire in Ancient Rome*. Princeton.

———. 2005a. *The World of Roman Song: From Ritualized Speech to Social Order*. Baltimore.

———. 2005b. "Slavery and Class." In S. Harrison, ed., *A Companion to Latin Literature*, 385–393. Malden, Mass. and Oxford.

———. 2005c. "Latin Literature Between Text and Practice." *TAPhA* 135: 83–9.

———. 2007. "Probing the Entrails of the Universe: Astrology as Bodily Knowledge in Manilius' *Astronomica*." In J. König and T. Whitmarsh, eds., *Ordering Knowledge in the Roman Empire*, 229–240. Cambridge.

Hartmann, M. 2005. *Die frühlateinischen Inschriften und ihre Datierung: eine linguistisch-archäologisch-paläographische Untersuchung*. Münchener Forschungen zur historischen Sprachwissenschaft Bd. 3. Bremen.

Haslam, M. 1992. "Hidden Signs: Aratus *Diosemeiai* 46ff., Vergil *Georgics* 1.424ff." *HSPh* 94: 199–204.

Harris, W. V., ed. 1993. *The Inscribed Economy: Production and Distribution in the Roman Empire in the Light of* Instrumentum Domesticum: *The Proceedings of a Conference Held at the American Academy in Rome on 10–11 January, 1992*. Journal of Roman Archaeology, Supplementary Series 6. Ann Arbor.

Hedeager, L. 1992. *Iron-Age Societies: From Tribe to State in Northern Europe, 500 BC to AD 700*. Trans. J. Hines. Oxford.

Horsfall, N. 1979. "Stesichorus at Bovillae?" *JHS* 99: 26–48.

———. 1983. "The Origins of the Illustrated Book." *Aegyptus* 63: 199–216.

Iacoboni, M. 2005. "Understanding Others: Imitation, Language, and Empathy." In S. Hurley and N. Chater, eds., *Perspectives on Imitation: From Neuroscience to Social Science*, vol. 1, 76–100. Cambridge, Mass. and London.

Jacques, J.-M. 1960. "Sur un acrostiche d'Aratos." *REA* 62: 48–61.

Johnson, M. 1990. *The Body in the Mind: The Bodily Basis of Meaning, Imagination, and Reason*. Chicago.

——— and G. Lakoff. 1999. *Philosophy in the Flesh: The Embodied Mind and Its Challenge to Western Thought*. New York.

Johnson, W. A. 2000. "Towards a Sociology of Reading in Classical Antiquity." *AJPh* 121: 593–627.

Kidd, D. 1997. *Aratus: Phaenomena*. Cambridge Classical Texts and Commentaries 34. Cambridge.

Kristeva, J. 1989. *Language—the Unknown: An Initiation into Linguistics*. Trans. A. M. Menke. New York.

Kurke, L. 1999. *Coins, Bodies, Games, and Gold: The Politics of Meaning in Archaic Greece*. Princeton.

Lamer, H. 1927. "Lusoria tabula." *RE* 13.2: 1900–2009.

Levitan, W. 1979. "Plexed Artistry: Aratean Acrostics." *Glyph* 5: 55–68.

———. 1985. "Dancing at the End of the Rope: Optation Porfyry and the Field of Roman Verse." *TAPhA* 115: 245–69.

Lombardo, S. 1983. *Sky Signs: Aratus' Phaenomena*. Berkeley.

Mair, A. W., and G. R. Mair. 1955. *Callimachus: Hymns and Epigrams. Lycophron. Aratus*. Loeb Classical Library 129. Cambridge, Mass.

Meyer, E. A. 1990. "Explaining the Epigraphic Habit in the Roman Empire: The Evidence of the Epitaphs." *JRS* 80: 74–96.

Morrison, K. 1987. "Stabilizing the Text: The Institutionalization of Knowledge in Historical and Philosophical Forms of Argument." *Canadian Journal of Sociology* 12: 242–74.

Olson, D. R. 1994. *The World on Paper: The Conceptual and Cognitive Implications of Writing and Reading*. Cambridge.

Peruzzi, E. 1998. *Civiltà greca nel Lazio preromano*. Accademia toscana di scienze e lettere, "La Colombaria," Studi 165. Florence.

Piccaluga, G. 1965. *Elementi spettacolari nei rituali festivi romani*. Studi e materiali di storia delle religione, Quaderni 2. Rome.

Purcell, N. 1995. "Literate Games: Roman Urban Society and the Game of *Alea*." *P&P* 147: 3–37.

Reay, B. 2003. "Some Addressees of Vergil's *Georgics* and their Audience." *Vergilius* 49: 17–41.

———. 2005. "Agriculture, Writing, and Cato's Aristocratic Self-Fashioning." *ClAnt* 24: 331–61.

Ridgway, D. 1996. "Greek Letters at Osteria dell'Osa." *ORom* 20: 87–97.

Riese, A., ed. 1894. *Anthologia Latina: Carmina in codicibus scripta*. Leipzig.

Rosenmeyer, T. 1989. *Senecan Drama and Stoic Cosmology*. Berkeley.

Rüpke, J. 2000. "Raüme literarischer Kommunikation in der Formierungsphase römischer Literatur." In M. Braun, ed., *Moribus antiquis res stat Romana: Römische Werte und römische Literatur im 3. und 2. Jh. V. Chr.*, 31–52. Munich.

Sadurska, M. 1964. *Les Tables Iliaques*. Warsaw.

Sambursky, S. 1959. *Physics of the Stoics*. London.

Scaffai, M. 1982. *Baebii Italici Ilias Latina*. Introduzione, edizione critica, traduzione italiana e commento. Bologna.

Schiesaro, A. 1997. "The Boundaries of Knowledge in Virgil's *Georgics*." In T. Habinek and A. Schiesaro, eds., *The Roman Cultural Revolution*, 63–89. Cambridge.

Sciarrino, E. 2004. "Putting Cato the Censor's *Origines* in Its Place." *ClAnt* 23: 323–57.

Small, J. P. 1997. *Wax Tablets of the Mind: Cognitive Studies of Memory and Literacy in Classical Antiquity*. London.

Smith, C. J. 1996. *Early Rome and Latium: Economy and Society, c. 1000 to 500 BC*. Oxford.

Starobinski, J. 1979. *Words upon Words: The Anagrams of Ferdinand de Saussure*. Trans. O. Emmet. New Haven. (Original title: *Les mots sous les mots: Les anagrammes de F. de S.*)

Stibbe, C. M., G. Colonna, C. De Simone, and H. S. Versnel. 1980. *Lapis Satricanus: Archaeological, Epigraphical, Linguistic and Historical Aspects of the New Inscription from Satricum*. Archeologische Studiën van het Nederlands Instituut te Rome. Scripta minora 5. Gravenhage.

Stoddart, S. and J. Whitley. 1988. "The Social Context of Literacy in Archaic Greece and Etruria." *Antiquity* 62: 761–72.

Taylor, D. 1978. "*Ordo* in Book X of Varro's *De Lingua Latina*." In J. Collart, ed., *Varron: Grammaire antique et stylistique latine*, 71–4. Paris.

———. 1996. *Varro. De Lingua Latina X: A New Critical Text and English Translation with Prolegomena and Commentary*. Amsterdam Studies in the Theory and History of Linguistic Science 85. Amsterdam.

Valette-Cagnac, E. 1997. *La lecture à Rome: rites et pratiques*. L'Antiquité au Présent. Paris.

Versnel, H. S. 1980. "Historical Implications." In Stibbe et al. 1980: 95–150.

Wachter, R. 1998. "'Oral Poetry' in ungewohntem Kontext: Hinweise auf mündliche Dichtungstechnik in den pompejanischen Wandinschriften." *ZPE* 121: 73–89.

Watkins, C. 1976. "Observations on the 'Nestor's Cup' Inscription." *HSPh* 80: 25–40.

Whitley, J. 2001. *The Archaeology of Ancient Greece*. Cambridge.

Wilcox, S. 1999. "The Invention and Ritualization of Language." In Barbara King, ed., *The Origins of Language: What Nonhuman Primates Can Tell Us*, 351–84. Santa Fe, N.M.

Willcock, M. M., ed. 1987. *Plautus: Pseudolus*. Bristol.

Wilson, E. O. 1975. *Sociobiology: The New Synthesis*. Cambridge, Mass.

Woolf, G. 1996. "Monumental Writing and the Expansion of Roman Society in the Early Empire." *JRS* 86: 22–39.

Part II

BOOKS AND TEXTS

7

The Corrupted Boy and the Crowned Poet

or, The Material Reality and the Symbolic Status
of the Literary Book at Rome

Florence Dupont
Translated by Holt N. Parker

WRITING AND THE BOOK

What is a book in Roman antiquity? Even if we confine ourselves to literature—to what the ancients called *litterae*—a book in Cicero's library, a book sent as a present from Horace to Augustus, and a book for sale in a bookstore in the Vicus Tuscus were different cultural realities.[1] Not because their realizations sometimes drew on different techniques—papyrus, parchment, tablets—but because their symbolic status and functions were different according to the social uses that were made of them.

The very practice of having books needs to be resituated in Roman civilization and put into proper relationship with other practices of writing. In Greece and in Rome, one can write on an object—for example, a drinking cup, a tripod, or a funerary stele.[2] The object that serves as a support (a medium or vehicle) for the writing has in this case its own reason for existing, and the writing is parasitic on it: the writing uses the person who manipulates the object to get itself read. The drinker reads the pederastic proclamation on the cup, the passerby reads the name of the deceased on the stele or of the dedicator of the ex-voto. The writing is spread on the object, taking its form or following the design painted on the vase.[3] It often happens that the engraver or the painter, having miscalculated the space, is forced to reduce the size of the letters or to tighten the spacing. The text reduced to itself is formless.

---

1. For the stores on the Vicus Tuscus and the other locations mentioned in this paper, see Peter White, ch. 11, this volume.
2. Svenbro 1988.
3. Lissarrague 1987.

The book therefore differs from the other supports for writing in that it is autonomous. What is written on it is read for itself and not because it is written or scratched on an object. One can therefore already classify Roman books according to what motivates their reading and so distinguish the literary book from the others.

By the end of the Republic, Rome is full of books. Public archives—political, judicial, and religious—pile up in Rome as well as the provincial capitals. Families have their own archives in which they store the political careers of their ancestors and their private cults. To these are added, first in the great families and then in Rome itself starting at the beginning of the Principate, certain private and public libraries that gathered books in Greek and Latin.

Roman books do not all have the same reasons for existence. Annals, sibylline books, *fasti*, and books of prayers have a form of reading and writing that are regulated by the ritual that is their reason for existence. So, too, for the archives and all the administrative documents that flourished at Rome, such as the legal rulings preserved in large books in the form of enormous collections of tablets, the *codex*.[4] Such books served as a sort of data bank.

The status of literary books is less evident. To what social practice do they respond? To what do they serve as supports?

We should recall that at Rome literary activities in the broad sense—*studia*—are "Greek" because they belong to the space of leisure, the nonpolitical, *otium*.[5] The literary activities to which the Roman elite are devoted are written in Greek as well as Latin. The *litterae latinae* are, so to speak, *litterae graecae* in Latin. Rome, like every Hellenistic city, adopts the Alexandrian book preserved in a library whether public or private. It also inherits its use, because the Alexandrian book was used in a quite particular process of reading and writing which should be recalled. To the question, "What made people read or write literary books at Rome?" the initial answer is Greek practice, more precisely Alexandrian.

However, there is not complete continuity between Alexandria and Rome. Though the book remains a Greek practice even when it speaks Latin, it can allow inclusion of Greek culture in the Roman world that can be negotiated, like other inclusions, in multiple ways.[6] To the Alexandrian use of the books in libraries, new social practices are added involving the book as autonomous object. Given by a client to his patron, the book can bring its author glory and riches even though it has only a few readers. On the other hand, sold at the stall of the booksellers, it may bring some money to its author, but it will pass from hand to hand and finally disappear, victim of the brittleness of the papyrus, without leaving a trace in the memory. The value of the text plays no role.

4. Nicolet 1994.
5. Cordier 2005.
6. Dupont 2005.

THE LIBRARY IN THE MUSEUM OF ALEXANDRIA:
READING FOR WRITING

The Alexandrian book, like that of classical Greece, is a papyrus roll, which is a simple support and accommodates a text preformed according to rules of production independent of that support. What was new to the Hellenistic era is, first, the multiplication of books and the mania for preservation of writing; and secondly, the establishment of primary texts from which future generations are supposed to write in their turn.

The reason for the creation of libraries—of which the one at Alexandria would go on to accumulate bookrolls by the thousands (500,000 at the time of Callimachus)—is to preserve in this form all the knowledge of the world. This foundation is integral to the general project of the Ptolemies, who want to make their capital "a city-museum" gathering the intellectual heritage of Hellenism, and a "mirror city" which will reflect the whole world. The king gives a concrete form to the dream of universality of Aristotle, called "the Reader."[7] Alexandria puts the "world into scrolls"[8] in the course of the third century B.C. under the first three Ptolemies. They order copies made of all the books that arrive in the port of Alexandria, and have them translated if necessary, and they send for every possible version of the Greek authors.

The library is inseparable from the Museum, an invention of the first Ptolemy on the advice of Demetrius of Phaleron, a disciple of Aristotle and statesman (governor of Athens from 317 to 307 B.C.). What changes, then, is not the relationship with the book but the relationship with the text whose letter is made sacred and definitively fixed, instead of being, as previously, a stage between two oralities and thus a variable stage. The collected texts for the most part are no longer intended for a ritual oralization, any more than they are the monumental traces of those performances. They become autonomous objects, which need to be preserved in an authentic and unique form.

Alexandrian scholars perform textual criticism to recover "the true text." They classify the texts according to genre, establish the biographies of the authors and set up their busts. The text, having become autonomous, is not always understandable by itself, and it needs to be commented on. The book thus merges with its author.

Nevertheless, the bookrolls of the library of Alexandria continue to be no more than a support for a text that owes them nothing. There are translations of foreign texts such as the Septuagint, poems that are originally oral, or finally recopied inscriptions such as epigrams. Of course, beginning with this first generation of books, new books are written, but

7. Aristotle, nicknamed "the Reader" by Plato (*Vita Marciana*, 6), was a great collector of books; see Athen. 1.3a–b.
8. Canfora 1992, 49.

these are only compilations, anthologies, commentaries, or imitations of
the ancient authors whose original utterances[9] they then go on to reproduce in writing. They can then function as a virtual utterance of their
texts, of which they would be only the transcription.

The figure of Callimachus is the model of the new relationship with the
books maintained by the members of the Museum.[10] He organizes
the library for their use, draws up catalogues so that books can be
found, outlining all sorts of possible approaches. Who are the readers?
The scientists of the Museum who are going to write using the library, and
no one else. "Thus, the poets, the antiquarians, the scholiasts, and para-
doxographers find the raw materials ready to be reused in new literary
constructions."[11] The texts produced are thus montages of quotations
of other books. Callimachus himself, for example, writes a collection of
Customs of the Barbarians. "It is a matter of building treatises by taking
materials from other books, and the form of the catalogue—geographical
or thematic—lends itself to this discontinuous writing, closer to a 'data
base' than a structured book."[12] We must emphasize once again that the
book is not an autonomous construction but is presented in the form of a
"collection."

In addition, Callimachus creates poetic works of two types. He composes
"true" poems to order on the occasion of real events, for example,
following the tradition of hymnic poetry, such as the *Hymn to Apollo*
for the festival of the Carnalia at Cyrene (his fatherland), circa 246 B.C.
during the reign of Ptolemy Euergetes. Or else he writes purely bookish
mythological poems, such as the *Hecale.* In this case, the poetic language
of Callimachus is artificial, made of a mixture of various dialects,
stuffed with mythological details and allusions to vanished realia: these
works consequently call for commentaries, lexicons, and scholia.[13] The
edition of his poems will be thus similar to that of Homer or Hesiod.
Callimachus in this way creates a trompe l'oeil effect, having introduced
an artificial distance between his work and his readers based on the model
of archaism. This esthetic of polymathy and of scholarship has been
much commented on, and we will add only that it is in this way that
Callimachus gives form and legitimacy to his books of poetry. They have
the same status as the books that collected the ancient oral poems, recently
fixed in writing, whose linguistic and semantic obscurity is due to their

9. In structuralist linguistics *énonciation* is an utterance, the process of speaking,
distinguished (by Benveniste) from the *énoncé*, that which is said. *Énonciation* involves the
speaker adopting a first person stance ("I"), addressing a second person ("you," stated or
implied), about a third. [–Trans.note].
10. Jacob 1992.
11. Jacob 1992, 105–106.
12. Jacob 1992, 106.
13. Jacob 1992, 107.

temporal distance. Callimachus publishes written texts that are like the transcription of virtual oral works, uttered in another world in which they were transparent.

This is what we will call a "fictive utterance," one that gives form to an utterance whose written reality pretends to be a transcription of it. This fictitious utterance also justifies the use of a metalanguage that knows only inspiration, the Muses, the Castalian spring, and Helicon.

During the classical era, written texts are presented often in the form of the fixation of ritualized or socially codified oral performances, that is, poems, or dialogues, or speech. This is a fiction that fools nobody and that does not seek to—its reader can be addressed as such—but which allows form to be given to a text which otherwise would not have had any. Even when it is not presented in the form of a transcription of an oral performance, the written text is supposed to be the transcription of another form of writing having its own proper status: for example, epigrams, letters, or inscriptions of any type associated with objects, or legal texts and public inscriptions, sacred or not.

The library of Alexandria changed nothing except for developing the fictive utterance. The book continues to be a support without ever performing writing. To read these books is to recover the trace of a fictive event or a preceding text to which the book can only allude.

The epigrams of the Palatine Anthology are an example. The book gathers short inscriptions. This gathering in—as the word anthology signifies—is necessary because they cannot be published individually. They are therefore gathered according to varying principles, for example by subject: some talk about animals, some describe works of art, or are erotic epigrams. Originally perhaps consisting of "true" poems—short inscriptions on walls, objects, or monuments in public spaces—the anthology continues to enlarge itself with virtual epigrams. Written on the model of the "true" epigram, they imitate its form, its subject and tone, like a series of duplicates of the original. Take, for example, "Myron's Cow." The famous Greek artist sculpted a heifer so realistic that it seemed alive.[14] Nearly forty epigrams of the Palatine Anthology are devoted to it.[15] All take the form of an epigram engraved on the sculpture of the animal, which praises its perfect resemblance to a live heifer. Some are "realistic," such as this one, which is a simple signature proclaiming the skill of the artist (9.733):

> Myron, O stranger, sculpted this cow (τὰν βοῦν τάνδε), at which
> this calf wags its tail as if it were alive, thinking it's his mother.

A number of others in the series voluntarily declare themselves to be imitations, while keeping the formal schema of an inscription celebrating

14. Pliny *HN* 34.57.
15. *AP* 9.713–742, 793–8.

the *kleos* of the artist, such as this one, which is addressed to a bull instead of a passerby (9.734):

> O bull, in vain you mount the heifer, for it is without breath.
> The cow-sculptor, Myron, has deceived you.

Furthermore, by naming Myron as the sculptor of the cow, the text is set after the fame of the heifer has traveled the world; it is, one might say, an apocryphal epigram. One addresses a gadfly (9.739). Another does not even mention the name Myron (9.740), calling him simply "the artist" (ὁ τεχνίτας).

We can therefore understand the central place of imitation in Alexandrian poetic culture. It is essential to the writing of books, because only it allows a text to have a form. Writing books within this framework allows playing with the "book-as-support." If the fictive utterance (*énonciation*) takes the form of that which has been uttered (*énoncé*), the act of signification takes this fiction into ludic account.

GREEK BOOKS IN LATIN: WHAT KIND OF SOCIALIZATION?

The play between fictive utterance and writing will become permanent in Rome, where all literary production is set in continuity with a Greek culture of book-as-support. We cannot here make an inventory of all the fictive utterances used by Latin authors, both oral and written, both prose and verse. We can cite, for example, Livy's *Annals*, Caesar's *Commentaries*, Cicero's dialogues, letters in various forms, both prose and verse; to which we can add Horace's *Odes*, Catullus's epigrams, Vergil's *Eclogues*, and all the poems collected and published in books whose ambiguous status is doubled because all are subject both to a fictive utterance as well as a real utterance: so odes of Horace sung in Roman banquets but also imitation Greek symposium song; the *Eclogues* enacted as mimes on stage during the festival of the Floralia, but also imitation poetic competitions in the manner of Theocritus; epigrams of Catullus or Martial recited at banquets, but also imitation Alexandrian epigrams. At a third level, these texts proclaim that they are written, and what is more, in a book, and thus in turn are intended for a reader.

THE BOOK AS GIFT

Paradoxically, if the book does not have a reality as utterance, because it is merely a support for a written text whose reading recalls an utterance, either fictive or real, that performed it, nevertheless the object as such in its material reality as *volumen* is very much present at Rome, associated with the erotic imagination because of its Greek connotations.

The material beauty of the book is frequently evoked in Roman poetry. Thus Catullus (22.1–11) gives a meticulous description of the materiality of a splendid book with pitiful contents, even though the author is charming (*uenustus*), cultivated (*urbanus*), and witty (*dicax*):

> Suffenus iste, Vare, quem probe nosti,
> homo est uenustus et dicax et urbanus,
> idemque longe plurimos facit uersus.
> puto esse ego illi milia aut decem aut plura
> perscripta, nec sic ut fit in palimpsesto
> relata: cartae regiae, noui libri,
> noui umbilici, lora rubra membranae,
> derecta plumbo et pumice omnia aequata.
> haec cum legas tu, bellus ille et urbanus
> Suffenus unus caprimulgus aut fossor
> rursus uidetur:

> (That Suffenus, whom you know so well, Varus,
> is a charming, witty, and cultivated man;
> he also makes by far the greatest number of verses.
> I think he's written out ten thousand or more
> and not, as is usually done, set down on palimpsests.
> Royal sheets, new books,
> new rollers, scarlet binding cords, parchment covers,
> everything ruled with lead and smoothed with pumice.
> But when you read them, this handsome and cultivated
> Suffenus seems to be a goat-milking yokel or ditch digger.)

Suffenus is a prolific poetaster (4–5). He has written (*perscripta*) thousands of lines. But when one reads these verses (*cum legas*), the author (Suffenus) seems a goat milker or ditch digger. This dissociation between the contents of a text and its appearance—so odd in the eyes of antiquity, because for them speech (*parole*) is the continuation of the man—insists precisely on the fact that writing is *not* speech. As in this case, a Roman can publish verses without subjecting them to social control. They will not to have to undergo the test of any ritual, not have to be engaged in any performance, unless the author voluntarily offers himself to the criticism of his friends by publicly reading them in front of a chosen public at a *recitatio*.[16] A bad book does not disqualify its author socially. Suffenus remains a man who is a delight to visit. The author of a book thus does not have a social reality as such, and the authorial figure that the book creates will have the status that the social, and variable, practice of the book allots to him.

If the book (*volumen*) at Rome is an object whose material reality is ceaselessly recalled, that is because it is so often integrated into the social practice of the gift. Its value then lies as much, if not more, in its material beauty as in the texts that it contains. Like any symbolic gift, a book can

---

16. Valette-Cagnac 1997, 111–70.

circulate from friend to friend. Here is what Catullus writes in an epigram in the form of letter addressed to his friend Calvus about a book of poems which Calvus's client, the poet Sulla, had given him, and which Calvus in turn had given Catullus (14):

Ni te plus oculis meis amarem,
iucundissime Calue, munere isto
odissem te odio Vatiniano:
nam quid feci ego quidue sum locutus,
cur me tot male perderes poetis?
isti di mala multa dent clienti,
qui tantum tibi misit impiorum.
quod si, ut suspicor, hoc nouum ac repertum
munus dat tibi Sulla litterator,
non est mi male, sed bene ac beate,
quod non dispereunt tui labores.
di magni, horribilem et sacrum libellum!
quem tu scilicet ad tuum Catullum
misti, continuo ut die periret,
Saturnalibus, optimo dierum!
non non hoc tibi, false, sic abibit.
nam si luxerit ad librariorum
curram scrinia, Caesios, Aquinos,
Suffenum, omnia colligam uenena.
ac te his suppliciis remunerabor.

(If I didn't love you more than my eyes,
Calvus, you very funny fellow, because of this gift
I would hate you as much as Vatinius does.
What have I said or done
that you should kill me with so many poets?
May the gods give many curses to the client
who sent you so many abominations!
If, as I suspect, the critic Sulla gave you
this newly discovered gift,
then I'm not sad but happy and delighted
that you've not wasted your efforts.
Dear gods! What a horrible and monstrous book!
Which you, of course, had to send to your friend, Catullus,
so that he die immediately on that day,
the Saturnalia, the best of all days.
No, no, you won't get away with it!
The moment it's dawn, I'll run
to the shelves of the bookshops for the likes of Caesius, Aquinus,
even Suffenus! I'll collect all the poison
and pay you back for this torture.)

The book (*libellus*) was given as a gift (*munus*) during the Saturnalia by his client, Sulla, to Calvus, who had defended him in a lawsuit, who sends it (*misti*) in turn to Catullus. Catullus as a joke says he will get his revenge by buying bad books at a bookseller, which he will give in return (*remunerabor*) to Calvus. The poems written in the book are unfortunately offered as a gift with it.

This is just how Catullus thanks his friend Allius for his services (*officiis*) in a poem written in a book (*munus carmine confectum*) that celebrates those *officia* (Cat. 68). But the value of this gift is not separable from the book that contains it. *Haec carta loquatur anus* (68.46): this poem is a gift because it is a written papyrus (*carta*), and it will live as long time as it has a support. It will ward off forgetfulness from Allius, whose friendly generosity will bring him glory as long as Catullus's book finds a place in libraries, a form of social recognition that will earn being copied and recopied (Cat. 68.41–46, 149–52):

> Non possum reticere, deae, qua me Allius in re
> iuuerit aut quantis iuuerit officiis,
> ne fugiens saeclis obliuiscentibus aetas
> illius hoc caeca nocte tegat studium:
> sed dicam uobis, uos porro dicite multis
> milibus et facite haec carta loquatur anus.
>
> . . .
>
> hoc tibi, quod potui, confectum carmine munus
> pro multis, Alli, redditur officiis,
> ne uestrum scabra tangat rubigine nomen
> haec atque illa dies atque alia atque alia.

> (I cannot keep silent, goddesses, about how Allius
> helped me and all the services with which he helped me,
> so that fleeting time in its forgetful cycles will not
> cover his service in blind night.
> But I shall tell you Muses, and you in turn tell it to many
> thousands and see to it that this page speaks when it is an old woman.
>
> . . .
>
> This gift for you, made from song, as much as I could,
> is given back to you for your many services,
> so that no corroding rust will touch your name
> today and the next and the next.)

Sent as a gift, it is also the occasion for the book to proclaim itself as a *xenion*. One can see this in an epigram of Catullus that accompanies the gift of a book of epigrams to an influential friend, Cornelius Nepos (Cat. 1):

> Cui dono lepidum nouum libellum
> arida modo pumice expolitum?
> Corneli, tibi.

> (To whom should I send this charming new little book
> freshly polished with dry pumice?
> To you, Cornelius!)

The dedication defines at the same time a recipient (the reader) and a beneficiary of the gift. The *volumen*, polished with pumice on its edges, is the occasion of the usual erotic joke on "lepidum novum"; the adjective *lepidus* is synonymous with *venustus*. *Novus*, in other words, new on the market, like the diminutive "little book," underlines its assimilation to a *puer delicatus* still young and fresh. The book is new because it presents new epigrams written by Catullus. Its new aspect points out the fragility of books and the rapid wearing out of *volumina*. The book is a gift offered to Cornelius Nepos: how will he treat this young boy?

THE LIBRARY OR THE BOOKSTORE?

When the gift of a book is inscribed in the client-patron relationship, and the giver is the poet himself and his patron accepts the gift, he could have it read in public to gain glory for himself. At that point the poet has a chance to obtain both financial reward and a certain social cachet. But for that to happen it is necessary that his capacity to make verse takes the shape of a material gift, which alone can ensure the book-as-object. No ritual of song or recitation exists in Rome that can take its place. The book, unless it is placed on the market of the bookstore, loses any possibility for evaluation.[17] The book's value lies in the success of the exchange.

One can see this very clearly in a passage from the *Letter to Augustus* (Hor. *Ep.* 2.1, and cf. *Ep.* 1.13). Horace brings a book (*liber*) to Augustus (220) and reads the verses aloud to him (223: *recitata revoluimus*), expecting from him a subsidy sufficient to live and further orders to write (225–8). Why should Augustus reward this? Because the books of Horace will come to fill the library that he has founded on the Palatine next to the temple of Apollo in 28 B.C. Two glories are offered to the versifier: the theater or the library (214–8).

> Verum age et his, qui se lectori credere malunt
> quam spectatoris fastidia ferre superbi
> curam redde breuem, si munus Apolline dignum
> uis complere libris et uatibus addere calcar,
> ut studio maiore petant Helicona uirentem.

> (But come, and give a little attention to those who prefer
> to entrust themselves to a reader rather than endure the disdain of the proud viewer,
> if you wish to fill the gift worthy of Apollo
> with books and to spur on the poets
> to seek with greater zeal verdant Helicon.)

17. See Cat. 95, quoted below.

There, says Horace, he will be raised to the ranks of the *vates*, the Greek singers, inspired (*calcar*) like Hesiod by the Muses of Helicon.

How should we understand this assimilation of a Latin poet to one of the mythical figures of great Greek poetry? Is this a tasteless hyperbole, a conventional comparison? If one focuses on the function of books and the library, Horace will occupy in the *litterae latinae* the place of a canonical author of the *litterae graecae*. It is as if the poems of Horace, a great and inspired Latin singer of ages past, had been collected and fixed in books piously deposited in the library of Apollo. In fact, no Roman poet composes while possessed by the Muses, but it has that status. This is the origin of new poetry, Greek poetry in Latin, such as that of Vergil, Varius, Propertius, or Tibullus. The book thus has a possible double destiny, based both on its materiality and on its symbolic status, which it owes to its fictive utterance.

This double destiny is presented very clearly by one of Horace's *Letters* (1.20). The *Letters* are poems that use a fictive epistolary utterance and thus have human recipients, who are addressed in the first or the second line. This is the only poem of Book 1 that is not addressed to a human, but rather to the book itself; it exposes the epistolary fiction by reminding us that the letters are in fact a collection of poems. This poem retains nothing of the epistolary form except the address to its recipient. The book has the choice of one of two destinies. In its first destiny, the book is reduced to the mere materiality of support. It is metamorphosed into a young debauched boy, following the same metaphor as in Catullus. The book whose edges had been smoothed by pumice is compared to a young boy with a smooth body. He is eager to be read/loved by the greatest number. Its other destiny is to remain hidden for the author's sake (*Ep.* 1.20.1–5):

> Vortumnum Ianumque, liber, spectare uideris,
> scilicet ut prostes Sosiorum pumice mundus.
> Odisti clauis et grata sigilla pudico,
> paucis ostendi gemis et communia laudas,
> non ita nutritus.

> (You seem, my book, to be looking at the temples of Vertumnus and Janus,
> no doubt so you can offer yourself for sale, polished with the pumice of
> Sosius & Sosius, Booksellers.
> You hate the keys and seals that please the modest.
> You chafe at being shown to just a few and praise a public life.
> That's not how I raised you!)

It wants to live as a *puer delicatus*, to attend the banquets, instead of remaining modestly in the bosom of the family. It refuses to be locked up in a box for bookrolls and deposited in a library, as a young "well-bred" book should; it wants to be seen/read and appreciated by a greater number of people. So it leaves and soon will regret it, because the papyrus is delicate and a succession of lovers (*amator*) is enough to ruin the book (*laeserit*), and then the Romans will quickly get tired of it (5–10). Sold, repurchased, resold, the book circulates not as a precious gift in a system of symbolic gifts but merely as a piece of merchandise (*Ep.* 1.20.11–13):

> contrectatus ubi manibus sordescere uolgi
> coeperis, aut tineas pasces taciturnus inertis
> aut fugies Uticam aut uinctus mitteris Ilerdam.

> (When you begin to get grubby from being fondled by the hands of the crowd,
> you will either silently feed the uncultured bookworms
> or escape to Utica or be sent bound to Ilerda.)

He will be passed from hand to hand (*contrectatus*) loved by all and sundry (*uulgi*); he will become ugly and dirty (*sordescere*) like a wretched vagrant. Vermin will get hold of him. He will no longer have a lover, that is, a reader; he will be dumb (*taciturnus*). He will be too ugly to find a buyer in Rome and the bookseller will have to send him to the provinces of Africa or Spain, in such bad shape that he has to be tied up with string to keep from falling to pieces—employing an image of a fugitive (and therefore valueless) slave, dispatched to remote markets (17–18):

> Hoc quoque te manet, ut pueros elementa docentem
> occupet extremis in uicis balba senectus.

> (This fate, too, awaits you: as you teach the boys their ABC's
> babbling old age will overtake you in some remote village.)

He will finish his life in a primary school, where he/it will be used to teach the children the rudiments of reading (*elementa*). Its text will be nothing more than a series of syllables to be pronounced (*balba senectus*).

The papyrus book is not made to be opened and read frequently, or to be sold to amateurs. This corresponds closely to its symbolic status. The book is a beautiful, fragile object whose beauty deserves a reading reduced to the minimum. The book is only a support, but valuable as such. Its existence consecrates the author *as* an author, provided that it is preserved, and preserved in a library. This is its second destiny.

The second part of the poem shows without transition—in an asyndeton marking a strong opposition—the book being read publicly on a soft summer's evening, during a *recitatio* among friends (19):

> Cum tibi sol tepidus pluris admouerit auris...

> (When the warm sun brings you more ears...)

This reading does not have the effect of either informing the listeners or of pleasing them; what the book makes heard (*loqueris*) is the poet's career as an author of verse letters. This is in keeping with the life of a poet of the

epistolary genre, according to the Alexandrian canon, a genre connected
to satire but more mild. The poet's glorious career—attested by the
abundance of first person personal and possessive pronouns—is opposed
to the degradation of the book in the bookstore (*maiores pinnas nido
extendisse*).

Thanks to his qualities (*uirtutibus*) and not to an aristocratic family
(*generi*), in fact, the son of a freedman (*libertino patre*), he has become the
friend, that is, the client, of the leading men of the city, Maecenas and
Augustus (*primis placuisse*; 20–23):

> . . . me libertino natum patre et in tenui re
> maiores pinnas nido extendisse loqueris,
> ut quantum generi demas, uirtutibus addas;
> me primis urbis belli placuisse domique,

> (. . . you will say that I, born to a freedman father and in straitened circum-
> stances,
> have spread my wings too wide for my nest,
> so that whatever you take from my lineage you add to my merits;
> that I have pleased the leading men of the city in both peace and war.)

He himself has a poor physique, a plebeian accustomed to work in the
fields (*solibus aptum*), no longer young, with the temperament necessary
for a mild satirist: quick to get angry (*irasci celerem*) but easily calmed
(*placabilis*; 24–25):

> corporis exigui, praecanum, solibus aptum,
> irasci celerem, tamen ut placabilis essem.

> (thin-bodied, prematurely gray, fond of the sun,
> quick to get angry but I'm quick to forgive.)

This portrait of the poet ends on a very Roman note—his age indicated by
reference to the civic calendar: during the consulates of Lollius and
Lepidus (21 B.C.), he was forty-four years old (26–28).

Admittedly, this signature of a book by a final poem is nothing remarkable;[18] what is remarkable is that the poet signs not a work but a book, a
scroll, materially indicated in its concrete reality. It is the object itself and
its destiny that consecrates, or not, the existence of the poet.

One finds, although differently formulated, the same alternative in an
epigram of Catullus (95). It opposes the *Zmyrna*, a short epyllion by his
friend Cinna, the fruit of long and painful work, with the botched and
numerous verses—500,000—of Hortensius. *Zmyrna* will be sent throughout the whole world and people will take care of the *volumen*, for even

18. Cf. *Odes* 3.30.

when the epic is very old (*cana*), people will still unroll the scroll, because it has been recopied and preserved thanks to his friends.

On the other hand, the innumerable verses of the *Annales* of Hortensius, handed over to the people (*populus*), which will undoubtedly like his swollen style (*tumido*), will provide masses of "paper" to wrap fish. Once again, the goal of the poet is not to please the greatest number, with his books sold and resold in the bookstores, because afterward he will be forgotten (Cat. 95):

> Zmyrna[19] mei Cinnae[20] nonam post denique mensem
> quam coepta est nonamque edita post hiemem,
> milia cum interea quingenta Hortensius[21] uno
> . . .
> Zmyrna cavas Satrachi penitus mittetur ad undas,
> Zmyrnam cana diu saecula pervolvent.
> At Volusi Annales Paduam morientur ad ipsam
> et laxas scombris saepe dabunt tunicas.
> Parva mei mihi sint cordi monumenta sodalis,
> at populus tumido gaudeat Antimacho.[22]

> (The *Zmyrna* of my Cinna, nine summers
> and nine winters after it was begun, has been made public!
> While in the meantime, Hortensius five hundred thousand in one
> . . .
> *Zmyrna* will be sent as far as the hollow waves of the Satrachus
> The white-haired ages will long unroll the *Zmyrna*.
> But the *Annals* of Volusius will die beside the Padua
> and make loose jackets for mackerel.
> Let me love my friend's little monument;
> and let the crowd enjoy swollen Antimachus.)

DESPERATELY SEEKING A LIBRARY

Ovid in exile combines the different meanings of the *volumen*, both as a support of a fictive utterance and as a material object, in the *Tristia* and the *Ex Ponto*. Further, he gives to the book an epistolary function, in keeping with its ability to serve as a support.

The *Tristia* is a collection of books gathering poems in the form of letters. The poet, exiled on banks of the Black Sea, sends books composed of letters to Augustus in order to obtain his return. The book acts as a gift in an exchange of *beneficia*. It is also the messenger of its master who

19. Also called Myrrha, who fell in love with her father Cinyras, king of Cyprus.
20. C. Helvius Cinna, the orator.
21. *Annales* of Q. Hortensius Hortalus, perhaps on the Marsic War.
22. Greek poet (end fifth cent.–beginning sixth cent. B.C.), author of a *Thebaid* and a *Lydia*; criticized by Callimachus.

cannot come to plead his cause himself. Ultimately, the destiny that Augustus allots to it will ensure (or not) the safety of its master, depending on whether he is recognized as a poet (or not) and placed in the library of Apollo.

In the first poem of the *Tristia*, the book on its way to Rome is physically the image of its exiled master: *incultus*, that is, without any of the ornaments that make an object beautiful, without the oil which protects the papyrus from insects and dyes it yellow, without a title in red, without having been polished with pumice, without the edges of its pages being dyed in black.

Like Horace's book, it speaks to the poet's friends who are worried about him (*Trist.* 1.1–12):

Parue—nec inuideo—sine me, liber, ibis in urbem:
  ei mihi, quod domino non licet ire tuo!
uade, sed incultus, qualem decet exulis esse;
  infelix habitum temporis huius habe.
nec te purpureo uelent uaccinia fuco—
  non est conueniens luctibus ille color—
nec titulus minio, nec cedro charta notetur,
  candida nec nigra cornua fronte geras.
felices ornent haec instrumenta libellos:
  fortunae memorem te decet esse meae.
nec fragili geminae poliantur pumice frontes,
  hirsutus sparsis ut uideare comis.

(Little book, without me—and I'm not jealous—you will go to Rome,
  alas, something your master's not allowed to do!
Go, but go unadorned, as it is right that an exile's book should be.
  Unhappy one, wear the clothing of this time.
No vellum will veil you in dark purple,
  That color is not suitable for mourning;
Your title will not be marked with scarlet or your pages with cedar oil.
  You may not wear white knobs next to your dark edges;
These are the trappings of happy books.
  It is fitting that that you be a reminder of my fate.
Nor should your two edges be polished by friable pumice:
  you should appear unkempt with your tangled locks.)

The goal of the voyage is to meet Augustus and to take its place in the library where the other books of Ovid are already locked away (*penetrale nostrum,* "our sanctuary") by obtaining a box (*scrinia*) in order to be lined up there beside its "brothers," that is, Ovid's previous books that bear *tituli*—their titles and the name of the author (105–10):

cum tamen in nostrum fueris penetrale receptus,
  contigerisque tuam, scrinia curua, domum,

aspicies illic positos ex ordine fratres,
    quos studium cunctos euigilauit idem.
cetera turba palam titulos ostendet apertos,
    et sua detecta nomina fronte geret;

(Nevertheless, when you have been received back in my sanctuary,
    and you make it back to your home, the round bookcases,
there you will see your brothers set out in order,
    all of whom identical carefulness worked on without sleeping.
The rest of the crowd will display their titles openly
    bearing their names on their exposed edges.)

Echoing this poem at the beginning of Book 1, the opening of Book 3 is the account by the *liber* of its voyage to Rome. Once again, it is the book-as-object and not the text that has speech. It addresses a *lector* (*Trist.* 3.1.2) and speaks about its papyrus (*in hac charta*, 4) as the support of its *versus*. Ultimately, it is always an object which speaks through writing, but the *book* in order to speak needs to be metaphorized in a double fiction built on the basis of its materiality as a roll of papyrus covered with letters. The book is a letter and the letter is a traveler.

Here, too, its physical appearance is that of an *incultus* (14): the papyrus has not been coated with cedar oil; it was not polished with pumice (13). Its letters are sometimes erased and its paper stained. The verses are uneven, that is, they are elegiac couplets; it limps because it has walked too far (9–16). A stranger in the city, it seeks someone to take it in. A man takes it to see Rome; when it gets to the Palatine, in front of the house of Augustus, the book is panic-stricken. Its letters shake with fear, the papyrus goes pale, and the verses tremble (54–56).

From there they go to the nearby temple of Apollo and visit the library where the ancient and modern authors live together (63). The book seeks its brothers, Ovid's previous books, in vain, and it must leave (65–69). It cannot find a place there, or in any other public library of Rome, not in the Portico of Octavia, or in the oldest, Asinius Pollio's in the Atrium Libertatis. The condemnation of Ovid means at the same time the public disappearance of his books; he disappears as a canonical author. He no longer forms a part of the *litterae latinae*. His last hope is refuge in a private library (79–82).

THE FICTIVE UTTERANCE OF THE *TRISTIA*

The *Tristia* takes the trope of remote address from the epistolary mode (*Trist.* 5.1.1–2):

Hunc quoque de Getico, nostri studiose, libellum
    litore praemissis quattuor adde meis.

(This book, also from the Getic shore, O you who care for me,
    Add to the four sent on ahead.)

But their poetic form is justified by a second fictive utterance: they are songs of mourning. Ovid is the new Orpheus sent on a voyage that brings him not far from Thrace. He thus finds legitimacy as the *qui primus* (the discoverer of a genre) on the Greek model of the mythical singer (3–5):

> Hic quoque talis erit, qualis fortuna poetae:
>> inuenies toto carmine dulce nihil.
>
> Fleblis ut noster status est, ita flebile carmen.

> (This one, too, will be like the poet's fortunes:
>> You will find nothing sweet in the whole of my song.
>
> Pitiable is my state, pitiable therefore is my song.)

And in another poem (*Trist.* 4.1.5–7, 15–19):

> hoc est cur cantet vinctus quoque compede fossor,
>> indocili numero cum grave mollit opus.
>
> cantat et innitens limosae pronus harenae . . .
>> fertur et abducta Lyrneside tristis Achilles
>
> Haemonia curas attenuasse lyra.
>> cum traheret silvas Orpheus et dura canendo
>
> saxa, bis amissa coniuge maestus erat.
>> me quoque Musa levat Ponti loca iussa petentem.

> (This is why even the ditch-digger in chains sings,
>> as he lightens his heavy work with untrained meter.
>
> Even the barge-hauler sings, straining bent over the slimy sand . . .
>
> They say that when Briseis was taken away, sad Achilles
>> reduced his cares by the Haemonian lyre.
>
> When Orpheus drew forests and harsh rocks to him by his singing
>> he was weeping for his twice-lost wife.
>
> The Muse will lighten my lot, too, as I seek the places commanded
>> me in Pontus.)

A fiction, of course, but one that gives value and legitimacy to the *carmina* and that makes Ovid the virtual ancestor of elegies of a new type: poems of exile (87–88):

> et tamen ad numeros antiquaque sacra reverti
>> sustinet in tantis hospita Musa malis.

> (And yet to her meters and to her ancient rites
>> my Muse can bear to return as a guest in such great evils.)

But this new hoped-for status requires that the collected book of poems be published in a *recitatio*, which is impossible among the ignorant Sarmates and Getes. He is therefore alone with his poems; and so their voyage to Rome (89–92):

sed neque cui recitem quisquam est mea carmina, nec qui
  auribus accipiat verba Latina suis.
ipse mihi—quid enim faciam?—scriboque legoque,
  tutaque iudicio littera nostra meo est.

(But there is no one here to recite my songs, no one
  whose ears understand Latin words.
I write and read for myself (what else can I do?)
  and my letters are safe in my own judgment.)

The first poem of Book 1 of *Ex Ponto*, in a letter to Brutus, picks up this theme of a desperate search for a library. His books are foreigners (*libellos peregrinos*) in need of hospitality (*hospitio*). They do not dare to enter the public libraries after the condemnation of *Ars Amatoria*, and so he asks a private person for a place where they can hide themselves (*sub Lare priuato latere*). There's a free place, formerly occupied by *Ars Amatoria*. They will be beside their fellow books.

THE BOOK CONSECRATES THE GREEK AND LATIN POET

The book deposited in the library consecrates a poet in the same way as the *qui primus*, the Roman equivalent of the πρῶτος εὑρετής. Paradoxically it confers on him the aura of the inspired poet. In effect, once he has been placed in a public library, just like the canonical authors of Greek literature have previously been, a poet such as Horace becomes a new Alcaeus, not because of his manner of producing poetry but because of the status that he has from now on in the *litterae Latinae*. He will be quoted by the speakers and the philosophers; he will be imitated by the poets. He offers a new form, a new fictive utterance to the Roman poets who in turn will write collections of the same type. Each innovator of the age of Augustus introduces a new Greek fictive utterance: Vergil for Homeric epic, didactic epic, and bucolic; Propertius for elegy; Horace for the *Odes* and *Letters*. This is what the most famous ode of Horace says so clearly (*Odes* 3.30.1–5):[23]

Exegi monumentum aere perennius
regalique situ pyramidum altius,
quod non imber edax, non Aquilo inpotens
possit diruere aut innumerabilis
annorum series et fuga temporum.

(I have built a monument more enduring than bronze
higher than the royal mass of the pyramids,
which no devouring rain, no raging north wind

23. See the comments of Lowrie 2002.

can tear down, not even the innumerable succession
of years and the flight of time.)

The beginning of this text is strange to say the least. The publication of a
book whose fragility we have seen and which could only with difficulty
claim to be more solid than bronze or the pyramids of Egypt, can this
bring the poet immortality? Of course, everyone knows the eternal glory
granted the Greek *aoidos*, but that is perpetuated by means of oral
performances, rituals that are missing from Rome. It is therefore not the
liber which is the *monumentum*.

Then Horace elaborates: he will not entirely die, a part of him will not
go in the tomb; quite the contrary, a glory always new (*recens*) will
accompany him in the future. *Recens* makes us think of a renewed ritual.
And in fact this eternal glory is related to the perenniality of the Capitoline cults, that is, with the survival of Rome as the city of Jupiter (6–9):

> Non omnis moriar multaque pars mei
> uitabit Libitinam; usque ego postera
> crescam laude recens, dum Capitolium
> scandet cum tacita uirgine pontifex.

> (I shall not wholly die and the greater part of me
> will evade Libitina; continually I
> shall grow fresh with added praise, as long as
> the Pontifex climbs the Capitoline with the silent virgin.)

In what then will his glory consist? Not in the perenniality of his verses
eternally sung. Rather, that people will say of him that he was the first
Roman (*princeps*, 13) to have brought in Aeolic poetry, that is, the Alcaic
or Sapphic stanza, integrating it with the old Italian rhythms, that is to
say, by creating a Latin metrics. And in fact the poetic revolution of the
age of Augustus consisted of imposing on the Latin language a true
metrical system on the Greek model that can make itself heard and
replaces the ancient *versus quadratus* of Ennius (10–14):

> Dicar qua uiolens obstrepit Aufidus
> et qua pauper aquae Daunus agrestium
> regnauit populorum, ex humili potens
> princeps Aeolium carmen ad Italos
> deduxisse modos.

> (I shall be spoken of where the raging Aufidus roars
> and where Daunus, short of water, ruled
> his rustic people, I, powerful from a humble birth,
> as having been the first to bring Aeolian verse
> to Italian measures.)

He thus deserves the same glory as the other melic poets in the heart of
the libraries and the same laurel wreath (14–16):

Sume superbiam
quaesitam meritis et mihi Delphica
lauro cinge uolens, Melpomene, comam.

(Take the pride
you have so richly earned and with Delphic laurel
kindly circle my hair, Melpomene.)

What makes a book literary in Rome? It is to recopy in a *volumen* texts
already composed. The *volumen* is always a collection in the Alexandrian
style; the *volumen* is a container of a fixed dimension in which one packs
all that one can, just like a box. The object is valuable in itself because it
created the poet, who had no other social expectation, no other consecration than to attach his name to a box deposited in a library. The book in
Rome is really a container and the text the contents. The interaction
between the contents and the container defines an "author" who is not
the subject of a writing.

There are three possible statuses for Roman literary books: there is the
book that one gives as a gift, the book that libraries preserve, and the book
that bookshops sell and resell. These three statuses are all deduced from
its material fragility and its exclusive function as a support. They owe
nothing to the value of the writings that they contain; only the occasion
and the genre play a part. It must make its addressee famous. As for the
occasion, best is that which makes it possible for the poet to be a *qui
primus*, to create the foundational text of a Greek genre at Rome. Only
thus can he hope for the consecration, in the Alexandrian style, of his first
text, preserved to be imitated. The text escapes the book and its fragility:
Monumentum aere perennius.

BIBLIOGRAPHY

Canfora, Luciano. 1992. "Le monde en rouleaux." In Jacob and de Polignac 1992:
    49–62.
Cordier, Pierre. 2005. "Les habits grecs du baigneur romain." In Dupont and
    Valette-Cagnac 2005: 81–102.
Dupont, Florence. 2005. "L'altérité incluse." In Dupont and Valette-Cagnac
    2005: 255–77.
—— and Emmanuelle Valette-Cagnac, eds. 2005. *Façons de parler grec à Rome.*
    L'Antiquité au Présent. Paris.
Jacob, Christian. 1992. "Callimaque: un poète dans le labyrinthe." In Jacob and de
    Polignac 1992: 100–12.
—— and François de Polignac, eds. 1992. *Alexandre IIIᵉ siècle av. J.-C.: tous les
    saviors du monde ou le rêve d'universalité des Ptolémées.* Série Mémoires 19.
    Paris.
Lissarrague, François. 1987. *Un flot d'images: une esthétique du banquet grec.* Paris.
Lowrie, Michèle. 2002. "Beyond Performance Envy: Horace and the Modern in
    the *Epistle to Augustus*." In Michael Paschalis, ed., *Horace and Greek Lyric
    Poetry*, 141–71. Rethymno.

Nicolet, Claude. 1994. "À la recherche des archives oubliées: une contribution à l'histoire de la bureaucratie romaine." In *La mémoire perdue: à la recherche des archives oubliées, publiques et privées, de la Rome antique*, v–xviii. Série Histoire Ancienne et Médiévale 30. Paris.

Svenbro, Jesper. 1988. *Phrasikleia: anthropologie de la lecture en Grèce ancienne*. Textes à l'Appui: Histoire Classique. Paris.

Valette-Cagnac, Emmanuelle. 1997. *La lecture à Rome: rites et pratiques*. L'Antiquité au Présent. Paris.

8

The Impermanent Text in Catullus and Other Roman Poets

Joseph Farrell

To us, who have lived our entire lives in a culture saturated with print, it seems obvious that the survival of a verbal artifact for any length of time would be impossible without material texts. To a writer, getting published is the necessary first step toward a potentially limitless *Nachleben*. The fact that, *ceteris paribus*, a new book is more likely to be pulped within a few years than to survive into the following century doesn't really enter into consideration. In a general way, publication itself is considered a form of immortality.

If we consider the past, the importance of material texts looms even larger. Virtually all our knowledge about ancient poetry, fiction, and other genres depends on what was written down, so that the importance of material texts seems self-evident; and it is easy to assume that it was evident to the ancients as well. Exhibit A is the elder Pliny's well-known remark that a civilized way of life, and particularly any knowledge of the past, actually depends on the use of papyrus (*NH* 13.21.68):

> Nondum palustria attingimus nec frutices amnium; prius tamen quam digrediamur ab Aegypto, et papyri natura dicetur, cum cartae usu maxime humanitas vitae constet, certe memoria.

> (So far I have said nothing about the plants that grow in wetlands or along rivers; but before I leave Egypt, I will say something about the papyrus plant, since civilized life, and above all our memory, depends upon its use.)

Pliny's perspective on material texts seems identical to our own, so that we may easily infer that all literate people of his time shared it with him, and so with us. And of course, many did so. But there is another side to the story.

Roman poets during the first century B.C. did recognize the importance of material texts as the medium in which their poetry would circulate most widely and for the longest time. Catullus, for instance, in presenting a *libellus* to Cornelius Nepos expresses the wish that the poetry that he has had copied into this volume might possibly outlive its author (*carm.* 1), and he elsewhere imagines future generations reading the *Zmyrna* of C. Helvius Cinna even on the banks of the river Satrachus, far from where the poem was composed (*carm.* 95). Horace envisions the book containing his *Odes*, enshrined in Maecenas's library, as proof of his inclusion among the canon of lyric poets (*carm.* 1.1.35–36). Yet these same poets—indeed, some of these same passages—also draw deliberate attention to the fragility of material texts. And in this way, such passages embody a paradox. Alongside the idea that poetry depends on some physical instantiation if it is to gain a wide and lasting audience, we find a countervailing concern that material texts, precisely because they are material, expose their contents to degradation, corruption, and destruction in ways that render them consummately impermanent, particularly in comparison to the spoken word.[1] The roots of this idea are in archaic and classical Greece, a period when literacy was still young. This material is fairly well understood, so that I can forgo discussion of it here.[2] But, paradoxically perhaps, this attitude became prominent again in Rome during the two centuries that span the turn of the era—that is, roughly speaking, in the age that produced Pliny, an age that depended heavily on texts in their material form. Indeed, the evidence from this period, which I have not seen discussed from this point of view, is too extensive to permit comprehensive treatment or adequate summary in a brief essay, so that I will have to be selective. For that reason, I will focus my discussion mainly on Catullus, with only brief consideration of some passages in Vergil and Horace.[3]

As we have learned from Peter Bing and others, one of the key contributions of the Hellenistic period to the poet's craft was a self-consciousness, an acceptance, and a celebration of the poet specifically

---

1. For a survey of the natural predators that threatened books in the ancient world and of texts that comment on these threats, see Puglia 1991. I am grateful to George Houston for calling this book to my attention.

2. Greek distrust of the written word in the archaic and classical periods focuses less on the material aspect of these texts than on their fixedness. The *locus classicus* for this attitude is of course Plato, *Phaedrus* 274e–277a. In Roman times, voice remains a privileged category and as such owes quite a lot to developments in the Hellenistic period, but its precise significance is not identical with that of any period of Greek culture.

3. On the opposition between the written and spoken word as a theme in Latin poetry, see McCarthy 1998, Farrell 1999, Roman 2001, and Farrell 2007. A more comprehensive survey, Roman 2006, came into my hands just as I was putting the final touches on this chapter. Roman cites, and builds upon, the argument of McCarthy 1998, 184, that Ovid's handling of this theme "separates out the poet's transcendent art from . . . the material instruments that might seem to affect its success" and that he thereby "implies that his voice (and subjectivity) transcend the material carriers of his words, that he can speak to us without the intervention of wood and wax." Where Ovid (and, for that matter, Horace) is concerned, this is an important part of the story, but only a part: see, for instance, Fitzgerald 2000, 62, on Ovid's "anxieties about the adequacy of the written word." Catullus's anxieties, however, are still more pressing, as I will show. Whereas Roman 2006, 353, asserts that

as a writer instead of a singer.[4] If we turn to Rome, we might expect these attitudes to continue, especially during the first century B.C., when Rome had become comparatively literate and when the ideas of Callimachus and his contemporaries were having their greatest impact on Roman poets. What we find instead is a tendency to treat the material text as a thing that is weak in itself and that becomes a focus for all those forces that threaten to consign a poet's work to oblivion. Catullus in particular is quite chary of predicting a long literary afterlife, at least for himself; and when poets such as Horace do so, they do not stake their immortality on the fact that they write, but rather imagine themselves as singers—and this in spite of the fact that their work is consummately literary, and that they were utterly dependent on libraries, copyists, and booksellers for both the production and the circulation of their works. Living in a world and practicing a profession in which Pliny's encomium of papyrus was shown to be valid every single day, these poets nevertheless emphasized and exaggerated the disadvantages of textual materialism, and occasionally asserted their claims to literary immortality in terms that to us seem anachronistic if not downright whimsical.

We can get a good idea of this perspective by looking closely at some familiar poems of Catullus. What is conventionally known as poem 1 focuses prominently, as is well known, on the material condition of the book that it introduces. This book is graceful (*lepidum*), new (*nouum*), small (Catullus uses not *liber*, but the diminutive *libellum*), and nicely finished (*arida modo pumice expolitum*). Commentators uniformly read these physical descriptors as metaphors for the style of the poetry that the book contains; and so they are. But this reading has become so familiar that we risk losing sight of other effects that these opening lines produce. Some of these effects were surely unintended and arose accidentally as the methods and conventions of book production developed over the centuries. A modern reader, holding in his hands a printed edition of Catullus, one that is identical with thousands of others, has to make a big effort to think himself back into the tactile world of Catullus's first readers, each of whom read, in effect, a unique text, defined as such by accidental errors as

The author's *ingenium* and deathless, immaterial voice must be differentiated from the mere matter (*materia*) he molds, animates, and finally transcends. It is not accidental, then, that the tablets disappear: their loss enables the emergence of the poetic author.

I agree that materiality and immaterial voice are the right terms of opposition, but find Catullus much less confident that his poetry and his reputation will outlive him or transcend their material condition. In what follows, I have tried to indicate in passing the most important points of similarity or difference between Roman's reading of Catullus and my own.

4. Bing 1988, esp. ch. 1, "Poetic Inspiration and the Poet's Self Image in Hellenistic Greece," 10–48.

well as by more deliberately controlled factors such as the *mise en page*. But even in a world before printing existed but long after the obsolescence of the bookroll, the reader who is told to imagine himself as reading a *libellus* ought to experience just a bit of cognitive dissonance. This particular effect will perhaps have been most pronounced for the first readers to encounter Catullus in codex form; but the word *libellus* itself should remind us that no one for most of the last two thousand years has read Catullus in a format similar to the one that he envisioned in poem 1; and, for that matter, apart from the fact that the form envisioned there is a scroll or bookroll, all else about that *libellus*—its exact dimensions, the number of poems it contained, whether its contents were determined and arranged by the poet himself or by someone else—are matters of scholarly debate.[5]

Even for Catullus's contemporaries, though, poem 1 has the potential to provoke a sense of alienation. This sense will be mild, for the most part, but might be quite sharp as well. In any case, we cannot suppose that all readers were in an equally advantageous position to appreciate the perfect congruity of form and content that we are accustomed to find in Catullus's description of his *lepidum nouum libellum/arida modo pumice expolitum*. In the first place, the condition of the book that Catullus describes is one that is guaranteed not to last very long. No one who owns and uses books of any kind has to be convinced of this. But bookrolls lose their youthful bloom in a particular way. Because of the way in which they are handled, the outer part of the roll is especially liable to damage of every kind.[6] If it is not actually torn away, it is very likely to become soiled through constant handling. This unassuming fact forms part of the background to the description of the *libellus* in poem 1. As the first poem in the collection, it will have been written very close to the front of the bookroll. It will therefore have found itself on that portion of the roll that became shopworn most rapidly.[7] This presents us with

5. On the shape of Catullus's oeuvre see Baehrens 1885, vol. 2, 57–61; Quinn 1972, 12 and 16; Wiseman 1985, 265–6, with reference to Wiseman's earlier work on the subject; Skinner 1992 and 2003, xxii–xxviii.

6. This is the point of Martial's references to the soiling of the outer edge of a bookroll from being held under the chin as the reader rewound it from the inside out (1.66.8, 10.93.5–6). Of course, it stands to reason that the beginning and the end of a roll would be more liable to damage of all sorts, including tearing, than other parts.

7. Presumably this is the case. The issue is complicated by the fact that a collection of Catullus's poetry circulated in antiquity under the name of *Passer*—an informal title based on the first word(s) of the collection, just as the *Aeneid* might be referred to as *Arma uirumque*. The question is whether there was a separate collection in which our poem 2 stood first. I know of no other poem or collection that takes its titular *incipit* from the first words of its second poem; but neither do I know of a poem or collection referred to as *Cui dono?* or anything remotely similar. On the other hand, we do have collections, such as Ovid's *Amores*, that are preceded by an epigram that is clearly meant as preliminary to the collection as a whole. In this case, the epigram is treated as supernumerary in modern editions. Moreover, the first words of *Am.* 1.1, *arma graui numero*, clearly allude to the

something of a paradox: the more the *libellus* was read, the shabbier the beginning of the roll will have looked, even though the first poem that the reader will have encountered there is one in which the author boasts of the book's fresh, new appearance.

Of course, at least one reader will have appreciated a perfect concinnity between the book described in poem 1 and the book that he held in his hands. That reader was Cornelius Nepos, the dedicatee of the *libellus*. In view of this fact, one might try to insist that the observations contained in my previous paragraph are beside the point. But in reality, this line of argument just raises another paradox. It is true that the book described in poem 1 is the book that Nepos read; at the very least, we must assume that this was the case. But Catullus expresses a wish for other readers at the end of this poem, when he wishes that his *libellus* will last. Clearly he is writing with readers besides Nepos in mind. But of course, the more readers he reaches, and the longer his work continues to be read, the greater the number of readers whose material experience of his poetry will be distant from the one described in poem 1, and the longer he is read, the greater that distance will become.[8]

Not to labor the point, I make these observations to underline the fact that the material references in this poem are not just symbolic references to the author's literary ideals. They situate the act of reading in a set of practices rooted in a specific cultural-materialist milieu that will be more or less familiar to any actual reader according to his or her distance from the reading experience that the poem assumes and partially describes.

In the last two lines of poem 1, as I noted briefly above, Catullus prays that his volume may remain immortal beyond a single generation (*quod...plus uno maneat perenne saeclo*, 9–10). This is an appealing bit of modesty, and it is unconventional.[9] Catullus does not claim hyperbolically that his poetry, now that he has "published" it, will live forever; he merely hopes that it will outlive him, at least for a while.[10] Perhaps he is

first words of the *Aeneid*, *arma uirumque cano*, and so to their titular character. (More on this relationship in Farrell 2004.) On balance, then, the situation that we face in Catullus would be probably be clearer if our poem 1 were treated as *extra ordinem*, and if the numbering of the poems began with our poem 2, *Passer deliciae meae puellae*.

8. This is the material aspect of an important thematic element in the poem, that of ownership or property, in regard to which Fitzgerald 1995 has well observed that "Nepos is welcome to the book (this attractive, smooth little volume)...but, as the poet prays for the same book that the Muse may preserve it fresh throughout posterity, he withdraws it from its dedicatee" (41).

9. Excellent commentary on Catullus's stance here in Fitzgerald 1995, 39, and Roman 2001, 120–1; see also Roman 2006, 356.

10. Contrast Catullus's more realistic request with the boast of Horace at the end of *Odes* 1–3 that he has created a *monumentum aere perennius*, and that of Ovid, who has a close eye on Horace, at the end of the *Metamorphoses*. Ovid, having staked his claim to poetic immortality in these lines, made undoing and ironizing it a major theme of his exile poetry (Farrell 1999, with further references; cf. Roman 2001, 121).

only being realistic: as a self-conscious exponent of novelty in literature, Catullus may have understood that he would be fortunate to remain popular even until the end of his own life, let alone beyond. But it is noteworthy that he makes this self-deprecating wish at the end of a poem that begins by commenting on the physical condition of the book that contains it.

I will return to poem 1 from time to time throughout this essay; for Catullus's references there to the appearance of his *libellus*, and his hope that the thing will last a while, announce textual materiality as a major theme of his poetry. In fact, it is one of the very first themes that Catullus sees fit to announce, along with the theme of gift exchange (*Cui dono?*)— and, by extension, that of reciprocal obligation more generally—as well as those themes that are metaphorically conjured by the words used to describe the physical *libellus* (which refer both to literary and social ideals). Critics have long been active in exploring the presence of the other themes announced here throughout Catullus's oeuvre. The facts would suggest that, by comparison, the theme of textual materiality has been overlooked.

Elsewhere in Catullus, just as in poem 1, the material text appears mainly in contexts in which its durability, and hence the survival of its contents, is open to doubt. Let us here return to poem 95, in which, as we have seen, Catullus predicts long life for the book that contains the *Zmyrna* of C. Helvius Cinna (5–8):

> Zmyrna cauas Satrachi penitus mittetur ad undas,
>   Zmyrnam cana diu saecula peruoluent.
> at Volusi Annales Paduam morientur ad ipsam
>   et laxas scombris saepe dabunt tunicas.
> (*Zmyrna* will travel far to the deep-watered channels of the Satrachus,
> the white-haired generations will long read *Zmyrna*;
> but Volusius's *Annales* will die right on the banks of the Po
> and provide comfortable tunics for many mackerel.)

Cinna's book will travel far and will be rolled and unrolled "for a long time" (*diu*) by "white-haired generations" (*cana . . . saecula*). Note the occurrence of *saecula* here and of *saeclo* in poem 1. In the earlier poem Catullus hopes that his *libellus* will outlast at least a single generation (10); here he predicts confidently that multiple generations will enjoy the *Zmyrna* (6). He graciously appears more certain about Cinna's posthumous reception than he is about his own. And, once

---

I use the word "published" with some hesitation and merely for convenience. The Roman realities that corresponded to modern "publication" involved a much more gradual dispersion of a text, mainly through social networks rather than a primarily commercial release in quantity to an anonymous reading public. On the ancient process see Starr 1987 (with Starr's caution against the use of words like "publish" at 215 n. 18).

again, we are talking about a *libellus*: the image introduced by *peruoluent* (6) requires that we think of an actual object, a scroll that the white-haired generations will wind and unwind as they read and reread the *Zmyrna*. This durable scroll is directly contrasted in the next line with one that contains another book, Volusius's *Annales*. That poem will not travel as far as the *Zmyrna* or last as long. Instead, it will never get past the Po and will be used to wrap fish (7–8). Here the vector of influence in the relationship between the physical book and its literary content becomes clear. Volusius, here as elsewhere, is for Catullus the paradigmatically bad poet. His work is so bad that the papyrus on which it is written is more valuable as wrapping paper than as a vehicle for preserving Volusius's work.

Catullus's thrust at Volusius is amusing, but it reflects uncomfortably on poem 1. In that poem Catullus shows little confidence that his beautifully finished *lepidus nouus libellus*—by which I mean the physical book—will itself ensure the survival of the poetry that it contains. Rather, the converse is true. We learn as much from poem 95, in which the book that contains Volusius's poem will be used for wrapping paper. We learn elsewhere, from the example of the poetaster Suffenus, that the beautiful outer form of a *libellus* does not necessarily guarantee the beauty of the poetry that lies within. We first meet Suffenus in poem 14, in which Catullus threatens to send poems by him and other insufferables to his friend Calvus in retaliation for the miscellany of bad poetry that Calvus sent Catullus as a mock Saturnalia present (16–23):

> non non hoc tibi, false, sic abibit.
> nam si luxerit ad librariorum
> curram scrinia, Caesios, Aquinos,
> Suffenum, omnia colligam uenena.
> ac te his suppliciis remunerabor.
> uos hinc interea ualete abite
> illuc, unde malum pedem attulistis,
> saecli incommoda, pessimi poetae.

(You won't get away with it, traitor! For when it's day I will run to the booksellers' stalls and buy poets like Caesius and Aquinus, even Suffenus himself, every form of poison there is. And in the meantime, goodbye and go back where you began your hapless journey, burden of our generation, worst poets.)

I note in passing the occurrence once again of the word *saeculum*, this time in the phrase *saecli incommoda* (23). Here there is no question of any *Nachleben* at all: these poets, and the misery (or mirthful derision) that they supply to their readers remains confined to the current generation. But that is not the end of Suffenus. In poem 22, Catullus tells us how the man composes, not only writing too much, but always writing everything on the best quality papyrus, carefully laid out as if he were not a poet but a scribe producing luxury copies for sale to the carriage trade (4–8):

puto esse ego illi milia aut decem aut plura
perscripta, nec sic ut fit in palimpsesto
relata: cartae regiae, noui libri,
noui umbilici, lora rubra membranae,
derecta plumbo et pumice omnia aequata.

(I suppose he's written out ten thousand or more, not jotted in the usual
way on reused stock: the best papyrus, new books, new roller ends, new red
ties for the wrapper, ruled with lead and smoothed with pumice all around.)

The satire works on different levels, but one simple point Catullus is
making is that Suffenus never revises; he doesn't use palimpsest, which
Catullus describes as the normal way to compose, and which is itself
emblematic of erasure, both in the process of composition and in that
unhappy stage of reception when a book becomes more valuable for its
materials than for its contents. The misguided Suffenus overrates his own
work by assuming that it will ever be worth writing down on top-quality
goods.[11] Perhaps he is deluded as well in thinking that these goods will
ensure that his poetry survives. More likely some right-thinking poet will
make use of Suffenus's volume by scraping off his scribblings and con-
verting his *cartae regiae* into the very palimpsests that Suffenus eschews.

Catullus marvels that Suffenus, whom he paints as a sympathetic
and urbane fellow, was nevertheless such a bad poet, and he wonders
at Suffenus's sheer cluelessness. But the end of this poem is surprising
(18–21):

nimirum idem omnes fallimur, neque est quisquam
quem non in aliqua re uidere Suffenum
possis. suus cuique attributus est error;
sed non uidemus manticae quod in tergo est.

(We probably all make the same mistake, and there's no one you couldn't
regard somehow or other as a Suffenus. Everyone has his own besetting sin;
we don't see the pack on our own back.)

We all have a bit of Suffenus in us, says Catullus. It is not like Catullus to
soften a blow in this way.[12] What in the world does this mean?

Is it possible that Catullus fears that he himself, in his satisfaction with
his own *lepidus novus libellus*, may not be so different from the deluded

---

11. Catullus's *cartae regiae*, a latinization of χάρται βασιλικοί (cf. Heron *De automatis*
26.3.5), is usually identified with the *carta Augusta* (called *carta Augustea regia* by Suetonius
ap. Isid. *Orig.* 6.10.2). According to Pliny (*NH* 13.74) this highest grade of papyrus was
originally known as *carta hieratica*.

12. The *mantica* is proverbial (Otto 1971, 209, no. 1032), but also specifically Aesopic
(Perry 1936, 266). As such, it may emblematize Catullus's ironic adoption of the satirist's
habitual stance of abjection, as is suggested to me by Ralph Rosen.

Suffenus? I think there is little question but that this is so. If we look among Catullus's poems for a correlative to Suffenus's pretentious volume, we will find one in Catullus's description of his own. Catullus calls his own book a *nouum libellum* (1.1); Suffenus writes on *noui libri* (22.6). The edges of Catullus's papyrus have been nicely finished with pumice stone (1.2); ditto Suffenus's (22.8). It is true, at least, that Catullus doesn't actually write his first and only draft of a poem on this beautifully finished papyrus, as Suffenus does. Still, Catullus's ridicule of Suffenus's delight in his beautiful book casts an uncomfortable light on poem 1.

Viewed from one angle, of course, the bad poets whom Catullus mocks exist only to set off the good poets—friends of his, like Calvus and Cinna—whom he approves. Viewed from another angle, they may exemplify the fate to which Catullus fears his own work might be consigned. And this fate is regularly expressed as the fate of the poet's book as a physical object. At least two distinct aspects are visible.

First, after the poems have been finished and arranged, and the collection copied out into multiple *libelli* for presentation or sale, there is the question of what will happen to these books. In this regard Volusius, to return to that worst of poets, is not merely Catullus's opposite; he is a kind of *Doppelgänger*, or even an emblem of the failed poet that Catullus fears he himself may turn out to be. In poem 95, Volusius's books are used to wrap fish. In poem 36, they fare even worse. When Catullus ridicules Volusius's *Annales* as *cacata carta*, he metaphorically equates with excrement the inferior poetry that has befouled what had been perfectly good papyrus, and suggests the kind of degrading use for which those books might now be fit. But Catullus envisions a more complete annihilation of Volusius's books. His *puella* and he are about to burn them in fulfillment of a vow that she took to Venus and Cupid to burn the choicest products of the worst of poets if Catullus would only stop writing nasty things about her. By "worst of poets," of course, she meant at the time Catullus himself; but now that she has made up with him, he cheerfully joins her in fulfilling her vow by burning Volusius instead. It is a funny poem, but our enjoyment of it should not mask the fact that Volusius is being burned *in Catullus's place*, thus narrowly saving Catullus's own work from annihilation.

The form of Volusius's poem that Catullus envisions here is evidently a bookroll. The word *carta*, "papyrus," suggests as much; and because Catullus is so hostile to Volusius's poetry, and does nothing to suggest that the two of them were on intimate or even friendly terms, it is reasonable to assume that Catullus knew the *Annales* not in draft, but in the form in which Volusius had made the poem public. I make the point just to underline the fact this poem dramatizes the destruction of a "published" text.[13] But the vow of the *puella* brings into view a second

---

13. This fact underlines one difference between Roman's approach and my own. Whereas Roman argues that the published work symbolizes the release of the poet's voice, in

aspect of Catullus's anxiety over his books' fate, one that is prior to any concerns he may have about the reception of the finished product. Even before it is finished, the book's condition as a physical object exposes it to hazards that threaten its existence. For the vow to burn Catullus's books is not merely a symbolic threat: the actual, physical possession of Catullus's work is thematized in poem 42, in which a *moecha* (3) has got hold of some of his poems, leaving him in a state over how to get them back. Specifically, what the *moecha* has got hold of are *pugillaria* and *codicilli*, or a number of tablets bound together as leaves in a quire.[14] This is the form in which one would expect a poet to keep his work prior to public circulation in the form of a scroll (*liber* or *libellus*).[15] Catullus, as I have said, in this respect, at least, is no Suffenus. But the more humble *codex* form is no less material than a scroll, and it is just as liable to destruction as a finished book, if not more so. Catullus does not say explicitly that the *moecha* has acquired what appear to be the *only* copies he had of at least some of his poems, but it does seem possible that she now has the power to destroy his notebooks and prevent at least some poems not only from surviving into the next generation, but from surviving long enough to be made public.

If we put this poem together with the one in which Volusius gets burned instead of Catullus, it seems likely that destroying the poems is what the *moecha* of 42, like the *puella* of 36, has in mind.[16] But we can imagine other malicious possibilities as well, like the circulation of poems that Catullus himself would have decided not to make public; the circulation of Catullus's poems under someone else's name; or the circulation under Catullus's name of texts altered for the worse, expressly to embarrass him. Catullus does not mention these possibilities, but all are real.[17]

my view Catullus never regards his poetry, or any poetry, as transcending the limitations of the physical materials on which they are written. Certainly here, at any rate, the imagined destruction of Volusius's work in its material form is not to be taken as symbolizing the release of his voice and the survival of his work as a classic.

14. On these words and the kinds of books that they denote see Birt 1882, 85–7 and 95–6; Kenyon 1932, 89–91.

15. Birt 1882, 12–14.

16. The point of putting these poems together is not to construct a single, coherent confessional or novelistic account of the love affair between "Catullus" and "Lesbia." There is nothing that requires the reader to identify the *puella* of 36 and the *moecha* of 42 with Lesbia or even with each other, and nothing to prevent the reader from imagining that "Catullus" had this sort of trouble with a series of girlfriends. But I would suggest that the situations of poems 36 and 42 speak to one another in a way that invites the reader to construct a narrative not of "what actually happened," but an exemplary one, and one that is not confessional but speculative. On this question in general see Fitzgerald 1995, 27–9.

17. In fact, such things did happen in one way or another to a number of ancient authors, some of whose complaints we have. Out of the scores of plays that circulated under the name of Plautus, M. Terentius Varro identified only twenty-one as definitely genuine (Gellius *NA* 3.3). When Cicero's *Academica* were released (by a well-meaning Atticus) in a two-book edition, the author had to work to suppress the first edition and to replace it with a second in four books (*Att.* 13.13.1). (Result: the text that we have combines book 1 of the second

There is, however, a larger point. The theft of Catullus's notebooks stands for the inevitable moment that every author eventually confronts, namely, that of the alienation of his text from his personal ownership and control.[18] For that is what the wider circulation of his text—or to use the anachronistic modern term, its publication—fundamentally entails. In order to be read, the author has to give his text away, and this fact, too, is tied to the image of the book as a material artifact.

The moment of alienation is the process that Catullus thematizes and in fact dramatizes in the poem with which we began, his dedication poem. Here the *libellus* is an object, a physical thing that the poet has to give to someone. Poem 1 begins with Catullus wondering who should get it. When he lights upon Cornelius Nepos, he enacts the formal presentation of the dedication copy with the words *habe tibi* (8); and, as commentators point out, the idiom *sibi habere* "is a regular phrase of Roman law in reference to the disposal of property" even if the colloquial *tibi habe* "often implies a certain indifference which is here in keeping with the following words."[19] As such, the phrase is perfectly chosen. Presenting the dedication copy to someone represents the alienation of the book and its contents from the author as a piece of property and the placing of his work into the public domain. Catullus's lighthearted and somewhat high-handed attitude in performing this ceremonial act may be felt to mask an element of anxiety. "To whom am I giving my book?" he asks, or better, "To whom am I making a gift of my book?" The language underlines the idea of exchange, because gift giving is a practice that circulates throughout society: Catullus, like everybody else, gives in order to get. Like other writers, he gives his work to some patron in the hope of getting a favorable reception. Of course, Catullus in choosing Cornelius Nepos puts himself in a position that is hardly abject. First of all, even to assume the right of choosing who will receive the dedication copy implies a certain freedom that Roman poets did not always have.[20] Second, in choosing Nepos,

---

edition, the *Academica posteriora*, with book 2 of the first edition, the *Academica priora*.) Cicero's oration against Clodius and Curio was also published without his approval (*Att.* 3.12.2, 3.13.3; fragments and discussion in Crawford 1994, 227–63). The *Aeneid*, of course, was edited to some extent and released against Vergil's deathbed wishes, according to the ancient *vita* tradition. Martial repeatedly complains, or boasts, of being plagiarized (1.29, 38, 52, 53, 63, 66, 72, 2.20, 10.100, 11.94, 12.63). Perhaps the most extreme case is that of Galen, who in his treatises "On My Own Books" and "On the Order of My Own Books" documents the various ways in which unauthorized works ascribed to him circulated through the Roman book trade, creating difficulties for the author himself in his effort to establish the canon of his own works. Cf. Pliny, *Epist.* 2.10.2–3. On the poetic thematization of this problem by Ovid, see Farrell 1998, 307–38, esp. 329–38.

18. Fitzgerald 1995, 44–55 and 93–104; Roman 2001; Roman 2006, 354 n. 9.

19. Fordyce 1961, 86 *ad* 1.8.

20. Catullus's independent-minded question is not unprecedented, however, but echoes that of Meleager in the dedication poem of his *Garland* (*AP* 4.1). Horace, too, having once addressed Maecenas as his first dedicatee and as destined to be his last (*Epist.* 1.1.1), nevertheless addresses his later epistles to Augustus, to Florus, and to the Pisones.

Catullus selects a dedicatee who might be seen as worthy of the poet in various ways—as a fellow *transpadanus*, as a learned writer in his own right, and so forth—rather than one on whose patronage in the traditional sense Catullus might depend.[21] It makes sense to think of their relationship as a friendship of the sort defined in particular by Peter White.[22] But another occasion in the Catullan corpus when we hear about the gift of a book is, again, in poem 14, in which someone has presented Calvus with a miscellany of bad poetry as a Saturnalia present. That someone is designated as one of Calvus's *clientes* (6), meaning someone whom Calvus had defended in court; but the word, like the textually suspect *patrona* in poem 1, or like *patronus* in 49, hints at the patron/client relationship that lurked beneath unequal friendships between poets and their addressees.[23] The sharp edge of explicit deference involved in the client's presentation of a Saturnalia present to his patron Calvus, in poem 14, is blunted somewhat when Calvus immediately sends the same present to Catullus, his social equal. Still, the precise meaning of the client's act of fealty remains visible, and his presenting Calvus with the gift of a book reflects upon Catullus's gift to Cornelius Nepos. When Catullus, despite the relative independence that he shows in poem 1, nevertheless submits to the formal ritual of presenting a dedication copy to a patron, he acknowledges, even if ironically, the patron's social role in the reception and survival of the poetry with which he is presented. And both the patron's role in this process and the fate of the poetry itself are bound up with the fate of the physical book that Catullus presents to Nepos, praying that it might remain everlasting, at least beyond a single generation.

At this juncture I would like to expand the focus of this essay from the written word alone to include that other medium in which poetry is experienced: the spoken word or, as so often in the ancient world, song. And I want to begin by pointing out a fact that, when I first realized it, surprised me a lot. Unlike so many ancient poets, Catullus almost never represents himself as a singer. Indeed, he is relatively uninterested in singing generally. He does mention singing by others several times, but only in mythical or ritual contexts.[24] The single time when Catullus imagines himself as a singer is in poem 65, in which he says that, although he will never see his dead brother again, he will always love him, and will

---

21. Cairns 1969; Wiseman 1979, 171; Gibson 1995.

22. White 1978 and 1993.

23. The treatment of the Muse by Catullus's model, Meleager (see note 20 above), is worth bearing in mind. Meleager addresses the Muse immediately, asking her to whom he ought to dedicate his *Garland*. At the beginning of Catullus's poem, it is not clear to whom the question, "*Cui dono...?*" is addressed, but comparison with Catullus's source suggests that it may be the Muse. Nepos, of course, is then apostrophized in lines 3–7; but the phrase *patrona uirgo* in line 9 may signal a return to the original addressee of lines 1–2.

24. The devotees of Cybele sing (63.11, 27–29) as do the Fates (64.306, 382–83); there is singing by choruses in poem 34, a hymn to Diana, and in 61 and 62, the epithalamia.

forever sing songs of mourning like the nightingale, mourning the death of
Itys. This is a poem that requires a closer look.

> Etsi me assiduo confectum cura dolore
>   seuocat a doctis, Ortale, uirginibus,
> nec potis est dulcis Musarum expromere fetus
>   mens animi, tantis fluctuat ipsa malis—
> namque mei nuper Lethaeo in gurgite fratris
>   pallidulum manans alluit unda pedem,
> Troia Rhoeteo quem subter litore tellus
>   ereptum nostris obterit ex oculis.
>
> * * * * * * * *
>
>   numquam ego te, uita frater amabilior,
> aspiciam posthac? at certe semper amabo,
>   semper maesta tua carmina morte canam,
> qualia sub densis ramorum concinit umbris
>   Daulias, absumpti fata gemens Ityli—
> sed tamen in tantis maeroribus, Ortale, mitto
>   haec expressa tibi carmina Battiadae....

(Although I am beset with constant sorrow and heartache keeps me from the
learned maidens, Hortalus, and my mind is unable to bring forth the sweet
children of the Muses, so great is the sea of troubles on which it floats—for
waters that run in the pool of Lethe have just now bathed my brother's pallid
little foot, my brother whom the Trojan land, under the shore of Rhoeteum,
treads upon, hidden from my sight. *** Shall I never again see you, brother
more loveable than life? But surely I will always love you, always will I sing
songs that are mournful because you are dead, like those Daulius's daughter
sings, bewailing the fate of the murdered Itylus, under the dense shadows of
branches—nevertheless, in the midst of such sorrow, Hortalus, I send you
these versions of poems by Callimachus, scion of Battus....)

Like poem 1, poem 65 is a dedication poem. It introduces poem 66,
the *Coma Berenices*, which Catullus, as we are told, has produced at
the request of his friend Hortalus. In this dedication poem, Catullus is
concerned to explain how difficult it has been for him to fulfill Hortalus's
request. The death of Catullus's brother has left him paralyzed and has
severed his relationship to the Muses (1–4); nevertheless, he has managed
to translate a poem of Callimachus, the *Coma Berenices*, which follows.
Poem 66 is of course a major statement about Catullus's literary ideals
and, as a translation, an extraordinary masterpiece.[25] But Catullus presents it in a rather particular light. First, as we have just seen, it is characterized as a piece that was written to order. Second, although the
translation is certainly Catullus's work, he refers to it as *carmina Battiadae*
(65.16), a poem of Callimachus. It is therefore, we might say, alienated

---

25. Marinone 1997.

from Catullus in two senses, both as something that belongs to Hortalus, and as something that belongs to Callimachus. Third, the poem that Catullus has chosen to translate, or that Hortalus has chosen for him, is itself an example par excellence of poetry written in honor of a patron.[26] And finally, as a translation, it stands at an extreme point on the spectrum of bookish poetry. I take it that this statement needs no elaboration.

It is very significant, then, that this literary tour de force is implicitly contrasted with a very different sort of poem, not poem 65 itself, but the unwritten and unwritable poem that Catullus would prefer to sing and that almost prevented him from translating the *Coma* for Hortalus. This would be a poem of mourning for Catullus's brother—a poem that would mean little to Hortalus or any other patron, but that would mean everything to the poet—like the song of the nightingale, which listeners might find beautiful, but which the bird sings to and for itself. And, like the nightingale's song, Catullus's lament would never end. Just how this could be so, Catullus does not make clear. Even though he declares that he will always sing songs of mourning for his brother, we have to take his declaration as more of a wish. Still, it is notable that he links his wish to produce this most personal of poems with an image of himself as a singer rather than as a writer, and with an obsessive desire to indulge himself in this song forever, while contrasting this desire with the need to write out a translation of another poet's work for some third party.

There is one other passage that must enter into this discussion. Poem 68 seems to fall into two more or less distinct parts that nevertheless go together much in the way that poem 65 goes with poem 66.[27] The first part, lines 1–40 (poem 68a), introduce the proto-elegiac narrative that follows in the second part, lines 41–160 (poem 68b). Like poem 65, poem 68a addresses itself to a friend who has asked Catullus to write him a poem. Catullus explains that the request is difficult to answer: as in poem 65, here, too, the death of his brother is a major psychological obstacle. And on a more mundane level, Catullus represents himself as being in Verona, where he has no books. This of course is interesting because it is so different from the situation to which we are introduced in poem 65,

---

26. Callimachus's *Coma Berenices* was of course the conclusion to his *Aetia*. Standing as it did at the end of the fourth and last book, it balanced the *Victoria Berenices* at the beginning of Book 3, working together with that episode as a frame for the second half of the collection and inscribing the poet's patron into the structure of the work in a most forceful and obvious way. On the structure of the *Aetia* see Fantuzzi and Hunter 2004, 44–9 and 83–8.

27. The text of poem 68 and the relationship between parts a and b remains controversial. The most significant problem is that in the manuscripts part a, the dedicatory epistle, addresses one Manius (*Mani* 11 [v.l. *Manli* R], 30), whereas part b, the elegiac narrative, expresses a great debt to someone named Allius (41, 50, 66 [*Mallius* O in marg. *Manlius* GR]), who is addressed in the vocative at the end of the poem (*Alli* 150). The simplest remedy is to accept Schöll's emendation *mi Alli* for *Man(l)i* "in spite of the unique elision in the sixth foot in 1. 11" (Fordyce 1961, 342).

which introduces a translation of the *Coma Berenices*—a consummately bookish poem in every sense. By contrast, Catullus implies in poem 68a, anything that he manages to produce on this occasion will be a kind of improvisation—certainly not a translation, and probably free of the elaborate, sometimes recondite, learning and allusiveness for which Catullus is known.

In any case, having concluded these preliminaries, Catullus launches into the poem that he has managed to compose. His friend Allius, who has been such a help to him, is not actually addressed until near the end of the poem (150); he is first introduced in a third-person reference while Catullus addresses the Muses in order to ensure that his poem, and so memory of Allius, will last (41–50):

> Non possum reticere, deae, qua me Allius in re
>   iuuerit aut quantis iuuerit officiis,
> ne fugiens saeclis obliuiscentibus aetas
>   illius hoc caeca nocte tegat studium:
> sed dicam uobis, uos porro dicite multis
>   milibus et facite haec carta loquatur anus.
>
> * * * * * * * *
>
>   notescatque magis mortuus atque magis,
> nec tenuem texens sublimis aranea telam
>   in deserto Alli nomine opus faciat.

> (I cannot remain silent, goddesses, about the favor Allius did me,
> —either the kind of favor or how great it was—
> lest the passage of time in the forgetful succession of generations
> cover his good offices in the darkness of night.
> But I shall speak to you, and you in turn speak to many
> thousands and cause this page of mine to speak even when it is old.
>
> * * * * * * * *
>
> and even in death may he become more and more famous,
> and may no spider, spinning its delicate web on high,
> perform its work on the name of a forgotten Allius.)

Once again, several features link this poem to the dedication of the *libellus* as a whole. One is, in fact, the address to the Muses. For it is difficult to imagine what other goddesses (*deae* 41) Catullus has in mind here, just as no one has convincingly refuted the idea that the *patrona* addressed at 1.9 is also a Muse.[28] In poem 1, the apostrophe to the Muse is surprising. Catullus has been addressing Cornelius Nepos, who is to receive the presentation copy of his *libellus*, when he suddenly turns to the Muse, his *patrona*, and prays that his book may outlast his own generation (*saeclo* 1.10). As we have seen, the word *saeculum* is linked in several other

---

28. For a recent committed attempt to oust the Muse from poem 1, see Gratwick 2002.

passages to the idea of poetic reputation, and is used to express the idea that a poem (or poet) is or is not likely to last. Here, as well, Catullus prays to the Muses that his poem for Allius will not merely outlive the current generation, but that it will survive the passage of many "forgetful generations" (*obliuiscentibus saeclis* 43). So here the idea of composing a work that will last is as much on Catullus's mind as it was when he composed the dedication poem to the *libellus* itself.

There is, however, an important difference between poems 1 and 68. The former, as I hope to have shown, is deeply implicated in an anxious discourse of materiality. The very handsomeness of the presentation copy that Catullus bestows upon Nepos is an aspect of its materiality. The appearance of this book may be an accurate reflection of its contents, and Catullus clearly means to suggest that it is. But he knows this may not be the case. His beautiful book may, in the eyes of readers, be as much a failure as that of Suffenus; and if so, it will not remain *plus uno . . . perenne saeclo*, but it will be regarded as one of the *saecli incommoda*. In either case, the survival of the poetry is linked to the survival of the book that contains it; and although circulation in material form may be a poet's best chance for winning a reputation that will outlive him, it is also true that a material existence exposes poetry, like that of Volusius and, very nearly, that of Catullus himself, to all sorts of mistreatment, including degradation and destruction. For this reason, the ritual presentation of a poetry book to some patron is but one of the ways in which a poet must alienate his work from himself. Of course, he must do so in order to gain a wide and long-lasting readership. But readers can do with books as they please, and Catullus depicts himself and others in the act of ridiculing, misusing, and destroying books. When viewed in this light, the ritual of presenting one's patron with a new *libellus* represents a loss of control and an acceptance of the fact that the fate of the new work and one's own reputation are now in the hands of someone else. Or rather, of many. For books circulate, and even one that finds an initial reader who is well disposed may be passed on by that reader to someone else who will find the book risible, as happens in poem 14. Small wonder, then, that when Catullus imagines poetic immortality, he imagines himself in poem 65 as singing an eternal song, not to please a patron but to indulge his own sorrow. So perhaps the remarkable conflation in poem 68 of these two modes of poetic expression, singing and writing, is as far as Catullus can go in hoping that any product of his pen can last, as he predicts Cinna's poetry will, for generations. He can only do so, however, not by praying to the Muse or Muses, as he does in poem 1, but by enlisting their aid: he will sing (*dicam* 45) to the Muses, and they in turn will sing (*dicite* 45) to many thousands, so that the page may continue speaking when it is an old lady (*carta loquatur anus* 46).

The speaking page is a paradoxical image with which to close, but perhaps an apt one. If Catullus is obsessed with and anxious about textuality, and utopian in his sparing claims to be a singer, the paradox

of the singing page, along with singing and writing as sharply defined
alternatives, are themes that future generations of Roman poets would
enthusiastically explore. That is a topic for another occasion. I hope here
to have shown first that the materials of textuality are an important theme
in the poems of Catullus, and second that what seem to us commonsen-
sical assumptions about the relationship between materiality and the
survival of texts are contradicted in the work of this highly literate poet.
The image of the physical book remains closely linked to conditions of
patronage in post-Republican literature. A telling example is found in
Vergil's sixth eclogue, which, like Catullus's dedication poem, walks a fine
line in managing the poet's relationship to his patron. It does so by carefully
observing the two modalities of poetic communication, writing and singing.

> Prima Syracosio dignata est ludere uersu
> nostra, neque erubuit siluas habitare, Thalia.
> Cum canerem reges et proelia, Cynthius aurem
> uellit, et admonuit: 'Pastorem, Tityre, pinguis
> pascere oportet ouis, deductum dicere carmen.'
> Nunc ego (namque super tibi erunt, qui dicere laudes,
> Vare, tuas cupiant, et tristia condere bella)
> agrestem tenui meditabor harundine Musam.
> Non iniussa cano. Si quis tamen haec quoque, si quis
> captus amore leget, te nostrae, Vare, myricae,
> te nemus omne canet; nec Phoebo gratior ulla est
> quam sibi quae Vari praescripsit pagina nomen.
> —*Eclogue* 6.1–12

(My Muse was the first to deign to dabble in Syracusan verse and not to
blush at living in the woods. When I was trying to sing of kings and battles,
Apollo tugged at my ear and told me, "A shepherd, Tityrus, should feed his
sheep fat, but sing a slender song." Now (for you will have many wanting to
sing your praises, Varus, and to compose poems of bitter war), I cultivate a
country Muse with my thin reed. I sing under orders. But if someone should
be enticed to read these things as well, the arbutes, Varus, and the whole
grove will sing you, you, you; nor is any page more welcome to Phoebus
than one with Varus's name at the top.)

The speaker of this poem, Tityrus, has been asked to compose a poem on
the military exploits of one Varus, who is identified as either Quintilius or
Alfenus Varus. Tityrus excuses himself on the grounds that Apollo of
Cynthus has advised him not to attempt that sort of thing. Now, Tityrus,
in keeping with the prevailing attitude of bucolic poetry, represents himself as a singer. This would be less striking if he did not also, as is well
known, paraphrase a passage in which Callimachus received a similar
injunction from Apollo Lycius, altering one important detail. Both
Callimachus and Tityrus recall an earlier attempt to compose poetry.
For Callimachus, the attempt in question seems to be his very first: he
specifies the moment "when he first put a writing tablet on his knees." For

Tityrus, it is not clear whether the occasion was his first; the really important point, however, is that he was not writing but singing. In fact, Tityrus alters Callimachus a second time, because Apollo Lycius advises Callimachus in metaphorical and material terms: his sacrificial offering is to be plump, but he is to keep his Muse slender. In Vergil, Apollo Cynthius tells Tityrus similarly to make his flock nice and fat, but to sing (*dicere*) a *deductum carmen*. For my purposes, *dicere* is the important word. Again, this is a remarkable alteration. Callimachus and his contemporaries, as Peter Bing and others have shown, embraced their role as writers and made the fact of writing along with its implications and symbolism an important part of their respective poetic identities. Now Vergil's Tityrus, alluding unmistakably to a foundational passage of Callimachus's literary credo, signally alters the poet's role from that of writer to that of singer. This is certainly unexpected. By the time of the triumviral period, when the eclogues were composed, the idea of poet as writer was not the novelty that it had seemed to be in Alexandria two hundred years before. And Catullus, who obviously knew his Callimachus, just a few years before the eclogues had represented himself primarily as a writer, too. Why does Vergil's Tityrus prefer to present himself as a singer instead?

I think we can answer this question. Although Catullus was a writer, we have seen that for him the material text was a locus of anxiety at least as much as of empowerment. Moreover, we have traced this anxiety to several moments in which the text becomes alienated from the poet as a piece of property. This nexus of ideas is put into play immediately in Catullus's dedication poem to the patron figure Cornelius Nepos. Vergil, too, represents Tityrus as negotiating with a patron. I infer from all this that, in Roman culture, one crucial and emblematic role played by the physical text was to supply the presentation copy that the poet presented to his patron in acknowledgment of the patron's social superiority. If this is right, then it makes sense for Vergil to have converted Callimachus's writing tablet into a song precisely in the context of a *recusatio*. For in this passage a poet says no to a patron. Or at least, he pretends to say no, ostensibly refusing to celebrate his military victories in heroic verse, but instead commemorating them gracefully and perhaps more effectively in bucolic verse. At any rate, I take it that Tityrus's representation of himself as a singer, and not as a writer, has something to do with his ability to refuse Varus's request. He can refuse to write for Varus because he must sing for Apollo. He has, we might say, a higher calling.

This higher calling clearly has something to do with the poet's own ambition and with his preferences. In this sense it resembles Catullus's song of mourning for his brother. If we turn now to Horace, we find that his odes corroborate this impression.

The first of the odes invites comparison with Catullus's dedication poem. What attracts attention in Horace's ode are factors such as the treatment of Maecenas, so much more prominent and hyperbolically complimentary

than Catullus's address to Nepos, and the elaborate priamel of occupations
that occupies the majority of the poem's lines. The important thing for our
purposes, though, is the very end of the poem, in which Horace speaks of his
ambition to join the canon of Greek lyric poets:

> Me doctarum hederae praemia frontium
> dis miscent superis, me gelidum nemus
> Nympharumque leues cum Satyris chori
> secernunt populo, si neque tibias
> Euterpe cohibet nec Polyhymnia
> Lesboum refugit tendere barbiton.
> Quod si me lyricis uatibus inseres,
> sublimi feriam sidera uertice.
> —*Carm.* 1.1.29–36

(An ivy crown, the reward of learned brows, places me among the
gods above, the cool grove and the nimble dancing of Nymphs with Satyrs
removes me from the crowd, if Euterpe does not withhold her pipes and
Polyhymnia refuse to offer the harp of Lesbos. But if you will insert me
among the lyric bards, I shall strike the stars with my towering head.)

Horace's language, as I have said elsewhere in another connection, is
extremely bookish and material.[29] *Quodsi me lyricis inseres uatibus/sublimi
feriam sidera uertice*. It is the word *inseres* that we must give its full weight.
Nisbet and Hubbard compare it to the Greek *egkrinein* and emphasize the
act of judgment by which Horace will gain inclusion within the lyric
canon. But the word is more straightforward than that. In fact, the English
derivative captures the basic sense nicely: "but if *you will insert* me among
the lyric poets, I will strike the stars with my towering head." What does
this mean? It is helpful to remember that the "you" in *inseres* is Maecenas,
and that we are to imagine Maecenas not just as the addressee of this poem
and the dedicatee of *Odes* 1–3 as a whole, but also, in this capacity, as the
recipient of a ceremonial presentation copy. Accordingly, Horace says in
this opening poem of the collection that he hopes Maecenas likes his gift
well enough to find it a place in his library next to the works of Sappho,
Alcaeus, and the other poets of the Greek lyric canon. The patron's act of
judgment is figured as the concrete act of storing the three *libelli* that make
up this corpus of lyric poems in the same *capsa* or *scrinium* in which he
keeps the Greek lyric poets.

So, as in Catullus, the physical presentation copy that Horace gives
his patron symbolizes their relationship in the economy of gift exchange;
at the same time, Horace makes clear the idea latent in Catullus that
whatever the patron does with the book has an important bearing on

---

29. For what follows cf. Farrell 2007, 188–92.

the poet's reputation. The relationship represented here is clearly asymmetrical, with the patron having a key advantage over the poet.

Horace develops this idea just a few poems later in *Odes* 1.6, in which he suggests that his friend Varius would be a much better choice to compose an epic on the exploits of M. Vipsanius Agrippa. *Scriberis Vario*, Horace tells Agrippa, "you will be written by Varius." This opening phrase has long provoked puzzled comment, directed mainly at *Vario*: the dative of agent would be a bit unusual, but an instrumental ablative almost insulting. What is seldom noticed is that the verb *scribere*, and indeed any word or image that points specifically to writing, is rare in the *Odes*. It occurs twice in this poem. This makes the ode a useful pendant to *Eclogue* 6—like it, a *recusatio*—in which, remember, Vergil *suppresses* the idea of writing that is so prominent in the Callimachean passage that he imitates. Here Horace, unusually in the *Odes*, introduces the idea of writing, but in connection with a different poet, Varius, and with a genre that is alien to Horace. He instead associates his own poetry and his chosen themes with vocal performance (*dicere* 5, *cantamus* 19).

To return briefly to Maecenas, a number of scholars have shown that, over the three books of odes, Horace's position vis à vis his patron changes decisively.[30] Whereas in the first poem Maecenas is superior to Horace in all respects, the poet gradually assumes a position of equality with the patron, and then at last even asserts his own superiority in some respects. The poet's self-esteem reaches its climax in the final two poems of book 3. Poem 3.30, famously, is a matching bookend to poem 1.1, the only other ode of this collection composed in the first Asclepiadian meter. It is, then, surprising to find Maecenas, in his last appearance, "demoted" from the final ode to the penultimate one, the opening of which (*Tyrrhena regum progenies*) clearly recalls that of the dedication ode. By relegating Maecenas to this inferior station, Horace reserves the place of honor to himself, and takes the opportunity to express pride in his achievement. The final poem declares that it will outlast all material monuments, precisely because it is immaterial: neither bronze, nor of stone like the pyramids, and thus impervious to the elements and to time, Horace will not die altogether, but will grow in posthumous praise, because his poetry will live in viva voce performance (*dicar* 10).

A lot more could be said, but I hope that this much makes clear a few basic points. First, in Catullus the image of the physical book is associated not only with permanence, but also with various possibilities for theft, corruption, destruction, ridicule, and oblivion. It is also associated with the alienation of the poet's work from his control, whether by theft, by public circulation, or by gift to a patron. Further, the patron's reception of a physical book in the form of a ceremonial presentation copy represents the all-important first stage of public reception, which conventionally and,

---

30. Zetzel 1982 and Santirocco 1984.

perhaps normally, in fact as well sets the tone for all future stages. For all these reasons, the image of the book serves as a magnet for the poet's anxiety about his immediate reception and posthumous reputation.

Against such images of the material book, Catullus presents himself only once as a singer; the subject of his song will be intensely personal, a lament for his dead brother; and significantly, on that occasion he imagines that his song will be eternal. Later in Vergil and then more clearly in Horace we find immaterial song opposed to material text in ways that suggest both the poet's assertion of independence from the demands of a patron and, in Horace, in ways that instantiate the poet's claim to immortality through his work. The oppositions between images of material and immaterial texts continue to inform the works of later poets, but investigation of these developments must await another occasion.

BIBLIOGRAPHY

Baehrens, A. 1885. *Catulli Veronensis Liber.* Leipzig.
Bing, Peter. 1988. *The Well-Read Muse: Present and Past in Callimachus and the Hellenistic Poets.* Hypomnemata 90. Göttingen.
Birt, Theodor. 1882. *Das antike Buchwesen in seinem Verhältniss zur Litteratur, mit Beiträgen zur Textgeschichte des Theokrit, Catull, Properz, und anderer Autoren.* Berlin, rpt. Aalen 1974.
Cairns, Francis. 1969. "Catullus 1." *Mnemosyne* 22: 153–8.
Crawford, Jane W. 1994. *M. Tullius Cicero, the Fragmentary Speeches.* 2nd ed. Atlanta.
Fantuzzi, Marco, and Richard Hunter. 2004. *Tradition and Innovation in Hellenistic Poetry.* Cambridge.
Farrell, Joseph. 1998. "Reading and Writing the *Heroides.*" HSPh 98: 307–38.
———. 1999. "The Ovidian *Corpus*: Poetic Body and Poetic Text." In P. R. Hardie, A. Barchiesi, S. E. Hinds, eds., *Ovidian Transformations: Essays on the Metamorphoses and its Reception.* Cambridge Philological Society, Supplement 23, 127–41. Cambridge.
———. 2004. "Ovid's Virgilian Career." *MD* 52: 41–55.
———. 2007. "Horace's Body, Horace's Books." In S. J. Heyworth, ed., *Classical Constructions: Papers in Memory of Don Fowler, Classicist and Epicurean,* 174–93. Oxford.
Fitzgerald, William. 1995. *Catullan Provocations: Lyric Poetry and the Drama of Position.* Berkeley.
———. 2000. *Slavery and the Roman Literary Imagination.* Cambridge.
Fordyce, C. J. 1961. *Catullus: A Commentary.* Oxford.
Gibson, B. J. 1995. "Catullus 1.5–7." *CQ* 45: 569–73.
Gratwick, A. S. 2002. "*Vale Patrona Virgo*: The Text of Catullus 1.9." *CQ* 52: 305–20.
Kenyon, F. G. 1932. *Books and Readers in Ancient Greece and Rome.* Oxford.
Marinone, N. 1997. *Berenice da Callimaco a Catullo: testo critico, traduzione e commento.* 2nd ed. Bologna.
McCarthy, Kathleen. 1998. "*Servitium amoris: Amor servitii.*" In S. Murnaghan and S. Joshel, eds., *Women and Slaves in Greco-Roman Culture,* 174–92. London.

Otto, August. 1971. *Die sprichwörter und sprichwörtlichen Redensarten der Römer.* Hildesheim.

Perry, B. E. 1936. *Studies in the Text History of the Life and Fables of Aesop.* Haverford, Penn.

Puglia, Enzo. 1991. *Il libro offeso: insetti carticoli e roditori nelle biblioteche antiche.* Napoli.

Quinn, Kenneth. 1972. *Catullus: An Interpretation.* New York.

Roman, Luke. 2001. "The Representation of Literary Materiality in Martial's *Epigrams.*" *JRS* 91: 113–45.

———. 2006. "A History of Lost Tablets." *ClAnt* 25: 351–88.

Santirocco, Matthew. 1984. "The Maecenas Odes." *TAPhA* 114: 241–53.

Skinner, Marilyn B. 1992. *Catullus' Passer: The Arrangement of the Book of Polymetric Poems.* New York.

———. 2003. *Catullus in Verona: A Reading of the Elegiac Libellus, Poems 65–116.* Columbus.

Starr, Raymond J. 1987. "The Circulation of Literary Texts in the Roman World." *CQ* 37: 213–23.

White, Peter. 1978. "*Amicitia* and the Profession of Poetry in Early Imperial Rome." *JRS* 68: 74–92.

———. 1993. *Promised Verse: Poets in the Society of Augustan Rome.* Cambridge, Mass.

Wiseman, T. P. 1979. *Clio's Cosmetics.* Leicester.

———. 1985. *Catullus and his World: A Reappraisal.* Cambridge.

Zetzel, J. E. G. 1982. "The Poetics of Patronage in the Late First Century B.C." In B. K. Gold, ed., *Literary and Artistic Patronage in Ancient Rome,* 87–102. Austin.

9

Books and Reading Latin Poetry

Holt N. Parker

When Horace wrote,

> me Colchus et qui dissimulat metum
> Marsae cohortis Dacus et ultimi
>   noscent Geloni, me peritus
>   discet Hiber Rhodanique potor.

(The Colchian, and the Dacian who pretends not to be afraid of the Marsian cohort, and the Geloni at the end of the world will know me, the learnéd Spaniard will study me, and the drinker of the Rhône.)

he meant exactly what he wrote.[1]

THE ROMAN EXPERIENCE OF POETRY

> parve (nec invideo) sine me, liber, ibis in urbem,
>   ei mihi, quod domino non licet ire tuo!...
> vade, liber, verbisque meis loca grata saluta.
>   —Ovid, *Trist.* 1.1.1–2, 15

(Little book, without me—and I'm not jealous—you will go to Rome, alas, something your master's not allowed to do.... Go, book, greet with my words the places I long for.)

I am interested in how the Romans read and enjoyed poetry.[2] There is now a widely held consensus that for the poets of the Republican and

---

1. *Odes* 2.20.17–20. Nisbet and Hubbard 1978, 346–7: "*noscent* suggests less detailed study than *discet* ... *peritus*: the adjective goes further than *discet* and implies specialist knowledge." For *discet* "learn me in school," see Quinn 1980, 240.
2. This chapter focuses on Latin and poetry, primarily Republican and Augustan poetry, though some of the evidence adduced on this topic by me and others concerns prose or

Augustan periods, "The author's texts were intended primarily for a relatively small circle of hearers at recitations."[3] That is, they assume the audience was small, indeed intimate, and the medium of communication was oral and aural, an immediate "performance" of some sort to a literal "audience" of some sort. The poets, however, say that they wrote for people far away, both in space and in time. The writers therefore assumed that their audience was large, indeed potentially unlimited, and that the medium of communication was written, a text of some sort. These two ideas are at variance.

The doctrine that literature was intended for the ears is enshrined, for example, in the *Cambridge History of Classical Literature*:

> The literary life of Greece and Rome retained the characteristics of an oral culture. . . . Nearly all the books discussed in this history were written to be listened to. . . . In general it may be taken for granted that throughout antiquity books were written to be read aloud, and that even private reading often took on some of the characteristics of a modulated declamation. It might be said without undue exaggeration that a book of poetry or artistic prose was not simply a text in the modern sense but something like a score for public or private performance.[4]

The problem with this type of sweeping (and vastly influential) summation is that it unfortunately oversimplifies a more complex picture. As the evidence considered below and in other papers in this collection make clear, the Romans enjoyed poetry (and literature in general) in four basic ways, each with its own social parameters: in recitations, as entertainments at convivia, through professional lectors, and by private reading. The last has generally in the past received the greatest amount of attention. More recently, however, much important work has been done on the performance of Roman literature.

I am a bit concerned, however, that like Luther's drunken man on horseback, we may be in danger of slipping off the other side, and oddly enough losing sight of the role of books in the hands of individual readers. The recitations and other means of listening to literature were very important to the social life of the capital,[5] but what emerges from the

---

comes from later sources. The literary life of Cicero has been underutilized in this regard, with the exception of Rawson 1985, esp. 40–4. W. A. Johnson 2000, 625, has called for discussions of the vast topic of "reading" to be framed "within highly specific sociocultural contexts." He focuses on Greek literary prose texts (606) and rightly remarks that the "use of performative reading of certain types of texts may tell us little or nothing about how others handled these texts, or how the elite handled other types of texts" (625). See, too, Goldhill 1999, 118.

3. Holzberg 2001, 3: "Texte vom Autor zunächst für einen relativ kleinen Kreis von Zuhörern bei Rezitationen bestimmt waren."

4. Kenney 1982, 3, 12. The lumping together of Greece and Rome is symptomatic of an unnuanced approach.

5. How important they may have been outside Rome is a question for later.

many and detailed descriptions the Romans have left us of what William Johnson has called "reading events" (2000, 602) is a fairly clear picture showing that each of these other ways of enjoying literature was considered and presented as preparatory, ancillary, or supplementary to the main event, the unmarked case of private reading.

Each of these, it must be emphasized, was indeed a reading event. That is, each involved someone reading from a book. The first three merely use different types of mediation between the text and the audience in the strict sense. We do not find literature being performed from memory without a text in front of a reader. Indeed, one of the things that marks theatrical performance is not only the assumption of roles (pretending to be someone you are not), but precisely this absence of a visible text, and great pains were taken to distinguish the readers of texts from the actors of plays.

The purpose of this chapter is to reexamine this now widely accepted idea. It falls into four parts. The first analyzes in some detail the intellectual underpinnings of the idea that poets wrote primarily for performance. The second looks at some instances of the considerable evidence for solitary, private reading as the unmarked norm for how Romans experienced texts. The third examines the various occasions for public, communal readings of texts to see what they do, and do not, tell us about the Roman reading of literature. Finally, after this background, I turn to the questions that especially interest me: How did the poets themselves want their poetry to be experienced? Did they expect to be listened to or to be read? Did they write with listeners or with readers in mind? What does their poetry say about its own reception?

To state the conclusions at the beginning, I hope to show that the assumption that Rome can be considered an "oral" society in any meaningful sense because of certain types of vocal performance of certain types of literary texts in certain contexts (some rightly understood, some not) is mistaken. The testimony from Latin poets and other writers indicates quite clearly that poets intended their works to be read, by readers, in books. They wrote to tell us, quite explicitly, that they hoped to reach a readership larger than those who happened to be present at any particular performance, a readership extending through space and time, far beyond the confines of the city of Rome or the poet's own life.

I. THE STANDARD VIEW AND ITS UNDERPINNINGS

Some Recent Examples

First some quotes to illustrate the claims of this widespread view of how Roman literature circulated:

> Books were not the normal means by which the writer reached his audience.
>
> My argument is that . . . what makes the work known to the public is performance, not publication.

> The Romans even as late as the first century A.D. still felt that performance
> was the real thing and a written text ... was not in itself a substitute for
> performance.
>
> Romans were more accustomed to the sound than the sight of a literary text.
>
> In the Augustan age it seems clear that the written text continued to be felt
> as no more than the basis for a performance.[6]

This view of the primacy of performance leads to an odd conclusion:

> The "Aeneid" is in a sense an anachronism, a literary dinosaur even in its
> own day: its carefully planned plot-structure, its detailed craftsmanship,
> made it incompatible with performance, and there was no other way
> in which the poem could reach a large audience.[7]

Any theory that makes Vergil out of touch with the basis of successful
poetry probably needs to be looked at again.

This common view has not been without its critics: "For the student of
the Golden Age of Latin poetry, the reading of books is a particularly
important subject. It is commonly misrepresented, through romantic
preconceptions about oral culture."[8] However, such objections have
been largely overlooked in favor of the handbook formulation. Recent
examples might include such flat statements as the following:

> Many of the nineteenth- and twentieth-century readers of Roman elegy
> have read these poems [elegies] as if they were ancient versions of Romantic
> male confessions ... This approach ignores the conditions of poetic com-
> position, presentation, and response which prevailed in the late republic
> and early empire and which presuppose a dramatic, communal performance
> and response. Roman elegy and drama share more than themes, characters,
> situations, and vocabulary. Although works in these genres were recorded in

6. Quinn 1982, 82, 83 n. 23, 90, 91, and 145. I quote liberally from Quinn 1982 as not
only the most detailed treatment but also as the most influential (directly or indirectly).
Many studies however simply take the "orality" of Rome as a given. Examples will be cited
below. Cavallo, Fedeli, and Giardina 1993, and Cavallo 1999 are largely derivative. Quinn's
seminal essay tends toward imaginative reconstruction (e.g., 85, 149) and is oddly self-
contradictory. So contrast the last statement with (142): "In the Augustan age [which seems
to include Cinna's Zmyrna (Cat. 95)] the poet thinks of himself as a writer rather than a
performer." Fantham 1996, 38 (cf. 42, 214) shows similar formulations: "So we should
imagine the cultured book-lover listening to more often than perusing his texts"; however,
she rightly emphasizes the role of the book in transmitting literature outside of Rome (10).
7. Quinn 1982, 144. The contradictions of the purported chronology of orality are never
resolved. Roman literature was first oral (like Greece); then written (down to Catullus, with
some overlap into the Augustans); then oral (with the rise of the recitation), when apparently Romans forgot how to read books, leaving poor Vergil a whale beached on the sands of
time; and then written again (84–9). Part of the problem in many discussions is a confusion
between what has survived and what was there: thus, early Rome is thought to be all drama
(Plautus and Terence) and so labeled "oral."
8. Hutchinson 1984, 100, citing Kenney, above. So, too, Morgan 2001, 81, who, though
he believes that the Romans normally read aloud, writes, "The Roman upper classes who
were the core audience for this poetry ... still had an essentially bookish culture rather than a
performative one."

writing, they were produced for, and experienced primarily in, oral delivery
and performance—a format that much more accurately renders all the
dimensions of elegy than does silent reading. Every elegist composed with
the expectation that his poems would be performed in dramatic readings.
Tibullus, Propertius, Ovid, and Sulpicia could not have conceived of
the private, internalized forms of reading practiced by nineteenth- and
twentieth-century readers.[9]

A recent series of articles and a book has presented a picture of Catullus as
a performer of "dinner party recitals" in search of "upward mobility" and
"self-promotion":[10]

> The basic assumptions that Catullus' poetry is consciously composed for
> readers and that his texts were first disseminated, individually or collect-
> ively, in written form underlie almost all contemporary studies of the poet.

The author is sympathetic to those who have been misled by the "apparently straightforward evidence" of Cat. 1, 14b, 16, 32, 35, 36, 65, 68, and
116, "among others":

> It is not hard to understand, then, why such beliefs persist, even in the face
> of new investigative approaches that treat all Greco-Roman poetry as
> fundamentally oral and performative in nature.[11]

These common assertions rest on three interrelated presuppositions
that need to be questioned in turn. The first, and by far the most influential, is the persistent belief that the Romans regularly read aloud, or
perhaps *could* only read aloud.[12] The second is the idea that the practice
of reading aloud somehow made Rome an "oral," "oligoliterate," or "per-

---

9. Gamel 1998, 79–80, drawing on Quinn 1982, 81–3.

10. Skinner 1993, 62, 63. The belief that poetry had to be performed here mixes with
what I find to be a misunderstanding of Catullus's social world and an imposition of a
"patron" to "client" relationship.

11. Skinner 1993, 61; again note the lumping together of Greece and Rome. How 1, 14b,
16, 32, 35, 36, 65, 68, and 116 ought to be understood is not explained, and this approach
seems to privilege "new investigative approaches" over Catullus's own words. Cf. Skinner
2001, in which the proper interpretation of the poems turns on "stance, tone, gesture," "facial
expression" (58), "a sweeping gesture" (63), "body language" (66; see also 71). Both articles
are at odds with another set of studies, in which Skinner looks for complex patterning in
Catullus's poetry books and assumes that the interpretation of certain poems depends upon
their place in the collections. See Skinner 1981, and 2003: poems 69–92 need a "sequential
reading" (2003, 107–9), but Cat. 67 (dialogue with the door) depends on the audience
being able to see that the Catullus standing before them is a tall redhead (67.46–48). How
then could such a site-specific, audience-specific piece of performance art have ever been
published?

12. For example, *Brill's New Pauly* (2: 726–27 = *Der Neue Pauly* 2: 815), "Book: Private
and public reading" ("Lesen und Vorlesen") simply conflates the two: "In antiquity, the most
common way to read a book was to read it out aloud, which, particularly in public readings,
made it necessary for the reader to adapt his voice in intonation and modulation to the
specific character and rhythm of his text. A good reading was almost like the interpretation

formative" culture, although exactly how and exactly what is meant by these terms are never clearly stated.[13] Here we need a working definition of an "oral" culture. The third is a somewhat understandable reaction to generations of scholars who simply assumed that the ancients read exactly like we do. The impact of oral theory on the study of Greek literature has been enormous, and one effect has been a desire to try to find ways to apply the Greek model to Rome.[14] This has led in turn to a desire to exoticize ancient reading, to make the ancients as different from us as they can. The focus tends to be exclusively on the ways that the Romans experienced literature other than our supposed norm of private/silent reading. Three features in particular are singled out: the use of *lectores*, the institution of the *recitatio*, and the practice of readings as communal entertainment. These are examined below. This focus is combined with an exaggerated notion of what these different ways of experiencing literature might actually mean for cultures both ancient and modern.

Eyes and Ears

The first factor is the most fundamental, the most pervasive, the most persistent, and yet the most easily discredited. Knox, more than thirty-five years ago, showed that a reader reading alone, silently to himself, was unremarkable in the ancient world.[15] There is no need to repeat here the overwhelming evidence, and William A. Johnson's recent "Towards a Sociology of Reading in Classical Antiquity" (2000) traces the history of these persistent weeds and uproots them more thoroughly than ever before.[16]

of a musical score." So, too, Blanck 1992, 71, still relying on the same old proof text of Augustine's supposed wonder at Ambrose's silent reading (*Conf.* 6.3); n. 29, below.

13. "Oligoliterate": a nonce formation by Goody and Watt 1968, 36, "suggesting the restriction of literacy to a relatively small proportion of the total population," describing Egyptian, Sumerian, and (less accurately) Chinese societies with complex writing systems that required a trained priesthood or elite. This term has been misapplied to Rome by Barton 2001, 71 n. 189, and others. Note that the decision to label Rome as an oral society is curiously based entirely on the role of reading and literature.

14. The desire may not be confined to modern scholars. Joseph Farrell, at the Semple Symposium that was the origin of this volume, pointed out that part of the reason for Cato's stories of ancient *carmina*, which so influenced Macaulay, may have been a desire to create for themselves a heroic literary antiquity comparable to the Greeks (Cic. *Brut.* 71–75; cf. Varro, *De Vita Populi Romani*, fr. 84 = Non. 56 M, prob. the same source). The passage shows a palpable need to compete with Homer and to push Roman literary history back before Livius Andronicus and Ennius. For the history and influence of these supposed "ballads," see Momigliano 1957, Williams 1982, 55. For more recent work, see Habinek 2005, 39, 43–4.

15. Knox 1968, 421–35. Note the attempts by Quinn 1982, 91 n. 58, Gamel 1998 (quoted above), and Cavallo 1999, 76, to wriggle out of this fact.

16. Johnson 2000 has reviewed the arguments of Gavrilov 1997, Burnyeat 1997, and others. See also Busch 2002. Some discussions in New Testament studies may be less familiar to classicists: Achtemeier 1990, Slusser 1992; Gilliard 1993; Müller 1994, Burfeind 2002.

Although the view that the Romans were constrained to read aloud is untenable, it is, as the quotations above show, the most important foundation for the view that Roman literature had to be performed in order to exist.

The question I am interested in, however, is different. I am less concerned with *how* the Romans read, that is, whether they realized the words of the books before them silently, by moving their lips, muttering under their breath, reading aloud, or making the welkin ring. What I am concerned with (and by) is the now dominant view that because Romans sometimes read the words in front of them in an audible voice, it somehow follows that recitations and other forms of performance before a group were the usual or indeed the only way in which Romans experienced poetry.

There is still considerable confusion over what are three rather basic points. First, oral composition, oral communication, and oral transmission are three quite different things.[17]

Second, silent/aloud and private/public are two quite different contrasts, and none necessarily implies any other. One can read silently and privately (what we take to be the unmarked case). One can also read aloud and privately (rehearsing lines, memorizing or savoring a poem). One can read aloud and publicly (an academic lecture, an author's book tour), or silently and communally (everyone reading the same passage in a classroom or a church, a group of people looking up at a monumental inscription, the news crawl in Times Square, or movie subtitles).[18]

Third, most poetry—except parts of Ezra Pound—is better read aloud. That is, poetry has an *aural* element (sound patterning). This does not make it *oral* (properly understood and defined).[19] Further, the claim that all Greek and Roman poetry was intended for the ear is demonstrably false: there are poems intended only for the eye—acrostics, picture poems, and the like—from Nicander onward. Poems in the shape of eggs or wings, in which one has to read inward (first verse, then last, then second, then second to last, etc.), cannot be read aloud.[20]

---

17. See Finnegan 1977, 16–24; Gentili 1988, 4–5; Rosalind Thomas 1992, 6.

18. See the remarks of Chartier 1994, 17–18.

19. This is a common mistake. For example, Skinner 1993, 63, says rightly that some poems "cry out for oral delivery." But so do Lindsey's "The Congo," Noyes's "The Barrel Organ," and Fearing's "Dirge." Skinner 2001, 65, insists that in Cat. 10, "the dialogic quality of the narrative . . . indicates that the poem must have been composed for performance." But Frost's "The Death of the Hired Man," is more dialogic still.

20. See Habinek, ch. 6, in this volume. For Roman examples: "Q. ENNIUS FECIT" as an acrostic in a poem by Ennius (Cic. *Div.* 2.111); the first and last eight lines (with 1,056 in between) of *Ilias Latina* (Neronian or Julian) spelling out ITALICUS SCRIPSIT; a poem in the shape of wings by Laevius (22 FPL-Blänsdorf, imitating Simias, *AP* 15.24). See Lombardo 1989, Courtney 1990, Ernst 1991; OCD^3 s.v. "acrostic" (the promised article on "pattern poetry" will be found instead under "technopaignia").

What Do You Mean "Oral"?

The second presupposition is that Rome was an oral culture, at least in some sense. We first need to define the term. The differences between Rome and a predominantly oral culture such as archaic Greece can be shown in one important fact, which I have not seen mentioned in the various treatments of the oral performance of poetry at Rome. In an oral culture, X sings a poem to Y, *who in turn sings it to Z*. It is this last stage of oral *transmission* that marks an oral culture proper. So burning Sappho loved and sang, and later Solon heard his nephew singing one of her songs and asked the young man to sing it again so that he might learn it (Ael. ap. Stob. *Flor.* 3.29.58).

We can get a better idea of the differences between written and oral by examining with some suspicion the recurring and misleading metaphor of reading as the interpretation of a musical "score."[21] Those who maintain that for the Romans "performance was the real thing and a written text...was not in itself a substitute for performance" must necessarily maintain that for the Romans to read to themselves was a failed reading, a poor second best, that they read to themselves only when they could not get a better performer to read to them, as is the case with drama. If we are to continue with music as a metaphor, the only proper and obvious analogy is folk song.[22] Here it is important to realize that we are speaking about oral *circulation*. Did the audience (in the strict sense) for Roman poetry go to hear a performance, learn the song/poem by ear, and then go home with it in their memories, to perform it later for others?

It is clear that they did not. There is no example known to me of any person who performed a Latin poem or a speech before a second person, who in turn transmitted it orally it to a third.[23] Instead authors or other performers read from written texts to audiences, who, if they wished to experience that text again, obtained a written copy.[24] Because this point

21. Originating with Hendrickson 1929, 184 (Johnson, 2000, 597 n. 10), who, however, deploys the metaphor to indicate the wonder of the earliest listeners to the earliest readers; cf. Saenger 1982, 371. Quinn 1982, 91, defends the notion of a "score" against the text of a drama; repeated by Cavallo 1999, 73.

22. For a brilliant analysis of the intertwining of oral, manuscript, and print in even the oldest layer of English ballads, see Fox 2000, 1–10.

23. The two nearest cases I know are instructive. (a) One of the Elder Seneca's anecdotes of remarkable feats of memory that tells of a man (Greek or Roman is not specified) who heard a poem and recited it back to its author, who could not himself repeat it (*Cont.* 1. pref.19). (b) Horace *Sat.* 2.4, his witty parody of the *Phaedrus*, in which Catius is in a hurry to write down the rules of the gourmet lecture he's just heard—yet despite Catius's phenomenal memory (6–7) it's just not the same as being there (90–91). See below for Mart. 7.51, in which Pompeius who has memorized Martial's poetry still reads it to another fan out of books.

24. See the examples below. For the written text, which distinguishes a recitation from an oration, see Pliny 2.19.2; and Dupont 1997, 45; Markus 2000, 144, 152. The process is laid out by Starr 1987, esp. 213–16; Valette-Cagnac 1997, 111–69, esp. 140–7.

has been misunderstood so often, it may be necessary to repeat that performance is not the same as an oral culture. Though literature at Rome could be (but need not be) *presented* orally on occasion, literature at Rome did not *circulate* orally.[25] Rather, Roman authors explicitly directed their books to a group of men and women who could read them.[26]

Reading Aloud Now

> Don't you read or get read to?
>
> —Dickens, *Bleak House*, ch. 21

The third factor is an odd forgetfulness of the fact that the features that are held to have made Rome an "oral" or "performative" culture are not the exotic practices of a distant land and time but things we are all familiar with, both in how people read books in the recent past, and how we read them today. The evidence that is used to conclude that Rome was an oral society, that books were merely scores for performance and so on, is richly available for most of history without such overstatements being drawn. The Romans, in short, show the same mixture of private reading and shared reading that has been a feature of literate Europe from the Hellenistic Age through the Middles Ages to the Renaissance and to the present day. The practice of public reading does not indicate a lack of private reading, nor does private reading cancel out communal enjoyment.[27]

Let me offer three scenes from English literature to query the sorts of arguments being made for Rome.

> Goldsmith one day brought to THE CLUB a printed Ode, which he, with others, had been hearing read by its authour in a publick room at the rate of five shillings each for admission. One of the company having read it aloud,

---

25. For examples of quasi-oral composition, which always involved writing, see Horace's condemnatory picture of Lucilius, for what it's worth (*Sat.* 1.4.9–10, 1.10.59–61; Quinn 1982, 84–5, is somewhat credulous). For dictation, see Horsfall 1995, 51–2. Contrast Hor. *Sat.* 1.10.72: "saepe stilum vertas" and the picture of Vergil's method of composing the Georgics (*Vit. Don.* 22). For "circulation," see Starr 1987, Cavallo et al. 1993.

26. Two famous statements: Lucil. 592–5 Marx (Cic. *De orat.* 2.25): "Persium non curo legere, Laelium Decumum volo" ("I'm not interested in Persius reading me, I want Laelius to read me"); Hor. *Sat.* 1.10.72–90: "contentus paucis lectoribus" ("I'm content with a few readers").

27. For this mixture, see the sensible remarks of Chartier 1989, 103–20, and 1994, esp. 1–17 (both primarily on early modern France). See also Darnton 1990, esp. 165–7) and the revised version 2001, esp. 164–5 for his critique of Engelsing's proclamation of a *Leserevolution* c. 1750 (Engelsing 1969 and 1974). For English literary history, see the stimulating study by Fox 2000, esp. the opening essay, 1–50. Coleman 1996, in an effort to redress the balance for Chaucer, effectively ignores all private reading, and rules out at the beginning many possible counterexamples from her survey. Saenger 1982, frequently adduced by scholars in Early Modern Studies, believes that Latin was always written without word divisions, as do Fantham 1996, 37, and Gamel 1998, 81.

Dr. Johnson said, "Bolder words and more timorous meaning, I think never were brought together."
> —*Boswell: Life of Johnson*, ed. R. W. Chapman; 3. ed. corr.
> J. D. Fleeman (Oxford, 1970), 1074 (anno 1780)

"Mr. Martin, I suppose, is not a man of information beyond the line of his own business? He does not read?"

"Oh yes!—that is, no—I do not know—but I believe he has read a good deal—but not what you would think any thing of. He reads the Agricultural Reports, and some other books that lay in one of the window seats—but he reads all them to himself. But sometimes of an evening, before we went to cards, he would read something aloud out of the *Elegant Extracts*, very entertaining. And I know he has read the *Vicar of Wakefield*."
> —Jane Austen, *Emma* (1815), ch. 4

"For I aint, you must know," said Betty, "much of a hand at reading writing-hand, though I can read my Bible and most print. And I do love a news-paper. You mightn't think it, but Sloppy is a beautiful reader of a news-paper. He do the Police in different voices."
> —Charles Dickens, *Our Mutual Friend* (1865), bk. I, ch. 16

In Boswell, we have a *recitatio;* in Austen, reading aloud as a form of entertainment; in Dickens, a *lector.*

The problem is that, speaking broadly, scholars have tended to ignore the fact that reading aloud to others both publicly and privately has long been (and still is) a common activity.[28] It is incorrect to claim that the bad "printed ode" was "something like a score for public or private performance," though it was indeed performed both publicly and privately; that the *Elegant Extracts* were "felt as no more than the basis for a performance," though Mr. Martin gave a very entertaining performance; that reading a Victorian newspaper was "almost like the interpretation of a musical score," no matter how many voices he do the police in. The mistake comes in assuming that one of the ways in which a text could be used (recitation) was the only or primary way it could be used, and furthermore assuming that recitation represented the author's intention or expectation of the only way in which it could be used.

II. READING WITHOUT AN AUDIENCE

Alia vero audientis, alia legentis magis adiuvant.
(You get more out of some things by listening, others by reading.)
> —Quintilian 10.1.16

---

28. For a satiric scene from early-twentieth-century domestic life, see Virginia Woolf, *Night and Day* (1919), ch. 7. We today continue to enjoy books in a number of different ways, many of which correspond closely to Roman practices. It is curious that this mono-lithic view of what "we" mean by "reading" remains so popular in an age of public readings, book groups, radio broadcasts, audio CDs, and iPods.

Thanks to Valette-Cagnac, Dupont, Johnson, and others, a more balanced picture has emerged, and we can begin from two obvious facts. First, the Romans read to themselves; second, the Romans read to each other. Because the first fact oddly enough seems to be in danger of being forgotten or ignored, it needs to be pointed out that Romans did in fact read books while alone. We discover people reading all the time, with no need for, or mention of, company. I have chosen a few examples, out of potentially hundreds, in which the circumstances are sufficiently detailed to let us know that the reader had the book in his own hands and was reading by himself.[29] So, Cicero goes down to young Lucullus's villa to consult some books of Aristotle. There he bumps into Cato, who is sitting in the library, surrounded by piles of Stoic philosophers, reading all by himself.[30] In a later anecdote, Cato reads the *Phaedo* all alone just before he commits suicide. He does not read aloud to friends; he does not get a *lector* to read to him. He reads and rereads the book by himself inside his tent and then stabs himself.[31] Several jokes by Martial crucially depend on the social fact that people regularly read alone. In 3.68.11–12 after a warning to the *matrona* that the poems are now going to get a little blue:

Si bene te noui, longum iam lassa libellum
    ponebas, totum nunc studiosa leges.

29. Most examples of *legere* (and its derivatives) do not, of course, specify that the reader is alone, because reading alone is the unmarked case. Two examples. Sen. *Ep.* 46: Seneca has received a new book from Lucilius; he has read it himself and is going to reread it; the style and the effect are *as if* he had heard it: "De libro plura scribam cum illum retractavero; nunc parum mihi sedet iudicium, tamquam audierim illa, non legerim." Note the contrast between *legerim* and *audierim*. So, too, in the famous misunderstood anecdote about Ambrose *Conf.* 6.3: "cum quibus quando non erat, quod perexiguum temporis erat, aut corpus reficiebat necessariis sustentaculis aut lectione animum" ("When he was not with the crowds, which was only for the briefest of moments, he refreshed his body with the minimum of necessary food or his mind with reading"); that is, reading is *assumed* to be solitary. The marked case of reading aloud has its own proper term: *recitare*. See Valette-Cagnac 1997, 26–7, on etymology and semantics: "D'où l'emploi privilégié du verbe *legere* en contexte privé, pour désigner une lecture individuelle, solitaire."
    30. Cic. *Fin.* 3.7–10 (the setting for the third dialogue): "quo cum venissem, M. Catonem, quem ibi esse nescieram, vidi in bibliotheca sedentem multis circumfusum Stoicorum libris. erat enim, ut scis, in eo aviditas legendi, nec satiari poterat, quippe qui ne reprehensionem quidem vulgi inanem reformidans in ipsa curia soleret legere saepe, dum senatus cogeretur. . . . quo magis tum in summo otio maximaque copia quasi helluari libris, si hoc verbo in tam clara re utendum est, videbatur." ("When I got there, I saw M. Cato, . who I didn't know was there, sitting in the library surrounded by many books of the Stoics. His zeal for reading was so great, you know, and unsatisfiable, that disdaining the empty censure of the mob, he was accustomed to read even in the Curia while the senate was assembling. . . . All the more then, when at complete leisure and with such a supply, he seemed to be having a veritable orgy of books, if one can use such an expression of so important a matter.") Cf. Plut. *Cat. Min.* 19. The whole scene shows how common were reading, reading to oneself, and reading silently to oneself (Cicero does not mention hearing Cato vocalizing as he snuck up on him).
    31. Plut. *Cat. Min.* 68–70, App. *BC* 2.98–99, Dio 43.11.2–5.

(If I know you well, you were tired of this long book and about to put down it, but now you'll read the whole thing eagerly.)

The matrona is explicitly said to hold the book in her own hands; there is no *lector*. He follows it up with 3.86.1–2:

Ne legeres partem lasciui, casta, libelli,
    praedixi et monui: tu tamen, ecce, legis.

(I warned you not to read this part of my naughty book, O chaste lady, and yet here you are, reading it.)

He makes the same joke (and the same point) in 11.16.9–10:

Erubuit posuitque meum Lucretia librum,
    sed coram Bruto. Brute, recede: leget.

(Lucretia blushed and put down my book, but that was when Brutus was present. Go away, Brutus: she will read.)

No audience, no *lector*, only the matron alone with her dirty book in her own hands.[32]

A number of descriptions of the daily round mention the same thing: a quiet morning spent reading by oneself. Cicero describes how after the morning crowd recedes, he reads or writes, provided he is not holding office hours; then exercise.[33] Horace describes his modest life: sleep till ten, then in silence, all by himself (*tacitum*), he reads or writes; then exercise.[34] Seneca's ideal day is the same: bed, reading; then exercise.[35] On a less than ideal day, when he is sick, he progresses from reading to writing. He does both of these activities alone; only later do friends arrive.[36] Pliny imagines his own perfect day: reading, and writing, with

32. Cf. Ov. *Trist.* 2.243–80 on women and reading. For other examples in which the individual reader is explicitly said to hold the book in his/her hands, see Cat. 44.19, Hor. *Ep.* 1.19.34, *Ars* 446–9, Prop. 3.3.19–20, Pliny 9.22.2, cited below.

33. Cic. *Fam.* 9.20 (193 SB): "ubi salutatio defluxit, litteris me involvo; aut scribo aut lego. veniunt etiam qui me audiant quasi doctum hominem quia paullo sum quam ipsi doctior. inde corpori omne tempus datur." Reading is for time when one is alone.

34. *Sat.* 1.6.122–23: "ad quartam iaceo; post hanc vagor, aut ego lecto / aut scripto quod me tacitum iuvet, ungor olivo." That is, he reads or writes in bed or on his couch, cf. *Ep.* 2.1.112 (rightly Kiessling and Heinze 1958, 127; see n. 44, below). Morris 1968, 110–11: "I.e. he finds pleasure in his reading or writing, without needing any companion to express it to." Serafini 1966, 94: "fra me e me, in silenzio." Fedeli is driven to desperation when his presuppositions encounter the plain sense of the text (1994, II.2, 461): "*tacitum* si riferisce qui solo alla scrittura, considerato che la lettura avveniva ad alta voce."

35. Sen. *Ep.* 83.3: "totus inter stratum lectionemque divisus est; minimum exercitationi corporis datum."

36. Sen. *Ep.* 65.1: "Hesternum diem divisi cum mala valetudine... Itaque lectione primum temptavi animum; deinde, cum hanc recepisset, plus illi imperare ausus sum, immo permittere: aliquid scripsi... donec intervenerunt amici... In locum stili sermo successit."

no one to bother him; then exercise. He loves his villa precisely because he can read by himself.[37]

Not only did Romans read silently to themselves, they read silently to themselves *even when other people were present*.[38] So a famous anecdote:

> During a leisure moment, Caesar was reading one of the books about Alexander and became lost in thought for a long time, and then be began to cry. His friends were amazed and asked the reason: "Doesn't it seem to you worthy of grief that when Alexander was my age he had already ruled for so long, but I've never done anything remarkable?"[39]

Cato the Younger, as the other senators shuffled into the Curia, used to while away the time with a book, reading to himself.[40] Cicero and Trebatius read side by side in silence each with his own books at Tusculum.[41] Pliny read a volume of Livy to himself, sitting quietly beside his mother, while Vesuvius erupted on the horizon (6.20.5). Severus used to enjoy Martial's poetry so much that he took the books to parties and the theater.[42]

---

37. 1.9.4: "in Laurentino meo aut lego aliquid aut scribo aut etiam corpori vaco"; 1.22.11: "sollicitudine . . . qua liberatus Laurentinum meum, hoc est libellos et pugillares, studiosumque otium repetam"; 2.17.8: "Parieti eius in bibliothecae speciem armarium insertum est, quod non legendos libros sed lectitandos capit"; 8.9: "Olim non librum in manus, non stilum sumpsi, olim nescio quid sit otium quid quies." Cf. 1.3, 2.2, 2.8, 5.6, 6.20.2, 8.19 (using *studium, studeo*, or the like). So, too, for Bassus in retirement (4.23.1): "multum disputare, multum audire, multum lectitare"; *audire* here means "listen to philosophical conversation" rather than "listen to books being read"; see the discussion of the opposition by Valette-Cagnac 1997, 62–71.

38. As Gavrilov 1997, 63, points out, this is the point of the misused anecdote about Augustine finding Ambrose reading silently: "What puzzled Augustine is not Ambrose's method of reading [silently] in and of itself, but his resorting to that method *in the presence of his parishioners*" (his emphasis).

39. Plut. *Caesar* 11.5–6: σχολῆς οὔσης ἀναγινώσκοντά τι τῶν περὶ Ἀλεξάνδρου γεγραμμένων σφόδρα γενέσθαι πρὸς ἑαυτῷ πολὺν χρόνον, εἶτα καὶ δακρῦσαι· τῶν δὲ φίλων θαυμασάντων τὴν αἰτίαν εἰπεῖν· "οὐ δοκεῖ ὑμῖν ἄξιον εἶναι λύπης, εἰ τηλικοῦτος μὲν ὢν Ἀλέξανδρος ἤδη τοσούτων ἐβασίλευεν, ἐμοὶ δὲ λαμπρὸν οὐδὲν οὔπω πέπρακται;" The situation is clear: Caesar read silently to himself, while surrounded by friends, who noticed the tears but did not hear the text.

40. Cic. *Fin.* 3.7 (quoted above, n. 30); Plut. *Cat. Min.* 19.1; also Val. Max. 8.72, who specifies Greek books.

41. Cic. *Top.* 1.1.1: "Cum enim mecum in Tusculano esses et in bibliotheca separatim uterque nostrum ad suum studium libellos quos vellet evolveret, incidisti in Aristotelis Topica quaedam, quae sunt ab illo pluribus libris explicata. Qua inscriptione commotus continuo a me librorum eorum sententiam requisisti." ("When you were with me in the Tusculum villa, and each of us separately in the library for our own study were unrolling the books we wanted, you happened upon something called *Topics* by Aristotle, which had been explicated by him in several books. Intrigued by the title, you immediately asked me for the subject of the books"). The picture is clear: Cicero and Trebatius in the same room, reading their own books silently; then Trebatius breaks the silence to ask Cicero a question.

42. Mart. 2.6: "haec sunt, singula quae sinu ferebas/per conuiuia cuncta, per theatra"; the implication is that he read them there in preference to the regular entertainments or conversation on offer; cf. 7.76 for *conuiuia* and *theatra*. Nauta 2002, 93, interprets this

III. READING WITH AN AUDIENCE

> Sunt qui audiant, sunt qui legant.
> —Pliny 4.16.3

Lectores

One practice in particular has been used to exoticize the Romans and to claim for them the status of an oral culture, and that is the use of professional readers (*lectores*, *anagnostae*).[43] So for example, Pliny describes another ideal day, that of Spurinna (3.1):

> In the morning he keeps to his study couch,[44] at the second hour he calls for his shoes, walks three miles and exercises his mind no less than his body. If there are friends present, serious conversations are expounded; if not, a book is read, sometimes even when friends are present, but only if they do not mind. Then he sits down, and the book again or conversation in preference to the book....Having bathed, he lies down and postpones dinner for a while. Meanwhile he listens to someone reading something lighter and easier. During all this time, his friends are free to do the same or something else if they prefer.[45]

That is, Spurinna, like Horace, begins the day in solitary reading or writing. Later, in company, he enjoys listening to books, both serious and light. But as Sloppy and others show, having someone read to you while you do something else was (and is) a common practice, and hardly implies that the society in question was oral or performative in any meaningful sense.[46]

---

passage differently, as referring to friends who "re-use" the epigrams "at various types of social gatherings": "Of course the symposiast will not read the book in silence, but will recite it out loud to his drinking companions." The interpretation seems to depend on the idea that silent reading was impossible. Further, although this idea might work for the dinner party, it does not for the theater, unless Severus is supposed to be an actor reciting on stage.

43. The evidence is assembled in *RE* XII.1 (1924), 1115–6, and Starr 1991, who rightly remarks (337): "Roman society was not, of course, an 'oral' society in the sense in which anthropologists use the term. Roman literature is profoundly dependent on books and access to them by both writers and readers."

44. Not with the Loeb, "stays in bed." Sherwin-White 1985, 206: "Couch or sofa; he is not still under the blankets"; *OLD* s.v. *lectulus* C. "used for study"; see *RE* 23 (1924) 1101–3, and n. 47 below.

45. "Mane lectulo continetur, hora secunda calceos poscit, ambulat milia passuum tria nec minus animum quam corpus exercet. Si adsunt amici, honestissimi sermones explicantur; si non, liber legitur, interdum etiam praesentibus amicis, si tamen illi non gravantur. Deinde considit, et liber rursus aut sermo libro potior . . . Lotus accubat et paulisper cibum differt; interim audit legentem remissius aliquid et dulcius. Per hoc omne tempus liberum est amicis vel eadem facere vel alia si malint." See Johnson 2000, 621–2, for Spurinna's day. *Liber legitur* seems to be a set phrase; cf. Pliny 9.36.4 and n. 65 below.

46. Other modern literary examples of the house *lector* could include Marya Dmitrievna Akhrosimova's day in *War and Peace* (Bk. 8, Ch. 6), or Mademoiselle Bourienne, whose ambition extends beyond reading aloud to Nicholas Bolkonski.

Spurinna's use of a *lector* does not, of course, mean that he was unaccustomed to the sight of a book. Indeed, Pliny tells us that Spurinna spends the first hour of the day reading by himself.[47] Pliny's account allows us to see exactly what the *lector* was for. The *lector* fills in those periods when it would be inconvenient or impossible for the master to read by himself. Spurinna's *lector* reads to him while the master is trotting round the walking path, and during the rest break after the walk and the bath. This desire to improve the shining hour with literature marks Spurinna as a man of exceptional culture.[48]

The role of the *lector* has sometimes been misunderstood. The use of a *lector* was not in place of reading by oneself; it was in addition to reading by oneself. Pliny makes this point clear. He has an eye infection and is confined to bed in a dark room: "Here I'm abstaining not only from the pen but even from reading—with difficulty, but I'm doing it—and I'm studying with ears alone." In other words, Pliny considers solitary reading the norm; a *lector* is handy when he cannot read by himself.[49] The *lector* was part of the entertainment staff of great households, but the presence of a *lector* no more indicates that upper-class Romans were incapable/unwilling/unaccustomed (the exact claim is often not clear) to read for themselves than the presence of secretaries shows that they were incapable/unwilling/unaccustomed to write for themselves.[50]

Places for Hearing Poetry

Romans could both read poetry for themselves and have it read to them. The question now is which was more important. Did the people who

47. Rightly Westcott 1898, 174, "studies on his reading couch"; Sherwin-White 1985, 206: "So too Pliny who keeps to his room studying much longer than Spurinna, ix.36.2." Cf. Hor. *Sat.* 1.6.122–23, quoted above (n. 34). Later in the day, Spurinna retires to compose Greek and Latin poetry, which as Catullus and Ovid show, cannot be divorced from reading (see n. 105). The two are frequently conjoined under *studia* (see n. 37).

48. Pliny the Elder used the *lector* precisely to fill in all those moments when he could not read himself (cf. Pliny *Ep.* 3.5.8, 14); see Horsfall 1995, 52. What is "evidently unusual" (rightly Johnson 2000, 605) is his mania about wasting time.

49. 7.21.1: "hic non stilo modo verum etiam lectionibus difficulter sed abstineo, solisque auribus studeo." Rightly Nauta 2002, 137.

50. For the use of secretaries and readers, see Horsfall 1995. For *lectores* at dinner parties, see below. Further, in the effort to co-opt the presence of *lectores* to make Rome into an oral culture, there is a tendency on the part of some scholars to exaggerate the difficulties of reading a manuscript (e.g., Quinn 1982, 82, 91; Starr 1991, 343). In fact, everyone did quite well with manuscripts for thousands of years, and even today all of us routinely read letters scrawled in a wide variety of hands, without the need of "professional" readers. Nor does anyone comment on the lack of professional readers among the Greeks, who did without word divisions, or the Semites, who did without vowels. In short, unless one is prepared to claim that Cicero, for example, wasn't "much of a hand at reading writing-hand," and found the task of making out a book written in his native language simply too difficult to undertake without the assistance of trained slaves, it is best to drop this particular line of argument.

knew Horace and other poets come to know them *primarily* through listening or through reading? That is, did Roman poetry circulate orally? As we have seen, it did not.

At first glance the question about the relative importance of reading or being read to seems difficult to answer, a matter of unrecoverable percentages of reading to oneself versus attending recitations perhaps. However, a clear answer emerges once we examine more closely and critically the actual role of reading aloud in the production and circulation of Latin poetry. We need to be more precise about the circumstances in which Romans heard verse read to them.

Most previous discussions distinguished two areas: staged public performance by professionals, people other than the author; and formal readings by the poet, that is, *recitationes* proper.[51] Besides these more formal venues, Johnson has recently and rightly turned our attention to a third area, that of private, intimate entertainments, dinner parties and the like, as a site for the performance of poetry.[52]

We have only a few uncertain instances of the first type of performance. The anecdotes about Vergil are clearly treated as exceptions due to his enormous success.[53] The vagueness of the tales does not allow us to know whether these performances were staged readings of Vergil's text or mimes based on Vergilian matters.[54] Ovid said that his own poems were

51. Quinn 1982, 146. Precise definitions by Pennacini 1993, 254, and Dupont 1997, 46 n. 5.

52. Johnson 2000. Quinn (1982, 146–7, 154) adds two other venues, by creating a type of formal poetic competition in the Temple of the Muses on the basis of Hor. *Sat.* 1.10.37–39, and makes a distinction between large and small recitations based on misreading of Hor. *Ep.* 1.19.41–42 (150, 154; Horace is merely saying he does not write plays for the theatre; see Quinn's own remarks: 1982, 146, 147, 155; and nn. 144, 145 below).

53. The only solid evidence is Tac. *Dial.* 13: "populus, qui auditis in theatro Virgilii versibus surrexit universus et forte praesentem spectantemque Virgilium veneratus est sic quasi Augustum"; this seems to refer to Vergil's verses inserted into some theatrical piece rather than a reading as such. *Vit. Don.* 26: "Bucolica eo successu edidit, ut in scena quoque per cantores crebro pronuntiarentur," the *quoque* making it clear that public recitation on stage was unusual. The only other piece of evidence is so dubious that even Servius (*E.* 6.11) guarded it about with many a "dicitur": "It is said that the line was recited by Vergil to great acclaim, so much so that later when Cytheris (who was ultimately called Lycoris) sang (cantasset) it in the theater, Cicero was amazed and asked whose it was. Later when he finally saw him, he is said to have said (to his own praise and that of Vergil), 'O second hope of great Rome,' which Vergil later transferred to Ascanius (*Aen.* 12.168). So the commentators say." Any modern scholar capable of believing this farrago (Cicero in the theater with Cytheris, Cicero having to ask who the author of the *Eclogues* might be, Cicero bursting out with a particularly useful half-line) will believe anything. See Quinn's discussion 1982, 152–4.

54. Bell 1999 chooses the *Aeneid* as proof that "the public performance of poetry enabled its dissemination to audiences that did not necessarily possess a wealth of inter-textual knowledge acquired from libraries and the mellifluous lips of slaves" (264). For him, "although there is no certainty that this incident ever happened, the anecdote offers a good reminder that some excerpts of Vergilian verse could be made accessible to an audience simply through performance" (266–7). Apparently *ben trovato* is preferable to *vero*.

"danced" publicly, and his language points to adaptation rather than recital.[55] Whatever form these stage shows may have taken, they are far from showing the primacy of performance over text. Instead, the staging of poetry by people other than the author could only have occurred after there was an independently circulating, written text.[56] Further, the fact that a book (nearly any book) is capable of being read aloud or adapted for the stage is not in itself significant. Cervantes has furnished ballets; T. S. Eliot has been turned into a musical; Joyce has been turned into films. Despite the fact (if it is a fact) that the *Eclogues* were put on stage, they remain a book, intended for readers. Vergil says so (Ecl. 3.84–85):

> Pollio amat nostram, quamuis est rustica, Musam:
> Pierides, uitulam *lectori* pascite uestro.

> ("Pollio loves my Muse, though she is rustic.
>   Pierides, feed up a calf for your *reader*.")

Recitationes

The second venue, the recitation, is the most familiar.[57] That a work could become known—in the first instance, in any case—by the poet reading aloud to a limited audience (in the strict sense) is not at issue.[58] Famous occasions include Vergil reading the completed *Georgics* to Augustus and parts of books 2, 4, and 6 of the *Aeneid* to the imperial family.[59] One of Vergil's recitations was the occasion for someone in

---

55. *Tr.* 2.519–20: "Et mea sunt populo saltata poemata saepe / saepe oculos etiam detinuere tuos [Augustus]"; 5.7.25–28: "Carmina quod pleno saltari nostra theatro, / uersibus et plaudi scribis, amice, meis, / nil equidem feci (tu scis hoc ipse) theatris, / Musa nec in plausus ambitiosa mea est." For later incidents, Suet. *Nero* 54: Nero threatened that "proditurum se . . . histrionem saltaturumque Vergili Turnum" ("he would exhibit himself as an actor and dance Vergil's Turnus"). Macr. 5.17.5 points to adaptation for mime or the like (actors along with painters and sculptors all use Dido). See White 1993, 53, for a list of incidents; however, Pliny 7.4.9 and Hor. *Sat.* 1.10.17–19 (contrast *legit* in the previous line) do not indicate staged performance; see Markus 2000 on the meaning of *cantare*.

56. *Vit. Don.* 26: *edidit* (quoted above, n. 53); cf. Dupont 1997, 46 n. 5.

57. Pliny 8.21 for a detailed description of the purpose and physical setting. This two-day affair is carefully distinguished from dinner entertainment: "et in triclinio . . . positis ante lectos cathedris amicos collocavi." See Roller 1998, esp. 90–3.

58. For two excellent surveys, see Salles 1994, 93–110, and Dupont 1997. The fullest set of data is still Funaioli 1914 (*RE* I A 435–46). In exceptional circumstances the poet, though present, could rely on someone else to read for him, if he did not feel up to the task. So Vergil is said to have asked Maecenas to take over (*Vit. Don.* 27); and Pliny (9.34) thinks about using a stand-in (see n. 62).

59. *Vit. Don.* 27, 32, Serv. *A.* 4.323, 6.861; cf. Serv. *Ecl.* 6.11. All marked as hearsay in the sources (*fertur, dicitur, constat*). A famous anecdote has been consistently misunderstood (*Vit. Don.* 29): "Seneca reported that Julius Montanus the poet used to say that he'd steal Vergil's verses, if he could steal his voice (*vocem*), facial expression (*os*), and way of

the audience to cap "Nudus ara, sere nudus..." with "habebis frigore febrem."[60] Macer, Horace, and Propertius, among others read their verses to audiences that included the young Ovid (*Trist.* 4.10.44–50, *Vit. Hor.*).

Even here, however, the notion of "performance" needs to be interrogated. Elaborate precautions were taken to avoid tainting the poet-performer with the *infamia* of the actor.[61] The reciter was always seated; he always had a text open before him; he did not use his hands; he avoided facial expressions.[62] The poet must not be mistaken for an actor.

Convivia

About readings at private functions we are oddly ill-informed. That books could be read aloud as dinner entertainment is clear from several sources.[63] Atticus employed a *lector* for the task.[64] Pliny says that at his small dinners the choices are a reader, a lyre player, or a comedy troupe;

performing (*hypocrisin*), for the verses sounded good when Vergil recited them, but the same ones were empty and mute without him." This is so obviously a case of sour grapes (who exactly found or finds Vergil's verses *inanes mutosque?*), that I am surprised anyone takes it seriously. If Vergil's success depended on his personal appearances, it is difficult to explain the stage shows, much less the survival of the author's work after his death. Juvenal says quite the opposite about the performance of Vergil's verses (11.182): "quid refert, tales versus qua voce legantur?" Quinn is so dominated by the idea of the recitation that he can ask (1982, 93): "How many people in the generation after Vergil's death ever attained what one could call a working knowledge of the poem?" Thousands upon thousands would be a good answer. Vergil became an instant classic. If Ovid (*Am.* 1.15.25–26: "Tityrus et segetes Aeneiaque arma *legentur*, / Roma triumphati dum caput orbis erit") won't do for the "generation after," perhaps one might glance at Q. Caelius Epirota, who began lecturing (*praelegere*: Suet. *Gram.* 16) on Vergil almost immediately, or at the elder Seneca: Vergil is already providing taglines (*Con.* 7.1.27, 7.5.9, *Suas.* 3.7, 4.4–5: all *Aen.*); learned men argue about his style (*Suas.* 1.12, 2.20), and show a knowledge of his prose works [!] (*Con.* 3 pr. 8). Quotations in the younger Seneca are too numerous to list.

60. *Vit. Don.* 43; *G.* 1.299; cf. Serv. ad loc. and ad *Ecl.* 6.11. Not "the waggish pen of some anonymous parodist" (Thomas 1988, ad loc.). Also not proof of "the high sophistication of the literary public" (Morgan 2001, 81), even if the story is true.

61. Dupont 1997, 46–7; Markus 2000, 140–4.

62. Pliny 2.19.1–4. Pliny 9.34 has been misunderstood. Pliny is wondering whether to use a *lector* to deliver his next recitation: "Ipse nescio, quid illo legente interim faciam, sedeam defixus et mutus et similis otioso an, ut quidam, quae pronuntiabit, murmure oculis manu prosequar?" ("I don't know what I am to do while he is reciting. Should I sit there fixed and mute and like someone at leisure, or as some do, should I accompany what he is going to say with murmur, eyes, hand?") The actions are not those of the reciter (how could he speak *and* accompany his own words with a murmur?), but of certain audience members, the equivalent of those who beat time to the music during concerts.

63. Hor. *Ep.* 2.1.109–10 *dictant* refers to dictation (composition) rather than recitation: Brink 1982, 3: 147–50; cf. what seems to be the situation at Mart. 9.89.

64. Nepos *Att.* 14: "Nemo in convivio eius aliud acroama audivit quam anagnosten; quod nos quidem iucundissimum arbitramur: neque umquam sine aliqua lectione apud eum cenatum est, ut non minus animo quam ventre convivae delectarentur." See below, on Cic. *Att.* 16.2, 16.3.

sometimes only the book at dinner, with the music and comedy later.[65] His uncle also had books read at dinner.[66] Martial as host says he will *not* read a thick book (*crassum volumen*) at his modest party (5.78.25). Only Seneca mentions a genre, the philosophy of Quintus Sextius, but there seems to be a prejudice toward the philosophical and the "useful."[67]

Poetry might, of course, be read aloud at banquets, but it is curious how little we hear of it. Cicero and the republican and Augustan poets write about many parties but they never once write about poetry being performed at parties.[68] Later poets and prose authors are quite clear that poetry was occasionally read aloud during dinners,[69] but the general

65. 1.15.2: "Audisses comoedos vel lectorem vel lyristen vel—quae mea liberalitas—omnes." 9.36.4: "Cenanti mihi, si cum uxore vel paucis, liber legitur; post cenam comoedia aut lyristes." Cf. 9.17.3 (cited below).

66. 3.5.12: "super hanc [mensam] liber legebatur": clearly prose.

67. Sen. *Ep*. 64.2: "lectus est liber." So Varro (*Men. Sat.* 340 Astbury = Gell. 13.11.5): "In convivio legi non omnia debent, sed ea potissimum, quae simul sint βιωφελῆ et delectent"; for this use of βιωφελής, cf. Sex. Emp. *Adv. Math.* 1.296 (on the uselessness of poets and grammar). Spurinna's choices for morning readings also seem to have been on the didactic side, though the afternoon readings are "remissius aliquid et dulcius"; see Johnson 2000, 621–2. Quinn maintains, 1982, 83, n. 23: "In the case of a literary work (as opposed, e.g., to a didactic work), what makes the work known to the public is performance, not publication." In fact we have more examples of "didactic" works being read aloud in social settings than "literary" works. The distinction, however, is special pleading to eliminate the fact that no one can imagine any social setting in which the 142 books of Livy were read aloud. For didactic works, Macer read about snakes to Ovid (*Trist*. 4.10.43); Calpurnius Piso gave a recitation of his *Catasterismi* (Pliny 5.17).

68. Cicero enjoys parties but never mentions any readings at them apart from the single instance of his own *De Gloria* (see below); the pleasures are those of conversation, for example, *Fam*. 9.24.2–3 (362 SB), 9.26 (197 SB, the famous dinner with Cytheris), *Att.* 2.14.1 (34 SB, dinner with Clodia), 2.18 (38 SB), 9.1.3 (167 SB), 13.52 (353 SB: a huge dinner party for Caesar: "σπουδαῖον οὐδὲν in sermone, φιλόλογα multa": not then the recitation of poetry, but literary conversation, with the assumption that guests had already read poetry); cf. *Off*. 1.144: reciting your upcoming court speech is not appropriate for parties.

69. The best evidence is Pers. 1.30–40 (and even here the goal is to leave behind a book: 40–43); Juv. 11.179–82 (*Iliad* and *Aeneid* rather than Spanish dancing girls at Juvenal's modest dinners); Mart. 3.44.15, 3.45, 3.50 (the bad poet Ligurinus who recites *everywhere*), 4.8.7–12 (Martial's books suitable for Caesar's dinners), 5.16.9, 7.51 (quoted below), 7.97, 10.20 (a book for Pliny), 11.52 (two friends alone: Martial won't recite but Cerealis may); Gell. 2.22.1–2: "Apud mensam Favorini in convivio familiari legi solitum erat aut vetus carmen melici poetae aut historia partim Graecae linguae, alias Latinae. Legebatur ergo ibi tunc in carmine Latino 'Iapyx' [of a wind in Hor. *Odes* 1.3.4, 3.27.20, Verg. *A.* 8.710]." Note that even here Latin poetry does not seem to feature prominently and is missing from the initial list. Further evidence might be the musical settings of Pliny's poetry (4.19.4, 7.4.9), and Statius's (*Silv.* 3.5.65), but no specifics are given as to where these were performed. Julianus recites from memory several early Latin love poems (Gell. 19.9), but this again is part of dinner conversation, meant to triumph over some snooty Greeks, not entertain them (see n. 94).

There are also the parodies of dinner entertainments at Trimalchio's: Trimalchio composes (pretends to improvise?) three verses with the aid of *codicilli* and recites from memory verses he claims are by Publilius Syrus (Petr. *Sat.* 55). He also reads aloud from a Latin book during the Greek performance by the *Homeristae*. Habinnas's slave declaims in a

impression left by the sources is that poetry, even in the houses of the learned, played little part in entertainment and took second place to dramatic and musical performances.[70]

Performance at banquets and the like must be sharply distinguished from the upper-class social ritual of the *recitatio*. It is clear that the job of reading as entertainment was given over to professionals who were slaves or freedmen, while the host and guests remained reclining at table. Neither host nor guest stood up and "performed" at parties.[71] Here, of course, we must distinguish between formal performance of texts as dinner entertainment and the informal exchange of poetry between learned persons, in other words, poetry as part of the conversation and φιλόλογα that Cicero praises.[72] So Martial makes it clear that it is bad manners for a host to subject his guests to his verses, much less compel a guest to perform.[73]

The popular picture of poets "singing for their supper"—more or less literally—is backed by no evidence. The reasons for this are not far to seek. Just as the Romans took elaborate precautions to separate the noble reciter from the ignoble actor, so they avoided any hint of acting for another's pleasure. Such a role would have been an insult to any freeborn man and runs the danger of tainting him with the *infamia* of the stage.[74] It would rank him with the *comoedi*, *lyristes*, and *lector* whom Pliny actually employs to entertain his guests, and only a step above the *scurrae*, *cinaedi*, and *moriones*, whom he decries in others.[75]

singsong style (*canora voce*) a farrago of Vergil and Atellane farce. For commentary see Horsfall 1989; Courtney 2001, 106–7. Some examples occasionally cited (for example, by Mayor 1872, I, 173–82, in his massive note on Juv. 3.9) are not germane. Hor. *Odes* 3.11.6, a hymn to Mercury, cannot be used as a description of Roman daily life. Mart. 4.82: nothing about other people being present and everything points to private reading. Mart. 11.52: see above. Stat. *Silv.* 2.1.117–19: a talented dead favorite boy. *AP* 9.141: philologists wrangling over dinner.

70. So Augustus (Suet. *Aug.* 74): "et aut acroamata et histriones aut etiam triviales ex circo ludios interponebat ac frequentius aretalogos." His *lectores* were to read him to sleep (78). Cf. Pliny 6.31.13: Trajan's modest dinners include *acroamata*, but no mention of reading. Spurinna's *lector* is not part of a dinner entertainment; that slot is reserved for the performance of a comedy (Pliny 3.1.9). Nep. *Att.* 14 makes clear that readings were not the first thing that one thought of under the heading *acroamata*.

71. Starr 1991; cf. Plut. *Quest. Conv.* 7.8 (*Mor.* 711e–712f).

72. For example, Cat. 50; Mart. 2.71, 11.52; Gell. 19.9; Quint. 10.7.19. Again, Trimalchio provides the parodic limits.

73. Mart. 3.44.15, 3.45, 3.50, 9.89; n. 69 above. Ligurinus's recital is not "entertainment"; it is merely a failure of the poetic mutuality that ought to attend an intimate party; so, too, Mart. 1.63.

74. Tacitus makes clear the revulsion that Romans felt for the degradation of performance: *Ann.* 14.14–16, and esp. 14.20: Nero and senate force noble Romans to pollute themselves with the stage under the pretext of speeches and poems ("ut proceres Romani *specie orationum et carminum* scaena polluantur").

75. Pliny 1.15.2, 9.17.3: "Quam multi, cum lector aut lyristes aut comoedus inductus est, calceos poscunt." Not everyone appreciates readings.

Accordingly, nowhere in Catullus, Horace, Propertius, Tibullus, or Ovid do we find a single suggestion that the poets ever "performed" at their own or anyone else's *convivia*. They all issue numerous invitations to parties of various sorts, to friends of various standings (including their "patrons"), but never once do they say that they will perform.[76] They describe going to numerous parties, but never once suggest that their duties included performing there. Neither Persius nor Juvenal was reticent about the horrors of the literary life, but they never mention being forced to provide dinner-theater entertainment as one of them.[77] Martial, too, never shows a single case, and as Nauta rightly observes (2002, 96):

> Indeed, it must be doubted whether Martial ever held full-dress recitations. Whenever he boasts of his popularity as a poet, he refers not to his hearers but to his readers. There are only a few passages where he represents himself as reciting, and there the situation seems to be one informal social exchange rather than performance for large invited audiences: he always recites to one specified person, who sometimes reciprocates by reciting in turn.[78]

No guest is ever made to sing for his supper.[79]

The Role of Performance in the Circulation of Roman Poetry

Ubi sunt qui aiunt ζώσης φωνῆς?
(What nonsense that is about the living voice!)
—Cic. *Att.* 2.12.2 [30 Shackleton Bailey; his trans.]

---

76. For example, Cat. 10, 13; contrast the informal mutuality of poetic exchange in Cat. 50 and Martial (below). This is the point of Tacitus's picture of Nero attempting to force into existence dinner parties of poets (*Ann.* 14.16).

77. The poet in Persius 1.30–40 is dead and derives no benefit from the professional reader who performs his works (rightly Korfmacher 1933, 283). For Bramble (1974, 100–5) the poet is only "metaphorically dead." Juvenal 7 has the bad patron rent a lousy house for his poet client, but does not have him summon the poet to perform at his home.

78. Nauta goes on to say (96–7), "However, there is some evidence, both circumstantial and internal, that there was one social occasion at which Martial gave oral presentation of his poetry throughout his career. This occasion is the dinner party or symposium." However, he offers no evidence from Martial (his other examples are Greek and do not speak about a poet performing his own works), apart from the two passages in which Martial says he will *not* perform (5.78.25, 11.52.16). This leads to a weak and speculative conclusion: "If Martial's satiric epigrams were indeed performed at symposia, they would fulfil the same function (but on a higher level of sophistication) as the *scurrae, cinaedi, moriones*, mentioned by Pliny," showing exactly why Martial did not perform such tricks.

79. The nearest case is Tac. *Ann.* 14.48: Antistius, a praetor, recites verses against Nero when dining at house of Ostorius Scapula (*vulgavitque celebri convivio*). This is, however, not a "performance." The praetor is a guest, not the entertainment. In *Ann.* 3.49 read *iecerat*: Koestermann 1963, I: 512; cf. Furneaux 1896, I: 450.

When we look closely at what actually happened at these various types of performances, six very important facts emerge.

1. Not only did Romans not go to performances in order to hear poetry and pass it on to others in the manner of folk songs, it is quite clear that they did not learn, or expect to learn, any poetry there themselves. This can be illustrated by two telling anecdotes from Pliny. He writes to a friend after attending a three-day-long *recitatio* (4.27). From all of this he manages to remember a mere eight lines (all about him, and he is a trifle hazy about line 2). But when the poems are published in a book, he will send his friend a copy.[80] In another letter (3.21), he announces that Martial is dead. He recalls part of a poem (again about himself; Mart. 10.20.12–21): "You ask what are the verses that won my gratitude. I would refer you to the very book-roll, if I did not have some of them by heart. If you like these, *you can look up the rest in the book.*"[81]

A poem of Martial shows the same thing (2.6.1–10):

I nunc, edere me iube libellos.
Lectis uix tibi paginis duabus
spectas eschatocollion, Seuere,
et longas trahis oscitationes.
Haec sunt, quae relegente me solebas
rapta exscribere, sed Vitellianis;
haec sunt, singula quae sinu ferebas
per conuiuia cuncta, per theatra;
haec sunt aut meliora si qua nescis.

(Now go and tell me to publish my poetry books. You've only read two pages and you're already looking for the final sheet, Severus, and heaving up long sighs. But these are the very poems that, when I reread them to you, you grabbed and copied out and on Vitellian tablets. These are the ones you used to carry as individual poems in the fold of your toga to every dinner party to every theater. These are those poems or even better ones you don't know about.)

Martial's friend asked him to read his poems and called for encores at the time (*relegente*), but in order to enjoy them later Severus copied them out on special tablets and read them to himself.[82] Pliny and Martial make it clear. Poetry did not circulate orally. It circulated in books.

---

80. 4.27.5: "ad hunc gustum, totum *librum* repromitto, quem tibi, ut primum *publicaverit*, exhibebo."

81. 3.21.4: "Quaeris, qui sint versiculi, quibus gratiam rettuli? Remitterem te ad ipsum volumen, nisi quosdam tenerem; tu, si placuerint hi, ceteros in libro requires." Martial himself is explicit that these very verses arrived at Pliny's house in the form of a book (10.20).

82. Cf. 7.51, in which Pompeius Auctus has memorized and will recite Martial's verse. Note: (a) the usual way to learn about a poet's verse is to buy his books; (b) Pompeius has learned and memorized Martial, not by attending lectures, but by reading his books;

2. A recitation gave only the penultimate draft of a work in progress. Pliny, for example, is explicit about the role of books *after* the recitation: "And so, if any of those who were present [at my recitation] care to read these same things, he will understand that I have changed or eliminated some things, perhaps in keeping with his judgment, even though he said nothing to me."[83] The role of the recitation, says Pliny, is to get criticism from men of taste before releasing his book.[84] In numerous passages he makes plain a standard sequence of events: there is studying, then writing, followed by a shakedown recitation; after that, circulating drafts to friends, followed by correction, all of which culminates in a written, public book.[85] Again, the evidence is clear. The polished final thoughts of the poet circulated only in books.

3. The performances usually consisted only of bits and pieces of a full work. Cicero mentions reading aloud at dinner only a single time in his entire correspondence, and his description has important implications for understanding the way books were used for these entertainments. Cicero is sending Atticus a revised draft version of his *De Gloria*, which he describes in two letters.

> "De Gloria" misi tibi. custodies igitur, ut soles, sed notentur eclogae duae quas Salvius bonos auditores nactus in convivio dumtaxat legat. mihi valde placent, mallem tibi. (16.2.6 = 412 SB)

> ("I am sending you my 'On Glory.' You will keep it safe, as you always do,[86] but make sure to mark the two selections for Salvius to read, but only to kind listeners at a banquet. They please me enormously; I'd rather they pleased you.)

> sed tamen idem σύνταγμα misi ad te retractatius et quidem ἀρχέτυπον ipsum crebris locis inculcatum et refectum. hunc tu tralatum in macrocollum lege

(c) though he has the books he has read down cold, when it comes time to recite them to another, he turns back to the published text.

83. 5.3.10–11: "Atque adeo si cui forte eorum qui interfuerunt curae fuerit eadem illa legere, intelleget me quaedam aut commutasse aut praeterisse, fortasse etiam ex suo iudicio, quamvis ipse nihil dixerit mihi." Cf. Severus in Martial 2.6 discussed above.

84. Pliny 5.12, 7.17, 8.21: so, too, Ovid *Pont.* 2.4.13–18, 4.2.35–38. Cf. Cic. *Off.* 1.147. See Dupont 1997, Roller 1998, 290–8.

85. For example, 1.5.2: *recitaret et publicaret* (two distinct stages), 1.8, 2.5, 3.10, 3.13, 3.15 (Pliny has heard the poetry recited, but he cannot give a final judgment till he has read the book), 4.5, 4.7, 4.20, 5.3, 5.5 (Fannius was at work on a fourth volume, encouraged by how many people were reading the first three), 5.12, 5.17, 7.4 (his verses composed, recited to friends, written out, copied, then *read* by others and even set to music by Greeks), 7.17 (spelled out, step by step), 7.20, 8.3, 8.4, 8.7, 8.15, 8.19, 8.21, 9.1, 9.13, 9.18, 9.20, 9.26, 9.28, 9.34, 9.35, 9.38. Ovid's difficulties in exile show the same sequence (*Trist.* 3.14.37–52): first comes reading, then writing, then a trial recitation.

86. In other words, keep it from being made public, as Atticus had failed to do before (*Att.* 13.21a.1 = 327 SB); see Shackleton Bailey 1965–70, ad loc.

arcano convivis tuis sed, si me amas, hilaris et bene acceptis, ne in me stomachum erumpant cum sint tibi irati. (16.3.1 = 413 SB)

("I am sending you the same old treatise in a revised state, in fact the original, with things rewritten or stuck between the lines in numerous places. Once it is copied onto special sheets,[87] read it privately to your dinner guests, but, please, only when they are happy and well-fed, so they don't get angry at me, when they should be angry at you.")

Cicero still has not finished with the book, and he asks that Atticus have his slave Salvius read portions at a dinner party.[88] For this particular performance a clean copy is made of two selections on special large-size papyrus in order to make a reading script. In short, although it was always possible to create a performance copy from a book, not all books were intended as performance copies.[89]

Pliny makes clear that this sort of excerpting was standard. A friend's recitation consisted only of selections. Pliny will give detailed criticisms when he gets the chance to read the entire book.[90] After subjecting his friends to a two-day recitation of his own poetry, he claims:

The audience agreed on calling for this, despite the fact that others skip various things and claim credit for skipping, while I skip nothing and tell them that I am skipping nothing. I read everything so that I can correct everything, which those who read selections cannot do. Their way is more modest and maybe more respectful. Mine is more open and friendly.[91]

87. For the cubit-broad *macrocollum*, see Pliny *HN* 13.80, Cic. *Att.* 13.25.3 (333 SB); Johnson 1994.

88. That Cicero further refined the text is clear from the fact that this version seems to be a single volume work, whereas the published *De gloria* was in two volumes (*Off.* 2.31). See Shackleton Bailey 1965–70, ad loc. For Salvius, see also Cic. *Att.* 9.7.1 (174 SB), 13.44.3 (336 SB). This reading seems to be envisioned less an entertainment than as a further tryout *recitatio* (though *in absentia*) before a critical (but not too critical) audience.

89. Johnson 2000, 616, also uses the metaphor of scripts: "Bookrolls were not, in gross terms, conceptualized as static repositories of information (or of pleasure) but rather as vehicles for performative reading in high social contexts" and writes of "the conceptualization of the bookroll as a performance script." Though I agree with his observations, I will venture to disagree with this particular formulation. This is certainly *one* of the ways and *one* of the settings in which a bookroll could be read. But, as Johnson notes (600–6, 618), reading aloud among friends was not the only way in which a text could be enjoyed, and literature was, of course, read in contexts other than the "high social."

90. 3.15: "Videor autem iam nunc posse rescribere esse opus pulchrum nec supprimendum, quantum aestimare licuit *ex iis quae me praesente recitasti* . . . Igitur non temere iam nunc de universitate pronuntio, de partibus experiar *legendo*."

91. 8.21.4: "Hoc assensus audientium exegit; et tamen ut alii transeunt quaedam imputantque quod transeant, sic ego nihil praetereo atque etiam non praeterire me dico. Lego enim omnia ut omnia emendem, quod contingere non potest electa recitantibus." For *electa*, cf. 3.5.17, and 4.14.6 (of written texts). The full paragraph shows how close Pliny's situation is to Cicero's. Cf. also Pliny 9.27, an interrupted reading, cited below.

We are faced with an unmistakable fact. Recitations and private readings could be counted on to supply only fragments of a poet's work.[92]

4. There seem to be no recorded instances of a restaging of a recitation. Pliny, for example, goes to many such but each one is for a single author, for a single work, for a single time. Poets never seem to present the same work (or same section of a work) twice in a series of recitations. A recitation is a strictly one-off performance.

5. There are no recorded instances of a public recitation of the ancient Greek poets.[93] We do, however, hear of a few occasions on which Greek poetry was performed at Roman banquets by professional entertainers.[94]

6. There was no Dead Poets Society. Living authors read their own works, but there seem to have been almost no opportunities for hearing the poetry of any previous generation.[95] One of the few examples deserves to be examined closely because it has been misused. Quinn (1982, 91) claims that books were read only by "professionals," that everyone else got their poetry by listening to others read (publicly or privately), and that "those who were not in some way professionals probably consulted a text only to clear up a particular point, or to get a better impression of a work which they had heard performed." The following incident is cited as proof.

92. As indeed they would have to. It is difficult to imagine (and more to the point, there are no records of) a twelve-day recital for the *Aeneid* at a book a day, fifteen days for the *Metamorphoses*, or an eighteen-day marathon for Ennius's *Annales*.
93. Contrast Cicero's contemporary, Philodemus; Cic. *Pis.* 70–71: "multa a multis et lecta et audita"; that is, both studied (*lecta*) and lectured on (*audita*).
94. Plut. *Mor.* 622c, 711b, Gell. 19.9.1–5, all mention Anacreon and Sappho, and Gellius adds other more recent erotic elegies; Gell. 2.22.1–2: "vetus carmen melici poetae." An example of bad behavior: Sen. *Ep.* 27.5–8, Calvisius Sabinus, the ignorant freedman, who has eleven slaves, nine assigned to memorize each of the lyric poets plus two more for Homer and Hesiod. He occasionally exhibits them to the annoyance of his guests. Luc. *Adv. Indoc.* should be compared throughout.
95. Suet. *Gram.* 2.3 mentions two activities of the early grammarians who followed Crates of Mallos: making commentaries, and popularizing through recitation: "ut carmina parum adhuc divulgata vel defunctorum amicorum vel si quorum aliorum probassent, diligentius retractarent ac legendo commentandoque etiam ceteris nota facerent" ("They carefully went over poems that had not yet circulated widely either of dead friends or others of whom they approved, and by reading and commenting they made them known to others"). As an example of reading to an audience, Suetonius mentions only "ut postea Q. Vargunteius *Annales* Ennii, quos certis diebus in magna frequentia pronuntiabat" ("Q. Vargunteius read aloud the *Annales* of Ennius on fixed days to a large audience"). Even here, note that for Suetonius the grammarians' activities center on a written text: "ut C. Octavius Lampadio Naevii Punicum bellum, quod uno volumine et continenti scriptura expositum divisit in septem libros... ut Laelius Archelaus Vettiasque Philocomus Lucilii saturas familiaris sui, quas legisse se apud Archelaum Pompeius Lenaeus, apud Philocomum Valerius Cato praedicant." The product was also a written text: Suet. *Gramm.* 8 (M. Pompilus Andronicus on Ennius), 14 (Curtius Nicias on Lucilius), 18 (Crassicius on Cinna), 24 (Probus on the early poets). See Kaster 1995, 60, 63–7.

Gellius (18.5) tells of an occasion in his youth when Antonius Julianus heard that a professional reader (*anagnostes*), who preferred to be called by the neologism *Ennianista*, was reading aloud in a theater.[96] They listen and have a lively debate to prove that Ennius wrote the word *eques* not *equus*. Afterward Julianus goes and consults a very old and expensive edition to verify the reading.[97]

There are three things to notice, each of which has been misunderstood. First, Gellius shows that such an occurrence was not common. Someone trying to create a Latin version of a *Homerista* by doing shows of Ennius was a novelty act.[98] Second, these were not people getting to know Ennius through an oral performance. These were people who have already read and studied a classic text with professional teachers.[99] Third, what was rare about Julianus's action was not the act of consulting a text, for people in Gellius read and compare published texts all the time.[100] What was rare is the antiquity of the volume consulted. Quinn's "professionals" are simply the educated population of the Latin-speaking world.[101]

The Role of Books in the Circulation of Roman Poetry

Tolle, lege, tolle, lege.

—Augustine, *Confessions* 8.29

96. 18.5: "Atque ibi tunc Iuliano nuntiatur anagnosten quendam, non indoctum hominem, voce admodum scita et canora Ennii annales legere ad populum in theatro. 'Eamus' inquit 'auditum nescio quem istum Ennianistam': hoc enim se ille nomine appellari volebat. Quem cum iam inter ingentes clamores legentem invenissemus—legebat autem librum ex annalibus Ennii septimum—hos eum primum versus perperam pronuntiantem audivimus."

97. Cicero does the same; he does not summon an *Ennianista* to recite to him; he reads the books (*Orat.* 48: "antiqui...libri"). Gellius is disappointed to discover that Julianus seems to have cribbed his whole show of erudition from old commentaries on the passage. Again, commentaries are for texts, not oral performances.

98. Rightly pointed out by Starr 1989. Ennius is also read aloud on the occasion of a public holiday (Gell. 16.10.1).

99. 18.5.7: "Cumque aliquot eorum, qui aderant, 'quadrupes ecus' apud suum quisque grammaticum *legisse* se dicerent..."

100. For example, texts of Cato (2.14.1, 10.13.3), Claudius Quadrigarius (9.14), Catullus (6.20.6), Cicero (1.7.1, 1.16.15), Fabius Pictor (5.4.1), Sallust (9.14.26, 20.6.14), and Vergil (1.21.2, 9.14.7).

101. There is a certain circularity of argument: anyone who reads a book is a professional; therefore only professionals read books. The very distinction between "professionals" and others is tendentious and anachronistic. In what sense are the literary miscellanies, showing profound reading, listed by Gellius (praef. 6–7) of Pliny the Elder, Masurius Sabinus, Alfenus Varus, Suetonius, not to mention Pollio, Varro, or Gellius himself, the work of "professionals"?

The picture we are given of Roman poetry (and literature in general), therefore, is very curious. It is a poetry rich in intertextuality, one that relies on a profound knowledge of previous Greek and Latin literature, but there seem to be no opportunities to hear that literature, which we are told is the only way most people encounter it.

On the contrary, the Latin poets themselves are very clear about how they came to know the great body of Greek and Latin poetry. They read it in books.[102] Horace read Lucilius.[103] Horace read the authors of Old Comedy.[104] Catullus 68.33 ought to be decisive: I can't write, he says, *nam, quod scriptorum non magna est copia apud me*, "because I don't have a large number of books with me." Catullus is paralyzed; his library is back in Rome and he only brought a single box of books. The very creation of poetry depends on reading literature in books.[105]

If we now ask our question in a slightly more emphatic form—Did the people who knew (not knew of, but really knew) Roman poetry come to know it primarily through listening or through reading?—there is a clear answer. If you wanted to hear poetry *once*, there were plenty of opportunities (too many, said Pliny).[106] Making an initial acquaintance of a poet at a recitation was easy. However, if you wanted to enjoy the same poem *twice*, you had to resort to the written text. Even in the case of private gatherings, anyone who had the text read to him, should he wish to reexperience the reading, got hold of the text. He did not ask the host to restage the reading.

The six observations made above entail six important conclusions about the role of books.

(1) If you wanted to learn, memorize, or even merely reexperience a poem, you studied the book.
(2) If you wanted to know the poem in the final form that its author intended, you bought the book.
(3) If you wanted to experience the complete work, you had to get the book.
(4) If you wanted to hear that strain *again*, there was only one possibility, and that was reading the book.
(5) If you wanted to know the poetry of Callimachus, or any other Greek, you went and found the book.
(6) If you wanted to know the poetry of Martial, or any other dead poet, you had to hunt for the book.

102. Even the Emperor Augustus himself, though fond of reciting his works to friends and reading improving works to the Senate (Suet. *Aug.* 85), reads Greek and Latin literature with his own hands (89: "In *evolvendis* utriusque linguae auctoribus").
103. *Sat.* 1.10.56: "nosmet Lucili scripta *legentis*."
104. Unlike Hermogenes (*Sat.* 1.10.18): "Illi, scripta quibus comoedia prisca viris est, / hoc stabant, hoc sunt imitandi; quos neque pulcher / Hermogenes umquam *legit*."
105. So, too, Ov. *Trist.* 3.14.35–37, 5.12.53.
106. *Epist.* 1.13.

In short, performance was a lousy way of getting to know literature. Pliny has read the poetry of Cicero, Calvus, Pollio, Messala, Hortensius, Brutus, Sulla, Catulus, Scaevola, Sulpicius, Varro, various Torquati, Memius, Lentulus, Seneca, and Verginius Rufus, not to mention those non-senators, Accius, Ennius, Vergil, and Nepos; he has no idea if they gave recitations or not.[107] "Nearly all the books discussed in this history were written to be listened to," says the handbook.[108] Cicero says the exact opposite: "One can derive much greater pleasure from reading lyric poetry than hearing it."[109] Going to a recitation was not a substitute for reading. It was a (sometimes tedious and socially obligatory) prelude to reading. Listening to someone else recite a book at a dinner party was not a substitute for reading. It was a (mostly pleasant) entertainment for the highly literate who already loved and read books. Pliny praises a youth for being *litteratus*, "well-read."[110] Neither Pliny, nor anyone else, praises someone as cultured because he attended a lot of recitations or went to a lot of dinner parties.[111]

Dupont rightly labels the recitation "An event of little consequence."[112] Of little consequence, but not completely unimportant. It is merely that their import has been generally misunderstood. The public reading of verse had only a very limited role in the *circulation* of literary texts. Instead, it was part of the process of the *production* of Roman poetry. Performance was not a substitute for the publication of the written text; it was merely one possible (and far from mandatory) precursor to it.[113]

Mime offers an instructive contrast. We read a great deal about the circulating *texts* of poets, the older playwrights, orators, historians, and prose writers of various sorts. We read nothing about the circulating texts of the mimes, despite their staggering popularity. This is because the mime genuinely was "a score for public or private performance."[114]

---

107. Pliny 5.3.5–7.

108. Kenney 1982, 3.

109. *Tusc.* 5.116: "et si cantus eos forte delectant, primum cogitare debent, ante quam hi sint inventi, multos beate vixisse sapientis, deinde multo maiorem percipi posse legendis iis quam audiendis voluptatem." The remark is the more telling because Cicero is not writing to inform us about Roman modes of reading; this is an offhand remark to show that deafness is not that bad. Contrast Quint. 11.3.4 on the ability of actors to make even great verse better and mediocre verse seem great.

110. 6.26.1: "ipse studiosus litteratus etiam disertus."

111. This is the whole point of Lucian's satire on the ignorant book collector. Quintilian never mentions attending parties or recitations as a source of learning; he does, however, mention reading books.

112. Dupont 1997, 48.

113. See Fantham 1996, 16, 64, 218; Starr 1987, 213–14; Valette-Cagnac 1997, 116–39 (though she does label recitations "indispensable"); Dupont 1997, 48. Hor. *Ars* imagines both an author reading his lines to a critic (438: *recitares*) and a critic marking up a book of those lines (445–50); the budding author (385–90) is to write (*scripseris*), let qualified judges hear his work, then put the written text (*membranis*) away for nine years before publishing it (*edideris*).

114. Kenney 1982, 12.

Once performed, its life was over. That is one of the reasons we do not have any texts of Roman mimes, except precisely for the "literary" mimes of Liberius and Syrius.[115]

The Romans read aloud to each other. That is not in dispute. However, as the examples from English literary culture make clear, reading aloud does not take the place of other forms of reading. No one is (or at least should be) arguing that the *only* books were the luxury display items ridiculed by Catullus, Seneca, and Lucian;[116] that books could be brought out only at recitations or parties; that any time Romans wanted to read poetry they had to hire a hall or invite friends over for dinner.[117] In sum, even as Cicero did not owe his detailed knowledge of Latin drama solely to attending plays,[118] so the occasional performance of poems on the stage, at recitations, and parties was not the vehicle for the circulation of Latin verse, and cannot account for the detailed knowledge of previous Greek and Latin poetry that educated Romans evinced and that the understanding of contemporary Latin poetry demanded.[119]

I want to draw attention away from the figure that currently seems to fascinate us—the performer—to the book he held in his hand. What happened to a book of poetry once it reached the *ultimos Britannos*—read silently or aloud to oneself, read aloud by a professional *lector*, read aloud to a small group of friends, read aloud to a vast crowd—is not as important as the fact that it had first to reach Britain.[120] And it did not get there through the medium of wandering bards, nor by repetitions from memory

115. Again, a comparison with modern society may be illuminating. It is easy to buy a novel, a book of poetry, even many plays. However, only a very few movie scripts (generally classics) are published, primarily to be studied by professionals. This is because movies *are* meant only for performance.

116. Cat. 22, Sen. *Tranq.* 9.4–7, Luc. 31 (*Adv. Indoc.* "The Ignorant Book-Collector"). As Johnson shows (2000, 614–15), one of Lucian's complaints is precisely that the man treats reading (reading aloud at banquets) solely as an occasion for showing off and does not read the texts by himself with any understanding (2, 3, 18, 20, 28). Cf. Seneca's story about Calvisius Sabinus (*Ep.* 27.5–8).

117. Though certain scholarly formulations seem headed in this direction.

118. Wright 1931, 31–79; *Brut.* 71: The plays of Livius Andronicus are not worth *rereading.*

119. Thus the *Homeristae* can "stage" Homer, yet no one asserts that such performances can account for the detailed knowledge of all forty-eight books of Homer evidenced by Roman writers (see *RE Suppl.* 3 [1918], 1158). Equally, the tasteless vogue at Rome (decried by Plut. *Mor.* 711c) for turning some of Plato's dialogues into little plays was not the way in which most Romans learned Plato.

120. See Fantham 1996, 10; Starr 1987, 213–16. Milesian tales are carried in the baggage of the Romans killed at Carrhae in 53 B.C. (Plut. *Crass.* 32); Gallus's elegies are in Egypt by round 20 B.C. For literature at the ends of the world: Vergil (*Aen.* 9.473) is at Vindolanda (Tab. Vindol. II.118); Catullus might have been copied, too (Tab. Vindol. II.119); *libros* in a fragmentary context (Tab. Vindol. II.333). See Bowman 1994, 91–2; Bowman at al. 1994, 65–8, 315: "There is no reason to doubt the availability of books." By the first century Vergil is in Egypt and atop Masada: Gallazzi 1982; Cotton and Geiger 1989, 31–5 (no. 721); Bowman 1994, 92; Bowman et al. 1994, 66.

by people who happened to have been present at some distant *recitatio* or mime adaptation at Rome. It arrived in the form of a written text.[121]

A Textual Society

Literate Rome was a textual society. A few further examples from Pliny the Younger, so frequently trotted out as chief witness to the domination of the *recitatio* and the oral dissemination of literature, reveal how much.

- There are people waiting for Pliny's speeches, first to hear them and then to read them (4.16.3).
- It is not the case that the written text is considered a copy or record of the oral presentation. Pliny explicitly states that the opposite is true: the written text is the model and archetype for the speech as actually delivered.[122]
- Poetry is read out of books. If you take the elegies of Passenus Paulus (descendent of Propertius) in hand, you will read a polished work.[123]
- Poetry exists in books, which an individual reader picks up; parts can be memorized after the book is read.[124]
- Pliny will gather his hendecasyllables into a book, which he will label and send to his friend (4.14); later the book is being read and copied, and *even* performed (*legitur, describitur, cantatur etiam*: 7.4.9). Notice the force of *etiam*: being read and being copied are the proofs of popularity; performance is an unexpected bonus.
- Pliny is proud his books are on sale in Lyon (9.11).
- A man in from the provinces has read Pliny out there (4.7).
- The Spaniard who came to Rome just to catch a glimpse of Livy came because a *text* of Livy had made it out to Cadiz (2.3).
- Pliny urges a poet to publish his works: recitations are all very well, and individual poems may circulate without the author's permission, but only publication will allow them to spread as far as the Roman language has spread.[125]

121. So, too, prose. Cic. *Sulla* 42–43: the testimony of the Catilinarian witnesses is copied and sent throughout the world ("Itaque dico locum in orbe terrarum esse nullum, quo in loco populi Romani nomen sit, quin eodem perscriptum hoc indicium pervenerit"). Pliny *HN* 35.11: even so difficult a work as Varro's group of 700 portraits—a difficult work to read aloud—was distributed "in omnes terras." Pliny 4.7: Regulus recites a life of his son, then has a thousand (*mille*) copies transcribed and sent throughout Italy and the rest of the Empire with a request to have it read to the people there.
122. 1.20.9: "est enim oratio [the text] actionis [the delivered speech] exemplar et quasi ἀρχέτυπον.... sequitur ergo, ut actio sit absolutissima, quae maxime orationis similitudinem accipiat."
123. 9.22.2: "Si elegos eius *in manus sumpseris*, leges opus tersum molle iucundum, et plane in Properti domo scriptum." No lector, no audience; a reader with a book in his hands.
124. 3.21.4: "quaeris qui sint versiculi, quibus gratiam rettuli. remitterem te ad ipsum *volumen*, nisi quosdam tenerem. tu, si placuerint hi, ceteros in *libro* requires." Cf. 9.22.
125. 2.10.1: "hominem te patientem vel potius durum ac paene crudelem, qui tam insignes *libros* tam diu teneas! Quousque et tibi et nobis invidebis, tibi maxima laude, nobis

- Pliny writes to a friend about a comedy that he heard the poet recite. He does not write, "Come to Rome and hear it," or "I'll recite it to you the next time we meet," or "Have your lector read it to you," not even "This book will recreate for you the atmosphere of the original reading"; but simply "I'll force him to cough up a copy and send you the book to read, or rather to learn by heart; for I know once you pick it up you won't be able to put it down."[126]
- Pliny comments after the two-day recitation of the *Panegyric*: "Of course, I am well aware that I have recited for a few what I wrote for everyone."[127]
- Pliny writes, "I don't want to be praised when I recite, but when I'm read."[128] He could not be more explicit: the goal of literature is not a transitory recitation but the permanent text.

One short letter should be quoted more fully (9.27):

Quanta potestas, quanta dignitas, quanta maiestas, quantum denique numen sit historiae, cum frequenter alias tum proxime sensi. Recitauerat quidam uerissimum librum, partemque eius in alium diem reseruauerat. Ecce amici cuiusdam orantes obsecrantesque, ne reliqua recitaret. Tantus audiendi quae fecerint pudor, quibus nullus faciendi quae audire erubescunt. Et ille quidem praestitit quod rogabatur (sinebat fides); liber tamen ut factum ipsum manet manebit legeturque semper, tanto magis quia non statim. Incitantur enim homines ad noscenda quae differuntur.

("I have often been aware of how much power, dignity, majesty and even divinity there is in history, and just lately I have realized it again. A man had been reciting a very honest book and left part of it for another day. Up come the friends of so-and-so, begging and pleading him not to recite the rest. So great is the shame of hearing what they had done, though there was none at doing what they now blush to hear. And he did what they asked; his loyalty to the truth allowed it. *But the book, like their deeds, remains; it will remain and will be read forever.* All the more for not being read immediately; for what is withheld only makes people want to know it more.")[129]

voluptate? sine per ora hominum ferantur isdemque quibus lingua Romana spatiis pervagentur." The allusion in *per ora hominum* is to Ennius's supposed epitaph. Notice the way in which being "spoken" is a metaphor for an explicitly *textual* dissemination. 2.10.6: "Et de editione quidem interim, ut voles. recita saltem, quo magis libeat emittere." Cf. 9.1 on prose works.

126. 6.21.7: "In summa extorquebo ei *librum legendumque*, immo ediscendum mittam tibi; neque enim dubito futurum, ut non *deponas* si semel *sumpseris*." Again, a reader with the book in his hands as the norm.

127. 3.18.9: "memini quidem me non multis *recitasse* quod omnibus *scripsi*."

128. 7.17.7: "Nec uero ego dum *recito* laudari, sed dum *legor* cupio."

129. Cf. the anecdote in Sen. *Contr.* 10 praef. 8 on Labienus and his soon-to-be-burned books and Tacitus on the survival of Cordus's burned books (Ann. 4.35: *sed manserunt, occultati et editi*). This is not *Fahrenheit 451*: the way to stop a work circulating is to burn it and if it escapes destruction it is because *texts* have survived.

The evidence from Pliny and others is overwhelming: literature is, and is meant to be, disseminated in books.[130] Pliny in writing to his friend Suetonius makes it plain: "Allow me to see your name on the title; allow me to hear that the books of my dear Tranquillus are being copied out, read, and sold."[131] Not a word about performance. Martial in A.D. 101 assumes the book trade to be worldwide (12.2). His own books are doing quite nicely in Vienne (7.88), are being read in Britain (11.3), and carried throughout the Roman Empire (8.3.4–8).[132]

Thus, although any given work may have made its initial appearance before the public at a recitation in Rome, it owed its existence to books. This is true even of the most oral of all Latin literary arts, that of oratory.[133] When someone who had not been present at a trial wished to know what was said, he did not ask Cicero or any member of the original audience to rerecite the speech for him. He read the written text.[134] Even those who had been present but wanted to reexperience his oratory read the author's written text.[135] Much that was written was not recited; nothing was recited that was not written.[136]

---

130. White 1993, 59 and this volume. The poets are keen to have copies of their works in the public libraries of Rome: Hor. *Ep.* 2.1.214–18, 2.2.92–94; Ov. *Tr.* 3.1.59–72, *Pont.* 1.1.5–10; Mart.5.5, 12.2.78. Again, this is hard to reconcile with a society in which poetry is supposedly disseminated orally.

131. 5.10.3: "Patere me uidere titulum tuum, patere audire describi legi uenire uolumina Tranquilli mei." Harris 1989, 225–6, claims that Tac. *Dial.* 10.1–2 shows that "it is assumed to be the *recitatio*, not the book, which will make the man famous." However, the contrast in this rhetorical set piece is between the lasting effects of the orators' speeches (laws, convictions) and the evanescent effects of the poets'. Just a little later (*Dial.* 12.5), the argument is countered: "nec ullus Asinii aut Messallae *liber* tam inlustris est quam Medea Ovidii aut Varii Thyestes": speeches and plays are all in books. In fact, *Dial.* 10.3 shows that people are indeed coming in from Spain, Asia, and Gaul, and asking to see Saleius Bassus. The tragedy *Cato* that starts the *Dialogus* is a book (*librum* 3.1), soon to be published (*emitteres*).

132. Mart. 1.2: a special traveling edition is available for sale so you can take his books on a long journey. His books have traveled with the army to the Getae and Britain (11.3). Books normally are sent from Rome to Spain, not the other way round (12.2). Old Greek books for sale in Brundisium: Gell. 9.4.1. Romans circulated outside Rome; so did their books; see n. 120. See Salles 1994, 153–6; Nauta 2002, 91–141 (a detailed and nuanced review).

133. Even drama may have been more textual than we imagine. Like speeches, plays circulated in scripts; they were read as well as staged and restaged. So Ambivius Turpio says he worked *ne cum poeta scriptura evanesceret* (Ter. *Hec.* 13). For the textualization of Shakespeare, see Erne 2003.

134. *Att.* 1.13.5, with Cicero adding embellishments. See Fantham 1996, 8. Cf. Ov. *Pont.* 3.5.7.

135. So Cicero's young fans begging for his omnibus volume of consular speeches of 60 BC: *Att.* 2.1.3: "oratiunculas autem et quas postulas et pluris etiam mittam, quoniam quidem ea quae nos scribimus adulescentulorum studiis excitati te etiam delectant." Not that an author himself might not choose to reread his polished, written speech before an audience of especially tolerant friends, for example, Pliny 7.17.

136. Cf. Pliny 3.10.2: Pliny recites only part of a eulogy that he has written.

IV. MONUMENTUM AERE PERENNIUS

We can now finally turn to the poets. Here is what Catullus wrote in a book (36.1): "Annales Volusi cacata charta." Notice, not "a waste of an afternoon, having to listen to someone read it," not "displeasing to the ear," not "poorly performed," but "shitty *sheets*." Catullus read (not heard) the poets he then loved or hated. Calvus sends him a horrible book (*libellum*), in revenge Catullus will send him the full content of the bookshops (*librariorum ... scrina*) containing Caesus, Aquinus, Suffenus (14). "Aurelius and Furius had *read* the kiss poems (16.13, *legisti*). Of course; Catullus was a poet, and wrote to be read."[137] Suffenus writes bad books, which you, alas, must read (22). Caecilius's girlfriend has read the draft of his epic (35). Catullus read the speech of Sestius and so caught cold; he will never pick up another in his hands (*recepso*) (44).[138] Cinna's *Zmyrna* is now published (*edita*), and as a written book it will travel the entire world (95), a book so complex that it soon acquired a commentary by Crassicius Pansa (Suet. *Gramm.* 18). The writing of commentaries is impossible to reconcile with a supposed primacy of oral performance (see nn. 95, 107).

Going to recitations seems to play remarkably little part in the poets' literary life, though they write much about that part of their existence. Catullus, as Wiseman notes, never tells us of a single one. Though Horace is forced to go to some recitations out of duty (*Ep.* 2.2.67, 95, 105), and to give some himself (*Sat.* 1.4.73–74, *Ep.* 1.19.35–49, 2.1.214–17), they have no part in his ideal life in Rome (*Ep.* 2.2.2.67, 105). Instead he prefers to read (*Sat.* 1.6.122). Propertius reads a lot of poets (2.34.85–92); he goes to a lot of parties, but never mentions a recitation. Ovid heard the poets in his youth (*Trist.* 4.10.44–50), but writes about recitations mostly to say that he cannot give them in exile (*Trist.* 3.14.39–40, 4.1.89–90, 4.10.113, 5.12.53, *Pont.* 4.2.35–38). In short, though recitations undoubtedly occurred, they were of little interest to the poets who flourished around the turn of the millennium.

---

137. Wiseman 1985, 124, his emphasis. But so strong is the stranglehold of Quinn 1982 (cited in support of this statement), that on the same page he claims for Catullus, "What mattered artistically was the oral performance." These two statements are irreconcilable. Two pages later Wiseman is surprised to find that "Catullus has plenty to say about poetry, his own and that of his friends and enemies. It is striking that he never refers to public performance or an audience of listeners, but only to poems written down on writing tablets, to be read." Nor does Cicero refer to recitations of poetry (*Off.* 1.147 refers to public approval). One might get by with claiming that Catullus and Cicero were before the age of the recitation (see n. 7, on the chronological difficulties), appealing to the Elder Seneca's testimony (*Cont.* 4 praef. 2) that Pollio was the first to give recitations, which, however, is incorrect; see Dalzell 1955; Rawson 1985, 52.

138. See Quinn 1973, ad Cat. 44.12 on *legi*.

We can now answer our question: Did the republican and Augustan poets write with readers or listeners in mind? The evidence is overwhelming. Because Rome was not an oral culture, and because literature did not get passed down by oral transmission in unbroken succession from generation to generation or place to place, all claims to poetic immortality or worldwide fame must rest on the existence of written, physically enduring texts. That books—not performances—were the medium through which all poets make themselves known to the world is the unmistakable testimony of Catullus (14, 22, 95), Horace (*Sat.* 1.10.72–74; *Ars* 6, 372–73, 386–90), Propertius (2.34.87–90: *scripta Catulli . . . pagina Calvi*), and Ovid (*Am.* 1.15.25–30).[139]

Let us turn to the poets' own works. Quinn claims, "He [the poet] refers to his audience sometimes as his 'readers' (*lectores*) and sometimes as his 'listeners' (*auditores*)."[140] In fact, the republican and Augustan poets never use *auditor* of the audience of their finished verse.[141] The poets never speak of people "listening" to their books. There is not a single example of Catullus, Horace, Propertius, Tibullus, or Ovid writing of the reception of their poetry: "When you hear my lines . . . As you sit listening to my poetry . . . When you next attend a party and someone recites my poetry to you . . . ."[142] Instead they write, again and again, about their readers.

139. Starr 1987, 223, seems to imply that publication was something new on the scene: "Authors in Pliny's time may have wanted to reach further beyond the narrow circles of their own friends and their friends' friends. It would be misleading to think of this as an increase in authors' ambitions, because this might seem to imply that earlier writers were men of modest ambitions. Rather, the change may have represented a somewhat broader conception of the potential audience for a literary work"; so, too, Fantham 1996, 64, dating the change to the Augustan poetry book. However, the broadest possible conception of the potential audience had been present in Roman literature since its beginning. Ennius hoped for (*Annales* 1.12 Skutsch) and achieved (Lucr. 1.119) fame throughout Italy; Lucretius hoped for an *aeternum leporem* on his words (1.28); Catullus modestly hoped his book would last for more than one generation, whereas Horace and Ovid looked forward to the entire civilized and yet to be civilized world as their readership.

140. Quinn 1982, 87.

141. The word *auditor* is used exactly five times by the Augustan poets (never by Catullus or Lucretius): once in Ovid *Pont.* 4.2.35 of the kind of trial recitations before friends that he cannot now stage in exile; four times in Horace: *Sat.* 1.10.7, of the mimes of Liberius contrasted with polished poetry; *Ars* 100 and 149 of the theater (see esp. 112–3, and n. 144 below). In Hor. *Ep.* 1.19.39, *auditor* has nothing to do with recitations; see n. 145 below.

142. Even the few places in which they do use *audio* or the idea of "listening" are revealing. Catullus and Tibullus never write of "hearing" poetry, their own or others', only reading and writing. Horace asks people to "listen" only when picturing himself as a singing bard (*Odes* 3.25.4, 4.2.45) or within the fictive conversational setting of the *Sermones*, and the fiction of a fiction of conversation in *Epistles* (*Ep.* 1.14.31, 1.17.16; cf. *Ars* 153), and these are always when Horace is delivering a moral "lecture." Being listened to is not for lyric poetry but for the theater (*Ep.* 2.1.187, *Ars* 100, 149, 153, 180, etc.; n. 145). Propertius uses "listening" twice, once in the fiction of conversation (1.1.37–38); the other instance is telling: Prop. 2.13.11–12, a reading to be sure, but a private one in Cynthia's lap (Cf. Ov. *Ars* 2.283–84). So, too, Ov. *Trist.* 3.7.18–26: private lessons with Perilla, reading their verses to

So Catullus assumed he would be read, and in books, by people far away in time:

Libelli . . . quod . . . / plus uno maneat perenne saeclo. (1.10)
(May this book last through the years for more than one age.)

sed dicam uobis, uos porro dicite multis
milibus et facite haec carta loquatur anus. (68.5–6)

(But I shall tell you Muses [how Allius helped me], and you in turn tell it to many thousands and see to it that this page speaks when it is an old woman.)

Catullus has readers (*lectores*, 14b.2), not listeners.

Horace had readers (*Ep.* 1.19.35). He assumed that he would be read and in books (*Sat.* 1.10.4, *Ep.* 1.20, *Odes* 2.20, 3.30). Used copies of his books will be sent to the provinces (*Ep.* 1.20.9–13). He wants readers with his book open in their hands (*Ep.* 1.19.34):

iuuat immemorata ferentem
ingenuis oculisque legi manibusque teneri

(I rejoice that I bring things previously unknown and that I am read by free eyes and held by free hands.)[143]

He goes on to say explicitly that he writes for the eye not the ear, for the private reader not the theatrical public (*Ep.* 1.19.35–40):[144]

scire velis, mea cur ingratus opuscula lector
laudet ametque domi, premat extra limen iniquus:
non ego ventosae plebis suffragia venor
inpensis cenarum et tritae munere vestis;
non ego nobilium scriptorum auditor et ultor
grammaticas ambire tribus et pulpita dignor.

(You want to know why the ungrateful reader praises and loves my little works at home, but unfairly disparages them out of doors? I do not buy

---

each other (cf. Cat. 50) but his published verse is in *libelli* (27). Ovid (*Am.* 1.8.2, *Trist.* 4.9.23–24, *Pont.* 2.2.95, 3.9.39, 4.15.39) speaks of "listening" only within the fiction of conversation or letters (e.g., *Pont.* 4.5.1–2: "Ite, leues elegi, doctas ad consulis aures / uerbaque honorato ferte legenda uiro"). *Pont.* 2.5.33 is interesting: "Qui si forte liber uestras peruenit ad aures"; it does not mean "if someone has read my book to you," but "if you have heard about the existence of a previous book." Salanus, the addressee, is reading the poetic letter of Ovid before him ("versus / legis et lectos," 19–20).

143. Mayer 1994, 266: "H.'s ideal reader . . . 'gets to grips with' the text personally, without the services of an *anagnostes*, who was a slave."

144. For Horace the contrast is not between reading and recitation, but between poetry (for readers with books) and drama (for spectators with seats): "qui se lectori credere malunt / quam spectatoris fastidia ferre superbi" (*Ep.* 2.1.214–15).

the votes of the fickle public with the expense of dinners and the gift of worn-out clothes. I do not—for I am the disciple and protector of great writers—think it worthy to suck up to the tribes of literary expounders and their lecture platforms.)[145]

Readers love Horace's books when they read them in private, but they carp at him for not currying their favor. Horace wants readers not listeners. Horace's *monumentum aere perennius* (*Odes* 3.30.1) is not a voice reciting a poem. It is a book.

Propertius assumed that he would be read, and in books:

et turpis de te iam liber alter erit. (2.3.4)

(And now there will be a second cruel book about you.)

sat mea, sat magna est, si tres sint pompa libelli,
    quos ego Persephonae maxima dona feram. (2.13.25–26)

(My funeral procession will be enough, big enough, if it is only three books that I can bear as the greatest gifts to Persephone.)

ista meis fiet notissima forma libellis. (2.25.3)

(Your beauty will become the most famous of all because of my books.)

at Musae comites et carmina cara legenti,
    nec defessa choris Calliopea meis.
fortunata, meo si qua's celebrata libello!
    carmina erunt formae tot monumenta tuae. (3.2.15–18)

(Yet, the muses are my comrades and my songs are dear to the reader, nor has Calliope tired of my choruses. Fortunate woman, whoever is celebrated by my book. My songs will be so many memorials to your beauty.)

"Tu loqueris, cum sis iam noto fabula libro
    et tua sit toto Cynthia lecta foro?" (2.24.1–2)

("Is that how you talk, when you are a piece of gossip as a result of your famous book and your Cynthia is read all over the forum?")

Holzberg claims, "the author's texts were intended primarily for a relatively small circle of hearers at recitations."[146] The author himself, however, says the exact opposite. His Cynthia is being read all over town. The

---

145. This passage has been misunderstood since Lambinus, but Fraenkel (1957, 348–9) pointed out the correct meaning long ago: "*auditor* appears often as synonymous with *discipulus*." Horace disdains two distinct groups: the bribable public and the professors.
    146. Holzberg 2001, 3.

people who had read Propertius's first book were not all friends of the poet.[147] They did not attend his readings because they knew about his private life. Total strangers were speculating about his private life because they had read his book.[148]

The picture Propertius paints of his reader in 3.3.19–20 is quite precise:

> ut tuus in scamno iactetur saepe libellus,
>   quem legat exspectans sola puella virum.

(So that your book, which a girl reads all alone as she waits for her man, may get often tossed aside onto the bench.)[149]

She is not at a lecture, not at a party, not being read to. She is alone (*sola*) and holding the book in her hands and reading it to herself.

Propertius intended his verses for readers far away in time and space (1.7.13–14):

> me legat assidue post haec neglectus amator
>   et prosint illi cognita nostra mala.

(Let the neglected lover in years to come *read* me studiously and may he profit from learning about my misfortunes.)

Propertius got his wish. The witty lover who parodied his verses, and the neglected lover who scrawled his verses years later on walls in Pompeii had read his books.[150]

Ovid assumed that he would be read, and in books, books that could be promulgated in a second edition (*Am.* epigr.). He hoped that he would be read throughout time and throughout space, everywhere that Latin was read:

147. Skinner 1993, 63, for example, makes the proper interpretation of Catullus 4 limited to "listeners personally acquainted with the author."

148. Propertius is very clear: he had become a topic of gossip (*fabula*), because total strangers (*toto foro*) had read (*lecta*) his successful book (*noto libro*). See Allen 1950, 257. To this list add Prop. 2.7.17–18: his fame for erotic servitude has traveled to the ends of the earth.

149. For the correct interpretation of the first part, see Rothstein 1920–24, 2: 23: "und sie wirft sie [the book] fort in den Augenblicke, wo der Erwartete erscheint." For *in* with abl., Kühner 1912–4, 2.1: 595, §114 a(ε), cf. Cic. *de Or.* 1.28. Valckenaer (cited from Brunck 1772–76, 2: 370) had already pointed to Strato *AP* 12.208.5–6: ἢ παρὰ δίφρους / βληθέν.

150. *CIL* 4.1520: *Candida me docuit nigras odisse puellas* (cf. Prop. 1.1.5) and *CIL* 4.4491 = Prop. 2.5.9–10: *nunc est ira recens, nunc est discedere tempus. / si dolor afuerit, crede, redibit amor.* The evidence from Pompeii has been carefully analyzed by Franklin 1991, esp. 87–8; see also Gigante 1979, 163–83, and Milnor, ch. 12, this volume. The people who wrote the opening lines of the *Aeneid* (more or less successfully) on the walls of Pompeii were not bragging that they had been to a recitation in which someone had read to them. They were bragging that they themselves knew how to read. Whether they were good at it or not is another matter.

nomenque erit indelebile nostrum,
quaque patet domitis Romana potentia terris,
ore legar populi, perque omnia saecula fama,
siquid habent veri vatum praesagia, vivam. (*Met.* 15.876–79)

(My name will be never be erased, and wherever Roman power spreads
itself over conquered lands, I shall be read by the mouth of the people,
and through all ages, if the prophets' predictions have any truth, in fame
shall I live.)

His name can never be blotted out (*indelebile*) from the page.[151] His
immortality is guaranteed by the physical existence of his books.

dumque suis uictrix omnem de montibus orbem
      prospiciet domitum Martia Roma, legar. (*Trist.* 3.7.51–52)

(And while from her hills Mars' own Rome surveys the conquered world,
I shall be read.)

Quanta tibi dederim nostris monumenta libellis,
      o mihi me coniunx carior, ipsa uides.
Detrahat auctori multum fortuna licebit,
      tu tamen ingenio clara ferere meo;
dumque legar, mecum pariter tua fama legetur,
      nec potes in maestos omnis abire rogos. (*Trist.* 5.14.1–5)

(How great are the monuments I have given you in my books, you can see
for yourself, my wife, dearer to me than myself. Fortune may take away
much from the author, but you will be made famous by my talent. While
I am read, your fame will be read equally with me.)[152]

Ovid is the most widely read author in the whole world (*Trist.* 4.10.128:
et in toto plurimus orbe legor).[153]

151. This text demonstrates an important methodological point. Whereas the
metaphors of listening, speaking, singing, and so on are available to all poets, the act of
reading (in literary contexts) is not a metaphor. So one can speak of the "audience" for a
silent film; Yeats can urge Irish poets to sing whatever is well made without intending
them to take actual harps in actual hands ("Under Ben Bulben"); Whitman writes "I sing
the body electric" in a published poem (in fact an addition to that poem). See Nauta
2002, 137–8 on metaphors of "listening"; and n. 142 above.
      152. And cf. *Am.* 1.3.25, 1.15.7–8, *Ars* 2.740, *Rem.* 363, *Trist.* 2.118, 4.9.17–26. His
claims to immortality grow more insistent precisely as books become his only possible means
of contact with his readership.
      153. So, too, Mart. 1.1: "Hic est quem legis ille, quem requiris, / toto notus in orbe
Martialis / argutis epigrammaton libellis" ("Here is the one you read, the one you want,
Martial, known throughout the world for his clever books of epigrams.") Cf. 5.13.3,
5.60.4–5, 6.60 (contrast 6.61), 11.3, 12.2.

Ovid in exile shows one of the many problems with any theory that the only real poetry for the Romans was performed poetry. If so, we should then expect to find a clear difference between "normal" poetry, meant for performance by the poet in front of an audience, and "abnormal" poetry, which the author was forced to send to unknown readers. In short, the *Amores* (in this theory written for recitation at Rome) ought to have not just a different subject but ought to be an utterly different kind of composition from the *Tristia* or the *Ex Ponto*.[154] We ought to be able to hear the difference in the *Fasti* between verses written at Rome to be performed and those written from Tomis to be read. We ought to be able to hear at once that Martial Book 12, sent from the ends of the earth to Rome, is utterly different from his other books of epigrams, sent from Rome to the ends of the earth (2.1, 11.3, 5.61, 12.2, 12.5).

That poets expected their poems to be read out of books is shown not only by the descriptions of presentation copies of the verses (Cat. 1; [Tib.] 3.1, Ov. *Trist.* 1.1, Mart. 4.10), but also by the fact that draft versions were sent to selected readers, even when some of the poems had been recited to the very person now receiving the finished volume or prepublication proofs.[155] Catullus's friend Caecilius sent him a draft of his *Magna Mater* (Cat. 35). Vergil sent drafts of portions of the *Aeneid* to Augustus when he was away on campaign (*Vit. Don.* 31; cf. Macr. *Sat.* 1.24.11). These poets could very well have recited these works.[156] They did. But they also chose to treat their verses as written words intended to be read by someone at a distance even in the earliest stages of dissemination. Quinn maintains (1982, 156):

> Performance is always implied. Even when contact with a writer takes place through a written text, that text was thought of as recording an actual performance by the writer . . . it is offered as, so to speak, a transcript of a performance which the reader recreates for himself.

But this is simply not the case. As often as poems offer themselves as fictive representations of the poet's speaking voice (e.g., Cat. 4, 5), they come in the guise of fictive letters, drawing deliberate attention

---

154. Cf. the opening of *Pont.* 4.1.

155. So for the finished volume: Cat. 1 to Nepos, though he has heard or read some of the poems; Horace's *Odes* to Augustus (*Ep.* 1.13). For a draft to be criticized: Pliny 3.15. Augustus *read* the first book of Horace's *Satires* (Suet. *Vit. Hor.*). So, too, for prose, for example, Cic. *Att.* 13.21a (SB 327), 15.14.4 (SB 402), 15.27.2 (SB 406), 16.11.1 (SB 420). For Pliny, see above, esp. 1.8, 9.28. See Starr 1987, 213; Valette-Cagnac 1997, 145.

156. Horace pictures the critic listening as the poet reads his verses (*Ars* 438–44), but also picking up the written book and reading, emending, annotating, and crossing out (445–50). Even in the case of *recitatio*, as Dupont notes (1997, 45): "We are dealing with a real 'writer,' that is someone who has entrusted his text to the page." Cf. Valette-Cagnac 1997, 116–25.

to their status as *written* texts (e.g., Cat. 14, 50). Even the *Sermones* ("Conversations") are written for readers.[157]

Accordingly, we must distinguish three different groups to whom the poet directed his verses: (1) the original addressee(s), (2) the immediate audiences (in the strict sense), and (3) the ultimate readership (in the strict sense).[158] There may or may not be an original addressee. The addressee may or may not be fictional.[159] There is a naive tendency on the part of some modern readers to accept the fictive situation (that we are reading a letter, overhearing a conversation or monologue or whatever) as real.[160] Catullus may have indeed written his variations on Sappho, and then read it aloud or sent it by messenger to Lesbia, but nothing compels us to this belief any more than we believe that— or, more to the point, have ever even wondered if—Lovelace actually wrote "To Althea from Prison" to an Althea from a prison.[161] As to the immediate audience—the happy few who happened to be friends of the poet or to be in Rome at the moment of a recitation— who heard the poems as they were being worked over, we know nothing about them or about the words they heard apart from a few stray anecdotes.[162]

Only the readers remain, to whom the Roman poets explicitly addressed their books. What Horace's *Odes* looked or sounded like before publication is beyond all conjecture. What we do know, and the only thing we and *all* the poet's intended readers were meant to know, is the written, published, public text.[163]

157. *Sat.* 1.10.72–4: "saepe stilum vertas, iterum quae digna legi sint / scripturus, neque te ut miretur turba labores, / contentus paucis *lectoribus.*"

158. Cf. Fantham 1996, 8: "A reading public can be assumed among the elite in Cicero's day, but most works of this period will have had both an immediate audience and a subsequent readership." Dupont 1997, 48–9: "The publication of a text gives it a new status in society: from private discourse it becomes public discourse. The book that emerges from the recitatio has as its potential audience the Roman people in their entirety." So Ov. *Trist.* 5.1.23; these are now *publica carmina.* For what was involved in "publication," see also Van Groningen 1963; Quinn 1982, 169–71; Kenney 1982, 3–32, esp. 10–12, 19–22; Starr 1987, 215; Valette-Cagnac 1997, 140–58.

159. Who were Flavius (Cat. 6), Veranius (9, 12, 28, 47), Varus (10, 22), Furius (11, 16, 23, 26), Aurelius (11, 15, 16, 21), or Asinius Marrucinus (12)? Does it really matter?

160. Scholars speak of "letters in verse," for example, Kroll 1923, 89, or Quinn 1973, 235, on Cat. 50.

161. The prison in any case was real; Westminster Gatehouse from April 30 to June 21, 1642.

162. Note how Pliny (5.3.5–7) says he has no idea if any of his distinguished predecessors in light verse gave readings or not.

163. I hope to deal with the consequences of the circulation of Roman poetry for its interpretation in future articles.

BIBLIOGRAPHY

Achtemeier, Paul J. 1990. "Omne Verbum Sonat: The New Testament and the Oral Environment of Late Western Antiquity." *JBL* 109, 3–27.

Allen, A. W. 1950. "Elegy and the Classical Attitude toward Love: Propertius I.1." *YCS* 11: 255–77.

Barton, Carlin A. 2001. *Roman Honor: The Fire in the Bones*. Berkeley.

Bell, A. J. E. 1999. "The Popular Poetics and Politics of the *Aeneid*." *TAPhA* 129: 263–79.

Blanck, Horst. 1992. *Das Buch in der Antike*. Beck's archäologische Bibliothek. München.

Bowman, Alan K. 1994. *Life and Letters on the Roman Frontier: Vindolanda and Its People*. London.

—— , J. David Thomas, and J. N. Adams. 1994. *The Vindolanda Writing-Tablets*. Tabulae Vindolandenses II. London.

Bradley, Keith R. 1978. *Suetonius' Life of Nero: An Historical Commentary*. Bruxelles.

Bramble, J. C. 1974. *Persius and the Programmatic Satire: A Study in Form and Imagery*. Cambridge.

Brink, C. O. 1982. *Horace on Poetry*, vol. 3. *Epistles Book II: The Letters to Augustus and Florus*. Cambridge.

Brunck, Richard François Philippe. 1772–76. *Analecta Veterum Poetarum Graecorum*. 3 vols. Argentorati.

Burfeind, Carsten. 2002. "Wen hörte Philippus? Leises Lesen und lautes Vorlesen in der Antike." *ZNTW* 93: 138–45.

Burnyeat, Miles F. 1997. "Postscript on Silent Reading." *CQ* 47: 74–6.

Busch, Stephan. 2002. "Lautes und leises Lesen in der Antike." *RhM* 145: 1–45.

Cavallo, Guglielmo. 1999. "Between Volumen and Codex: Reading in the Roman World." In Guglielmo Cavallo and Roger Chartier, eds., *A History of Reading in the West*, 64–89. Studies in Print Culture and the History of the Book. Boston.

—— and Friedrich Hild. 1997. "Buch." In *Der neue Pauly* 2: 809–16. Stuttgart.

—— , Paolo Fedeli, and Andrea Giardina, eds. 1993. *Lo spazio letterario di Roma antica*. 2nd ed. Vol. II. *La circolazione del testo*. Roma.

Chartier, Roger. 1989. "Leisure and Sociability: Reading Aloud in Early Modern Europe." In Susan Zimmerman and Ronald F. E. Weissman, eds., *Urban Life in the Renaissance*, 103–20. Newark.

—— . 1994. *The Order of Books: Readers, Authors, and Libraries in Europe between the Fourteenth and Eighteenth Centuries*. Trans. Lydia G. Cochrane. Stanford.

Chesterton, G. K. 1936. *Autobiography*. London.

Coleman, Joyce. 1996. *Public Reading and the Reading Public in Late Medieval England and France*. Cambridge.

Cotton, Hannah M., and Joseph Geiger. 1989. *Masada II: The Yigael Yadin Excavations 1963–1965. Final Reports. The Latin and Greek Documents*. Jerusalem.

Courtney, E. 1990. "Greek and Latin Acrostichs." *Philologus* 134: 3–13.

—— . 2001. *A Companion to Petronius*. Oxford.

Cramer, Frederick H. 1945. "Bookburning and Censorship in Ancient Rome: A Chapter from the History of Freedom of Speech." *JHI* 6: 157–96.

Dalzell, Alexander. 1955. "C. Asinius Pollio and the Early History of the Public Recitation at Rome." *Hermathena* 86: 20–8.

Darnton, Robert. 1990. "First Steps Toward a History of Reading." In *The Kiss of Lamourette: Reflections in Cultural History*, 154–87. New York.

——. 2001. "History of Reading." In Peter Burke, ed., *New Perspectives on Historical Writing*, 157–86. 2nd ed. University Park, Penn. [Revised version of Darnton 1990.]

Dupont, Florence. 1997. "*Recitatio* and the Reorganization of the Space of Public Discourse." In Thomas Habinek and Alessandro Schiesaro, eds., *The Roman Cultural Revolution*, 44–59. Cambridge.

Engelsing, Rolf. 1969. "Die Perioden der Lesegeschichte in der Neuzeit: Das statistische Ausmass und die soziokulturelle Bedeutung der Lektüre." *Archiv für Geschichte des Buchwesens* 10: cols. 945–1002.

——. 1974. *Der Bürger als Leser: Lesergeschichte in Deutschland 1500–1800*. Stuttgart.

Erne, Lukas. 2003. *Shakespeare as Literary Dramatist*. Cambridge.

Ernst, Ulrich. 1991. *Carmen Figuratum: Geschichte des Figurengedichts von den antiken Ursprüngen bis zum Ausgang des Mittelalters*. Köln.

Fantham, Elaine. 1996. *Roman Literary Culture: From Cicero to Apuleius*. Ancient Society and History. Baltimore.

Fedeli, Paolo, ed. 1991–97. *Q. Orazio Flacco: Le opere*. 6 vols. Roma.

Finnegan, Ruth. 1977. *Oral Poetry: Its Nature, Significance and Social Context*. Cambridge.

Fox, Adam. 2000. *Oral and Literate Culture in England, 1500–1700*. Oxford Studies in Social History. Oxford.

Fraenkel, Eduard. 1957. *Horace*. Oxford.

Franklin, James L. 1991. "Literacy and the Parietal Inscriptions of Pompeii." In J. H. Humphrey, ed., *Literacy in the Roman World*, 77–98. Journal of Roman Archaeology, Supplementary Series 3. Ann Arbor.

Funaioli, G. 1914. "Recitationes." *RE* 1A, cols. 435–46.

Furneaux, Henry. 1896. *The Annals of Tacitus*. 2nd ed. 2 vols. London.

Gallazzi, C. 1982. "P. Narm. Inv. 66.362: Vergilius, *Eclogae* VIII 53–62." *ZPE* 48: 75–8.

Gamel, Mary-Kay. 1998. "Reading as a Man: Performance and Gender in Roman Elegy." *Helios* 25: 79–95.

Gavrilov, A. K. 1997. "Techniques of Reading in Classical Antiquity." *CQ* 47: 56–73.

Gentili, Bruno. 1988. *Poetry and its Public in Ancient Greece from Homer to the Fifth Century*. Trans. A. Thomas Cole. Baltimore.

Gigante, Marcello. 1979. *Civiltà delle forme letterarie nell' antica Pompei*. Napoli.

Gilliard, Frank D. 1993. "More Silent Reading in Antiquity: *non omne verbum sonabat*." *JBL* 112: 689–94.

Goldhill, Simon. 1999. "Body/Politics: Is There a History of Reading?" In Thomas M. Falkner, Nancy Felson, and David Konstan, eds., *Contextualizing Classics: Ideology, Performance, Dialogue: Essays in Honor of John J. Peradotto*, 89–120. Greek Studies: Interdisciplinary Approaches. Lanham, Md.

Goody, Jack and Ian Watt. 1968. "The Consequences of Literacy." In Jack Goody, ed., *Literacy in Traditional Societies*, 27–68. Cambridge.

Habinek, Thomas. 2005. *The World of Roman Song: From Ritualized Speech to Social Order*. Baltimore.

Harris, William V. 1989. *Ancient Literacy*. Cambridge, Mass.

Hendrickson, G. L. 1929. "Ancient Reading." *CJ* 25: 192–6.

Holzberg, Nicklas. 2001. *Die römische Liebeselegie: Eine Einführung.* 2nd ed. Darmstadt.
Horsfall, Nicholas. 1989. "'The Uses of Literacy' and the *Cena Trimalchionis:* I & II." *G&R* 36: 74–89 and 194–209.
——. 1995. "Rome without Spectacles." *G&R* 42: 49–56.
Hutchinson, G. O. 1984. "Propertius and the Unity of the Book." *JRS* 74: 99–106.
Johnson, William A. 1994. "Macrocollum." *CPh* 89: 62–4.
——. 2000. "Towards a Sociology of Reading in Classical Antiquity." *AJPh* 121: 593–627.
Kaster, Robert A., ed. 1995. *De Grammaticis et Rhetoribus: C. Suetonius Tranquillus.* Oxford.
Kenney, E. J. 1982. "Books and Readers in the Roman World." In E. J. Kenney, ed., *The Cambridge History of Classical Literature,* II. 3–50. Cambridge.
Kiessling, Adolf and Richard Heinze. 1958. *Q. Horatius Flaccus: Briefe.* 5th ed. Berlin.
Knox, B. M. W. 1968. "Silent Reading in Antiquity." *GRBS* 9: 421–35.
Koestermann, Erich. 1963. *Cornelius Tacitus. Annalen.* 4 vols. Heidelberg.
Korfmacher, William Charles. 1933. "Persius as a Literary Critic." *CJ* 28: 276–86.
Kroll, Wilhelm. 1923. *C. Valerius Catullus.* Leipzig.
Kühner, Raphael. 1912–14. *Ausführliche Grammatik der lateinischen Sprache.* 2. Aufl. Hannover.
Lombardo, Stanley. 1989. "Technopaegnia: Hellenistic Pattern Poetry." *Temblor* 10: 200–4.
Markus, Donka D. 2000. "Performing the Book: The Recital of Epic in First-Century C.E. Rome." *ClAnt* 19: 138–79.
Mayer, Roland. 1994. *Horace: Epistles. Book I.* Cambridge.
Mayor, John E. B. 1872. *Thirteen Satires of Juvenal.* London.
Momigliano, Arnaldo. 1957. "Perizonius, Niebuhr and the Character of Early Roman Tradition." *JRS* 47: 104–14.
Morgan, Llewelyn. 2001. "Creativity Out of Chaos: Poetry between the Death of Caesar and the Death of Virgil." In Oliver Taplin, ed., *Literature in the Roman World,* 75–118. Oxford.
Morris, Edward P. 1968. *Horace: Satires and Epistles.* Repr. Norman, Okla.
Müller, Peter. 1994. *"Verstehst du auch, was du liest?" Lesen und Verstehen im Neuen Testament.* Darmstadt.
Nauta, Ruurd R. 2002. *Poetry for Patrons: Literary Communication in the Age of Domitian.* Leiden.
Nisbet, R. G. M., and Margaret Hubbard. 1978. *A Commentary on Horace: Odes, Book II.* Oxford.
Pennacini, Adriano. 1993. "L'arte della parola." In Guglielmo Cavallo, Paolo Fedeli, and Andrea Giardina, eds., *Lo spazio letterario di Roma antica.* Vol. II. *La circolazione del testo,* 215–67. 2nd ed. Roma.
Quinn, Kenneth. 1973. *Catullus: The Poems.* 2nd ed. New York.
——. 1980. *Horace: The Odes.* New York.
——. 1982. "The Poet and His Audience in the Augustan Age." *ANRW* II.30.1: 75–180.
Rawson, Elizabeth. 1985. *Intellectual Life in the Late Roman Republic.* Baltimore.
Roller, Matthew. 1998. "Pliny's Catullus: The Politics of Literary Appropriation." *TAPhA* 128: 265–304.
Rothstein, Max. 1920–24. *Die Elegien des Sextus Propertius.* 2. Aufl. 2 vols. Berlin.

Saenger, Paul. 1982. "Silent Reading: Its Impact on Late Medieval Script and Society." *Viator* 13: 367–414.

Salles, Catherine. 1994. *Lire à Rome*. Paris.

Serafini, Augusto, ed. 1966. *Orazio: Satire et Epistole*. Torino.

Shackleton Bailey, D. R. 1965–70. *Cicero: Letters to Atticus*. 7 vols. Cambridge.

——— . 1977. *Cicero: Epistulae ad Familiares*. 2 vols. Cambridge.

Sherwin-White, A. N. 1985. *The Letters of Pliny: A Historical and Social Commentary*. Oxford.

Skinner, Marilyn B. 1981. *Catullus' Passer: The Arrangement of the Book of Polymetric Poems*. New York.

——— . 1993. "Catullus in Performance." *CJ* 89: 61–8.

——— . 2001. "Among Those Present: Catullus 44 and 10." *Helios* 28: 57–73.

——— . 2003. *Catullus in Verona: A Reading of the Elegiac Libellus, Poems 65–116*. Columbus.

Slusser, Michael. 1992. "Reading Silently in Antiquity." *JBL* 111: 499.

Starr, Raymond J. 1987. "The Circulation of Literary Texts in the Roman World." *CQ* 37: 213–23.

——— . 1989. "The Ennianista at Puteoli: Gellius 18.5." *RhM* 132: 411–2.

——— . 1991. "Reading Aloud: *Lectores* and Roman Reading." *CJ* 86: 337–43.

Thomas, Richard. 1988. *Virgil: Georgics. Volume 1: Books I–II*. Cambridge.

Thomas, Rosalind. 1992. *Literacy and Orality in Ancient Greece*. Key Themes in Ancient History. Cambridge.

Valette-Cagnac, Emmanuelle. 1997. *La lecture à Rome: rites et pratiques*. L'Antiquité au Présent. Paris.

Van Groningen, B. 1963. "*ΕΚΔΟΣΙΣ*." *Mnemosyne* 16: 1–17.

Westcott, J. H. 1898. *C. Plini Secundi Epistulae Selectae*. Boston.

White, Peter. 1993. *Promised Verse: Poets in the Society of Augustan Rome*. Cambridge, Mass.

Williams, Gordon. 1982. "The Genesis of Poetry at Rome." In E. J. Kenney, ed., *The Cambridge History of Classical Literature*, II, 53–9. Cambridge.

Wiseman, T. P. 1985. *Catullus and His World*. Oxford.

Wright, Frederick Warren. 1931. *Cicero and the Theater*. Smith College Classical Studies 11. Northampton, Mass.

Part III

INSTITUTIONS AND COMMUNITIES

10

Papyrological Evidence for Book Collections and Libraries in the Roman Empire

George W. Houston

Working primarily with literary, archaeological, and epigraphical evidence, modern scholars have recovered a great deal of information about Roman libraries and book collections. From Ephesus, Timgad, and other sites, we have an idea of their physical appearance; inscriptions and literature provide information on staffing and management; and we know something of the existence, building history, or both, of dozens of libraries in Rome, Italy, and the provinces of the Roman Empire.[1] From the Villa of the Papyri at Herculaneum, we have the actual contents of a private library, and some (not very helpful) information about its physical arrangement.[2] Apart from the collection of volumes in the Villa of the Papyri, however, our knowledge of the contents of Roman book collections—what exactly was in them, how they were organized, and how they came to be—is, so far, very limited.[3] In this chapter, I will set out and analyze various types of papyrological evidence—materials not previously exploited in this context—in an attempt to shed further light on the question of the contents and organization of Roman book collections. As we will see, the evidence pertains largely to personal, rather than to more or less public collections, and the nature of the evidence imposes a

1. The literature is vast, but there is no need here for an extended bibliography. A good recent study of these questions, with earlier bibliography, is Blanck 1992, 190–222. On staff, see Houston 2002 (public libraries), and Dix 1986, 133–7 (private libraries). For the physical appearance, see, for example, Strocka 1981, 322–9 (Ephesus) or Pfeiffer 1931 (Timgad). Many particulars remain in doubt.

2. Cavallo 1983 provides an analysis of the collection in the Villa of the Papyri, Gigante 1979 a catalogue of the papyri found in the Villa, and Longo Auricchio and Capasso 1987 a description of what can be known at present about the physical arrangement of the books.

3. It is largely limited to chance references to specific items in particular libraries. For some examples, see Blanck 1992, 215–22.

number of other limitations as well.[4] We will deal primarily with two kinds of evidence: first, lists of books that appear in papyri and have some claim to represent the contents of actual book collections; and second, concentrations of papyrus fragments that were found together and so probably belonged originally to the same collection. No attempt will be made here to provide an exhaustive treatment of this material. Instead, my goal is to set out the evidence and provide some examples of ways in which it can be exploited.

1. LISTS OF BOOKS THAT HAVE BEEN PRESERVED IN PAPYRI

A considerable number of papyri containing lists of books survive. Nineteen of them have recently been gathered and republished, with some commentary (primarily on textual problems and questions of literary history), by Rosa Otranto.[5] Some of the lists are so short or limited in content that they are of no use in the present context.[6] Others are letters in which books are mentioned, but with no indication that we are dealing with a complete or coherent book collection.[7] Two of the papyri are pre-Roman.[8] A number of the papyri, however, may well be surviving portions of what were originally lists or inventories of individual book collections or libraries, but every one of them presents problems of interpretation. To illustrate the nature of these lists and the problems they present, we can consider Otranto no. 16 (*PSI Laur.* inv. 19662v = MP^3 2087).[9]

Like most such lists, this one is broken at beginning and end. We thus cannot know how long it was originally, nor can we do more than guess at the size of the complete contents of the book collection it represents.[10]

---

4. An obvious one is geography: all of the papyri relevant to our study come from Egypt or Herculaneum. Will conclusions drawn from this material be valid in other areas of the Empire? The answer seems to be yes: the patterns of collecting and use that we will find in the papyri can often be paralleled in literary sources pertaining to the city of Rome, providing some reassurance. Other problems will arise and be discussed in the course of our study.

5. Otranto 2000. Harrauer 1995 includes most of these and many additional lists. Harrauer's materials range much later in date than those in Otranto's collection and include ostraka, Coptic texts, and lists of Christian texts. All of these fall outside the scope of this study, which is a study of Roman library history, and I will use the later materials only for comparative purposes.

6. For example, Otranto 2000, nos. 8 (titles of six comedies by Cratinus), 9 (19 comedies of Menander), and 10 (18 tragedies of Euripides).

7. Otranto 2000, nos. 4, 5, 11, and 19.

8. Otranto 2000, nos. 1 and 2.

9. This papyrus has been studied in detail by Puglia 1996. Puglia provides extensive earlier bibliography and a thorough discussion of a number of problems not dealt with here.

10. A few letters survive in a column to the left of the list, but they cannot be restored, and we do not know whether they formed part of the list or not.

Otranto, no. 16 = *PSILaur.* inv. 19662v

	Oxyrhynchus, 3rd century A.D.	English equivalents at the right
	Συμ[πό]σιο[ν]	Symposium
	διάλογοι κ′	dialogues 20
	Σοφιστής α′	Sophist 1
	Πρὸς Καλλικλέα γ′	Against Callicles 3
5	Πρωταγόρας α′	Protagoras 1
	Εὐθύδημος α′	Euthydemus 1
	Παρμενίδης Ἀνάχαρσις	Parmenides Anacharsis
	Χαρμίδης	Charmides
	Ἀλκιβιάδης ἢ Λύσις	Alcibiades or (?) Lysis
10	Μένων Μενέξενος	Meno Menexenus
	Ἱππίαι β′ καὶ Εὔδημος	Hippias (Maior and Minor) Eudemus
	Τίμαιος	Timaeus
	Πολιτικός	Politicus
	Κρατύλος	Cratylus
15	Ἀλκιβιάδ(ης)	Alcibiades
	Φίληβος	Philebus
	Φαίδων	Phaedo
	Λάχης	Laches
	Ἀλκιβιάδης	Alcibiades
20	Γοργίας	Gorgias
	Πρωταγόρας	Protagoras
	Φίληβος	Philebus
	Ξενοφῶ(ντος) Παιδ(είας) η′	Xenophon's (Cyro)paedia 8
	Ἀνάβασις	Anabasis
25	Ἀγησίλαος	Agesilaus
	Κυνηγετικ(ός)	Cynegeticus
	Συμ[πό]σιον	Sym[po]sium
	Ὁμήρου ὅσα εὑρίσκ(εται)	Of Homer, as much as is found
	Μενάνδ(ρου) ὅσα εὑρίσ(κεται)	Of Menander, as much as is found
30	Εὐριπίδου ὅσα εὑρίσκ(εται)	Of Euripides, as much as is found
	Ἀρ[ιστ]οφά(νους) [	Of Ar[ist]ophanes
	.[...]εινου	Of [...]inus
	[....]	[...]
	[....].ινου	Of [...]inus

It begins in line 1 with *Symposium*, then in line 2 tells us "dialogues," followed by the number kappa, or 20. There follow 20 lines, down to the *Philebus* in line 22, and we can probably infer that each line represents the contents of one papyrus roll and that the number 20 in line 2 is intended to give the total number of rolls that follow in this section of the list. Almost all of the titles represent works of Plato.[11] After the *Philebus* in line 22

11. There are exceptions, all of them much discussed. In line 7, the *Anacharsis* is a work of the second-century A.D. satirist Lucian, and in line 11 the *Eudemus* is by Aristotle. These may have been volumes with works written on both sides of the roll, and this may be the case also with the roll mentioned in line 10. For full discussions, see Puglia 1996, 56–8.

there is a *paragraphus*—a horizontal line indicating a break—followed by works of Xenophon and then, after a second break indicated simply by a space, the phrase (in line 28) ῾Ομήρου ὅσα εὑρίσκ(εται), "Of Homer, as much as is found." That phrase (of uncertain significance, and to which we will return) then recurs with the works of Menander and Euripides, and was perhaps intended to be understood with the names of Aristophanes and at least three other authors that appear, in very fragmentary form, at the bottom of the list. Such, then, is the list. What, though, was its purpose? Since its title, if it had one, does not survive, we can only guess at its exact nature, and scholars have advanced a number of theories: this might be a list of books in a book collection or library, or in a bookseller's shop, or perhaps it was a list of *desiderata*, works someone wanted to buy, or maybe it was the reading assigned by a teacher to his students.[12] For my purposes, the crucial question here, and for all of these lists, is this: does the list give us the contents of an actual, existing book collection, or does it give us a list of books that did not exist as an actual collection, such as a shopping list, or assigned readings, or a scholar's bibliography of, say, the works of Plato?

Scholars working on these papyri have developed a number of criteria to help determine the nature and purpose of the lists: (1) If titles are repeated, we can probably assume that we are not dealing with a scholar's bibliography, a teacher's assignments, or a list of *desiderata*, because in each of those cases there would be no logical reason to repeat titles. (2) If a list devoted to a single author omits titles that should have been known to any scholar, we can probably rule out a scholarly bibliography.[13] (3) If a list includes what appear to be opisthographs (rolls written on both sides), we can safely rule out teacher's assignments and scholarly bibliographies, neither of which would be likely to specify or record such volumes. Our list includes repetitions (*Alcibiades* in lines 9, 15, and 19, *Protagoras* in 5 and 21, *Philebus* in 16 and 22), and probably some opisthographs (lines 7, 10, and 11), so that it most likely represents an actual collection.

In addition, this papyrus, like some others, contains peculiarities that can best be explained on the assumption that the compiler of the list was looking at and recording actual physical volumes. To take one example: in line 4, the only known ancient works *Against Callicles* are orations by Lysias and Demosthenes, not dialogues of Plato, and several scholars have accordingly suggested that this title might represent the third book of Plato's *Gorgias*, in which Socrates' opponent is the philosopher Callicles, or per-

---

12. These and other theories are set out clearly in summary form by Carlini 1989, 94–7. He notes that at least nine different explanations of the list have been proposed so far.

13. Such bibliographies, or lists of an author's works, were often appended to the end of the biography of an author. See Otranto 2000, XIV–XV, and cf. the remarkably full lists of an author's works that Diogenes Laertius attached at the end of each of his biographies.

haps the entire *Gorgias*.[14] If this is correct, we would seem to have the compiler looking at an actual volume, examining it, and puzzling a bit about what it might be: perhaps the usual title was lacking, or the papyrus was fragmentary, forcing the compiler to try to identify the work. Seeing the name of Callicles, he decided, perhaps, that he was dealing with a dialogue called the *Against Callicles*. The last lines of the papyrus, in which authors' names are given together with the phrase "as much as is found," have occasioned much discussion. Although no scholarly consensus has yet emerged, most scholars take the phrase as a Greek equivalent of *omnia quae extant* ("complete extant works"), and I accept that suggestion here.[15]

I take this, then, as the inventory of a real collection of books. The occasion of such an inventory might be, for example, a purchase or sale (as in Cic. *Fam.* 16.20), a gift (such as those made by the ephebes to the Ptolemaion at Athens, attested in *IG* 2^2.1009, 1029, etc.), an inheritance, or perhaps an owner simply wanting a list of his books in order to determine what he lacked and needed to buy (as in Cic. *Hortensius* frg. 8 Grilli).[16] In the case of a large collection or a library, a list of this sort could help a user, whether that user was the owner, a friend of the owner, or a scholar given permission to use the collection,[17] to determine if a given book was present and so avoid a lengthy and perhaps frustrating search among the rolls themselves.

If we apply such criteria to each of the lists in Otranto, we end up with eight likely inventories (or what survives of inventories) of actual book collections. I set these out, insofar as possible in chronological order, in table 10.1.[18]

We can make some preliminary observations, none of them very surprising. We would expect most papyri to date primarily from the second and third centuries, and they do; and the provenance of most of our

14. Puglia 1996, 52–4 and 58–9, provides a full discussion of this problem.

15. The matter, however, is quite uncertain. Harrauer 1995, 66, arguing that ὅσα εὑρίσκεται is not the way a Greek would say "complete works," took lines 28–30 as constituting a commission or order ("*Desiderataliste*," "*Suchliste*"). In favor of his suggestion is the fact that we find the verb εὑρίσκω used in connection with a request for books in *P.Oxy.* 2192, lines 41–3: "If you find (ἐὰν εὑρίσκῃς) any books I don't have, have copies made and send them to me." On the other hand, it is almost impossible to take the first 27 lines of this list as a list of desiderata, given such items as the odd opisthograph of line 7, which must surely be an existing volume, and it seems very unlikely that someone who owned so much of Plato would not already own Homer, Menander, and Euripides. See Puglia 1996, 59–60, for a full discussion.

16. Johnson forthcoming points out that some such list is implicit in the request for books in *P.Oxy.* 2192, cited in the previous note.

17. We find such users in the library of Lucullus: Cato and Cicero as friends (Cic. *Fin.* 3.2.7), Greek scholars granted the run of the place (Plut. *Luc.* 42.1–2).

18. Each of the eight contains its own peculiarities, problems, and uncertainties. Space precludes a full discussion here, although we will consider some of them, and the reader is referred to Otranto for further discussion and earlier bibliography.

Table 10.1. Lists of Book Collections Preserved in Papyri

No.	Publication	Date and Provenance	Size	Brief Description[1]
1	Otranto 3 = *P. Vindob.Gr.* inv. 39966, column 1	Mid-first century A.D., Arsinoite nome	About 9 titles and 75 rolls are present or implied	List of poets and titles. For each work, the individual books are listed by number.[2] Poets named: Homer, Callimachus, Pindar, Hesiod. Traces of others. Broken at beginning and end, but we are probably not lacking much.
2	Otranto 3 = *P. Vindob.Gr.* inv. 39966, column 2	Mid-first century A.D., Arsinoite nome	About 17 titles and 85 rolls are present or implied	List of poets and titles, followed by "Selections from the Orators."[3] For each of the poetic works, the individual books are listed by number.[4] Poets named: Homer, Hesiod, Callimachus. For the rhetorical works, book numbers are sometimes provided, sometimes just the title. Orators named: [?]dorus, Dionysius, Aelianus, Aeschines, Demosthenes.
3	Otranto 6 = *P. Oxy.* 2659	Second century A.D., Oxyrhynchus	63 titles	Eleven writers of comedy, in alphabetical order, from Amipsias to Epicharmus. Beneath each name, the author's works, also in alphabetical order. At least 27, and probably 39, comedies of Aristophanes were listed.
4	Otranto 14 = *P. Turner* 39	Early third century A.D., Apollinopolis Magna	5 works, then household items	Philemon, Eratosthenes, lexicon of Platonic words, commentary on Priscus, encomium of Rufus.
5	Otranto 15 = *P. Ross.Georg.* I.22	Third century A.D., Memphis	About 14 authors and at least 22 works	Philosophical works and one medical writer. No discernible order; four authors appear at more than one place in the list. Authors (or works) named: collection of letters of the Socratics, Aristotle, Posidonius, Theodas (a medical writer), Theophrastus, Dio of Prusa, Crito, Nigrinus, Diogenes, Simon, Chrysippus, Cebes,[5] Apion, Hippias, Archimedes.
6	Otranto 16 = *PSILaur.* inv. 19662 *verso*	Third century A.D., Oxyrhynchus	6 authors, at least 24 rolls, and possibly an uncertain number of codices[6]	For details, see the text of Otranto no. 16, given above. In sum: dialogues of Plato, with some other works mixed in; Xenophon, Homer, Menander, Euripides, Aristophanes, and traces of other names.
7	Otranto 17 = *P. Vars.* 5 *verso*	Third century A.D., Arsinoite nome	13 authors named (but many names are lost in lacunae),	List of philosophical and medical writers. No titles are given. To the right of the authors' names, a column of numbers probably

(*Continued*)

Table 10.1. (*Continued*)

No.	Publication	Date and Provenance	Size	Brief Description[1]
			and 296 rolls, it seems	indicates the number of rolls of each author's works present in the collection. Philosophical authors named: Geminus, Diogenes of Babylonia, [?] "a Socratic," [Zeno?] of Tarsus, [Zeno?] of Citium, Hierocles. Medical authors named: Glaucon, Xenophon, Chrysippus, Thessalus (?), Erasistratus, Themison, Harpocration. Summary numbers state how many of the mss. were opisthographs (at least 51 of the philosophical works, it appears) and what appear to be the total number of rolls in each category: 142 philosophical, and 296 (medical, or perhaps the total collection).
8	Otranto 18 = *P. Turner* 9	Early fourth century A.D., Hermopolis Magna	About 15 authors or commentaries on authors	Five or six works, probably commentaries, are followed by several fragmentary names of authors and then a number of historical works. The commentaries are on Archilochus, Callimachus, Aeschines, Demosthenes (two different ones), and Homer. The fragmentary names include Callinichus and Ru[fus?]. Then follow: Herodotus, Xenophon, Aristotle, Thucydides, Xenophon again, and Callinichus.

1. There are numerous problems in reading authors and titles. For the sake of consistency, I follow Otranto's readings, and in the discussion that follows I avoid drawing inferences from names or titles that are uncertain.

2. In the listing of what appears to be Homer's *Odyssey*, Book 7 may be omitted. If so, it is possible that that book was not present in this collection of volumes, or misshelved, or perhaps the compiler of the list omitted it by mistake.

3. We cannot tell if "Selections from the Orators" is the title of a specific work or a heading in the list similar to the "dialogues" in line 2 of the list of Plato's works that we looked at above.

4. In the listing of the books of the *Odyssey*, Books 3 and 4 are listed after Book 24. Because of a lacuna in the preceding line, we cannot know if these were second copies of Books 3 and 4, or if the compiler had omitted them at their proper place and inserted them only here, at the end. Either explanation implies an actual collection of books.

5. Each of the names Crito, Simon, and Cebes is modified by the adjective "Socratic." It is not clear whether these are authors or titles.

6. Puglia 1996, 64-5, suggested that the last lines of the list, which are separated from the works of Xenophon by a space and which give not the names of individual works but rather the names of authors only (Homer, Menander, etc.), might record not rolls but codices. As Puglia noted, the "complete extant works" of an author—the meaning we have tentatively assigned to the Greek ὅσα εὑρίσκ(εται)—might have been contained conventionally in a set number of codices, one or more depending upon the author. While there are problems with this—as Joseph Farrell has pointed out to me, the phrase ὅσα εὑρίσκ(εται) is certainly not the most obvious way to specify "codex"—it should be considered a possible explanation of the unusual nature of this list.

papyri, where it is known, is a city of some size, also as one would expect. The sizes of the various collections cannot be determined with any precision, but the lists do indicate a wide range of sizes. Thus number 4 (from Apollinopolis Magna), which may well be complete, includes just five books among other household items.[19] Several collections may well have been quite small, perhaps a few dozen or a hundred volumes: thus nos. 1, 2, 4, 5, and 8. Others, such as no. 7, included perhaps several hundred rolls, and no. 3, which as we will see may be part of the booklist of a library, might originally have numbered several thousand volumes.

The authors represented in this small group of lists are a mixture of the most popular and the obscure. Of the eleven authors who occur most frequently in Greek papyri from Oxyrhynchus, ten are mentioned in one or more of our lists.[20] Some of the authors or works, such as Nigrinus in no. 5, are attested in no other source, and many of the philosophical and medical authors named in no. 7 are little known, hard to identify, or both. None of the lyric poets, no novels or romances, and only three authors certainly of Roman imperial date (Theodas and Dio of Prusa in no. 5, and Lucian in no. 6) appear.[21] The collections tend to be homogeneous: nos. 1, 2, 6, and 8 are composed largely of standard, widely read authors or commentaries on such authors. No. 3 is all comedy (but see further below), whereas nos. 5 and 7 could be specialist collections of philosophy and philosophy/medicine respectively. Only the extremely brief list of no. 4 has no apparent coherence. We can explain the homogeneity of any given list in either of two ways. First, we may have a specialist's professional collection of books on a particular topic or topics, such as philosophy or medicine,[22] or a collection of the classics (nos. 1, 2, 6, 8). Second, we may be dealing with just one section of a much larger and more comprehensive collection, given that our lists are fragmentary parts of larger wholes. This may well be the case with our no. 3, the list of comic writers, to which we can now turn.

19. For similar small collections elsewhere, cf. House B17 at Karanis (four or five texts, van Minnen 1998, 132–3), or the highly miscellaneous collection—in Coptic and Greek, on wood and papyrus—from three houses at Roman-era Kellis. In one case, some twenty-one texts were found scattered through nine rooms of a house: Gardner 1996.

20. Homer, Hesiod, Callimachus, Plato, Euripides, Menander, Demosthenes, Thucydides, Herodotus, and Pindar. Of the top eleven, only Aeschylus is not mentioned in any list. For the frequency figures (valid for Oxyrhynchus, not necessarily all of Egypt), see Krüger 1990, 214–15.

21. Several other authors or works, however, are either possibly or probably of imperial date: Priscus and the encomium of Rufus in no. 4, Nigrinus in no. 5, Hierocles and Harpocration in no. 7, and Callinichus in no. 8. Aelianus (if that is the correct reading) in no. 2 sounds like a Roman name, but this list is early (mid-first century A.D.), so Aelianus must have lived very early in the Empire (or before).

22. For a specialist scholarly collection in philosophy, cf. the papyri from the Villa of the Papyri at Herculaneum. A professional collection of astronomical texts from Oxyrhynchus has recently been identified: Jones 1999.

List no. 3, written on the *verso* of *P.Oxy.* 2660, which is a Greek-to-Latin glossary dating from the first or second century, was carefully prepared, arranged, and copied, as can be seen in figure 10.1. It gives every impression of being a formal booklist from a library of some size. The writers mentioned are all authors of comedy, beginning with Amipsias, whose name must be supplied at the upper left, then continuing down to Aristophanes, and after a lacuna resuming at the top of column 2 with Archippus and continuing down to Epicharmus. Authors and titles are arranged in single-letter alphabetical order, and the text is written clearly and carefully. It seems reasonable to assume that the list continued through the alphabet, providing similar coverage for other comic writers and their works, and on that assumption it is very unlikely that this was a list of *desiderata* or of assigned readings: it is simply too long and complete for that. Nor is it likely to be a scholar's bibliography on, say, the subject of comedy, because it omits some well-known works, among them the *Women of Lemnos* and *Pelargoi* of Aristophanes, and the title given specifically as *Plutus A* shows that the compiler was well aware that there was a *Plutus B* as well, yet he omits that title from his list.[23] In addition, there appear to be some repetitions among the plays of Epicharmus in column 2: the *Harpagai* at lines 15 and 17, *Dionysoi* at lines 21 and 22, and *Epinicius* at lines 24 and 25. The repetition of these titles could be due to scribal error,[24] but they may well represent duplicate copies of works in the collection.[25] Taken together, the possible duplicates, the omissions, and the careful presentation of the text all argue for this being the surviving part of an actual library booklist.

If we now look at our no. 3 as a list of the books in a library,[26] we are struck first of all by how little information it provides. We find authors and titles only: no dates (of composition, say, or of when this copy was made,

23. These omissions, as well as that of the *Ichthues* of Archippus, were all noted by John Rea, who edited the text for *The Oxyrhynchus Papyri* XXXIII. He concluded that the fragment is quite probably "the catalogue of some provincial library or a reading list." I believe its length rules out the latter possibility.

24. Rea, *ad P.Oxy.* 2659, took the first pair as due to scribal error. Only the first six or seven letters of each title survive, and Rea accordingly assumed that the second titles in the second and third pairs were different, and previously unattested, works. The matter is quite uncertain. It is unsatisfying to explain a problem by assuming a previously unattested work, but on the other hand it is disconcerting to find these duplicate copies, if that is what they are, all concentrated within the space of ten lines in a list that otherwise has no repetitions at all.

25. Otranto 2000, 37, took them as duplicates. We know from the Villa of the Papyri at Herculaneum that libraries could and sometimes did have duplicate copies: Gigante 1979, 59, provides a list of the works present in the Villa collection in two or more copies.

26. There is no way to know if this was purely a private collection or a "public" library. Nor is there likely to be much difference: any owner of books was likely to make his collection, or specific books in it, available to his friends and to scholars. We see this both in Egypt (*P.Oxy.* 2192 = Otranto 11, cf. the discussion by Johnson forthcoming; *P.GettyMus.* acc. 76.AI.57 = Otranto 4; and *P.Mil.Vogliano* 11 = Otranto 5) and in Italy, where Lucullus threw open his library to his friends and to Greek scholars (Plut. *Luc.* 42.1–2). That is, any such library could be made available, though privately owned, to much of the reading public.

Figure 10.1 P.Oxy. 2659. A list of writers of comedy and titles of their works

or of acquisition), no bibliographical information whatever. There is no catalogue number of any sort, no reference to which cabinet the roll was stored in. This is true of our other lists as well, and of the surviving *sillyboi* (the tags or labels that were attached to papyrus rolls to identify them), on which we regularly find author and title, but never any indication of where the book was to be shelved or stored.[27]

All of this is consistent with what we know of the organization of Roman libraries generally. There is no evidence for an ancient equivalent of the modern call number or catalogue.[28] Rather, as previous scholars have argued, ancient booklists were very probably organized first by literary genre (epic, say, or lyric) or, where literary genres did not apply, by subject (medicine, astronomy), and then alphabetically by author.[29] Presumably this system derives ultimately from categories defined by Aristotle and employed in the library at Alexandria, and it probably also reflects the physical organization of the actual book collections themselves.[30] All of this is now generally accepted.[31] What has not been

And, on the other hand, any "public" library in a provincial town would almost certainly be a gift from an individual to the town, like those in Ephesus and Timgad, and open to virtually the same group of readers as a "private" library in that town would be. Libraries in gymnasia might conceivably have had restricted access, but we have no clear evidence on such libraries and cannot even prove they existed in Egypt. See Funghi and Messeri Savorelli 1992a, 59–61, for a general discussion, and cf. van Minnen 1998, 106–8, on the question of whether we can assume that high-quality texts might have come from gymnasia.

27. On *sillyboi*, see Dorandi 1984, and add Stephens 1985, and Hanson 2004, 209–19. Dorandi's no. 1 can serve as an example. It reads in its entirety, "Hermarchus, *Against Empedocles*, Book 9."

28. Probably the closest we come is a statement in the *Historia Augusta*. The author, here called Flavius Vopiscus, claims that his reader could find a certain book in the "sixth bookcase" (*in armario sexto*) in the Ulpian library at Rome (*HA Tac.* 8.1). This has been taken (e.g., by Blanck 1992, 218) as an indication that the bookcases were numbered—implying a kind of elementary cataloguing system—but it is not convincing evidence. This whole passage in the *HA* is not to be trusted (Paschoud 2002, 276–7), and the author of this section of the *HA* is quite willing to invent documents and bogus sources, even ones that could readily be checked, so that we cannot even assume that he was striving for verisimilitude (Chastagnol 1994, cxxi–cxxii). Given that no known *sillybos* indicates the bookcase in which the book was shelved, we are entitled to doubt that such a cataloguing system existed. It should be noted, however, that the number of known *sillyboi* is very small, and the discovery of even a single example with a bookcase number could change the picture we have substantially.

29. For a useful summary of the thesis, the ancient evidence on which it is based, and references to some of the secondary literature, see Otranto 2000, XII–XV.

30. Otranto 2000, XVI–XVII, with a useful distinction between the booklist of the library and the *Pinakes* compiled by Callimachus. The *Pinakes*, it appears, did not include all of the books in the Alexandrian library, and so were not the kind of booklist we are concerned with. They were, rather, a scholarly bibliography, with biographies of authors as well as *incipits* and line counts of their various works, precisely the kind of information that we do not find in, for example, our no. 3.

31. Cf. Blanck 1992, 217–8. For book retrieval in practice in second-century Rome, see Houston 2004.

noticed, so far as I know, and what is particularly interesting about the lists in table 10.1, is that these inventories allow us to move beyond this general principle and observe the system at work, as ancient compilers dealt not with theory but with actual books in real collections. We find clear reflections of the genre/author organization,[32] but there are variations and idiosyncrasies as well.[33] We will consider several examples, at varying levels of detail.

Small collections, of course, need no organization. You simply riffle through your volumes until you find what you want. Thus, in all likelihood, nos. 4 and 8, and perhaps no. 1, where the owner might keep all of the volumes of the *Iliad* in one *capsa* (carrying case) or on one shelf, and other works or authors each in its own case or shelf, as a kind of informal and practical organization. In no. 1, the owner was interested in (or at least owned) standard, widely read poetry,[34] and the fact that he groups four poets who wrote in three different genres together, rather than organizing by genre, probably means that he did not own a wide selection of poetry, perhaps no more than we have here: this was not an extensive or sophisticated collection. List no. 2 is a particularly interesting example, in part because it is probably complete or nearly so.[35] There is an obvious distinction between poetry and prose, and an awareness of genre is implicit in line 14, in which we have the phrase Ἐγλογαὶ Ῥητ[όρων], followed by works that all seem to deal with rhetoric or oratory, first probably reference works, then titles of speeches by Aeschines and Demosthenes.[36] This

32. Obviously, we must be careful to avoid circular reasoning at this point. Otranto claimed some of her lists as probable library booklists precisely because they seem to have been arranged by genre and author: Otranto 2000, XXX, citing her nos. 8, 9, and 10. In assembling table 10.1, I included only lists that can be classed as booklists of actual collections on the basis of other criteria—duplicate copies, omissions, opisthographs, length, and particular details in the list—in order to avoid circularity insofar as possible.

33. The lists may or may not be organized exactly as the physical books were. Certainly the easiest way to inventory a collection would be to go along your cabinets and shelves, listing items as you came to them, and in that case the written list would reflect the physical arrangement. But even if in some instances the books themselves were arranged in a manner different from the way they are presented in the lists, the latter still help us see how the ancients conceptualized collections and chose to organize them on paper.

34. He owned Homer, Hesiod, Callimachus, and Pindar. These authors rank first, second, third, and eleventh in order of frequency of attestation among the papyri from Oxyrhynchus: Krüger 1990, 214.

35. To the left of it is an open space of 20 cm, so that no column of titles seems to have preceded what we have; we thus have the beginning (though it is fragmentary). At the bottom of list no. 2 is a third, completely unrelated, text. It apparently was written in an open space below the list, so that our list probably came to an end at this point.

36. Exactly what is meant by Ἐγλογαὶ Ῥητ[όρων], how to fill the lacuna, and how to interpret the lines that follow immediately, cannot be determined with certainty. See Puglia 1998, 81–2; he posits, among other things, a lexicon in line 15. What is clear is that this part of the list consists of works in prose, and that they are all either certainly or probably related to rhetoric or oratory.

collector, then, possessed a small library of a hundred volumes or so, which he organized in three groups: poets (standard: Homer, Hesiod, Callimachus), then probably reference works on rhetoric, and, finally, a small collection of speeches.

No. 5 (philosophical works and one medical writer) is a list of unknown length, the papyrus being broken on all sides. Two columns survive, the left one nearly complete, the right one nearly all lost. The compiler generally provides quite full information: author, title, and in two cases (lines 8 and 21) a book number. That, plus the fact that the list is written on the *recto*, and not, as is usual with our lists, on the *verso* of a document, indicate that this list was prepared with some care. It certainly implies an awareness of genre: either it was a specialist collection of philosophy, or it represents the philosophy section of a larger collection organized by genre. It is, then, surprising to find clear signs of disorganization. Four authors appear more than once and at random spots in the list: Theophrastus appears once in each column, Chrysippus once in column 1 and twice in column 2, Diogenes once in each column, and Aristotle appears four times. Even similar works are not grouped together, for Aristotle's *Constitution of the Athenians* appears in column 1, and his *Constitution of the Neapolitans* in column 2. We are left with several impressions. The book collection itself does not seem to have been arranged alphabetically, because any such arrangement would presumably be reflected in the inventory. Nor were the rolls sorted before the compiler went through them to record authors and titles. We might then infer a smallish collection, stored in no particular order. Given the task of making an inventory of this collection, one or two persons (we might reasonably suppose) worked through the rolls, picking up one at a time and recording it, then moving on.[37] It is possible, of course, that this list served only as a first draft, a kind of counting up, and that a better organized list was subsequently prepared from it, but we cannot know if that was the case.[38]

37. Such a scenario (obviously conjectural) might help to explain the problematic ενοικια in line 3, which has been taken by several editors as ἐν οἰκίᾳ, "in the house." Those editors have suggested that the book collection was kept in more than one place, and that the items following this phrase were stored "in the house." That would be consistent with the scenario suggested here for the creation of the inventory. On the phrase, see further Otranto 2000, 82–3, citing earlier bibliography and alternative explanations.

38. This suggestion emerged in discussion of these papyri at the University of Pennsylvania. My thanks to Joseph Farrell and Ann Kuttner for pointing out the possibility of draft lists: any given list that survives might have been a first draft, a final draft, or some intermediate stage. A first draft, compiled directly from the book collection (as appears to have been the case with our no. 5 and most of the others), might represent more or less faithfully the degree of organization of the collection. A revised and more carefully organized later draft might present us instead with an ideally organized collection, more systematically arranged than the actual volumes on the shelves were. Such might be our no. 3, which we will consider further below. Even final lists intended for consultation, however, might well

In no. 6, we have an interesting variation on the genre/author organization: the basic distinction seems to be between prose, arranged by author (Plato, then Xenophon), and poetry, beginning with Homer. Plato's works, though, were apparently subdivided by genre: the *Symposium* (line 1) is not classed as a dialogue, but separately, and perhaps some other genre had been specified earlier.[39] Thus the basic and traditional system of classification here was applied flexibly, in a way that took account of the contents of the individual collection and, perhaps, the particular interest of the owner.

Finally, no. 3 (writers of comedy), as we have seen, may be all that survives of a comprehensive booklist from a library. If so, we have just part of the library's holdings in comedy—primarily old comedy at that, so we must assume that new comedy had its own section—and we may well have a list, our only such, that actually follows with some care the rule of organization by genre and authors arranged alphabetically. If this is correct, and if the library provided coverage of other genres (tragedy, epic, lyric; history, oratory, etc.) and miscellaneous works (among them works of reference) at the same level of completeness as it did comedy, then we might easily posit a collection of several thousands of volumes, impressively large for antiquity.[40]

In sum, these lists provide information that allows us to probe several aspects of book collections in Roman Egypt. In many particulars what we see is very similar to what we know of contemporary collections in Rome and Italy. We can see how the collectors conceptualized their collections by genre, subject, or both, in some cases the subcategories they used, and whether they were rigorous or casual in compiling the inventories. The lists we have often imply only the most rudimentary sorting and organization, and the goal in most cases seems to have been simply to count the

---

have been left disorganized or even chaotic to our eyes. There are examples of such from the libraries of monasteries in late antiquity. See, for example, Coquin 1975, a catalogue in which there are some logical groupings (New Testament texts, say), but the same groups reappear at more than one place in the list, and unrelated works are mixed in with them. So, too, Crum 1893, 60–2, no. 44, in which, as Crum noted, the books "are not arranged according to their contents." Both of these lists are in Coptic.

39. Puglia 1996, 52. The symposium itself may well have been thought of as a genre. Or perhaps Plato's *Symposium*, dominated as it is by long speeches, was considered as rhetoric.

40. For some comments on the capacities of Roman libraries, and the many uncertainties involved, see Dix and Houston 2006. Also, van Minnen 1998, 100, provides comparative numbers from medieval and Renaissance libraries. They are invariably small by modern standards. Similarly, booklists from Anglo-Saxon libraries in England range in size from a few books to a maximum of 65 (Lapidge 1985). These were codices, and thus the largest libraries would have contained the equivalent of about 250 to 300 papyrus rolls. What I would emphasize here is that we have in our lists from Egypt reasonably clear evidence for what common sense would suggest: that Roman-era libraries varied in size along a wide range from just a few volumes to several thousands, and that collections of even a few dozen volumes might well be considered, and in fact were, impressive.

volumes present in a given collection. In several cases we see the specific contents, which can vary from collections of basic classical authors to highly specialized or professional collections, and we can make rough guesses about the sizes of these collections. The evidence we have points, as we would have expected, to a wide range of sizes and in general to collections small by our standards.

2. CONCENTRATIONS OF PAPYRI FOUND TOGETHER IN PARTICULAR SITES

I turn now to our second kind of papyrological evidence, namely concentrations of papyri found together in specific and identifiable archaeological sites. Except for the Villa of the Papyri at Herculaneum, all of the sites are in Egypt. In general, these concentrations consist of hundreds or thousands of papyrus fragments, ranging in size from just one or a few letters to several dozen more or less complete columns of text, that were found together by excavators, mostly in the early years of the twentieth century. The assumption is that these concentrations were found together because in antiquity they were thrown out together,[41] and that the papyri in any given concentration thus originated in a single ancient book collection.[42] The most famous of these finds were the "three great literary finds" made by Bernard Grenfell and Arthur Hunt in the winter of 1905–1906.[43] It should be noted that it is by no means easy to reconstruct exactly what was in these finds. The excavators did not keep accurate records of precisely where they found things, and the reports they published are frustratingly vague. Grenfell and Hunt themselves never provided a complete list of the papyri in any of their great finds. They did assign inventory numbers to the papyri they found, but many of those numbers have now been lost.[44] One consequence is that we cannot be sure we can identify all the texts Grenfell and Hunt found in any one concentration,

41. In a few cases, it should be noted, the fragments were found not in a dump, but in a house: below, table 10.2, nos. 1, 2. Most, however, and all of those from Oxyrhynchus, were found in trash dumps, commingled with all the other rubbish (much of it long since decomposed) that ancient Egyptians might throw out.

42. If we do not assume they were thrown out together, we must assume that for some reason various people, from various houses, all (by a rather remarkable coincidence) decided to throw out literary texts at one time, and in one spot, in the dump. This seems a much less likely scenario, and I believe it is more probable that someone was clearing texts, old or no longer wanted, out of his library, and had them taken out together and thrown on the dump. Support for the possibility of coherent collections being preserved in dumps comes from the large numbers of similar bodies of documentary materials, in which specific names and dates often prove that the papyri in the concentration belonged together and came from a single original archive. A list of such archives is given in Montevecchi 1973, 248–61.

43. For further information on the excavations, both in general and specifically on the second and third finds, see Turner 1982 and Houston 2007.

44. Jones 1999, 56–60, gives an excellent account of the records, both as Grenfell and Hunt kept them, and as they are today.

and we thus should not ordinarily draw conclusions based on the absence of, say, a given author in a given concentration.

There are problems of another sort, too, in dealing with this material, leading to similar uncertainties. Once the papyri were placed in the dump, they (or detached fragments of them) might blow from one spot to another, thus contaminating or at least confusing our concentrations. Nor do dumps provide the kind of stable stratigraphy, especially when the archaeologist is concerned only to find papyri, that other kinds of sites do: sections of material can slide down slopes, and other trash can be deposited within a concentration before it is sealed.[45] Even so, such concentrations provide, as we will see, remarkably coherent collections of material, and if we work with what is there, rather than with what is missing, we can draw some useful conclusions. The concentrations and other collections attested archaeologically that I have been able to identify so far are presented in table 10.2.

Considered thus in summary form, these concentrations are reassuringly similar to the collections represented by the lists in table 10.1. They range later in date, nos. 8, 9, and 10 all being later than any of the lists in table 10.1, but there is a clear preference for classical authors, as opposed to writers of the Roman imperial period; we find both specialized libraries (nos. 1 and 6) and more general collections; the probable number of volumes varies widely along a range from fewer than twenty (nos. 2, 3, and 10) to well over a thousand (no. 1); and most collections, however small, include one or more "subliterary" items, such as grammatical works, commentaries, glossaries, and author's drafts (nos. 2, 4, 5, and 7, respectively, as examples). All of this is similar to what we saw in the lists of books. The variations in types of text, and the relatively high frequency of classical literature, are in both cases simply a reflection of what we find in the papyrological record generally and not at all surprising. The real question about these concentrations of papyri can be simply put: what do we learn when we thus divide papyri into their probable original collections? In what follows, I will suggest five things that we can learn by doing this.

1. *The useful life of manuscripts.* Within the concentrations of papyri, we frequently find manuscripts that were two or more centuries old at the time the collections to which they belonged were thrown out or destroyed. A few examples will suffice. In no. 4 (Breccia 1932), which was discarded sometime around A.D. 300,[46] there were three manuscripts

45. I am grateful to Nikolaos Gonis for discussing with me the problems involved in identifying the specific papyri that were found in any given concentration.

46. This collection was found intermingled with documents pertaining to a man named Sarapion alias Apollonianus, two of which have dates of A.D. 265 (*PSI* 1249 and 1250). Even if the books did not belong to Sarapion, it is quite clear that the books and the documents were discarded at roughly the same time, in other words, probably about a generation after the latest dated document, and so around 300.

Table 10.2. Concentrations of Papyri Found Together in Egypt and at Herculaneum

No.	Name or Publication	Dates of Mss. and Provenance	Size	Brief Description
1	Villa of the Papyri, Herculaneum.	Third B.C.-first A.D., Herculaneum	Estimated 1,100 rolls	Core of Epicurus's *On Nature*. Second group of second-century mss. Many first-century mss. of works by Philodemus. Some post-B.C. 40. Scattered others, including Latin.
2	Karanis, House B17. van Minnen 1998, 132–3.	Mid-second A.D.	5 rolls known	Two grammatical works, Menander, Callimachus's *Aitia*, *Acta Alexandrinorum*.
3	Grenfell and Hunt's first find. Cockle 1987, 22 n. 14; add *P.Oxy*. 1607, 1608, and 1612.	Early second to mid-third A.D., Oxyrhynchus	15 rolls	Lyric, tragedy, history, philosophy, oratory; commentary on Thucydides, treatise on literary composition, oration on the imperial cult. Six of 15 texts are on the *verso*.
4	Breccia 1932 find (*PSI* vols. 11 and 12)	first–third A.D., Oxyrhynchus	52 mss.	Numerous authors of the fifth to third centuries B.C. Also Ninus romance, another romance, Philo (a codex), mimes of Sophron, two commentaries, and a few others.
5	Grenfell and Hunt's third find (i.e., most of *P.Oxy*. XVII)	Late first–third A.D., Oxyrhynchus	25 mss.	Numerous authors of the fifth to third centuries B.C. Also glossary, commentary, treatise on rhetoric, two items in Latin.
6	*P.Oxy*. XVI "Group A." Jones 1999.	c. A.D. 200-fourth or fifth, Oxyrhynchus	45 in core group, with 11 more possibly belonging	Astronomical texts. A majority are codices. Of the rolls, at least 11 are on the *verso*.
7	Grenfell and Hunt's second find	First B.C.-mid-third A.D., Oxyrhynchus	35 mss. and two one-page compositions	See table 10.3 below for a complete list.
8	Codex library. See comments *ad P.Oxy*. 1369.	Fifth or 6th A.D., Oxyrhynchus	Between 11 and 14 codices	*Iliad, Odyssey, Oedipus Tyrannus, Medea, Orestes*, Aristophanes, unidentified tragedy.
9	Johnson 1913[1]	Sixth A.D.? Antinoopolis	Perhaps 20	Theocritus, a botanical work (probably Dioscurides), *Iliad, Odyssey*, Euripides (probably a student's exercise), comedy, history, theology, grammar, medicine.

(*Continued*)

Table 10.2. (*Continued*)

No.	Name or Publication	Dates of Mss. and Provenance	Size	Brief Description
10	Archive and codex collection of Dioscorus of Aphrodito[2]	Sixth A.D., Aphrodito	About 7 codices, found in a jar	Menander, Eupolis, *Iliad* (Bk. 2 at least), biography of Isocrates, Greek-Coptic glossary, Dioscorus's own compositions, archival materials.

Note: The concentrations are arranged roughly in chronological order. I list here only those collections that include at least some Greek or Latin non-Christian texts. Thus I exclude, for example, the collection of 21 Manichean and other religious texts (some in Coptic) from House 3 in Roman Kellis, even though they are fourth century and a coherent collection. I will use such collections for comparative purposes only. I also do not include the collection of books owned, in all likelihood, by Aurelia Ptolemais late in the third century, as reconstructed by Bagnall 1992, because they were not recovered together archaeologically. What we know so far as belonging to Aurelia was one or two copies of the *Iliad*, a history of Sicyon, and Julius Africanus's *Cestoi*. She may have owned many more.

1. Johnson 1914, 176, summarized the contents, but except for the Theocritus (MP^3 1487), Euripides (MP^3 415), and botanical work (*P.Ant.* 123 or following), the specific papyri Johnson found cannot now be identified.

2. These materials were found together in a jar, but as far as I can tell they have never been completely described or published. The list of the works Dioscorus owned given here derives from Clarysse 1983, 56–7. Calderini 1921, 150, mentions also Aristophanes and metrological tables.

datable to the first century and so at least two hundred years old.[47] In no. 7 (Grenfell and Hunt's second find), which was discarded about A.D. 400,[48] there are several manuscripts of the first century A.D., and one that may date from the second century B.C. and so have been more than five hundred years old when it was discarded.[49] And, of course, the collection in the Villa of the Papyri still possessed, when it was destroyed by Vesuvius in A.D. 79, a number of manuscripts of the second century B.C. and earlier, and so two hundred or more years old.[50] Thus papyrus manuscripts could quite clearly remain in use for two centuries or more, and often did. On the other hand, a considerable majority of volumes in our concentrations were not that old when they were discarded or (in the case of the Villa of the Papyri) destroyed. Many of the texts in concen-

47. *PSI* 1213 (Eupolis), 1214 (Sophron, *Mimes*), and 1305 (Novel of Ninus).

48. The manuscripts in Grenfell and Hunt's second find were intermingled with many fourth- and fifth-century documents, so they must have been thrown out in the fourth or fifth century. See further Houston 2007.

49. See below, table 10.3, nos. 1, 7, 8, 10, and 28, all of the first century A.D. The oldest would be the text of Ibycus, no. 16.

50. Cavallo identified seven manuscripts in the Villa (his Group A) as similar to Egyptian texts of the third century B.C.: Cavallo 1983, 28–9 and 50. He assigned the sixteen manuscripts in his Groups B and C to the second century: Cavallo 1983, 29–30, 50, and 56–7. And five manuscripts not assigned to any group are, Cavallo thought, similar to Egyptian texts of the third century B.C.: Cavallo 1983, 57, with notes 442 and 443.

trations nos. 3, 4, 5, and 7 were written in the second century and discarded in or around the end of the third century. Although we cannot know exactly why they were discarded (change of taste? or interest? replacement by *codices*? or simply worn out), the simple fact remains that the concentrations indicate a useful life of between one hundred and two hundred years for a majority of the volumes, with a significant minority lasting two hundred years or more.[51]

2. Did novels remain in vogue for more than a brief period? In 1996, Guglielmo Cavallo published a most useful article on what the Italians call the "letteratura di consumo," in the case of this particular article meaning novels and romances.[52] Cavallo noted that most romances known from papyri are attested only in copies produced within a limited period of time, often less than a century. The Novel of Ninus, for example, is known only from papyri written in the middle and second half of the first century A.D.[53] Cavallo inferred from this that such works enjoyed a brief period of popularity, but then were dropped in favor of new stories.

Looking at books sorted by collection, however, allows us to suggest a more nuanced picture. The Breccia 1932 find (table 10.2, no. 4) was thrown out, as we have seen, in about A.D. 300, but it includes a first-century copy of the Novel of Ninus. In this case, that is, the novel was either passed along in a collection for some two hundred years, or purchased as a used copy long after it was originally written. It is possible, of course, that this particular manuscript is an intruder in this collection, blown hither by the wind, but that it does belong to the collection is indicated by the presence in this same concentration of a second novel and of a first-century copy of the mimes of Sophron, not to be sure a novel, but certainly relatively light reading.[54] In any case, this should keep us alert to the possibility that extended works of prose fiction might be kept in collections, and perhaps read and reread, long after they were first produced.

3. The formation of collections. If we examine the concentrations closely, we can begin to formulate some hypotheses on how they came into being. Although we cannot here deal with all of the concentrations, we can look at one of them—Grenfell and Hunt's second find—in some detail. In table 10.3

51. A few anecdotes in literature similarly document items lasting two or three hundred years. Gellius, for example, reports finding an autograph manuscript of Aelius Stilo in the library of the Temple of Peace (Gell. *NA* 16.8.2). The manuscript must have been more than 200 years old, and probably about 250.

52. Cavallo 1996, 29. I will refer to these works as novels, following Stephens and Winkler 1995, 3.

53. A complete list of the known papyrus copies of novels is provided by Stephens and Winkler 1995, 480–1. Their list clearly supports Cavallo's point. Only two novels are known from copies produced over a period of 150 years or more: Achilles Tatius (150–300) and Chariton (150–600), and in Chariton's case we have three papyrus rolls all dated in the period 150–200, and one parchment codex of about A.D. 600.

54. *PSI* 1220 (novel) and 1214 (Sophron).

Table 10.3. Grenfell and Hunt's "Second Great Find" of Literary Papyri

Catalogue and MP^3 Numbers	Date (all A.D. unless noted)	Contents	Comments	Scribe, if Known
1. MP^3 55	First	Alcaeus	At least two later hands provide variants. Glosses. Exegetic notes. Myrsilus cited, frg. 12.9.	
2. MP^3 56	Second	Alcaeus (Book 1?)	Corrections by *diorthotes*.	A32
3. MP^3 59	Late second	Alcaeus	Exegetic notes, perhaps by *diorthotes*.	
4. MP^3 61	Late second	Alcaeus	Exegetic notes, one on the myth of Sisyphus. Didymus cited, frg. 15.	A20
5. MP^3 65	late second	Alcaeus	Glosses. Exegetic notes. Myrsilus cited, frg. 40.[1]	A5
6. MP^3 177	Second	Bacchylides	*Sillybos* attached[2]	
7. MP^3 179	First	Bacchylides	One hand added variants, a second exegetic notes. Ptol(emaeus?) cited for variant, frg. 5.	
8. MP^3 216	First	Callimachus, *Aitia*	Corrections by *diorthotes*.	
9. MP^3 218 (on *verso*)	Second–third	Callimachus, *Iambi*		
10. MP^3 237	First	Cercidas, *Meliambi*	One or two hands added glosses, variants, and exegetic notes. Hesiod cited, frg. 1, col. 3.20.	A4
11. MP^3 256	Early second	Demosthenes *Olynth.* 1–3, *Phil.* 1, *De Pace*		
12. MP^3 357	Second–third	Ephorus Book 12 (or 11)		
13. MP^3 473	Late second	Herodotus Book 2	5 lines added by corrector from another ms.	A5
14. MP^3 474	First-early second	Herodotus Book 3	At least two later hands added variants and perhaps exegetic notes.	A7
15. MP^3 525	Second–third	Hesiod, *Catalogue?*	Corrections by *diorthotes*.	

16. MP^3 1237	c. 130 B.C.[3]		Ibycus	Later hand (first A.D.?) added diacriticals. Exegetic note cites [...] imachus.	
17. MP^3 1363[4]	Early second		Pindar, *Paeans* 6, 12, others?	Corrections by *diorthotes*.	
18. MP^3 1367	Late second		Pindar, *Dithyrambs*	At least three later hands. Variants. Glosses. Exegetic notes.	A20
19. MP^3 1368	Late second		Pindar, *Dithyrambs?* and perhaps other poets and works. Probably more than one roll is represented.	Variants. Exegetic notes on grammar (frg. 27.6), myth (frg. 8).	A20
20. MP^3 1360	Third		Pindar, *Hymns*, *Paeans*, others? Probably 3 to 5 rolls are represented.	Scholarly notes, some by the original scribe, on myth (frg. 29.4–6), historical questions, obscure references, orthography. Didymus cited, frg. 97.	A30
21. MP^3 1421	Late second		Plato, *Republic* Book 8	Extensive scholarly notes, some using tachygraphic symbols.	
22. MP^3 1445	Second		Sappho Book 1	Corrections by *diorthotes*.	
23. MP^3 1449	Third		Sappho Book 4?		A30
24. MP^3 1456	Second		Satyrus, *Life of Euripides* (from Book 6 of his *Lives*)		
25. MP^3 1472	Late second		Sophocles, *Eurypylus*	Companion ms. to no. 26: same scribe and corrector. Variants, with refs. to other mss. Perhaps exegetic notes.	B1
26. MP^3 1473	Late second		Sophocles, *Ichneutae*	Companion ms. to no. 25: same scribe and corrector. Variants, with at least three other mss. or sources cited.[5]	B1
27. MP^3 1471	Late second		Sophocles, *Trachiniae*	Variant, exegetic note.	

(Continued)

Table 10.3. (*Continued*)

Catalogue and MP³ Numbers	Date (all A.D. unless noted)	Contents	Comments	Scribe, if Known
28. MP³ 1495	Late first	Theocritus	Corrections by *diorthotes*.	A28
29. Parts of MP³ 1445[6]	Second	Lyric, perhaps Sappho	One marginal note.	
30. MP³ 1739	Second	Satyr play	Exegetic notes, perhaps by the original scribe.	A11
31. MP³ 1321	Early second	*Hypotheseis* of comedies of Menander		
32. MP³ 2195 *recto*	Late second	Anonymous work on Alexander the Great	Correction by *diorthotes*. On *verso* is no. 33.	
33. MP³ 2127 *verso*	Second–third	Lexicon of rare words	Mistakes, but no corrections.	
34. MP³ 2070	Second–Third	Biographies (Sappho, Simonides, Aesop, Thucydides, Demosthenes, and others)		
35. MP³ 2290	Early third	Problems in literary criticism[7]	Corrections by *diorthotes*.	

Note: This concentration also included two single-sheet drafts of short works: a verse panegyric on the gymnasiarch Theon, and a prose encomium on the fig (MP³ 1847 and MP³ 2527 respectively). The first is probably the author's own copy, because it contains erasures and corrections that appear to be those of an author's draft. Turner 1971, 90–1, no. 50, discusses the nature of this document. The erasures and revisions are easily visible in the photograph he provides.

1. McNamee 2007, chapter 3, takes this text, in which text and annotations are by the same scribe, as "conceivably a copy used by [a] grammatical student or [his] teacher."

2. The surviving fragment comes from Bacchylides *Dithyramb* 17, but the *sillybos* simply says "Bacchylides, Dithyrambs," so the volume presumably contained all of the dithyrambs.

3. For the date: Barron 1969, 119 with n. 3, citing E. G. Turner. It had been dated to the first century B.C. by Grenfell and Hunt.

4. This manuscript includes *P.Oxy.* 1604 and *P.Oxy.* 2445 frg. 1. For the assignment of this latter fragment to the manuscript represented by *P.Oxy.* 1604, see E. Lobel, *ad P.Oxy.* 2445.

5. The two Sophocles mss., nos. 25 and 26, were professionally prepared, as shown by the inclusion of stichometric counts in the *Ichneutae*. The corrector was different from the original scribe, but the same for the two manuscripts. There were not many exegetic notes, if any, in what survives, and the notes seem aimed at providing a correct text, not elucidating Sophocles. The sources cited for alternate readings in no. 26 are The(on), Ar or Arn (possibly Aristophanes or Aristarchus), and N with a vertical stroke, perhaps for Nicanor.

6. Lobel and Page 1955, 25, distinguished a number of the lyric fragments that Grenfell and Hunt had published together as *P.Oxy.* 1231 as belonging to a separate manuscript. To my knowledge, Lobel and Page did not include the fragments within their text of Sappho and Alcaeus, so I have classed them simply as lyric, perhaps Sappho. The particular fragments, all of them very small, are *P.Oxy.* 1231 (= MP³ 1445) 24, 32–34, 37 + 47, 39, 40, 46, and probably 8. What survives of a note is in frg. 33.

7. This work is not unlike a series of exegetic annotations. It takes up in turn a series of problems, such as obscure allusions, and elucidates them by reference to a wide range of authors in both poetry and prose.

I list the papyri that can be assigned to that find, arranged alphabetically, with *adespota* (works of which the author is not known) and various miscellaneous works added at the end. A few preliminary comments will be useful.

I follow the consensus opinion on the production of literary works on papyrus rolls as it has emerged in the past few years. Briefly put, the consensus holds that most literary works were prepared, probably on commission, by professional, trained scribes. One scribe would copy the text from a master copy, perhaps correcting some of his own mistakes as he went. Before the papyrus was turned over to the purchaser, it was often checked against the master copy by a second scribe, the *diorthotes*. Both the original scribe and the *diorthotes* were, naturally enough, sometimes very careful, sometimes not careful at all, and usually somewhere in between. Annotations could be included in the text: the purchaser might ask the original scribe to include whatever notes were already in the master copy, or a second scribe could be commissioned to add notes, or they might be added at some later stage.[55] (More on this later.) The "Comments" column of table 10.3 gives a brief summary of the kind of annotations to be found in each manuscript. By "gloss" I mean a definition or clarification, usually by means of a synonym, of a single word or phrase, and by "exegetic note" I mean a more extensive note, one that explains the material at hand, for example by elaborating on a myth, providing background information, or drawing on similar passages elsewhere. I mention the corrections done by a *diorthotes* only in cases in which those are the *only* additions.

This concentration was found by Grenfell and Hunt over a period of weeks (January to March 1906) in one particular mound, a part of the dump of ancient Oxyrhynchus that is (or was in 1906) known as the kôm Ali El Gamman. The list of manuscripts found at that time is based on that of Funghi and Messeri Savorelli 1992b, 77 n. 16, but with both additions and deletions; in the appendix, I give the evidence that shows that each of these papyri was a part of this "second find," as well as the *P.Oxy.* numbers of each manuscript.

Obviously, the collection includes manuscripts that were written over a considerable arc of time, from as early as 130 B.C. (no. 16, Ibycus) through the first century A.D. (nos. 1, 7, 8, 10, and 28) to around A.D. 200 (nos. 9, 12, 15, and 23, with others written in the middle or second half of the second century A.D.). No single scribe predominates, even if we consider a limited period of time. For example, many of the manuscripts in the collection were produced in the middle or the latter half of the second century, and within this period we find copies made by at least five, and surely several more, professional scribes: scribe A5 (nos. 5, 13); scribe A11 (no. 30), scribe A20 (nos. 4, 18, and 19), scribe A32 (no. 2), and

---

55. For the process of production, with much more detail, see Johnson 2004, 157–60 (scribes and commissions), Turner 1980, 93–6 (editing and correcting), and McNamee 2007. Kleberg 1989, 45–54, working more with literary than papyrological evidence, and primarily with evidence from the city of Rome, presents a very similar picture.

scribe B1 (nos. 25, 26).[56] Work of at least four of these scribes is known
from other archaeological contexts as well,[57] indicating that they worked
not just for this book collector, but for a number of collectors. All of this is
consistent with the picture of books produced by trained copyists as
outlined above, although this evidence does not allow us to rule out
other scenarios, such as purchase of some items at auction or from used-
book dealers.[58] In any case, this collection does not seem to have been
created by reliance upon any one copyist; rather, the owner(s) patronized a
series of copyists.

4. *Personalities of the collections.* We saw above that the lists of books in
papyri (table 10.1) allow us to assess the contents and organization of book
collections, and to learn something of the interests of their owners. The
concentrations of literary works enable us to push even further in this
direction, for here we have the manuscripts themselves, and we can see
what types of literature each collector favored, and how he treated and
worked with his volumes.[59] I will make a few quick observations about
some of the concentrations, and we will then study Grenfell and Hunt's
second find (table 10.3) in more detail. One important preliminary note:
I will often, for convenience, refer to "the collector," as though only one
person owned each set of books. It should be understood, though, that any
given set of books might have been, and probably was, owned by a succession of collectors, with additions and deletions occurring over time. We will
discuss precisely this matter below, under point 5, "life of the collection."

The Villa of the Papyri at Herculaneum (table 10.2, no. 1) is, of course,
the most obvious and complete example of a private library in which the
collector's interests are made clear by the identity of the books. Even if
the Villa possessed general collections of Greek and Latin literature,[60] it is
very clear that philosophy, and in particular Epicurean philosophy, was of
great interest to the Villa's book collector(s), and continued to be so for

---

56. The manuscripts assigned to various scribes are conveniently set out in Johnson
2004, 61–5, drawing on and expanding Krüger 1990, 193–5. I say that there were several
additional scribes at work because other manuscripts in the collection are dated in the same
period but not (yet) assigned to any particular scribe. These are nos. 3, 6, 22, and 29 (all lyric
poetry, and probably professionally produced), 27 (Sophocles), 21, 24, and 32.

57. These are A5, A11, A20, and A32. See Johnson 2004, 61–5, for lists of all their
known manuscripts. B1, too, may have done other work, in prose: Turner 1971, 66 (noted by
Johnson 2004, 64, *ad* scribe B1).

58. It is also possible that the book collector owned one or more of the scribes (who
might be slaves), and that the slave scribe produced books both for his own master and to be
sold to others. We cannot know the exact mechanisms.

59. The concentrations do not, of course, give us any information about the organization
or physical arrangement of the collections.

60. The suggestion that a great villa such as this must have had general collections of
Greek and Latin classics in addition to its philosophical collection has been made frequently,
but is quite uncertain. See, for discussion of the matter and some bibliography, Johnson
2006, 496.

more than a century.[61] For our purposes, this library is important above all because it shows that a coherent collection could continue to exist for an extended period, well beyond a single person's lifetime, and that its essential contents and integrity as a specialized collection might remain intact throughout that period.

Grenfell and Hunt's first find (table 10.2, no. 3) contains 15 manuscripts. At least six of these, or 40 percent, are written on the *verso* of documents,[62] and such recycling of documentary rolls is usually taken as a sign of an economy-minded collector, one who was trying to save money by having his copies made on secondhand rather than new papyrus.[63] Strikingly different in this regard is concentration no. 4, the Breccia 1932 find. Here, of fifty-two rolls, only two, both of them books of the *Iliad*,[64] are certainly written on the *verso*, so this collector was apparently less concerned with cost. Thus various characteristics can be identified when we treat papyri neither one at a time nor *en masse*, but rather sorted into the book collections from which they seem to have come. A closer look at Grenfell and Hunt's second find (table 10.3) will illustrate this further.

One notes immediately that this collection is heavy on poetry, especially but not exclusively lyric. There are at least five different manuscripts, by at least four different scribes, of parts of Alcaeus (nos. 1–5). Whether these combined to form a single and perhaps complete edition of Alcaeus's works (which in antiquity were collected in ten books) we cannot tell, because it is also possible that the collection possessed duplicate copies of one or more of the books of his poetry.[65] There are two works, *Dithyrambs* and perhaps the *Encomia*, of Bacchylides (nos. 6, 7),

61. The collection as we know it was presumably assembled in the first instance by the philosopher Philodemus. Cavallo 1983, 65, suggested that at least a few books on Epicureanism were added to the collection even after Philodemus's death in about 40 B.C. Parsons 1989, 360, expressed doubts about Cavallo's dating of these later manuscripts, because Cavallo's only evidence was paleographical, but in any case the library continued to exist, and seems to have preserved its essential focus on Epicureanism, until the destruction of the Villa in A.D. 79.

62. *P.Oxy.* 984 (Pindar), 918 (*Hellenica Oxyrhynchia*), 985 (Euripides), 986 (a commentary on Thucydides), 1045 (treatise on literary composition), and 1044 (Plato): thus both literature and subliterary works.

63. So Lama 1991, 93 (though noting that there are many variables to consider). Krüger 1990, 161, provides the statistical norms for papyri from Oxyrhynchus. Of all the papyri recovered there, 17.9% have, like our six examples, documents on one side and literary or subliterary works on the other. Thus Grenfell and Hunt's first find had something more than twice as many reused documents as Oxyrhynchus papyri in general. It should be noted that, despite the use of old documents, the texts appear to have been professionally copied, because stichometric (line) counts appear in the Pindar and Euripides. On the implications of the presence of such counts, see Montevecchi 1973, 338–9.

64. *PSI* 1185 (*Iliad* 6) and 1188 (*Iliad* 10). The latter has wide margins and handsome letters, and was no doubt done by a professional scribe.

65. We have already noted probable duplicates in the lists of papyri, for example, among the Platonic dialogues (table 10.1, no. 6) and the works of Epicharmus (table 10.1, no. 3). Cf. also n. 25 above for duplicates in the Villa of the Papyri collection.

two of Callimachus (nos. 8, 9), plus single rolls (so far as we know) of Cercidas, Hesiod, and Ibycus (nos. 10, 15, and 16). Pindar (nos. 17–20) is represented by a large but uncertain number of rolls, probably at least seven and perhaps a dozen, and two of them were copied by scribe A20, who also did one of the Alcaeus texts.[66] There are two manuscripts, probably of different books and perhaps parts of a complete edition, of Sappho (nos. 22, 23). Two of the plays of Sophocles (nos. 25, 26) were copied by the same scribe, then annotated by the same second hand, and so probably formed a set, which may well have included other plays as well. A third play of Sophocles (no. 27), a relatively early text of Theocritus (no. 28, first century A.D.), more lyric, and a satyr play (nos. 29, 30) complete the list of poetic works attested in the collection. The absence of Homer in this concentration is striking. As we noted above, the nature of the finds made by Grenfell and Hunt forbids us from reading too much into the absence of any given author, but Homer is so ubiquitous in the papyrological record that his absence in this collection, which is otherwise so strong in poetry, should at least be noted, even if it cannot be explained.[67]

There is also some prose. No. 14 is a text of Herodotus that was carefully written and then annotated by at least two nearly contemporary hands, who provided variants and, perhaps, explanatory notes. Demosthenes, Ephorus, and Satyrus all appear (nos. 11, 12, and 24), all of them in manuscripts that have no annotation. The Plato text (no. 21, a section from the *Republic*) is, in stark contrast, heavily annotated with exceptionally learned notes.[68]

It is, in fact, the frequency, density, and content of marginal notes that are the most striking characteristic of this collection. Of the thirty-five manuscripts or groups of manuscripts into which it can be divided, at least sixteen, or some 45 percent, contain marginal notes that cite other sources for variant readings, explicate matters in the text, or both.[69] Not only is this percentage very different from that of the Breccia 1932 collection (table 10.2, no. 4), in which only three of fifty-two manuscripts, or about 6 percent, certainly contain such marginalia, it is also a much higher figure than the average for all papyri: Kathleen McNamee

66. The Pindar texts and their copyists have been carefully studied by Funghi and Messeri Savorelli 1992a. Johnson 2004, 63, *ad* scribe A20, did not accept all of their suggestions concerning that scribe.

67. Not that we can't take a guess. The absence of Homer in Grenfell and Hunt's second find may indicate not that the person who assembled this collection disliked Homer, but rather that the person who threw out the lyric texts Grenfell and Hunt found *did* like Homer and wanted to keep his Homer volumes. He also may have wanted to keep Euripides, another very popular author not represented in this concentration. Or perhaps the original collector, a scholarly reader as will emerge in what follows, was less concerned with such standard authors as Homer and Euripides.

68. The notes, written in part in shorthand and extremely difficult to read, let alone understand, have now been largely deciphered and explicated by McNamee and Jacovides 2003.

69. Nos. 1, 3, 4, 5, 7, 10, 14, 16, 18, 19, 20, 21, 25, 26, 27, 30.

estimates that only some 5 percent of all literary manuscripts have significant marginal notes.[70] Of the Alcaeus papyri listed in the Mertens-Pack database, seven have annotations,[71] and of those seven, four—more than half of all the known annotated copies of Alcaeus—come, remarkably, from this one collection. We cannot, of course, know exactly who added these notes, or when, although we can identify several possibilities. Some seem to have been added by the original scribe in the course of the production of the text (no. 20); others were probably added by a second hand, but still in the course of production of the text, as in the case of our matched set of two plays of Sophocles (nos. 25, 26); and some were probably added by the owner/reader of the text (no. 21, Plato).[72] William Johnson, noting that annotations are often written by hands that are roughly contemporary in date, has suggested plausibly that many such additions were the result of friends sharing texts with one another, discussing them, and adding comments or corrections.[73] We cannot know the exact process, but it seems safe to conclude that the collection of books from which Grenfell and Hunt's second find derived was owned by one or more persons who were interested in knowing about variant readings, establishing correct texts, and adding helpful notes, and that they were willing to have such information added to their texts or to commission or purchase such texts with the notes already included. This, then, is a serious reader (or series of readers), and accordingly we should note the presence in the collection also of an edition of the *hypotheseis* of the plays of Menander (no. 31), of a series of biographies (no. 34), and of at least part of Satyrus's *Lives* (no. 24).[74] All of these would provide background information on writers that would be particularly welcome to our collector, given that ancient texts did not include prefaces or introductions of the sort that we take for granted in editions of our classical authors (such as, for example, the Folger Shakespeare Library).

    5. *The life of the collection.* How did this collection—Grenfell and Hunt's second find—come into existence, and how long did it continue

---

70. McNamee 2007, 5. The figure is only approximate because there are many variables (in definition of marginal notes, for example) and uncertainties in the texts themselves.

71. MP^3 59, 60, 61, 63, 67, 69, and 71.1.

72. McNamee 2001 suggested, very cautiously, that the notes in the Plato manuscript might have been added by the owner/reader of the volume, and that the presence of a number of shorthand symbols in the notes might even suggest that he added the notes in the course of listening to a lecture on the passage.

73. Johnson forthcoming. As Johnson points out, such a scenario is consistent with the kind of sharing and commenting implicit in scholars' letters such as *P.Oxy.* 2192. This should not be taken as implying that these various readers added their personal reactions or comments, for virtually all surviving annotations consist of material that derived from earlier scholarly work on the texts and consisted of variant readings, explanations of obscure myths and names, and the like.

74. Perhaps relevant here is the inclusion in this same concentration of what was apparently an author's copy of a panegyric on the gymnasiarch Theon (MP^3 1847) and the (epideictic?) encomium on the fig (MP^3 2527), both of which imply an owner involved in an active literary life.

to exist as a coherent and identifiable collection? We cannot answer these questions with any certainty, for there are too many variables and possible scenarios, but we can observe what we have and draw at least some useful inferences. Let us start with what we know.

First, seventeen, or just under half, of the manuscripts were written in the middle or second half of the second century A.D.[75] Several of these second-century manuscripts relate to what seems to have been the owner or owners' particular interest: two of the Alcaeus manuscripts were heavily annotated (nos. 4, 5), as were several rolls of Pindar (nos. 18, 19), the Plato (no. 21), and two of the plays of Sophocles (nos. 25, 26). Second, from that period of about seventy years, we have manuscripts copied by at least six different scribes: A5, A11, A20, A32, B1, and one or more unidentified scribes who copied manuscripts nos. 3, 6, 22, and others. It seems reasonable to infer from these two observations that one or two (or more) owners commissioned copies, or bought ready-made copies, from a range of scribes over the course of this period.

Third, we can note that eight of the thirty-five manuscripts (nos. 9, 12, 15, 20, 23, 33, 34, and 35) date from about A.D. 200 or the early part of the third century. These include texts that form part of the central interest of the concentration: Callimachus (no. 9), Hesiod (no. 15), the extensive edition of Pindar (no. 20, at least three rolls), and Sappho (no. 23). From this I would infer that the collection was maintained, and in some cases augmented, well into the third century. Its life as a recognizable collection, then, may well have lasted for about three generations, and possibly a good deal longer.

Beyond this it is difficult to go. Assuming a mid-second-century collector interested above all in poetry, we could posit that he inherited or purchased the earlier materials *en bloc*, thus acquiring the core of his collection; or that he bought them individually on the used-book market;[76] or some combination of such procedures. The history of our collection, then, would look something like this: toward the middle of the second century, our collector began to assemble a collection strong in poetry.[77] He may have inherited a preexisting collection, or perhaps he bought a number of rolls (hence the volumes copied in the first century and earlier); he certainly purchased or commissioned a number of new rolls (thus the large number of texts copied in the middle and second half of the second century). The collection so formed reflected its originator's interest in poetry and maintained its shape over time, being added to even when it passed to other owners. At some point toward the middle of the third century, the collection seems to have stopped growing and fallen out of use, and within two or three generations

75. Nos. 2, 3, 4, 5, 6, 13, 18, 19, 21, 22, 24, 25, 26, 27, 29, 30, and 32.

76. Starr 1990 argued that there was no significant used-book trade in the Roman Empire, but see Peter White, ch. 11, in this volume.

77. For the sake of simplicity, I will state the history as if there were a single owner, but of course there may have been more than one, both at any one time and over the course of the years.

after that the fragments we now have were discarded. A history of this sort, which is suggested by the manuscripts we have, would be quite similar to the history of the Herculaneum collection as reconstructed by Cavallo: Philodemus, Cavallo suggested, purchased the core collection of about two dozen third- and second-century texts while in Athens in the early part of the first century B.C., then settled at Herculaneum and added the majority of the texts while there. The collection then passed down, maintaining its basic shape and emphasis, until its destruction in A.D. 79.[78]

Although such histories cannot be proved, they are reasonable enough, and they are consistent with such evidence as we have.[79] Probably the most likely, and the most important, aspect of the history of Grenfell and Hunt's second find is that, on almost any reading of the evidence, this concentration of volumes continued in existence for several generations as a recognizable whole. No doubt some volumes were discarded, and others added, over time.[80] Presumably the collection passed down from generation to generation, either within a single family or passing from one family to another by sale, gift (from teacher to student, for example), or inheritance. Quite possibly, the manuscripts represented by our fragments formed part of a larger collection, the nature of which must remain unknown to us. But that it did exist as a coherent group of volumes, and for an extended period of time, seems highly likely, because otherwise we would have to assume that one person purchased all of these texts on the used-book market in the third century, a much less likely scenario. It is the segregation of papyri into distinct collections that allows us to study all of these phenomena. For the first time, we can draw upon evidence more detailed than the anecdotes about libraries in literature and more varied than the single collection in the Villa of the Papyri at Herculaneum. This allows us, as we have seen, to formulate useful hypotheses and to move forward, however carefully, toward a more complete understanding of ancient book collections.

78. Above, n. 50, for the earlier texts. For his summary comments on the post-Philodemus history of the library, see Cavallo 1983, 65, but note also the reservations of Parsons (above, n. 61).

79. Not all concentrations of papyri fit neatly into the same pattern, however, although I know of none that is significantly different. In the case of the concentration of manuscripts found by Evaristo Breccia in 1932, there is no clear pattern of acquisitions concentrated within a given period of, say, fifty years. Of the fifty-two manuscripts represented in that collection, as many as eleven may date to the first century or early in the second century; thirty are dated to the second century, but to no more specific date than that; and the other eleven are later in date, c. 200 or early third century. That is, we cannot demonstrate for the Breccia 1932 concentration a single period of development comparable to those that appear in the collections from the Villa of the Papyri and in Grenfell and Hunt's second find. If the second-century manuscripts in the Breccia 1932 find could be dated more precisely, however, it might well turn out that that collection, too, had a history similar to that of the other two collections. See further on the Breccia 1932 collection Houston 2007.

80. As we have seen, eight new manuscripts—nearly a quarter of the concentration—were added c. A.D. 200 or in the early third century. We need not assume that the collection remained static, even if it appears that it maintained a single primary focus over a period of a century or more.

APPENDIX: EVIDENCE FOR THE COMPOSITION OF GRENFELL AND HUNT'S "SECOND GREAT FIND" OF LITERARY PAPYRI

I provide here references to the statements provided by Grenfell and Hunt (and Lobel) that show that each of the papyri listed above in table 10.3 was found in the "second find." The catalogue numbers are as in table 10.3; I add here the *P.Oxy.* numbers as well.

Catalogue, MP³, and P.Oxy. Numbers	Contents	Reference to Evidence Showing that the Fragments Came from the Second Find
1. MP³ 55 = P.Oxy. 1789 + 2166(e) + XXI Addenda, 146–7	Alcaeus	P.Oxy. XV preface
2. MP³ 56 = P.Oxy. 1233 + 2081(d) + 2166(b) + XXI Addenda, 127–30	Alcaeus (Book 1?)	P.Oxy. X preface
3. MP³ 59 = P.Oxy. 1234 + 1360 + 2166(c) + XVIII Addenda, 182 + XXI Addenda, 130–4	Alcaeus	P.Oxy. X preface
4. MP³ 61 = P.Oxy. 1788 + 2166(e) + XXI Addenda, 139–47 + XXIII Addenda, 105–6	Alcaeus	P.Oxy. XV preface, cf. introduction to 1788
5. MP³ 65 = P.Oxy. 2297	Alcaeus	Introduction to P.Oxy. 1092 (Herodotus): Hunt says that the Herodotus was found together with another text (which he does not identify) in a virtually identical hand. In the introduction to P.Oxy. 2297, he says that the Alcaeus is in the same hand as the Herodotus text.
6. MP³ 177 = P. Oxy. 1091	Bacchylides, *Dithyrambs*	P.Oxy. VIII preface, and *EEF Archaeological Reports 1905–1906*, p. 12
7. MP³ 179 = P. Oxy. 1361 + 2081.e	Bacchylides	P.Oxy. XI preface: "the lyric pieces." Cf. introduction to P.Oxy. 1361, distinguishing it from P.Oxy. 1091 but noting that it comes from the great find of 1906.

8. MP³ 216 = P. Oxy. 1362	Callimachus, *Aitia*	*P.Oxy.* XI preface: "the lyric pieces." Grenfell and Hunt seem to include this among those pieces, because they do not refer to elegiacs as a separate category.
9. MP³ 218 = P. Oxy. 1363	Callimachus, *Iambi*	*P.Oxy.* XI preface: "the lyric pieces." Grenfell and Hunt seem to include this among those pieces, because they do not refer to the iambics as a separate category.
10. MP³ 237 = P. Oxy. 1082	Cercidas, *Meliambi*	*P.Oxy.* VIII preface, and *ad P.Oxy.* 1082
11. MP³ 256 = P. Oxy. 1810	Demosthenes, *Olynth.* 1–3, *Phil.* 1, *De Pace*	*P.Oxy.* XV preface
12. MP³ 357 = P. Oxy. 1610	Ephorus Book 12 (or 11)	*P.Oxy.* XIII preface, and introductions to *P.Oxy.* 1610 and 1619
13. MP³ 473 = P. Oxy. 1092	Herodotus Book 2	*P.Oxy.* VIII preface
14. MP³ 474 = P. Oxy. 1619	Herodotus Book 3	*P.Oxy.* XIII preface, and introduction to *P.Oxy.* 1619
15. MP³ 525 = P. Oxy. 1359	Hesiod, *Catalogue of Women?*	*P.Oxy.* XI preface
16. MP³ 1237 = P. Oxy. 1790 + 2081(f)	Ibycus	*P.Oxy.* XV preface
17. MP³ 1363 = P. Oxy. 1792 + 2442 frgs. 32–37	Pindar, *Paeans* and perhaps other works	*P.Oxy.* XV preface
18. MP³ 1367 = P. Oxy. 1604¹	Pindar, *Dithyrambs*	Introduction to *P.Oxy.* 1604²
19. MP³ 1368 = P. Oxy. 2445, frgs. 2–32	Pindar, *Dithyrambs?* and perhaps other works	Introduction to *P.Oxy.* 2445: fragments found together with those of *P.Oxy.* 1604 (Pindar); frg. 1 probably came from the ms. represented by *P.Oxy.* 1604
20. MP³ 1360 = P. Oxy. 2442	Pindar, *Hymns, Paeans,* and perhaps other works	Introduction to *P.Oxy.* 2442: found commingled with the fragments of *P.Oxy.* 1787 (Sappho)
21. MP³ 1421 = P. Oxy. 1808	Plato, *Republic* Book 8	*P.Oxy.* XV preface
22. MP³ 1445 = P. Oxy. 1231 + 2081(c) + 2166(a).³	Sappho Book 1	*P.Oxy.* X preface
23. MP³ 1449 = P. Oxy. 1787 + 2166(d) + *P. Halle* 2	Sappho Book 4?	*P.Oxy.* XV preface
24. MP³ 1456 = P. Oxy. 1176	Satyrus, *Life of Euripides*	Introduction to *P.Oxy.* 1619.
25. MP³ 1472 = P. Oxy. 1175 + 2081 (b)	Sophocles, *Eurypylus*	Introduction to *P.Oxy.* 1619. Cf. the introduction to *P.Oxy.* 1174: these fragments were found close to those of the *Ichneutae.*

(*Continued*)

Catalogue, MP³, and P.Oxy. Numbers	Contents	Reference to Evidence Showing that the Fragments Came from the Second Find
26. MP³ 1473 = P. Oxy. 1174 + 2081a	Sophocles, *Ichneutae*	Introduction to P.Oxy. 1619, but cf. the introduction to P.Oxy. 1174: most of the fragments were found not in 1906, but in 1907.
27. MP³ 1471 = P. Oxy. 1805 + 3687	Sophocles, *Trachiniae*	P.Oxy. XV preface
28. MP³ 1495 = P. Oxy. 1806	Theocritus	P.Oxy. XV preface
29. Parts of MP³ 1445 = P.Oxy. 1231 frgs. 24, 32–34, 37 + 47, 39, 40, 46 (and 8?)	Lyric, perhaps Sappho	P.Oxy. X preface for P.Oxy. 1231 (Sappho). See note 6, table 10.3, for these fragments as belonging to a separate manuscript
30. MP³ 1739 = P. Oxy. 1083 (+ 2453?)	Satyr play	P.Oxy. VIII preface, and *ad* P.Oxy. 1082
31. MP³ 1321 = P. Oxy. 1235	*Hypotheseis* of comedies by Menander	P.Oxy. X preface
32. MP³ 2195 = P. Oxy. 1798 + 2081(g)	Anonymous work on Alexander the Great	P.Oxy. XV preface. On *recto* of P. Oxy. 1802 (the lexicon of rare words)
33. MP³ 2127 = P. Oxy. 1802	Lexicon of rare words	P.Oxy. XV preface (this text is on the verso of P.Oxy. 1798, the work on Alexander the Great)
34. MP³ 2070 = P. Oxy. 1800 + 2081(h) + 1611 frg. 44[4]	Biographies (Sappho etc.)	P.Oxy. XV preface
35. MP³ 2290 = P. Oxy. 1611	Problems in literary criticism	P.Oxy. XIII preface, and introductions to P.Oxy. 1610 and 1619

Note: MP³ 1847 = P.Oxy. 1015. Not a whole volume, but rather a single-sheet panegyric on the gymnasiarch Theon. Probably the author's own copy. Belongs to the second find: *EEF Archaeological Reports 1905–1906*, p. 12.

MP³ 2527 = P.Oxy. 2084. A single-sheet panegyric on the fig. The introduction to P.Oxy. 2084 states that it was found in the same find as 1015 (the panegyric on Theon), and it therefore belongs to the second find. It was not, however, a whole volume.

1. Probably to be added here is P.Oxy. 2445, frg. 1.

2. Grenfell was not sure that the fragments of this manuscript should be assigned to the rest of the collection represented by the second find. See, however, Funghi and Messeri Savorelli 1992a, 55, n. 63. To their observations, one can add that Grenfell thought the marginalia in this manuscript "very similar" to those in another text from the second find, P.Oxy. 1234 (Alcaeus).

3. Cf. also P.Oxy. XXI, Addenda, pp. 122–6, for some fragments now reassigned and additional new fragments.

4. For P.Oxy. 1611 frg. 44 as belonging to P.Oxy. 1800 etc., see *ad* P.Oxy. 2081(h).

ACKNOWLEDGMENTS

I would like to thank William Johnson, Holt N. Parker, and their colleagues at the University of Cincinnati for organizing the conference and the stimulating discussions that followed the papers. A second version of this paper was given at the University of Pennsylvania in September 2006; I thank Sheila Murnaghan and Joseph Farrell for inviting me to present the paper there, and the audience for helpful comments. I owe particular thanks to Kathleen McNamee and William Johnson for sharing with me drafts of forthcoming publications and answering many questions; Peter van Minnen for numerous helpful suggestions, especially on bibliography; and the late John Oates, together with Josh Sosin and John Bauschatz at Duke, for providing me with convenient access to the Duke Papyrology Room. The photograph of *P.Oxy.* 2659 (figure 10.1) is reproduced here courtesy of the Egypt Exploration Society.

BIBLIOGRAPHY

Bagnall, Roger. 1992. "An Owner of Literary Papyri." *CP* 87: 137–40.
Barron, J. P. 1969. "Ibycus: *To Polycrates*." *BICS* 16: 119–49.
Blanck, Horst. 1992. *Das Buch in der Antike*. Beck's archäologische Bibliothek. Munich.
Calderini, A. 1921. "Piccola letteratura di provincia nei papiri." *Aegyptus* 2: 137–54.
Carlini, A. 1989. "Elenco di opere filosofiche e letterarie." *Corpus dei papiri filosofici greci e latini* 1.1: 94–8.
Cavallo, G. 1983. *Libri scritture scribi a Ercolano: introduzione allo studio dei materiali greci*. Cronache ercolanesi 13. Supplement 1. Naples.
——— . 1996. "Veicoli materiali della letteratura di consumo: maniere di scrivere e maniere di leggere." In O. Pecere and A. Stramaglia, eds., *La letteratura di consumo nel mondo greco-latino*, 11–46. Cassino.
Chastagnol, A. 1994. *Histoire Auguste: Les empereurs romains des IIe e IIIe siècles*. Paris.
Clarysse, W. 1983. "Literary Papyri in Documentary 'Archives.'" In E. Van't Dack [et al.], eds., *Egypt and the Hellenistic World: Proceedings of the International Colloquium, Leuven, 24–26 May 1982*, 43–61. Louvain.
Cockle, W. E. H. 1987. *Euripides. Hypsipyle. Text and Annotation Based on a Reexamination of the Papyri*. Rome.
Coquin, R.-G. 1975. "Le catalogue de la bibliothèque du couvent de saint-Élie 'du rocher' (ostracon IFAO 13315)." *BIFAO* 75: 207–39.
Crum, W. E. 1893. *Coptic Manuscripts Brought from the Fayyum by W. M. Flinders Petrie*. London.
Dix, T. Keith. 1986. Private and Public Libraries at Rome in the First Century B.C.: A Preliminary Study in the History of Roman Libraries. Unpublished PhD Diss., University of Michigan.
——— and George W. Houston. 2006. "Public Libraries in the City of Rome: From the Augustan Age to the Time of Diocletian." *MEFRA* 118.2: 671–717.
Dorandi, Tiziano. 1984. "Silloboi." *S&C* 8: 185–99.

Funghi, M. Serena, and Gabriella Messeri Savorelli. 1992a. "Lo 'scriba di Pindaro' e le biblioteche di Ossirinco." *SCO* 42: 43–62.

——. 1992b. "Note papirologiche e paleografiche." *Tyche* 7: 75–88.

Gardner, Iain. 1996. *Kellis Literary Texts*. Vol. 1. Oxford.

Gigante, Marcello. 1979. *Catalogo dei Papiri Ercolanesi*. Naples.

Hanson, Ann Ellis. 2004. "A Title Tag: PCtYBR inv. 4006." In Isabella Andorlini, ed., *Testi medici su papiro: Atti del Seminario di studio* (Firenze, 3–4 giugno 2002), 209–19. Florence.

Harrauer, Hermann. 1995. "Bücher in Papyri." In Helmut W. Lang [et al.], eds., *Flores litterarum Ioanni Marte sexagenario oblati: Wissenschaft in der Bibliothek*, 59–77. Vienna.

Houston, George W. 2002. "The Slave and Freedman Personnel of Public Libraries in Ancient Rome." *TAPhA* 132: 139–76.

——. 2004. "How Did You Get Hold of a Book in a Roman Library? Three Second-Century Scenarios." *CB* 80: 5–13.

——. 2007. "Grenfell, Hunt, Breccia, and the Book Collections of Oxyrhynchus." *GRBS* 47: 327–59.

Johnson, J. de M. 1914. "Antinoë and Its Papyri: Excavation by the Graeco-Roman Branch, 1913–14." *JEA* 1: 168–81.

Johnson, William A. 2004. *Bookrolls and Scribes in Oxyrhynchus*. Studies in Book and Print Culture. Toronto.

——. 2006. "The Story of the Papyri of the Villa dei Papiri." *JRA* 19: 493–6. Review of David Sider, 2005, *The Library of the Villa dei Papiri at Herculaneum*, Los Angeles.

——. (forthcoming). "The Ancient Book." In Roger Bagnall, ed., *The Oxford Handbook of Papyrology*. Oxford.

Jones, Alexander. 1999. *Astronomical Papyri from Oxyrhynchus (P.Oxy. 4133–4300a)*. Vols. 1 and 2. Philadelphia.

Kleberg, Tönnes. 1989. "Commercio librario ed editoria nel mondo antico." In Guglielmo Cavallo, ed., *Libri, editori e pubblico nel mondo antico: guida storica e critica*, 25–80. Rome.

Krüger, Julian. 1990. *Oxyrhynchos in der Kaiserzeit: Studien zur Topographie und Literaturrezeption*. Europäische Hochschulschriften III 441. Frankfurt am Main.

Lama, Mariachiara. 1991. "Aspetti di tecnica libraria ad Ossirinco: copie letterarie su rotoli documentari." *Aegyptus* 71: 55–120.

Lapidge, Michael. 1985. "Surviving Booklists from Anglo-Saxon England." In M. Lapidge and H. Gneuss, eds. *Learning and Literature in Anglo-Saxon England*, 33–89. Cambridge.

Lobel, Edgar, and Denys Page. 1955. *Poetarum Lesbiorum Fragmenta*. Oxford.

Longo Auricchio, Francesca, and Mario Capasso. 1987. "I rotoli della Villa ercolanese: dislocazione e ritrovamento." *CronErcol* 17: 37–47.

McNamee, Kathleen. 2001. "A Plato Papyrus with Shorthand Marginalia." *GRBS* 42: 97–116.

——. 2007. *Annotations in Greek and Latin Texts from Egypt*. American Studies in Papyrology 45. Cincinnati.

——, and Michael L. Jacovides. 2003. "Annotations to the Speech of the Muses (Plato *Republic* 546B–C)." *ZPE* 144: 31–50.

Montevecchi, Orsolina. 1973. *La Papirologia*. Turin.

Otranto, Rosa. 2000. *Antiche liste di libri su papiro*. Sussidi eruditi 49. Rome.

Parsons, P. J. 1989. *CR* 103: 358–60. Review of Cavallo 1983.

Paschoud, François. 2002. *Histoire Auguste 5.1: Vies d'Aurélien et de Tacite*. Paris.
Pfeiffer, Homer F. 1931. "The Roman Library at Timgad." *MAAR* 9: 157–65.
Puglia, Enzo. 1996. "Il catalogo di un fondo librario di Ossirinco del III d. C. (PSILaur. inv. 19662)." *ZPE* 113: 51–65.
——. 1998. "Gli inventari librari di PVindob. Gr. 39966." *ZPE* 123: 78–86.
Starr, Raymond J. 1990. "The Used-Book Trade in the Roman World." *Phoenix* 44: 148–57.
Stephens, Susan A. 1985. "The Ancient Title of the *Ad Demonicum*." *YCS* 28: 5–8.
——, and John J. Winkler. 1995. *Ancient Greek Novels: The Fragments: Introduction, Text, Translation, and Commentary*. Princeton.
Strocka, Volker Michael. 1981. "Römische Bibliotheken." *Gymnasium* 88: 298–329.
Turner, E. G. 1971. *Greek Manuscripts of the Ancient World*. Oxford.
——. 1980. *Greek Papyri: An Introduction*. 2nd ed. Princeton.
——. 1982. "The Graeco-Roman Branch." In T. G. H. James, ed., *Excavating in Egypt: The Egypt Exploration Society 1882–1982*, 161–78. Chicago.
van Minnen, Peter. 1998. "Boorish or Bookish? Literature in Egyptian Villages in the Fayum in the Graeco-Roman Period," *JJurPap* 28: 99–184.

11

Bookshops in the Literary Culture of Rome

Peter White

—*In grateful appreciation of Joseph O'Gara and Jack Cella*

Our knowledge of the ancient book trade has benefited little from modern discoveries of inscriptions and papyri. The evidence remains mostly as it was when Theodor Birt and others compiled it a century and more ago: a few dozen allusions scattered in predominantly literary sources.[1] But one feature of it that is underappreciated is that the majority of references to the activity of booksellers happens to be tied specifically to the city of Rome. This coincidence carries two advantages. The first is that, instead of having to synthesize data from disparate places and periods, we gain a view of the book trade in one city over several centuries, as Rome became the Mediterranean center of that trade. The second advantage is that Rome is also the city for which we have the most abundant information about schools, public libraries, literary entertainment, and other text-based institutions of ancient life. We therefore have a reasonable expectation of being able to connect our information about bookshops with a broader literary culture. That possibility is further enhanced by the fact that our informants tend to be the same in all cases. Booksellers themselves have left almost no testimony. The only exceptions are a laconic tomb marker commemorating Sextus Peducaeus Dionysius *bybliopola* and an even more laconic subscription in a Greek papyrus that was arguably produced by Horace's bookseller Sosius.[2] For knowledge of the book trade, as for all other aspects of ancient culture, we depend on the authors who were the first-order producers of books, like

1. The standard treatments are Birt 1882, 353–60, and Birt 1913, 307–12, Dziatzko 1897, Haenny 1885, 24–88, and Schubart 1921, 146–70. Comparison with more recent compilations such as Kleberg 1967—an Italian translation of which is incorporated into Cavallo 1989—or Blanck 1992, 113–29, will show how little the evidentiary base has changed.

2. The inscription is CIL 6.9218. The subscription of Σωσου is found at the end of a papyrus containing Apollodorus's grammatical study of *Iliad* 14, Vogliano 1937, 174–5, no. 19 [*P. Mil. Vogl.* I.19]; Turner 1968, 51, and n. 21 endorses the suggestion that the subscriber is one of Horace's Sosii.

Catullus, Cicero, Horace, Martial, Quintilian, Pliny, Gellius, and Galen. As writers, they had engagements with the literary culture that put them on a different footing from their contemporaries who were not so intimately involved with books. They more than any should have been in a position to discern connections between the commerce and the culture of the book.

My approach to this subject will be organized under three headings: bookshops in the Roman cityscape, bookshops as businesses, and book-shops and literary performance. But first, it is necessary to acknowledge the difficulty of pinning down the activity of booksellers in our sources. The surest criterion is, of course, the Greek word *bibliopola*. But that word occurs fewer than a dozen times in sources concerned with Rome, it was not picked up by Latin writers before the time of Martial, and it eventually faded from use as a loan word.[3] In Latin, the most common term for someone who sold books was *librarius*.[4] Unfortunately, that word also covers a wide range of service providers who are not all, or even mostly, concerned with books or with commerce. For example, it denotes the private secretary to whom one dictates a letter, as often in the correspondence of Cicero. Another sort of functionary comes into view in a passage in which Cicero says that as consul he instructed several *librarii*, evidently not his own, to make him a copy of a bill that had been posted by a tribune.[5] In these cases, neither a book nor a sale is involved. By itself, then, the word *librarius* cannot pinpoint a bookseller unless the context supplies independent evidence that books are being offered for sale. Yet even when both those elements are present, they do not neces-sarily imply a book dealer, because the owner of a book can bypass the market and sell directly to another individual.[6] Apart from the occur-rence of the word *bibliopola* itself, there is no simple test for identifying

3. Strabo 13.1.54 [609], Mart. *Epigr.* 4.72.2, 13.3.4, 14.194.2, Pliny *Epist.* 1.2.6, *CIL* 6.9218, Porphyrio and Pseudo-Acro on Horace *Sat.* 1.4.71, *Epist.* 1.20.2, and *Ars* 345. (Pliny *Epist.* 9.11.2 and Sid. Apoll. *Epist.* 2.8.2, 5.15, and 9.7.1 concern *bibliopolae* in Gaul.) Βιβλιοπωλεῖον is the word for "bookstore" at Galen *Lib. Propr.* 19.8.4 Kühn and Athenaeus 1.1 d–e, both referring to Rome.

4. *Librarius* unmistakably refers to someone we would call a bookseller at Cat. 14.17, Sen. *Ben.* 7.6.1, Mart. *Epigr.* 2.8.3, Gell. *NA* 5.4.1, 18.4.1, Pseudo-Acro on Hor. *Epist.* 1.1.55, and Sulpic. Sev. *Dial.* 1.23.4, as does its disparaging by-form *libellio* at Stat. *Silvae* 4.9.21, and probably *librariolus* at Cic. *Leg.* 1.2.7. *Libraria* (for *libraria taberna*) is clearly a bookshop at Gell. *NA* 5.4.1 and 13.31.1. I have found no case in which the term *scriba* is applied to someone engaged in the ancient book trade, probably because from an early date that word was reserved for the higher-status category of those who clerked for Roman magistrates (compare Festus's remark "scribas proprio nomine antiqui et librarios et poetas vocabant; at nunc dicuntur scribae equidem librarii, qui rationes publicas scribunt in tabu-lis," 446.26–9 Lindsay).

5. Cic. *Agr.* 2.13. The range of meanings in literary sources can be seen from Collassero's *TLL* article (7.1347–8); an even more elaborate array of meanings can be found in Rossi's survey of the epigraphic evidence in *Dizionario Epigrafico* (4.955–65).

6. As for example at Pliny *Epist.* 3.5.17 and Suet. *Gr.* 8.3.

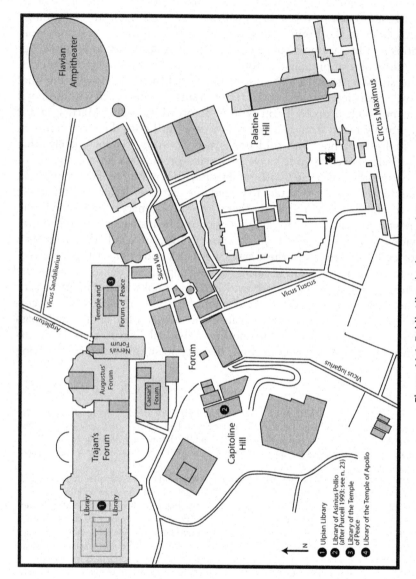

Figure 11.1 Public Libraries in central Rome.

Flavian Ampitheater

Palatine Hill

Circus Maximus

Vicus Sandaliarius

Argiletum

Temple and Forum of Peace

Sacra Via

Vicus Tuscus

Nerva's Forum

Augustus' Forum

Forum

Caesar's Forum

Vicus Iugarius

Trajan's Forum

Library

Library

Capitoline Hill

N

① Ulpian Library

② Library of Asinius Pollio
(after Purcell 1993: see n. 23)

③ Library of the Temple
of Peace

④ Library of the Temple of Apollo

market transactions. We rely on more or less plausible inferences from context, and not every context can be brought into sharp focus.

But although the particular activities of booksellers often elude us, we can say something about them in the aggregate. At Rome it was possible to purchase Greek books and Latin books, newly authored works and established titles, recently copied manuscripts and antiquarian ones, books written to order as well as books ready made, and by the time of Martial, codices as well as bookrolls.[7] This range of offerings implies that collectively, booksellers were able to organize a variety of resources in terms of materials, bibliographic information, and production techniques.

BOOKSHOPS IN THE ROMAN CITYSCAPE

As described by our informants, bookselling at Rome was a retail trade carried on almost exclusively in indoor shops. In that respect, their experience may seem not so far removed from our own, at least until recently, but some details bear thinking about. All evidence suggests that, unlike baths or bars or food markets, Roman bookshops were not dispersed throughout the city, but concentrated in and around the center. The places in which books were sold are mentioned in about ten cases, and those that can be mapped (see figure 11.1) lie immediately south of the central forum on the Vicus Tuscus, or north and east of it, near Nerva's Forum and along the Argiletum and its cross street, the Vicus Sandaliarius, where Galen says that "most" or "very many" bookshops were located in his day.[8] Like Galen in this instance, other sources indicate that a number of bookshops operated in proximity to one another.[9]

7. (Some examples only) Greek authors: Strabo 13.1.54 [609], Galen *Lib. Propr.* 19.8–10, Kühn; Latin authors: Cat. 14.17–19, Statius *Silvae* 4.9.20; new titles: Hor. *Epist.* 1.20, Quint. *Epist. ad Tryph.*; old titles: Sen. *Ben.* 7.6.1, Mart. *Epigr.* 14.194; new copies: Mart. *Epigr.* 1.66, 2.8.3–4; antiquarian (or perhaps pseudo-antiquarian) editions: Gell. *NA* 2.3.6, 18.5.11; books written to order: Cic. *QFr.* 3.4.5, Aug. *Conf.* 6.10.16; codices: Mart. *Epigr.* 1.2, 14.190. I cannot point to evidence that illustrated texts were also on sale in Roman shops. But because it required at least as much skill to illustrate a text as to write book hand, there can be little doubt that anyone who wanted a copy, say, of Varro's *Hebdomades* with its 700 portraits of famous men (Pliny *HNat.* 35.11) would have had to acquire it from a shop.

8. Bookshops on the Vicus Tuscus: Hor. *Epist.* 1.20.1–2 with Porphyrio's note; on the opposite side of the Forum, near Nerva's Forum and the Temple of Peace: Mart. *Epigr.* 1.2.7–8; along the Argiletum: Mart. *Epigr.* 1.3.1, 1.117.9–12; the Vicus Sandaliarius: Gell. *NA* 18.4.1, Galen *Lib. Propr.* 19.8.4 Kühn. If a medieval subscription has been correctly emended by De Bruyne 1913, it attests a late antique book dealer not far from the Argiletum, near the church of St. Peter in Chains. The location of the Sigillaria, associated with book sales in three passages (Gell. *NA* 2.3.5 and 5.4.1, Auson. *Cento Nupt. pr.*), remains unknown. For the sites, see Steinby *LTUR* 1: 125–6 (Argiletum), 4: 310 (Sigillaria), 5: 189 (Vicus Sandaliarius), and 5: 195–7 (Vicus Tuscus).

9. Other texts implying the presence of several bookshops in proximity to one another are Cat. 55.4, Mart. *Epigr.* 1.3.1, and Gellius *NA* 18.4.1. For the clustering of shops of a given

One fact implicit in these arrangements is that books had a distinct commercial identity. They were not lumped with other commodities available for purchase (say, furniture or artwork or writing materials), but sold separately. Their distinctive status emerges in other ways as well. Books were bundled together for import or export, they were sometimes disposed of separately in the division of estates, and, not coincidentally, they engaged the efforts of lawyers to define them in terms of format and content.[10] The product category denoted by the word *liber* thus acquired a sharper identity than the worker category described by the term *librarius*.

The difficulty of distinguishing booksellers from other *librarii* may shed light on the evolution of the trade in books at Rome, however. The location of many bookshops off the Forum, in combination with the variety of book types available for purchase, suggests that, as Phillips surmised, clerks "who otherwise made a living transcribing public or private documents had begun to take on the job of copying and selling literary works when a market developed."[11] There is an instructive comparandum for this hypothesis. Centuries later, when a commercial book trade revived in Paris after the Dark Ages, it was concentrated in a small area of the Ile de la Cité and an adjacent area of the Left Bank. Not only did this location put booksellers in close proximity to the court, church, and university circles who made up their clientele, it was also an area in which tradesmen involved in the production of individually commissioned books—parchment and paper dealers, scribes, illuminators, and binders—were already established. The Paris book trade coalesced as *librarii* assumed an entrepreneurial role in the coordination of book-making services.[12]

To focus again on the trade in Rome, however, a further implication of an organized market is that there must have been a regular demand for books from some part of the buying public. Who these book buyers were can be indirectly plotted by a sampling of what they bought: scien-

type in the same area, see Morel 1987, 136 and, for a comparatist perspective, Sjoberg 1960, 101, 189, and 201 (a reference I owe to George Houston).

10. The parcels of old Greek books which Gellius found in the port of Brundisium (*NA* 9.4.1–5) were surely being imported to Rome, and Horace implies at *Epist.* 1.20.13 that his own book will eventually be packed with others for export to North Africa or Spain. Book collections are the subject of bequests at Cic. *Att.* 1.20.7, 2.1.12, *vita Persi* p. 38.36–41 Clausen, and *HA Gord.* 18.2–3. Ulpian's analysis of books is at *Dig.* 32.52. For book auctions, see Kleberg 1973.

11. Phillips 1981, 24.

12. Rouse and Rouse 2000, vol. 1, pp. 11–49—I am greatly indebted to Paul Gehl of the Newberry Library for guiding me to this work. Several elements of the situation described by the Rouses invite comparison with ancient Rome: the clustering of bookshops near the haunts of the elite, the initial lack of a clear-cut term for "bookseller," the production of books for sale to the public in tandem with private orders, and a disdain for booksellers on the part of the educated as crass and uncultured.

tific treatises by Aristotle and Galen, the poetry of Horace, Lucan, and Martial, Pliny's speeches, and Quintilian's opus on the training of the orator.[13] In range and sophistication, these texts blend with the literary fare consumed by the elite generally, and so it seems reasonable to think that book buyers, too, presented a profile indistinguishable from the rest of the reading public. Nothing in the evidence suggests that the Roman market catered to tastes that were either more vulgar or more specialized than ordinary.

A remark by Cicero shows that booksellers were a primary resource even for those who had access to books through other channels. When his brother was out of the country and wanted Cicero to take charge of installing a library in his new town house, Cicero responded:

> As for filling the gaps in your Greek collection, trading in books, and purchasing Latin ones, I'm keen on getting it done, the more so as it will serve my interest too. But I don't even have anyone to handle that for *me*. There are not things for sale (nothing satisfactory, anyway), and they can't be made to order except by a painstaking professional. Still, I will put Chrysippus on it, and have a talk with Tyrannio. (*De bibliotheca tua Graeca supplenda, libris commutandis, Latinis comparandis, valde velim ista confici, praesertim cum ad meum quoque usum spectent. sed ego mihi ipsi ista per quem agam non habeo. neque enim venalia sunt, quae quidem placeant, et confici nisi per hominem et peritum et diligentem non possunt. Chrysippo tamen imperabo et cum Tyrannione loquar.*) QFr. 3.4.5

This passage has been used to argue that Rome was as yet ill served by bookshops in the mid-first century,[14] and it certainly does show that Cicero doubted they had the stock on hand to supply his brother's needs. Nevertheless, it presupposes the necessity of dealing with the market throughout. First, Cicero takes it for granted that the books for Quintus will have to be purchased somewhere, and that the market is the place to start. Not only that, he gives an impression that he has already some idea of what is available there.[15] The next alternative he

13. Strabo 13.1.54 [609], Galen *Lib. Propr.* 19.8–10 Kühn, Hor. *Epist.* 1.20, Mart. *Epigr.* 1.2 and 14.194, Pliny *Epist.* 4.26.1, Quint. *Epist. ad Tryphonem* 3.

14. Dix 2000, 444, n. 12, for example, infers from this passage that the Roman book trade was "relatively underdeveloped," while Kenney 1982, 20, writes "as one of Cicero's letters . . . illustrates, many of the books, especially Greek books, which a scholar or amateur might need for his library, were not commercially available." Not but what others drew precisely the opposite conclusion. Given this passage of Cicero, wrote Becker 1838, vol. 1, p. 175, "so kann dabei nicht wohl an etwas anderes als an eigentlichen Handel mit Büchern gedacht werden."

15. We should not let Cicero's dismissive tone mislead us into thinking that Roman bookstores would have been devoid of material that might have interested Quintus. As the words "quae quidem placeant" reveal, Cicero is thinking as much about quality as about inventory, and the standards he set for tradesmen were stiff. While supervising Quintus's builders, for example, he felt no hesitation about altering a blueprint (QFr. 3.1.1–2), and at

contemplates, which is to have the books made to order, also implies recourse to commercial sources. When he describes the level of expertise required, he is clearly talking about skills not to be found within his own or Quintus's household (or in Atticus's, evidently). He can only be alluding to professional book copyists. And finally, the strategy that Cicero adopts for handling his brother's request is not to dispense with booksellers, but to deal with them at a dignified remove. No doubt he himself was hardly more likely to set foot in a bookshop than in a butcher's shop. But he intends to turn over the legwork to people knowledgeable enough to negotiate purchases in his stead. Chrysippus was an educated slave whom Cicero manumitted for his learning, whereas Tyrannio was a *grammaticus* who had already organized two large private libraries in Rome and was an aggressive book collector in his own right.[16] In a follow-up letter written not long afterward (*QFr.* 3.5.6), Cicero is still fretting about the quality of books available from shops and copyists, and hoping for a capable agent to take the problem off his hands.

For those who, unlike Cicero, preferred to do their shopping in person, the market consisted of more than books. Because the streets on which bookstores clustered formed part of Rome's central shopping district, books were only one among many commodities available for a shopper's inspection. The premise of one of Statius's poems (*Silvae* 4.9.23–45) is that the friend who bought him a cheap used book would have pleased him more if he had stopped at a neighboring stall to buy him tableware or sausages or figs instead. A visit to the market did not necessarily mean that one was in quest of a book, or of anything in particular. Both Horace and Martial describe sauntering among shops and stalls as a pastime for people with nothing more pressing to do.[17] Bookstores, like barbershops, clubrooms (*scholae*), and porticoes, were places in which they were apt to loiter for a while. As known hangouts, they became points of encounter where it was possible to locate other people as well as books. Hence in a poem in which Catullus describes the haunts through which he went searching for a friend, he included a circuit of the bookshops.[18]

Presumably the denizens of bookshops were self-selecting. Certain people would more readily be found there, for example, and others in eating and drinking places. But one thing that bookshops had in common with taverns, and which set them apart from vendors of produce, tools,

more than one juncture, he made them demolish and redo work they had done (*QFr.* 3.1.1 and 2 and 3.4).

16. For Chrysippus, see *Att.* 7.2.8. For Tyrannio, see Wendel 1943. The two libraries were Sulla's (Strabo 13.1.54 [609] and Plut. *Sulla* 26.1) and Cicero's own (*Att.* 4.4a.1 and 4.8.2); for Tyrannio's book collecting, see *Suda* 4: 607.23 Adler. Cicero had at one point depended on Atticus to assemble a collection for him (*Att.* 1.7, 1.10.4, 1.11.3).

17. Hor. *Serm.* 1.6.111–14 and Mart. *Epigr.* 9.59.

18. Cat. 55.4. Two centuries later, Galen and a fellow physician ran into each other as they were on their way to shops in the Vicus Sandaliarius (*de praecogn.* 14.620.1 Kühn).

and many other goods, is that they more or less required loitering. It took longer to inspect a stock of books than of cabbages, especially in the era of the handwritten bookroll, when a closed book was tightly closed and when no two copies of a given work harbored the same set of defects. But apart from that, booksellers seem to have encouraged leisurely visits. In Gellius's tales of encounters in bookshops, customers are described as seated (*NA* 5.4.1 and 13.31.1), a detail worth noting because sitting down in public places was not widely encouraged in Rome. What is more, the shops that Gellius and Galen frequented were spacious enough to accommodate several loungers at a time.[19]

Four of the anecdotes that Gellius connects with the book market revolve around the presence of *grammatici*.[20] In one (*NA* 2.3.5), a grammarian has purchased an ancient copy of the *Aeneid* that guarantees a particular spelling variant. In another (*NA* 5.4), a prospective purchaser brings in a grammarian to examine an old copy of Fabius Pictor's history. In both cases, the *grammatici* figure as book specialists, which was the same role that, two centuries earlier, Cicero hoped Tyrannio would undertake. This affinity with grammarians suggests that, in addition to the experience of sociability, customers could look to bookshops for bibliographic expertise.

Their initial source of information had to have been the shop proprietors themselves, however. Not that booksellers—by contrast with grammarians—could pretend to liberal learning: commerce and culture were reckoned contradictory pursuits. In fact, to judge by their names, Roman booksellers were often freedmen, like other vendors.[21] It was because booksellers lacked a liberal education that Lucian could assert that they were ignorant of books (*Ind.* 4). Yet even in antiquity, as certainly today,

19. Gellius and at least two others at *NA* 5.4; Gellius, a *grammaticus*, and *complures alii* at *NA* 13.31.1–6; and a *coetus multorum hominum* at *NA* 18.4.1. Galen also describes browsing amid other customers at *Lib. Propr.* 19.8–10 Kühn. In the discussion that followed presentation of this paper, it was suggested that Roman bookstores offered a shopping experience less like that of a Barnes and Noble than of a Levantine bazaar.

20. *NA* 2.3.5, 5.4.1, 13.31.1, and 18.4.1–2. Gellius does not explicitly set *NA* 1.7 in a bookshop, but that is a likely setting for a discussion in which people argue about a reading they have found in an ancient copy of Cicero, and have their uncertainties resolved by an expert on grammar who is present. The φιλόλογος who takes center stage in a bookstore anecdote told by Galen (*Lib. Propr.* 19.8.4 Kühn) was surely a *grammaticus*, and "Ulpian of Tyre," the pedant and habitué of bookshops whom Athenaeus introduced as a symposiast at 1.1d–e, has the earmarks of being another (see Baldwin 1976, 29–36). Again, these vignettes are all set in Rome, which suggests that if Horace had cared to "canvass the tribes of the grammarians" (*Epist.* 1.19.40), he had only to resort to bookshops in order to find them.

21. Four of seven identifiable booksellers have Greek names (Atrectus [Mart. *Epigr.* 1.117.13)], Sextus Peducaeus Dionysius [*CIL* 6.9218], Dorus [Sen. *Ben.* 7.6.1], and Trypho [Quint. *Epist. ad Tryphonem*, Mart. *Epigr.* 4.72.2, 13.3.4]), whereas a fifth, Secundus, is identified as the *libertus* of Lucensis (Mart. *Epigr.* 1.2.7). The subject is discussed by Brockmeyer 1972.

they controlled information that the readers of books did not. Apart from knowing their own inventory, they knew something about the private collections of those they had bought from or sold to, and they must have been familiar with the range and quality of books in neighboring shops. The concentration of shops in certain areas can only have enhanced the function of the market as a clearing house of information. The earliest report about booksellers in Rome shows them mobilizing to take joint advantage of commercially relevant news. When they heard that the remnants of Aristotle's library had been installed in Sulla's house in Rome, they smuggled in copyists to transcribe the texts and started marketing them.[22]

Bookshops were thus able to pool information possessed by merchants, by individual sellers and purchasers of books, and by professional scholars. In the period before Rome's first public library opened in the 30s B.C., they formed the deepest institutional reservoir of bibliographic knowledge in the capital. And after that, they were in a position to draw libraries as well into their network of intelligence. The streets on which bookshops were located passed close to four of the most important: Pollio's library on the Forum, the library of the Temple of Apollo above the Vicus Tuscus, the library of the Temple of Peace at the northeast corner of the Forum, and the Ulpian Library in Trajan's Forum (see figure 11.1).[23] Moreover, the administrators who organized and ran the libraries were sometimes recruited from the ranks of *grammatici* who haunted bookshops.[24]

22. Strabo 13.1.54 [609] and Plut. *Sulla* 26.1. Tyrannio appears to have been peripherally involved in this escapade.

23. For the location of Pollio's library, I follow Purcell 1993, who argues that the Atrium Libertatis in which the library was housed should be identified with the building commonly known as the Tabularium. According to the traditional view, it stood no great distance away, behind the Temple of Venus on Caesar's Forum.

So far as I am aware, no ancient source links Roman bookshops with the public libraries, but it is not merely their physical proximity that suggests a cooperative relationship. The libraries must have acquired the bulk of their holdings through purchase, as Cicero expected to do in the case of his brother's new library, and as Julius Caesar expected when he charged Varro to "purchase and organize" a collection of Greek and Roman books for the public library he hoped to found (Suet. *Jul.* 44.2). Whether the copies already existed or had to be newly made, it is hard to imagine how the librarians could have procured them without the services of booksellers.

24. Three library heads are identified as *grammatici*: Hyginus (Suet. *Gr.* 20.2), Melissus (Suet. *Gr.* 21.3), and Dionysius of Alexandria (*Suda* 2: 109–10 Δ 1173 Adler). The *Suda* is probably mistaken in claiming that Suetonius, who also gained a library appointment, was a *grammaticus*, because there is no evidence that he ever taught school. But Suetonius's scholarly profile is otherwise indistinguishable from that of a *grammaticus*, and so it was a natural mistake. See Wallace-Hadrill 1983, 30. By late antiquity if not before, the presence of important schools of rhetoric and grammar around the imperial fora gave *grammatici* another link to the area: see Marrou 1976.

BOOKSHOPS AS BUSINESSES

Having traced the pattern of human traffic set up by Roman bookshops, let me return now to the fact that they were businesses. Their commercial aims in one way or another color much that is reported about them, which can make it difficult to distinguish between prejudice and fact. For the most part, our informants belong to an elite educated to think the worst of all who engaged in commerce, including booksellers. Nowhere does the stigma emerge more plainly than in the valedictory Horace attached to his first book of *Epistles* when he sent it to market (1.20). The poem is conceived as a farewell to a house-born slave boy eager to escape the master's protection and to attract admirers in the world outside. Horace characterizes the move from private to commercial distribution as prostitution, and his booksellers as pimps.[25]

One thing that lent itself to the prostitution metaphor was that books had to be physically manipulated in order to be read. As Horace tells his own book, "you will be mauled and sullied by the hands of the rabble" ("contrectatus... manibus sordescere volgi / coeperis").[26] A bookroll suffered wear every time it was pulled open and coiled up again, and that concern perhaps contributed to a characteristic form of advertising that booksellers practiced. A shop consisted of inside and outside space. Whereas inside, the closed rolls were stacked on tables and shelves or in cabinets or scroll cases,[27] the storefront was plastered with excerpts that passersby could browse at a glance. One of Martial's poems directs a book seeker to a shop whose doorposts, he says, "are covered in writing on right and left, so that you can scan all the poets quickly" ("taberna / scriptis postibus hinc et inde totis, / omnis ut cito perlegas poetas," Mart. *Epigr.* 1.117.10–2). Horace alludes to pillars appropriated for displays of the latest poetry.[28]

That merchants advertised only confirmed their vulgarity in the eyes of the elite. Seneca complained that their advertising was deceptive as well. He says that the eye-catching samples (*ocliferia*) they hung out were only a lure, and that customers found nothing inside a shop to equal what they

---

25. The prostitution metaphor again lurks in Horace's reference to a book which "meret aera... Sosiis" at *Ars* 345. The equation of publication with prostitution is discussed by Oliensis 1995 and Myers 1996, 16–17.

26. *Epist.* 1.20.11–12; similarly "nulla taberna meos habeat neque pila libellos, / quis manus insudet volgi Hermogenisque Tigelli," *Serm.* 1.4.71–2. Mart. *Epigr.* 1.66.8 speaks of bookrolls being rubbed by readers' chins, with a still more salacious insinuation.

27. Tables: Pseudo-Acro on Hor. *Epist.* 1.20.2; shelves: Mart. *Epigr.* 1.117.15; cabinets: Porphyrio and Pseudo-Acro on Hor. *Serm.* 1.4.71 and Sid. Apoll. *Epist.* 2.9.4; scroll cases: Cat. 14.10 and Stat. *Silvae* 4.9.21.

28. Hor. *Serm.* 1.4.71 and *Ars* 373. As Brown 1993, 133 comments, "the pillar belongs to a public building or arcade, and is either the site of a bookstall or stands in front of a bookshop in the arcade and is utilised to advertise its wares." But it was not only booksellers who posted verse: compare Prop. 3.23.23–24 and Gell. *NA* 15.4.3.

saw outside.[29] But by far the most frequent complaint raised against booksellers was that they took insufficient care over the quality of what they manufactured.[30] In their concern for profit, they were apt to dispense with the step of proofing and correcting copies against the master text.

If a desire to increase profits motivated both storefront displays and shortcuts in production, it played a still greater part in another area of operations. Some booksellers acted aggressively to acquire material they could market. Unlike their modern counterparts, they were not able to order books ready made from publishing houses or jobbers. Except for items they purchased from private hands, they had to manufacture every book they sold. Furthermore, the distinction between "in print" and "out of print" that largely differentiates new bookstores from secondhand or antiquarian bookstores for us was obviously meaningless to the Romans. A hundred-year-old title was no more or less complicated to copy and market than a modern author's newest work.

Because Roman booksellers could not count on being automatically supplied with books, they had to exercise initiative in order to acquire them. How they acquired the works of Aristotle has been mentioned earlier. But calculations of profit are described as guiding decisions about what to market, too,[31] and they evidently expected new titles to sell more briskly than old. At any rate, it is usually new work that we find them pursuing. Quintilian's opus on the *Training of the Orator* is a case in point. The text is headed by a letter to the bookseller Trypho in which Quintilian writes that he is acceding to the clamor of the public and to repeated requests from Trypho that he deliver the manuscript for publication. We have every reason to take his word that Trypho did press to acquire this work. Quintilian enjoyed unrivaled prestige in his field. After a career as the first officially appointed rhetor of the city of Rome, he had been called to the palace, where he was tutoring the princes who were to be Domitian's heirs.[32] Moreover, Trypho's interest in the *Training of the Orator* should be seen against the background of Quintilian's publication history. Two of his earlier essays and several forensic speeches had been transcribed from oral presentations and published without his permission.[33] By the time Trypho approached him, therefore, he was an author for whom there was a certified demand.

29. *Epist.* 33.3. Although Seneca does not say explicitly that the shops he has in mind are bookshops, booksellers are elsewhere described as making use of outside displays, and books are what Seneca is talking about before and after his remark about *ocliferia*.

30. Strabo 13.1.54 [609], Cic. QFr. 3.4.5, 3.5.6, Livy 38.55.6, Quint. *Inst.* 9.4.39, Mart. *Epigr.* 2.8, Suet. *vita Luc.* p. 300.6 Roth, Galen *In Hipp. Off. Med. comment.* 18.2.630 Kühn.

31. For booksellers' concern about the profitability of their inventory, see Hor. *Ars* 345, Mart. *Epigr.* 13.3, 14.194, and Sulp. Sev. *Dial.* 1.23.4.

32. The details of Quintilian's career are set out in *PIR*² F 59 (Stein) and Schwabe 1909. Mart. *Epigr.* 2.90 also guarantees Quintilian's prestige at this time.

33. *Inst.* 1 *pr.* 7 and 7.2.24.

Quintilian was far from being the only writer whom Roman booksellers attempted to recruit. Martial refers to marketing arrangements he had with four separate shops, including Trypho's.[34] Pliny writes that he at least discussed the circulation of his books with booksellers (*Epist.* 1.2.6). Horace evidently consigned the manuscript of *Epistles I* to the Sosius brothers for publication. And Ovid entreated his bookseller to keep his work in circulation while he was in exile.[35]

However, booksellers on the lookout for fresh material were also prepared to bypass authors if they could. According to Quintilian, the unauthorized editions of his speeches were the work of stenographers who transcribed them, as he says, "for profit" ("in quaestum," *Inst.* 7.2.24). He does not stipulate that booksellers were responsible, but the production of books for profit indicates the activity of booksellers more often than not. And the recording of Quintilian's speeches is only one example of a widespread practice. When Julius Caesar was praetor in 62 B.C., he delivered a controversial address of which a flawed text was subsequently put into circulation. Suetonius attributed it to stenographers unable to keep pace with Caesar's words (Suet. *Jul.* 55.3). A decade later, a text of the stumbling, unsuccessful speech that Cicero actually gave in defense of Milo came into circulation before the improved version that Cicero published himself (Asc. in Cic. *Mil.* 42.2–4 Clark).

What these episodes have in common is a well-known personality, a speech given in a public venue, and an utterance recorded on the spot rather than a written text released by the speaker. There are signs that other speeches circulated similarly, although the agency of stenographers is not expressly mentioned.[36] In late December of the year 50, during the

---

34. Mart. *Epigr.* 1.2 (Secundus), 1.113 (Pollius Valerianus), 1.117 (Atrectus), and 4.72 and 13.3 (Trypho).

35. The anonymous addressee of *Tr.* 3.14 is hailed as "cultor et antistes doctorum sancte virorum" (1) and "vatum studiose novorum" (7), and is exhorted to "produce" (*conficere*) 5) Ovid's oeuvre and to ensure that it remains publicly available (*sit palam,* 18). As Haenny 1885, 58, recognized, the addressee must be the man who published Ovid's poems.

36. Marshall 1987 gathered most of the references cited in this and the preceding paragraph, but resisted the conclusion that the speeches must have been taken down in shorthand. He believed that in the late Republic, at least, Roman shorthand was not yet developed enough for the recording of speeches, and he preferred to think that what circulated were summaries drawn from the *acta diurna.* But this hypothesis seems dubious on several counts. To invoke the *acta diurna* is to seek a solution in an institution about which we know even less than we do about Roman shorthand. Nor does Marshall elaborate on the recording process by which he thinks detailed summaries of speeches containing verbatim quotations, but not full transcripts, were obtained for the *acta diurna.* But the most important counter-consideration is this: if in the year 63, Cicero could rely on four senators who were expert recorders to produce a transcript of the Catilinarian hearing (*Sull.* 41–44), we can hardly suppose that the professional *librarii* who normally assisted magistrates were incapable of recording speeches. That *librarii* of the Republic were capable of capturing live utterances in shorthand also seems implied by a notice preserved in Isidore of Seville, *Etym.* 1.22.1: "notarum usus erat ut, quidquid pro contione aut in iudiciis diceretur, librarii scriberent conplures simul astantes, divisis inter se partibus, quot quisque verba et quo ordine exciperet."

run-up to the civil war, Cicero in his villa on the coast was able to read a *contio* that had been given at Rome by Mark Antony four or five days earlier (*Att.* 7.8.5). A few years later, as the assassination of Caesar was about to cause a new outbreak of civil war, Cicero was down on the Bay of Naples, studying addresses given by the consul Dolabella, by Antony's brother, and by Octavian only a few days earlier.[37] For a last example, when Cicero's friend Sestius was tried in the year 56 for inciting public violence as tribune in the previous year, his enemy Vatinius was able to supply the prosecution with texts of the harangues that Sestius had delivered while in office.[38]

So far as I know, the publication of these speeches has not been tied to booksellers before, but that is a plausible source for them. In several if not all cases, the initiative clearly proceeded from someone other than the speech giver. The fact that only speeches delivered in public and not those delivered in the senate, whose meetings were closed, are said to have circulated in this way suggests that the recording was done by persons outside government. Most speeches brought out in rush editions seem to be linked with crises or controversies of interest to a broad public, which in turn makes a commercial motive likely. But above all, it is the method of obtaining texts that points to booksellers. The ability to transcribe a speech from oral delivery was a specialized skill possessed by a small subset even of the literate population. Few private persons would have commanded a clerical staff with the necessary training.[39]

I have been arguing the unremarkable claim that booksellers had commercial aims, and that their commercial practices underlie complaints about shoddy workmanship, deceptive advertising, and bootleg editions. Yet that was not the worst of it. It is likely that Roman booksellers sometimes connived in perpetrating book frauds. In one of the publicity pieces that Martial wrote to puff his books (*Epigr.* 1.113), he announces that his youthful work can be found on sale at the shop of Pollius Valerianus, who he says "does not let my trifles pass away" ("per quem perire non licet meis nugis"). Valerianus himself surely offered bona fide verse of Martial. But in making available the early work of a best-selling author, he was catering to a demand that was as familiar in Rome as it is today, and

---

37. Cic. *Att.* 14.17a.7, 14.20.2 and 5, 14.21.4, and 15.2.3. Later in the year, when Cicero was again out of Rome, he received copies of *contiones* delivered by Antony and Octavian respectively, *Phil.* 1.8 and *Att.* 16.15.3.

38. Cic. *Vat.* 3. Note that Cicero refers to Vatinius's copies of Sestius's speeches as "books" (*libri*).

39. It is precisely this specialty that seems to be depicted in a relief from Ostia, inv. no. 130, a photograph of which may be found as plate VI in Turner 1968, reproduced opposite (figure 11.2). The interpretation of this image, which has yet to be adequately published, is controversial. But in size and format it resembles shop signs that have been found at Ostia. The center is occupied by a man on a platform in the characteristic stance of a public speaker. In the foreground on either side of him, two men sit at tables before open codices in

it is certain that in other cases, the demand was satisfied with spurious compositions.[40] Few readers nowadays credit Vergil with authorship of the *Catalepton*, for example, a brochure edition that in poem 15 presents itself to the public as a collection of the poet's first fruits.[41]

In another form of book fraud, the target of fabrication was not the substance of a text but the material support on which it was written. Zetzel 1973 drew attention to variant readings in Vergil and other classics that he argued cannot be author variants, but which ancient critics nevertheless claimed to have discovered in author copies or in other manuscripts of exceptional age and authority. Given that the readings are false,

Figure 11.2 Relief from Ostia, inv. no. 130.

which they are writing, while in the background the heads of listeners are visible. Because the composition is dominated by the two recorders, it can be plausibly interpreted as the shop sign of a *librarius*, and connected with a note at Asc. *in Milon.* 29, p. 33, Clark, describing how a mob in the Forum cremated Clodius's body "subselliis et tribunalibus *et mensis et codicibus librariorum.*"

40. As Fraenkel 1952, 7, noted in this connection, "When there is an urgent desire for a particular commodity, it will be satisfied in one way or another. The missing juvenile works of the great poets did at last turn up."

41. Another fake put into circulation was a letter of Horace introducing himself to Maecenas (Suet. *vita Hor.* 298.24–28 Roth). The juvenilia that circulated under the name of Julius Caesar may not have been bogus, although Augustus disavowed them (Suet. *Jul.* 56.7).

he concluded that the manuscripts that carried them must have been fakes.[42] And from anecdotes in Aulus Gellius showing that such manuscripts were sold for exorbitant prices in Roman shops, he made a case that the prime beneficiaries of the fraud would have been booksellers.[43] Dealers inevitably knew more than most customers about the provenance and physical attributes of manuscripts, and it would be surprising if they never manipulated their advantage in order to increase profits.

BOOKSHOPS AND LITERARY PERFORMANCE

I want now to connect the two strands of my argument, and to suggest that the business orientation of Roman bookshops impinged on the sociability they fostered to produce a distinctive mode of engagement with texts. But the point will be clearer if I begin with some alternative models of socioliterary intercourse.

One such model is the public presentation at which an author delivers a reading from his work. The phenomenon of recitation has been so well studied that the salient features will be quickly recalled.[44] At a recitation, a single person reads while others listen, having no textual material to orient or distract them. The reader's script is not only unfamiliar to most of the audience, it is not yet publicly available; as a rule, it is not yet a finished book. The reader occupies a physically distinct space from everybody else, a platform or open area that marks him as a performer. Yet in his performance, unlike an actor's or an orator's, the written text serves as a crucial prop and accompaniment. The audience does not gather casually but has been recruited by invitation, and predominantly from members of the capital elite. Among dozens of anecdotes about Roman recitations, not one points to the presence of cultural professionals such as Greek literati, or grammarians, or booksellers. The reciter's performance is not normally interrupted except by applause, nor is it followed by critical discussion. Although the purpose of the occasion is ostensibly to try out work in progress before a live audience, what the reciter looks for is not an explicit critique, but signs of enthusiasm or ennui from listeners during

---

42. Timpanaro 1986, 33–42 and 200–9, defending the value of the indirect tradition for establishing the text of Vergil, prefers to take the more charitable view that these manuscripts were indeed old, just not as old as their dealers and purchasers believed. In that case, the booksellers profited from their honest mistakes.

43. The practice of booksellers in Rome would thus parallel what is reported of their practice elsewhere. Lucian *Ind.* 1 accuses them of peddling phony antiquarian manuscripts, and other sources (*Comm. in Aristot. Graec.* 18.128.5–9 and D.Chr. *Or.* 21.12) describe the antiquing of papyrus by sellers of fakes.

44. Recent treatments of recitation at Rome include Binder 1995, Dupont 1997, and Valette-Cagnac 1997, 111–69, but Funaioli 1914 has not been superseded.

the performance.[45] The recitation is an event characterized by radically asymmetrical inputs on the part of reciter and audience respectively.

At another extreme is a scene of socioliterary interaction described by Plutarch. In his *Life of Lucullus* he writes as follows about Lucullus's generosity in sharing his books:

> His use of his books did him more credit than his getting of them. He opened up every corner of his libraries. The porticoes and rooms surrounding them afforded unlimited hospitality to the Greeks who flocked there as to a haven of the Muses, sharing one another's company and happily slipping away from other cares. Lucullus himself often joined them, dropping in on the scholars in the porticoes, and he helped those in politics with anything they needed. All in all, his house served as hearth and headquarters of Greece for all who had come to Rome. (ἥ τε χρῆσις ἦν φιλοτιμοτέρα τῆς κτήσεως, ἀνειμένων πᾶσι τῶν βιβλιοθηκῶν, καὶ τῶν περὶ αὐτὰς περιπάτων καὶ σχολαστηρίων ἀκωλύτως ὑποδεχομένων τοὺς Ἕλληνας, ὥσπερ εἰς Μουσῶν τι καταγώγιον ἐκεῖσε φοιτῶντας καὶ συνδιημερεύοντας ἀλλήλοις, ἀπὸ τῶν ἄλλων χρειῶν ἀσμένως ἀποτρέχοντας. πολλάκις δὲ καὶ συνεσχόλαζεν αὐτὸς ἐμβάλλων εἰς τοὺς περιπάτους τοῖς φιλολόγοις, καὶ τοῖς πολιτικοῖς συνέπραττεν ὅτου δέοιντο· καὶ ὅλως ἑστία καὶ πρυτανεῖον Ἑλληνικὸν ὁ οἶκος ἦν αὐτοῦ τοῖς ἀφικνουμένοις εἰς τὴν Ῥώμην.)[46]

Let me sidestep the question whether Plutarch is here describing a historical reality or instead concocting a fantasy of how Roman grandees should treat Greek scholar-statesmen like himself. His description can serve a purpose even if it is taken simply as an imagined model of intercourse. The comfortable appointments of Lucullus's library are the magnet on which persons of culture converge. Yet Plutarch does not offer a glimpse of books actually being consulted, and although it may be implicit that they are the subject of conversations, that, too, is not made explicit. The books remain in the background. What is foregrounded is the liberal give-and-take among intellectual peers, among whom the most striking oddity is the absence of all Roman interlocutors but Lucullus himself.

With these paradigms in mind, we may now revisit the Roman bookshop, by way of a story that Galen tells in order to explain what led him to compose his own bio-bibliography:

> In the Vicus Sandaliarius, where a great many of the bookshops in Rome are located, I observed some people arguing whether a book being sold was mine or written by somebody else. It was inscribed "Galen the physician." The purchaser took it for mine, but a scholarly individual, struck by the

---

45. Pliny puts much more emphasis on the body language ("ex vultu oculis nutu manu murmure silentio") of a recitation audience than on explicit comment (*Epist.* 5.3.9).

46. Plut. *Luc.* 42. For a discussion of this and other sources on the library of Lucullus, see Dix 2000.

oddness of the inscription, wanted a look at the foreword. After reading
the first two lines, he cast the text aside, declaring flatly, "This is not
Galen's style, and this book has been falsely labeled." (ἐν γάρ τοι τῷ
Σανδαλαρίῳ, καθ' ὅ δὴ πλεῖστα τῶν ἐν 'Ρώμῃ βιβλιοπωλείων ἐστιν, ἐθεασάμεθά
τινας ἀμφισβητοῦντας, εἴτ' ἐμὸν εἴη τὸ πιπρασκόμενον αὐτό βιβλίον εἴτ' ἄλλου
τινός· ἐπεγέγραπτο γὰρ 'Γαληνὸς ἰατρός'. ὠνουμένου δέ τινος ὡς ἐμὸν ὑπὸ τοῦ
ξένου τῆς ἐπιγραφῆς κινηθείς τις ἀνὴρ τῶν φιλολόγων ἐβουλήθη γνῶναι τὴν
ἐπαγγελίαν αὐτοῦ· καὶ δύο τοὺς πρώτους στίχους ἀναγνοὺς εὐθέως ἀπέρριψε τὸ
γράμμα, τοῦτο μόνον ἐπιφθεγξάμενος, ὡς οὐκ ἔστιν ἡ λέξις αὕτη Γαληνοῦ καὶ
ψευδῶς ἐπιγέγραπται τουτὶ τὸ βιβλίον.) *Lib. Propr.* 19.8 Kühn

By contrast with the vignette of Lucullus's library, books, or a particular
book, is at the center of this anecdote. It does not call into play a literary
culture that assimilates those present, however, but exposes interests
that set them at odds: the shop owner who hopes to make a sale, one or
more customers, a bibliographic expert with a reputation to uphold, and
coincidentally, the supposed author of the book in question. Although the
episode features an ostentatious act of reading, the expert's performance
is the very opposite of a reciter's performance. What he puts on show is
his ability to size up a book at a glance, without regard for substantive
content. The histrionic flourish he makes comes not in reading the book,
but in tossing it aside.

Encounters like the one Galen describes, minus participation by the
authors of books, also figure in anecdotes that Aulus Gellius relates. But in
Gellius, the agonistic emphasis is even more pronounced. In one story
that is typical (*NA* 13.31), he hears a grammarian in a bookshop boasting
about his knowledge of Varro's *Menippean Satires*. Gellius happens to
have in hand an early copy of that very text, which he passes to the
grammarian, inviting him to read a certain passage aloud. With an ill
grace, the grammarian complies, but bungles the reading. The rankest
schoolboy would have done no worse, says Gellius. Having scored off his
victim once, Gellius then challenges him to explain an idiom in what he
just read. But this time the grammarian forestalls exposure by declaring
that he does not teach for free, and flees the shop. Whereupon Gellius
explains the idiom himself.

In both Galen's and Gellius's stories, the participants have come to
bookstores for reasons related to the business carried on there. A purchase
is the explicit occasion of Galen's story, whereas the antiquarian text that
Gellius holds in the second is more likely to be something he contemplates buying than a book he brought with him to the shop. Grammarians, too, had practical motives for being present, if it is correct to think
that they touted their services as consultants. In any case, their profession
gave them a more than ordinary appetite for the acquisition of books. The
truncated readings that take place are likewise appropriate to a place of
business—customers do not normally read entire books when browsing—
and the focus on accidentals like appearance, age, and provenance rather

than on the substance of a book acknowledges the reality that a book in a shop is, before anything else, a commodity.

Nevertheless, it seems unmistakable that in the scenes described by Galen and Gellius, a commercial situation has been transformed into something else. Perhaps in part because the venue is quasi-public, and because commerce is intrinsically competitive, a personal exchange turns into a contest. The preoccupation with bibliological details steers talk toward arcana that can only be the province of specialists. As Gellius and Galen present it, the literacy of bookshops is a hyperliteracy that is not equally shared by all, and which can therefore be exploited to develop a social advantage. And although grammarians come off badly in most of the stories Gellius tells, our evidence about bookshops suggests that from the beginning, they found there a microenvironment in which they could shine by advertising and applying their peculiar knowledge of books. Bookshops may thus hold part of an answer to the question, how did *grammatici* gain entry into Roman literary circles? Suetonius's *De grammaticis* shows that many did in fact gain entry, and yet apart from the lessons they taught to children, they seem to have had no obvious venue in which to engage the cultured public. They did not offer show performances of oratory like rhetors, for example, or have the support of institutions like the *collegium poetarum* and the recitation that supported poets.[47] But in bookshops they discovered a social niche in which they could be challenged only by those—like Gellius—prepared to try to top them at their own game.

Finally, I want to suggest that each of the situations I have described in this section is a case of hyperliteracy converted into social performance. To be sure, the tone and style of the respective interactions vary greatly. But in each case, the principals possess a level of literacy far exceeding anything that would be captured in a standard definition of the term, and they operate in settings that privilege their expertise: the segregated space of recitations, the hothouse Hellenism of Lucullus's library, and the commerce in books. That literacy is a tool with many uses is an unremarkable fact. But one thing that is interesting about its use in Roman society is how often the practitioners I have been describing—as well as others like rhetors, stenographers, and the clerical category known as *scribae*—were able to convert niche skills into positions of broader public or social authority.

47. Kaster 1988, 208–9, has emphasized the problem: "[The grammarian's] expertise did not lend itself to public displays from which stellar reputations could be won, and in fact the evidence for such displays of the skills and knowledge specific to his profession is virtually non-existent. Instead, his expertise lent itself to displays in private settings and accumulated its reputation less dramatically through contacts made face to face."

ACKNOWLEDGMENT

I am grateful to the editors and to Robert Kaster for good advice about preparing this chapter for publication.

BIBLIOGRAPHY

Baldwin, B. 1976. "Athenaeus and His Work." *AClass* 19: 21–42.
Becker, W. A. 1838. *Gallus, oder Römische Scenen aus der Zeit Augusts*. Leipzig.
Binder, G. 1995. "Öffentliche Autorenlesungen: zur Kommunikation zwischen römischen Autoren und ihrem Publikum." In G. Binder and K. Ehlich, eds., *Kommunikation durch Zeichen und Wort*, 265–332. Bochumer Altertumswissenschaftliches Colloquium 23. Stätten und Formen der Kommunikation im Altertum 4. Trier.
Birt, T. 1882. *Das antike Buchwesen in seinem Verhältniss zur Litteratur, mit Beiträgen zur Textgeschichte des Theokrit, Catull, Properz, und anderer Autoren*. Berlin.
———. 1913. *Kritik und Hermeneutik nebst Abriss des antiken Buchwesens*. 3rd ed. Handbuch der klassischen Altertumswissenschaften I.3. Munich.
Blanck, H. 1992. *Das Buch in der Antike*. Beck's archäologische Bibliothek. Munich.
Brockmeyer, N. 1973. "Die soziale Stellung der 'Buchhändler' in der Antike." *AGB* 13: 237–48.
Brown, P. M. 1993. *Horace: Satires I*. Warminster.
Cavallo, G., ed. 1989. *Libri, editori e pubblico nel mondo antico: guida storica e critica*. Rome.
de Bruyne, D. 1913. "Gaudiosus: un vieux libraire romain." *RBen* 30: 343–45.
Dix, T. K. 2000. "The Library of Lucullus." *Athenaeum* 88: 441–64.
Dupont, F. 1997. "*Recitatio* and the Reorganization of the Space of Public Discourse." In T. Habinek and A. Schiesaro, eds., *The Roman Cultural Revolution*, 44–59. Cambridge.
Dziatzko, K. 1897. "Buchhandel." *RE* 3: 973–85.
Fraenkel, E. 1952. "The *Culex*." *JRS* 42: 1–9 = *Kleine Beiträge zur klassischen Philologie*, vol. 2 (Rome, 1964): 181–97.
Funaioli, G. 1914. "Recitationes." *RE* 1A: 435–46.
Haenny, L. 1885. *Schriftsteller und Buchhändler im alten Rom*. 2nd ed. Leipzig.
Kaster, R. A. 1988. *Guardians of Language: The Grammarian and Society in Late Antiquity*. The Transformation of the Classical Heritage 11. Berkeley.
Kenney, E. J. 1982. *The Cambridge History of Classical Literature*. Vol. 2: *Latin Literature*. Cambridge.
Kleberg, T. 1967. *Buchhandel und Verlagswesen in der Antike*. Trans. by E. Zunker. Darmstadt.
———. 1973. "Book Auctions in Ancient Rome." *Libri* 23: 1–5.
Marrou, H.-I. 1976. "La vie intellectuelle au Forum de Trajan et au Forum d'Auguste." In *Patristique et humanisme: Mélanges*, 65–80. Patristica Sorbonensia 9. Paris. (Reprint; first published 1932 in *MEFR* 49: 93–110.)
Marshall, B. A. 1987. "*Excepta Oratio*, the Other *Pro Milone* and the Question of Shorthand." *Latomus* 46: 730–6.

Morel, J.-P. 1987. "La topographie de l'artisanat et du commerce dans la Rome antique." In *L'Urbs: espace urbain et histoire (Ier siècle av. J.-C.—IIIe siècle ap. J.-C.)*, 127–55. Rome.

Myers, K. S. 1996. "The Poet and the Procuress: The Lena in Latin Love Elegy." *JRS* 86: 1–21.

Oliensis, E. 1995. "Life after Publication: Horace, Epistles 1.20." *Arethusa* 28: 209–24.

Phillips, J. J. 1981. "The Publication of Books at Rome in the Classical Period." Diss. Yale University.

Purcell, N. 1993. "Atrium Libertatis." *PBSR* 61: 125–55.

Rouse, R. H., and M. A. Rouse. 2000. Manuscripts and Their Makers: Commercial Book Producers in Medieval Paris 1200–1500. *Illiterati et uxorati*. Turnhout.

Schubart, W. 1921. *Das Buch bei den Griechen und Römern*. 2nd ed. Berlin.

Schwabe, L. 1909. "M. Fabius Quintilianus (Fabius 137)." *RE* 6: 1845–64.

Sjoberg, G. 1960. *The Preindustrial City, Past and Present*. Glencoe, Ill.

Steinby, E. M. 1993–2000. *Lexicon topographicum urbis Romae*. 6 vols. 2nd ed. Rome.

Timpanaro, S. 1986. *Per la storia della filologia virgiliana antica*. Quaderni di filologia critica 6. Rome.

Turner, E. G. 1968. *Greek Papyri: An Introduction*. 2nd ed. Oxford.

Valette-Cagnac, E. 1997. *La lecture à Rome: rites et pratiques*. L'Antiquité au Présent. Paris.

Vogliano, A. 1937. *Papiri della R. Università di Milano*. Vol. 1. Milan.

Wallace-Hadrill, A. 1983. *Suetonius: The Scholar and His Caesars*. London.

Wendel, C. 1943. "Tyrannion 2." *RE* 7A: 1811–9.

Zetzel, J. E. G. 1973. "Emendavi ad Tironem: Some Notes on Scholarship in the Second Century A.D." *HSPh* 77: 225–43.

12

Literary Literacy in Roman Pompeii

The Case of Vergil's *Aeneid*

Kristina Milnor

A couple of years ago, I came across a page in the upscale clothing catalogue put out by the J. Peterman Company. It advertises a certain blouse, called "the Satin Doll," which the company sold at the time for $128. Like almost every page in the J. Peterman catalogue, this is not just an advertisement but a narrative, one that, in this case, seems to have been inspired by a line from the 1950s jazz song "Satin Doll" (music by Duke Ellington and Billy Strayhorn, lyrics by Johnny Mercer), which is printed at the top of the page: "Careful, amigo, you're trippin': Speaks Latin, that Satin Doll." The narrative, printed next to an artist's rendition of the blouse, runs like this:

> She walked into the club alone around midnight.
> Duke looked up from the bar as she approached. His face lost that world-weary look.
> "Arma virumque cano," she said, using her cigarette holder like a baton to mark the rhythm. It was some gambit.
> "Troiae qui primus ab oris..." he continued, not missing a beat. He pulled out his Dunhill. Their eyes met over the flame. Her blouse shimmered. So did she.
> They talked for hours, until Billy Strayhorn shut down the piano for the night; the subjunctives flowed like champagne.
> "Utinam te mox videam!" he finally blurted out.
> "Quod tibi libet, mihi libet," she replied, writing her phone number on a napkin. She turned, looked over her shoulder. "Tuesday."
> Strayhorn heard the end of the conversation. "Man, what was *that*?" he asked.
> "That," said Duke, "was one smooth lady."

Details of material, construction, and price of the blouse follow. Aside from its role in representing an entertaining collision of classics and American popular culture, though, this page from the catalogue also makes an interesting case study of (what I would call) "literary literacy" in the average American consumer. Obviously the joke of the piece turns on the "Latin" spoken by the "satin doll," which, in Mercer's original lyrics, did not actually signify the classical language. But lest we think this is some kind of snobbish put-down of people who can't tell the difference between the use of "Latin" in "Latin America" and the language spoken by the Romans, note that the hero of our story seems to be Duke Ellington himself, who not only is able to cap the mysterious lady's quotation from the *Aeneid* but subsequently produces a perfectly service-able Latin sentence all on his own. I would argue rather that the joke here is at least partially on the reader, who thinks that she knows what Latin is spoken in the world of the satin doll; but instead of a living, and lively, "Latin rhythm" or perhaps "Latin lovin'," we get a dead ancient Medi-terranean language—so dead, in fact, that the smooth lady is reduced to quoting someone else for her opening "gambit" rather than saying some-thing of her own. Indeed, the function of *arma virumque cano* here is not actually to communicate anything at all except the fact that the lady in question speaks classical Latin, something that is at once funny and mysteriously learned; within the narrative, the opening phrase of the *Aeneid* functions as a pick-up line, but outside of it, as part of the discourse of advertisement, it simultaneously captures our attention with its humor and lends a certain air of educated classiness to the jazz-and-smoke-filled bar that notionally gave birth to the satin blouse.

Of course, as citizens of the modern United States and products (to whatever extent) of its educational system, we have a very different relationship to Vergil's *Aeneid* from the one which people enjoyed in antiquity. But I think the page from the J. Peterman catalogue illustrates the ways in which *arma virumque cano* continues in the modern day to have both mobility and meaningfulness; it is a phrase that simultaneously says more and less than the sum of its words and which is able to communicate significance without relying on sense. This is something, I will argue below, that we also see in the use and abuse of Vergil's opening tag in Pompeian wall writing. Vergilian quotation in Pompeian graffiti has, over the years, been variously interpreted. As long ago as 1837, Christopher Wordsworth compared the wall-writing practices of Pompeians favorably with those of his own day: "I should much question whether all the walls of all the country towns in England, would, if Milton were lost, help us to a single line of the Paradise Lost. *Our* Pompeiis do not yet exhibit the words of *our* Virgils, nor does it seem probable that they soon will" (6; emphasis in original). On the other hand, it has been pointed out that the vast majority of the Vergilian quotations are limited to the first words of *Aeneid* books 1 and 2—little more than "school tags" and thus not necessarily indicative of a wide-ranging knowledge of Latin literature.[1] In its original context, *arma virumque* is a phrase full of weight and meaning, the opening of (some would say) the greatest work of

1. Harris 1989, 261; Franklin 1996–7, 182.

Rome's greatest poet; yet its appearance in the Pompeian graffiti seems to reduce it to simple words, scratches on a wall with no more meaning than *Marcellus Praenestinam amat.*

Like the appearance of the *Aeneid*'s opening in the J. Peterman catalogue, therefore, the quotations from Vergil in Pompeian graffiti seem at once to demand and deny explication. Part of the difficulty here would seem to be that the practice of literary quotation in Pompeian wall writing generally is poorly understood. Although Marcello Gigante made a concerted effort to use the graffiti to prove that Pompeii possessed a widespread, "Hellenistic" literary culture,[2] his approach seems overly optimistic; although it is true that there are a surprising number of quotations from canonical literature found in the graffiti, the vast majority of wall texts are much more mundane. Moreover, although it is tempting to try to find a uniform explanation of Pompeian graffiti writers' and readers' motivations, I would argue that this is a mistake, insofar as it necessarily treats Pompeians as a homogenous group that possessed common tastes, interests, and levels of knowledge. In a community as socially and economically diverse as Pompeii, this is clearly an error. In order to do justice to the differences among both writers and readers, therefore, I think we must accept the possibility that even a single text might mean different things to different people: *arma virumque* might appear to one as a "learned" quotation, to another as a hackneyed and ridiculous tag, to a third, barely literate, person as uninterpretable words on a wall. For this reason, I have not here attempted to come up with an explanation for every instance in which a reference to the *Aeneid* appears on a Pompeian wall, let alone formulate a single, overarching theory of what inspired Pompeians to quote Vergil when inscribing the walls of their city. Rather, my aim is to look at a few specific instances of Vergilian quotation in the graffiti and to consider how each of them reveals different modes of reading and writing this most canonical of Latin texts in this least canonical of ancient written forms. What will emerge is not a comprehensive account of literary quotation in early imperial Pompeii, but one account of the complicated ways in which "literary literacy" could be displayed and deconstructed in ancient Roman wall writing.

We have known for many years that the story of Aeneas enjoyed a "popular" following under the early Roman empire. This is illustrated in Pompeii by the wide variety of representations of the hero found there, which range from panel paintings in elite houses to small decorative terracotta statuettes.[3] But the proliferation around Pompeii of images of Aeneas does not actually tell us anything about familiarity with the words of Vergil's *Aeneid*; for answering this question, the graffiti provide an

---

2. Gigante 1979.
3. A summary of the evidence appears in Galinsky 1969, 3–61.

invaluable, albeit not entirely transparent, set of data. From them, it is clear that *arma virumque cano*, at the very least, was a well-known phrase: often shortened simply to *arma virumq*, it is found quoted at least fifteen times in the graffiti from Pompeii, in material contexts that range from the walls of cook shops to the interiors of wealthy houses.[4] Indeed, the phrase was so well-known that it might be construed as a kind of common language, as is suggested in *CIL* 4.2361, where it is found preceded by the words *carmina communemne*. The grammar of this comment is difficult to construe, and because the plaster fragment has long since disappeared we must trust the nineteenth-century excavators for the reading of the text. Still, the words would seem to imply something about "common" or "vulgar song," which, given the number and geographical spread of *arma virumque* quotations in the graffiti, would seem to be a legitimate description at least of the first words of Vergil's text.

The volume of textual graffiti from the ancient Roman city of Pompeii has long both fascinated and frustrated critics. Indeed, the presence of literally thousands of fragments of text—written in charcoal, scratched with a stick or stylus, painted with a brush—led some scholars in the past to characterize ancient Pompeians as a people amongst whom wall writing was wide spread as a leisure-time activity: "one of their [sc. Pompeians'] favorite ways of amusing themselves . . . was by idly scribbling on any convenient surface, a temptation furnished by the stucco walls."[5] In later years some effort was made to distinguish different kinds of (what has been called) graffiti from one another, so that important and useful work has been done specifically on election notices[6]—"vote for so-and-so"—on prosopographical inscriptions[7]—"so-and-so slept here"—and on graffiti with erotic content[8]—"so-and-so slept here with so-and-so." The corpus of Pompeian wall writings, moreover, has been seen as a window onto the language of everyday life in the ancient Roman world, one of our few opportunities to read words written by ordinary people performing an activity (writing graffiti) that we in the modern day do not associate with the cultural elite.[9] But perhaps precisely because of this

4. See the appendix for a complete list. Cf. della Corte 1940, the appendix to Hoogma 1959, and Franklin 1996/7.
5. Tanzer 1939, 83. Cf. Lindsay 1960, 115: "Our [sc. Pompeii's] walls bear witness to the crowds of citizens who like to scribble verses." Estimates vary, but as one scholar notes, *CIL* 4 contains almost 11,000 pieces of text that survive from the walls of Pompeii and Herculaneum, and that includes only material excavated before 1956: Mouritsen 1988, 9.
6. For example, Franklin 1980; Mouritsen 1988; Franklin 2001.
7. For example (most famously), della Corte 1965; cf. Franklin 1985/6.
8. For example (among many others), della Corte 1958; Varone 2002.
9. Herman 2000, 18–20. The social status of Pompeian wall writers is still very much an open question, because, as William Harris correctly observes, "almost all graffiti leave the status, sex and occupation of the writer and of the expected reader or readers indeterminate" (Harris 1989, 261). One view of the issue is famously represented by Augustus Mau: "the cultivated men and women of the ancient city were not accustomed to scratch their names

distinction, scholars have found it difficult to define exactly what the wall texts meant to an ancient writer or reader, and how their presence in the ancient urban environment should be judged. What we might call Pompeian graffiti culture thus remains deeply enigmatic, and we have been left with some of our most basic questions unanswered: who was writing Pompeian graffiti? Why did they write it? What did they think it was for?

One way in which scholars have attempted to answer these questions is by looking at the role that writing played in ancient culture as an aspect of canonical literature—an important and complex issue in the Latin poets. Again, however, there are clearly both material and generic differences between a poem by Vergil and one found written on a wall in Pompeii: on the most fundamental level, the graffito is by definition an autograph and has not as a text passed through the hands of thousands of readers, rereaders, copyists, and critics. Indeed, this circumstance—that there is an intimate connection between a graffito and the hand of its author—has led scholars in the past to see the language of the wall texts as closely representing Latin as it was spoken in the streets of the ancient city.[10] Although not disputing this claim, I would point out that it is curious, therefore, how thoroughly the graffiti authors embrace their role as "writers." We have numerous instances of signatures to graffiti texts that employ forms of the verb *scribo* ("so-and-so wrote this")[11] and others that clearly allude to the creation of a graffito text as writing: for example (following an obscene joke), "he writes it who knows about it";[12] "as many times as I wrote, you also once and for all are reading (it)";[13] "Lesbianus, you shit and you write 'hello.'"[14] In addition, we have a

upon stucco . . . We may assume that the writers were as little representative of the best elements of society as are the tourists who scratch or carve their names upon ancient monuments to-day" (Mau 1902, 491). On the other side, those who, like William Harris, think that even male literacy was restricted to "well below the 20–30% range" (Harris 1989, 259) conclude that the writers must have been among the elite. To my mind, the sheer volume of graffiti and its wide variation in style, orthography, and placement would seem to argue for a community of both writers and readers from a fairly wide range of social and educational backgrounds. For a critique of Harris's position on the Pompeian wall texts, see Franklin 1991.

10. An approach most famously represented in Väänänen 1966, but cf. Wachter 1998. A more fanciful version is represented in Maiuri 1986 (quoted in Varone 2002, 103): the graffiti are an "echo of that lively, noisy, uproarious life in the open air which turned human relationships in a Campanian city, as it still does in the old quarters of Naples, into the life of a single immense household, where all feel themselves to be housemates and acquaintants, conversing and debating loudly as if within the walls of their own houses" (136).

11. For example (among many others), CIL 4.1520, *scripsit Venus Fisica Pompeiana;* 4.1841 *scribit Narcissus;* 4.2395, *scribet Sabinus;* 4.4925, *Anteros hoc scripsit;* 4.8259, *scribit rivalis;* and so forth.

12. *Scribit qui novit* (CIL 4.4239).

13. *Quot scripsi semel et legis* (CIL 4.1860).

14. *Lesbiane, cacas scribisque [sa]lute(m)* (CIL 4.10070). Cf. Martial (12. 61. 7–10): *quaeras, censeo, si legi laboras, / nigri fornicis ebrium poetam, / qui carbone rudi putrique creta / scribit carmina, quae legunt cacantes* ("I tell you, if you want to be read about, you should look

number of texts that play on the written materiality of the graffito text, perhaps most famously the couplet found scratched several times in different parts of the city: *Admiror o paries te non cecidisse ruinis / qui tot scriptorum taedia sustineas* ("I'm amazed, wall, that you haven't fallen down in ruins, / since you bear the tedious outpourings of so many writers," *CIL* 4.1904).[15] Unlike canonical Latin poets, who seem to have a certain ambivalence about the material aspects of book production,[16] graffiti authors repeatedly call attention to the written aspect of their work.

This is not to insist on a strong distinction between the vocabulary of authorship in the Pompeian graffiti and that found in canonical Latin literature—prose authors such as Livy and Cicero, after all, often speak of themselves and their literary models as *scriptores* without any apparent hesitation. Yet it is important to consider the ways in which the appellation "writer" signifies differently in a graffito text and, for example, in the preface to Livy's 142-book history. That is, when Livy refers to his relationship to other "writers" (*novi . . . scriptores; in tanta scriptorum turba: AUC* pref. 2–3) and their practice of "writing" (*scribendi:* pref. 2), he underscores both the materiality of his own work and the material tradition of which it is a part; the *Ab Urbe Condita* thus takes its place as a book in a long line of books on the subject of Roman history. The materiality of the graffito text, by contrast, is much more local and immediate; when a wall text tells us that "so-and-so wrote this" it deliberately calls attention not just to the words themselves but to the act that created them. In this sense, to quote critic Susan Stewart on the modern day, "graffiti is not a crime of content," or, in other words, what often signifies about graffiti is the material fact of their existence and not what they actually say.[17] Fundamentally, graffiti are meaningful not just as texts qua texts but as traces of the act of inscribing them. They serve to document not simply the sentiments their words express but the practice of writing those words on the wall.

---

for a drunk poet of the dark brothel, who, with crude charcoal and crumbling chalk, writes poems which people read while they shit").

15. Other examples include *CIL* 4.1234, *pupa quae bela is, tibi / me misit qui tuus es[t]. vale* ("girl, you who are lovely: he who is yours sends me to you. farewell"). The epistolary form here—seen in the verb *misit* and the final *vale*—is the rather feeble joke, because the text is stationary and the girl (any beautiful girl who comes by, presumably) must come to it. More sophisticated is *CIL* 4.2360, which plays with the relationship between writer, text, and reader: *Amat qui scribet, pedicatur qui leget, / qui opsultat prurit, paticus est qui praeterit. / Ursi me comedant; et ego verpa qui lego* ("He loves, the one who writes; the one who reads is fucked, / The critic wants it bad. Who passes by? He sucks. / Bears eat me! I'm the reader and a dickhead too"). The joke in this instance is compounded if we imagine someone reading this text aloud and ending with the statement in the final line.

16. See Farrell, ch. 8, in this volume.

17. Stewart 1987, 174.

We need not, however, prioritize the graffiti's role as artifacts over their role as texts in an attempt to take their materiality seriously. Rather, I would underscore the ways in which graffiti foreground the act of writing and must, therefore, be understood in relation to the various other writing practices that gave structure to social interactions in Roman culture. We should see the graffiti in relation to other written texts that make up the "literate landscape" of the ancient city, texts that range from notices advertising rental properties, to the painted street signs that enjoin the passerby not to foul the footpath, to inscriptions on the bases of honorific statues in the forum.[18] Graffiti share with these other writings both a fixed, material place in the urban environment and the sense that they speak to a casual, almost accidental reader, rather than someone who has deliberately chosen to encounter a text. At the same time, however, the graffiti also reflect, reformulate, and represent more formal and "elite" kinds of literature. One of the first examples of wall writing published in the reports from the Bourbon excavations was a fragment of Euripides found in 1743 painted on a wall in Herculaneum;[19] subsequently quotations from a number of different canonical authors, more Roman than Greek, emerged painted or scratched into the ancient plaster. In addition to the direct quotations from canonical authors, moreover, there is other evidence of a connection between the wall texts and elite literature: uses of meter such as dactylic hexameter, the elegiac couplet, and iambic senarii; invocations of mythological characters like Pasiphae, Danae, and Dionysus with his Bacchantes; the use of "literary" words, figures, and modes of expression.[20] The Pompeian wall texts thus represent, in a certain sense, the meeting point between two genres of writing, between pragmatic, urban, everyday texts and those that emerged from the sphere of elite cultural production.

In this context it is worth taking note of one instance in which the first words of the *Aeneid* are found not scratched but painted on a wall in Pompeii. On a wall to the south of the city, in Regio 1, was found a

18. "For rent" signs: *CIL* 4.138, 1136; *cacator cave malum* ("shitter beware!"): *CIL* 4.3782, 3832, 4586, 5438. For a discussion of the different ways in which texts framed the experience of the urban environment, see Kellum 1999.

19. Pannuti 1983, 213. The fragment in question is a version of a line from the *Antiope* (frg. 220 Nauck). Because it was excavated so early, we have little information on the exact findspot other than that it was painted on a wall on a street corner in large black and red letters. The painting itself has long since vanished. It seems clear that a significant percentage of wall writers and readers were literate in Greek, although the common practice of transliteration suggests that there may have been more speakers than writers/readers. For a discussion of the different ways in which Greek mingles with Latin in the graffiti, and what it signifies about the literate population of Pompeii, see Biville 2003.

20. For an excellent description of the literary range of Pompeian graffiti, see Gigante 1979. As noted above, I disagree with some of his conclusions, but his book remains the only attempt to offer a systematic explanation for this aspect of the graffiti, which makes it an invaluable resource.

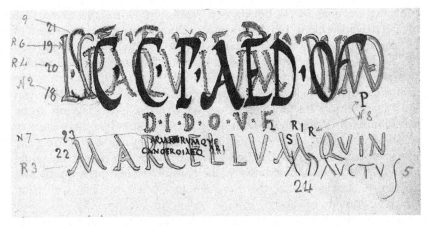

Figure 12.1 M. Della Corte, drawing of CIL 4. 7129–7131.

programma that supports a certain Gaius Cuspius Pansa for aedile (*CIL* 4.7129)—a notice that was painted over a number of others that are difficult to disentangle from one another. From Matteo della Corte's line drawing in his 1911 excavation notebook (figure 12.1), it is clear that the notice supporting Cuspius Pansa was the freshest when the city was destroyed; on the basis of this and other evidence, it has been concluded that he was standing for aedile in the elections of 79.[21] Below it in the same black paint is a small, two-line phrase written neatly in block letters that reads *arma virumque / cano Troiae q(ui) arm[*—that is, the first four words of the *Aeneid*, an abbreviation of the fifth (*qui*), and another *arma* to start the quotation all over again. It is difficult to be certain exactly what relation these words have to the programmata above them, but a few circumstances lead me to connect them at least tangentially with the one supporting Cuspius Pansa. First, like that advertisement, they were written in black paint. Instances of "random" painting in Pompeii are rare; unlike the modern day, private or unauthorized graffiti tended to be scratched into plaster rather than presented in the more elaborate medium of the professional sign writers. Secondly, the words were written over an advertisement for a certain Marcellus, who was standing for the senior post of *quinquennalis*. Although the bare cognomen makes it difficult to identify the exact candidate, the quinquennial elections were only held once every five years. It is possible that this notice is left over

---

21. Franklin 1980, 61–2, with table 6; cf. 48. The situation is slightly confused by the fact that there were actually three C. Cuspii Pansae who were active in Pompeian politics, the candidate for aedile in 79, his father and his grandfather. *CIL* 4.7129, however, was painted over an advertisement for Paquius for Duovir—this must be P. Paquius Proculus, who stood for that office in 74 (Franklin 1980, 67, and table 6).

from the elections of 70, but its neat placement below the second line of the advertisement for Paquius for Duovir (from the election of 74) makes it seem more likely that it dates to the quinquennial elections of 75. Thus, the words from the *Aeneid* would have to have been painted between 75 and the city's destruction in August of 79; the only other painting activity, also in black, on this section of wall during that time was the advertisement for Cuspius Pansa, which must have gone up in the first months of 79. Finally, it is important to remember that this section of wall—admittedly the site of quite a flurry of painting activity over the years before Pompeii's destruction—was surrounded by untouched white plaster, so that, had the painter wished simply to leave the words as a random unattached trace, there were many meters of open wall from which he could have chosen.

But exactly what function does the *Aeneid* quotation have here? By way of background to this question, it is worth noting that sign writers in other contexts seem to have been guilty of filling in space with words and phrases unrelated to the candidate or event they were hired to advertise. Often these relate to the activities of the sign painter himself, as, for example, in CIL 4.3884 where, beside a notice advertising a gladiatorial combat, we are offered the information that "Aemilius Celer wrote this, alone, by the light of the moon" (*scripsit Aemilius Celer singulus ad lunam*). More puzzling is CIL 4.7679, an advertisement for "Gavius" for aedile. Painted beneath the usual GAVIUM AED, however, is the neatly lettered sentence *Marcellus Praenestinam amat et non curatur* ("Marcellus loves Praenestina and isn't cared for [by her?]"). It seems doubtful that this last sentiment has anything to do with Gavius's candidacy, although it neatly fills in the space that in traditional programmata is used to express the candidate's qualifications and the name or names of his supporters. Although this "local gossip" may have had meaning to some readers, it seems likely that to others—especially those whose literacy was minimal—the words would simply function as part of the apparatus of the sign, less significant for what they say than the fact that someone paid to have them said.

It is perhaps in this vein that we should see the quotation from the *Aeneid* in the advertisement for Cuspius Pansa: although it is possible that certain readers might recognize the words as a "learned" quotation, others might simply see them as words and nothing more. They might—and in the case of those whose literacy reached only to being able to pick out the letters of names and offices, surely did—simply extend visually the space of the sign supporting Cuspius Pansa. Here again it is important to note that the black color of the paint used in the programma for Cuspius Pansa and the words of the *Aeneid* serves both to connect these two texts to one another and to differentiate them from the earlier writing on this part of the wall, which was all done in red. I would argue, however, that in addition to this basic visual and pragmatic reading of the *Aeneid* quotation, there is also a second, more "literary," interpretation that should be seen. As I noted above, the first words of Vergil's text are written below the second line of the advertisement for Paquius for Duovir, the first line (reading simply "Paquium") lying underneath the letters of the pro-gramma for Cuspius Pansa. The second line consists of a series of letters that abbreviate some standard words and formulae: D. I. D. O. V. F., which stands for *duumvirum iure dicundo oro vos faciatis* ("I ask that you make [Paquius] duovir for declaring the law"). There is nothing terribly remarkable about this, but an examination of della Corte's drawing of the wall shows that the *Aeneid* quotation is placed neatly under the first four letters—which, it will be noted, spell DIDO, the name of Aeneas's doomed lover in Book 4 of Vergil's text.[22] In other words, the *Aeneid* quotation here does seem to have both context and some content, al-though it is noteworthy that the painter did not quote Book 4 or any other lines from the epic that directly relate to Dido. Rather, he provided the most remembered and easily recognizable words from the text as a whole, so that the joke, if we may call it that, is still fairly basic, requiring only the ability to recognize *arma virumque* as the first words of Vergil's text and "Dido" as the name of a central character within it.

The programma for Cuspius Pansa thus neatly illustrates my earlier point about Pompeian wall writing: that it represents the meeting of two very different kinds of writing practice, what we may term the pragmatic and the literary.[23] We need not attribute to the Pompeian sign writer a great knowledge of Vergil's text; far from it, because one way of reading the final, repeated *arma* is to suppose that the writer could not continue the quotation past *Troiae qui* and so started over again at the beginning to fill in the remaining space. Rather, the opening words of the *Aeneid* have here been redeployed as part of the discourse of advertisement: on the one hand, the words function simply as words, verbiage that both displays the sign writer's skill in writing and his ability to construct a visually appealing notice; on the other hand, the literariness of the phrase, and the joke it expresses, must have been visible to some readers, who might then see an association between the "learned" gesture and the candidate being supported. In other words, a fragment like *arma virumque cano* is significant here precisely because the words no longer say what they purport to say. The

---

22. Play on the practice of abbreviating words in programmata is attested in Cicero's *De Oratore* (2. 59. 240), in which the letters LLLMM in a political notice from Terracina, which might have stood for something like *Lege Laetus Lubens Merito Memmium*, are interpreted as *Lacerat Lacertum Largi Mordax Memmius*—an insult to the candidate rather than a recommendation.

23. Indeed, it may be worth noting that this Cuspius Pansa is also the subject of another programma that incorporates poetry, in this second instance much more systematically. Nearby, also in Regio 1, we find another notice which supports him for aedile, again adding a slightly misconstructed couplet: C. *Cuspium Aed. Si qua verecunde viventi gloria danda est / huic iuveni debet gloria digna dari* ("C. Cuspius for Aedile: if any honor should be given to one living modestly / fitting honor ought to be given to this young man": *CIL* 4.7201).

writer is not actually attempting to communicate that he himself is singing about arms and the man, or even necessarily that he agrees with Vergil that singing arms and the man is an important or illustrious thing to do. On the other hand, he also did not write a series of random or simply banal words like "man wood dog" or "sheep are fat," nor did he write a message that could be construed as a personal sentiment even if it was not, for example, "I love you" or "power to the people." Instead, he selected a phrase that, as a function of its literary heritage, seems to say something important beyond what the words themselves signify; as in the J. Peterman catalogue, the opening of Vergil's *Aeneid* is here useful because what it means goes beyond what the words actually say.

The association between the words and Vergil's text produces, then, a sense of meaningfulness. Still, the quotation does not depend solely on recall of the *Aeneid* to signal its origins: its literariness is additionally expressed in its dactylic rhythm, its invocation of Troy, and especially by the verb *cano*. Among Pompeian wall texts, which, as I noted above, frequently foreground the fact that they are part of a written medium, "I sing" necessarily invokes a different discourse: other than in quotations of the first line of the *Aeneid*, the word is found in only two other places on walls in the ancient city, both of which (I would argue) are deliberately employing literary language. The irony here is that, by writing a word for verbal performance (*cano*), the writer of the Pompeian text sounds book-ish, by which I do not just mean he sounds learned but rather as though he has been reading something other than walls in Pompeii. One of the things that serves to signal the quotation as a quotation, of a literary medium, is the fact that it represents in writing an imagined oral event.[24] This is not, I hasten to add, to say that Vergil's text was under-stood to be a "real" song that people actually sang. Rather, the idea of a sung poem is, within the context of the graffiti, anomalous, so that the use of *cano* necessarily invokes the high literary tradition represented by Vergil rather than the general discourse of graffiti.

Perhaps the important question is not so much why people wrote the first line of the *Aeneid* on walls in Pompeii, but rather why they wrote the first line of the *Aeneid* as opposed to something else. Again, the answer to this question probably varies from instance to instance, but as a general observation it is worth noting the wide mobility of *arma virumque*—words that especially when quoted without the governing verb *cano*, as very frequently occurs in the Pompeian graffiti, are literally meaningless except as a reminder of Vergil's text. This reflects, of course, the popularity of the *Aeneid* particularly, but it is also true that poetic quotation far

---

24. We might compare *CIL* 4.9848, which is a rare instance of the verb *cano* used in Pompeian wall writing outside of a quotation of the first line of the *Aeneid*. Here the phrase *hic duo rivales ca[n]ont* ("here two rivals sang") appears beneath two lines of verse quoted from Ovid and Propertius.

outstrips citations from prose in ancient wall writing. Because so much ancient literature has been lost, it is of course possible that there are citations or parodies in the graffiti that we cannot recognize, but it is remarkable how few references to known Latin prose works there are in all Pompeian wall texts.[25] In contrast, Pompeian walls preserve direct quotations from a number of different canonical Latin poets, from Ennius (*CIL* 4.3135 and 7353) to Propertius (*CIL* 4.1520, 1894, 4491, 9847) and Ovid (*CIL* 4.1324, 1893, 1895, 1520, 3149, 9847). Vergil's *Eclogues* are also in evidence (see appendix), although I am not convinced that what della Corte (1940, 175) describes as the single "quotation" from the *Georgics* actually is one.[26] As I mentioned above, we have yet to formulate a viable explanation of what function such quotations had in Roman popular culture generally or Pompeian graffiti particularly, although it seems likely that poetry was more popular than prose because of the former's prominence in elementary education: Quintilian notes that passages from poetry are useful because "learning them is more pleasing to children" (*namque eorum cognitio parvis gratior est*: *Inst.* 1. 1. 36), and we have numerous instances in the papyri of phrases from canonical poets being used as copy models.[27] But, again, the fact that someone may have memorized the first line of Vergil's *Aeneid* in school does not on its own explain why he or she would write that line on a particular wall in Pompeii, or what a reader might have been imagined to take away after stopping to peruse the text.

We are fortunate, therefore, to have one instance in the Pompeian graffiti in which an author is more explicit about the relationship of his/her text to Vergil's original. Outside of the so-called house of Fabius Ululitremulus appears a painted version of Aeneas, Ascanius, and Anchises that flanks the main door on one side; across from it in a parallel painting is the figure of Romulus bearing the *spolia opima*.[28] Nearby was found scratched a witty hexameter (see figure 12.2): *fullones ululamque cano, non arma virumque* ("I sing the fullers and the screech owl, not arms

---

25. There are, in fact, no direct quotations, and only a few vague allusions. One such is *CIL* 4.1261, a poorly spelled inscription from the outside wall of the "House of the Tragic Poet": *futebatur inquam futuebatur civium Romanorum atractis pedibus cunus, in qua nule aliae veces erant nisissei dulcisime et pissimae* ("Fucked, I say, fucked with legs drawn back was the cunt of the citizens of Rome, during which there was no sound except moans sweet and respectful"). It has been hypothesized that this is a parody of a passage from one of Cicero's *Verrines*, in which a man under torture refuses to make any sound except to say "I am a Roman citizen" (*civis Romanus sum*: *Verr.* 2. 5. 162). See Cugusi 1985. For a fairly exhaustive catalogue of all quotations from, and references to, Greek and Latin literature in Pompeian graffiti, see Gigante 1979.

26. *Matris Eleusinae*, in *CIL* 4.8560 and 8610, but this is simply a name for Demeter, which could have been common. When the two words appear in *Georgics* 1. 163, moreover, they are in reverse order (*Eleusinae matris*).

27. Cribiore 2001, 134–5.

28. On the space, see Spinazzola 1953, 147–55.

Figure 12.2 Line drawing of hexameter outside House of Fabius
Ululitremulus (CIL 4. 9131).

and the man"). Matteo della Corte, among others, suggested that the
screech owl was a bird sacred to the fullers and associated with them,
probably because of the connection between the bird and their patron
goddess Minerva.[29] On the other hand, a fragment of Varro's *Menippean
Satires* offers the proverbial phrase *homines eum peius formidant quam
fullo ululam* ("men fear him worse than the fuller fears the screech owl":
Sat. Men. 86.4 [539 Astbury]), which suggests a particular aversion
between the bird and the woolworker—although it has been suggested
that the "fear" here is more of a sense of religious awe.[30] The name of the
building on whose face the graffito was found, moreover, arises from a
programma found written below the image of Romulus and above the
fullones ululamque graffito; it announces that Fabius Ululitremulus ("owl
fearer") recommends Gaius Cuspius Pansa and Popidius Secundus for the
position of aediles. It seems legitimate that we should take this Ululitremulus as a fuller, on the basis both of his cognomen (which seems to
allude to the proverbial phrase above) and the fact that the word "fullones" was scratched several times on both sides of the *programma*. The
fullers and their screech owl, therefore, seem to have a popular, proverbial connection, expressed in both Ululitremulus's name and in the graffito
cited above.

It should be noted here that the traditional assumption, originated by
Matteo della Corte, that the *programmata* provide us with the names of a
house's inhabitants has been largely discredited, especially in cases such as
this one in which excavation was halted before the interior of the
building could provide any more information. We do not know whose
house this was—or, indeed, that it was a house at all[31]—so that the
presence of the *programma* by Fabius Ululitremulus in this particular
place could be due to a number of different factors. What is curious,
however, and (I would argue) significant for the question of "literary
literacy" in Pompeii is the way that the *fullones ululamque* graffito
may be seen as responding to and connecting the painting of the Trojan
group and the *programma*. That is, one way of understanding the "witty"

29. Della Corte 1965, 336.
30. Moeller 1976, 89–90, but cf. Courtney 1995, 281.
31. Moeller 1976, 51, assumes that it was a fullery.

hexameter is as a response to both paintings, one that expresses a preference for Ululitremulus and his profession over Aeneas and his story:
"I sing the fullers and their screech owl, NOT arms and the man." On
one level, then, the graffito may be understood as engaging the visual
competition between the programma and the painting—between, that
is, the formal decorative element represented by the Trojan group and
the much more informal and "popular" advertisement embodied in the
election notice.[32]

In addition, however, I would argue that there is also a sense of poetic
competition embedded in the graffito. Like the line from the *Aeneid* that
it parodies, the graffito has the form of a hexameter. That is, it gives its
song of "the fullers and their owl" the same poetic form that Vergil
had given his "arms and the man," so that the graffito has a kind of
tongue-in-cheek grandiosity that serves as part of its humor. But equally
significant is the fact that the *fullones ululamque* graffito appears immediately below another fragment of a hexameter line written in what della
Corte, at any rate, thought was the same hand. This graffito reads *quisquis
amat valeat pereat* or "whoever loves let him be well; let him perish.…"
Although the four words are, at first glance, somewhat enigmatic in
meaning, it is still possible to see in them the beginning of a hexameter
(the first three and a half feet); this is confirmed, and their meaning
clarified, when we recognize them, like the fullones parody written
below, as a quotation—not necessarily, this time, of a canonical author,
but of a poetic line that we know only from Pompeian graffiti.
More extensive forms of the verse are found several other places in the
city, such as *CIL* 4.3199, inscribed on a wall near the doorway of house
9. 7. 17: *cuscus amat valeat pereat qui noscit amare* ("whoever loves,
let him be well; let him perish who does not know how to love").[33]
In fact, the words *quisquis amat* are found numerous other places in
Pompeii, more than twelve times in various material contexts and attached to various subsequent words and lines: it is occasionally rendered
as *quisquis amat veniat* ("whoever loves let him come"), or even (probably a joke) *quisquis amat pereat* ("whoever loves, let him die").[34] In sum,
however, it is clear that the phrase is a stock one in Pompeian graffiti

32. It is perhaps also worth noting that the *programma* here is again supporting C.
Cuspius Pansa for aedile, as was the notice above, which employed the quotation from
Vergil. Especially taken along with the notice that supports him with an attempted elegiac
couplet (see above, note 23) it seems that his supporters were a rather "literary" crowd.

33. *Noscit* seems to be written here as a variant of *nescit*. The error also appears in *CIL*
4.1173 (on which see below).

34. Other instances of *quisquis amat* generally but not always followed by a jussive verb:
CIL 4.1824, 3200d, 4091, 4659, 4663, 5186, 5272, 6782, 9202, and several times in the
House of Fabius Rufus (Giordano 1966, nn. 24, 40, 46 = Solin 1975, nn. 18, 65, 66). See
Varone 2002, 62–3 n. 83.

writing—and one that is not, it should be added, ever found in the elite Latin poets.[35]

The appearance of *quisquis amat valeat* on the wall here in company with *fullones ululamque cano* suggests a further dimension of "literary literacy" in Pompeian wall writing. That is, the latter text indicates a fairly high level of knowledge about Vergil's text, especially if we connect it with the painting of Aeneas and see it as a "reading" of the decorative elements on the wall. As a parody, moreover, it is effective, particularly because the author possessed enough knowledge to compose his or her own hexameter. *Quisquis amat*, however, is quoted directly, not apparently in jest but simply as a quotation, not unlike the use of the first line of the *Aeneid* we saw in the earlier advertisement for Cuspius Pansa. And as I remarked of that instance, the quoted words here are significant precisely because they do not mean what they say; their function is to look and sound like something important rather than to convey information or meaning. In fact, *quisquis amat* appeared elsewhere in Pompeii in a context that underscores this function of the (pseudo-)literary quotation. Early in the excavation history of the site, when it was still called Città and considered an annex of Herculaneum, a panel painting was found which depicted various objects associated with writing: a wax tablet, an inkwell, a stylus, and a scroll (see figure 12.3). On the scroll is written a poem, whose later lines are difficult to decipher but which clearly begins *quisquis / ama(t) valia(t) / peria(t) qui n/oscit ama[re]*.[36] Here, then, we have the tag otherwise only known to us from graffiti represented as "literature," or, at any rate, as something that might legitimately be found written on a bookroll. *Quisquis amat* in this context is not simply words, or simply poetry, but rather is given weight by the artist as "poetry"—a couplet familiar from a more popular context re-presented here in the place of a canonical text.[37] *Quisquis amat* may have sometimes just been a convenient tag, therefore, but the painting indicates the ways in which it might be imagined as part of a larger literary tradition.

35. Although it is true that similar phrases (*quisquis amas, si quis amat*) are found in Ovid and Propertius, they are never followed by the jussive verb as in the graffiti. For a list of parallels, see Wachter 1998.

36. See the entry in *CIL* 4.1173, with pp. 204 and 461, for a discussion of the text and interpretations of the later lines.

37. Note that the poem in the painting appears on the scroll, a reasonably permanent medium, rather than on the wax tablet where one would expect lower-level exercises or drafts to be completed. It is, of course, perfectly possible that *quisquis amat* is a quotation from some famous poem by a canonical author that is lost to us. This would in no way vitiate anything I say here: indeed, if this were true it would make the association with the Vergilian parody more meaningful. We cannot be sure one way or the other—the words' appearance on the bookroll certainly makes them look "canonical," but their absence from the surviving canonical poetry does not—but my point here is simply to emphasize the way that, like *arma virumque cano*, *quisquis amat* is able to move between graffiti and a more overtly "literary" context.

Figure 12.3 Painting of writing materials from Pompeii (MANN 4676).

The act of literary quotation on Pompeian walls generally, I would argue, trades on this sense of "poetry," on a self-conscious sense of writing in a distinct, more formal mode. In this way, there is not a vast difference between quoting the first line of the *Aeneid* and quoting *quisquis amat*, even though the canonization of Vergil had already under the early Roman empire far outstripped that of the nameless author who left us the latter text. Yet if we look back to the inscriptions outside the "house" of Fabius Ululitremulus, it is worth noting that, here, the quotation of the *Aeneid*'s first words has been given content and context by both the parodic change to the line and the surrounding environment in which it appears. Rather than representing a slavish repetition of the canonical text, the parody invests Vergil's text with meaning, as the thing against which the new "song of the fullers" will be measured. The earliest commentators on the graffito spent some energy imagining the real song that is reflected here—was it a sort of guild chant or something more like a popular ditty? This, to my mind, is missing the obvious joke of the text, which is encapsulated in *cano* as it is transferred from the epic "arms and the man" to the much more pedestrian "fullers and the screech owl." The point is that in neither case is anyone actually singing; *cano* is funny here because it evokes a world of elite literary performance—perhaps in contrast with the "song" of the owl that gave the *ulula* its name—whereas its written form reminds us that even Vergil's song had long since been circulating as a material text.

In a certain sense, the play between spoken and written word animates a great deal of ancient poetry—even, it might be argued, Vergil's original *arma virumque cano*. The opening of *Aeneid* 2 with *conticuere omnes* ("everyone was silent"), moreover, makes a neat contrast with the poet's emphatic speaking that commenced Book 1. In fact, this latter phrase is quoted almost as frequently in the Pompeian graffiti as *Aeneid* 1.1, a circumstance that has been taken to indicate the particular reading and memorizing patterns of the ancient populace (see appendix for a list of

instances). It may well be true that Books 1 and 2 of Vergil's epic poem
were the most popular in early imperial Rome, but I would also point to
the ways in which *conticuere omnes*, like *arma virumque cano*, underscores
itself as a quotation by representing in writing a spoken act, or, rather, an
unspoken one, which does the opening of the *Aeneid* one better. The joke
of writing "everyone was silent" on a wall—especially a wall that most
of the time also contained other graffiti—is not just to nudge the reader to
recall happy days in the schoolroom consuming Vergil's poem; it also
serves to call attention to the lack of silence, or the lack of a lack of speech,
which is represented by the presence of the words on the wall. In the same
sense that *arma virumque cano*, when quoted out of context, does not
mean anyone is actually singing, so *conticuere omnes* does not mean anyone
is in reality silent. Again, the point of the quoted words is not to mean what
they say, but rather to call attention to themselves as quotations, in part by
invoking the world of poetic spoken communication that is external to the
written world of graffiti.

The Vergilian quotations above stand out from the other wall writings
because they do not sound like locally authored graffiti. But their discursive difference does not just lie in their vocabulary or metrical form; it is
also visible in the speech acts they describe and the way they describe
them. Thus far, however, we have been focusing on the opening phrases
of the first books of the *Aeneid*, phrases that seem to have enjoyed
significant popularity in many different contexts and locations. *Arma
virumque cano*, especially, probably circulated as a phrase almost independently from the rest of Vergil's text, and was probably consumed and
reproduced by people who had only the vaguest notion of what connection it had with the great epic poem. Yet the Pompeian graffiti also offer
us a selection of other quotations from the *Aeneid* whose "popularity" is
not so easily identified or understood. That is, we know that the *Aeneid*
played a significant role in ancient education, as one of the standard texts
for learning everything from syntax to ethics; Robert Kaster famously
offered a vivid description of the "sacredness" of Vergil's text among
the Latin grammarians in the third and fourth centuries, who used him
to create an educated elite "as superior to the uneducated as they are to
cattle."[38] The further quotations—that is, those that are neither *arma
virumque cano* nor *conticuere omnes*—from Vergil's text that we find in
Pompeii have usually been attributed to the priority that the *Aeneid* was
given in the ancient schoolroom. At the same time, however, these are
often passages whose thematic or educational significance are not immediately obvious, and they are generally not lines to which the later grammarians—who, admittedly, represent a much later period in ancient
education—give much attention.

38. Kaster 1988, 17.

There is, however, one noticeable unifying theme amongst the Pompeian graffiti quotations from the *Aeneid*—again, setting aside the first words of Books 1 and 2.[39] This is a marked preference for lines that come from speeches in the original text: thirteen of seventeen citations are spoken not in Vergil's narrative voice but by one character or another. Moreover, there is a surprisingly high concentration of vocatives, imperatives, and second person verbs in the Vergilian graffiti: six of the seventeen quotations contain at least one of these grammatical forms that explicitly point to the words as a communication from one individual to another. Indeed, we might consider this, rather than narrative or thematic importance to Vergil's text, as an explanation for the choice of the particular lines. For example, one line scratched into the wall of the palaestra is *vade, age, nate, vocas Zepirios* ("come now, son, you call the Zephyrs"), a version of *Aeneid* 4.223 (which has *voca* in place of *vocas* and the spelling *Zephyros*). The line opens Jupiter's address to Mercury, when he orders him to retrieve Aeneas from the arms of Dido—the speech as a whole is certainly thematically important, but this particular line seems more significant for its representation of the mechanics of direct address. Similarly, scratched into the plaster of the atrium in house 1. 10. 8 were the words *Entelle heroum*, or the opening of Acestes's reproach at *Aeneid* 5. 389—a phrase that, like *arma virumque*, is meaningless on its own but does offer an unambiguous vocative form. The basilica offers the beginning of Priam's reassuring words to Sinon in Book 2 (148) *Quisquis es, amissos hinc iam obliviscere Graios* ("whoever you are, here and now forget the departed Greeks"). And quoted on two different walls in Pompeii is Ascanius's oddly decontextualized remark to Nisus in Book 9 (269), *vidisti quo Turnus equo, quibus ibat in armis* ("you saw on what horse, with what arms, Turnus went"). Although it is true there are a number of quotations from the *Aeneid* on Pompeian walls that do not contain internal evidence that they were spoken from one character to another, it is nonetheless suggestive that so many (particularly of the fragments that are longer than three words: four of seven) contain internal grammatical evidence that they were originally spoken from one individual to another.

Given these parallel examples, we might then wish to revisit the traditional understanding of other instances that, on the surface, seem to point to greater narrative or "literary" understanding—thus, for example, a line from Nisus's prayer to the moon in Book 9 (404) was found scratched on a wall outside a cook shop in Pompeii's seventh region: *tu Dea, tu pr(a)ese(ns), nostro succurre labor(i)* ("you, goddess, be present, assist [us] in our work"). Della Corte sees it in its graffiti form as an invocation of the goddess to look after the shop's business, which is by no means impossible. Yet, like the other quotations above, it represents a

39. See my appendix for a list.

vividly spoken moment in Vergil's text, a point that is emphasized by the fact that the line contains both a vocative and an imperative. Of course, a line from the *Aeneid* learned in another context might be reused here for a different, more local, purpose. Still, this quotation fits well with the others in prioritizing a moment when the sober, factual, narrative voice of Vergil's text recedes and a character engages in direct discourse. In this sense, Nisus's prayer from Book 9 may have been less significant for an ancient Pompeian as a prayer than as a moment of emotionally charged communicative speech.

The idea that the fragments of the *Aeneid* found on Pompeian walls may attest a particular interest in communication is borne out by one further example. This is a line that was found scratched into the plaster of a room off of the peristyle in the so-called House of Fabius Rufus. The space itself is somewhat puzzling, the more so because (despite the fact that the work on the site was done in the 1970s) the excavation report has yet to be published; fortunately, Carlo Giordano and subsequently Heikki Solin were independently able to work on and publish the substantial graffiti remains from several walls within the house.[40] At any rate, it was here in a small but finely decorated room off of the peristyle that the *Aeneid* quotation was found, Book 1, lines 242 and part of 243: *Antenor potuit mediis elapsus Achivis / Illiricos penetrare sinus* ("Antenor, having escaped from among the Greeks, was able to make his way into the Illyrian bays"). As above, the line itself does not, on the surface, seem spectacularly significant for understanding the *Aeneid*, nor do its meter or grammar seem particularly worthy of note. This line, however, is one significant exception to the rule that the Pompeian quotations are not those of particular interest to the late antique grammarians. In fact, Book 1 line 242 shows up repeatedly, in Donatus, Diomedes, Charisius, and others. There is, moreover, universal agreement about its role as a paradigm: it represents an example of *adhortatio* or encouragement, so that Antenor's unlikely escape from the Greeks and ultimate success in Italy may be used to buck the spirits of someone else faced with a difficult situation.[41] Indeed, Marius Plotius Sacerdos (*Art. Gram.* 1. 180) uses it as an example of something "not brought up except either by people asking for something or (in response) to people asking for something" (*non inducitur nisi aut a petentibus aut ad petentes, ut "Antenor potuit"* ...).

In this sense, the quotation from the House of Fabius Rufus is an exception that proves the rule: although it contains no second-person

40. Giordano 1966 and Solin 1975.

41. Charisius, *Art. Gram.* 4. 277; Diomedes *Art. Gram.* 2. 464; Donatus *Ars Gram.* 3. 6. 402 and *Aen.* 1. 245–50; Marius Plotius Sacerdos, *Art. Gram.* 1. 166 and 180; Iulianus Toletanus, *Art. Gram.* 2. 19. 109; Marius Victorinus, *Explanationes in Ciceronis rhetoricam* 1. 30.

verbs or other deictic words, the later educational treatises understand it primarily as an example of a particular kind of direct address. In its original textual context, moreover, it is found (like the other quotations above) in a speech: in addressing Jupiter, Venus uses the contrasting example of Antenor to point out that Aeneas is at least as deserving of rescue. It is perhaps curious that, there, it is not actually used in the manner later recommended by the grammarians: although Venus certainly wants Jupiter to do something, the example of Antenor is brought up as a kind of negative example, to show how much greater have been the sufferings of Aeneas. Such "misreadings" are common in the grammarians, but if we may transpose their interpretations back to the Pompeian graffito, it should again give us some pause in seeing the "Antenor" quotation as evidence of knowledge about the *Aeneid* generally as a text. Instead, perhaps like many of the other lines from the *Aeneid* found in Pompeii, its significance lies in its role as a means of communication from one person to another.

In fact, the particular context of the Antenor graffito from the House of M. Fabius Rufus adds, I would argue, another layer to our understanding of the *Aeneid*'s role in the "literate landscape" of Roman Pompeii. The Vergilian line was actually found written beneath two other fragments apparently in the same hand:[42] the first reads, *Secundus Onesimo fratri suo p[lu]rimam perpetuamque salutem* ("Secundus [gives] the most and eternal salutations to his brother Onesimus"); second, and immediately above the quotation from the *Aeneid*, *occasionem nactus non praetermisi tibi scribendi ut scires me recte valere* ("Having obtained the opportunity of writing, I have not let it go by in order that you should know that I am very well"). In other words, the Antenor quotation appeared along with fragments of text that are clearly from a personal letter—although, I would say, probably not an actual letter but one written for practice, because elsewhere on the same wall we also have written *Onesimus Secundo fratri suo, Secundo plurimam amabiliter salutem*, and further repetitions of the phrase *occasionem nactus*. Scholars have long theorized that letter writing was a skill taught in the ancient school,[43] and the Pompeian graffiti provides some of our best evidence of this. Indeed, the basilica—home to many "learned" jokes such as the neologism *irrumabiliter*—offers us what is to my mind clearly a parody of a practice letter: *Pyrrhus Chio conlegae sal / moleste fero quod audivi / te mortuom itaque val.* ("Pyrrhus [gives] salutation to his associate Chius. I am sorry to hear that you are dead. Therefore farewell"). Similarly, CIL 4. 1237 runs in part *Prime-*

---

42. See Giordano 1966, nn. 9–11 for line drawings of the original texts. Unfortunately, although other fragments from the space have been preserved in Pompeii's antiquarium, these particular texts have been lost.

43. Cribiore 2001, 215–19: "The practice of epistolary skills in education has not been investigated extensively" (216).

*genius...Mystiis communi suo salute(m) vidisti quo Turnum aequoribus eibat in arm[is—*that is, "Primegenius...[gives] salutation to his comrade Mystii; 'have you seen Turnus, where he goes on the seas in arms....'"[44]

It may be argued that the connection in these cases between the graffi-tied *Aeneid* quotations and letter fragments is merely coincidental, or at least may simply be traced to the fact that these happened to be two of the most important subjects learned in school: how to write a letter and how to quote from Vergil. But I would suggest that we should also recognize a connection with the preference seen in the Vergilian quotations for lines that emphasize the act of communication—on a narrative level, by focus-ing on lines that were originally delivered by characters in speeches, and grammatically, through vocatives, imperatives, and second-person verbs. That is, as Thomas Augst has noted of the nineteenth-century American middle class, letter writing is significant because it puts the emphasis on literacy as a social practice, a means of articulating and reinforcing rela-tionships through the creation of a written document.[45] This is also, in a slightly different way, what is being performed in the quotations from Vergil's *Aeneid* in the Pompeian graffiti, as the great canonical text is mined for fragments that mimic the forms of spoken communication. Again, I will say that I am resistant to looking for a single, overarching explanation for all Vergilian quotation in Pompeian graffiti, and the fact of the matter is that there are numerous fragments that do not fit this pattern, perhaps most notably the long quotation found in the palaestra (*CIL* 4.8630b) of *Aeneid* 1. 192–3: *nec prius absistit quam septem ingentia victor / corpora fundat humi* ("nor did he cease before he laid seven huge bodies on the ground"). The line is neither from a speech in the original text nor does it contain any of the grammatical forms that signal communication that I noted above; it is, however, particularly appropriate to its material

44. The quotation is *Aeneid* 9. 269, although the writer's memory and/or grammar are faulty. Vergil's original is *vidisti quo Turnus equo, quibus ibat in armis*; the writer has transformed *equo quibus* into *aequoribus* and *Turnus* into *Turnum*. Cipriotti 1975, 273, sees these errors as reflecting the fact that the writer originally heard the line, probably in school. There is another word below the name Primegenius (SOES[?]), which may be intended to be read before Mystiis or may be the beginning of the second line of the inscription: see appendix for the full text.

45. Augst 2003, 71–9. Augst emphasizes the ways in which personal letters in the nineteenth century functioned as a literate performance of personal emotion, that is, young men and women learned to express their love for their families by writing to them. The situation is very different in Rome, at least partially because the Romans were operating with different models of "private" intimacy and its expression. On the other hand, it seems significant to my mind that Roman letters generally, and many of the practice or mock fragments from them on Pompeian walls, open with a salutation that explicitly describes the relationship between the writer and supposed reader: "to his brother," "to his associate," "to his comrade," and so on.

context (the palaestra, where wrestling matches and other athletic contests took place), which may explain why it is quoted here. This is an example of the kind of "local" explanations, which, like the letters spelling DIDO above the painted quotation of *Aeneid* 1.1 in the programma for Cuspius Pansa, would have been immediately visible to some ancient viewers, but which are all too frequently overlooked in a modern scholarly quest for more global interpretations.

In other words, one of the things that we must always bear in mind when discussing the Pompeian graffiti is the importance of the local; although on some level the mass of graffiti texts offers us a kind of window onto the Pompeian populace, it cannot be forgotten that each text is unique, written by a single hand, in a single place, at a single moment in time. For this reason, any general assertion about the function of literary literacy in Pompeii is going to be vulnerable to individual exceptions. On the other hand, what I hope I have shown here are some of the ways in which local interpretations of individual wall texts can provide us with a view of how some wall writers saw the relationship between Vergil's text and their own. For these Pompeians, the *Aeneid* is not so much a stable, idealized, cultural product, as a means of cultural production; like graffiti generally, Vergilian quotations on Pompeian walls are less facts than acts and are aware of themselves as such. As has been written of "sampling"—the practice in contemporary music of quoting passages from others' compositions—"it is a longstanding practice for consumers to customize their commodities."[46] That Vergil's great epic poem was simply one such commodity in the streets of Pompeii is an important fact to remember as we try to peel away the layers of canonization which had already begun to accrue to the *Aeneid* in antiquity. Moreover, it also allows us to see how canonization itself was a useful tool, in that it could give certain people a kind of common language overtly distinct from the discourse of everyday life. In this sense, therefore, like its use by the mysterious "satin doll" with whom I began, the literary Latin on Pompeian walls speaks less to a specific taste for the canon than a desire, and an ability, to put the canon to work in the ancient urban environment.

APPENDIX: QUOTATIONS FROM VERGIL ON POMPEIAN WALLS

Aeneid

1.1: Arma virumque cano, Troiae qui primus ab oris

1. *CIL* 4.1282: ARMA VIRUS (perhaps m)
size: 6.5 cm long × 2 cm high

---

46. Sanjek 1994, 343.

location: 6. 7. 20–1, probably in the peristyle (*CIL* 4.1281 and 1283 came from there, although 1282 is simply listed as being from the same house)

2. *CIL* 4.2361: CARMINA / COMMUNEMNE / ARMA • VIRUMQUE CANO TRO
size: 31 cm long × 13 cm high
location: 9. 1. 4, on the western wall of the taberna, to the left of the door as you go in
other notes: Mommsen thinks that this is probably all the same hand, although the letters are somewhat differently formed.

3. *CIL* 4.3198 ARMA VIRU
size: 1.5 cm high
location: the wall of the street between 9. 7. 17 and 18
other notes: Mommsen in *CIL* gives the location as on the eastern side of the Vico di Tesmo between the fourth and fifth door from the Via Diadumenorum (the old name for the Via dell'abbondanza); della Corte 1940, 175 n. 23, which gives the location "IX, VII, lato S. tra gl'ingressi 4 e 5" is misleading.

4. *CIL* 4.4757 ARMA VIR
size: 1 cm high
location: 7. 7. 5 in the peristyle, on the column to the extreme right rear

5. *CIL* 4.4832 [A]RMA VIRUMQUE CANO TROIA(E) QUI PRIMUS AB ORIS
size: 27 cm long
location: 7. 15. 8, on the rear wall of the atrium, to the left as you go in near the corner of the door

6. *CIL* 4.5002 ARMA VIRUMQUE
size: 26 cm long
location: 9. 2. 26, on the wall of the atrium, to the right

7. *CIL* 4.5337 ARM VIR
size: unknown
location: 9. 9. c, on the right post of the door

8. *CIL* 4.7131 ARMA VIRUMQUE / CANO TROIAE Q(UI)   ARM[
size: 1.5 cm high (each line)
location: 1. 6. 1, on the wall of the street to the left of the door
other notes: Della Corte 1940, 175 n. 16, which lists the location as 1. 4. 1, is incorrect.

9. *CIL* 4.8320 e–f ARM(A) / . . . QUI PR(IM)US
size: (arm) 1.9 cm long × 0.4–0.8 cm high; (qui primus) 3.1 cm long × 0.3–0.22 high
location: 1. 10. 4, in the peristyle

10. *CIL* 4.8416 ARMA VIRUMQUE CAN / . . . ARM (written under "que");
size: 12 cm long × 0.5–.1.1 cm high
location: 1. 11. 1, on the wall of the street to the right of the door

11. *CIL* 4.8831 ARMA VIRUMQUE / QUI P(RIMUS) / [VIRU]MQ(UE) VIR(UMQUE);
size: 18 cm long
location: 3. 2. 1, on the outside wall to the left (west) of the house

12. *CIL* 4.9131: FULLONES ULULAMQUE CANO, NON ARMA
VIRUMQ[UE
size: 29.5 cm long
location: 9. 13. 5, on the outside wall to the left of the door

13. *CIL* 4.10055c QUI PR(IMUS?) . . . / U
size: 10 cm long × 10 cm high
location: 1. 12. 16, on the outside wall to the left of the door above a bench
other notes: The location given by della Corte in *CIL* (2. 2. 16) is incorrect
according to the system of numbering regiones and insulae currently used.

14. *CIL* 4.10059 ARMA VIR(UMQUE)
size: 10 cm long × 6 cm high
location: 1. 13. 1, on the eastern wall of the atrium
other notes: The location given by della Corte in *CIL* (2. 3. 1) is incorrect
according to the system of numbering regiones and insulae currently used.

15. *CIL* 4.10086a ARMA VIRUMQUE
size: 24 cm long × 3 cm high
location: 2. 1. 10, on the wall of the street to the right of the door
other notes: The location given by della Corte in *CIL* (2. 4. 10) is incorrect
according to the system of numbering regiones and insulae currently used.

16. *CIL* 4.10111a CAELUS / [A]RM[A VI]R[UMQUE]
size:14 cm long × 10 cm high
location: 2. 3. 3, in the space off of the portico to the east
other notes: Below is written CAM (*CIL* 4.10111b), which might be interpreted
as CAN[O]. The location given by della Corte in *CIL* (2. 6. 3) is incorrect
according to the system of numbering regiones and insulae currently used.

1.126 stagna refusa vadis, graviter commotus; et alto

17. *CIL* 4.2066, w. add. pp. 215, 465, 704: (MOLES?) MULTA MIHI CURAE
CUM [PR]ESSERIT ARTUS, / HAS EGO MANCINAS, STAGNA REFUSA,
DABO.
size: 14.5 cm long × 3 cm. high
location: 8. 4. 4, in the hallway which runs along the west side of the tablinum, on
the left-hand wall.
other notes: The inscription can be translated as "When the weight of cares
oppresses my limbs, I use my left hand to let the liberating gushes spurt out"
(Varone 2002, 94). The author has taken the phrase *stagna refusa* from Vergil and
redeployed it as part of his own couplet. The supplement of MOLES at the
beginning is by Bücheler in *CLE* n. 956.

1.135 Quos ego—sed motos praestat componere fluctus

18. *CIL* 4.4409 QUOS EGO SED
size: unknown
location: 5. 5. 3, to the right of the exedra that opens off of the back of the
peristyle near the right corner
other notes: Della Corte 1940 also includes *CIL* 4.8798 (sever(us): / ego quos /
Pompei(i)s) and 8641 (QUOS) as quotations of *Aeneid* 1.135. To my mind,

however, there is not enough in these inscriptions to connect them specifically with Vergil's text.

1.192–3: nec prius absistit, quam septem ingentia victor / corpora fundat humi, et numerum cum navibus aequet

19. CIL 4.8630b
NEC PRIUS / ABSISTIT QUA[M] / SEPTE(M) INGENTIA / VICTOR CORPORA / FUNDA(T) HUM(I)
size: 8 cm long × 6.5 cm high (overall)
location: the portico of the palaestra (2. 7), on column 62

1. 234: Certe hinc Romanos olim, volventibus annis

20. CIL 4.5012: CERTE HINC ROMANOS OLIM / VOLVENTIBUS ANNEIS
size: first line = 10 cm high, second = 6 cm high
location: 9. 2. 26, in the portico, on the second pillar from the right

1.242–3: Antenor potuit, mediis elapsus Achivis, / Illyricos penetrare sinus, atque intima tutus

21. CIL 4.1531: ANTENOR POTU(IT)
size: 33cm long × 7.5 cm high
location: 6. 14. 43 (NOT 6. 16 as in della Corte 1940, 176 n. 33), on the left wall of the tablinum, not far above the floor

22. Giordano 1966 n. 11 (= Solin 1975 n. 11): OCCASIONEM NACTUS NON PRAETERMISI TIBI SCRIBENDI, UT SCIRES ME RECTE VALERE / ANTENOR POTUIT MEDIIS ELAPSUS ACHIVIS ILLIRICOS PENETRARE SINUS, APPULIT(?)
size: unknown. A line drawing appears in Giordano 1966, but the plaster on which the graffito was preserved has been destroyed
location: 6. Ins. Occ. 22 (= Casa di M. Fabius Rufus), from a room on the second floor (below) down a flight of steps to the west of the portico on the house's southern end

1.468–9: hac Phryges, instaret curru cristatus Achilles / Nec procul hinc Rhesi niveis tentoria velis

23. CIL 4.8624b: NEC PHRYGAS / EXTABANT. QUID / AGIT APEX DESTER?
size: 6 cm long × 4.5 cm. high
location: the portico of the palaestra (2. 7), on col. 61
other notes: It is difficult to interpret the text's meaning, and its connection with the *Aeneid* seems a bit tenuous.

24. CIL 4.8757: I NEC VE(LIS) / VELIS
size: 4.2 cm long by 0.4–1.4 cm high
location: in the portico of the palaestra (2. 7), on col. 105

2.1 *Conticuere omnes intentique ora tenebant*

25. *CIL* 4.1672 CONTICUER(E)
size: 7. 5 cm long × 2.5 cm high
location: 7. 2. 35, on one of the eastern columns in the tetrastyle atrium

26. *CIL* 4.2213 CONTIQUERE
size: 16 cm long × 7.5 cm high
location: 7.12.18–20, on the eastern wall to the left of the door as you enter

27. *CIL* 4.3151 CONTI(QUERE)
size: 6 cm long × 8 cm high
location: 9. 2 on the wall of the street between door 16 and the southeastern
corner of the insula

28. *CIL* 4.3889 CONTICUERE OMNES / OMN(ES) / INTENTIQ[. .]S
size: 0.6 cm high (each line)
location: 1. 2. 6, on the rear wall of the atrium, to the right as you enter

29. *CIL* 4.4036 CONTI[C]U[E]RE O(MNES)
size: unknown
location: 5. 1. 18, on the wall to the right of the door
other notes: Inscription continues, below and off to the side: SIQUA /
C[. .]TIT QUATIT.

30. *CIL* 4.4191 CONTIQUERE / OMNES
size: 0.8 cm high
location: 5. 2. i, on a column on the right to the rear of the peristyle

31. *CIL* 4.4212 CONTICU(ERE)
size: 4.5 cm high
location: 5. 2. i, in the exedra that is in the middle of the back side of the
peristyle, on the right wall in the middle

32. *CIL* 4.4665 CONTIQUERE
size: 6 cm high
location: 6. 15. 9, between two doors on the back wall of the atrium

33. *CIL* 4.4675 CONTIQ(UERE)
size: 2.2 cm high
location: 6. 15. 16, on the right wall of the taberna

34. *CIL* 4.4877 CONT(ICUERE) / CONT(ICUERE)
size: 7 cm and 6 cm high
location: 8. 2. 20, on the north wall of the entrance

35. *CIL* 4.6707 CONTICUERE OMNES
size: 35 cm long
location: 5. 3. 9, on the street wall outside

36. *CIL* 4.8222 CON[TI]QUERE OMN(ES)
size: 41 cm long
location: 1. 8. 17, on the northern wall of the garden
other notes: Written in charcoal.

37. *CIL* 4.8247 CONTIQ(UERE)
size: 4 cm long
location: 1. 10. 2, in the "Thermopolium Primae," where there are many
inscriptions on the western wall that adjoins house 3

38. *CIL* 4.10096b CONTICUERE OM(NES)
size: 12.7 cm long × 0.5–3.4 cm high
location: 2. 1. 11, on the exterior wall to the right of the door
other notes: Found near a number of graffitied caricatures, including a gladiator
and a bird. The location given by della Corte in *CIL* (2. 4. 11) is incorrect
according to the system of numbering regiones and insulae currently used.

2.14: ductores Danaum tot iam labentibus annis

39. *CIL* 4.5020: DUCTORES DANAU(M)
size: unknown
location: 9. 2. 26, in the portico that is in front of the garden, on the second
pillar from the right

2.148: Quisquis es, amissos hinc iam obliuiscere Graios

40. *CIL* 4.1841: QUISQUIS ES, AMISSOS HIN[C IAM OB]/LIVISCERE
GRAIOS / SCRIBIT NARCISS / ER
size: 31.5 cm long × 24 cm high
location: basilica

2.324: Venit summa dies et ineluctabile tempus

41. *CIL* 4.1251, w. add. p. 206: VENIT SUMMA (DIES)
size: 4 cm long
location: 6. 5. 19, on the left post of the entrance to the house
other notes: The words above are followed by a number of uninterpretable letters/
words.

3.286: aere cauo clipeum, magni gestamen Abantis

42. *CIL* 4.1069a: BARBARUS AERE CAVO TUBICEN D[E]DIT [HORRIDA
SI]GNA
size: unknown
location: 9. 1. 22, in the tablinum which is between the two peristyles, on the left
wall in the lower margin of a picture representing Hesione being freed from the
rock (by Hercules)
other notes: The supplements at the end of the line are suggested by Bücheler,
CLE n. 350. Like n. 30 above, the Vergilian phrase has been inserted into a "local"
composition.

4.223: Vade age, nate, uoca Zephyros et labere pennis

43. *CIL* 4.8768: VADE / AGE NATE / VOCAS ZE / PIRIOS
size: 5.2 cm long × 0.8–0.3 cm high (each line)
location: portico of the palaestra (2. 7), col. 106

5.389: *Entelle, heroum quondam fortissime frustra*

44. *CIL* 4.8379: ENTELLE HEROUM
size: 11.1 cm long × 0.5–6.6 cm high
location: 1. 10. 8, in the atrium, on the pillar to the right as you go into the cubiculum/tablinum

6.119: *si potuit manis accersere coniugis Orpheus*

45. *CIL* 4.3183: SI POTUIT
size: 16 cm long × 8 cm high
location: 9. 1. 22, on the wall of the fauces to the left
other notes: It is not clear to me that there is enough of this inscription to see a direct quotation of Vergil.

6.823: *uincet amor patriae laudumque immensa cupido*

46. *CIL* 4.3681: VINCET AMU
size: unknown
location: 9. 3. 18–19, on the wall of the street between the two doors
other notes: Unusually, done in white paint rather than scratched, and thus probably to be connected with the surrounding programmata.

7.1: *Tu quoque litoribus nostris, Aeneia nutrix*

47. *CIL* 4.3796: AENEIA NUTRIX
size: 1.4 cm high
location: 9. 9. g, on the outside wall to the right of the door
other notes: This house is known as "the house of Aemelius Celer" (a well-known sign painter) on the basis of a painted inscription that reads "Aemelius Celer hic habitat" (*CIL* 4. 3794). The words above were also painted, in black, along with the name Aemelius Celer (*CIL* 4.3790, 3792).

48. *CIL* 4.4127: AENEIA
size: 2.5 cm high
location: 5. 2. 10, on the right wall of the atrium

49. *CIL* 4.4373: AAAENEA
size: 3.5 cm high
location: 5. 5. 3, on a column in the peristyle (fourth on the right side, from the south)

9.269: *uidisti, quo Turnus equo, quibus ibat in armis*

50. *CIL* 4.1237 w. add. p. 205: PRIMI[G]ENIUS . . . MYSTIIS COMMUNI SUO SALUTE VIDISTI QUO TURNUM AEQUORIBUS EIBAT IN ARM[IS] / SOES . . . VIRTUTIS MERCES PALMAM PRETIUM GLORIAE VICTORIAE SPEM CAUSAS
size: 54 cm long × 3 cm high
location: 6. 1. 24, on the street wall to the left of the door
other notes: It is not clear what connection the second line has to the first, although Zangemeister in *CIL* thinks it may be senarii. He suspects the author was a schoolboy.

51. *CIL* 4.8292: VIDISTIQUO TURNUS EQUO Q[
size: 20 cm long
location: 1. 10. 4, among the tituli to the right of the door

9.404: Tu, dea, tu praesens nostro succurre labori

52. *CIL* 4.2310k: TU DEA TU PRESENOS TRO SUCCURRE LABORE;
size: unknown
location: 7. 3. 24, on the street between the house door and the SE corner of
the insula

Eclogues

2.21: Mille meae Siculis errant in montibus agnae

53. *CIL* 4.8625c: MILLE MEAE / SICULIS ERRANT
size: 6 cm long × 0.4–1.6 cm high
location: the portico of the palaestra (2. 7), col. 62

54. Giordano and Casale 1990, 293 n. 71: SEVERUS / MILLE MEAE
SICULIS ERRANT IN MONTIBUS AG
size: unknown ("caratteri minuti")
location: 1. 15. 3, in the atrium

2.56: Rusticus es, Corydon; nec munera curat Alexis

55. *CIL* 4.1527: RUSTICUS EST CORYDO[N]
size: 7 cm long × 2 cm high
location: 6. 14. 12, in the atrium

56. *CIL* 4.1524: RUSTICUS
size: unknown
location: 6. 14. 12, in the atrium

57. *CIL* 4.9208: RUSTICUS
size: 23 cm long × 3.1–7.3 cm high
location: Villa of the Mysteries, on the far wall to the left of the door through
which you enter the tetrastyle atrium

58. *CIL* 4.4660: CORUSTICUS
size: 4 cm long × 4 cm high
location: 6. 15. 9, on the right wall of the door

59. *CIL* 4.8801: CORI/DON
size: 5 cm long × 1.9–4.3 cm high
location: portico of the palaestra (2. 7), col. 110

3.1: Dic mihi, Damoeta, cuium pecus? An Meliboei?

60. *CIL* 4.5007: DET MIHI DAMOETA FELICIOR QUAM PHASIPHAE
HAEC OMNIA SCRIPSIT ZOSIMUS
size: 35 cm long

location: 9. 2. 26, in the portico that is before the garden, on the second pillar from the right

61. *CIL* 4.9987: D]IC MIHI / DAM]OET[A
size: 20 cm long × 4 cm high (each line)
location: 1. 6. 12, on outside of the northern wall

7.44: Ite domum pasti, si quis pudor, ite, iuuenci

62. *CIL* 4.8701: SI PUDOR QUIS
size: 3.5 cm long × 0.3–1.5 cm high
location: the portico of the palaestra (2. 7), col. 83

8.70: carminibus Circe socios mutavit Ulixi

63. *CIL* 4.1982: CARMINIBUS / CIRCE SOCIOS / MUTAVIT / OLYXIS
size: unknown
location: on the outside of the north wall of the Chalcidicum of Eumachia (7. 9. 1), opposite 7. 9. 62–6.
other notes: The line drawing provided in *CIL* is from Wordsworth 1837 and is certainly not to scale.

64. *CIL* 4.4401: CARMIN[
size: unknown
location: 5. 5. 3, on the sixth column on the left side in the peristyle
other notes: In both this instance and the one below, I am doubtful that there is enough inscribed to be sure of a quotation from Vergil.

65. *CIL* 4.5304 CARM[
size: 1.2 cm high
location: 9.9.d–e, on the wall of the street at an equal distance between the doors
other notes: see above, n. 63

Georgics

1.163 tardaque Eleusinae matris uoluentia plaustra

66. *CIL* 4.8560: MATRIS ELEUSINAE
size: 16. 5 cm long × 2.25 high
location: the portico of the palaestra (2. 7), col. 17
other notes: I am doubtful that we should see this as an allusion to the *Georgics*, as the epitaph may have become standard, and the words appear here in the reverse order from the way they are used in Vergil's text.

67. *CIL* 4.8610: MATRIS HELEUSINAE
size: 5.2 cm long × 0.5–1.2 cm high
location: the portico of the palaestra (2. 7), col. 33
other notes: see above, n. 65

BIBLIOGRAPHY

Alföldy, G. 1991. "Augustus und die Inschriften: Tradition und Innovation: Die Geburt der imperialen Epigraphik." *Gymnasium* 98: 289–324.

Augst, Thomas. 2003. *The Clerk's Tale: Young Men and Moral Life in Nineteenth-Century America*. Chicago.

Biville, F. 2003. "Le latin et le grec 'vulgaires' des inscriptions pompéiennes." In H. Solin, M. Leiwo, and H. Halla-aho, eds., *Latin vulgaire–latin tardif. 6, Actes du VIe colloque international sur le latin vulgaire et tardif, Helsinki, 29 août–2 septembre 2000*, 219–35. Hildesheim.

Bowman, A. K. and G. Woolf, eds. 1994. *Literacy and Power in the Ancient World*. Cambridge.

Cipriotti, P. 1975. "Brevi note su alcune scritte Pompeiane." In Bernard Andreae and Helmut Kyrieleis [et al.], eds., *Neue Forschungen in Pompeji und den anderen vom Vesuvausbruch 79 n. Chr. verschütteten Städten*, 273–6. Recklinghausen.

Courtney, Edward. 1995. *Musa lapidaria: A Selection of Latin Verse Inscriptions*. Atlanta.

Cribiore, Raffaella. 2001. *Gymnastics of the Mind: Greek Education in Hellenistic and Roman Egypt*. Princeton.

Cugusi, P. 1985. "Spunti di polemica politica in alcuni graffiti di Pompei e di Terracina." *ZPE* 61: 23–9.

de Vos, Mariette. 1991. "La fuga di Enea in pitture del I secolo d. C." *KJ* 24: 113–23.

Degrassi, A. 1937. "Elogia Pompeiana." *Inscriptiones Italiae*. Vol. 13, *Fasti et elogia*. Fasc. 3, *Elogia*, 68–70. Rome.

della Corte, Matteo. 1940. "Virgilio nell'epigrafia pompeiana." *Epigraphica* 2: 171–8.

——. 1958. *Amori e amanti di Pompei antica. Antologia erotica Pompeiana*. Naples.

——. 1965. *Case ed abitanti de Pompei*. 3rd ed. Naples.

Franklin, J. L. 1980. *Pompeii: The Electoral Programmata, Campaigns, and Politics, A.D. 71–79*. Papers and Monographs of the American Academy in Rome 28. Rome.

——. 1985/6. "Games and a *Lupanar*: Prosopography of a Neighborhood in Ancient Pompeii." *CJ* 81: 319–28.

——. 1991. "Literacy and the Parietal Inscriptions of Pompeii." In Humphrey 1991: 77–98.

——. 1996/7. "Vergil at Pompeii: A Teacher's Aid." *CJ* 92: 175–84.

——. 2001. *Pompeis difficile est: Studies in the Political Life of Imperial Pompeii*. Ann Arbor.

Galinsky, G. Karl. 1969. *Aeneas, Sicily, and Rome*. Princeton.

Gigante, M. 1979. *Civiltà delle forme letterarie nell'antica Pompei*. Naples.

Giordano, Carlo. 1966. "Le iscrizioni della casa di M. Fabio Rufo." *RAAN* 41: 73–89.

—— and Angelandrea Casale. 1990. "Iscrizioni pompeiane inedite scoperte tra gli anni 1954–1978." *AAP* 39: 273–378.

Harris, William. 1989. *Ancient Literacy*. Cambridge, Mass.

Herman, József. 2000. *Vulgar Latin*. Trans. by Roger Wright. University Park, Penn.

Hoogma, R. P. 1959. *Der Einfluss Vergils auf die Carmina Latina Epigraphica: Eine Studie mit Besonderer Berücksichtigung der metrisch–technischen Grundsätze der Entlehnung*. Amsterdam.

Humphrey, J. H., ed. 1991. *Literacy in the Roman World.* Journal of Roman Archaeology, Supplementary Series 3. Ann Arbor.

Kaster, Robert A. 1988. *Guardians of Language: The Grammarian and Society in Late Antiquity.* Berkeley.

Kellum, Barbara. 1999. "The Spectacle of the Street." In B. Bergmann and C. Kondoleon, eds., *The Art of Ancient Spectacle,* 283–99. Studies in the History of Art 56. Washington, D.C.

Lindsay, J. 1960. *The Writing on the Wall: An Account of Pompeii in Its Last Days.* London.

MacMullen, Ramsay. 1982. "The Epigraphic Habit in the Roman Empire." *AJPh* 103: 233–46.

Maiuri, A. 1986. *Mestiere d'archeologo: antologia di scritti.* 2nd ed. Ed. by M. Belli. Milan.

Mau, A. 1902. *Pompeii: Its Life and Art.* Trans. by F. W. Kelsey. New York.

Moeller, W. A. 1976. *The Wool Trade of Ancient Pompeii.* Leiden.

Mouritsen, H. 1988. *Elections, Magistrates and Municipal Élite: Studies in Pompeian Epigraphy.* Analecta Romana Instituti Danici, Supplement 15. Rome.

Pannuti, U. 1983. "Il Giornale degli Scavi di Ercolano 1738–1756 (SNSP Ms. 20. B.19bis)." *MAL* 26: 159–410.

Sanjek, David. 1994. "'Don't Have to DJ No More': Sampling and the 'Autonomous' Creator." In Martha Woodmansee and Peter Jaszi, eds., *The Construction of Authorship: Textual Appropriation in Law and Literature,* 343–60. Durham, N.C.

Solin, Heikki. 1975. "Die Wandinschriften im sog. Haus des M. Fabius Rufus." In Bernard Andreae and Helmut Kyrieleis [et al.], eds., *Neue Forschungen in Pompeji und den anderen vom Vesuvausbruch 79 n. Chr. verschütteten Städten,* 243–66. Recklinghausen.

Spannagel, Martin. 1999. *Exemplaria principis: Untersuchungen zu Entstehung und Ausstattung des Augustusforums.* Archäologie und Geschichte 9. Heidelberg.

Spinazzola, Vittorio. 1953. *Pompei alla luce degli scavi nuovi di Via dell'Abbondanza (anni 1910–1923).* Rome.

Stewart, S. 1987. "Ceci Tuera Cela: Graffiti as Crime and Art." In John Fekete, ed., *Life After Postmodernism: Essays on Value and Culture,* 161–80. New York.

Tanzer, H. 1939. *The Common People of Pompeii: A Study of the Graffiti Evidence.* Baltimore.

Väänänen, Veikko. 1966. *Le latin vulgaire des inscriptions pompéiennes.* 3rd augmented ed. Berlin.

Varone, Antonio. 2002. *Erotica Pompeiana: Love Inscriptions on the Walls of Pompeii.* Trans. by R. Berg, with revisions by D. Harwood and R. Ling. Studia archaeologica 116. Rome.

Wachter, Rudolf. 1998. "'Oral Poetry' in ungewohntem Kontext: Hinweise auf mündliche Dichtungstechnik in den pompejanischen Wandinschriften." *ZPE* 121: 73–89.

Woolf, Greg. 1996. "Monumental Writing and the Expansion of Roman Society in the Early Empire." *JRS* 86: 22–39.

Wordsworth, Christopher. 1837. *Inscriptiones Pompeianae; or Specimens and Facsimiles of Ancient Inscriptions Discovered on the Walls of Buildings at Pompeii.* London.

13

Constructing Elite Reading Communities in the High Empire

William A. Johnson

A reading community in Antonine Rome is described in some detail by Aulus Gellius in his sole surviving work, the *Attic Nights*. Gellius's work is one of those from antiquity that is more often cited than studied, so a few introductory remarks are in order. The *Attic Nights* is a miscellany, in the sense that it is a series of about four hundred short essays—often no more than a page or so—on miscellaneous topics. The storytelling varies in its narrative aims and strategies, but the twin ideas of "fun stories" and "fun facts to know and tell" is by far the dominant mode. The miscellany gains coherence through consistency in the topics of interest: the fun facts and fun stories, as it happens, are mostly about words, their etymology and meaning and proper usage; or exempla culled from literature, especially that "archaic" literature of the Republic.

But this sober summary doesn't do justice to the work, which describes a very unusual—one wants to say perfectly insane—community. Or at least I think most people who are not scholars would judge it so. In Gellius's world, we the readers are trained to think nothing of even absurdly esoteric discussions. At 1.7, for example, it is natural that a learned friend, when presented with an unusual reading in a Tironian manuscript(!) of Cicero's *in Verrem*, not only has a strong opinion about that reading, but also is able to adduce in support of his opinion an obscure speech of Gaius Gracchus, parallel constructions in Greek, the *Annales* of Claudius Quadrigarius and of Valerius Antias, the *Casina* of Plautus, the *Gemelli* of Laberius, and a minor speech of Cicero himself. And, of course, the friend is able to give this evidence off the cuff. As readers of Gellius, we acclimate even to the idea that in a public square a youth in Gellius's group can make a comment on the antiquity of the word *spartum* ("Spanish broom") that is then challenged by a couple of the half-educated men (the *male litterati*) who hang around the squares. In argument, these *male litterati* quote Homer with an ease of learning almost inconceivable today and laugh at the youth's reply, and "they would have only laughed more at him" (we are told, 17.3) had he not been able to pull out of the pocket of his toga the twenty-fifth book of Varro's *antiquitates rerum humanarum*, whose authority as an antiquarian text wins the day. This is a community that lives and breathes texts, literary texts, *classical* texts.

It may be justly doubted that this community "truly" existed—idealized details strain credulity at every turn—but the fiction is nonetheless important as, at the least, an ideal that Gellius expects to be able to live in the minds of his readers. The fact that this world is a literary depiction is a problem to which we will return at the end.

In earlier work,[1] I have argued for the need to consider ancient literacy within the context of a broad system of interlocking social behaviors, and I have also emphasized the need to consider the "reading system" or "reading culture" (both terms I have used) within a particular time and place. I concede, of course, that reading systems have continuity: that conventions become traditions, and that reading and writing systems are prone to conservative treatment. But as a point of methodology and of fact, there are important differences that arise among communities as we move in time and place, even among communities in the same time and place. The "reading system," that is, turns out to be an ever-changing thing; like all social systems, the details and even the structure of interactions are subject to continual negotiation by the community. Despite a general sense of continuity, the ways that people interact with texts are no more stable than other social conventions. Just as, for example, the meaning and use of words can change over time and place, so, too, can the significances associated with the use of text. In this chapter I want therefore to focus not so much on the broader system of reading, but on the individual community. In what follows, I will concentrate on two complementary aspects: (1) the sociology of text-centered events, that is, the nuts and bolts of how the community makes use of texts; and (2) the cultural construction of text-centered events, that is, the ideological and other encumbrances that the community attaches to its use of texts.

GELLIUS'S WORLD: THE READING COMMUNITY

Let us turn first to consider a characteristic encounter in the reading community that I have chosen as my example—that is, "Gellius's world," that Antonine community, dating from roughly the 140s to the 170s A.D., described by Gellius. The chapter is 19.10, and the scene is the house of Cornelius Fronto, famously the tutor of Marcus Aurelius and a leading orator and intellectual of his day. The story here told is particularly rich in typical elements, but it is not otherwise unusual: each of the elements recur, *mutatis mutandis*, again and again in the scenarios

---

1. Johnson 2000, 2002.

depictcd in Gellius, and so the whole of the scene has a richly representative feeling for Gellius's readers.[2] Gellius comes in company with his friend Julius Celsinus to visit Fronto, ill with gout. We are presented with a fascinating tableau. Fronto reclines on a little Greek sickbed (*in scrimpodio Graeciensi*) "surrounded on all side by men renowned for intellectual capacity, birth, or wealth." Fronto is busy with some builders, discussing plans for adding a new bath complex. To a remark by one of the builders, one of Fronto's friends interjects a comment that, as it happens, contains the expression, *praeterpropter*, "more or less." Fronto stops all conversation at once, looks at his friend, and asks what *praeterpropter* means. The friend demurs, referring the question to a celebrated grammarian sitting nearby. The grammarian dismisses the question—*honore quaestionis minime dignum*: "hardly deserving the honor of the inquiry"— because the word is an "utterly plebeian expression," the idiom of workers rather than of cultivated men. Fronto objects: how can *praeterpropter* be a lowly expression when Cato and Varro and other early writers use it? Gellius's friend Julius Celsinus now interposes the information that the word is used in the *Iphigeneia* of Ennius, and asks that the bookroll itself be produced. It is, and the chorus containing the word is read. The defeated grammarian, sweating and blushing, beats a hasty exit to the loud laughter of many; whereupon a general exodus ensues.

Note how swiftly the social scene shifts, by catalysis from some chance remark, into a literary event. The movement from social converse to bookishness to actual reading is seamless. When we unpack the event, we see the following elements. The marked social group is composed generally of powerful men, but as a matter of course includes the intellectually powerful. A topic, introduced serendipitously, immediately leads to a philological challenge: what exactly does a given word mean? The challenge is passed along to a specialist—*present because the social group is constructed in that way*—who is then able to assert his expert knowledge. But the expert falls prey to the superior knowledge of the master, Fronto, and his aristocratic friend, Celsinus. As final arbiter, the literary texts themselves are ushered in: first, by reference and then literally (as the text of Ennius is summoned to be read). The bookroll itself delivers the decisive evidence. The episode now over, the group breaks up—which signals indirectly that the literary event, fortuitous though it was, was *the reason why the social group was constituted*. In Gellius's world, elite society seems to exist for literary events of exactly this type: this is what the crowd of distinguished men is waiting *for* as they watch Fronto deal with his builders.

Gellius's reading community is, then, exclusionary in some special ways. The group is not the elite-at-large, but a self-selected collection of the ambitiously bookish. The *raison d'être* of the group seems to be to play a particular sort of learned game, in which the participants make comments on language and literature with reference to antiquarian texts and their commentators before an appraising but largely unparticipating crowd. The masters both participate in and act as final authority for these interactions, which are frequently in the mode of challenges to knowledge. That the textual material be abstruse is an important criterion. Those uninterested in these texts, or uninterested in the game played with these texts, or not educated in the particulars necessary to appreciate the interactions, are excluded from the group. Implicit is a "crowd" that works hard at gaining the knowledge necessary to have even marginal understanding of the esotericism that here plays out.

READING ALONE

To us, the scholar's acquisition of knowledge is constructed as a solitary activity. The world of Gellius maps differently—we have already had a glimpse of how intermeshed scholarly reading and society can be, and we will see more just below—but for Gellius, too, the scholar alone with his studies is clearly a defining image. The very title, *Attic Nights*, refers to the winter nights that Gellius spent as a student creating the knowledge set necessary to participate in this erudite community. In the preface, Gellius defines the invited readers of his work as "those who find pleasure and keep themselves busy in reading, inquiring, writing and taking notes, who spend wakeful nights in such work"[3]—an image that recurs. Sociologically, reading alone does different duty from working with texts in the context of the group. At 14.6, a *familiaris* presents to Gellius "a fat bookroll overflowing with every sort of knowledge" (*librum grandi volumine doctrinae omnigenus praescatentem*) as a resource in writing his *Nights*. Gellius eagerly takes the book and shuts himself deep within the house (*recondo me penitus*) in order to read it *sine arbitris*—"without any onlookers," that is, without the distracting presence of the peer group. Gellius's emphasis on lucubration in the preface is, then, not simply an issue of concentration, but a reflex of the need to protect himself from onlookers, that is, from the competitive pressures of the supporting society. Implicit in this is the assumption that literate events like reading and writing commonly occur within deeply social contexts. In Gellius's depiction, removal from the group appears the less usual, *marked* circumstance for reading—exactly the inverse of our society.

---

3. Paraphrasing praef. 19; cf. *hibernarum vigiliarum*, praef. 10, *lucubratiunculas*, praef. 14.

We can go further.[4] "Burning the midnight oil" remains a contemporary expression, but in second-century Rome the *topos* of lucubration had been long established as a mark of serious intellectual endeavor, including especially writing poetry, oratorical study, and "scholarly" pursuits—as we see from examples in Lucretius, Cicero, Seneca, Pliny the Elder, Quintilian, Tacitus, Juvenal.[5] The lucubration theme is a way of signaling that the work is important, and involves immense and concentrated effort. That effort, unusually, requires removal from others. But lucubration also typically signals work culled from leisure time, work done during times like the evening so as not to interfere with the business of the day (*negotium*, in Roman terms). At issue is the very valuation of leisure, *otium*: what *should* elite Romans spend their leisure hours doing? Strong moralistic overtones come into play. Counterpoised in the Roman cultural schematic is the other expected way to spend one's evening, that is, in entertainments with varying degrees of idleness or debauchery. The anxiety to position the scholar's nighttime *otium* as one worthy of a dutiful Roman comes out in a variety of sources in the early empire (such as the preface to Pliny's *Natural History*, or *Epistle* 8 of Seneca). Gellius, who hardly mentions his *negotium* otherwise, nonetheless feels compelled to stress in the preface that he "made himself busy and weary by rolling and unrolling many a bookroll in every break from *negotium* in which I could steal some *otium*" (praef. 12; cf. 23). For archaizing conservatives of Gellius's era, lucubration took on associations with hard work and duty, and it is no coincidence that these same elite chose to overlook the elegancies of Augustan and Silver Age literature to concentrate on the hardy texts of the Republic. What at first seems a simple case of a scholar needing to be alone to concentrate on reading and writing turns out to be far more: a cultural construction of *otium* that carries with it essentialist notions of what it is to be "Roman."

READING IN THE GROUP

I have already remarked that in Gellius, reading and other text-centered events commonly occur within social contexts, much more so than in our own culture. A systematic presentation of evidence is not possible here, but even a few further examples will serve both to flesh out that statement and to delineate some characteristic behaviors.

4. Far the best general study of the Romans' cultural construction of reading by lamplight is Ker 2004, on which this paragraph in part depends.
5. Writing poetry: Lucretius 1.142; Juvenal 1.51 on Horace; Tacitus, *Dial.* 9. Oratorical study: Cicero, *Cael.* 45; Q. Cicero *Fam.* 16.26.1; Quintilian *Inst.* 10.3.25–27. "Scholarly" pursuit: Varro *Ling. Lat.* 5.9; Cicero, *Parad.* praef. 5; Seneca *Ep.* 8.1; Pliny *NH* praef. 18, 24, 18.43.

Because the *magister* is an informing figure in Gellius, let us begin with a scene from his school days. A passage at the front of 11.13 is remarkable enough to quote in full:

> At the home of Titus Castricius, a teacher of the discipline of rhetoric and a man of weighty and solid judgment, a speech of Gaius Gracchus was being read aloud. At the beginning of that speech, the words were arranged with more precision and musicality than is usual for the early orators. These are the words, composed just as I have indicated: *quae uos cupide per hosce annos adpetistis atque uoluistis, ea si temere repudiaritis, abesse non potest, quin aut olim cupide adpetisse aut nunc temere repudiasse dicamini (if you now rashly reject the things which all these years you have earnestly sought and longed for, it must be said either that you sought them earnestly before, or that you have now rejected them without consideration).*
>
> The flow and sound of the well-rounded and smooth sentence delighted us extremely, to an unusual degree, and all the more since we saw that a composition of this sort had been pleasing to Gracchus, a distinguished and austere man. But when those same words were read over and over again at our request, Castricius admonished us to consider what was the force and value of the thought, and not to allow our minds as well as our ears to fill up with empty pleasure, charmed by the music of the well-cadenced speech.

The passage serves as vivid reminder that the educated audience of antiquity was trained to a very different sensibility for the rhythm and sounds of oratory. Gracchus's sentence is striking for its repetition of words and sounds, for the balance in clauses,[6] and for the overall rhythm. Yet it hardly rises to the level that it seems reasonable—to us—that students ask it to be read again and again (*saepius lectitarentur*). Importantly, our students wouldn't ask that *anything* be read again and again; nor do modern instructors need to worry that students will pay too much attention to the musicality of a sentence! The very experience of hearing the words when read aloud to the group—what one listens to, what one listens for—is utterly unfamiliar to modern perceptions. This is not news: Norden's *Die antike Kunstprosa* eloquently described the ancient reader's attitudes toward literary prose a century ago.[7] The differences are not, however, solely interior. Sociologically, even the brief scene here implies a situation in which someone reads the text performatively; the students ooh and aah and demand an encore; the text is read again; more clamor and discussion; after several iterations the teacher finally intervenes. The rest of the chapter is taken up with Castricius's demonstration, at length, of logical and stylistic problems with Gracchus's expression in this sentence. The way in which a small section of text is held up *by the*

---

6. A good example of isocolon, as Norden saw (1915, 1.172): *quae ... repudiaritis* = 32 syllables; *abesse ... dicamini* = 31 syllables; *aut* in each case introduces a phrase of 10 syllables.

7. Norden 1915.

group to intense scrutiny, repeatedly and interactively, is not easy to parallel in modern society.[8]

That this habit of turning over a passage in a group setting is not mere schoolroom behavior is readily established. Let us take as example a reading event depicted in extraordinary detail in chapter 3.1, this time involving Favorinus and back in Rome. Gellius and others were with Favorinus on a temperate late-winter day, taking a stroll in the courtyard of the Titian baths. As they were walking, the *Catilina* of Sallust was being read aloud (*legebatur*); Favorinus had noticed the book in the hand of a friend and ordered it to be read. Once a short passage on avarice[9] is reached, Favorinus then looks at Gellius and asks him a pointed question on the content ("How exactly does *avarice* make a man's body *effeminate?*"). Gellius gains time for himself (*cunctabundus*) by answering: "I too have been on the verge of posing this question for some time now, and, if you hadn't beat me to it, I would have asked you this very thing." Immediately, one of the *sectatores* of Favorinus, an old hand in things literary (*in litteris veterator*), butts in to remark what he had heard the grammarian Valerius Probus say on the topic. Favorinus dismisses the remark, and now turns attention to an unnamed man of considerable learning (*homo quispiam sane doctus*) who is with them on the walk. After the learned gentleman opines, Favorinus orders that the same four lines of Sallust be read aloud again, and once the lines have been reread he finishes his argument with this learned companion. As the scene unfolds, we get a gradual sense of the hangers-on involved in this ambulation around the baths: in addition to Gellius, friends (*amici*), followers (*sectatores*), and at least one *doctus* of rank more or less equal to the great teacher. None aside from Gellius are named: here as everywhere in Gellius, the great teacher brings along with him a large, anonymous crowd.

Several aspects of the scene in 3.1 merit our close attention. First is Favorinus's reaction to finding an interesting book in the hands of a friend: he orders that the book be read aloud to himself and his entourage. The ease of movement from discovery of the book to a group reading event is arresting. Equally striking is the ease with which the reading event moves from discussion, back to the passage, and onward to more discussion—in the end, Gellius records two pages of discussion concerning four lines of text. Consider also the *way* that the text is used. As indicated, the book is read until a passage of interest is discovered. Once discovered, the reading is suspended while the passage and its implications are scrutinized. The discussion characteristically combines urgent philological investigation into the meaning of the antiquarian text with optimism that proper interpretation will lead to more refined thinking: the engagement is

8. Perhaps the closest analogue in modern society is the group study of religious texts, for example, the Talmud or the Bible.
9. *Catilina* 11.3: four lines.

simultaneously with "Sallust" and with one's contemporaries. The *combination* of inquiry and discussion is what makes the text enduringly vital to the community—what makes the text a "classic."[10] Finally, there is the negotiation of the intellectual challenge that Favorinus mounts to the text. The text cannot be interrogated unless it has an advocate to speak for it: who, then, will interpret and defend the text? Favorinus's attention first falls on Gellius; a *sector* tries unsuccessfully to step in; a learned companion is then found willing to engage. One has the clear sense of a pecking order among the entourage, and of a continual vying to maintain or better one's place. Personal competition for status forms one of the principal bounds within the community. Because the community defines itself in bookish terms, that competition plays out in relation to texts and to the masters of texts.

When one looks at what the group gets together to do, much of the behavior seems driven by the negotiation of authority with reference to a particular group of texts. For reasons that are partly idiosyncratic[11] and partly ideological, the "classics" that this community looks to are in the main the archaic texts. The urgency, as Gellius depicts it, is to determine who can act as a proper spokesman for these texts; in what ways are the texts properly discussed; and how much one can properly extract from them. This can get down to seemingly trivial matters—whether, for instance, the use of a word like *praeterpropter* in one of these "classics" is enough to qualify it for refined society. The *Attic Nights* is packed with commentary on what are the right ways to speak, to think; who are the right voices from the past to attend; who are the arbiters—commentators and masters—of this rightness. At a remove, the commentary on commentators may seem tiresome, and the wrangling over *minutiae* absurd; but in its context this sort of learned disputation is critical, because the battle over these details determines who will be the cultural gatekeepers for the society. The *Nights* itself, by my reading, is self-consciously advocating its own circle as those gatekeepers—gatekeepers, again, not simply of trivia, but of the right ways, as a "proper" Roman, of speaking and thinking and behaving and remembering the past.

LITERATURE AND THE CONSTRUCTION OF THE READING COMMUNITY

In looking at some typical reading events in this ancient community, I have tried to highlight the cultural and sociological encumbrances.

10. On what made a "classic" in antiquity, see Porter 2006.
11. Perhaps going back to the oddball literary tastes of Hadrian, who famously preferred "Cato to Cicero, Ennius to Vergil, Caelius to Sallust" (*SHA Hadr.* 16). It should be noted that Fronto (and others: e.g., Apuleius) did not share Gellius's celebration and advocacy of archaism.

The question I wish to pose is not, "Did the Romans read silently?"—of course they did[12]—but how they *constructed* the significance of the circumstances in which reading took place. The Romans no doubt read silently and alone in a variety of circumstances, but the circumstance this author chooses to remark upon is, as we have seen, the lucubration or vigilation, that idea of reading and writing by lamplight, an image that instantiates the virtuous and productive Roman who, like Lucretia in the paradigmatic folktale,[13] works hard even in *otium* while other aristocrats indulge in debauchery. The scholarly reading necessary to be a validated member of the exclusionary group is thereby *constructed* not simply as entertainment, or as an expedient to intellectual or social advancement, but as an upright behavior important to the moral underpinnings of the society.

Similarly, I do not here pose the question of whether Romans read and otherwise made use of literary texts in groups—again, of course they did—though I am interested in the social mechanics of how that happens, and we have seen along the way that in Gellius's world texts are used in a variety of group circumstances that distinguish the society broadly from our own. Thus, the habit of *rereading* a text aloud to one another, the habits of interrogating the text, of locating an advocate for the text, of using the text as a springboard to discussion but returning to it as an arbiter—all these are characteristic of this community. More essentially, though, I am interested in the ways in which texts are central to the self-construction and self-validation of the group: these texts are *constructed* as "classic" texts that can be used to guide speech and thought and behavior, and thus require authoritative voices to direct others in their interpretation; this *constructed need for authority* then drives many of the group behaviors.

Lurking underneath all this is a Big Question: why is literature important to the elite in this society in a way that it is not in others? It is easy to observe that literature was important to the wealthy and powerful in antiquity in a way that it is not to today's political or economic elite. But in trying to address the question of the social functioning of literature, we should avoid stepping too swiftly toward generalization; we need to be careful not, say, to toss together fifth-century Athens and Antonine Rome, six hundred years removed. The goal, as I see it, is a more thorough exploration of the rich *variety* of ways that literature can function within societies.

In any case, I think we have to start with particulars. In that strange place that I have called "Gellius's World," which reflects at least in part

---

12. See Johnson 2000 and bibliography collected there, especially Gavrilov 1997 and Burnyeat 1997.
13. Livy 1.57. Further at Ker 2004, 222–4.

certain tendencies in Antonine society, literature, taken as a whole, seems to function in the following ways:

- as an exclusionary device: admitted into the community are only those with the education to be able to understand, let alone participate in, the learned exchanges
- as a social mechanism: this is what the community gets together to do, and serves as the means by which the members of the community establish a hierarchy
- as an ideological statement: these are cultured people who buy into a certain idea of Romanness: these are the virtuous, who see the present as heir to a particular Roman paradigm—harder and simpler and more upright
- as an aesthetic statement, which (in this case) is self-consciously archaizing
- as the basis on which to assert a gatekeeper role: the controllers of these (central) texts become the arbiters of what is "correct,"[14] and thus the (central) importance of this subgroup among the elite is asserted

Finally, I return, however briefly and inadequately, to the question of the literary text. As with any carefully controlled fiction, it is difficult to say how much of what we see is ideal or traditional or simply imaginative and how much is reflective of a real society. In this case, it seems clear enough from the letters of Fronto and other contemporary witnesses[15] that the scenes we have visited have some concrete basis, even if they are (as I suppose) highly idealized. But in any case the codes of behavior seem to be what the author chooses to highlight, what the author endorses. An interesting and important feature of this sort of literature is that the text itself seems at least in part designed so as to *assist in the construction of the reading community*; that is, the literary text not only invites a defined readership (which is exclusive in a way parallel to the community), but also advocates through its fiction certain types of community behavior, including "best practice" ways of interacting with texts. The literary text of Gellius is intrinsically self-serving, and it seems to me that in this respect it is not only not unique but represents a fairly broad class of writings. The text, that is, does not merely reflect or serve its readers, but projects and thereby *actively seeks to create* the (ideal) reading community to which the writing aspires.

BIBLIOGRAPHY

Burnyeat, Miles F. 1997. "Postscript on Silent Reading." *CQ* 47: 74–6.
Gavrilov, A. K. 1997. "Techniques of Reading in Classical Antiquity." *CQ* 47: 56–73.

14. In language, of course, but also literary criticism, textual criticism, history (at least biographical history: e.g., 13.20), ethics, philosophy; there is aspiration even to subjects like anatomy and law, though the group seems to find its limits there.

15. On the Greek side, the *loci classici* are Lucian, *Indoct.* and *Symp.*, but we see much of the same in Plutarch, Galen, Athenaeus.

Johnson, William A. 2000. "Towards a Sociology of Reading in Classical Antiquity." *AJPh* 121: 593–627.

——. 2002. "Reading Cultures and Education." In Peter C. Patrikis, ed., *Reading between the Lines: Perspectives on Foreign Language Literacy*, 9–23. Yale Language Series. New Haven.

——. 2010. *Readers and Reading Culture in the High Empire: A study of Elite Reading Communities*. Oxford.

Ker, James. 2004. "Nocturnal Writers in Imperial Rome: The Culture of *Lucubratio*." *CPh* 99: 209–42.

Nordon, Eduard. 1915. *Die antike Kunstprosa vom VI. Jahrhundert v. Chr. bis in die Zeit der Renaissance*. Vol. I. 3rd ed. Leipzig.

Porter, James I., ed. 2006. *Classical Pasts: The Classical Traditions of Greece and Rome*. Princeton.

Part IV

BIBLIOGRAPHICAL ESSAY

14

Literacy Studies in Classics

The Last Twenty Years

Shirley Werner

Twenty-five years ago a distinguished historian could write, "There are plenty of studies on literacy, none on its use, that I know of" (MacMullen 1982: 233). Nothing could be further from the truth today. Discussions of material evidence—some of it long known, some more recently discovered (including *instrumentum domesticum*, the *lapis Satricanus*, the wooden tablets from Vindolanda, a handful of lead letters[1])—have gone hand in hand with theoretical analyses bearing on the broader functions and cultural significance of these written materials within their societies. The collected work by Detienne (ed.) 1988a, *Les savoirs de l'écriture*, was organized around the hypothesis that writing, as a social practice, is a way of thinking that functioned at the center of social life in classical Greece and opened up new possibilities for the intellect. Thomas 1989, *Oral Tradition and Written Record in Classical Athens*, sought to provide an "extensive reinterpretation of the place of writing in Greek culture and its relation to oral communication." The publication of Harris 1989a, *Ancient Literacy*—often cited as the most comprehensive treatment of the levels of Greek and Roman literacy to date—prompted scholars to pursue topics which had not been taken up in that book. Humphrey (ed.) 1991, *Literacy in the Roman World*, adopted Harris's study as a starting point for contributors' discussions of literacy in the Roman world. Thomas 1992 continued her groundbreaking work on the interaction between writing and oral tradition in ancient Greece with the publication of *Literacy and Orality in Ancient Greece*, which contained chapters on oral poetry; the coming of the alphabet; the relationship between literate and oral; orality, performance, and the written text; and literacy and the state. Pébarthe 2006, *Cité, démocratie et écriture: histoire de l'alphabétisation*

---

1. Lapis Satricanus: Stibbe et al. 1980. On other kinds of primary evidence see the bibliographical index under the relevant topics (e.g., "Instrumentum Domesticum," "Lead Letters," "Ostraka," "Tablets," and "Vindolanda").

d'Athènes à l'époque classique, examined the uses of public and private writing in Athens.

New theoretical perspectives have also arisen concerning the uses of writing on materials and in texts that do not in large part survive. The study of archives has proven to be very productive: see Woolf, chapter 3, in this volume for discussion of the multivolume collection entitled *La mémoire perdue* (Demougin 1994, Moatti 1998, 2000). This ambitious collection addresses the use of written records in such areas of Roman public life as banking, politics, the Senate, law, the administration of public lands, and religion—to name only some of the topics covered in the first volume (Demougin 1994). The second volume (Moatti 1998) delves into two broad areas of investigation: first, the use of archives in Roman religious contexts, and second, the production of records connected with the grain distribution. The third volume (Moatti 2000) is concerned with judiciary archives. Another collection of essays on concepts of record keeping in the ancient world was compiled by Brosius (ed.) 2003. Census archives have supplied the subject for yet another substantial collective work, *Les archives du census* (Moatti 2001).

Our goal in this essay is to give an overview—given the volume of scholarship it can be no more than skeletal—of the many-faceted and stimulating work on ancient literacy published in the last generation. Although the bibliography in Harris 1989 is taken as a point of rough chronological departure, this essay (following the direction of the chapters in this book) adopts a perspective rather different from that of Harris: our aim is not so much to define the levels of literacy in ancient populations but rather to ponder the cultural and social significances of literacy and literate behavior. Thus, major scholarship from earlier decades is occasionally included in this bibliography as we touch on areas not covered by Harris.

A logical starting point is recent work on the origins and diffusion of the alphabet in Greece and its adaptation in Italy into the Etruscan and Roman alphabets. Baurain, Bonnet, and Krings (eds.) 1991, *Phoinikeia Grammata,* address the genesis of the Phoenician alphabet, the transfer of the alphabet to Greece, and writing in Phoenicia, Cyprus, Greece, and the western Mediterranean. Even within the covers of this collection a long-standing controversy on the moment of and reasons for the introduction of the alphabet into the Greek world continues. Whereas Powell 1991 argues that the Greek alphabet was created by a single man at a single time for the purpose of writing down the *Iliad* and the *Odyssey,* Isserlin 1991 believes that the hypothesis that the Greek alphabet had multiple origins extending over a range of time is worth considering. The origins of the alphabet are discussed in other books and articles that take a variety of perspectives: Thomas 1992 (above) discusses the origins of the Greek alphabet within the context of literacy and orality; Robb 1994, *Literacy and Paideia,* discusses the spread of literacy in its relation to *paideia* in Greece; in an article, Ruijgh 1995 considers the introduction of the alphabet within the context of the dialect of Homeric language (cf. Ruijgh 1997). Woodard 1997, *Greek Writing from Knossos to Homer*, makes a linguistic argument for the continuity of literacy from syllabic to alphabetic scripts: "The Linear B syllabic script, the syllabary of the Cypriot Greeks and the alphabet each stand as points along an unbroken continuum of Greek literacy." The study of the evolution of the alphabet is in any case inextricably tied up with questions concerning literacy (Bodson 1991). This development has received much attention within the field of Greek epigraphy. In a review article, Walbank 1993 discusses the challenges of interpreting the evidence, remarking that "the preponderance of Attic inscriptions, as well as of Athenian literary material, has led to an undeserved emphasis upon Athens in the history of the Greek alphabet." Recent work (Guarducci 1987, Jeffery 1990 [1st ed. 1961], Immerwahr 1990) shows that "literacy was by no means the invention of the Athenians." Rather, as Immerwahr 1990: 29 suggests, the paucity of the epigraphical documentation from Attica in the late eighth and first three quarters of the seventh century indicates that "Athens seems to have been a cultural backwater, at least so far as writing is concerned." Pandolfini and Prosdocimi 1990 discuss the rise of alphabetic literacy in Etruria and archaic Italy; Camporeale 2004: 192–208 conveniently surveys this topic and provides further bibliography. The cultural significance of Linear B has continued to be assessed. Whereas Palaima 1987 argues that writing in the Mycenaean world was the almost exclusive province of the palace administration, Godart and Tzedakis 1989 reconsider the history of Linear B in light of recent discoveries of inscribed vases. Driessen 1992 reflects on possible links between Linear B documents and other Aegean scripts, and asks whether the Mycenaeans had an oral epic poetry and whether the Homeric poems show any knowledge of it. For further comparanda with Aegean and other Mediterranean scripts—such as cuneiform and hieroglyphic Hittite—see A. Davies 1986. Sherratt 2003 raises the question of whether a link may be found between the introduction of alphabetic literacy in Greece and the reemergence of syllabic literacy in Cyprus. Chrisomalis 2003 discusses the Egyptian origin of the Greek alphabetic numerals.

The study of the bookroll—of its material and social contexts, of its physical and conceptual structure—has undergone a renaissance, thanks in part to an outpouring of dedicated scholarship that has benefited from developing technology that allows investigation of the carbonized papyrus bookrolls discovered at Herculaneum without causing disastrous further damage, partly also to dramatic recent discoveries such as the Posidippus epigram book (*P.Mil.Vogl.* VIII 309), and partly to other new work. The typology and material aspects of the ancient book were first studied systematically by Birt 1882 before the spectacular discovery, in the late nineteenth and early twentieth centuries, of fragments of thousands of Greek literary bookrolls preserved at Oxyrhynchus and elsewhere in Egypt. Fundamental contributions of the twentieth century to

our understanding of physical aspects of the ancient Greek book are
Turner 1980 (1st ed. 1968), *Greek Papyri*, and Turner and Parsons 1987
(1st ed. Turner 1971), *Greek Manuscripts of the Ancient World*. More
recent book-length studies include Cavallo 1983, *Libri scritture scribi
a Ercolano*, Capasso (ed.) 1994, *Il rotolo librario*, and Capasso 1995,
Volumen. Johnson 2004, *Bookrolls and Scribes in Oxyrhynchus*, recon-
structs the typology of the papyrus bookroll by examining the literary
papyri from Oxyrhynchus that contain works preserved in fuller form in
the medieval manuscript tradition. On the codex, Turner 1977, *The
Typology of the Early Codex*, and Roberts and Skeat 1983, *The Birth of
the Codex*, were followed by *Les débuts du codex*, edited by Blanchard
1989. The collection by Martin and Vezin (eds.) 1990, *Mise en page et
mise en texte du livre manuscrit*, surveys page layout in both bookrolls and
codices from Mediterranean antiquity through the Middle Ages. Willy
Clarysse's impressive Leuven Database of Ancient Books at http://www.
trismegistos.org/ldab/index.php "attempts to collect the basic information on [the oldest preserved copies of] all ancient literary texts" from
which the user may "get a view of the reception of ancient literature
throughout the Hellenistic, Roman and Byzantine period: which author
was read when, where and by whom throughout Antiquity."

Book production, publication, and circulation receive comprehensive
and/or general treatment in Cambiano, Canfora, and Lanza (eds.) 1992–
1996, *Lo spazio letterario della Grecia antica*, Cavallo, Fedeli, and Giardina
(eds.) 1989–1994, *Lo spazio letterario di Roma antica*, and Cavallo 1989a
(ed.), *Libri, editori e pubblico nel mondo antico*. Dorandi 2000, *Le stylet et la
tablette* (revised and translated 2007), attempts to reconstruct the working methods of ancient authors (cf. Dorandi 1991, 1993). On other
aspects of publication in Rome, see the articles by Starr 1987 on the
circulation of literary texts, and McDonnell 1996 on writing, copying,
and autograph manuscripts. Dortmund 2001, *Römisches Buchwesen um
die Zeitenwende*, poses the question of whether Atticus was a publisher.
The publication and dissemination of individual authors' works have been
examined in many studies, only a few of which can be included here (e.g.,
Murphy 1998 [on Cicero], Fowler 1995 and White 1996 [on Martial]).
On bookselling and book buying in Rome, see J. Phillips 1985, Starr 1990,
Fedeli 1992. Studies on publication in the Greek world seem to be fewer
(but see Porciani 2005 [on Herodotus]; Cerri 1991 [on Theognis]); a
significant exception is Finkelberg 2006, who ambitiously tries to demonstrate that in the Hellenistic, Roman, and Byzantine periods the production, circulation, and transmission of books concentrated around
four self-contained regional centers, one for each of the major Hellenistic
kingdoms.

The structures and purposes of ancient libraries, the nature and extent
of private book collections, the availability of books, and similar questions
seem always to inspire interest. Book-length studies of libraries often
cover a wide chronological and geographical sweep: see Baratin and

Jacob 1996, *Le pouvoir des bibliothèques: la mémoire des livres en Occident;* Gratien and Hanoun 1997, *Lire l'écrit: textes, archives, bibliothèques dans l'antiquité;* Cavallo 1998, *Le biblioteche nel mondo antico e medievale;* Casson 2001, *Libraries in the Ancient World;* Hoepfner 2002, *Antike Bibliotheken.* More specialized studies are Pesando 1994, *Libri e biblioteche* (in Rome); Sider 2005, *The Library of the Villa dei Papiri at Herculaneum;* Dix and Houston 2006, "Public Libraries in the City of Rome." The fate of the library of Alexandria exercises a particular fascination over biblio-philes: Canfora 1986, *La biblioteca scomparsa* = 1989 *The Vanished Library*, is a novel written with a vivid historical imagination; on this topic see also El-Abbadi 1992 (1st ed. 1990), *Life and Fate of the Ancient Library of Alexandria.* Scholars have striven to create a more definite outline or to establish significant details of how libraries originated and functioned, what resources they may have contained, and how they may have been used in other places throughout the ancient world (to list a limited number of examples—Carthage: Baurain 1992; Roman Africa: Tlili 2000; Pergamon: Mielsch 1995, Wolter von dem Knesebeck 1995; Rome/Italy: Fedeli 1988, Canfora 1993, Strocka 1993, Meneghini 2002, Houston 2002, 2004). Papyrological and material evidence for personal collections of books open up further intriguing areas of inquiry (e.g., Longo Auricchio and Capasso 1987, Bagnall 1992, Funghi and Messeri Savorelli 1992, Puglia 1996, 1998, Otranto 2000, Houston 2007). Readers' interactions with books are examined from a material perspec-tive by, for example, McNamee 2001, 2007 (on readers' annotations in literary papyri), and Johnson 2005 (on readers' marks in the Posidippus epigram collection).

Broader questions in the realm of literacy studies concern the cultural aspects of reading. To attain perspective on positions classical scholars of the last century have taken on ancient reading, we may mention the controversy—by now largely moribund—about reading aloud. An argu-ment that readers almost always read aloud, and that silent reading was marked and unusual in antiquity, was first put forth emphatically in the earlier part of the twentieth century (Balogh 1927; this view was largely demolished by Knox 1968 but has been marvelously tenacious; it was revived by Saenger 1997 in the context of medieval reading and writing; for bibliography and analysis of the issues see Johnson 2000). Recent work on reading, writing, and oral tradition—which promises to provoke con-tinuing and productive discussion—has challenged "the static definitions of oral and literate as mutually exclusive modes of creation" (as formu-lated by Yamagata 2001, reviewing Mackay 1999, *Signs of Orality;* Tho-mas 1989 has already been mentioned; Worthington [ed.] 1996, *Voice into Text*) and has stressed the role of oral practices even within the literate culture of Rome (Vogt-Spira [ed.] 1990, *Strukturen der Mündlichkeit in der römischen Literatur;* Benz 2001 [ed.], *Die römische Literatur zwischen Mündlichkeit und Schriftlichkeit;* Habinek 2005, *The World of Roman Song).* And although Horsfall 2003, *The Culture of the Roman Plebs,* "is careful not to mention" literacy—minimally defined in terms of "the distinct abilities to read, write and count"—he discusses Roman oral practices as he develops his thesis that "literacy is not essential to the whole range of those social or cultural pastimes dear to a Roman plebeian which required some degree of intellectual engagement." Scholars have sought to define the performative aspects of writing (Habinek 1998, *The Politics of Latin Literature*) and of reading (Johnson 2000 argues that an appreciation of the social aspects of reading in the early empire is essential for a proper understanding of the production of elite prose). Campbell 2001, *Performing and Processing the Aeneid*, contemplates the relationship between reading, listening, and writing, arguing that "the performance and processing" of the *Aeneid* "retained a massive residue of orality": "When people felt the need to process or compose a graphic text, they functioned as listeners and dictators." In many ways the focus has shifted to the reader and the act of reading rather than, or in addition to, the writer. Svenbro 1988b, *Phrasikleia*, observes that the Greeks regarded the reader as passive in that he is subjected to the writing; an analogy can thus be drawn between the relationship that binds the writer to the reader and the social practice of pederasty. Salles 1992, *Lire à Rome*, asks: "History of the book, history of the writer, or history of the reader? An object, a creator, a consumer: these three components of reading are inseparable." Valette-Cagnac 1997, *La lecture à Rome*, goes further in maintaining that Roman reading should not simply be thought of in terms of the opposition between reading aloud and reading silently, which depends on a purely technical view of the act of reading. Although previous scholarship has concentrated on the use of writing from a sociological perspective, "this book's perspective is different: it is not a sociology of Roman readers, any more than it takes an interest in the monuments of classical literature. It seeks instead to demonstrate that Roman reading constitutes a subject in its own right, an act separable from writing, which has cultural specificity." Cavallo and Chartier (eds.) 1999: 3, *A History of Reading in the West*, state:

> A comprehensive history of reading and readers must . . . consider the historicity of ways of using, comprehending and appropriating texts. It must consider the 'world of the text' as a world of objects, forms and rituals whose conventions and devices bear meaning but also constrain its construction. It most also consider that the 'world of the reader' is made up of what Stanley Fish calls 'interpretive communities' to which individual readers belong. In its relation to writing, each of these communities displays a shared set of competences, customs, codes and interests. This means that throughout this book we will be looking at both the physical aspects of texts and their readers' practices.

Olson 1994a, *The World on Paper* (discussing the conceptual and cognitive implications of writing and reading in the early modern period), stresses recognition of the reader's contribution to the text, rather than the autonomy of textual meaning: thus, an altered practice and under-standing of reading and interpretation, rather than of writing, was respon-sible at that time for changing the relationship between what was said to what was meant by it.

These approaches point to an understanding of reading not as a simple, isolated act but as a set of cultural practices: in the words of Johnson 2000: 603 "reading is not simply the cognitive process[ing] by the indi-vidual of the 'technology' of writing, but rather *the negotiated construction of meaning within a particular sociocultural context.*" We can and perhaps should compare the role of *mousike* as an "endlessly variegated, rich set of cultural practices" that "lies at the very heart of," and in a sense defines, "culture" in Greece (Murray and Wilson [eds.] 2004: 1, *Music and the Muses*). Such a perspective is relevant to the very concepts of literate culture, of literary culture, and of literature. No honest attempt can be made in this essay to come to terms with the flood of publications on the literary cultures, cultural identities, and cultural histories of the Greek and Roman worlds: for a selective listing of writings in these areas that have a bearing on literacy, the reader may consult the rubric "Literate/ Literary Culture" in the bibliographical index. Some illustrative examples are mentioned here. Of scholarship with a particular focus on the social relationships of writers, and on writers and intellectuals in society, one may point to work on the relations of the poet with people of power (White 1993, *Promised Verse*, on Augustan poets; Nauta 2002, *Poetry for Patrons*, on Martial and Statius); and on the intellectual life of public figures and the role of intellectuals in public life (N. Lewis 1981, Dillon 2002, Reay 2005). In contrast to elite literature and literary prac-tices, there arose a "literature of consumption" produced for people sufficiently literate to enjoy entertainment and escapist literature (Pecere and Stramaglia [eds.] 1996, *La letteratura di consumo*).

Scholarship exploring the relationship between literate and oral prac-tices and memory includes both work with a highly theoretical focus (Connerton 1989, *How Societies Remember*) and work focusing on the role of memory, remembering, and recording (Rossi [ed.] 1988, *La memoria del sapere*, Small 1997, *Wax Tablets of the Mind*, Corbier 2006, *Donner à voir, donner à lire*, Rodríguez Mayorgas 2007, *La memoria de Roma*; cf. above on archives and below on ancient scholarship and tech-nical writing) and on techniques of memory training in antiquity (for an older study see Blum 1969, *Die antike Mnemotechnik*; Pelliccia 2003 argues in detail against "the unsupported dogma that the culture [of the late archaic and classical periods] possessed no concept or practice of verbatim accuracy in the reproduction of poetic texts"). There are book-length studies of communication in Greece (Coulet 1996, *Commu-niquer en Grèce ancienne*, Nieddu 2004, *La scrittura "madre delle muse"*) and Rome (Achard 1991, *La communication à Rome*). The power dynam-ics in which literacy is implicated have been variously tackled by Bowman and Woolf (eds.) 1994a, *Literacy and Power in the Ancient World*; Habinek

1998, *The Politics of Latin Literature*; Too and Livingstone (eds.) 1998, *Pedagogy and Power*; and Haines-Eitzen 2000, *Guardians of Letters*.

The invention and role of writing has been pondered in relation to the development of genres of poetry or of thought: lyric poetry (Ford 1993), philosophy (for a range of views on this topic see the collection edited by Robb 1983a, *Language and Thought in Early Greek Philosophy*; more recently, Kahn 2003), science (Olson 1994b, Horowitz 1996). The role of writing within—as well as its absence from—Greek and Roman religious practice and thought have been explored (Beard 1991, Scheid 1997, Henrichs 2003b, de Polignac 2005; Moatti 1998 has a section on religious documents). Within a given culture a continuous engagement with the written word inevitably gives rise over time to scholarship. Alexandria is the focus of Jacob and de Polignac (eds.) 1992, *Alexandrie IIIe siècle av. J.-C.* The collection by MacDonald, Twomey, and Reinink (eds.) 2003, *Learned Antiquity: Scholarship and Society in the Near East, the Greco-Roman World, and the Early Medieval West*, ranges broadly in chronological and geographic terms. Ancient poetic theory is discussed by Ford 2002, *The Origins of Criticism*. Reynolds and Wilson 1991 (1st ed. 1968), *Scribes and Scholars*, give a history of the transmission of Greek and Latin literature, while Zetzel 1981, *Latin Textual Criticism in Antiquity*, sheds light on the methods of ancient textual scholarship (cf. Zetzel 1973, 1980). The titles of Timpanaro 1986, *Per la storia della filologia virgiliana antica*, and Kaster 1988, *Guardians of Language: The Grammarian and Society in Late Antiquity*, speak for themselves. The collections by Kullmann and Althoff (eds.) 1993, *Vermittlung und Tradierung von Wissen*, and Kullmann, Althoff, and Asper (eds.) 1998, *Gattungen wissenschaftlicher Literatur*, embrace both scholarship and technical writing. These topics bring us back to memory (cf. above) and to the intersection of orality and written practices in technical writings within such areas as medicine, geography, and other realms of professional activity (for comprehensive treatments of which see Nicolet 1996, *Les littératures techniques*, Meissner 1999, *Die technologische Fachliteratur*, and Horster and Reitz [eds.] 2003, *Antike Fachschriftsteller*).

It would be a mistake to conclude without mentioning some of the valuable theoretical approaches and comparanda from cultures other than those of ancient Greece and Rome. In the last half century the cultural significance of writing has been subject to theoretical analysis in a number of disciplines. An overview is given by Jahandarie 1999, *Spoken and Written Discourse: A Multi-Disciplinary Perspective*, who discusses the views of Milman Parry, Albert Lord, Eric Havelock (1962, *A Preface to Plato*; 1982, *The Literate Revolution in Greece*), Harold Innis, Marshall McLuhan, Walter Ong (1982, *Orality and Literacy*), Jack Goody (1986, *The Logic of Writing and the Organization of Society*; 1987, *The Interface between the Written and the Oral*), David Olson, and others; for further bibliography and discussion see Harris 1989. Street 1984, *Literacy in Theory and Practice*, should not be overlooked for its own analysis as well as its critique of some of the theories just mentioned. Olson and Torrance (eds.) 2001, *The Making of Literate Societies*, discuss the role of literacy in social development, shifting away from the traditional focus on personal literacy to a focus on what makes a society a literate society, and including comparanda from Africa, Asia, Europe, and the Americas with one chapter on ancient Greece (by Thomas 2001a). Other theoretical work includes Barton, Hamilton, and Ivanič (eds.) 2000, *Situated Literacies: Reading and Writing in Context*, and Collins and Blot 2003, *Literacy and Literacies: Texts, Power, and Identity*. Memory in medieval societies has been addressed by Carruthers 1990, *The Book of Memory* (cf. the anthology by Carruthers and Ziolkowski [eds.] 2002, *The Medieval Craft of Memory*), Clanchy 1993 (1st ed. 1979), *From Memory to Written Record*, Stock 1983, *The Implications of Literacy: Written Language and Models of Interpretation in the Eleventh and Twelfth Centuries*, and Mostert 1999, *New Approaches to Medieval Communication*. Scribner and Cole 1981, *The Psychology of Literacy*, describe the unique writing system invented by the Vai people in Liberia for their commercial and personal affairs. Boone and Mignolo (eds.) 1994, *Writing Without Words: Alternative Literacies in Mesoamerica and the Andes*, discuss ancient systems of record keeping in the New World that did not make use of writing, and argue interestingly that our conception and definition of literacy should take these wordless archival systems into account. The massive, two-volume collection *Schrift und Schriftlichkeit*, by Günther, Ludwig, et al. (eds.) 1994–1996, contains both theoretical and comparative work on the material, formal, general, psychological, and linguistic aspects of writing and its use; the history of writing; literate cultures; functional and social aspects of literacy; the acquisition of literacy; and special writing systems.

Inevitably there remain areas and topics related to literacy that cannot be addressed here. There is insufficient space to include work on Roman recitation. Nor have I tried to embrace comprehensively the abundant scholarship on performance—in whatever theoretical sense the word is intended (although the rubric "Performance" in the bibliographical index points to some work having specific relevance to literacy or to the genesis of written texts). The same statement holds for literacy as a component of "Education," a large topic not adequately covered here. Orality in terms of the Homeric Question could not be treated here: for a lucid, helpful discussion of this vast subject, see the bibliographical essay in Thomas 1992. Also not discussed is "song culture" (a term invented by C. J. Herington, *Poetry into Drama: Early Tragedy and the Greek Poetic Tradition* 1985: 3–4; cf. "Literate/Literary Culture" in the bibliographical index and my remarks on *mousike* above). Editions of primary sources are not generally cited unless they explicitly address issues pertaining to literacy (as do, e.g., a number of publications on the Vindolanda tablets): for a discussion of primary sources on the uses of writing in Greece, see again Thomas 1992. The rubric "Bibliography" in the index points to scholarship in disciplines not covered here or to useful earlier compilations in the areas of ancient Greek and Roman literacy.

The bibliography that follows is arranged alphabetically for ease of reference. It is preceded by a topical index in order to give shape to the mass.

INDEX

Alexandria

Alphabet

Archives

Bibliographies

Beil 1983; Bouquiaux-Simon 2004; Camassa and Georgoudi 1988; Canfora 2004; Detienne 1988a; Didderen 2004; Didderen and Marganne 2007; Ehlich, Coulmas, and Graefen 1996; Istasse 2004; Melve 2003; Mostert 1999; Thomas 1992; Turner and Parsons 1987.

Bilingualism

Adams 1994, 2003b; Adams, Janse, and Swain 2002; Baslez and Briquel Chatonnet 1991; Clarysse 1993; Coldstream 1993; de Hoz 2006; Dupont and Valette-Cagnac 2005; Falivene 1991; Hanson, A. 1991; Kearsley 2001; Kraus 2000; Rochette 1997; Sosin and Manning 2003; Swain 2004; Thompson 1992b.

Books

See also: Tablets. Bartolomé Gómez, Cruz González Rodríguez, and Quijada Sagredo 2004; Blanck 1992; Bouquiaux-Simon 2004; Cavallo 1999a, 1999b; Cavallo and Hild 1997; Clarysse (LDAB); Didderen 2004; Didderen and Marganne 2007; Dorandi 1997; Fehrle 1986; Fredouille et al. 1997; Gamble 1995; Ipert and Marty 2005; Irigoin 2001; Kenney 1982; Marganne 2004; Martin and Vezin 1990; Petrucci 1995; Zelzer 2001.

Books: Bookroll   Bastianini 1995; Birt 1882, 1907; Blanchard 1993; Capasso 1994, 1995, 1996, 1997b, 1998; Cavallo 1983; De Luca 2007; Del Corso 2006, 2007; Delattre 2005; Harrauer 1995; Johnson 2004, 2009; Manetti 2006; McNamee 2001, 2007; McNamee and Jacovides 2003; Palme 2007; Suerbaum 1992; Turner 1980; Turner and Parsons 1987; Williams 1992; Zanker 1993.

Books: Buying; Selling   Fedeli 1992; Kleberg 1989; Marganne 2007; Phillips, J. 1985; Starr 1990.

Books: Codex   Autenrieth 1995; Blanchard 1989; Haran 1996; Harris, W. 1991; Hurtado 2006; Resnick 1992–3; Roberts and Skeat 1983; Turner 1977; Voss 1997.

Books: Production; Publication   See also: Libraries/Collections. Božič and Feugère 2004; Cambiano, Canfora, and Lanza 1992–6; Cavallo 1989a, 1992, 1996; Cavallo, Fedeli, and Giardina 1989–94; Cerri 1991; Dorandi 1991, 1993, 2000; Dortmund 2001; Fedeli 1992; Finkelberg 2006; Fowler 1995; Heyworth and Wilson 1997; Kleberg 1989; Lama 1991, 2007; McDonnell 1996; Murphy 1998; Phillips, J. 1981; Pinto 2006; Porciani 2005; Rouse and Rouse 2000; Salles 1992; Starr 1987; Stephens 1988; White 1996.

Britain

See also: Vindolanda. Evans 1987; Hanson, W. and Conolly 2002; Ingemark 2000–1; Mann 1985; Raybould 1999; Willis 2005.

Christianity/Christian Writings

Gamble 1995; Grafton and Williams 2006; Haines-Eitzen 2000; Hurtado 2006; Osiek 1998; Resnick 1992–3; Schaeffer 1996.

Commerce

Andreau 2001; Aubert 1994a, 2004; Cohen 2003; Harris, W. 1993; Jordan 2003; Lawall 2000; Lombardo 1988; Matthews, R. 1995; Moatti 1998; Nissen, Damerow, and Englund 1993; Pébarthe 2000; Rodríguez Somolinos 1996; Rodríguez-Almeida 1993; Sanmartí and Santiago 1987; Santiago and Sanmartí 1988; Uchitel 2003; Van Berchem 1991; Virlouvet 1995; Wilson 1997–8.

Communication

Achard 1991; Citroni 1995; Corbier 2006; Coulet 1996; de Polignac 2006; Lewis, S. 1992; Longo 1992; Mostert 1999; Nieddu 2004; Wallace 1995; Worthington and Foley 2002.

Comparanda

Amodio 2004; Baumann 1986; Boone and Mignolo 1994; Brosius 2003; Carruthers 1990; Carruthers and Ziolkowski 2002; Cavallo 1998, 1999a; Chartier 1989, 1994; Clanchy 1993; Coleman 1996; Davies, A. 1986; D'Errico 1995; Ehlich, Coulmas, and Graefen 1996; Finnegan 1988; Fox 2000; Gamble 1995; Goody 1987; Günther, Ludwig, et al. 1994, 1996; Haarmann 1995; Holmes 2002; Holmes and Waring 2002; Horowitz 1996; Innes 1998; Invernizzi 2003; Irigoin 2001; Irvine 1994; Jacob 1998; Kallendorf 2007; Lalou 1992; Legras 2002; Lewis, D. 1994; Lloyd 2003; MacDonald, Twomey, and Reinink 2003; Marcus 1995; Martin 1994; Matthews, R. 1995; Melve 2003; Mostert 1999; Nissen, Damerow, and Englund 1993; Olson and Torrance 2001; Petrucci 1995; Postgate, Wang, and Wilkinson 1995; Reichler-Béguelin 1992; Resnick 1992–3; Rouse and Rouse 2000; Saenger 1989, 1997; Schaefer 1997; Scribner and Cole 1981; Sherratt 2003; Stock 1983; Street 1993; Vansina 1985; Waring 2002; Waschkies 1993.

Crete

Papakonstantinou 2002; Whitley 1997, 1998.

Cyprus

Sherratt 2003.

Education

Cribiore 1996, 2001; Frasca 1996; Johnson 2002; Manacorda 1992; Meissner 2003; Morgan 1998, 1999; Pandolfini and Prosdocimi 1990; Poehlmann 1989; Robb 1994; Too and Livingstone 1998; Wear 2006.

Egypt

See also: Alexandria; Oxyrhynchus. Bowman 2006; Bucking 2007; Canfora 1992; Capasso 1997a; Chrisomalis 2003; Clarysse 1993, 2003; Cribiore 1996, 2001, 2002; De Luca 2007; Falivene 1991; Hanson, A. 1991; Hopkins 1991; Jacob 1992a; Jacob and de Polignac 1992; Kraus 1999, 2000; Lallot 1992; Lama 2007; Legras 1997, 2002; Manfredi 1985; Marganne 2003; McNamee 2007; Nightingale 1999; Sosin and Manning 2003; Thompson 1992a, 1992b, 1992c, 1994; van Minnen 1998.

Epigraphical Evidence

See also: Instrumentum Domesticum; Lead Letters; Ostraka; Tablets. Adams 1999; Agostiniani 1992; Bartoněk 1996; Bats, Michel 2004; Bing 2002; Boffo 1995; Brandt 1990; Briquel 1989, 1991; Brosius 2003; Camporeale 2004; Charlier 2004; Colonna 1980a; Cooley et al. 2002; Cornell 1991; Curchin 1995; Davies, J. 2000, 2005; de Hoz 2006; de Simone 1980; Delage 2004; Derderian 2001; Deru 2004; Evans 1987; Franklin 1991; Guarducci 1987; Hannah, P. 2001; Hedrick 1999, 2000; Immerwahr 1990; Ingemark 2000–1; Jeffery 1990; Kearsley 2001; Kilmer and Develin 2001; Langdon 1991; Laubenheimer 2004; Lawall 2000; Liddel 2003; MacMullen 1982; Mann 1985; Meyer 1990; Osborne 1999; Papakonstantinou 2002; Pébarthe 2000; Peruzzi 1998; Piérart 1991; Poucet 1989; Powell 1988; Pucci 1988; Raybould 1999; Rebillard 1991; Rhodes and Osborne 2003; Ridgway, D. 1996; Robert 1987; Sechi 1990; Sickinger 1994; Slater 1999; Steinhart 2003; Stibbe 1980; Stibbe et al. 1980; Svenbro 1988a; Thomas 1994; Versnel 1980; Wachter 1998; Walbank 1993; Woolf 1996.

Etruscan/Etruria

Agostiniani 1992; Briquel 1989, 1991; Camporeale 1992, 2004; Coldstream 1993; Cornell 1991; Gleirscher 1993; Haarmann 1995; Lejeune 1989; Pandolfini and Prosdocimi 1990; Poucet 1989; Sandoz 1991; Stoddart and Whitley 1988.

Greek Authors (selected)

Athenaeus Braund 2000; Braund and Wilkins 2000; Davies, J. 2000; Jacob 2000; Too 2000.

Herodotus Ceccarelli 2005; Giangiulio 2005; Johnson 1994; Luraghi 2001; Murray 1987, 2001; Nenci 1998; Porciani 2005; Thomas 1993, 2001b.

Hesiod Scodel 2001.

Homer Brillante 1996; Driessen 1992; Finkelberg 2006; Kullmann 1999; Peliccia 2003; Powell 1991; Robb 1994; Ruijgh 1995; Saussy 1996; Thomas 1992.

Pindar   Scodel 2001.

Plato   Havelock 1962; Naddaf 2000; Nightingale 1999; Tarrant 1999; Trabattoni 2005; Yunis 2003c.

Solon   Loraux 1988.

Theognis   Cerri 1991; Pratt 1995.

Thucydides   Nicolai 2001; Yunis 2003c.

Herculaneum

Cavallo 1983; Delattre 2005; Dorandi 1995; Johnson 2006; Longo Auricchio and
   Capasso 1987; Sider 2005.

Instrumentum Domesticum

Aubert 1993; Bémont 2004; Colonna 1980b; Harris, W. 1993; Rodríguez-
   Almeida 1993.

Judaism/Jewish Writings

Hezser 2001; Thatcher 1998.

Latin Authors (selected)

Apuleius   Keulen 2004; Swain 2004.

Fronto   Swain 2004; Zetzel 1980.

Gellius   Binder 2003; Dillon 2002; Holford-Strevens and Vardi 2004; Keulen
   2004; Swain 2004; Vardi 2004.

Martial   Fowler 1995; Nauta 2002; White 1996.

Petronius   Brandt 1990; Horsfall 1989.

Pliny (C. Plinius Caecilius Secundus)   Fantham 1999.

Pliny (C. Plinius Secundus)   Naas 1996; Nikitinski 1998.

Law

Camassa 1988; Cohen 2003; Fezzi 2004; Gagarin 2003; Hölkeskamp 1992, 1992;
   Moatti 2000; Loraux 1988; Maffi 1988; Matthews, J. 1998; Meyer 1988,

2004; Naddaf 2000; Nightingale 1999; Osborne 1999; Papakonstantinou 2002; Perlman 2002; Robb 1994; Ruzé 2001; Sickinger 2002; Thomas 1995; Volonaki 2001; Whitley 1997, 1998.

Lead Letters

Chadwick 1990; Harris, E. 2005; Jordan 2000, 2003; Rodríguez Somolinos 1996; Sanmartí and Santiago 1987, 1988b, 1988; Wilson 1997–8.

Libraries/Collections

Bagnall 1992; Baratin and Jacob 1996; Baurain 1992; Bellier-Chaussonnier 2002; Blanchard 1993; Cambiano, Canfora, and Lanza 1992–6; Canfora 1989b, 1992, 1993, 2004; Casson 2001; Cavallo 1998; Chartier 1994; Daris 1995; Del Olmo Lete 2005; Dix 1988, 2000, 2002; Dix and Houston 2006; Dorandi 1995; El-Abbadi 1992; Fedeli 1988; Funghi and Messeri Savorelli 1992; Grafton and Williams 2006; Gratien and Hanoun 1997; Hoepfner 1996, 2002; Houston 2002, 2004, 2007; Jacob 1991, 1997, 1998, 2000; Johnson 2006; Legras 1997; Longo Auricchio and Capasso 1987; Marganne 2003; Meneghini 2002; Mielsch 1995; Neudecker 2004; Nicolai 2000; Otranto 1996, 2000; Pesando 1994; Puglia 1996, 1998; Sider 2005; Staikos 2005; Strocka 1993, 2000; Tlili 2000; Too 2000; Vössing 1997; Waring 2002; Wolter-von dem Knesebeck 1995.

Linear A

Haarmann 1995; Michailidou 2000–1; Uchitel 2003.

Linear B

Davies, A. 1986; Driessen 1992; Godart 2001; Godart and Tzedakis 1989; Haarmann 1995; Palaima 1987, 2003.

Literacy/Illiteracy

(i.e., the uses of literacy, significance of literacy, extent and spread of literacy). *See also: Bilingualism, Epigraphical Evidence, Writing/Writers.* Adams 1999; Andersen 1989; Bartoněk 1996; Bowman 1991, 1994b; Brandt 1990; Burns 1985; Campbell 1995; Camporeale 1992; Corbier 1991; Cornell 1991; Curchin 1995; Dubuisson 1991; Goody 1994; Günther, Ludwig, et al. 1994; Haarmann 1995; Hannah, R. 2001; Hanson, A. 1991; Harris, W. 1989a, 1989b; Havelock 1986; Horsfall 1989, 1991; Humphrey 1991; Jahandarie 1999; Konishi 1993a; Kraus 2000; Pébarthe 2006; Purcell 1995; Santirocco 1986; Slater 2002; Thomas 1992, 2001a; Waring 2002; Woolf 2000.

Literate/Literary Culture

See also: Scholarship (Ancient). Amodio 2004; Baumann 1986; Benz 2001; Binder 2003; Birt 1882; Braund 2000; Braund and Wilkins 2000; Bulloch, Gruen, Long, and Stewart 1993; Capasso 1997a; Cavallo 1988a, 1989b, 1991; Cavallo and Chartier 1999; Cavallo, Fedeli, and Giardina 1989–94; Chartier 1994; Citroni 1995; Detienne 1988a; Dillon 2002; Dubuisson 1991; Dupont 1999; Fantham 1996; Fein 1994; Ford 1999; Ford 2002; Fox 2000; Goldhill and Osborne 1999; Günther, Ludwig, et al. 1994; Havelock 1962; Holford-Strevens and Vardi 2004; Holmes 2002; Holmes and Waring 2002; Horster 2003; Humphrey 1991; Hunter 2003; Irvine 1994; Jacob and de Polignac 1992; Johne 1991; Johnson 2000, 2002, 2009; Kaster 1988; Keulen 2004; Kilmer and Develin 2001; Krüger 1990; Kullmann and Reichel 1990; Lanza 1988; Lewis, N. 1981; MacDonald, Twomey, and Reinink 2003; Manfredi 1985; Mazal 1999; Morgan 1999; Most 1990; Nauta 2002; Nicks 2000; Obbink 2007; Oesterreicher 1997; Olson and Torrance 2001; O'Sullivan 1996; Phillips, C. 1990–1; Powell 2002; Purcell 1995; Quinn 1982; Reay 2005; Renate 1991; Rosen 1997; Rösler 1994; Rüpke 2000; Sciarrino 2004; Sechi 1990; Sousa 1989; Stock 1983; Stoddart and Whitley 1988; Tarrant 1999; Thatcher 1998; Thomas 1989, 2001a; Too 2000; van Minnen 1998; Vardi 2004; Vegetti 1992; Vogt-Spira 1994; White 1993; Wise 1998; Worthington 1993, 1996; Yunis 2003a; Zanker 1993; Zorzetti 1990–1.

Literature of Consumption

Bowie 1994, 1996; Cavallo 1996, 2001; Hägg 1994; Pecere and Stramaglia 1996; Stephens 1994.

Mathematics

Cambiano 1988a; Raible 1993; Waschkies 1993.

Medicine

Althoff 1993; Asper 1998; Barras 2003; Cavallo 2002; Dean-Jones 2003; Flemming 2007; Kollesch 1992; Marganne 2003, 2004, 2007; Miller 1990; Pigeaud 1988; Von Staden 1998, 2000.

Memory

Blum 1969; Carruthers 1990; Carruthers and Ziolkowski 2002; Cavallo 1988a; Clanchy 1993; Connerton 1989; Corbier 2006; Horsfall 1991; Innes 1998; Kullmann 1999; Moreau 1994; Pelliccia 2003; Rodríguez Mayorgas 2007; Rossi 1988; Small 1995, 1997.

Music/Mousike/Song

Ford 2003; Gentili 1992b; Goldhill and Osborne 1999; Habinek 2005; Konishi 1993a; Murray and Wilson 2004; Ruzé 2001.

Orality/Oral Culture

See also: Music/Mousike/Song. Adkins 1983; Amodio 2004; Bakker 1999; Barras 2003; Beil 1983; Benz 2001; Campbell 2001; Cavallo, Fedeli, and Giardina

1989–94; Clanchy 1993; Detienne 1988a; Finnegan 1988; Ford 2003; Gagarin 1999; Gentili 1992a; Gentili and Paioni 1985; Goody 1987; Günther, Ludwig, et al. 1994; Habinek 2005; Hägg 1994; Havelock 1962, 1982, 1986; Horsfall 2003; Jahandarie 1999; Kirk 1983; Kullmann and Reichel 1990; Labarbe 1991; Lentz 1989; Mackay 1999; Melve 2003; Murray 1987, 2001; Nicolai 2001; Oesterreicher 1997; Osiek 1998; Pelliccia 2003; Pratt 1995; Robb 1994; Rodríguez Mayorgas 2007; Santirocco 1986; Schaefer 1997, 1996; Scodel 2001; Thomas 1989, 1992, 2001b; Trabattoni 2005; Vansina 1985; Vegetti 1992; Vogt-Spira 1990; Von Ungern-Sternberg and Reinau 1988; Watson 2001; Wear 2006; Willard 1983; Worthington 1996; Worthington and Foley 2002; Yamagata 2001.

Ostraka

Adams 1994; Lang 1982, 1990; Phillips, D. 1990.

Oxyrhynchus

Bowman et al. 2007; Houston 2007; Johnson 2004; Krüger 1990; Lama 1991; Obbink 2007; Puglia 1996.

Performance

Bakker and Kahane 1997; Boone and Mignolo 1994; Campbell 2001; Canfora 1988; Demont 1993; Fantham 1999; Ford 1999; Gagarin 1999; Goldhill and Osborne 1999; Habinek 1998; Johnson 2000; Marcus 1995; Naddaf 2000; Nauta 2002; Osborne 1999; Rosen 1997; Thomas 1992, 1993, 2003; Valette-Cagnac 1995; Worthington 1993.

Philosophy/Science

Adkins 1983; Brisson 1990; Carlini 1989; Dillon 2002; Donovan 1993; Erler 1993, 1998; Ferrari 1984; Geier 1994; Havelock 1983; Hershbell 1983; Horowitz 1996; Jacob 1988; Kahn 1983, 2003; Kullmann, Althoff, and Asper 1998; Laks 2001; Lloyd 2003; Margolis 1983; Nieddu 1993, 2004; Olson 1994b; Robb 1983a, 1983b; Tarrant 1999; Wear 2006; Wöhrle 1993.

Poetry

Adams 1999; Bing 2002; Campbell 2001; Citroni 1995; Driessen 1992; Ford 1993; Hershbell 1983; Nagy 2000; Phillips, C. 1990–1; Quinn 1982; Reitz 2003; Wachter 1998; Wenskus 1998; Zorzetti 1990–1.

Politics/State/Public Life

See also: Archives; Power. Andreev 1994–5; Clark and Ivanič 1997; Coudry 1994; Detienne 1988b, 1988c; Falivene 1991; Frost 1987; Harris, W. 1989b; Hedrick 1994, 1999, 2000; Langdon 1991; Lewis, N. 1981; Liddel 2003; Palaima 1987; Pébarthe 2000; Rhodes 2001; Ruzé 1988; Thompson 1992c; White 1997.

Pompeii

Franklin 1991; Wachter 1998.

Power

Bowman 1994b; Bowman and Woolf 1994a, 1994b; Collins and Blot 2003; Habinek 1998; Haines-Eitzen 2000; Lewis, D. 1994; Martin 1994; Most 1990; Ruzé 1988; Thompson 1994; Too and Livingstone 1998; Woolf 1994.

Reading/Readers

Balogh 1927; Baurain, Bonnet, and Krings 1991; Bowie 1994, 1996; Campbell 2001; Canfora 1989a; Cavallo 1995, 1999b; Cavallo and Chartier 1999; Chartier 1989; Christmann 2003; Coleman 1996; Del Corso 2005; Gavrilov 1997; Goldhill 1999; Jacob 2000; Johnson 2000, 2002, 2005, 2010; Kallendorf 2007; Kenney 1982; Knox 1968; Legras 1997, 2002; Manguel 1996; Mazal 1999; McNamee 1981, 1992, 2001, 2007; McNamee and Jacovides 2003; Nagy 2000; Obbink 2007; Olson 1994a; Petrucci 1995; Saenger 1989, 1997; Salles 1992; Starr 1998; Svenbro 1988b; Usener 1994; Valette-Cagnac 1993, 1997, 2002; Yunis 2003c.

Religion

Beard 1991; Bremmer 1982; de Polignac 2005; Henrichs 2003a, 2003b; Hershbell 1983; Moatti 1998; Müller 1993; Pucci 1988; Scheid 1994, 1997.

Scholarship (Ancient)

Cambiano 1988b; Cavallo 1988a; Delvigo 1990; Ford 2002; Istasse 2004; Jacob 1992a, 1992b, 1997; Jacob and de Polignac 1992; Kaster 1988; Kullmann and Althoff 1993; Kullmann, Althoff, and Asper 1998; La Penna 1992; Lallot 1992; MacDonald, Twomey, and Reinink 2003; McNamee 1981, 2001, 2007; McNamee and Jacovides 2003; Nikitinski 1998; Raible 1993; Reynolds and Wilson 1991; Rossi 1988; Timpanaro 1986; Zetzel 1973, 1980, 1981.

Sparta

Andreev 1994–5; Millender 2001.

Tablets

See also: Vindolanda. Degni 1998; Haran 1996; Hurschmann 2001; Lalou 1992; Lewis, D. 1994; Meyer 2004; Wilson 1997–8.

Technical Writing

Campbell 1995; Christmann 2003; Demont 1993; Dihle 1998; Fögen 2003; Horster 2003; Horster and Reitz 2003; Krenkel 2003; Kullmann, Althoff, and Asper 1998; Meissner 1999, 2003; Nicolet 1996; Podossinov 2003; Reitz 2003; Wenskus 1998.

Theoretical Perspectives

Barton, Hamilton, and Ivanič 2000; Brandt 1990; Clark and Ivanič 1997; Connerton 1989; D'Errico 1995; Finnegan 1988; Ford 2002; Forrester 1996; Goody 1968, 1987; Günther, Ludwig, et al. 1994, 1996; Halverson 1992; Longo 1992; Manguel 1996; Oesterreicher 1997; Olson 1994a, 1994b, 2002; Olson and Torrance 2001; Olson, Torrance, and Hildyard 1985; Ong 1982; Raible 1993; Saussy 1996; Schaefer 1997; Schousboe and Larsen 1989; Scribner and Cole 1981; Small 1997; Street 1984; Vansina 1985.

Vindolanda

Adams 1995, 2003a; Bowman 1994a, 1994b, 2006; Pearce 2004.

Women

Capomacchia 1991; Cavallo 1995; Cribiore 2002; Flemming 2007; Glazebrook 2005; Haines-Eitzen 1998; Steinhart 2003.

Writing/Writers

Adams 2003a; Allen and Dix 1991; Andersen 1989; Bartolomé Gómez, Cruz González Rodríguez, and Quijada Sagredo 2004; Bats, Michel 2004; Baurain, Bonnet, and Krings 1991; Beard 1991; Beltrán Lloris 1998–9; Božič and Feugère 2004; Bucking 2007; Cardona 1988; Cavallo 1983, 1991, 1995; Cerri 1991; Christmann 2003; Clarysse 1993; Colonna 1988; Cordano 1984; Cribiore 1996; de Polignac 2006; D'Errico 1995; Desbordes 1985, 1990; Dorandi 1991, 1993, 2000; Ehlich, Coulmas, and Graefen 1996; Fedeli 1992; Feugère 2004; Feugère and Lambert 2004; Flemming 2007; Giovè Marchioli 1993; Goody 1986, 2000; Günther, Ludwig, et al. 1994, 1996; Habinek 1998; Haines-Eitzen 1998, 2000; Hartog 1989; Johnson 2004; Ker 2004; Kraus 1999; Ledentu 2004; Lewis, S. 1992; Marshall 1987; Marty 2005; Matthews, R. 1995; McDonnell 1996; Naas 1996; Nauta 2002; Nieddu 2004; Olson 1994a, 2002; Ong 1986; Palaima 2003; Petrucci 1996; Poehlmann 1989; Postgate, Wang, and Wilkinson 1995; Poucet 1988; Purcell 2001; Reichler-Béguelin 1992;

Reynolds and Wilson 1991; Salles 1992; Steiner 1994; Svenbro 1988a; Wachter 1991; White 1993; Willis 2005; Woolf 1994; Yunis 2003b, 2003c.

BIBLIOGRAPHY

Achard, Guy. 1991. *La communication à Rome*. Paris.

Adams, James N. 1994. "Latin and Punic in Contact? The Case of the Bu Njem Ostraca." *JRS* 84: 87–112.

———. 1995. "The Language of the Vindolanda Writing Tablets: An Interim Report." *JRS* 85: 86–134.

———. 1999. "The Poets of Bu Njem: Language, Culture and the Centurionate." *JRS* 89: 109–34.

———. 2003a. "The New Vindolanda Writing-Tablets." *CQ* 53: 530–75.

———. 2003b. *Bilingualism and the Latin Language*. Cambridge.

———, Mark Janse, and Simon Swain, eds. 2002. *Bilingualism in Ancient Society: Language Contact and the Written Text*. Oxford.

Adkins, Arthur W. H. 1983. "Orality and Philosophy." In Robb 1983: 207–27.

Agostiniani, Luciano. 1992. "Contribution à l'étude de l'épigraphie et de la linguistique étrusques." In *LALIES: actes des sessions de linguistique et de littérature, XI (Cortona, 20–31 août 1990)*, 37–74. Paris.

Allen, Marti Lu, and T. Keith Dix. 1991. *The Beginning of Understanding: Writing in the Ancient World*. Ann Arbor.

Althoff, Jochen. 1993. "Formen der Wissensvermittlung in der frühgriechischen Medizin." In Kullmann and Althoff 1993: 211–23.

Amadasi Guzzo, Maria Gulia. 1991. "'The Shadow Line': Réflexions sur l'introduction de l'alphabet en Grèce." In Baurain, Bonnet, and Krings 1991: 293–311.

Amodio, Mark C. 2004. *Writing the Oral Tradition: Oral Poetics and Literate Culture in Medieval England*. Notre Dame.

Andersen, O. 1989. "The Significance of Writing in Early Greece: A Critical Appraisal." In Schousboe and Larsen 1989: 73–90.

Andreau, Jean. 1994. "Pouvoirs publics et archives des banquiers professionels." In Demougin 1994: 1–18.

———. 2001. *La banque et les affaires dans le monde romain (IVe siècle av. J.-C.—IIIe siècle ap. J.-C.)*. Paris. Trans. by J. Lloyd from *Banking and Business in the Roman World*. Cambridge, 1999.

Andreev, Yury. 1994–5. "A Greek Polis without Bureaucracy and Literature (The Role of Literacy within Spartan Society)." *Hyperboreus* 1: 9–18.

Asper, Markus. 1998. "Zu Struktur und Funktion eisagogischer Texte." In Kullmann, Althoff, and Asper 1998: 309–40.

Aubert, Jean-Jacques. 1993. "Workshop managers." In W. Harris 1993: 171–81.

———. 1994. *Business Managers in Ancient Rome: A Social and Economic Study of Institores, 200 BC–AD 250*. Leiden.

———. 2004. "De l'usage de l'écriture dans la gestion d'entreprise à l'époque romaine." In Jean Andreau, Jérôme France, et Sylvie Pittia, eds., *Mentalités et choix économiques des Romains*, 127–47. Scripta antiqua/Ausonius 7. Bordeaux.

Autenrieth, Johanne. 1995. "Bücher im Übergang von der Spätantike zum Mittelalter." *Scriptorium* 49: 169–79.

Bagnall, Roger. 1992. "An Owner of Literary Papyri." *CP* 87: 137–40.

Bakker, Egbert J. 1999. "How Oral Is Oral Composition?" In Mackay 1999: 29–47.

—— and Ahuvia Kahane, eds. 1997. *Written Voices, Spoken Signs: Tradition, Performance, and the Epic Text*. Cambridge, Mass.

Balogh, Josef. 1927. "*Voces paginarum*: Beiträge zur Geschichte des lauten Lesens und Schreibens." *Philologus* 82: 84–109; 202–40.

Baratin, Marc, and Christian Jacob, eds. 1996. *Le pouvoir des bibliothèques: la mémoire des livres en Occident*. Bibliothèque Albin Michel: Histoire. Paris.

Barras, Vincent. 2003. "Remarques sur l'usage des recettes antiques dans l'histoire de la médecine: rationalité et thérapeutique." In Nicoletta Palmieri, ed. *Rationnel et irrationnel dans la médecine ancienne et médiévale: aspects historiques, scientifiques et culturels*, 251–64. Mémoires: Centre Jean-Palerne 26. Saint-Étienne.

Bartolomé Gómez, J., M. Cruz González Rodríguez, and Milagros Quijada Sagredo, eds. 2004. *La escritura y el libro en la antigüedad*. Madrid.

Barton, David, Mary Hamilton, and Roz Ivanič, eds. 2000. *Situated Literacies: Reading and Writing in Context*. Literacies. London.

Bartoněk, Antonín. 1996. "Literacy in Archaic Latium." In Hannah Rosén, ed. *Aspects of Latin: Papers from the Seventh International Colloquium on Latin Linguistics, Jerusalem, April 1993*, 19–26. Innsbrucker Beiträge zur Sprachwissenschaft 86. Innsbruck.

Baslez, Marie-Françoise and Françoise Briquel Chatonnet. 1991. "De l'oral à l'écrit: le bilinguisme des Phéniciens en Grèce." In Baurain, Bonnet, and Krings 1991: 371–86.

Bastianini, Guido. 1995. "Tipologie dei rotoli e problemi di ricostruzione." In M. Capasso, ed., *Atti del V Seminario internazionale di Papirologia (Lecce 27–29 giugno 1994)*. Papyrologica Lupiensia 4. Lecce.

Bats, Maria. 1994. "Les débuts de l'information politique officielle à Rome au premier siècle avant J.-C." In Demougin 1994: 19–43.

Bats, Michel. 2004. "Grec et gallo-grec: les graffites sur céramique aux sources de l'écriture en Gaule méridionale (IIe–Ier s. av. J.-C.)." In Feugère and Lambert 2004: 7–20.

Baumann, Gerd, ed. 1986. *The Written Word: Literacy in Transition*. Oxford.

Baurain, Claude. 1992. "La place des littératures grecque et punique dans les bibliothèques de Carthage." *AC* 61: 158–77.

——, Corinne Bonnet, and Véronique Krings, eds. 1991. *Phoinikeia grammata: lire et écrire en Méditerranée: actes du colloque de Liège, 15–18 novembre 1989*. Collection d'études classiques 6. Namur.

Beard, Mary. 1991. "Writing and Religion: *Ancient Literacy* and the Function of the Written Word in Roman Religion. Question: What Was the Rôle of Writing in Graeco-Roman Paganism?" In Humphrey 1991: 35–58.

Beil, Joanne. 1983. "Select Bibliography on Orality and Literacy." In Robb 1983: 277–81.

Bellier-Chaussonnier, Maud. 2002. "Des représentations de bibliothèques en Grèce classique." *REA* 104: 329–47.

Beltrán Lloris, Francisco. 1998–9. "Writing, Language and Society: Iberians, Celts and Romans in Northeastern Spain in the 2nd and 1st Centuries BC." *BICS* 43: 131–51.

Bémont, Colette. 2004. "L'écriture à la Graufesenque (Millau, Aveyron): les vaisselles sigillées inscrites comme sources d'information sur les structures professionnelles." In Feugère and Lambert 2004: 103–31.

Benz, Lore, ed. 2001. *Die römische Literatur zwischen Mündlichkeit und Schriftlichkeit.* ScriptOralia 29. Tübingen.

Bernal, Martin. 1987. "On the Transmission of the Alphabet to the Aegean before 1400 BC." *BASO* 267: 1–19.

Binder, Vera. 2003. "*Vir elegantissimi eloquii et multae undecumque scientiae*: Das Selbstverständnis des Aulus Gellius zwischen Fachwissen und Allgemeinbildung." In Horster and Reitz 2003: 105–20.

Bing, Peter. 2002. "The Un-Read Muse? Inscribed Epigram and Its Readers in Antiquity." In M. A. Harder, R. F. Regtuit, and G. K. Wakker, eds., *Hellenistic Epigrams*, 39–66. Hellenistica Groningana 6. Leuven.

Birt, Theodor. 1882. *Das antike Buchwesen in seinem Verhältniss zur Litteratur, mit Beiträgen zur Textgeschichte des Theokrit, Catull, Properz, und anderer Autoren.* Berlin.

———. 1907. *Die Buchrolle in der Kunst: archäologisch-antiquarische Untersuchungen zum antiken Buchwesen.* Leipzig.

Blanchard, Alain, ed., with a preface by Jean Irigoin. 1989. *Les débuts du codex: actes de la journée d'étude organisée à Paris les 3 et 4 juillet 1985 par l'Institut de papyrologie de la Sorbonne et l'Institut de recherche et d'histoire des textes.* Bibliologia 9. Turnhout.

———. 1993. "Les papyrus littéraires grecs extraits de cartonnages: études de bibliologie." In Marilena Maniaci and Paola F. Munafò, eds., *Ancient and Medieval Book Materials and Techniques. Erice, 18–25 September 1992*, 1: 15–40. Studi e testi 357. Città del Vaticano.

Blanck, Horst. 1992. *Das Buch in der Antike.* Beck's archäologische Bibliothek. München.

Blum, Herwig. 1969. *Die antike Mnemotechnik.* Spudasmata 15. Hildesheim.

Bodson, Liliane. 1991. "Aspects techniques et implications culturelles des adaptations de l'alphabet attique préliminaires à la réforme de 403/2." In Baurain, Bonnet, and Krings 1991: 591–611.

Boffo, Laura. 1995. "Ancora una volta sugli 'archivi' nel mondo greco: conservazione e 'pubblicazione' epigrafica." *Athenaeum* 83: 91–130.

Boone, Elizabeth Hill, and Walter D. Mignolo, eds. 1994. *Writing without Words: Alternative Literacies in Mesoamerica and the Andes.* Durham, N.C.

Bouquiaux-Simon, Odette, with the collaboration of Marie-Hélène Marganne et al. 2004. *Les livres dans le monde gréco-romain.* Followed by Jean-Christophe Didderen, "Liber antiquus: bibliographie générale." Cahiers du CEDOPAL 2. Liège.

Bowie, Ewen. 1994. "The Readership of the Greek Novels in the Ancient World." In James Tatum, ed., *The Search for the Ancient Novel*, 435–59. Baltimore.

———. 1996. "The Ancient Readers of the Greek Novels." In Gareth Schmeling, ed., *The Novel in the Ancient World*, 87–106. Mnemosyne Supplementum 159. Leiden.

Bowman, Alan K. 1991. "Literacy in the Roman Empire: Mass and Mode." In Humphrey 1991: 119–31.

———. 1994a. *Life and Letters on the Roman Frontier: Vindolanda and Its People.* London.

——. 1994b. "The Roman Imperial Army: Letters and Literacy on the Northern Frontier." In Bowman and Woolf 1994: 109–25.

——. 2006. "Outposts of Empire: Vindolanda, Egypt, and the Empire of Rome." *JRA* 19: 75–93.

—— and Greg Woolf, eds. 1994a. *Literacy and Power in the Ancient World.* Cambridge.

—— and Greg Woolf. 1994b. "Literacy and Power in the Ancient World." In Bowman and Woolf 1994a: 1–16.

——, R. A. Coles, N. Gonis, D. Obbink, and P. J. Parsons, eds. 2007. *Oxyrhynchus: A City and its Texts.* Graeco-Roman Memoirs 93. London.

Božič, Dragan, and Michel Feugère. 2004. "Les instruments de l'écriture." In Feugère and Lambert 2004: 21–41.

Brandt, Olle. 1990. "Lapidariae litterae." *Eranos* 88: 163–5.

Brandt, Deborah. 1990. *Literacy as Involvement: The Acts of Writers, Readers, and Texts.* Carbondale, Ill.

Braund, David. 2000. "Learning, Luxury and Empire: Athenaeus' Roman Patron." In Braund and Wilkins 2000: 3–22.

—— and John Wilkins, eds. 2000. *Athenaeus and His World: Reading Greek Culture in the Roman Empire.* Exeter.

Bremmer, J. 1982. "Literacy and the Origins and Limitations of Greek Atheism." In J. den Boeft and A. H. M. Kessels, eds., *Actus: Studies in Honour of H. L. W. Nelson,* 43–55. Utrecht.

Brillante, Carlo. 1996. "La scrittura in Omero." QUCC 52: 31–45.

Briquel, Dominique. 1989. "La mode de l'écriture dans l'Étrurie des VII–VI siècles avant J.-C." In *Les phénomènes de mode dans l'antiquité: actes du colloque organisé par la MAFPEN et l'ARELAD,* 56–70. Dijon.

——. 1991. "L'écriture étrusque. D'après les inscriptions du VIIe s. av. J.-C." In Baurain, Bonnet, and Krings 1991: 615–31.

Brisson, Luc. 1990. "Mythes, écriture, philosophie." In Jean-François Mattéi, ed., *La naissance de la raison en Grèce: actes du congrès de Nice, mai 1987,* 49–58. Paris.

Brixhe, Claude. 1991. "De la phonologie à l'écriture: quelques aspects de l'adaptation de l'alphabet cananéen au grec." In Baurain, Bonnet, and Krings 1991: 313–56.

Brosius, Maria, ed. 2003. *Ancient Archives and Archival Traditions: Concepts of Record-Keeping in the Ancient World.* Oxford Studies in Ancient Documents. Oxford.

Bucking, Scott. 2007. "On the Training of Documentary Scribes in Roman, Byzantine, and Early Islamic Egypt: A Contextualized Assessment of the Greek Evidence." *ZPE* 159: 229–47.

Bulloch, Anthony, Erich S. Gruen, A. A. Long, and Andrew Stewart, eds. 1993. *Images and Ideologies: Self-Definition in the Hellenistic World. Papers Presented at a Conference Held April 7–9, 1988 at the University of California, Berkeley.* Hellenistic Culture and Society 12. Berkeley.

Burns, Alfred. 1985. "The Role of Literacy in Ancient Greece." In Πρακτικά του xii Διεθνούς συνεδρίου κλασικής αρχαιολογίας, Αθήνα 4–10 Σεπτεμβρίου 1983, I: Ρίζες, έννοια, εξέλιξη και απόψεις του κλασικου. Πληροφορική και κλασική αρχαιολογία. Διεθνή αρχαιολογικά προγράμματα. Αθήνα : Υπουργείο πολιτισμού και επιστημών, 69–83. Athens.

Camassa, Giorgio. 1988. "Aux origines de la codification écrite des lois en Grèce." In Detienne 1988: 130–55.

Camassa, Giorgio and Stella Geourgoudi. 1988. "Traces bibliographiques." In Detienne 1988: 525–38.

Cambiano, Giuseppe. 1988a. "La démonstration géométrique." In Detienne 1988: 251–72.

———. 1988b. "Sapere e testualità nel mondo antico." In Rossi 1988: 69–98.

———, Luciano Canfora, and Diego Lanza, eds. 1992–6. Lo spazio letterario della Grecia antica. Vol. 1: La produzione e la circolazione del testo. Tomo 1: La polis. Tomo 2: L'Ellenismo. Tomo 3: I greci e Roma. Vol. 2: La ricezione e l'attualizzazione del testo. Vol. 3: Cronologia e bibliografia della letteratura greca. Roma.

Campbell, J. B. 1995. "Sharing Out Land: Two Passages in the Corpus agrimensorum romanorum." CQ 45: 540–46.

Campbell, B. G. 2001. Performing and Processing the Aeneid. Berkeley Insights in Linguistics and Semiotics 48. New York.

Camporeale, Giovannangelo. 1992. "Rapports entre Grèce et Étrurie: faciès villanovien et orientalisant." In LALIES: actes des sessions de linguistique et de littérature, XI (Cortona, 20–31 août 1990), 83–92. Paris.

———. 2004. Gli Etruschi: storia e civiltà. 2nd ed. Torino. (1st ed. 2000.)

Canfora, Luciano. 1988. "Discours écrit/discours réel chez Démosthène." In Detienne 1988: 211–20.

———. 1989a. "Lire à Athènes et à Rome." Annales (ESC) 44: 925–37.

———. 1989b. The Vanished Library: A Wonder of the Ancient World. Berkeley. Trans. by Martin Ryle from La biblioteca scomparsa. Palermo, 1986.

———. 1992. "Le monde en rouleaux." In Jacob and de Polignac 1992: 49–62.

———. 1993. "Nascita delle biblioteche a Roma." Sileno 19: 25–38.

———. 2004. La bibliothèque d'Alexandrie et l'histoire des textes. Followed by Nathaël Istasse, "Alexandria docta: bibliographie générale." Cahiers du CEDOPAL 1. Liège.

Capasso, Mario, ed. 1994. Il rotolo librario: fabbricazione, restauro, organizzazione interna. Papyrologica Lupiensia 3. Galatina.

———. 1995. Volumen: aspetti della tipologia del rotolo librario antico. Cultura 3. Napoli.

———. 1996. "I titoli nei papiri ercolanesi. 3: I titoli esterni (PHerc 339, 1491 e 'scorza' non identificata." In Corrado Basile and Anna Di Natale, eds., Atti del II Convegno Nazionale di Egittologia e Papirologia. Siracusa, 1–3 dicembre 1995, 137–55. Quaderni dell'Istituto Internazionale del Papiro 7. Siracusa.

———. 1997a. "Libri, autori e pubblico a Bakchias: contributo alla storia della cultura letteraria del Fayyum in epoca greca e romana." In Corrado Basile and A. Di Natale, eds., Archeologia e papiri nel Fayyum: storia della ricerca, problemi e prospettive: atti del convegno internazionale, Siracusa, 24–25 maggio 1996, 261–83. Quaderni del Museo del Papiro, Siracusa 8. Siracusa.

———. 1997b. "I titoli nei papiri ercolanesi. 2: Il primo esempio di un titolo iniziale in un papiro Ercolanese (PHerc. 1457)." In B. Kramer et al., eds., Akten des 21. Internationalen Papyrologenkongresses: Berlin, 13.–19. 8. 1995. Vol. 1: 146–54. Berlin.

———. 1998. "I titoli nei papiri ercolanesi. 4: Altri tre esempi di titoli iniziali." PapLup 7: 41–73.

Capomacchia, Anna Maria G. 1991. "La scrittura delle donne." In Baurain, Bonnet, and Krings 1991: 533–8.

Cardona, Giorgio Raimondo. 1988. "Il sapere dello scriba." In Rossi 1988: 3–28.

Carlini, Antonio. 1989. "Elenco di opere filosofiche e letterarie." *Corpus dei papiri filosofici greci e latini* 1.1: 94–8.
Carruthers, Mary J. 1990. *The Book of Memory: A Study of Memory in Medieval Culture*. Cambridge.
—— and Jan M. Ziolkowski, eds. 2002. *The Medieval Craft of Memory: An Anthology of Texts and Pictures*. Philadelphia.
Casson, Lionel. 2001. *Libraries in the Ancient World*. New Haven.
Cavallo, Guglielmo. 1983. *Libri scritture scribi a Ercolano: introduzione allo studio dei materiali greci*. Presentazione delle tavole illustrative e indici a cura di Mario Capasso e Tiziano Dorandi. Cronache ercolanesi 13: Supplement 1. Naples.
——. 1988. "Cultura scritta e conservazione del sapere: dalla Grecia antica all'Occidente medievale." In Rossi 1988: 29–67.
——, ed. 1989a. *Libri, editori e pubblico nel mondo antico: guida storica e critica*. Roma.
——. 1989b. "Libro e cultura scritta." In Emilio Gabba and Aldo Schiavone, eds., *Storia di Roma, 4: Caratteri e morfologie*, 693–734. Torino.
——. 1991. "Gli usi della cultura scritta nel mondo romano." In *Princeps urbium: cultura e vita sociale dell'Italia romana*, 169–251. Antica madre. Milano.
——. 1992. "Alfabetismo e circolazione del libro." In Vegetti 1992: 166–86.
——. 1995. "Donne che leggono, donne che scrivono." In Renato Raffaelli, ed., *Vicende e figure femminili in Grecia e a Roma: atti del convegno di Pesaro 28–30 aprile 1994*, 517–26. Ancona.
——. 1996. "Veicoli materiali della letteratura di consumo: maniere di scrivere e maniere di leggere." In Pecere and Stramaglia 1996: 11–46.
——, ed. 1998. *Le biblioteche nel mondo antico e medievale*. Biblioteca Universale Laterza 250. 5th ed. Roma.
——. 1999a. "Tracce per una storia del libro e della lettura tra antichità e medioevo." In Giancarlo Reggi, ed., *La cultura materiale antica: aspetti, problemi e spunti per la scuola d'oggi: atti del Corso d'aggiornamento per docenti di latino e greco del Canton Ticino, Lugano 17–18–19 ottobre 1996*, 29–48. Lugano.
——. 1999b. "Between *Volumen* and Codex: Reading in the Roman World." In Cavallo and Chartier 1999: 64–89.
——. 2001. "L'altra lettura: tra nuovi libri e nuovi testi." *AntTard* 9: 131–8.
——. 2002. "Galeno e la levatrice: qualche riflessione su libri e sapere medico nel mondo antico." *MedSec* 14: 407–16.
—— and Roger Chartier, eds. 1999. *A History of Reading in the West*. Studies in Print Culture and the History of the Book. Boston. Trans. by Lydia G. Cochrane from *Histoire de la lecture dans le monde occidental*. Roma, 1995 and Paris, 1997.
—— and Friedrich Hild. 1997. "Buch." In *Der Neue Pauly* 2: cols. 809–16. Stuttgart.
——, Paolo Fedeli, and Andrea Giardina, eds. 1989–94. *Lo spazio letterario di Roma antica*. Vol. 1: *La produzione del testo*. Vol. 2: *La circolazione del testo*. Vol. 3: *La ricezione del testo*. Vol. 4: *L'attualizzazione del testo*. Vol. 5: *Cronologia e bibliografia della letteratura latina*. Roma.
Ceccarelli, Paola. 2005. "Messaggio scritto e messaggio orale: strategie narrative Erodotee." In Giangiulio 2005: 13–60.
Cerri, Giovanni. 1991. "Il significato di sphregis in Teognide e la salvaguardia dell'autenticità testuale nel mondo antico." *QS* 17 no. 33: 21–40.
Chadwick, John. 1990. "The Pech-Maho Lead." *ZPE* 82: 161–6.

Charlier, Fabrice. 2004. "La pratique de l'écriture dans les tuileries gallo-romaines." In Feugère and Lambert 2004: 67–102.

Chartier, Roger. 1989. "Leisure and Sociability: Reading Aloud in Early Modern Europe." In Susan Zimmerman and Ronald F. E. Weissman, eds., *Urban Life in the Renaissance*, 103–20. Newark.

——. 1994. *The Order of Books: Readers, Authors, and Libraries in Europe between the Fourteenth and Eighteenth Centuries*. Stanford. Trans. by Lydia G. Cochrane from *L'ordre des livres: lecteurs, auteurs, bibliothèques en Europe entre XIVe e XVIIIe siècle*. Paris, 1992.

Chrisomalis, Stephen. 2003. "The Egyptian Origin of the Greek Alphabetic Numerals." *Antiquity* 77: 485–96.

Christmann, Eckhard. 2003. "Zum Verhältnis von Autor und Leser in der römischen Agrarliteratur: Bücher und Schriften für Herren und Sklaven." In Horster and Reitz 2003: 121–52.

Christol, M. 1994. "Pline l'Ancien et la *formula* de la province de Narbonnaise." In Demougin 1994: 45–63.

Citroni, Mario. 1995. *Poesia e lettori in Roma antica: forme della comunicazione letteraria*. Collezione storica. Roma.

Clanchy, M. T. 1993. *From Memory to Written Record, England, 1066–1307*. 2nd ed. Oxford. (1st ed. 1979.)

Clark, Romy, and Roz Ivanič. 1997. *The Politics of Writing*. London.

Clarysse, W., et al. LDAB. "Leuven Database of Ancient Books." http://www.trismegistos.org/ldab/index.php

——. 1993. "Egyptian Scribes Writing Greek." *CE* 68: 186–201.

——. 2003. "Tomoi synkollesimoi." In Brosius 2003: 344–59.

Cohen, David. 2003. "Writing, Law, and Legal Practice in the Athenian Courts." In Yunis 2003a: 78–96.

Coldstream, John Nicolas. 1990. "The Beginnings of Greek Literacy: An Archaeologist's View." *AH* 20: 144–59.

——. 1993. "Mixed Marriages at the Frontiers of the Early Greek World." *OJA* 12: 89–107.

Coleman, Joyce. 1996. *Public Reading and the Reading Public in Late Medieval England and France*. Cambridge.

Collins, James and Richard K. Blot. 2003. *Literacy and Literacies: Texts, Power, and Identity*. Cambridge.

Colonna, Giovanni. 1980. "L'aspetto epigrafico." In Stibbe et al. 1980: 41–52.

——. 1980. "Appendice: le iscrizioni strumentali latine del VI e V secolo a. C." In Stibbe et al. 1980: 53–70.

——. 1988. "L'écriture dans l'Italie centrale à l'époque archaïque." *Revue de la société des élèves, anciens élèves et amis de la section des sciences religieuses de l'EPHE*, 22–31. Paris.

Connerton, P. 1989. *How Societies Remember*. Themes in the Social Sciences. Cambridge.

Cooley, Alison E., with contributions by A. Burnett et al. 2002. *Becoming Roman, Writing Latin? Literacy and Epigraphy in the Roman West*. Journal of Roman Archaeology, Supplementary Series 48. Portsmouth.

Corbier, Mireille. 1991. "L'écriture en quête de lecteurs." In Humphrey 1991: 99–118.

——. 2006. *Donner à voir, donner à lire: mémoire et communication dans la Rome ancienne*. Paris.

Cordano, Federica. 1984. "L'uso della scrittura in Italia meridionale e Sicilia nei secoli VIII e VII a. C." *Opus* 3: 281–309.

Cornell, Tim. 1991. "The Tyranny of the Evidence: A Discussion of the Possible Uses of Literacy in Etruria and Latium in the Archaic Age." In Humphrey 1991: 7–34.

Coudry, Marianne. 1994. "Sénatus-consultes et *acta senatus*: rédaction, conservation et archivage des documents émanant du Sénat, de l'époque de César à celle des Sévères." In Demougin 1994: 65–102.

Coulet, Corinne. 1996. *Communiquer en Grèce ancienne: écrits, discours, informations, voyages*. Paris.

Cribiore, Raffaella. 1996. *Writing, Teachers and Students in Graeco-Roman Egypt*. American Studies in Papyrology 36. Atlanta.

———. 2001. *Gymnastics of the Mind: Greek Education in Hellenistic and Roman Egypt*. Princeton.

———. 2002. "The Women in the Apollonios Archive and Their Use of Literacy." In Henri Melaerts et Leon Mooren, eds., *Le rôle et le statut de la femme en Égypte hellénistique, romaine et byzantine: actes du colloque international, Bruxelles-Leuven, 27–29 novembre 1997*, 149–66. Studia Hellenistica 37. Leuven.

Culham, Phyllis. 1989. "Archives and Alternatives in Republican Rome." *CPh* 84: 100–15.

Curchin, Leonard A. 1995. "Literacy in the Roman Provinces: Qualitative and Quantitative Data from Central Spain." *AJPh* 116: 461–76.

D'Angour, Armand J. 1998–9. "Archinus, Eucleides and the Reform of the Athenian Alphabet." *BICS* 43: 109–30.

Daris, Sergio. 1995. "Realtà e fortuna d'una biblioteca ellenistica." In L. Belloni, C. Milanese, and A. Porro, eds., *Studia classica Johanni Tarditi oblata*. Vol. 2: 1123–39. Bibliotheca di aevum antiquum 7. Milano.

Davies, Anna Morpurgo. 1986. "Forms of Writing in the Ancient Mediterranean World." In Baumann 1986: 51–77.

Davies, John K. 2000. "Athenaeus' Use of Public Documents." In Braund and Wilkins 2000: 203–17.

———. 2003. "Greek Archives: From Record to Monument." In Brosius 2003: 323–43.

———. 2005. "The Origins of the Inscribed Greek Stela." In Piotr Bienkowski, Christopher Mee, and Elizabeth Slater, eds., *Writing and Ancient Near Eastern Society: Papers in Honour of Alan R. Millard*, 283–300. Journal for the Study of the Old Testament, Library of Hebrew Bible/Old Testament Studies 426. New York.

de Hoz, María Paz. 2006. "Literacy in Rural Anatolia: The Testimony of the Confession Inscriptions." *ZPE* 155: 139–44.

De Luca, Cosimo Damiano. 2007. "Il libro greco e latino del Fayyum: aspetti paleografici e bibliologici." In Palme 2007: 159–60.

de Polignac, François. 2005. "Usages de l'écriture dans les sanctuaires du haut archaïsme." In Véronique Dasen and Marcel Piérart, eds., Ἰδίᾳ καὶ δημοσίᾳ: *les cadres "privés" et "publics" de la religion grecque antique: actes du IXe colloque du Centre International d'Étude de la Religion Grecque Antique (CIERGA), tenu à Fribourg du 8 au 10 septembre 2003*, 13–25. Kernos, Supplément no. 15. Liège.

———. 2006. "Espaces de communication et dynamiques d'appartenance en Grèce archaïque." *REA* 108: 9–24.

de Simone, C. 1980. "L'aspetto linguistico." In Stibbe et al. 1980: 71–94.

Dean-Jones, Lesley. 2003. "Literacy and the Charlatan in Ancient Greek Medicine." In Yunis 2003a: 97–121.

Degni, Paola. 1998. *Usi delle tavolette lignee e cerate nel mondo greco e romano.* Ricerca papirologica 4. Messina.

Del Corso, Lucio. 2005. *La lettura nel mondo ellenistico.* Biblioteca universale Laterza 574. Roma-Bari.

——. 2006. "Libro e lettura nell'arte ellenistica: note storico-culturali." *S&T* 4: 71–106.

——. 2007. "Morfologia dei primi libri greci alla luce delle testimonianze indirette." In Palme 2007: 161–8.

Del Olmo Lete, G. 2005. "Les bibliothèques de l'antiquité." In Ipert and Marty 2005: 16–27.

Delage, Richard. 2004. "L'écrit en 'représentation': les marques de grand format au sein des décors sur sigillée du Centre de la Gaule." In Feugère and Lambert 2004: 145–52.

Delattre, Daniel. 2005. *La Villa des Papyrus et les rouleaux d'Herculanum: la bibliothèque de Philodème.* Cahiers du CEDOPAL 4. Liège.

Delvigo, Maria Luisa. 1990. "L'emendatio del filologo, del critico, dell'autore: tre modi di correggere il testo? (I)." *MD* 24: 71–110.

Demont, Paul. 1993. "Die *Epideixis* über die *Techne* im V. und IV. Jh." In Kullmann and Althoff 1993: 181–209.

Demougin, S., ed. 1994. *La mémoire perdue: à la recherche des archives oubliées, publiques et privées, de la Rome antique.* Publications de la Sorbonne. Série Histoire Ancienne et Médiévale 30. Paris.

Derderian, Katharine. 2001. *Leaving Words to Remember: Greek Mourning and the Advent of Literacy.* Mnemosyne Supplementum 209. Leiden.

D'Errico, Francesco. 1995. "A New Model and its Implications for the Origin of Writing: The La Marche Antler Revisited." *CArchJ* 5: 163–206.

Deru, Xavier. 2004. "Les estampilles littérales et anépigraphes sur céramique belge et le rapport à l'écrit des potiers belgo-romains." In Feugère and Lambert 2004: 133–43.

Desbordes, Françoise. 1985. *Signes graphiques et unités linguistiques: textes latins sur l'écriture, des origines à la fin du deuxième siècle de notre ère.* Thèse d'État, Paris IV.

Desbordes, Françoise. 1990. *Idées romaines sur l'écriture.* Lille.

Detienne, Marcel, ed., with the collaboration of Georgio Camassa et al. 1988a. *Les Savoirs de l'écriture: en Grèce ancienne.* Cahiers de philologie 14. Villeneuve-d'Ascq.

——. 1988b. "L'écriture et ses nouveaux objets intellectuels en Grèce." In Detienne 1988a: 7–26.

——. 1988c. "L'espace de la publicité: ses opérateurs intellectuels dans la cité." In Detienne 1988a: 29–81.

Didderen, Jean-Christophe. 2004. "Liber antiquus: bibliographie générale." In Bouquiaux-Simon 2004.

—— and Marie-Hélène Marganne. 2007. "Liber antiquus: bibliographie générale: avec mise à jour 2005–2007 par Marie-Hélène Marganne." http://www.ulg.ac.be/facphl/services/cedopal/pages/bibliographies/Liber%20antiquus.htm

Dihle, Albrecht. 1998. "Mündlichkeit und Schriflichkeit nach dem Aufkommen des Lehrbuches." In Kullmann, Althoff, and Asper 1998: 265–77.

Dillon, John. 2002. "The Social Role of the Philosopher in the Second Century C.E.: Some Remarks." In Philip A. Stadter and Luc Van der Stockt, eds., *Sage and Emperor*, 29–40. Leuven.

Dix, T. Keith. 1988. "Ovid Strikes Out: *Tristia* 3.1 and the First Public Libraries at Rome." *AugAge* 8: 27–35.

——. 2000. "The Library of Lucullus." *Athenaeum* 88: 441–64.

——. 2002. "A Survey of Ancient Libraries: Review Article." *JRA* 15: 469–78. Review of Casson 2001.

—— and George W. Houston. 2006. "Public Libraries in the City of Rome: From the Augustan Age to the Time of Diocletian." *MEFRA* 118.2: 671–717.

Donovan, Brian R. 1993. "The Project of Protagoras." *RSQ* 23: 35–47.

Dorandi, Tiziano. 1991. "Den Autoren über die Schulter geschaut: Arbeitsweise und Autographie bei den antiken Schriftstellern." *ZPE* 87: 11–33.

——. 1993. "Zwischen Autographie und Diktat: Momente der Textualität in der antiken Welt." In Kullmann and Althoff 1993: 71–83.

——. 1995. "La 'Villa dei Papiri' a Ercolano e la sua biblioteca." *CPh* 90: 168–82.

——. 1997. "Tradierung der Texte im Altertum; Buchwesen." In Heinz-Günther Nesselrath, ed., *Einleitung in die griechische Philologie*, 3–16. Einleitung in die Altertumswissenschaft. Stuttgart.

——. 2000. *Le stylet et la tablette: dans le secret des auteurs antiques*. L'âne d'or 12. Paris. Revised and corrected as *Nell'officina dei classici: come lavoravano gli autori antichi*. Frecce 45. Roma, 2007.

Dortmund, Annette. 2001. *Römisches Buchwesen um die Zeitenwende: war T. Pomponius Atticus (110–32 v. Chr.) Verleger?* Buchwissenschaftliche Beiträge aus dem Deutschen Bucharchiv München 66. Wiesbaden.

Driessen, Jan. 1992. "Homère et les tablettes en linéaire B: mise au point." *AC* 61: 5–37.

Dubuisson, Michael. 1991. "Lettrés et illettrés dans la Rome antique: l'importance sociale, politique et culturelle de l'écriture." In Baurain, Bonnet, and Krings 1991: 633–47.

Dupont, Florence. 1999. *The Invention of Literature: From Greek Intoxication to the Latin Book*. Baltimore. Trans. by Janet Lloyd from *L'invention de la littérature: de l'ivresse grecque au livre latin*. Textes à l'appui: Histoire classique. Paris, 1994.

—— and Emmanuelle Valette-Cagnac, eds. 2005. *Façons de parler grec à Rome*. L'Antiquité au présent. Paris.

Ehlich, Konrad, Florian Coulmas, and Gabriele Graefen, eds. 1996. *A Bibliography on Writing and Written Language*. Vol. 1. Trends in Linguistics: Studies and Monographs 89. Berlin.

El-Abbadi, Mostafa. 1992. *Life and Fate of the Ancient Library of Alexandria*. 2nd ed. Paris. (1st ed. 1990.)

Erler, Michael. 1993. "*Philologia medicans*: Wie die Epikureer die Texte ihres Meisters lasen." In Kullmann and Althoff 1993: 281–303.

——. 1998. "Einübung und Anverwandlung: Reflexe mündlicher Meditationstechnik in philosophischer Literatur der Kaiserziet." In Kullmann, Althoff, and Asper 1998: 361–81.

Evans, Jeremy. 1987. "Graffiti and the Evidence of Literacy and Pottery Use in Roman Britain." *AJ* 144: 191–204.

Falivene, Maria Rosaria. 1991. "Government, Management, Literacy: Aspects of Ptolemaic Administration in the Early Hellenistic Period." *AncSoc* 22: 203–27.

Fantham, Elaine. 1996. *Roman Literary Culture: From Cicero to Apuleius*. Ancient Society and History. Baltimore.

——. 1999. "Two Levels of Orality in the Genesis of Pliny's *Panegyricus*." In Mackay 1999: 221–37.

Faraguna, Michele. 2000. "A proposito degli archivi nel mondo greco: terra e registrazioni fondiarie." *Chiron* 30: 65–115.

——. 2005. "Scrittura e amministrazione nelle città greche: gli archivi pubblici." *QUCC* 80: 61–86.

Fedeli, Paolo. 1988. "Biblioteche private e pubbliche a Roma e nel mondo romano." In Cavallo 1988: 29–64.

——. 1992. "Autore, committente, pubblico in Roma." In Vegetti 1992: 77–106.

Fehrle, Rudolf. 1986. *Das Bibliothekswesen im alten Rom: Voraussetzungen, Bedingungen, Anfänge*. Schriften der Universitätsbibliothek Freiburg i. Br. 10. Freiburg.

Fein, Sylvia. 1994. *Die Beziehungen der Kaiser Trajan und Hadrian zu den litterati*. Stuttgart.

Ferrari, G. R. F. 1984. "Orality and Literacy in the Origin of Philosophy." *AncPhil* 4: 194–205. Review of Robb 1983.

Feugère, Michel. 2004. "L'*instrumentum*, support d'écrit." In Feugère and Lambert 2004: 53–65.

—— and Pierre-Yves Lambert, eds. 2004. "L'écriture dans la société galloromaine: éléments d'une réflexion collective." *Gallia* 61: 1–193.

Fezzi, Luca. 2004. "Il passagio da oralità a scrittura nel processo attico." *LEC* 72: 109–18.

Finkelberg, Margalit. 2006. "Regional Texts and the Circulation of Books: The Case of Homer." *GRBS* 46: 231–48.

Finnegan, Ruth H. 1988. *Literacy and Orality: Studies in the Technology of Communication*. Oxford.

Flemming, Rebecca. 2007. "Women, Writing and Medicine in the Classical World." *CQ* 57: 257–79.

Fögen, Thorsten. 2003. "Metasprachliche Reflexionen antiker Autoren zu den Charakteristika von Fachtexten und Fachsprachen." In Horster and Reitz 2003: 31–60.

Ford, Andrew. 1993. "L'inventeur de la poésie lyrique Archiloque le Colon." *Métis* 8: 59–73.

——. 1999. "Reading Homer from the Rostrum: Poems and Laws in Aeschines' *Against Timarchus*." In Goldhill and Osborne 1999: 231–56.

——. 2002. *The Origins of Criticism: Literary Culture and Poetic Theory in Classical Greece*. Princeton.

——. 2003. "From Letters to Literature: Reading the 'Song Culture' of Classical Greece." In Yunis 2003a: 15–37.

Forrester, Michael A. 1996. *Psychology of Language: A Critical Introduction*. London.

Fowler, Donald. 1995. "Martial and the Book." *Ramus* 24: 31–58.

Fox, Adam. 2000. *Oral and Literate Culture in England, 1500–1700*. Oxford Studies in Social History. Oxford.

Franklin, James L. 1991. "Literacy and the Parietal Inscriptions of Pompeii." In Humphrey 1991: 77–98.

Frasca, Rosella. 1996. *Educazione e formazione a Roma: storia, testi, immagini*. Bari.

Fredouille, Jean-Claude, Marie-Odile Goulet-Cazé, Philippe Hoffmann, Pierre Petitmengin, eds. 1997. *Titres et articulations du texte dans les oeuvres antiques: actes du Colloque International de Chantilly 13–15 décembre 1994*. Collection des Études Augustiniennes. Série Antiquité 152. Paris.

Frost, Frank J. 1987. "Attic Literacy and the Solonian σεισάχθεια." *AncW* 15: 51–8.

Funghi, M. Serena and Gabriella Messeri Savorelli. 1992. "Lo 'scriba di Pindaro' e le biblioteche di Ossirinco." *SCO* 42: 43–62.

Gagarin, Michael. 1999. "The Orality of Greek Oratory." In Mackay 1999: 163–80.

——. 2003. "Letters of the Law: Written Texts in Archaic Greek Law." In Yunis 2003a: 59–77.

Gamble, Harry Y. 1995. *Books and Readers in the Early Church: A History of Early Christian Texts*. New Haven.

Gavrilov, A. K. 1997. "Techniques of Reading in Classical Antiquity." *CQ* 47: 56–73.

Geier, Manfred. 1994. "Schriftlichkeit und Philosophie." In Günther, Ludwig, et al. 1994: 646–54.

Gentili, Bruno. 1992a. "Oralità e scrittura in Grecia." In Vegetti 1992: 30–52.

——. 1992b. "Poeta e musico in Grecia." In Vegetti 1992: 53–76.

—— and Giuseppe Paioni, eds. 1985. *Oralità: cultura, letteratura, discorso: atti del convegno internazionale (Urbino 21–25 luglio 1980)*. Quaderni urbinati di cultura class. Atti di convegni 2. Roma.

Georgoudi, Stella. 1988. "Manières d'archivage et archives de cités." In Detienne 1988: 221–47.

Georgountzos, Panayotis K. 1993. "L'alphabet création grecque." *Platon* 45: 3–12.

Giangiulio, Maurizio, ed. 2005. *Erodoto e il "modello erodoteo": formazione e trasmissione delle tradizioni storiche in Grecia*. Labirinti 88. Trento.

Giovè Marchiolli, Nicoletta. 1993. *Alle origini delle abbreviature latine: una prima ricognizione (I secolo a.C.–IV secolo d.C.)*. Ricerca papirologica 2. Messina.

Glazebrook, Allison. 2005. "Reading Women: Book Rolls on Attic Vases." *Mouseion* 5: 1–46.

Gleirscher, Paul. 1993. "Zum etruskischen Einfluss auf die Golaseccakultur und dessen Auswirkungen auf die Kulturverhältnisse im Alpenrheintal." *HA* 24: 51–68.

Godart, Louis. 2001. "L'histoire des écritures égéennes." *Ktèma* 26: 21–4.

—— and Iannis Tzedakis. 1989. "La storia della lineare B e le scoperte di Armenoi e La Canea." *RFIC* 117: 385–409.

Goldhill, Simon. 1999. "Body/Politics: Is There a History of Reading?" In Thomas M. Falkner, Nancy Felson, and David Konstan, eds., *Contextualizing Classics: Ideology, Performance, Dialogue: Essays in Honor of John J. Peradotto*, 89–120. Greek Studies: Interdisciplinary Approaches. Lanham.

—— and Robin Osborne, eds. 1999. *Performance Culture and Athenian Democracy*. Cambridge.

Goody, Jack, ed. 1968. *Literacy in Traditional Societies*. Cambridge.

——. 1986. *The Logic of Writing and the Organization of Society*. Cambridge.

——. 1987. *The Interface between the Written and the Oral*. Studies in Literacy, Family, Culture and the State. Cambridge.

——. 1994. "On the Threshold to Literacy." In Günther, Ludwig, et al. 1994: 432–6.

Goody, Jack. 2000. *The Power of the Written Tradition.* Smithsonian Series in Ethnographic Inquiry. Washington.

Grafton, Anthony, and Megan Williams. 2006. *Christianity and the Transformation of the Book: Origen, Eusebius, and the Library of Caesarea.* Cambridge, Mass.

Gratien, Brigette, and Roger Hanoune, eds. 1997. *Lire l'écrit: textes, archives, bibliothèques dans l'antiquité.* Ateliers: cahiers de la Maison de la recherche 12. Villeneuve-d'Asq.

Gros, Pierre. 2001. "Les édifices de la bureaucratie impériale: administration, archives et services publics dans le centre monumental de Rome." *Pallas* 55: 107–26.

Guarducci, Margherita. 1987. *L'epigrafia greca dalle origini al tardo impero.* Roma.

Günther, Hartmut, Otto Ludwig, et al., eds. 1994 and 1996. *Schrift und Schriftlichkeit: ein interdisziplinäres Handbuch internationaler Forschung = Writing and Its Use: An Interdisciplinary Handbook of International Research.* Handbücher zur Sprach- und Kommunikationswissenschaft, Bd. 10.1 and 10.2. Berlin.

Haarmann, Harald. 1995. *Early Civilization and Literacy in Europe: An Inquiry into Cultural Continuity in the Mediterranean World.* Approaches to Semiotics 124. Berlin.

Habinek, Thomas. 1998. *The Politics of Latin Literature: Writing, Identity, and Empire in Ancient Rome.* Princeton.

——. 2005. *The World of Roman Song: From Ritualized Speech to Social Order.* Baltimore.

Hägg, Tomas. 1994. "Orality, Literacy, and the 'Readership' of the Early Greek Novel." In Roy Eriksen, ed. *Contexts of Pre-Novel Narrative: The European Tradition,* 47–81. Approaches to Semiotics 114. Berlin.

Haines-Eitzen, Kim. 1998. "Girls Trained in Beautiful Writing: Female Scribes in Roman Antiquity and Early Christianity." *JECS* 6: 629–46.

——. 2000. *Guardians of Letters: Literacy, Power, and the Transmitters of Early Christian Literature.* Oxford.

Halverson, John. 1992. "Goody and the Implosion of the Literacy Thesis." *Man* 27: 301–17.

Hannah, Patricia A. 2001. "*TON AΘENEΘEN AΘΛON*: A Case Study in the History of a Label." In Watson 2001: 161–84.

Hannah, Robert. 2001. "From Orality to Literacy? The Case of the *Parapegma.*" In Watson 2001: 139–59.

Hanson, Ann Ellis. 1991. "Ancient Illiteracy." In Humphrey 1991: 159–98.

Hanson, William S., and Richard Conolly. 2002. "Language and Literacy in Roman Britain: Some Archaeological Considerations." In Cooley 2002: 151–64.

Haran, Menahem. 1996. "Codex, *Pinax* and Writing Slate." *SCI* 15: 212–22.

Harrauer, Hermann. 1995. "Bücher in Papyri." In Helmut W. Lang et al., eds., *Flores litterarum Ioanni Marte sexagenario oblati: Wissenschaft in der Bibliothek.* Wien.

Harris, Edward M. 2005. "Notes on a Lead Letter from the Athenian Agora." *HSPh* 102: 157–70.

Harris, William V. 1989a. *Ancient Literacy.* Cambridge, Mass.

——. 1989b. "Notes on Literacy and Illiteracy in Fifth-Century Athens." *Index* 17: 39–45.

——. 1991. "Why Did the Codex Supplant the Book-Roll?" In John Monfasani and Ronald G. Musto, eds., *Renaissance Society and Culture: Essays in Honor of Eugene F. Rice Jr.,* 71–85. New York.

——, ed. 1993. *The Inscribed Economy: Production and Distribution in the Roman Empire in the Light of* Instrumentum Domesticum. *The Proceedings of a Conference Held at the American Academy in Rome on 10–11 January, 1992.* Journal of Roman Archaeology, Supplementary Series 6. Ann Arbor.

Hartog, François. 1990. "Écritures, généalogies, archives, histoire en Grèce ancienne." In Marie-Madeleine Mactoux and Évelyne Geny, eds., *Mélanges Pierre Lévêque.* 5: *Anthropologie et société,* 177–88. Centre de Recherches d'Histoire Ancienne 101. Annales Littéraires de l'Université de Besançon 429. Paris.

Havelock, Eric A. 1962. *A Preface to Plato.* Oxford.

——. 1982. *The Literate Revolution in Greece and Its Cultural Consequences.* Princeton Series of Collected Essays. Princeton.

——. 1983. "The Linguistic Task of the Presocratics." In Robb 1983: 7–82.

——. 1986. *The Muse Learns to Write: Reflections on Orality and Literacy from Antiquity to the Present.* New Haven.

Hedrick, Charles W. 1994. "Writing, Reading, and Democracy." In Robin Osborne and Simon Hornblower, eds., *Ritual, Finance, Politics: Athenian Democratic Accounts Presented to David Lewis,* 157–74. Oxford.

——. 1999. "Democracy and the Athenian Epigraphical Habit." *Hesperia* 68: 387–439.

——. 2000. "Epigraphic Writing and the Democratic Restoration." In Pernille Flensted-Jensen, Thomas Heine Nielsen, Lene Rubinstein, eds., *Polis and Politics: Studies in Ancient Greek History Presented to Mogens Herman Hansen on His Sixtieth Birthday, August 20, 2000,* 327–35. Copenhagen.

Henrichs, Albert. 2003a. "*Hieroi logoi* and *hierai bibloi*: The (Un)written Margins of the Sacred in Ancient Greece." *HSPh* 101: 207–66.

——. 2003b. "Writing Religion: Inscribed Texts, Ritual Authority, and the Religious Discourse of the Polis." In Yunis 2003a: 38–58.

Hershbell, J. B. 1983. "The Oral-Poetic Religion of Xenophanes." In Robb 1983: 125–33.

Heyworth, S., and N. Wilson. 1997. "Auflage, zweite." In *Der Neue Pauly* 2: cols. 271–5.

Hezser, Catherine. 2001. *Jewish Literacy in Roman Palestine.* Texte und Studien zum antiken Judentum 81. Tübingen.

Hoepfner, Wolfram. 1996. "Zu griechischen Bibliotheken und Bücherschränken." *AA* 1996: 25–36.

——, ed. 2002. *Antike Bibliotheken.* Zaberns Bildbände zur Archäologie. Sonderbände der Antiken Welt. Mainz.

Holford-Strevens, Leofranc, and Amiel Vardi, eds. 2004. *The Worlds of Aulus Gellius.* Oxford.

Hölkeskamp, Karl-Joachim. 1992a. "Written Law in Archaic Greece." *PCPhS* 38: 87–117.

——. 1992b. "Arbitrators, Lawgivers and the 'Codification of Law' in Archaic Greece: Problems and Perspectives." *Métis* 7: 49–81.

Holmes, Catherine. 2002. "Written Culture in Byzantium and Beyond: Contexts, Contents and Interpretations." In Holmes and Waring 2002: 1–31.

—— and Judith Waring, eds. 2002. *Literacy, Education and Manuscript Transmission in Byzantium and Beyond.* The Medieval Mediterranean: Peoples, Economies and Cultures 400–1500, Vol. 42. Leiden.

Hopkins, Keith. 1991. "Conquest by Book." In Humphrey 1991: 133–58.

Horowitz, Michael G. 1996. "The Scientific Dialectic of Ancient Greece and the Cultural Tradition of Indo-European Speakers." *JIES* 24: 409–19.

Horsfall, Nicholas. 1989. "'The Uses of Literacy' and the *Cena Trimalchionis*." Pts. 1 and 2. *G&R* 36: 74–89; 194–209.

——. 1991. "Statistics or States of Mind?" In Humphrey 1991: 59–76.

——. 2003. *The Culture of the Roman Plebs*. London.

Horster, Marietta. 2003. "Literarische Elite? Überlegungen zum sozialen Kontext lateinischer Fachschriftsteller in Republik und Kaiserzeit." In Horster and Reitz 2003: 176–97.

—— and Christiane Reitz, eds. 2003. *Antike Fachschriftsteller: Literarischer Diskurs und sozialer Kontext*. Klassische Philologie. Palingenesia, Bd. 80. Stuttgart.

Houston, George W. 2002. "The Slave and Freedman Personnel of Public Libraries in Ancient Rome." *TAPhA* 132: 139–76.

——. 2004. "How Did You Get Hold of a Book in a Roman Library? Three Second-Century Scenarios." *CB* 80: 5–13.

——. 2007. "Grenfell, Hunt, Breccia, and the Book Collections of Oxyrhynchus." *GRBS* 47: 327–59.

Humphrey, J. H., ed. 1991. *Literacy in the Roman World*. Journal of Roman Archaeology, Supplementary Series 3. Journal of Roman Archaeology 19. Ann Arbor.

Hunter, Richard. 2003. "Reflecting on Writing and Culture: Theocritus and the Style of Cultural Change." In Yunis 2003a: 213–34.

Hurschmann, R. 2001. "Tabula." In *Der Neue Pauly* 11: col. 1195.

Hurtado, Larry W. 2006. *The Earliest Christian Artifacts: Manuscripts and Christian Origins*. Grand Rapids.

Immerwahr, Henry R. 1990. *Attic Script: A Survey*. Oxford Monographs on Classical Archaeology. Oxford.

Ingemark, Dominic. 2000–1. "Literacy in Roman Britain: The Epigraphical Evidence." *ORom* 25–26: 19–30.

Innes, Matthew. 1998. "Memory, Orality and Literacy in an Early Medieval Society." *P&P* 158: 3–36.

Invernizzi, Antonio. 2003. "They Did Not Write on Clay: Non-Cuneiform Documents and Archives in Seleucid Mesopotamia." In Brosius 2003: 302–22.

Ipert, Stéphane and Bruno Marty, eds. 2005. *Les trésors manuscrits de la Méditerranée*. Dijon.

Irigoin, Jean. 1990. "L'alphabet grec et son geste des origines au IX siècle après J.-C." In Colette Sirat, Jean Irigoin and Emmanuel Poulle, eds., *L'écriture, le cerveau, l'œil et la main*, 299–305. Bibliologia 10. Turnhout.

——. 2001. *Le livre grec des origines à la Renaissance*. Paris.

Irvine, Martin. 1994. *The Making of Textual Culture: "Grammatica" and Literary Theory, 350–1100*. Cambridge Studies in Medieval Literature 19. Cambridge.

Isserlin, B. S. J. 1991. "The Transfer of the Alphabet to the Greeks: The State of Documentation." In Baurain, Bonnet, and Krings 1991: 283–91.

Istasse, Nathaël. 2004. "Alexandria docta: bibliographie générale." In Canfora 2004: 33–82. http://www.ulg.ac.be/facphl/services/cedopal/pages/bibliographies/ALEXDOCT.htm

Jacob, Christian. 1988. "Inscrire la terre habitée sur une tablette: réflexions sur la fonction des cartes géographiques en Grèce ancienne." In Detienne 1988: 273–304.

——. 1991. "La leçon d'Alexandrie." In Richard Figuier, ed., *La bibliothèque: miroir de l'âme, mémoire du monde*, 23–32. Mutations 121. Paris.

——. 1992a. "Un athlète du savoir: Ératosthène." In Jacob and de Polignac 1992: 113–27.

——. 1992b. "Callimaque: un poète dans le labyrinthe." In Jacob and de Polignac 1992: 100–12.

——. 1997. "La bibliothèque et le livre: formes de l'encyclopédisme alexandrin." *Diogenes* 178 vol. 45: 64–85.

——. 1998. "Vers une histoire comparée des bibliothèques: questions préliminaires, entre Grèce et Chine anciennes." QS 48: 87–122.

——. 2000. "Athenaeus the Librarian." In Braund and Wilkins 2000: 85–110.

—— and François de Polignac, eds. 1992. *Alexandrie IIIe siècle av. J.-C.: tous les savoirs du monde ou le rêve d'universalité des Ptolémées*. Série Mémoires 19. Paris.

Jahandarie, Khosrow. 1999. *Spoken and Written Discourse: A Multi-Disciplinary Perspective*. Stamford, Conn.

Jeffery, Lilian Hamilton, with a suppl. by Alan W. Johnston. 1990. *The Local Scripts of Archaic Greece: A Study of the Origin of the Greek Alphabet and its Development from the Eighth to the Fifth Centuries* B.C. Oxford Monographs on Classical Archaeology. Oxford. (1st ed. 1961.)

Johne, Renate. 1991. "Zur Entstehung einer 'Buchkultur' in der zweiten Hälfte des 5. Jahrhunderts v. u. Z." *Philologus* 135: 45–54.

Johnson, Willliam A. 1994. "Oral Performance and the Composition of Herodotus' *Histories*." *GRBS* 35: 593–627.

——. 2000. "Towards a Sociology of Reading in Classical Antiquity." *AJPh* 121: 593–627.

——. 2002. "Reading Cultures and Education." In Peter C. Patrikis, ed., *Reading between the Lines: Perspectives on Foreign Language Literacy*, 9–23. Yale Language Series. New Haven.

——. 2004. *Bookrolls and Scribes in Oxyrhynchus*. Studies in Book and Print Culture. Toronto.

——. 2005. "The Posidippus Papyrus: Bookroll and Reader." In Kathryn Gutzwiller, ed., *The New Posidippus: A Hellenistic Poetry Book*, 70–80. Oxford.

——. 2006. "The Story of the Papyri of the Villa dei Papiri." *JRA* 19: 493–6. Review of Sider 2005.

——. 2009. "The Ancient Book," In Roger Bagnall, ed., *The Oxford Handbook of Papyrology*. Oxford.

——. 2010. *Readers and Reading Culture in the High Empire: A Study of Elite Reading Communities*. Oxford.

Jordan, David R. 2000. "A Personal Letter Found in the Athenian Agora." *Hesperia* 69: 91–103.

——. 2003. "A Letter from the Banker Pasion." In David Jordan and John Traill, eds., *Lettered Attica: A Day of Attic Epigraphy: Proceedings of the Athens Symposium, 8 March 2000*, 23–39 (Appendix A: Corpus of Personal Letters on Lead). Publications of the Canadian Archaeological Institute of Athens 3. Athens.

Jourdain-Annequin, Colette. 1995. "Genèse, fonctions, diffusion de l'écriture: les *Phoinikeia grammata*." *DHA* 21: 227–34. Review of Baurain, Bonnet, and Krings 1991.

Kahn, Charles H. 1983. "Philosophy and the Written Word: Some Thoughts on Heraclitus and the Early Greek Uses of Prose." In Robb 1983: 110–24.

———. 2003. "Writing Philosophy: Prose and Poetry from Thales to Plato." In Yunis 2003a: 139–61.

Kallendorf, Craig. 2007. *The Virgilian Tradition: Book History and the History of Reading in Early Modern Europe*. Variorum Collected Studies Series. Aldershot.

Kaster, Robert A. 1988. *Guardians of Language: The Grammarian and Society in Late Antiquity*. The Transformation of the Classical Heritage 11. Berkeley.

Kearsley, Rosalinde A., ed., with the collaboration of Trevor V. Evans. 2001. *Greeks and Romans in Imperial Asia: Mixed Language Inscriptions and Linguistic Evidence for Cultural Interaction until the End of AD III*. Inschriften griechischer Städte aus Kleinasien 59. Bonn.

Kelly, C. M. 1994. "Later Roman Bureaucracy: Going through the Files." In Bowman and Woolf 1994: 161–76.

Kenney, E. J. 1982. "Books and Readers in the Roman World." In E. J. Kenney and W. V. Clausen, eds., *The Cambridge History of Classical Literature*. Vol. 2: *Latin Literature*, 3–32. Cambridge.

Ker, James. 2004. "Nocturnal Writers in Imperial Rome: The Culture of *Lucubratio*." *CPh* 99: 209–42.

Keulen, Wytse. 2004. "Gellius, Apuleius, and Satire on the Individual." In Holford-Strevens and Vardi 2004: 223–45.

Kilmer, Martin F., and Robert Develin. 2001. "Sophilos' Vase Inscriptions and Cultural Literacy in Archaic Athens." *Phoenix* 55: 9–43.

Kirk, G. S. 1983. "Orality and Sequence." In Robb 1983: 83–90.

Kleberg, Tönnes. 1989. "Commercio librario ed editoria nel mondo antico." In Cavallo 1989a: 25–80.

Knox, B. M. W. 1968. "Silent Reading in Antiquity." *GRBS* 9: 421–35.

Kollesch, Jutta. 1992. "Zur Mündlichkeit hippokratischer Schriften." In J. A. López Férez, ed., *Tratados hipocráticos (Estudios acerca de su contenido, forma y influencia): actas del VIIe colloque international hippocratique (Madrid, 24–29 de septiembre de 1990)*, 335–42. Madrid.

Konishi, Haruo. 1993a. "Muse Goddess of Literacy." *LCM* 18: 116–21.

———. 1993b. "The Origin of the Greek Alphabet: A Fresh Approach." *LCM* 18: 102–5.

Kraus, Thomas J. 1999. "'Slow Writers'—βραδέως γράφοντες: What, How Much, and How Did They Write?" *Eranos* 97: 86–97.

———. 2000. "(Il)literacy in Non-Literary Papyri from Graeco-Roman Egypt: Further Aspects of the Educational Ideal in Ancient Literary Sources and Modern Times." *Mnemosyne* (Ser. 4) 53: 322–42.

Krenkel, Werner. 2003. "Sprache und Fachsprache." In Horster and Reitz 2003: 11–30.

Krüger, Julian. 1990. *Oxyrhynchos in der Kaiserzeit: Studien zur Topographie und Literaturrezeption*. Europäische Hochschulschriften III 441. Frankfurt am Main.

Kullmann, Wolfgang. 1999. "Homer and Historical Memory." In Mackay 1999: 95–113.

—— and J. Althoff, eds. 1993. *Vermittlung und Tradierung von Wissen in der griechischen Kultur.* ScriptOralia 61. Tübingen.

—— and Michael Reichel, eds. 1990. *Der Übergang von der Mündlichkeit zur Literatur bei den Griechen.* ScriptOralia 30. Tübingen.

——, Jochen Althoff, and Markus Asper, eds. 1998. *Gattungen wissenschaftlicher Literatur in der Antike.* Tübingen.

La Penna, Antonio. 1992. "Il letterato." In Vegetti 1992: 140–65.

Labarbe, Jules. 1991. "Survie de l'oralité dans la Grèce archaïque." In Baurain, Bonnet, and Krings 1991: 499–531.

Laks, André. 2001. "Écriture, prose, et les débuts de la philosophie grecque." *Methodos* 1. http://methodos.revues.org/document139.html

Lallot, Jean. 1992. "Zénodote ou l'art d'accommoder Homère." In Jacob and de Polignac 1992: 93–9.

Lalou, Élizabeth, ed. 1992. *Les tablettes à écrire, de l'antiquité à l'époque moderne: actes du colloque international du Centre National de la Recherche Scientifique, Paris, Institut de France, 10–11 octobre 1990.* Bibliologia 12. Turnhout.

Lama, Mariachiara. 1991. "Aspetti di tecnica libraria ad Ossirinco: copie letterarie su rotoli documentari." *Aegyptus* 71: 55–120.

——. 2007. "Aspetti di tecnica libraria: copie letterarie nel *verso* di rotoli documentari." In Palme 2007: 381–5.

Lang, Mabel. 1982. "Writing and Spelling on Ostraka." In *Studies in Attic Epigraphy, History and Topography Presented to Eugene Vanderpool by Members of the American School of Classical Studies,* 75–87. Hesperia Supplement 19.

——. 1990. *The Athenian Agora: Results of the Excavations Conducted by the American School of Classical Studies at Athens.* Vol. 25: *Ostraka.* Princeton.

Langdon, Merle K. 1991. "Poletai Records." In Gerald V. Lalonde, Merle K. Langdon, and Michael B. Walbank, eds., *The Athenian Agora: Results of the Excavations Conducted by the American School of Classical Studies at Athens.* Vol. 19: *Inscriptions: Horoi, Poletai Records, Leases of Public Lands.* Princeton.

Lanza, Diego. 1988. "Le comédien devant l'écriture." In Detienne 1988: 359–84.

Laubenheimer, Fanette. 2004. "Inscriptions peintes sur les amphores gauloises." In Feugère and Lambert 2004: 153–71.

Lawall, Mark Lewis. 2000. "Graffiti, Wine Selling, and the Reuse of Amphoras in the Athenian Agora, ca. 430 to 400 B.C." *Hesperia* 69: 3–90.

Ledentu, Marie. 2004. *Studium scribendi: recherches sur les statuts de l'écrivain et de l'écriture à Rome à la fin de la République.* Bibliothèque d'études classiques 39. Louvain.

Legras, Bernard. 1995. "Les lecteurs des bibliothèques grecques dans l'Égypte ptolémaïque." In *Usages des bibliothèques: lieux d'histoire et état des lieux: actes de la table-ronde organisée par Histoire au Présent et l'Institut Historique Allemand de Paris,* 7–20. = *Sources: Travaux historiques: Revue de l'Association Histoire au Présent,* 1995 [1997].

——. 2002. *Lire en Égypte, d'Alexandre à l'Islam.* Antiqua. Paris.

Lejeune, Michel. 1989. "Le jeu des abécédaires dans la transmission de l'alphabet, III." In *Secondo congresso internazionale etrusco, Firenze 26 maggio–2 giugno 1985: atti,* 1285–91. Studi etruschi Suppl. Roma.

Lentz, Tony M. 1989. *Orality and Literacy in Hellenic Greece.* Carbondale.

Lewis, D. M. 1994. "The Persepolis Tablets: Speech, Seal and Script." In Bowman and Woolf 1994: 17–32.

Lewis, Naphtali. 1981. "*Literati* in the Service of the Roman Emperors: Politics before Culture." In L. Casson and M. Price, eds., *Coins, Culture and History in the Ancient World: Numismatic and Other Studies in Honor of Bluma L. Trell*, 149–66. Detroit.

Lewis, Sian. 1992. "Public Information: News and Writing in Ancient Greece." *Hermathena* 152: 5–20.

Liddel, Peter. 2003. "The Places of Publication of Athenian State Decrees from the 5th Century BC to the 3rd Century AD." *ZPE* 143: 79–93.

Lloyd, Geoffrey. 2003. "Literacy in Greek and Chinese Science." In Yunis 2003a: 122–38.

Lo Cascio, Elio. 2001. "Il *census* a Roma e la sua evoluzione dall'età 'serviana' alla prima età imperiale." *MEFRA* 113: 565–603.

Lombardo, Mario. 1988. "Marchands, transactions économiques, écriture." In Detienne 1988: 159–87.

Longo, Oddone. 1992. "L'informazione e la comunicazione." In Vegetti 1992: 15–29.

Longo Auricchio, Francesca, and Mario Capasso. 1987. "I rotoli della Villa ercolanese: dislocazione e ritrovamento." *CronErcol* 17: 37–47.

Loraux, Nicole. 1988. "Solon et la voix de l'écrit." In Detienne 1988: 95–129.

Luraghi, Nino, ed. 2001. *The Historian's Craft in the Age of Herodotus*. Oxford.

MacDonald, Alasdair A., Michael W. Twomey, and Gerrit Jan Reinink, eds. 2003. *Learned Antiquity: Scholarship and Society in the Near East, the Greco-Roman World, and the Early Medieval West*. Groningen Studies in Cultural Change 5. Leuven.

Mackay, E. Anne, ed. 1999. *Signs of Orality: The Oral Tradition and Its Influence in the Greek and Roman World*. Leiden.

MacMullen, Ramsay. 1982. "The Epigraphic Habit in the Roman Empire." *AJPh* 103: 233–46.

Maffi, Alberto. 1988. "Écriture et pratique juridique dans la Grèce classique." In Detienne 1988: 188–210.

Manacorda, Mario Alighiero. 1992. "Scuola e insegnanti." In Vegetti 1992: 187–209.

Manetti, Daniela. 2006. "La terminologie du livre: à propos des emplois d'ὕφος et ἔδαφος dans deux passages de Galien." *REG* 119: 157–71.

Manfredi, M. 1985. "Cultura letteraria nell'Egitto greco e romano." In S. Curto and O. Montevecchi, eds., *Egitto e società antica: atti del convegno (Torino, 8–9 giugno e 23–24 novembre 1984)*, 271–85. Vita e pensiero. Milano.

Manguel, Alberto. 1996. *A History of Reading*. New York.

Mann, J. C. 1985. "Epigraphic Consciousness." *JRS* 75: 204–6.

Marcus, Joyce. 1995. "Writing, Literacy, and Performance in the New and Old Worlds." *CArchJ* 5: 325–31. Review of Boone and Mignolo 1994.

Marek, Christian. 1993. "Euboia und die Entstehung der Alphabetschrift bei den Griechen." *Klio* 75: 27–44.

Marganne, Marie-Hélène. 2003. "Bibliothèques et livres de médecine dans l'Égypte gréco-romaine." In *École Pratique des Hautes Études. Livret-annuaire 2001–2002*, 342–53. Paris.

——, with a preface by Danielle Gouravitch. 2004. *Le livre médical dans le monde gréco-romain*. Cahiers du CEDOPAL 3. Liège.

——. 2007. "La terminologie de la librairie dans la Collection hippocratique." In Véronique Boudon-Millot, Alessia Guardasole, and Caroline Magdelaine, eds.,

La science médicale antique: nouveaux regards. Mélanges en l'honneur de Jacques Jouanna. Paris.

Margolis, Joseph. 1983. "The Emergence of Philosophy." In Robb 1983: 228–43.

Marshall, B. A. 1987. "*Excepta Oratio,* the Other *Pro Milone* and the Question of Shorthand." *Latomus* 46: 730–6.

Martin, Henri-Jean. 1994. *The History and Power of Writing.* Chicago. Trans. by Lydia G. Cochrane from *Histoire et pouvoirs de l'écrit.* Paris, 1988.

—— and Jean Vezin, eds. 1990. *Mise en page et mise en texte du livre manuscrit.* Paris.

Marty, B. 2005. "Histoire de l'écriture." In Ipert and Marty 2005: 48–65.

Matthews, J. F. 1998. "Eternity in Perishable Materials: Law-Making and Literate Communication in the Roman Empire." In T. W. Hillard, R. A. Kearsley, C. E. V. Nixon, and A. M. Nobbs, eds., *Ancient History in a Modern University: Proceedings of a Conference Held at Macquarie University, 8–13 July 1993 to Mark Twenty-Five Years of the Teaching of Ancient History at Macquarie University and the Retirement from the Chair of Professor Edwin Judge. 2: Early Christianity, Late Antiquity, and Beyond,* 253–65. New South Wales.

Matthews, Roger. 1995. "Writing and Civilization in Early Mesopotamia." *CArchJ* 5: 309–14.

Mazal, Otto. 1999. *Griechisch-römische Antike.* Geschichte der Buchkultur 1. Graz.

McDonnell, Myles. 1996. "Writing, Copying, and Autograph Manuscripts in Ancient Rome." *CQ* 46: 469–91.

McNamee, Kathleen. 1981. "Greek Literary Papyri Revised by Two or More Hands." In R. S. Bagnall, ed., *Proceedings of the 16th International Congress of Papyrology,* 79–91. Chico, Calif.

——. 1992. *Sigla and Select Marginalia in Greek Literary Papyri.* Papyrologica Bruxellensia 26. Bruxelles.

——. 2001. "A Plato Papyrus with Shorthand Marginalia." *GRBS* 42: 97–116.

——. 2007. *Annotations in Greek and Latin Texts from Egypt.* American Studies in Papyrology 45. New Haven.

—— and Michael L. Jacovides. 2003. "Annotations to the Speech of the Muses (Plato *Republic* 546B–C)." *ZPE* 144: 31–50.

Meissner, Burkhard. 1999. *Die technologische Fachliteratur der Antike: Struktur, Überlieferung und Wirkung technischen Wissens in der Antike (ca. 400 v. Chr.– ca. 500 n. Chr.).* Berlin.

——. 2003. "Mündliche Vermittlung und schriftliche Unterweisung in der antiken Berufsausbildung." In Horster and Reitz 2003: 153–75.

Melve, Leidulf. 2003. "Literacy—Aurality—Orality: A Survey of Recent Research into the Orality/Literacy Complex of the Latin Middle Ages (600–1500)." *SO* 78: 143–97.

Meneghini, R. 2002. "Nuovi dati sulla funzione e le fasi costruttive delle biblioteche del Foro di Traiano." *MEFRA* 114: 655–92.

Meyer, Elizabeth A. 1988. *Literacy, Literate Practice, and the Law in the Roman Empire,* A.D. *100–600.* PhD diss., Yale University.

——. 1990. "Explaining the Epigraphic Habit in the Roman Empire: The Evidence of the Epitaphs." *JRS* 80: 74–96.

——. 2004. *Legitimacy and Law in the Roman World: Tabulae in Roman Belief and Practice.* Cambridge.

Michailidou, Anna. 2000–1. "Indications of Literacy in Bronze Age Thera." *Minos* 35–36: 7–30.

Mielsch, Harald. 1995. "Die Bibliothek und die Kunstsammlung der Könige von Pergamon." *AA* 1995 (4): 765–79.

Millender, Ellen Greenstein. 2001. "Spartan Literacy Revisited." *ClAnt* 20: 121–64.

Miller, Gordon L. 1990. "Literacy and the Hippocratic Art: Reading, Writing, and Epistemology in Ancient Greek Medicine." *JHM* 45: 11–40.

Moatti, Claude. 1993. *Archives et partage de la terre dans le monde romain (II siècle avant—I siècle après J.-C.)*. Collection de l'École française de Rome 173. Roma.

——. 1994. "Les archives des terres publiques à Rome (IIe s. av.–Ier s. ap. J.-C.): le cas des assignations." In Demougin 1994: 103–119.

——, ed. 1998. *La mémoire perdue: recherches sur l'administration romaine*. Collection de l'École française de Rome 243. Rome.

Moatti, Claudia, ed. 2000. *La mémoire perdue. 3: Recherches sur l'administration romaine: le cas des archives judiciaires pénales.* MEFRA 112.2: 647–779.

——, ed. 2001. *Les archives du census: le contrôle des homes. Actes de la table ronde, Rome, 1er décembre 1997.* MEFRA 113.2: 559–764.

——, ed. 2004. *La mobilité des personnes en Méditerranée de l'antiquité à l'époque moderne: procédures de contrôle et documents d'identification.* Collection de l'École française de Rome 341. Rome.

Moreau, Philippe. 1994. "La mémoire fragile: falsification et destruction des documents publics au Ier s. av. J.-C." In Demougin 1994: 121–47.

Morgan, Teresa J. 1998. *Literate Education in the Hellenistic and Roman Worlds.* Cambridge Classical Studies. Cambridge.

——. 1999. "Literate Education in Classical Athens." *CQ* 49: 46–61.

Most, Glenn W. 1990. "Canon Fathers: Literacy, Mortality, Power." *Arion* 1: 35–60.

Mostert, Marco, ed., with an introduction by Michael Clanchy. 1999. *New Approaches to Medieval Communication.* Turnhout.

Müller, Roland J. 1993. "Tradierung religiösen Wissens in den Mysterienkulten am Beispiel von Andania." In Kullmann and Althoff 1993: 307–16.

Murphey, T. 1998. "Cicero's First Readers: Epistolary Evidence for the Dissemination of His Works." *CQ* 48: 492–505.

Murray, Oswyn. 1987. "Herodotus and Oral History." In H. Sancisi-Weerdenburg and A. Kuhrt, eds., *Achaemenid History*. Vol. 2: *The Greek Sources*, 93–115. Proceedings of the Groningen 1984 Achaemenid history workshop. Leiden. Reprinted in Luraghi 2001: 16–44.

——. 2001. "Herodotus and Oral History Reconsidered." In Luraghi 2001: 314–25.

Murray, Penelope, and Peter Wilson, eds. 2004. *Music and the Muses: The Culture of "Mousikē" in the Classical Athenian City.* Oxford.

Naas, Valérie. 1996. "Réflexions sur la méthode de travail de Pline l'Ancien." *RPh* 70: 305–32.

Naddaf, Gérard. 2000. "Literacy and Poetic Performance in Plato's *Laws*." *AncPhil* 20: 339–50.

Nagy, Gregory. 2000. "Reading Greek Poetry Aloud: Evidence from the Bacchylides Papyri." *QUCC* N. S. 64: 7–28.

Nauta, Ruurd R. 2002. *Poetry for Patrons: Literary Communication in the Age of Domitian.* Leiden.

Nenci, Giuseppe. 1998. "L'introduction de l'alphabet en Grèce selon Hérodote (V 58)." *REA* 100: 579–89.

Neudecker, R. 2004. "Aspekte öffentlicher Bibliotheken in der Kaiserzeit." In B. Borg, ed., *Paideia: The World of the Second Sophistic*, 293–313. Berlin.

Nicks, Fiona. 2000. "Literary Culture in the Reign of Anastasius I." In Stephen Mitchell and Geoffrey Greatrex, eds., *Ethnicity and Culture in Late Antiquity*, 183–204. London.

Nicolai, Roberto. 2000. "La biblioteca delle Muse: osservazioni sulle più antiche raccolte librarie greche." *GB* 23: 213–27.

———. 2001. "Thucydides' Archaeology: Between Epic and Oral Traditions." In Luraghi 2001: 263–85.

Nicolet, Claude. 1994a. "À la recherche des archives oubliées: une contribution à l'histoire de la bureaucratie romaine." In Demougin 1994: v–xviii.

———. 1994b. "Documents fiscaux et géographie dans la Rome ancienne." In Demougin 1994: 149–72.

———, ed. 1996. *Les littératures techniques dans l'antiquité romaine: statut, public et destination, tradition: sept exposés suivis de discussions*. Fondation Hardt. Entretiens sur l'Antiquité classique 42. Vandoeuvres-Genève.

Nieddu, Gian Franco. 1993. "Neue Wissensformen, Kommunikationstechniken und schriftliche Ausdrucksformen in Griechenland im sechsten und fünften Jahrhundert v. Chr.: Einige Beobachtungen." In Kullmann and Althoff 1993: 151–65.

———. 2004. *La scrittura "madre delle muse": agli esordi di un nuovo modello di comunicazione culturale*. Lexis Supplemento 9. Amsterdam.

Nightingale, Andrea Wilson. 1999. "Plato's Lawcode in Context: Rule by Written Law in Athens and Magnesia." *CQ* 49: 100–22.

Nikitinski, Oleg. 1998. "Plinius der Ältere: Seine Enzyklopädie und ihre Leser." In Kullmann, Althoff, and Asper 1998: 341–59.

Nissen, Hans Jörg, Peter Damerow, and Robert K. Englund, eds. 1993. *Archaic Bookkeeping: Early Writing and Techniques of Economic Administration in the Ancient Near East*. Trans. by Paul Larsen. Chicago.

Obbink, Dirk. 2007. "Readers and Intellectuals." In Bowman et al. 2007: 271–82.

Oesterreicher, Wulf. 1997. "Types of Orality in Text." In Bakker and Kahane 1997: 190–214, 257–60.

Olson, David R. 1994a. *The World on Paper: The Conceptual and Cognitive Implications of Writing and Reading*. Cambridge.

———. 1994b. "Writing and Science." In Günther, Ludwig, et al. 1994: 654–7.

———. 2002. "What Writing Is." *Pragmatics and Cognition* 9: 239–58.

——— and Nancy Torrance, eds. 2001. *The Making of Literate Societies*. Malden, Mass.

———, N. Torrance, and A. Hildyard, eds. 1985. *Literacy, Language, and Learning: The Nature and Consequences of Reading and Writing*. Cambridge.

Ong, Walter J. 1982. *Orality and Literacy: The Technologizing of the Word*. London.

———. 1986. "Writing Is a Technology That Restructures Thought." In Baumann 1986: 23–50.

Osborne, Robin. 1999. "Inscribing Performance." In Goldhill and Osborne 1999: 341–58.

Osiek, Carolyn. 1998. "The Oral World of Early Christianity in Rome: The Case of Hermas." In Karl Paul Donfried and Peter Richardson, eds., *Judaism and Christianity in First-Century Rome*, 151–72. Grand Rapids.

O'Sullivan, Neil. 1996. "Written and Spoken in the First Sophistic." In Worthington 1996: 115–27.

Otranto, Rosa. 1996. "Per una storia delle biblioteche private a Roma: censi giuridici e fonte letterarie." *Bollettino del Museo del Papiro* 1: 57–65. Syracuse.

——. 2000. *Antiche liste di libri su papiro*. Sussidi eruditi 49. Rome.

Palaima, Thomas G. 1987. "Comments on Mycenaean Literacy." *Minos* 20–22: 499–510.

——. 2003. "'Archives' and 'Scribes' and Information Hierarchy in Mycenaean Greek Linear B Records." In Brosius 2003: 153–94.

Palme, Bernhard, ed. 2007. *Akten des 23. Internationalen Papyrologenkongresses. Wien, 22.–28. Juli 2001*. Papyrologica Vindobonensia 1. Wien.

Pandolfini, Maristella and Aldo Prosdocimi. 1990. *Alfabetari e insegnamento della scrittura in Etruria e nell'Italia antica*. Bibl. di Studi etruschi 20. Firenze.

Papakonstantinou, Zinon. 2002. "Written Law, Literacy and Social Conflict in Archaic and Classical Crete." *AHB* 16: 135–50.

Pearce, John. 2004. "Archaeology, Writing Tablets and Literacy in Roman Britain." In Feugère and Lambert 2004: 43–51.

Pébarthe, Christophe. 2000. "Fiscalité, empire athénien et écriture: retour sur les causes de la guerre du Péloponnèse." *ZPE* 129: 47–76.

——. 2006. *Cité, démocratie et écriture: histoire de l'alphabétisation d'Athènes à l'époque classique*. Culture et cité 3. Paris.

Pecere, Oronzo, and Antonio Stramaglia, eds. 1996. *La letteratura di consumo nel mondo greco-latino*. Cassino.

Pelliccia, Hayden. 2003. "Two Points about Rhapsodes." In Margalit Finkelberg and Guy G. Stroumsa, eds., *Homer, the Bible, and Beyond: Literary and Religious Canons in the Ancient World*, 97–116. Jerusalem Studies in Religion and Culture. Leiden.

Perlman, Paula J. 2002. "Gortyn: The First Seven Hundred Years. Part II: The Laws from the Temple of Apollo Pythios." In Thomas Heine Nielsen, ed., *Even More Studies in the Ancient Greek Polis*, 187–227. Papers from the Copenhagen Polis Centre 6. Historia Einzelschriften 162. Stuttgart.

Peruzzi, E. 1998. *Civiltà greca nel Lazio preromano*. Accademia toscana di scienze e lettere, "La Colombaria," Studi 165. Florence.

Pesando, Fabrizio. 1994. *Libri e biblioteche*. Vita e costumi dei Romani antichi 17. Roma.

Petrucci, Armando. 1995. *Writers and Readers in Medieval Italy: Studies in the History of Written Culture*. Ed. and trans. by Charles M. Radding. New Haven.

——. 1996. "Au-delà de la paléographie: histoire de l'écriture, histoire de l'écrit, histoire de l'écrire." *BAB* 6: 123–35.

Phillips, C. Robert. 1990–1. "Poetry before the Ancient City: Zorzetti and the Case of Rome." *CJ* 86: 382–9.

Phillips, David J. 1990. "Observations on Some Ostraka from the Athenian Agora." *ZPE* 83: 123–48.

Phillips, John Joseph. 1981. *The Publication of Books at Rome in the Classical Period*. PhD diss., Yale University.

——. 1985. "Book Prices and Roman Literacy." *CW* 79: 36–8.

Piérart, Marcel. 1991. "Écriture et identité culturelle: les cités du Péloponnèse nordoriental." In Baurain, Bonnet, and Krings 1991: 565–76.

Pigeaud, Jackie. 1988. "Le style d'Hippocrate ou l'écriture fondatrice de la médicine." In Detienne 1988: 305–29.

Pinto, Pasquale Massimo. 2006. "La biblioteca di Isocrate: note sulla circolazione dei libri e sul lavoro intellettuale nel IV secolo a.C." *S&T* 4: 51–70.

Podossinov, Alexander. 2003. "Die antiken Geographen über sich selbst und ihre Schriften." In Horster and Reitz 2003: 88–104.

Poehlmann, Egert. 1989. "Der Schreiber als Lehrer in der klassischen Zeit Griechenlands." In Johann G. von Hohenzollern and Max Liedtke, eds., *Schreiber, Magister, Lehrer: Zur Geschichte und Funktion eines Berufsstandes*, 73–82. Schriftenreihe zum Bayerischen Schulmuseum Ichenhausen 8. Bad Heilbrunn.

Porciani, Leone. 2005. "Allusioni Erodotee: a proposito della 'pubblicazione' delle *Storie*." In Giangiulio 2005: 1–12.

Postgate, Nicholas, Tao Wang, and Toby Wilkinson. 1995. "The Evidence for Early Writing: Utilitarian or Ceremonial?" *Antiquity* 69: 459–80.

Poucet, Jacques. 1988. "Écrit et écriture dans la Rome archaïque." *Revue de la société des élèves, anciens élèves et amis de la section des sciences religieuses de l'EPHE*, 32–50. Paris.

———. 1989. "Réflexions sur l'écrit et l'écriture dans la Rome des premiers siècles." *Latomus* 48: 285–311.

Powell, Barry B. 1988. "The Dipylon Oinochoe and the Spread of Literacy in Eighth-Century Athens." *Kadmos* 27: 65–86.

———. 1991. "The Origins of Alphabetic Literacy among the Greeks." In Baurain, Bonnet, and Krings 1991: 357–70.

———. 2002. *Writing and the Origins of Greek Literature*. Cambridge.

Pratt, Louise H. 1995. "The Seal of Theognis, Writing, and Oral Poetry." *AJPh* 116: 171–84.

Pucci, Pietro. 1988. "Inscriptions archaïques sur les statues des dieux." In Detienne 1988: 480–97.

Puglia, Enzo. 1996. "Il catalogo di un fondo librario di Ossirinco del III d. C. (PSILaur. inv. 19662)." *ZPE* 113: 51–65.

———. 1998. "Gli inventari librari di PVindob. Gr. 39966." *ZPE* 123: 78–86.

Purcell, Nicholas. 1995. "Literate Games: Roman Urban Society and the Game of *Alea*." *P&P* 147: 3–37.

———. 2001. "The *Ordo Scribarum*: A Study in the Loss of Memory." *MEFRA* 113: 633–74.

Quinn, Kenneth. 1982. "The Poet and His Audience in the Augustan Age." *ANRW* II 30.1: 75–180.

Raible, Wolfgang. 1993. "Die Entwicklung ideographischer Elemente bei der Verschriftlichung des Wissens." In Kullmann and Althoff 1993: 15–37.

Raybould, Marilynne E. 1999. *A Study of Inscribed Material from Roman Britain: An Inquiry into Some Aspects of Literacy in Romano-British Society*. BAR British Series 281. Oxford.

Reay, B. 2005. "Agriculture, Writing, and Cato's Aristocratic Self-Fashioning." *ClAnt* 24: 331–61.

Rebillard, Laurence. 1991. "Exékias apprend à écrire: diffusion de l'écriture chez les artisans du Céramique au VIe s. av. J.-C." In Baurain, Bonnet, and Krings 1991: 549–64.

Reichler-Béguelin, Marie-José. 1992. "Perception du mot graphique dans quelques systèmes syllabiques et alphabétiques." In *LALIES: actes des sessions de linguistique et de littérature, X (Aussois, 29 août-3 septembre 1988; 28 août-2 septembre 1989)*, 143–58. Paris.

Reitz, Christiane. 2003. "Dichtung und Wissenschaft." In Horster and Reitz 2003: 61–71.

Renate, Johne. 1991. "Zur Entstehung einer 'Buchkultur' in der zweiten Hälfte des 5. Jahrhunderts v. u. Z." *Philologus* 135: 45–54.

Resnick, Irven M. 1992–3. "The Codex in Early Jewish and Christian Communities." *JRH* 17: 1–17.

Reynolds, L. D., and N. G. Wilson. 1991. *Scribes and Scholars: A Guide to the Transmission of Greek and Latin Literature*. 3rd ed. Oxford. (1st ed. 1968.)

Rhodes, Peter John. 2001. "Public Documents in the Greek States: Archives and Inscriptions." Pts. 1 and 2. *G&R* 48: 33–44; 136–53.

—— and Robin Osborne, eds. 2003. *Greek Historical Inscriptions: 404–323 BC.* Oxford.

Ridgway, D. 1996. "Greek Letters at Osteria dell'Osa." *ORom* 20: 87–97.

Robb, Kevin, ed. 1983a. *Language and Thought in Early Greek Philosophy*. Monist Library of Philosophy. La Salle, Ill.

——. 1983b. "Preliterate Ages and the Linguistic Art of Heraclitus." In Robb 1983a: 153–206.

——. 1994. *Literacy and Paideia in Ancient Greece*. Oxford.

Robert, Guy. 1987. "Dourian Literacy." In Claude Bérard, Christiane Bron, and Alessandra Pomari, eds., *Images et société en Grèce ancienne: l'iconographie comme méthode d'analyse. Actes du Colloque international Lausanne 8–11 février 1984*, 223–5. Cahiers d'archéologie romande 36. Lausanne.

Roberts, Colin H., and T. C. Skeat. 1983. *The Birth of the Codex*. London.

Rochette, Bruno. 1997. "Bilinguisme, traductions et histoire des textes dans l'Orient grec (Ier–IVe siècle après J.-C.)." *RHT* 27: 1–28.

Rodríguez Mayorgas, Ana. 2007. *La memoria de Roma: oralidad, escritura e historia en la república romana*. BAR International Series 1641. Oxford.

Rodríguez Somolinos, Helena. 1996. "The Commercial Transaction of the Pech Maho Lead: A New Interpretation." *ZPE* 111: 74–8.

Rodríguez-Almeida, Emilio. 1993. "Graffiti e produzione anforaria della Betica." In Harris 1993: 95–106.

Rosen, Ralph M. 1997. "Performance and Textuality in Aristophanes' *Clouds*." *YJC* 10: 397–421.

Rösler, Wolfgang. 1994. "Die griechische Schriftkultur der Antike." In Günther, Ludwig, et al. 1994: 511–7.

Rossi, Pietro, ed. 1988. *La memoria del sapere: forme di conservazione e strutture organizzative dall'antichità a oggi*. Storia e società. Roma.

Rouse, Richard H. and Mary A. Rouse. 2000. *Manuscripts and Their Makers: Commercial Book Producers in Medieval Paris 1200–1500*. Illiterati et uxorati. Turnhout.

Ruijgh, Cornelis J. 1995. "D'Homère aux origines proto-mycéniennes de la tradition épique: analyse dialectologique du langage homérique, avec un *excursus* sur la création de l'alphabet grec." In Jan Paul Crielaard, ed., *Homeric Questions: Essays in Philology, Ancient History and Archaeology, Including the Papers of a Conference Organized by the Netherlands Institute at Athens (15 May 1993)*, 1–96. Amsterdam.

——. 1997. "La date de la création de l'alphabet grec et celle de l'épopée homérique." *BO* 54: 533–603.

——. 1998. "Sur la date de la création de l'alphabet grec." *Mnemosyne* 51: 658–87.

Rüpke, J. 2000. "Raüme literarischer Kommunikation in der Formierungs-phase römischer Literatur." In M. Braun, ed., *Moribus antiquis res stat Romana: Römische Werte und römische Literatur im 3. und 2. Jh. v. Chr.*, 31–52. München.

Ruzé, Françoise. 1988. "Aux débuts de l'écriture politique: le pouvoir de l'écrit dans la cité." In Detienne 1988: 82–94.

———. 2001. "La loi et le chant." In Jean-Pierre Brun and Philippe Jockey, eds., *Techniques et sociétés en Méditerranée (Hommage à Marie-Claire Amouretti)*, 709–19. Paris.

Saenger, Paul. 1989. "Books of Hours and the Reading Habits of the Later Middle Ages." In Roger Chartier, ed., *The Culture of Print: Power and the Uses of Print in Early Modern Europe*, 141–73. Princeton.

———. 1997. *Space between Words: The Origins of Silent Reading*. Figurae: Reading Medieval Culture. Stanford.

Salles, Catherine, with an appendix by René Martin. 1992. *Lire à Rome*. Realia 14. Paris.

Sandoz, Claude. 1991. "Le nom de la lettre et les origines de l'écriture à Rome." *MH* 48: 216–9.

Sanmartí, B. E., and Rosa A. Santiago. 1987. "Une lettre grecque sur plomb trouvée à Emporion (Fouilles 1985)." *ZPE* 68: 119–27.

———. 1988. "La lettre grecque d'Emporion et son contexte archéologique." *RAN* 21: 3–17.

Santiago, R. A., and B. E. Sanmartí. 1988. "Notes additionnelles sur la lettre sur plomb d'Emporion." *ZPE* 72: 100–2.

Santirocco, Matthew S. 1986. "Literacy, Orality, and Thought." *AncPhil* 6: 153–60.

Saussy, Haun. 1996. "Writing in the *Odyssey*: Eurykleia, Parry, Jousse, and the Opening of a Letter from Homer." *Arethusa* 29: 299–308.

Schaefer, Ursula. 1997. "The Medial Approach: A Paradigm Shift in the Philologies?" In Bakker and Kahane 1997: 215–31, 260–4.

Schaeffer, John D. 1996. "The Dialectic of Orality and Literacy: The Case of Book 4 of Augustine's *De doctrina christiana*." *PMLA* 111: 1133–45.

Scheid, John. 1994. "Les archives de la piété: réflexions sur les livres sacerdotaux." In Demougin 1994: 173–185.

———. 1997. "L'écrit et l'écriture dans la religion romaine: mythe et réalité." In Gratien and Hanoune 1997: 99–108.

Schousboe, Karen, and Mogens Trolle Larsen, eds. 1989. *Literacy and Society*. Copenhagen.

Sciarrino, E. 2004. "Putting Cato the Censor's *Origines* in Its Place." *ClAnt* 23: 323–57.

Scodel, Ruth. 2001. "Poetic Authority and Oral Tradition in Hesiod and Pindar." In Watson 2001: 109–37.

Scribner, Sylvia, and Michael Cole. 1981. *The Psychology of Literacy*. Cambridge, Mass.

Sechi, Antonietta. 1990. "Cultura scritta e territorio nella Sardegna romana." In Mastino Attilio, ed., *L'Africa romana: atti del VII Convegno di studio, Sassari 15–17 dicembre 1989*, 641–54. Sassari.

Segenni, Simonetta. 2005. "Frontino, gli archivi della *cura aquarum* e l'acquedotto tardo repubblicano di Amiternum (CIL, 12 1853 = ILLRP, 487)." *Athenaeum* 93: 603–18.

Shear, T. Leslie. 1995. "Bouleuterion, Metroon, and the Archives at Athens." In Mogens H. Hansen and Kurt Raaflaub, eds., *Studies in the Ancient Greek Polis*, 157–90. Historia Einzelschriften 95. Papers from the Copenhagen Polis Centre 2. Stuttgart.

Sherratt, Susan. 2003. "Visible Writings: Questions of Script and Identity in Early Iron Age Greece and Cyprus." *OJA* 22: 225–42.

Sickinger, James P. 1992. *The State Archive of Athens in the Fourth Century* B.C. PhD diss., Brown University.

——. 1994. "Inscriptions and Archives in Classical Athens." *Historia* 43: 286–96.

——. 1999. *Public Records and Archives in Classical Athens*. Studies in the History of Greece and Rome. Chapel Hill.

——. 2002. "Literacy, Orality, and Legislative Procedure in Classical Athens." In Worthington and Foley 2002: 147–69.

Sider, David. 2005. *The Library of the Villa dei Papiri at Herculaneum*. Los Angeles.

Slater, Niall W. 1999. "The Vase as Ventriloquist: *Kalos*-Inscriptions and the Culture of Fame." In Mackay 1999: 143–61.

——. 2002. "Dancing the Alphabet: Performative Literacy on the Attic Stage." In Worthington and Foley 2002: 117–29.

Slings, S. R. 1998. "*Tsade* and *he*: Two Problems in the Early History of the Greek Alphabet." *Mnemosyne* (Ser. 4) 51: 641–57.

Small, Jocelyn Penny. 1995. "Artificial Memory and the Writing Habits of the Literate." *Helios* 22: 159–66.

——. 1997. *Wax Tablets of the Mind: Cognitive Studies of Memory and Literacy in Classical Antiquity*. London.

Sosin, Joshua D., and Joseph Gilbert Manning. 2003. "Palaeography and Bilingualism: P. Duk. inv. 320 and 675." *CE* 78 no. 155–6: 202–10.

Sousa, Marion C. 1989. *Literacy and Classical Rhetoric*. PhD diss., University of South Carolina.

Staikos, K. Sp. 2005. "Les manuscrits grecs et les bibliothèques byzantines." In Ipert and Marty 2005: 112–127.

Starr, Raymond J. 1987. "The Circulation of Literary Texts in the Roman World." *CQ* 37: 213–23.

——. 1990. "The Used-Book Trade in the Roman World." *Phoenix* 44: 148–57.

——. 1998. "Reading Ancient Readers and Their Texts." *NECJ* 26: 32–8.

Steiner, Deborah Tarn. 1994. *The Tyrant's Writ: Myths and Images of Writing in Ancient Greece*. Princeton.

Steinhart, Matthias. 2003. "Literate and Wealthy Women in Archaic Greece: Some Thoughts on the 'Telesstas' Hydria." In Eric Csapo and Margaret Miller, eds., *Poetry, Theory, Praxis: The Social Life of Myth, Word and Image in Ancient Greece: Essays in Honour of William J. Slater*, 204–31. Oxford.

Stephens, Susan A. 1988. "Book Production." In Michael Grant and Rachel Kitzinger, eds., *Civilization of the Ancient Mediterranean. Greece and Rome. 1*, 421–36. New York.

——. 1994. "Who Read Ancient Novels?" In James Tatum, ed., *The Search for the Ancient Novel*, 405–18. Baltimore.

Stibbe, C. M. 1980. "The Archaeological Evidence." In Stibbe et al. 1980: 21–40.

——, G. Colonna, C. de Simone, and H. S. Versnel, with an introd. by M. Pallottino. 1980. *Lapis Satricanus: Archaeological, Epigraphical, Linguistic and Historical Aspects of the New Inscription from Satricum.* Archeologische Studiën van het Nederlands Instituut te Rome. Scripta minora 5. Gravenhage.

Stock, Brian. 1983. *The Implications of Literacy: Written Language and Models of Interpretation in the Eleventh and Twelfth Centuries.* Princeton.

Stoddart, Simon, and James Whitley. 1988. "The Social Context of Literacy in Archaic Greece and Etruria." *Antiquity* 62: 761–72.

Street, Brian V. 1984. *Literacy in Theory and Practice.* Cambridge Studies in Oral and Literate Culture 9. Cambridge.

——. 1993. *Cross-Cultural Approaches to Literacy.* Cambridge.

Strocka, Volker Michael. 1993. "Pompeji VI 17,41: ein Haus mit Privatbibliothek." *MDAI (R)* 100: 321–51.

——. 2000. "Noch einmal zur Bibliothek von Pergamon." *AA* 2000: 155–65.

Suerbaum, Werner. 1992. "Zum Umfang der Bücher in der archaischen lateinischen Dichtung: Naevius, Ennius, Lukrez und Livius Andronicus auf Papyrus-Rollen." *ZPE* 92: 153–73.

Svenbro, Jesper. 1988a. "J'écris, donc je m'efface: l'énonciation dans les premières inscriptions grecques." In Detienne 1988: 459–79 and Svenbro 1988b.

——. 1988b. *Phrasikleia: anthropologie de la lecture en Grèce ancienne.* Textes à l'Appui: Histoire Classique. Paris. Transl. by Janet Lloyd as *Phrasikleia: An Anthropology of Reading in Ancient Greece.* Ithaca, 1993.

Swain, Simon. 2004. "Bilingualism and Biculturalism in Antonine Rome: Apuleius, Fronto, and Gellius." In Holford-Strevens and Vardi 2004: 3–40.

Tarrant, Harold. 1999. "Dialogue and Orality in a Post-Platonic Age." In Mackay 1999: 181–97.

Teeter, Timothy M. 2004. "Papyri, Archives and Patronage." *CB* 80: 27–34.

Thatcher, Tom. 1998. "Literacy, Textual Communities, and Josephus' *Jewish War.*" *JSJ* 29: 123–42.

Thomas, Rosalind. 1989. *Oral Tradition and Written Record in Classical Athens.* Cambridge Studies in Oral and Literate Culture 18. Cambridge.

——. 1992. *Literacy and Orality in Ancient Greece.* Key Themes in Ancient History. Cambridge.

——. 1993. "Performance and Written Publication in Herodotus and the Sophistic Generation." In Kullmann and Althoff 1993: 225–44.

——. 1994. "Literacy and the City-State in Archaic and Classical Greece." In Bowman and Woolf 1994: 33–50.

——. 1995. "Written in Stone? Liberty, Equality, Orality, and the Codification of Law." *BICS* 40: 59–74.

——. 2001a. "Literacy in Ancient Greece: Functional Literacy, Oral Education, and the Development of a Literate Environment." In Olson and Torrance 2001: 68–81.

——. 2001b. "Herodotus' *Histories* and the Floating Gap." In Luraghi 2001: 198–210.

——. 2003. "Prose Performance Texts: 'Epideixis' and Written Publication in the Late Fifth and Early Fourth Centuries." In Yunis 2003a: 162–88.

Thompson, Dorothy J. 1992a. "Literacy in Early Ptolemaic Egypt." In A. H. S. El-Mosalamy, ed., *Proceedings of the 19th International Congress of Papyrology, Cairo, 2–9 September 1989,* Vol. 2: 77–90. Cairo.

——. 1992b. "Language and Literacy in Early Hellenistic Egypt." In P. Bilde et al., eds., *Ethnicity in Hellenistic Egypt,* 39–52. Studies in Hellenistic Civilization 3. Aarhus.

Thompson, Dorothy J. 1992c. "Literacy and the Administration in Early Ptolemaic Egypt." In Janet H. Johnson, ed., *Life in a Multi-Cultural Society: Egypt from Cambyses to Constantine and Beyond*. Studies in Ancient Oriental Civilization 51. Chicago.

———. 1994. "Literacy and Power in Ptolemaic Egypt." In Bowman and Woolf 1994: 67–83.

Timpanaro, S. 1986. *Per la storia della filologia virgiliana antica*. Quaderni di filologia critica 6. Roma.

Tlili, Noureddine. 2000. "Les bibliothèques en Afrique romaine." *DHA* 26: 151–74.

Too, Yun Lee. 2000. "The Walking Library: The Performance of Cultural Memories." In Braund and Wilkins 2000: 111–23.

—— and Niall Livingstone, eds. 1998. *Pedagogy and Power: Rhetorics of Classical Learning*. Ideas in Context 50. Cambridge.

Trabattoni, Franco. 2005. *La verità nascosta: oralità e scrittura in Platone e nella Grecia classica*. Roma.

Turner, Eric G. 1977. *The Typology of the Early Codex*. Haney Foundation Series 18. Philadelphia.

———. 1980. *Greek Papyri: An Introduction*. 2nd ed. Oxford. (1st ed. 1968.)

———, revised and enlarged by Peter J. Parsons. 1987. *Greek Manuscripts of the Ancient World*. London. (1st ed. Princeton, 1971.)

Uchitel, Alexander. 2003. "Local Differences in Arrangements of Ration Lists on Minoan Crete." In Brosius 2003: 139–52.

Usener, Sylvia. 1994. *Isokrates, Platon und ihr Publikum: Hörer und Leser von Literatur im 4. Jahrhundert v. Chr.* ScriptOralia 63. Tübingen.

Valette-Cagnac, Emmanuelle. 1993. *Anthropologie de la lecture à Rome*. Thèse de doctorat, École Pratique des Hautes Études, Ve section.

———. 1995. "La *recitatio*, écriture orale." In Florence Dupont, ed., *Paroles romaines*, 9–23. Travaux et mémoires, Université de Nancy II. Études anciennes 12. Nancy.

———. 1997. *La lecture à Rome: rites et pratiques*. L'Antiquité au présent. Paris.

———. 2002. "Corps de lecteurs." In Philippe Moreau, ed., *Corps romains*, 289–312. Collection Horos. Grenoble.

Van Berchem, Denis. 1991. "Commerce et écriture: l'exemple de Délos à l'époque hellénistique." *MH* 48: 129–45.

van Minnen, Peter. 1998. "Boorish or Bookish? Literature in Egyptian Villages in the Fayum in the Graeco-Roman Period." *JJurPap* 28: 99–184.

Vansina, Jan. 1985. *Oral Tradition as History*. Madison, Wisc.

Vardi, Amiel. 2004. "Genre, Conventions, and Cultural Programme in Gellius' *Noctes Atticae*." In Holford-Strevens and Vardi 2004: 159–86.

Vegetti, Mario, ed. 1992. *Oralità scrittura spettacolo*. 2nd ed. Torino.

Versnel, H. S. 1980. "Historical Implications." In Stibbe et al. 1980: 95–150.

Virlouvet, Catherine. 1995. *Tessera frumentaria: les procédures de la distribution du blé public à Rome*. Bibliothèque des Écoles françaises d'Athènes et de Rome 286. Roma.

Vogt-Spira, Gregor, ed. 1990. *Strukturen der Mündlichkeit in der römischen Literatur*. ScriptOralia 19. Tübingen.

———. 1994. "Die lateinische Schriftkultur der Antike." In Günther, Ludwig, et al. 1994: 517–24.

Volonaki, Eleni. 2001. "The Re-Publication of the Athenian Laws in the Last Decade of the Fifth Century B.C." *Dike* 4: 137–67.

Von Staden, Heinrich. 1998. "Gattung und Gedächtnis: Galen über Wahrheit und Lehrdichtung." In Kullmann, Althoff, and Asper 1998: 65–94.

———. 2000. "The Dangers of Literature and the Need for Literacy: A. Cornelius Celsus on Reading and Writing." In Alfrieda Pigeaud and Jackie Pigeaud, eds., *Les textes médicaux latins comme littérature: actes du VIe colloque international sur les textes médicaux latins du 1er au 3 septembre 1998 à Nantes*, 355–68. Nantes.

Von Ungern-Sternberg, Jürgen, and Hansjörg Reinau. 1988. *Vergangenheit in mündlicher Überlieferung*. Colloquium Rauricum 1. Stuttgart.

Voss, W. E. 1997. "Codex." In *Der Neue Pauly* 3: cols. 50–5.

Vössing, K. 1997. "Bibliothek." In *Der Neue Pauly* 2: cols. 634–47.

Wachter, Rudolf. 1991. "Abbreviated Writing." *Kadmos* 30: 49–80.

———. 1998. "'Oral Poetry' in ungewohntem Kontext: Hinweise auf mündliche Dichtungstechnik in den pompejanischen Wandinschriften." *ZPE* 121: 73–89.

Walbank, Michael B. 1993. "Review Article: Recent Work on Greek Inscriptions and the History of the Attic Alphabet." *AHB* 7: 28–36. Review of Guarducci 1987, Immerwahr 1990, and Jeffery 1990.

Wallace, R. 1995. "Speech, Song and Text, Public and Private: Evolution in Communications Media and Fora in Fourth Century Athens." In Walter Eder, ed., *Die athenische Demokratie im 4. Jahrhundert v. Chr.: Vollendung oder Verfall einer Verfassungsform?: Akten eines Symposiums 3.–7. August 1992, Bellagio*, 199–217. Stuttgart.

Waring, Judith. 2002. "Literacies of Lists: Reading Byzantine Monastic Inventories." In Holmes and Waring 2002: 165–86.

Waschkies, Hans-Joachim. 1993. "Mündliche, graphische und schriftliche Vermittlung von geometrischem Wissen im Alten Orient und bei den Griechen." In Kullmann and Althoff 1993: 39–70.

Watson, Janet, ed. 2001. *Speaking Volumes: Orality and Literacy in the Greek and Roman World*. Mnemosyne Supplementum 218. Leiden.

Wear, Sarah Klitenic. 2006. "Oral Pedagogy and the Commentaries of the Athenian Platonic Academy." *Dionysius* 24: 7–19.

Wenskus, Otta. 1998. "Columellas Bauernkalender zwischen Mündlichkeit und Schriftlichkeit." In Kullmann, Althoff, and Asper 1998: 253–62.

White, Peter. 1993. *Promised Verse: Poets in the Society of Augustan Rome*. Cambridge, Mass.

———. 1996. "Martial and Pre-Publication Texts." *EMC* 40: 397–412.

———. 1997. "Julius Caesar and the Publication of *Acta* in Late Republican Rome." *Chiron* 27: 73–84.

Whitley, James. 1997. "Cretan Laws and Cretan Literacy." *AJA* 101: 635–61.

———. 1998. "Literacy and Lawmaking: The Case of Archaic Crete." In Nick Fisher and Hans Van Wees, eds., *Archaic Greece: New Approaches and New Evidence*, 311–31. London.

Willard, Dallas. 1983. "Concerning the 'Knowledge' of the Pre-Platonic Greeks." In Robb 1983: 244–54.

Willi, Andreas. 2005. "Κάδμος ἀνέθηκε: zur Vermittlung der Alphabetsschrift nach Griechenland." *MH* 62: 162–71.

Williams, G. D. 1992. "Representations of the Book-Roll in Latin Poetry: Ovid, *Tr.* 1.1.3–14 and Related Texts." *Mnemosyne* (Ser. 4) 45: 178–89.

Willis, Steven. 2005. "The Context of Writing and Written Records in Ink: The Archaeology of Samian Inkwells in Roman Britain." *AJ* 162: 96–145.

Wilson, Jean-Paul. 1997–8. "The 'Illiterate Trader'?" *BICS* 42: 29–56.

Wise, Jennifer. 1998. *Dionysus Writes: The Invention of Theatre in Ancient Greece*. Ithaca.

Wöhrle, Georg. 1993. "War Parmenides ein schlechter Dichter? Oder: Zur Form der Wissensvermittlung in der frühgriechischen Philosophie." In Kullmann and Althoff 1993: 167–80.

Wolter-von dem Knesebeck, Harald. 1995. "Zur Ausstattung und Funktion des Hauptsaales der Bibliothek von Pergamon." *Boreas* 18: 45–56.

Woodard, Roger D. 1997. *Greek Writing from Knossos to Homer: A Linguistic Interpretation of the Origin of the Greek Alphabet and the Continuity of Ancient Greek Literacy*. New York.

Woolf, Greg. 1994. "Power and the Spread of Writing in the West." In Bowman and Woolf 1994: 84–98.

——. 1996. "Monumental Writing and the Expansion of Roman Society in the Early Empire." *JRS* 86: 22–39.

——. 2000. "Literacy." In A. K. Bowman, P. D. A. Garnsey, and D. W. Rathbone, eds., *The Cambridge Ancient History*. Vol. 11: *The High Empire*, A.D. *70–192*, 875–97. 2nd ed. Cambridge.

Worthington, Ian. 1993. "Once More, the Client/Logographos Relationship." *CQ* 43: 67–72.

——, ed. 1996. *Voice into Text: Orality and Literacy in Ancient Greece*. Mnemosyne Supplementum 157. Leiden.

—— and John Miles Foley, eds. 2002. *Epea and Grammata: Oral and Written Communication in Ancient Greece*. Orality and Literacy in Ancient Greece 4. Mnemosyne Supplementum 230. Leiden.

Yamagata, Naoko. 2001. "Orality." *CR* 51: 58–60. Review of Mackay 1999.

Yunis, Harvey, ed. 2003a. *Written Texts and the Rise of Literate Culture in Ancient Greece*. Cambridge.

——. 2003b. "Introduction: Why Written Texts?" In Yunis 2003a: 1–14.

——. 2003c. "Writing for Reading: Thucydides, Plato, and the Emergence of the Critical Reader." In Yunis 2003a: 189–212.

Zanker, Paul. 1993. "The Hellenistic Grave Stelai from Smyrna: Identity and Self-Image in the Polis." In Bulloch et al. 1993: 212–30.

Zelzer, Michaela. 2001. "Buch und Text von Augustus zu Karl dem Grossen." *MIÖG* 109: 291–314.

Zetzel, James E. G. 1973. "*Emendavi ad Tironem*: Some Notes on Scholarship in the Second Century A.D." *HSPh* 77: 225–43.

——. 1980. "The Subscriptions in the Manuscripts of Livy and Fronto and the Meaning of *Emendatio*." *CPh* 75: 38–59.

——. 1981. *Latin Textual Criticism in Antiquity*. New York.

Zorzetti, Nevio. 1990–1. "Poetry and the Ancient City: The Case of Rome." *CJ* 86: 311–29.

Part V

EPILOGUE

15

Why Literacy Matters, Then and Now

David R. Olson

> *I read myself in quotation marks.*
>   —Todorov

Few events in the evolution of modern culture rival the importance of writing and a written tradition. Yet just how and why writing and literacy play a supportive if not a controlling role in this evolution remain obscure. That literacy was a defining feature of social life in ancient Greece and Rome is elaborated in all of the chapters of this volume. Indeed, four themes stand out in their importance for reconstructing our understanding of literacy both then and now. The first is the common focus on literacy as a topic, that is, on the implications of writing and a written tradition; not only to trace the evolution of a tradition but to show how the evolution of that tradition was influenced by writing and the availability of written records.

A second theme is that of addressing literacy as a social practice, that is, addressing the uses of literacy rather than the simple fact of literacy. Whereas a conspicuous weakness of earlier theories of literacy and culture was the implicit assumption that if only a society had writing all else would fall into place, an important acknowledgment in current theories of literacy is that literacy may have important effects if and only if it is found to serve a valued function (Doronila 2001; Thomas, ch. 2, this volume). Indeed, literacy is "a social condition which can be defined only in terms of readership" (Havelock 1982, 57).

The third theme reflects the view that it is no longer in question as to whether or not literacy plays a role in social and cognitive change but rather just how it is that writing and literacy can serve to bring about such change. Conspicuous in many of the chapters in this volume that discuss literacy in ancient Greece and Rome is the reliance on quotation, whether from memory or from a document, in classical discourse. The very nature of quotation, I shall argue presently, gives the discourse surprising and important characteristics and may help to explain some of the legacies of literacy.

And the fourth, less developed than the other three, is the focus on readers and what they made of the documents they had access to. Who created and consulted documents is vital, of course, but just how persons read, cited, and interpreted documents and how those interpretive practices changed over time remains largely unexplored. It remains to be seen if such written documents were, in fact, an invitation to diverse modes of interpretation and modes of thought in ways that oral discourse was not—as many have conjectured beginning with Vico's *New Science* (1744/1970) and continuing through Havelock's more recent writing. It is a compelling fact that the religious heretics of the late medieval and early modern period were often, if not always, readers (Ginzburg 1982; Stock 1983).

Understanding literacy whether in classical antiquity or in modern times requires not only a grasp of the spread of literacy and its increasing use in social arrangement but also an understanding of how the conceptual and cognitive resources of those readers and writers evolved to take advantage of the resources offered by written documents. Although it is manifestly true that thought and discourse have become in some sense more abstract and elaborate as written documents have come to occupy a more important place in certain social practices, the more urgent question is to address just how writing something down could change our mental representation of it (Carruthers 1990). That is, we have only begun to examine how our literate practices in particular domains such as literature, science, and politics altered those domains and at the same time the intellectual habits of the persons who participated in them. In fact, this was the challenge set out by such theorists as Jack Goody and Ian Watt, Eric Havelock, Marshall McLuhan, and Walter Ong in the 1950s and '60s. Although somewhat tainted by a cultural chauvinism and an overemphasis on the uniqueness of the alphabet, the central claim was eloquently expressed by Eric Havelock in a lecture delivered at the University of Toronto in 1976 and later republished in his *The Literate Revolution in Greece and Its Cultural Consequences*:

> The civilization created by the Greeks and Romans was the first on the earth's surface which was founded upon the activity of the common reader; the first to be equipped with the means of adequate expression in the inscribed word; the first to be able to place the inscribed word in general circulation; the first, in short to become literate in the full meaning of that term and to transmit its literacy to us. (Havelock 1982, 40)

I shall refer to the general claim relating writing to particular forms of social organization and particular forms of discourse and thought as the "literacy hypothesis."

THE LITERACY HYPOTHESIS

The literacy hypothesis was the bold claim that the invention, adoption, and application of a new mode and technology of communication, namely writing, altered the social practices of the society as well as the cognitive processes of those so affected. The sponsors of that hypothesis produced a series of influential papers and books that explored the relations between an oral and a written tradition, between traditional and modern societies, and between oral and written language. The legacies of writing were seen as including, on the social side, the growth of complex social and bureaucratic organizations and, on the cognitive side, an accumulative and increasingly reflective and critical attitude to knowledge and belief, not to mention the invention of narrative fiction. The products of writing, they argued, were not only history but historians, not only philosophy but philosophers, not only record keeping but also accountants, laws but also lawyers, written narratives but also writers and readers. And so on.

The literacy hypothesis should not be confused with the traditional assumption about literacy. It is almost universally assumed that literacy is simply a good, a good of such value that it is appropriate to impose it on everyone whether through universal schooling or international literacy campaigns, and that a major responsibility of modern states is to guarantee universal literacy. This traditional assumption, going back at least to the Enlightenment, was that literacy has direct causal and utilitarian consequences; if people become literate they will necessarily make social and cognitive advances. The literacy hypothesis of the 1960s changed the topic in a subtle but important way. It turned the question away from that of how best to advance literacy into a set of scientific questions: what was the nature of literacy; what were the uses and legacies of writing and written culture? For whom and under what circumstances was it beneficial? The question is no longer how to extend our literacy but rather to ask about the implications of literacy. I take this to be the primary legacy of the literacy hypothesis.

Of course, these writers were not the first to see writing as of revolutionary significance. Seventeenth- and eighteenth-century writers such as Vico, Condorset, and Rousseau took the form of writing as indication of social evolution: those who wrote with pictures the most primitive, those with an alphabet the most developed. Although our modern literacy theorists lack an allegiance to the notion of linear progress, they nonetheless advocate the view that writing altered social practices and consequently, cognitive ones, and that these cognitive ones defined our modernity. Bureaucratic social structures and certain modes of thinking were proposed as consequences of literacy.

Some writers were quick to point out that the claims for literacy were overstated and its effects were context dependent. Others noted the close relation between speaking and writing and so have questioned the usefulness of the oral-literate formula. But the literacy hypothesis received a ringing endorsement from educators. It confirmed the long held belief that early education, centered on learning to read and write, was a universally valid goal. In fact this belief was endorsed by the UN charter in which learning to read is now enshrined as a universal human right. Although researchers, such as myself, are more guarded about the potential significance of learning to read and write, they have provided overwhelming evidence to show that children's thinking about language changes in important ways with the acquisition of literate skills in the early school years (Ferreiro and Teberosky 1982; Olson 2001). Precisely what is involved, of course, remains subject to ongoing research and debate. I shall argue that one can be a successful speaker of a language and yet lack to a remarkable degree any consciousness of certain aspects of language and that learning to read and write necessarily brings important aspects of language into consciousness. Writing serves up a very distinctive consciousness of one's language; writing, the claim is, turns language into an object of thought.

THE CRITICS

Aside from a generalized aversion to any theory that sounds monocausal, the central criticism of the literacy hypothesis is its apparent emphasis on the mere fact of writing rather than upon the diverse uses to which writing has been and may be put. The importance of the uses of writing is, of course, not controversial. Attention to the uses of writing has sponsored a great deal of important research that is directed to sorting out how precisely texts were created and read for various purposes including literature, history, and philosophy in various cultural contexts, including those of ancient Greece and Rome but also local contexts such as prayer meetings and reading groups. The more nuanced question is whether those functions are themselves distorted or altered by the facts of writing and literacy. How, for example, is a contract different from an agreement? And how the same?

Yet the critics have shown that literacy plays less a causal role than an ancillary or instrumental one in psychological and social change. Literacy played a role in the elaboration and adjustment of preexisting structures and practices more so than in the actual creation of novel ones. Thus writing extended the rule of law but did not bring it into existence (Clanchy 1979 [2nd ed. 1993]), writing preserved literature but did not create it (Powell 2002), and writing advanced debate in Classical Greece but did not give rise to it (Lloyd 1979; Thomas 1989). Even medieval religious discourse, although heavily reliant on written record, was carried out largely through oral means (Carruthers 1990). Further, empirical studies of the effects of knowledge of writing on the reasoning processes of individuals, once thought to be decisive (Luria 1976), often fail to replicate. In general, the effects of literacy, narrowly defined as the ability to read and write, were found to be modest, whereas literacy, more broadly defined as systematic induction into the traditions of literacy through schooling, was found to be dramatic (Scribner and Cole 1981; Bernardo 1995; Halverson 1992). Finally, the attempt to change individuals and societies through mass literacy campaigns such as those sponsored by UNESCO in the 1950s failed to produce the enduring effects that had been expected. Literacy, it seems, is not a primary engine of social change as its original proposers of the literacy hypothesis may or may not have thought but rather an instrument in particular social contexts for particular social uses (Elwert 2001; Street 1984; Doronila 2001).

Anthropologist Jack Goody is the best known and only living member of the original proposers of the literacy hypothesis. His numerous books, including *The Interface between the Written and the Oral* (1987) and *The Logic of Writing and the Organization of Society* (1986), are representative (for a current appraisal of the work and influence of Jack Goody see Olson and Cole 2006). Goody has also accrued the greatest number of critics. Halverson (1992), an anthropologist writing in *Man*, described what he called the "implosion of the literacy thesis" claiming that Goody's hypotheses consisted of "a thin tissue of vague suggestions, gratuitous assumptions and unsupported generalizations" (p. 305). The basis for his criticism was that the effects that Goody described did not obtain universally; there were readers who could not write, there were societies with writing who still lacked legal codes, written literature, and a scholarly tradition, and so on. Yet, in my judgment, the criticisms are misdirected.

Halverson claimed, for example, that an interest in what words mean (as opposed to what persons mean by them) is universal, that rules for analogy and formal reasoning are universal, and that it is academic discourse, not literacy, that is relevant to reasoning—as if it were merely a contingent fact that academic discourse is based on a documentary tradition carried out in large part through writing and reading. He drew the rather pedestrian conclusion that "the consequences of literacy depend entirely on the uses to which literacy is put" (1992, 314). Baines (1983, 593), another anthropologist writing in the same journal, *Man*, drew a similar conclusion, that writing "may be a necessary precondition for some social or cognitive change, but it does not cause such change." This conclusion is upheld by the oft-cited findings of Scribner and Cole (1981) on the cognitive effects of a limited and indigenous literacy among the Vai peoples of Liberia. Researchers found few differences between those able and those not able to write the Vai script on a variety of cognitive measures. Learning to read and write and study English in the school over a period of years, on the other hand, produced dramatic effects on a variety of cognitive measures: especially, they noted, in the ability to give reasons and to justify and make explicit their reasoning on cognitive tasks. These skills, they point out, are the very skills that were in fact taught in the schools. Scribner and Cole attributed such knowledge to schooling, again, in my view, ignoring the fact that schooling is essentially a literate enterprise—an induction to the literate practices of the dominant society. The debate revolves around the conception of literacy at play. To the critics it means simply the ability to read and write; to the literacy theorists it meant the elaboration and participation in a literate tradition, a culture of writing, in which schooling plays an essential part.

CRITICIZING THE CRITICS

In his critique of Goody and Watt (1968), Halverson (1992) claimed that "the 'cognitive' claims of the literacy thesis have no substance" (p. 301) although acknowledging that "a 'cumulative intellectual tradition' is unquestionably aided immensely by writing" (p. 303). But his reading of Goody and Watt lacked, to say the least, nuance. Goody and Watt's cognitive claims are more suitably read as metalinguistic ones, namely, that words, as distinctive conceptual entities that could be inventoried and analyzed, owe their existence to writing. "Are we to suppose that no one before Socrates ever asked the meaning of a word?" Halverson asked (p. 304). But that misinterprets Goody's claim. The appropriate anthropological question, not asked let alone answered, is whether or not there is a universal distinction between "he means" and "it means." It is only the latter that is, by hypothesis, linked to literacy. The distinction to be drawn is between meaning as reference and meaning as sense. To ask what one is referring to when one speaks is a far simpler matter than asking about the definition of a word; only the latter becomes the object of literate analysis and sets the stage for the formation of dictionaries and philosophical analysis of words and meanings. To think of a word independently of its reference is a complex cognitive task achieved in large part in learning to read and later elaborated through discussion, commentary, and criticism of written documents. Recall Dickens' *Gradgrind* explaining to rural children that a horse was not simply a horse but a "domesticated quadruped."

Different scripts represent language in different ways. Scribner and Cole's (1981) study of readers of the Vai syllabaries found that even proficient readers had limited notion of words as entities because the script did not represent isolated words but rather syllables. Bruce Homer and I (Homer and Olson 1999) did extensive studies on this topic and concluded that the units of print, whether word or Chinese character, determined the units that subjects articulated out of the stream of speech. Johnson (2000) noted that in Greek literary texts *scriptio continua* lacked spaces between words but that words at line end were divided according to strict syllabic rules, indicating the primacy of sound over meaning units (Daniels, forthcoming). But in a segmented script even function words such as articles and prepositions are separated off as words. Thus the young children that Bruce Homer and I studied had no difficulty judging that content words, nouns, are words but did have difficulty with other parts of speech: "two little pigs" is thought to contain two words, "a little pig" is thought to be one word, and so on. Contrary to Halverson's claim that "the consequences of literacy depend entirely on the uses to which literacy is put" (p. 314), the very fact of writing a certain type of script calls into consciousness certain properties of language that are otherwise largely overlooked. These include not only an awareness of the phonology of the language, so-called phonological awareness, but also word awareness. In fact, even the great Samuel Johnson, the maker of the first English dictionary, lacked an adequate notion of the meaning of words, appealing to what they referred to as a means of defining them. It was only with Frege, as we shall see, that sense or meaning came to be clearly distinguished from reference. Thus Halverson's conclusion that consciousness of language is simply a given, available to all, literate and nonliterate alike, is false.

Halverson follows Scribner and Cole in further claiming that formal reasoning is not strictly speaking a consequence of literacy but rather a consequence of academic discourse as experienced in Western-styled schooling. Few would disagree that formal reasoning is a key concern of the school; where one may disagree is in the assumption that schooling is something other than an induction into literate practices. The better question is, why is literacy so central to those practices of formal schooling? Why not throw books away and content oneself with talk? And the answer, I suggest, is that formal reasoning and schooling alike derive from the particular access to language as served up by texts fixed by writing and taken as significant by the society.

THE METALINGUISTIC THEORY OF LITERACY

It is by now well known that literacy, more specifically, learning to read and write, involves a degree or type of awareness of language quite distinct from that required for speaking. Let me cite some of the most obvious cases. It is well known that what is called "metalinguistic awareness," namely, reader's awareness of the phonological properties of their own speech, is largely unknown to nonreaders. This may seem anomalous in that children must know the phonology because they are competent speakers of English, say, rather than Swahili. But such linguistic knowledge is largely implicit, and to learn to read and write, at least some of that knowledge must be reorganized in terms of a set of explicit categories represented by the written signs. Children have to learn that the "b" sound in baby, ball, rabbit, and rub can all be represented by the letter *b*. This consciousness can of course be taught through oral methods—word and sound games of various sorts—but it is a specialized knowledge about language that is required for dealing with an alphabetic script. Such metalinguistic knowledge is ordinarily a consequence of acquaintance with letters.

This is not just a feature of childhood. In fact, adults who have had little or no exposure to an alphabetic writing system behave much as do the preliterate children. Morais, Alegria and Content (1987) and more recently Petersson, Ingvar, and Reis (forthcoming), set a number of phonological tasks known to distinguish reading from prereading children to a group of essentially illiterate Portuguese fishermen, half of whom had had some exposure to the alphabet while they were young children. Tasks required them to break words into the phonological constituents represented by letters of the alphabet. A simple example would be to ask them to say /fish/ without saying the /f/. Like prereading children, those never exposed to an alphabet were unable to carry out this task by reporting /ish/. The ability to analyze one's own speech into such phonological categories depended upon their prior exposure to an alphabet. It is the writing system that provides some of the categories for thinking about, indeed hearing and analyzing, one's own speech.

But there are several levels of structure in language beyond the phoneme. These, too, have to be discovered and brought into consciousness, in large part, though not exclusively, through the acquaintance with a writing system. These include knowledge of words, propositions, paragraphs, and the specialized genres of written language. Prereading children readily attend to the content of what is said, including tone of voice—that is, to the meaning intended by a speaker—but they take considerable time to learn to play off what was said, the very words, from the meanings conveyed. Even some adults, of course, continue to insist that they said what they meant and they meant what they said! But writing is a favored vehicle for preserving "what was said" in such a way that it is easily made into the subject of discourse. Conversely, a consciousness of what was said (as opposed to what was intended by it) is basic to understanding writing. A nice example of this growing consciousness comes from an interview I did with my prereading grandchild. I showed her a card on which I had written "Three little pigs." I read it to her and had her say back to me what it said. I then covered up the last word and asked her to tell me what it now said, to which she replied "Two little pigs." She assumed that the written marks represented objects, pigs, not words, a kind of picture writing. In fact such picture writing occurs in modern traffic signs as well as in some North American aboriginal scripts. The Blackfoot tribe of Alberta, Canada, used picture writing in an ingenious way to create chronicles, one picture to represent an event typical of that year. Thus "The year the horses got drowned" was depicted by a circle representing the pond and some stick figure horses in the circle. In such a script there were no signs for the words of the utterance and consequently, no sign for the negative "No" as would be required to write "No horses got drowned." In fact the major achievement in the history of writing was the invention of a means of representing utterances themselves rather than ideas or things the utterances were about. Indeed, it may be argued that the invention of writing was the discovery of these properties of language. All full writing systems are in fact representations of language rather than representation of ideas. Even so-called "ideographic" writing systems are in fact "logographic," that is, writing systems that represent words, *logos*, not ideas, *eidos*.

Another example of prereading children's assumptions about writing may be inferred from their early attempts at writing. If asked to write

"A cat," a child may make a scribble; if asked to write "Two cats," they may make two squiggles, and so on. But if asked to write "No cats," they may say, "I didn't write anything because there are no cats." Writing requires sustained attention to the linguistic form as opposed to what the language is about. To oversimplify somewhat, writing distinguishes what is said from what is meant, capturing only the former. American linguist Benjamin Lee Whorf (1956) suggested that we dissect nature along lines laid down by our native language to show how our thought tends to run in conventional linguistic ruts. I revised this claim to the context of literacy to say, "We introspect our language along lines laid down by our scripts" (Olson 1994, 90).

The literacy hypothesis, then, is the hypothesis that a writing system and a tradition of writing is not a neutral practice; it allows us, indeed invites us, to think about language and mind in some new ways. Eric Havelock (1982) pioneered some of these ideas, claiming that the fixity of text allowed writing to take over the mental functions previously carried by memory. He traced some of the properties of Homeric texts to their oral composition and contrasted that with the beginnings of written poetry and especially written prose, views that have been importantly elaborated and extended by Powell (2002). Certainly it remains an interesting project to trace the ways that writing influenced discourse and the specialization of genre in both speech and writing.

But it is also possible to examine how writing contributes to two very specialized uses of language, one that may be described as the isolation of "pure thought" and the second as the elaboration of subjectivity. For more than a century anthropologists and sociologists have associated cultural development with two features of language use: the increase of rational thought and rationalized practices on one hand and the growth of subjectivity, the consciousness of the mental states, on the other. My question, the central point of this chapter, is to ask how literacy could contribute to these two special properties of social and cultural evolution.

THOUGHTS WITHOUT THINKERS—LITERACY AND ABSTRACT PROSE

The unit of thought that a sentence expresses is a proposition, the unit of language first systematically analyzed by Frege (reprinted 1970) at the end of the last century. One of Frege's important contributions was to show that a simple declarative sentence is actually composed of two parts, an "assertoric force" and a "predicate." Thus, an utterance, Frege argued, does two things at once: it both mentions a thought, the predicate, and asserts it as true, its assertoric force. Thus there are two things hidden inside the utterance of an ordinary declarative sentence. His distinction later provided the basis for Austin's (1962) theory of speech acts (Lee

1997, 24), and most writers have adopted the later terminology, thereby distinguishing what is called "the illocutionary force" of an utterance—what one does in saying, such as asserting or commanding—from the propositional content mentioned. In ordinary discourse no distinction is made between the content mentioned and the belief of the speaker; there is a conflation of thought with belief. The theory that I wish to advance is that writing is instrumental in distinguishing thought from belief. The theory is composed of two claims. The first is that the propositional content can be isolated from its assertoric or illocutionary force only when it occurs in the embedded clause of indirect discourse, that is, through the linguistic device of quotation. Both direct and indirect quotation are means of representing an idea without oneself believing it or asserting it as true. In quoted speech the thought has become free of the thinker! The second is that writing is a form of quotation.

One could argue along with Frege that indirect discourse (roughly quotation of an expression) is what makes conceptual thought possible. Pure thought is entertaining some content without either asserting or denying it. Although there are complexities here (Davidson 1984; Dummett 1981) quotation, indirect quotation, and reported thought all require that special interpretive procedures be brought to bear on the quoted expression. What are these special procedures? They are ones that treat the quoted expression as exempt from the assertoric force or intention of the original speaker. All of these procedures direct attention to the linguistic properties of the expression rather than to, or in addition to, its situational or referential meaning, and in particular, the assertoric or illocutionary force of the original expression. Stated another way, speaker's meaning has been carved off to leave sentence meaning. Consequently, what quotation does is free an utterance from its original intention. Phrased yet another way, quoted expressions are mentioned rather than used; they have been rendered "off-line" and their function becomes metarepresentational.

What is the link to writing? My conjecture is that written texts inherit the properties of quoted expressions. As in the expression by Todorov cited in the epigram to this chapter, we read as if expressions are in quotation marks. Written texts are written and read as if they were merely mentioned rather than used. Written texts, like quoted expressions, are closed in the sense that they are no longer open to updating and revision. They are a corpse more than a corpus; in philosophical jargon the expressions are opaque. They have a structure more or less independent of what the speaker or writer meant by them. It requires a reader to reanimate them. What the reader does is add his or her own assertoric or illocutionary force to the quoted expression. Although texts, on occasion, may have originated as a simple alternative to speech, once preserved and fixed, they are read as if in quotation marks, as quoted rather than stated. Such expressions are overheard rather than heard, to use a distinction made by J. S. Mill in his article "What Is Poetry?" (cited by Banfield 1993,

339). Quoted speech, too, is closed, not open to negotiation and revision; it is fixed, it is not addressed to us, it is overheard by us.

Quotation is not a simple matter. Critic I. A. Richards found nineteen different uses in writing for quotation marks. But our concern is with one of them, reported speech and thought. Two features are of particular relevance, first, how quotation loses illocutionary force to become pure thought, and second, how the free play of "illocutionary force" elaborates possibilities of subjectivity. Thus my intention is to trace out two of the special properties of written documents by means of treating them as quoted speech.

WHAT UTTERANCES LOSE IN BECOMING TEXTS—REPORTED SPEECH

In her search for the literary basis for the rise of subjectivity in modern novels, Banfield (1993) has extensively analyzed the linguistic basis of what she calls "reported speech and thought." She examined the links between literature, psychology and linguistics: for literature it was the form of the modern novel as exemplified by Jane Austen, Katherine Mansfield, and Virginia Woolf; for psychology it was the workings of the conscious and unconscious mind; and for linguistics, it was what she calls "represented thought," what literary theorists have called "style indirect libre." She wrote, "It is no accident that the rise of the novel, the literary genre directed at the representation of the inner (nonspeaking) self, and...the central role accorded to the conscious, thinking subject in modern philosophy and an inarticulate ego in psychology, coincide historically with the linguistic realization of the nonspeaking, noncommunicating self of represented thought" (p. 360).

Banfield (1993) reminds us that speech is dominated by the social or communicative function that assumes an *I* and a *you*, a *here* and a *now*. Written literature, on the other hand, is dominated by the expressive function of language that allows the formation of compositions in which no *you* exists, the *I* may not be the speaker/writer, and the *now* may be cotemporal with the past (if the introductory clause is past). "When these conditions exist...represented thought is born" (p. 353), a style much exploited, she suggests, by such novelists as Austen, Woolf, and Joyce. Written composition, she writes, "frees language from the speech act" (p. 357) allowing a new use of pronouns and deixis. These are the properties that are borrowed into writing from quotation.

Represented thought is the thought expressed separate from the belief of any particular speaker, a sort of Fregean pure thought. Banfield produces eight linguistic features that distinguish this kind of writing from what is permissible in actual speech. Here is one example from the writings of Virginia Woolf:

"Yes, today," she said. "I lunched with him. We walked in the Park." She
stopped. They had walked in the Park. A thrush had been singing; they
had stopped to listen. "That's the wise thrush that sings each song twice
over..." he had said. "Does he?" she had asked innocently. *And it had
been a quotation.*

The mistake was in not recognizing it as a quotation and thinking it was an
assertion that could be questioned. Quotations have lost their assertoric
force; it is inappropriate to treat them as if they were being asserted by the
speaker. The speaker merely mentions the expression; he or she does not
assert it as true.

Consider another example from Franz Kafka's (1979) *A Little Fable.*[1]
"Oh!" said the mouse. "The world is getting smaller every day." "Oh!" is
an expression of illocutionary force or attitude, that of resignation
I suppose, whereas "The world is getting smaller every day" is an expression of the content of a belief. In direct quotation, one could perhaps say,
"The mouse said 'Oh, the world is getting smaller every day,'" but more
likely the marker of attitude would be deleted. In the case of indirect
quotation the illocutionary marker is obligatorily deleted: "The mouse
said that the world is getting smaller every day," thereby losing the marker
of illocutionary force; the quoted expression has become what I have
called pure thought. Or one could compensate for the loss by moving the
illocutionary force outside the quoted clause and indicating it by elaborating the speech act verb: "The mouse *bemoaned* that the world is getting
smaller every day." But notice that here it is the reporter who has assigned
the illocutionary force that may or may not coincide with that held by the
original speaker. The important point is that the quoted clause has lost its
illocutionary force to become a simple thought, no longer anyone's belief.

There are two results of quoting utterances, the increasingly sharp
distinction between a belief and a thought, and the heightened awareness
of personal, private perspectives or subjectivity. Let us consider them
in turn.

THE EMANCIPATION OF PURE THOUGHT

The first result is the new kind of meaning of the quoted expression once
divorced from the illocutionary force of the speaker. The meaning is no
longer the speaker's meaning but a kind of abstract sentence meaning or
literal meaning that I have described as pure thought. They have become
ideas for contemplation rather than assertions to be believed or denied.
Such language is what makes contemplative thought possible. What
I mean by contemplative thought as opposed to ordinary thought is that

---

1. Monica Smith first pointed out the difficulty of quoting such interjections. And thanks
to Keith Barton for providing me with the reference.

it is thought about thought rather than about what anyone believes. Deriving conclusions from premises, as in Aristotelean logic, would be an example. But further, it is the language that defines public, essentially authorless, documents. Quoted expressions are in a sense mentioned rather than used. Literal meaning, like the definition of a word, is the meaning of a quoted, decontextualized expression. The advantage of such a decontextualized or autonomous or authorless meaning is that one can work out rules for strict inference; inferences that follow from the verbal form rather than from the speaker's intention or from the local utterance meaning. If "the world is getting smaller every day" then it follows that it is reduced in diameter or mass. It does not necessarily follow, as the mouse presumably intended, that he feels that the world is closing in. Stated more generally, it is that strict implication, unlike paraphrase, is difficult, to the point of impossibility, to derive from utterance meaning. On the other hand, the logical implications of quoted expressions are relatively straightforward as they derive from the sense of the sentence, the verbal form, rather than the intended meaning of the utterance. All of formal logic depends upon the availability of such, as we say, timeless meanings. Speakers, on the other hand, rely upon the speaker's intentions, goals, contexts, as well as the utterance itself. Speakers express their beliefs and they rely on quotation to express what I have called "pure thought," that is, thought as distinguished from belief.

Educated persons take it as a matter of course to distinguish thoughts from beliefs. Havelock (1982) traced the distinction between knowledge and the knower to the growth of literacy in classical Greece. Knowledge could be distinguished from the knower not only because it could be stored in documents, but also because they had learned to think about ideas rather than or in addition to their beliefs. Our contemplative habits are not universal but, it may be argued, a by-product of our literacy. One may recall Luria's (1976) famous study of reasoning among nonliterate adults in which he found that subjects frequently failed to draw the expected inference as in 1.

1. All the bears in Novaya Zemla are white. Ivan went to Novaya Zemla and saw a bear there. What colour was the bear?

To which the subjects tended to reply as in 2.

2. I've never been to Novaya Zemla, you'll have to ask Ivan, etc.

The subject, an unschooled, illiterate peasant, tended to treat 1 as an expression of the speaker's belief rather than as a "pure thought." Consequently, he disagreed with the speaker's assertion and failed to draw what we would regard as a necessary implication of that pure thought. Stated another way, the subject failed to notice that the expression was to be treated as if in quotation marks; the subject failed to treat the statement as a premise. Premises are statements in quotation marks. Note, this is not to say that nonliterate subjects lack the ability to handle quotation but only that literacy and schooling make the recognition and interpretation of quoted expressions routine.[2]

Written texts invite discourse not only about what *he/she* means but, more importantly, about what *it means*. This distinction between the speaker's meaning and textual meaning reflects the fact that the text is detached from the author in just the way that quotation detaches expression from the speaker. Linguist Roy Harris (1989, 104) has made a similar claim, stating that writing opens a conceptual gap between sentence and utterance, a gap that allows an analysis of sentences as opposed to utterance. More recently he has added the following:

> With the arrival of "the sentence," a new forum is created for the discussion of human thinking, and along with that comes the concomitant demand or expectation that all thinking (reasoning) worth bothering about has to be presented in sentential form. (This expectation is already realized by the time of Aristotle, because the sentence is the basis of the Aristotelian syllogism.)
>
>   This new forum, however, is also an intellectual cage or enclosure imposing its own limitations. It cannot accommodate non-sentential modes of thought. (Harris, forthcoming)

Once created, this gap poses problems of interpretation for students and others who find it difficult to reassign a textual statement to an author, that is, to translate a sentence back into an utterance, and hence, to criticize a text (Peskin 2000).

To summarize, quotation strips off the author's illocutionary force, leaving a somewhat bare propositional content, an unowned thought. And it is that denuded propositional content that provides a basis for logic and philosophy as well as for much of modern literature. It is worth noting that quotation is a linguistic device; quoted expressions are not unique to writing but have become central to writing and reading in the literate contexts I have been describing. The argument is only that writers may seize upon this resource and expand it to create the forms of expression we identify as literary. Of course, a great deal of learning sponsored by the school is required if one is to participate in this literary tradition. So writing does not cause the development of diverse forms of literacy but of course they could not develop without writing either. Writing is a necessary condition, not a sufficient one, as Goody frequently pointed out. A historical process has to intervene; and a good deal of human ingenuity.

2. Derrida (1976) was, I believe, the first theorist to take quoted expressions as the basis of culture and cognition. His concept of the "free play of the signifiers," the kind of thinking involved when one ignores the signified, is based on an analysis of the sense rather than reference of expressions. Derrida examined the nature of writing as if what was written was enclosed in quotation marks (see Hobson 1998).

THE RISE OF SUBJECTIVITY: WHAT READING REQUIRES

The second consequence of dealing with the sentential nature of written texts may be considered. If written texts have the properties of quoted expressions, new means have to be found for expressing the illocutionary force that was lost in quotation. In reanimating quoted expressions one must find new ways of recapturing illocutionary force through an elaborate set of speech act verbs such as *state, claim, assert, imply, acknowledge, allege*, and the like. Note that such a characterization signals both how the author may have intended his utterance to be taken (as a suggestion or command, for example) but also how the reporter characterizes that illocutionary force. *Allege*, for example, signals both: that the original speaker believed what he said whereas the reporter has serious reservations. The language of speech acts is a fundamental part of the language of subjectivity and mastering that language is one of the major ways that writing and literacy affects cognition. In large part rationality involves knowing how to take, that is, characterize, utterances—as *suggestions*, as *claims*, as *conclusions*, and the like (see also Reilly, Baruch, and Berman 2002). The cognitive implications of literacy, in part, come from attempts to make up for what has been lost in the transcription of utterances (Olson 1994, chapter 5).

THE EVOLUTION OF WAYS OF READING

In order to understand ancient literacy, it is necessary to examine not only who read and wrote but also how they cited, interpreted, commented on, and criticized existing texts. Did they distinguish what texts meant from what their authors meant by them? What was their conception of meaning? The common or default assumption about reading is that the meaning is "always already" in the text prior to and independent of anything a reader brings to a text. But was this assumption held in classical times? How did it arise? And when and why did it change? Even when the theory of meaning was elaborated by Origen, an early Church father—the four-fold meaning of Scripture—those meanings were regarded as given by or intrinsic to the text (Smalley 1941, p. 5). Reader response theorists of our generation are rather extravagant in their denunciations of this "givenness" assumption but remain vague on what kinds of constraints a text puts on its correct or authorized readings and the traditions in which these constraints are invented and taught to new readers.

There are many ways of reading, but classifying those ways and tracing their development remains a task for the future. For some people read aloud, some silently; some read to a group, some with a group; some read to memorize the wording, some to extract the meaning; some read on the lines, some between the lines; some read in public, some in private; some to reconstruct the author's meaning, some to test out their own meanings. And it must be remembered that some, perhaps the majority of world's population, read nothing at all.

But there is also such a thing as learning to read competently, that is, to read according to the relevant cultural conventions, and we need to know how these conventions evolved historically and how they are learned. Teachers everywhere encounter students who adopt a completely supine orientation to texts, memorizing them, and holding themselves account-able to those texts without troubling to decide whether or not they actually believe them. We may think of this as the naïve stance or the naïve way of reading. The reader is unconscious of his or her own contri-butions to the resulting meaning. To read critically and with perspectival understanding requires that one distinguish the content from the force, that is, to distinguish what is being said from how the author intended it to be taken—as a hint or as an assertion, as a suggestion or a command, for example. Seeing written statements of fact as assertions by a writer is the first step to appropriately relativising factual statements. This stance is sometimes described as the willing suspension of disbelief; grasping the thought without necessarily agreeing with the author. And the third way of reading allows the reader to take up the assertions of the author in terms of the reader's own perspective and goal. This stance acknowledges that reading involves the freedom to characterize the assertions of the author relative to the beliefs and goals of the reader. The reader is allowed to use a text for his or her own purposes; it gives the reader the right to his or her own meanings and beliefs. The mechanism for this third way of reading involves not merely reporting the illocutionary force of the quoted expression but characterizing it in such a way as to indicate the speaker or writer's own perspective. Thus, what was offered as an assertion may be taken up by a reader as an allegation. Creating an appropriate attitude to texts is an important route to system-atic thinking.

As a preliminary taxonomy of ways of reading we have the following:

The world is getting smaller every day. Grasping content. *Naïve reading.*

The world is getting smaller every day. Mouse thinks so. Grasping content + author attitude. *Critical reading.*

The world is getting smaller every day. Mouse thinks so. I doubt it. Grasping content + author's attitude + reader's perspective. *Reflective reading.*

There is the universal dilemma between choosing whether to make up one's own meanings, the right Menochio insisted upon at his peril (Ginzburg 1982), and the responsibility to the forms of interpretation sanctioned by one's culture. Does one have the right to read "against the grain," or is it an obligation to read as tradition dictates? Students of literacy are concerned with how and why writing exploits these diverse roles.

CONCLUSION

I have attempted to show that writing is neither equivalent to speaking nor is it an utterly unique and distinctive mode of communication. Rather, writing may be thought of as a subclass of speech, specifically that of quotation, a move that allows one to separate the force or attitude of an utterance from the propositional content it expresses. Consequently, writing calls for a distinctive mode of interpretation. Writing exploits the recursive property of language, the property that allows language to be used to reflect on language. All speakers of a language have access to these basic linguistic resources, resources including direct and indirect quotation. However, in written cultures that rely heavily on texts and documents, the familiarity and competence with reflexive, or quoted, language is greatly elaborated. Stated another way, literate people in literate societies have developed expertise in dealing with a special class of expressions, expressions that are mentioned rather than used, and so fall into the quoted class. Such texts constitute a major archival resource in modern document-based societies and in learning to cope with them people acquire a distinctive kind of social competence not inappropriately described as literacy.

Reading and writing are now seen as embedded in social practices as law, economics, literature, and religion, as well as in more local literacy practices such as Internet blogs and reading groups. The more formal social practices tend to exploit the distinctive access that writing gives to metalinguistic knowledge, the technical and precise meanings of terms and expressions. Conversely, altered social practices give rise to new ways of writing and reading. But it is the consciousness of words and meanings stripped of their illocutionary force, the so-called timeless meanings of formal discourse, on the one hand, and the free play of subjectivities divorced from those timeless meanings, on the other, that make writing so important to modern thought and to the development of a literate tradition.

BIBLIOGRAPHY

Austin, J. L. 1962. *How to Do Things with Words*. Cambridge, Mass.

Baines, J. 1983. "Literacy and Ancient Egyptian Society." *Man* 18: 572–99.

Banfield, A. 1993. "Where Epistemology, Style, and Grammar Meet Literary History: The Development of Represented Speech and Thought." In Lucy, J., ed., *Reflexive Language: Reported Speech and Metapragmatics*, 339–64. Cambridge.

Bernardo, A. 1995. *Cognitive Consequences of Literacy: Studies on Thinking in Five Filipino Communities*. Quezon.

Carruthers, M. J. 1990. *The Book of Memory: A Study of Memory in Medieval Culture*. Cambridge.

Clanchy, M. T. 1993. *From Memory to Written Record: England, 1066–1307*. 2nd ed. London.

Daniels, P. Forthcoming. "The history of writing." In D. R. Olson and N. G. Torrance, eds., *Cambridge Handbook of Literacy*. Cambridge.

Davidson, D. 1984. "Quotation." In D. Davidson, ed., *Inquiries into Truth and Interpretation*, 79–92. Oxford.

Derrida, J. 1976. *Of Grammatology*. Trans. by G. Spivek. Baltimore.

Doronila, M. L. C. 2001. "Developing a Literate Tradition in Six Marginal Communities in the Philippines: Interrelations of Literacy, Education, and Social Development." In D. R. Olson and N. G. Torrance, eds., *The Making of Literate Societies*, 248–83. Oxford.

Dummett, M. 1981. *The Interpretation of Frege's Philosophy*. London.

Elwert, G. 2001. "Societal Literacy: Writing Culture and Development." In D. R. Olson and N. G. Torrance, eds., *The Making of Literate Societies*, 54–67. Oxford.

Ferreiro, E., and A. Teberosky. 1982. *Literacy before Schooling*. Exeter, N.H. Originally published as *Los sistemas de escritura en el desarrollo del niño*. 1979. Mexico D.F.

Frege, G. 1970. "Begriffschrift." In J. U. Heijenoort, ed., *Frege and Godel*, 5–82. Cambridge.

Ginzburg, C. 1982. *The Cheese and the Worms: The Cosmos of a Sixteenth-Century Miller*. Markham, Ont.

Goody, J. 1986. *The Logic of Writing and the Organization of Society*. Cambridge.

——. 1987. *The Interface between the Written and the Oral*. Cambridge.

——, and I. Watt. 1968. "The Consequences of Literacy." In J. Goody, ed., *Literacy in Traditional Societies*, 27–68. Cambridge. (Originally published in 1963 in *Contemporary Studies in Society and History* 5: 304–45.)

Halverson, J. 1992. "Goody and the Implosion of the Literacy Thesis." *Man* 27: 301–17.

Harris, R. 1986. *The Origin of Writing*. London.

——. Forthcoming. "Speech and Writing." In D. R. Olson and N. G. Torrance, eds., *The Cambridge Handbook of Literacy*. Cambridge.

Harris, W. V. 1989. *Ancient Literacy*. Cambridge, Mass.

Hobson, M. 1998. *Jacques Derrida: Opening Lines*. London.

Havelock, E. 1982. *The literate revolution in Greece and its cultural consequences*. Princeton.

Homer, B., and D. R. Olson. 1999. "Literacy and Children's Conception of Words." *Written Language and Literacy* 2: 113–40.

Lee, Benjamin. 1997. *Talking Heads: Language, Metalanguage, and the Semiotics of Subjectivity*. Durham, N.C.

Lloyd, G. E. R. 1979. *Magic, Reason, and Experience*. Cambridge.

Luria, A. 1976. *Cognitive Development: Its Cultural and Social Foundations*. Cambridge, Mass.

Morais, J., J. Alegria, and A. Content. 1987. "The Relationships between Segmental Analysis and Alphabetic Literacy: An Interactive View." *Cahiers de Psychologie Cognitive* 7: 415–38.

Olson, D. R. 1994. *The World on Paper: The Conceptual and Cognitive Implications of Writing and Reading*. Cambridge.

——. 2001. "What Writing Is." *Pragmatics and Cognition* 9: 239–58.

—— and M. Cole, eds. 2006. *Culture, Technology and History: Implications of the Work of Jack Goody*. Mahwah, N.J.

Peskin, J. 2000. "Rhetorical and Aesthetic Form: Poetry as Textual Art." In J. W. Astington, ed., *Minds in the Making*, 80–97. Oxford.

Petersson, K. M., M. Ingvar, and A. Reis. Forthcoming. "Language and Literacy from a Cognitive Neuroscience Perspective." In D. R. Olson and N. G. Torrance, eds., *The Cambridge Handbook of Literacy*. Cambridge.

Powell, B. 2002. *Writing and the Origins of Greek Literature*. Cambridge.

Reilly, J., E. Baruch, and R. Berman. 2002. "Propositional Attitudes in Written and Spoken Language." *Written Language and Literacy* 5: 183–218.

Scribner, S., and M. Cole. 1981. *The Psychology of Literacy*. Cambridge, Mass.

Smalley, B. 1941. *The Study of the Bible in the Middle Ages*. Oxford.

Stock, B. 1983. *The Implications of Literacy*. Princeton.

——. 1993. "Afterword." In J. Boyarin, ed., *The Ethnography of Reading*, 270–75. Berkeley, Calif.

Street, B. 1984. *Literacy in Theory and Practice*. Cambridge.

Thomas, R. 1989. *Oral Tradition and Written Record in Classical Athens*. Cambridge.

Todorov, T. 1995. *The Morals of History*. Trans. by A. Waters. Minneapolis.

Vico, G. 1744/1948. *The New Science of Giambattista Vico*. Trans. by T. G. Bergin and M. H. Fisch. Ithaca, N.Y.

Whorf, B. L. 1956. Science and linguistics. In *Selected writings of Benjamin Lee Whorf*. Cambridge, Mass.

Index Locorum

References to illustrations are in boldface type.
Citations are abbreviated according to the indices of *Thesaurus Linguae Latinae* (Latin) or
Diccionario Griego-Español (Greek).

Achilles Tatius
1.18: 103
4.4: 102–3

Aelian
NA
1.36: 102
1.50: 103

Aeschines
3.192: 24

Alciphron
1–5: 110

Andocides
1.77–79: 32–3
1.83–84: 36*n*51

Anthologia graeca
4.1: 174*n*20
9.141: 205*n*69
9.713–42: 147*n*15
9.733: 147
9.734: 147–8
9.739: 148
9.740: 148
9.793–8: 147*n*15
12.208.5–6: 222*n*149
15.24: 192*n*20

Anthologia latina
214: 131*n*54
498: 126
501: 126

Antiphon
1.28–30: 27
5.53: 25

Appendix Vergiliana
See **Ciris**; Vergil *catal.*

Appian
BC
2.98–9: 196*n*31

Aratus
783–7: 129–30
802–6: 129–30
807–10: 130–1

Aristophanes
Eq.
188–93: 23

Aristotle
(*See also* **Commentaria**
in Aristotelem
Graeca *and* **Vita**
Marciana)
Pol.
2.1266b31–35: 36*n*49
Rh.
2.1400a.32–36: 34

Asconius
Mil.
29.33 Clark: 281*n*39
42.2–4 Clark: 279

Athenaeus
1.1d–e: 269*n*3, 275*n*20
1.1e: 100
1.1e–f: 96
1.1f–2a: 96
1.3a: 96
1.3a–b: 145*n*7
1.4a: 100

1.4b: 96
1.4c: 111
5.201d: 82*n*37

Augustine
conf.
6.3: 191*n*12, 196*n*29
6.10.16: 271*n*7
8.29: 211

Ausonius
cento nuptialis
pr.: 271*n*8

Callimachus
Ap.
146
Coma Berenices
176–8
Hecale
146
Victoria Berenices
177*n*26

Cato
ORF 8.173–5: 123

Catullus
1: 151–2, 164–70,
172, 175–6,
178–9, 181, 190,
224
1.8: 174
1.9: 175, 178
1.9–10: 168–9
1.10: 178, 220
2.1: 167–8*n*7
4: 222*n*147

General Index